Fundamentals of

Financial Management

(3rd Edition)

By the Same Author

Dynamics of Indian Financial System: Market, Institutions and Services (2nd Edition)

Fundamentals of
Financial Management

(3rd Edition)

Dr. Preeti Singh
Associate Professor
Department of Commerce
Jesus & Mary College
University of Delhi

Ane Books Pvt. Ltd.
New Delhi ♦ Chennai

Fundamentals of Financial Management, *3rd Edn*

Dr. Preeti Singh

First Edition : 2008
Second Edition : 2009
Third Edition : 2026

Published by

Ane Books Pvt. Ltd.
4821, Parwana Bhawan, 1st Floor, 24 Ansari Road, Darya Ganj,
New Delhi - 110 002, India
Tel.: +91(011) 23276843-44, Fax: +91(011) 23276863
e-mail: kapoor@anebooks.com, Website: www.anebooks.com

Branch Office :

- Avantika Niwas, 1st Floor, 19 Doraiswamy Road, T. Nagar, **Chennai** - 600 017, Tel.: +91(044) 28141554, 28141209
e-mail: anebookschennai@gmail.com

ISBN : 978-93-8061-895-1

Printed at: Sagar Colorscan, New Delhi.

Preface to the Third Edition

The revised and enlarged third edition of this book is presented to students of financial management. Its unique special characteristic is that the book has been written like a class lecture. It has been written keeping in mind the needs of the different students so that it is easily understood. The basic financial management principles and concepts have been explained. My teaching experiences of three decades in a constituent college of University of Delhi and at many postgraduate centres of education have given me an insight into the requirements of students. In this book, I have put my class experience into practice. I have participated in management development programmes as trainer in this area and shared my experiences with corporate managers.

I acknowledge and appreciate the work of scholars and professors who have researched and written on various aspects of corporate finance. I have tried to contribute to an understanding of financial management concepts in a manner that students from engineering, economics and science background can also grasp the subject easily. After the bachelors level many students take up the challenge of taking finance as a subject in the postgraduate level. It is at this time that they require a book which is easily understandable and puts them at par with those who have already completed some topics in finance and have a basic understanding of the subject.

This edition has an increased and enlarged coverage. A new chapter has been written on Sources of Finance and many new solved illustrations have been added to cover questions from MBA, MFC, M.Com, ICWA and CA. The subject is covered in 18 chapters and VII units. The subdivisions of the units are made according to the classification and coverage of the topic. It is a simple, student friendly book with many examples, solved illustrations, objective type questions, important points and concepts of financial management.

It is a comprehensive coverage of all the basic concepts of financial management to suit the requirements of the BBA, B.Com (Hons.), CA, ICWA, CS, MBA, M.Com students of Finance and managers who are interested in the subject of financial management.

Unit I covers the basic concepts and provides an introduction to financial management by discussing Time Value of Money; Profit Maximization *vs.* Wealth Maximization and Valuation of Securities. Some additional concepts have been discussed in this unit. Unit II covers Statement of Changes in Financial Position and Financial Statement Analysis, and Sources of Finance. It gives the various long-term, medium-term and short-term financing sources. Unit III covers long-term capital decisions with important concepts and techniques of capital budgeting, analysis of risk and uncertainty and the

Cost of Capital. New problems have been added for students. Unit IV is on Financing Decisions such as Operating and Financial Leverage, and Planning of Capital Structure of a company. This unit analyses different companies and gives an insight into Break-Even Analysis, Financial Indifference Point and the Importance of Operating Leverage and Financial Leverage. Unit V is on Dividend Policies and Decisions. Unit VI is on Management of Current assets. It discusses the concepts of Working Capital Management, Cash Management, Receivables Management and Inventory Management. Unit VII has been incorporated in this edition to cover the new strategies of companies in the Indian and International scenario. This Section covers Mergers/Amalgamations, Acquisitions and Takeovers.

I acknowledge with thanks the good wishes of my well-wishers, friends and students who have contributed by giving they feedback and remarks on the first edition of the book I would be failing in my acknowledgements if I did not thank my husband Raminder Singh who was very supportive while I was writing the book.

I am extremely thankful to my publishers, Mr. S. Saxena and Mr. J.R. Kapoor, for providing feedback on the first edition and inputs for the second edition. I am thankful to Mr. Verma for providing support and information of latest books and materials. I must thank my technical support. Mr. Brajendra who supported my project whole heartedly by working hard and typing the text.

Finally, I would also like to thank teachers of different universities and management institutes and in particular Delhi University for sharing their views and giving suggestions on new topics in the various chapters that they wanted me to cover in the third edition.

I also acknowledge students from different universities for giving me their feedback and suggestions on the second edition of the book. I am indeed indebted to my student friends who are now teachers in reputed universities and management institutes. They have been supportive and have offered their comments and suggestions for improvements and changes in the third edition.

Preeti Singh

Preface to the First Edition

This book is written for students of financial management. An attempt has been made to make it simple and clear to read and understand. It is a reference and guide to managers as basic financial management principles and concepts have been explained. After teaching at the undergraduate and graduate level, and given several talks in this area, to managers in training programmes, I put together my class notes and labour of many years. Works of many scholars and professors of repute are already in the market and I acknowledge their work with merit that it deserves as most of them in this area are known to me and I value and appreciate their work. Since I have taught this subject for many years and tried to understand the needs of the students, my effort is a small contribution to the world of financial management.

This book covers the subject in 14 chapters and 5 units. The subdivisions of the units are made according to the classification and coverage of the topic. It is a simple, student friendly book with many examples, solved illustrations, objective type questions important points and concepts of financial management.

It is a comprehensive coverage of all the basic concepts of financial management to suit the requirements of the B.Com, BBA, CA, ICWA, CS, MBA, M.Com and managers who are interested in the subject of financial management.

Unit I covers the basic concepts and provides an introduction to financial management by discussing time value of money; profit maximization *vs.* wealth maximization and valuation of securities. Unit II covers long-term capital decisions with important concepts and techniques of capital budgeting, analysis of risk and uncertainty and the cost of capital. Unit III is on financing decisions such as operating and financial leverage, and planning of capital structure of a company. Unit IV is on dividend policies and decisions. Unit V is on management of current assets. It discusses the concepts of working capital management, cash management, receivables management and inventory management.

I acknowledge with thanks the good wishes of my well-wishers, friends and students who have borne with me during the hours I toiled while writing this book. I spent 16 hours a day on the book. In writing the book I would be failing in my acknowledgments if I did not thank my husband Raminder Singh who has indeed been very patient with me and supportive while I was writing the book. I was encouraged by my son Madhukar in United States of America, trying to send me inputs and ideas and also gifting me with a Laptop to make my life easier. I appreciate and thank him for all his care and thoughts for my work. Thanks are also due to my Ladi behna, who deserves this mention for her support and understanding, during my difficult moments.

I writing this book I am inspired by Prof L.C. Gupta Director, Society for Capital Markets Research and Development. I would like to thank Prof J.D. Aggarwal, Chairman Indian Institute of Finance for his library support and valuable suggestions and Dr. Sunil Sharma from the faculty of management studies Delhi University who gave me valuable inputs in book writing.

I am extremely thankful to my publishers M/s Ane Books India, Mr. Verma who introduced me to them, Mr. Sunil Saxena and Mr. J.R. Kapoor, who called up every week to find out about my health and progress of the book. I must thank my technical support Mr. Pramod Roy who helped me throughout with the typing and all kinds of running around and errands related with the book.

Finally, I would also like to thank teachers of different universities and management institutes and in particular Delhi University for supporting me in writing this book.

I also acknowledge all students who have continuously shown interest in the subject while teaching them and those student friends who are now teachers in reputed universities and management institutes. I welcome suggestions and comments by all readers and students.

Preeti Singh

Abbreviations

A

ARR Average Rate of Return

C

CA Current Assets
CAPM Capital Asset Pricing Model
CCD Compulsory Convertible Debenture
CE Certainty Equivalent Approach (CE)
CF Cash Flows
CFAT Cash Flow after Taxes
CL Current Liabilities

D

DDB Deep Discount Bonds
Depr. Depreciation
DPS Dividend per Share
DFL Degree of Financial Leverage
DOL Degree of Operating Leverage
DCL Degree of Combined Leverage

E

EBIT Earnings before Interest and Taxes
EPS Earnings per Share

F

Firm Company (synonymously used)
FL Financial Leverage

G

g Growth Rate

I

IRR Internal Rate of Return
I_{rf} Interest Free Rate of Risk

K

k_d Cost of Debt
k_e Cost of Equity
k_p Cost of Preference Capital
k_o Overall Cost of Capital
k_r Cost of Retained Earnings

M

MP Market Price

N

NWC Net Working Capital
NPV Net Present Value Method
NP Net Proceeds

O

OCD Optionally Convertible Debenture

P

P/E Price Earnings Ratio

PAT Profit after Tax

PB Payback Method

PBT Profit before Tax

PI Profitability Index

R

RADR Risk Adjusted Discount Rate

ROI Return on Investment

RV Redeemable Value

S

SLM Straight Line Method

T

TV Terminal Value

V

VBM Value Based Management

VC Variable Cost

Vu Value of Unlevered Firm

VL Value of Levered Firm

W

WC Working Capital

WDV Written Down Value

WMCC Weighted Marginal Cost of Capital

WACC Weighted Average Cost of Capital/Overall Cost of Capital

Y

YTM Yield to Maturity

Contents

PART III LONG-TERM CAPITAL DECISIONS

PART IV FINANCIAL DECISIONS

PART V DIVIDEND DECISIONS

PART VI MANAGEMENT OF CURRENT ASSETS

PART I

Understanding Financial Management Concepts

1 Basic Concepts of Financial Management

LEARNING OBJECTIVES

1.1 Introduction
1.2 Principles of Financial Management
1.3 Evolution of Financial Management
1.4 Scope and Functions of a Financial Management/Manager
Economic Value Added (EVA), Corporate Valuation Approach, Value Based Management
1.5 Financial Decision Making
1.6 Objectives of Financial Management
1.7 Problem of Agency Costs
1.8 Risk-Return Dimension of Financial Management
1.9 Financial Management and Financial Accounting
1.10 Financial Management and Other Areas of Study
1.11 Financial Environment

1.1 INTRODUCTION

Financial Management is concerned with raising of funds, creating value to the assets of the business enterprises by efficient allocation of funds. It is the study of the integration of the flow of funds in the most optimum manner to maximize the returns of a firm by taking proper decisions in utilizing the funds. This means that the raising of funds should involve a low cost and bring about a good return. Good financial management is essential to bring about economic health of a business enterprise. Financial management consists of decision making within a firm. It works in the environment of 'money and capital markets' and it is concerned with investments. Thus the three major interconnected areas of finance are:

- Money and Capital Markets
- Investments and Portfolio Management
- Financial Management

Financial management is recognized as a very important branch of management. It has broad-spectrum activities and it is continuously concerned with producing an adequate return on a company/firm's investments. Financial management is a dynamic subject and is responsible for operating a company efficiently. Traditionally, financial management subject was treated with a very narrow function but now the modern concept of financial management has wide coverage. It has turned into a subject for bringing about analysis, planning and controlling of funds. Financial management has to work among conflicting goals of liquidity and profitability in a company. Financial management covers different functional areas in a firm. It has to be part of supply function, production function, distribution function and personnel function. Financing management evolved traditionally with the approach of raising of funds for an enterprise. The modern approach to financial management consists of dealing with managerial problems both of long term and day-to-day nature of the company. Some of its functions include determining of financial requirement of a firm, determining sources of funds, financial analysis, establishing optimum capital structure, profit planning and control, project planning and evaluation and corporate taxation. Financial management is thus the subject for financial decision making of a corporate organization. The important decisions have been classified as dividend decision, financing decision and investment decision.

1.2 PRINCIPLES OF FINANCIAL MANAGEMENT

Financial management is based on the following important principles:

(*i*) **Risk and return:** Every financial decision has two aspects these are 'risk and return'. Every decision involves a risk. This risk may be broad spectrum or market risk, which is uncontrollable. It can be unsystematic risk, which is specific to the firm and can be controlled. The degree of risk will become different in each case depending on whether it is controllable or uncontrollable risk. Financial management decisions are taken to optimize returns through the calculations of risk and return.

(*i*) **Time value of money:** It refers to the mathematics of finance for calculating future values and present values of cash. Time value of money evaluates cash flows expected to be generated at different times. It is the timing of cash flows because money received today is worth more than the amount received at a future date.

(*iii*) **Cash flow concept:** Financial management is based on the inflows and outflows of cash. It does not deal with non-cash items like depreciation, amortization of preliminary expenses. It uses cash revenues and cash-expenses to find out the return on its investments. Its approach is different from the accounting concept where the return is measured by profits earned by the firm on its investments.

(*iv*) **Incremental cash flow analysis:** Cash flows are measured of those proposals, which are an addition to the already existing projects. This concepts help in judging whether the new project is good for the firm. It also helps to assess the additional working capital required and cash flows associated with the new proposal. The feasibility in terms of costs and benefits can be considered.

(*v*) **Wealth maximization:** Maximization of shareholders wealth considers all cash flows pertaining to futures decisions. It is the concept based on cash flows to measure the economic value of a firm. Profit maximization may be considered as a part of wealth maximization. It can be said that maximization of shareholders wealth is the objective of financial management. Very often profit maximization is compared with wealth maximization.

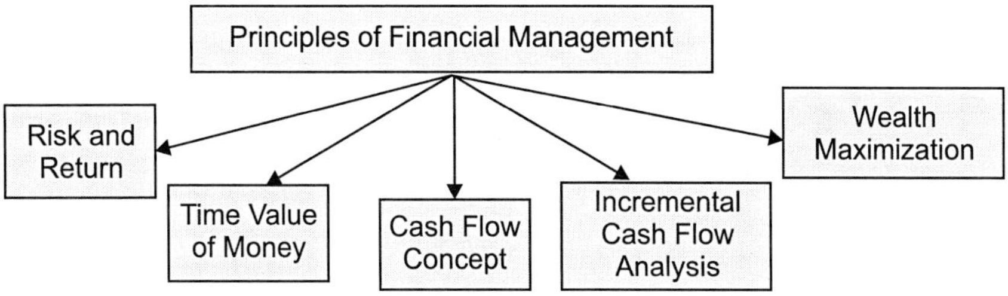

Fig. 1.1 Principles of Financial Management

The principles of financial management can be recapitulated as:

- **Risk and return**
- **Time value of money**
- **Cash flow concept**
- **Incremental cash flow analysis**
- **Wealth maximization**

1.3 EVOLUTION OF FINANCIAL MANAGEMENT

The evolution of financial management can be discussed under two distinct approaches—the traditional approach and the modern approach. The evolution of the subject started in the 20th Century. It can be divided into two periods. The traditional phase was from 1920 to 1950 and the modern phase that began in 1950. The traditional phase was called the 'outsider looking approach' and the modern phase is called the 'insider looking approach'.

Financial management was a part of economics, it began to grow into a distinct study as business began to grow and the functions of business required practical operational activities for managing cash, preparing reports and record keeping.

Traditional Approach

(*i*) **Procurement of funds:** This approach was concerned with the procurement of funds through an analysis of financial instruments, institutions and sources of funds.

(*ii*) **Outsider looking approach:** It had a limited scope because its emphasis was on the supplier of funds. It only considered the interest of the outsiders and there was no emphasis on the investment of funds.

(iii) **Capital budgeting:** The attention given by financial management was towards the procurement of funds for long-term use. Working capital was not considered at all. It ignored the day-to-day financial problems. Thus the scope of financial management was limited.

(iv) **Financial instruments:** The traditional approach considered the importance of procuring funds for the firm. Its function for procuring funds was through the issue of financial instruments like equity share, preference shares and debt securities.

(v) **Status of the subject:** Financial management was not part of the managerial functions. It was operational in nature, limited to preparing accounts, reports and procuring funds. Financial decision making was not part of the function of the subject tools and techniques that had not been developed.

Modern Approach: The modern approach to financial management gave the subject increased responsibilities and brought about an integrated and analytical scope of finance. The scope of finance was not only to cover the procurement of funds but also to the use of funds. This gave great importance to the subject. The following aspects show the coverage of financial management in the new role after 1950.

(i) **Integrated Finance Function:** Finance as a subject is a study of capital markets and institutions. It also covers security markets and studies security analysis and portfolio management. It has developed techniques for acquiring and investing funds in trading and manufacturing firms, covers fund management of government, profitable and non-profitable social oriented institutions like educational institutions, hospitals, clubs and non-government organizations (NGOs). It also provides coverage to international fund flow management, foreign exchange and risk management.

(ii) **Management Function:** Finance is no longer an outsider looking approach. It deals with decision-making process of a firm. It covers the allocation of funds not only in long-term usage but also in day-to-day routine matters. It deals with the three decision-making areas called investment decisions, financing decisions and dividend decisions.

(iii) **Status:** Finance has become a managerial position. Financial management has been conferred with the special position for obtaining funds as well as for their efficient allocation. It has become the lifeline of a firm. The work of a firm can be carried out only if the financial manager approves of an activity of expenditure. It is thus called an insider looking approach with the goal of wealth maximization of the shareholder.

(iv) **Techniques:** Modern financial management covers tool and techniques of evaluation in the following areas:

(a) ***Capital Budgeting:*** The techniques in capital budgeting are required for setting up a new project. These techniques are for long-term decisions and involve the techniques of calculation of the best project through payback period average rate of return, net present value, profitability index and internal rate of return.

(*b*) ***Cost of Capital:*** This technique helps in establishing the cutoff rate on investments made by the firm to reduce cost of capital and find optimum capital structure.

(*c*) ***Leverage*:** Operating and financial leverage assess risk of the firm. It also helps to increase the return to the shareholder.

(*d*) ***Working Capital*:** Working capital consists of day-to-day and short-term decisions involving cash, receivable and inventory management. Modern financial management for optimum utilisation of funds provides models, theories, concepts and practical applications.

1.4 SCOPE AND FUNCTIONS OF A FINANCIAL MANAGEMENT/MANAGER

Financial management is concerned with the integral part of management. It has the role of (*a*) Identifying the needs for funds and selecting the sources from which the funds can be obtained and (*b*) to use the funds in the business effectively by controlling it. The functions of financial management can be categorized as bringing about liquidity, profitability and proper management of funds. The functions of financial management are discussed here:

(*i*) **Liquidity of funds:** A financial manager has to match inflows and outflows and thus create liquidity continuously by managing the flow of the funds of the firm continuously. He has to plan the external borrowings by finding out the requirements. He has to ascertain the internal resources and raise funds from external sources for both long-term and short-term requirements.

(*ii*) **Profitability:** A financial manager is required to measure the cost of capital raised by him as a source for the funds of the company because cost of capital is linked with profitability of a company. He has to control costs in all operational areas of the company through costs control systems and costs accounting methods. The manager as a part of his duty formulates pricing policies, sales policies and marketing policies to bring about profitability in the company. He should continuously forecast future profits of the company and evaluate methods adopted to bring about profitability.

(*iii*) **Management:** The functions of a financial manager are to coordinate different activities of the company. The long-term and short-term requirements of the company have to be analysed, planned and controlled and the use of funds have to be justified. He has to be sure that the funds that he has acquired are functional, sufficient and economical. He must administer the funds in such a way that there is both profitability as well as liquidity in the firm. In all, he has to take an integrated approach for managing the funds of the company. While doing his tasks coordination with other department's like—production, marketing, sales and human resources is necessary.

(*iv*) **Balance conflicting goals:** Financial management has the scope of:

(*a*) ***Profitability and liquidity*** in a firm. The financial manager finds these conflicting goals. Cash does not have any return and if a firm increases its liquidity it will reduce its profitability. On the contrary if all the funds are invested, there will be no liquidity and this will also reduce profitability. In many situations, a financial manager faces the challenge of balancing the conflicting goals of profitability and liquidity. In a situation where an investment is profitable but the funds are locked for long periods of time, the financial manager may not take the option. The financial manager may consider this situation as risky because funds are locked up. The financial manager has to cope with the dilemma of his choice between profitability and liquidity. In this way he has to coordinate between difficult situations. The financial manager has to visualize the overall corporate goal.

(*b*) Conflict may also arise in the area of ***profit maximization and wealth maximization***. Profit maximization would be a measure of attaining profit in a firm and wealth maximization would consider the effect of earnings per share and dividends to shareholders. The objective of wealth maximization would be fulfilled by increasing the market price of shares through decisions on future cash flows, dividends and earnings per share. To maximize profits the financial manager may have to consider issues like—retained earnings, non-payment of dividends, investing funds in profitable outlets. The finance manager has to try and maximize profits without in any way affecting the shareholders wealth because the primary goal of financial decision making is to achieve wealth maximization.

(*c*) The third area of conflict is the decision to be taken regarding ***risk and return***. Return is required to maximize the market price of the share but return is associated with risk because the greater the return, higher the expectation of risk. Although high risk would be compensated with high return, the financial manager has to take the decision very carefully. He has to consider the risk of different financing patterns. He has to take a decision of a combination of risk and return where according to him it reaches the optimum level for the firm. Thus he has to balance his decision between risk and return.

(*v*) **Identification of groups:** The financial management has the scope of financial decision making for a large group of people. This group consists of shareholders, debt investors, employees, customers, suppliers, public, government and management.

The functions of the financial manager are to take decision to coordinate the interests of all the groups named above. The shareholders interests are primarily of priority and the financial manager has to take decisions to increase the wealth of the shareholders. The debt investors have provided funds to the company and they must be protected. Their interest should be paid in time. The employees of the company must be given their salaries in time and the financial manager should also provide schemes for employee welfare. The customers and suppliers should also be provided with proper policies of discounts on timely payment, commissions and payment terms should be clear. In the modern day management, the public interest has also to be considered because cost and benefit analysis is required for all new projects. Government has to be paid taxes and its policies have to be adhered. The management has to be apprised by the financial manager of the financial aspects of the company. However all these decisions have to be taken with the primary motive of providing the shareholders in maximizing their wealth? Hence their interest has to be protected by taking the important decisions of investment decision, financing decision and dividend decisions. The important aspect of financial decision making is discussed in the following section.

(*vi*) **Economic value added (EVA):** In order to maximize the goal of wealth maximization, a financial manager has the important function to create economic value to the organization. EVA is a financial tool, which provides to the organization knowledge of how much value the company is adding above the total cost of capital. It is also a performance measurement that accounts for changes in share values. The financial manager has the function of adopting EVA because 'EVA' makes managers act like shareholders. It is the true corporate faith for the 1990s[1]. EVA will provide the company after tax profits from operations minus the cost of all capital employed to produce those profits. If the financial manager uses EVA it will help all corporate decisions. EVA brings about financial discipline in a company. It will harmonize decisions to maximize the wealth of the firm. The financial manager may as a measure of performance also function to find out the return on equity, market, capitalization, and earnings per share by adding the concept of *Market Value Added*[2] *(MVA).* This works in close nexus to the economic value added concept. This concept shows the management the increase or decrease in the value of the capital through this principle the finance manager will be able to make the conflicting areas of conflict of the shareholders, debt investors and manager complementary.

(*vii*) **Corporate valuation approach:** This approach is used for estimating the economic value of a corporate organization. It also projects the market value of a company's financial assets and liabilities. The process is useful in analysing investments, planning for long-term horizon or investments of high volume and for valuing a business for merger or amalgamation.

The valuation techniques are used in taking long-term decisions of capital budgeting. This approach is also used for financial reporting, taxation and in cases of dispute.

It values the firm's price multiples. It calculates ratios of price to earnings or price to book values to value the firm by comparing prices of other companies.

Valuations are undertaken on a specific date like the end of the accounting quarter or year. It estimates the current value of assets or liabilities for the purposes of managing portfolios and associated financial risk. It is calculated by taking certain assumptions.

---

[1] Shawn Tully (1993, The Real Key to Creating Wealth, *Fortune 128,* no. 6, September: 38)

[2] Anne B. Fisher (1995, Creating Shareholders Wealth, *Fortune 132,* no. 12, December: 105,106)

It is a process and a set of procedures which calculates the worth of the company. Ratio analysis is done to find out whether stock is undervalued or overvalued. The discounted present value is used to value the going concern especially when a company is faced with financial stress or is planning to acquire another company.

Financial management also uses financial statements for projecting cash flows and estimating cost of capital. It considers valuation effects of capital structure and values equity shares, bonds and other securities.

There are three corporate valuation approaches to measure the value of an organization. These are asset approach, market approach and income approach.

(*a*) **Asset approach**

The asset approach considers the assets and liabilities to determine the value of the business. It determines the value of each asset and deducts the liabilities. This approach is complex because it is difficult to find out which assets and liabilities should be included in the valuation process.

(*b*) **Market approach**

This approach values the work of the business as it is in the market according to the fair market value.

(*c*) **Income approach**

This approach is based on discounting of cash flows. First the business income stream is projected over a future period of time then the discount rate is applied to reflect the risk. Finally the residual or terminal value is calculated to get the present value of the business. Therefore, a corporate organization values its business based on cash flows and risk. Valuation of securities is done to calculate the value of equity, preference and debt of the company.

Valuation approach is the general way which is followed to determine a value indication of a business, business ownership interest, security, or intangible asset using one or more valuation methods to do the same.

(*viii*) **Value Based Management (VBM):** It focuses on decision making at different levels in an organization. It determines the value of a company by its discounted future cash flows. Value is created when a company invests in capital and the return is greater than the cost of capital. This model focuses on analysing a company's management processes for decision making on the basis of value to the company. It is a measure of managing the balance sheet and income statement and balancing short and long-term perspective of a company. It brings about improved economic performance.

The focus of VBM is not on methodology to be used. It should be based on changing the corporate culture. It is useful in using valuation as a performance metric and decision-making tool.

VBM would provide a financial manager with the information to quantify and compare the value of alternative strategies and the incentive to choose the value-maximizing strategy. Such an incentive is created by specific financial targets set by senior management, by evaluation and compensation systems that reinforce value creation, and—most importantly—by the strategy review process between manager and superiors. In addition, the manager's own evaluation would be based on long and short-term targets that measure progress toward the overall value creation objective.

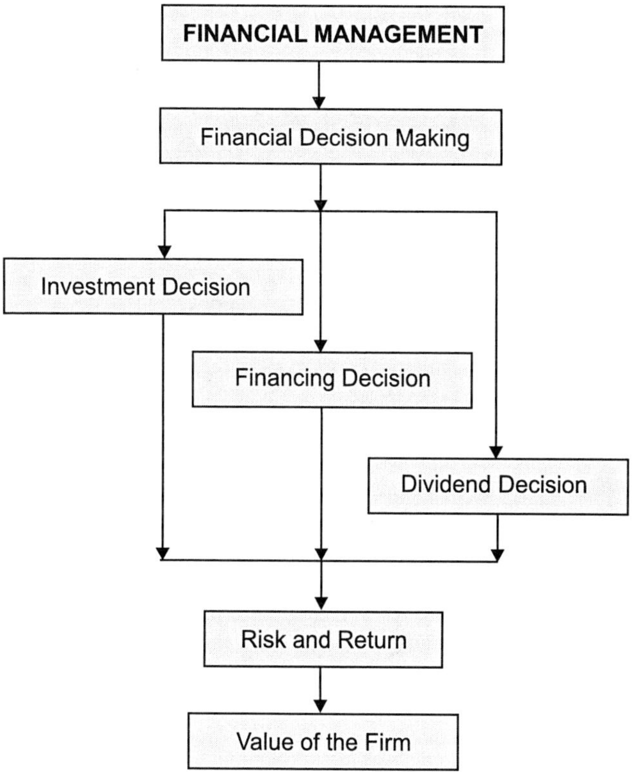

Fig. 1.2 Financial Management – Decision Making

1.5 FINANCIAL DECISION MAKING

Financial management is the study of the process of financial decision making. An organization should be effective in its management process to create and expand its operations. Financial Management is the art and skill of developing techniques to create effectiveness in this process. The decision-making process consists of ***investment decisions, financing decision and dividend decisions.***

Investment Decisions

Investment decisions deal with long-term and short-term finances of a firm. These can be termed as fixed assets and current assets. The long-term process covers the area of ***Capital Budgeting***. These decisions cover the firms budgeting for a vast outlay of funds and for long-term periods like 10 years or more. The fixed assets are cost intensive and the profitability of the firm depends on the composition of fixed assets. The financial manager has to be very careful in his decision-making process in the purchase of the assets. The decisions of the financial manager should be such that the purchase of the asset is at the correct price and useful for the organization because these decisions are irreversible. The cost is high and it is of long-term usage. The financial manager has to apply the techniques of capital budgeting to select the right project and then to apply the funds so that there is optimum allocation. Capital budgeting techniques have been discussed in chapters 7 and 8.

Short-term financing refers to the day-to-day coverage and usage of techniques for cash flows, inventory management and bills receivables and payments on a day-to-day basis. Financial management policies bring about effectiveness in managing such finances to maximize the amount used by a firm in its business practices. This is called ***Working Capital Management***. Financial manager has to take decision to be sure that there is adequate working capital in the firm. He has to see that liquidity is maintained and at the same time profitability of the firm is maximized. Chapters 14–17 of the book deal with working capital management.

Financing Decisions

Financial management also deals with financing issues, such as making the business profitable, by analysing break-even points, fixed costs and variable costs. This will not only help in assessing whether a company has been able to cover its costs but will also be useful in making future decisions when new projects or expansions of the operations is desired. This part of financial management is analysis of a company, through earnings before interest and taxes, variable costs, contribution. It is called a study of *Operating Leverage*. To complement this section the earnings per share to be given to shareholders is analysed through the techniques of *Financial Leverage*. When a study of both these aspects is made together, it is called *Combined Leverage*.

The techniques of financial management in a company can be usefully applied only when the capital structure is effectively constructed. Some of the questions relating to this aspect are how much ownership capital and what is the debt portion on the company's capital structure? That is equity capital *vs* debt. These are guided by capital structure theories. A study of capital and debt on the company's structure is called *Capital Structure Management*. The financing decisions to be taken by the finance manager are covered in chapters 10 and 11.

Dividend Decisions

Financial management is also applied to the requirement of the shareholders. It is concerned with the amount of profit that can and should be withdrawn to declare dividends to the owners of the capital of the company or the shareholders. The profits of the company have not only to be paid as dividend but also to be retained by the company as reserves. Dividend decision making is analysed in chapters 12 and 13 of the book. The financing manager has to take a decision as to whether all profits should be distributed or only a proportion should be paid as dividend. He has to determine the optimum dividend pay out ratio; he also has to take decision relating to bonus issues and interim dividend.

To quote Ezra Solomon (1969), "The function of the financial management is to review and control decisions to commit or re-commit funds to new or ongoing uses."[3] The techniques of capital budgeting, working capital management, financing decision, capital structure management are streamlined into three basic decision-making areas. These are called:

- Investment Decisions
- Financing Decisions
- Dividend Decisions

1.6 OBJECTIVES OF FINANCIAL MANAGEMENT

The objectives of financial management are:

(*i*) To have an efficient organization through proper sourcing and utilizing of funds.

(*ii*) To optimize the use of assets to maximize the profitability of the company.

(*iii*) To maximize wealth of the shareholder.

Profit Maximization

Profit maximization is concerned with appropriate selection of assets and its optimum utility thereof. An organization must be profitable to be an economic entity. Profitability shows efficiency and proper allocation of firm's resources. Thus profit maximization is measure of a firm's performance as it is a yardstick to measure the efficiency of a firm. It is a barometer which provides important financial information to help management in expansion and diversification programmes of a company. It also indicates the efficient use of funds and thereby it attracts investors to invest their savings in the firm. Profit maximization does not fulfil the complete goal of financial management. It has certain limitations.These are:

- Profit maximization concept ignores time value of money.
- The term 'profit' is not clear. Is it accounting profit or after tax profit? Would it be gross profit or net profit? Or is it indicative of earnings per share?
- It concentrates on profitability and it does not include the financing aspect.
- It does not analyse risks.

---

[3] Ezra Solomon—*Theory of Financial Management,* Columbia University Press, New York, 1969.

- It analyses the firm's utilization of resources rather than the interest of the shareholders. It does not reflect time value of money.
- Profit maximization is an accounting concept and does not consider the aspects of maximizing shareholders wealth. It does not show the internal position of the firm/company.

Maximisation of Shareholders Wealth

The shareholders wealth is reflected in the market value of its share. The shareholders economic value is the dividend that he receives presently and the future dividend benefits and capital appreciation of the share. In other words, the market price of the share is a present value of all the future cash flows in terms of benefits and dividends expected from the firm.

The market price of the share can be optimized by the three important decisions of the financial manager relating to the investment decisions, financing decisions and dividend decisions. These decisions are taken through the cash flow concept of finding out the present value of the share.

Wealth maximization has the advantage of considering the time value of money, which is the basic principle of financial management. The time value of money is considered by compound value calculations to find out future value of the shares and discounting to find out the present value of the share.

Wealth maximization concept measures risk and uncertainty. The value of the firm's share is measured through the net present value. This removes any doubt about the concept of risk, which is useful to understand the market value of the share. Thus wealth maximization can be considered to be consisting with the objective of maximizing owner's wealth.

Profit Maximisation *vs* Wealth Maximization

Profit maximization is an attempt to judge the performance of a firm by the profit that it is able to earn. It has a number of limitations because it looks into a firm's earnings but does not consider the shareholders earnings per share or any returns in the form of dividends paid to the shareholders. Therefore, profit maximization reflects the income of the firm but does not give any attention to the shareholders earnings. The wealth maximization objective recognizes the importance of shareholders' wealth by considering the decisions, which covers investment, financing and dividend decisions. It is a comprehensive term and includes profitability without which there can be no distribution of dividends. Wealth maximization is thus considered as the goal of financial management.

This discussion can be summarized in the following way:

- Profit maximization is important to judge and analyse the economic viability of a firm.
- Profit maximization is an important concept but profitability is an ambiguous term as it does not define whether the efficiency of the firm should be considered in terms of operating profit or net profit.

- It ignores the concept of time value of money.
- It considers the profit concept, but not the cash flow concept.
- The wealth maximization concept is a comprehensive term to include timing benefits, cash flow concept, as well as risk and return.
- The wealth maximization concept analyses the earnings per share, present and future dividends to be given to shareholders thus giving an indication of the maximum utility of the wealth of the shareholders.
- Wealth maximization is universally accepted due to the fact that it is able to achieve the objectives of a firm and take decisions to favour owners, institutions, employees and equity shareholders.

The objective of wealth maximization with profitability in a company has to be within the concept of risk and return. There is a relationship between return of an investment and risk associated with it. Returns should be expected after considering the different kind of risks surrounding in the market and the risks profile of an investor. Risk and return is the subject matter of Chapter 3 but being an important aspect of a study of financial management a basic introduction of risk is explained in this chapter.

Profit maximization is the narrow objective of financial management because profit is a test of economic efficiency but wealth maximization is comprehensive objective of financial management, it goes beyond the quantitative aspects as it also considers the qualitative benefits in a firm. Wealth maximization objective is therefore superior to the profit maximization concept.

1.7 PROBLEM OF AGENCY COSTS

We have discussed the concept of wealth maximisation and profit maximization. Therefore this appears to be for the benefit of the shareholders. However, in practice there are many conflicts that arise out of the conflict in the interest among different groups of people in a corporate organization. The conflicts are normally between shareholders who are the owners of the company/firm, the creditors of the firm and the internal management such conflicts cause problem of agency and costs are involved in such conflicting situations.

The shareholders expect that the maximum benefit should be in their favour. The debt-holders such as debenture holders of the company, banks and financial institutions giving long-term loans have given their funds and expect certain standards of financial discipline from the company. Any violation of principles of finance or borrowing in excess of the company's capacity creates a rift with the creditors of the company.

The management requires high perquisites for their work and involvement in company matters. Shareholders are in conflict with managers if their interests are not protected or the managers are more interested in increasing value to themselves rather than in creating profits or maximizing the wealth of the shareholders. They have been appointed for the welfare of the shareholders and they are answerable for any misdeeds and incorrect foresight in making the correct type of investments.

The company has to monitor the activities of the shareholders, debt-holders and management for proper utilization of resources suitable for all the three groups of people. This agency problem creates the costs of continuous evaluation and modifications in projects to get the best results.

Risk and Return—Basic Concepts

Risk is defined as the variability of the actual returns from expected returns associated with a given investment. Decisions taken by a finance manager relating to investment, financing and dividend have all to observe the maximum return on the money invested in the market presuming that risk-less decisions are not possible to achieve. Risks on investments like bank deposit are considered to be quite safe, but rates of interests can change depending on the policy of the Reserve Bank of India. Investments of a firm have a much higher degree of risk as they are surrounded by market risk, which is quite uncontrollable because they are broad spectrum depending on market forces. Certain risks, which pertain to individual firms problems, are controllable. A firm is surrounded by both controllable and uncontrollable risks which make its investments risky compared to government securities or bank deposits.

Return is associated with gain or loss on money invested in the market. The return is expected to be high when an investor purchases an equity share in the market, but such a return is associated with high risk. Government securities have a stable return but the return is very low. The investor has to pay the price of loss of interest or return when he wants to secure his investment.

A finance manager has to take a decision in investing the firm's funds in such a way as to optimize return and minimize risk. This combination is called the *risk return trade-off*. This is the level where the market price of a share is maximized. The balance brought about by matching risk and return helps in achieving the objectives of financial management which consists of wealth maximisation.

The financial manager has to find out the combination of risk and return in different areas of investment. In the case of capital budgeting projects, a financial manager has to choose the best project. The best project is that which gives the most attractive return. This has to be selected from a vast array of projects by using different capital budgeting techniques specially those of the *net present value and internal rate of return.* While choosing the projects it would not give the correct picture unless the financial manager considers an element of risk that he is surrounded with.

The financial manager has to take decisions relating to return while making arrangements for an issue of *equity capital and debt*. Debt is considered to be a low cost compared to equity capital. Debt capital increases the burden on the firm since it has to be returned. The decision of risk return trade-off is very important because financial risk increases with debt. There is a high risk associated with issuing equity capital as a return has to be earned for the owners of the company who have invested their capital trusting the firm's business. Thus the financial manager has to constantly consider risk and return in the *cost of capital decisions.*

Working capital management are decisions to be taken by the financial manager for running the business. These are decisions to be taken everyday in the normal course of business and involves a constant analysis of cash management, receivables management and inventory management. These decisions are crucial to the working of the business. If the decisions on risk and return are taken carefully, business will flourish. Business can fail if this decision is not taken rationally. Cash management involves a firm's liquidity position. If idle cash is maintained, then the firm will lose interest and also profitability or return. If cash is short for the firms running and maintenance, it will lose its reputation and also profitability. In both the situations, risk and return will have to be carefully calculated.

Working capital management also deals with credit sales. A firm cannot establish itself with profitability unless it enhances its sales. This is possible only through credit sales. A financial manager will have to take decisions as to whether he would like to sell and get immediate cash or sell on credit to increase sales in the firm. Credit sales involve delay in payments, bad debts and reduce profitability. Cash sales may reduce profits due to low sales. Thus the manager is surrounded with risks whether he takes cash policy or decides in giving credit. He has to take a decision to balance the returns with the risks in sales.

A financial manager is also surrounded with risk and return decisions while maintaining inventory of a firm. A high amount of inventory will lead to increased costs of maintaining the inventories but it will be a situation of low risk. However, if the firm is low on inventory it can lose the chance of making gains because of stock out position. The manager has to be careful in evaluating risk and return and taking the correct decision.

The relationship of risk and return also extends in taking decisions relating to dividends. Equity shareholders are the owners of a firm and they expect a return from the firm for the capital invested in it. The financial manager is faced with the objective of giving a good return to their shareholders. This is possible if he takes proper decisions for minimizing risk by trying to obtain funds for running the business at minimum cost and by reducing risk. The risk return trade-off is thus a continuous game, which the financial manager has to conduct to make a company profitable and to achieve wealth maximization for its shareholders.

The financial manager tries to reduce risk by understanding the risk environment. Risk consists of *systematic and unsystematic* exposures. Systematic risk is uncontrollable because it arises out of economic reasons backed by sociological and political factors in a country and they have an influence on the market conditions. Such risks are called 'market risk' and 'interest risk' and 'purchasing power risk'. Unsystematic risk pertains to the behaviour pattern or internal influences of a firm. These are controllable risks and can be minimized. An analysis of the risks influencing the investment decisions returns can be maximized. Risk can be minimized by analysing situations and using techniques of probability distribution, coefficient of variation and correlation of different factors of risk. Thus the manager should continuously balance his decisions of risk and return to get potential gains at minimum risk.

Financial management is also related to other areas of management and accounting. Its relationship with different branches of study is now discussed.

1.8 FINANCIAL MANAGEMENT AND FINANCIAL ACCOUNTING

Financial management and financial accounting have traditionally been expected to carry on similar functions. The modern concept in which financial management has developed brings about the fact that both financial management and financial accounting resemble each other. They are complementary, yet two different areas of study. Accounting is a resource or an input to financial management decisions. The financial accounting subject uses financial statement like balance sheet, profit and loss account; fund flow and cash flow statements are used to project to the public the profitability of the firm to ensure a good reputation of the firm. The same statements are used in financial management for taking decisions relating to investment, financing and dividends to reach the goal of wealth maximization. This is the complementary nature of both the subjects. It is often stated that the accounting manager is responsible for providing information to the finance manager.

Financial accounting and financing management have the following relationship:

(*i*) **Cash flow approach:** The financial accounting provides the value of a firm at a point of time. The information is given in the income statements and balance sheet of a firm. The financial management is a continuing process in providing value to the firm. It is based on cash flow approach or record of income and expenses are based on actual amounts received and paid. Accounting recognizes a sale or a purchase of goods when they are incurred and not when they have been paid. Thus a financial manager recognizes only cash inflows and cash outflows.

(*ii*) **Time value of money:** The accounting concept does not consider compounding and discounting techniques for finding out the value of the money. It provides the profits of the firm and also gives the assets and liabilities of a firm. It leaves the decisions of finding out the value of money in a time period as a decision area to be achieved through financial management concept.

(*iii*) **Treatment of funds:** Financial management emphasizes the cash flow approach to arrive at cash flows. It does not consider non-cash flow items like depreciation, amortization of preliminary and other expenses. In order to arrive at accounting profits these items are taken to find out accounting profits in financial accounting. It is often said that though finance and accounting are different they are compatible and complementary in nature as financial management begins when accounting ends. The accounting tools are an input to financial decision making.

(*iv*) **Activities:** A financial accountant is concerned with collection and presentation of financial data. The financial manager is responsible for decision making which is related with planning the finances in such a way that it brings about maximization of wealth of the shareholders. Accountancy is concern with information on profitability. Financial management deals with decision making relating to the broad spectrum of wealth maximization. The activities though different complement each other.

1.9 FINANCIAL MANAGEMENT AND OTHER AREAS OF STUDY

Financial management draws a relationship with many areas of study. It is related to economics, marketing, human resources management and production management.

(*i*) **Financial Management and Economics:** Financial management is closely related to macro and microeconomics. Financial management and macroeconomics are concerned with money and capital markets, financial intermediaries, banking system, monetary credit and fiscal policy. Macroeconomics prepares policies relating to the financial environment. The financial manager works and prepares policies for firms and other institutions depending upon the monetary and fiscal policies. He has to take financial decisions within these policies. He also has to make changes in his financing decisions if there are changes in macroeconomics policies.

Microeconomics consists of concepts and theories relating to supply and demand, price, profitability and profit maximization strategies. Financial decisions have to continuously evaluate price of a product, sales revenue and financing decisions of a firm. Thus it works in a complementary manner with both macro and microeconomics. A financial manager should have a good knowledge of economics. In fact financial management branched into its own discipline from economics.

(*ii*) **Financial Management and Marketing Management:** A financial manager has to play an integral part in marketing management of a company. He has to take financial implications of selling goods and services to its customers. He also has to participate in providing good credit and discount policies for customers to pay in time. He has to be part of advertisement budgets, brands, patents as it affects the liquidity position of a firm.

(*iii*) **Financial Management and Human Resources Management:** The financial manager of a company is constantly working towards profitability and wealth maximization of shareholders. This is possible only if the right number of people are working in the firm. Since the personnel department recruits, trains and places the staff, the financial manager works with them evaluating manpower. The financial manager has to provide financial implications on pay scales, incentive schemes, training programmes and employee's welfare programmes. Thus financial management and human resource department are connected with each other. Financial implications have an important bearing on recruitment and retaining policies of human resources in an organization.

(*iv*) **Financial Management and Production Management:** Financial management is also concerned with the production department in a firm. The production department procures material, machineries, spares and consumables it requires inventory, which is consistent because inventory has a 'cost of carrying' and 'cost of not carrying'. The financial manager has to work with the production department to determine the right quantity of materials to ensure smooth working in the department. Since materials are a large part of the production departments the financial manager has to support the department through preparation of policies. He has to provide a policy for economic order quantity of materials and the right storage through maximum level, re-order level and minimum level of stock. The financial manager also has to constantly make financial policies and their implications on decision-making areas like capacity utilization, replacement of machines, installation of safety systems and increase in production capacity to enhance sales.

Financial management is thus closely related to financial accounting, economics, marketing, human resources and production management.

1.10 ORGANIZATION OF FINANCE FUNCTION

Financial management is related to all the departments of a firm. It has to prepare financial policies for the working of a firm. All firms recognize its importance. Financial management function is now part of top management of the firm. On the board of directors there is usually a vice president or a director of finance. The finance function consists of the work of a controller and a treasurer. The vice president of finance looks after both the controlling function and the function of the treasurer. The controller function consists of making policies, evaluation and review relating to tax management, cost accounting management, credit administrating, investments and banking.

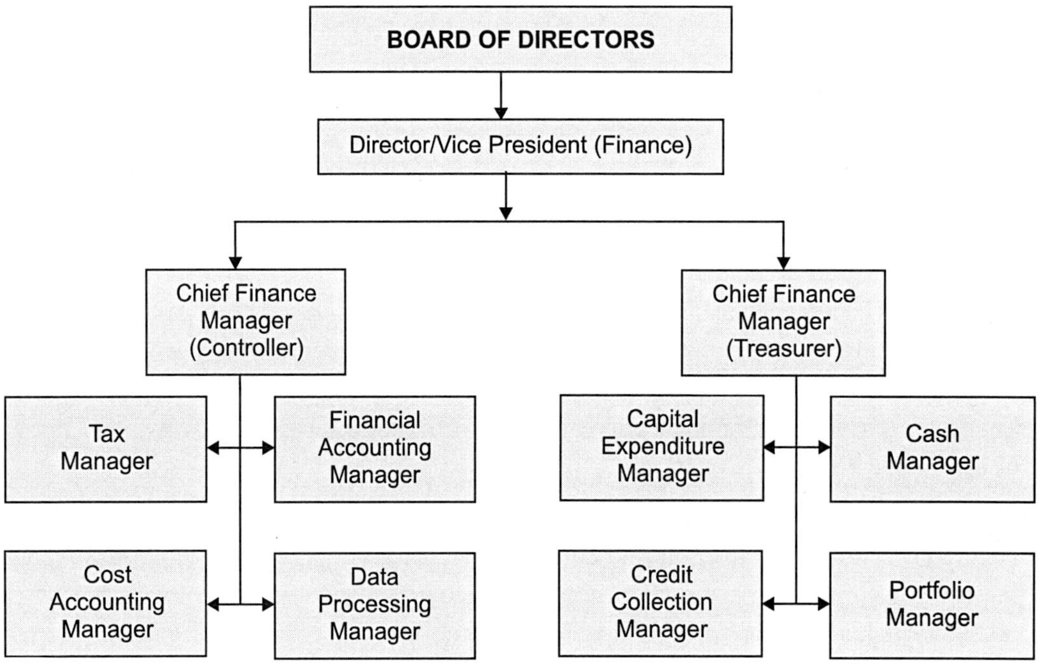

Fig.1.3 Organization of Finance Function

The treasury function of the vice president/director finance consists of financing planning and fund raising, cash management, credit management and foreign exchange management. Planning and fund raising is an important because it consists of providing a good cash balance and matching of cash inflows and cash outflows to meet liquidity requirements of the firm. It helps to maintain good relations with investors as well as shareholders. The treasury function also involves interaction of the firm with capital market and financial markets. Figure 1.3 shows the organization of the finance function.

The financial managers have to take a decision to satisfy various groups of people. The financial decisions cover the shareholders who have invested their funds in the firm. The primary concern has to be for the shareholders. Financial decision making also has to be responsible to government and pay the firm's taxes regularly. The financial manager is surrounded by those agencies from which funds have been borrowed by the firm. This category would cover both individuals and organizations providing funds. Thus the finance function is that of responsibility towards debt investors. Financing decisions have to be such that policies are satisfactory for the customers and suppliers of the firm. This will add value to the firm by enhancing its reputation. Financial decision-making thus affects shareholder, government agencies, customers, creditors and debtors of the firm and the general public. The finance director is responsible for taking decisions to suit the requirement of all these groups of people and institutions.

The finance function also covers functional areas such as marketing, human resources and production. The responsibility of the director in charge of fiannce is immense. He has many functions to perform. Thus a finance director has many finance managers working under him but these managers are sub-divided into treasury functions and controlling functions. Each manager looks after one of these functions. The ultimate authority is that of the finance director who makes policies on the basis of continuous review and evaluation.

1.11 THE FINANCIAL ENVIRONMENT

The financial environment is the interconnected group of financial institutions markets and instruments. This environment involves the transformation of savings into investment.

Financial Markets

There are three important segments of financial markets namely, **capital market, money market and government securities market.** The capital market is a market for long-term financial assets comprising the new issue market and the stock market. The new issue market is a primary market where financial instruments are sold for the first time. The stock market is the secondary market where the sale and purchase of securities and financial instruments are undertaken after they have been placed in the new issue market. The financial instruments in these markets consist of shares, bonds and debentures. The Securities Exchange Board of India (SEBI) regulates these markets and financial instruments.

The short-term financial market in India is the ***money market***. It has two segments. These are the market for formal and informal transactions. The formal markets have the Reserve Bank of India (RBI) as an important participant coupled with commercial banks, financial institutions, mutual funds and non-banking financial institutions. This market has RBI as its controller as it regulates transactions relating to treasury bills, inter-bank call money, commercial bills of exchange and inter corporate deposits. It has a control through reserve requirements and regulation of interest rates. This market is safe in its transactions but has very low rates of interest.

The informal segment of the money market has traditionally dominated the formal sector. These consists of moneylenders and chit funds who charge very high rates of interest but because of their flexible terms are able to attract people who require funds for short terms.

The government Securities Market is known for its gilt-edged securities. This means that the securities are as pure as gold because of their nature of safety. In this market trading takes place mainly of securities and loans of Central Government, state government and other government authorities. The participants in this market are commercial banks and provident funds. It is not able to attract other participants because of its low rate of interest.

Financial Assets

Financial investments consist of ownership securities debt securities and mutual fund units. Ownership securities consist of equity shares. Another type of security is the redeemable preference share in which the rate of dividend is fixed. It resembles the equity share as well as a debt. It is called a hybrid security.

Debt securities are debentures (Non-convertible), convertible debentures, deep discount bonds, bonds issued by financial institutions.

Mutual fund securities represent instruments for channellizing the savings of individuals. Mutual funds securities are called units. They have income schemes, growth schemes, equity schemes and money market schemes.

Financial Intermediaries

Financial intermediaries help in the process of flow of funds from savers to investors in an economy. They consist of a network of institutions in India. At the apex is the Reserve Bank of India. It frames monetary policies and has a large number of commercial banks, which help in the process of intermediation. The other financial intermediaries are the life insurance companies, general insurance companies, mutual funds, pension funds and the post offices. Financial institutions transform direct claims into indirect claims by purchasing primary securities and issuing their own secondary securities to the public. Savers deposit their funds with financial intermediaries and they lend to the ultimate investors.

The Indian Financial system has the following intermediaries:

Underwriters	Lead Managers
Share Brokers	Depositories
Portfolio Managers	Investment Bankers
Credit rating agencies	Mutual Funds
Investment Companies	Registrar and share transfer agents

The controlling agency in India is the Securities Exchange Board of India (SEBI).

POINTS TO REMEMBER

- Financial management is the processing of decision making for maximum utility of a firm/company's resources.
- The principle of financial management consists of cash flow approach, risk and return, incremental cash flow analysis and time value of money.
- It takes decisions for short-term and long-term funds to provide value to money invested in a firm.
- Financial management is complementary to important areas of study like—accounting, economics, marketing, production and human resources.
- Financial management was traditionally called the outsider looking approach. Its objective and functions were limited but in the modern approach it is called the insider looking approach, which includes all areas of internal working for providing maximum utility to the wealth of the shareholders.
- The objectives of financial management include profit maximization to achieve wealth maximization.
- The functions of financial management/manager consists of liquidity of funds, profitability, management, balance conflicting goals, identification of groups and to incorporate latest techniques of EVA and MVA.
- The financial manager has to take important decisions regarding investment decision, financing decision and dividend decision.
- The finance function is organized through a financial manager covering controlling functions and treasury functions.
- Financial management works within the financial environment consisting of financial markets, institutions and financial assets.

OBJECTIVE TYPE QUESTIONS

State whether the following statements are true (T) or False (F).

1. The traditional approach of financial management was 'insider looking' and modern approach is 'outsider looking'.
2. The financial manager has important decisions relating to long-term funds only.
3. The objective of the financial management is to maximize the wealth of the shareholder.
4. Risk and return must be balanced in a financial decision-making process.
5. Profit maximization approach considers the time value of money.
6. Financial management is related to accountancy, economics and marketing.
7. Accounting is an input for the use of financial management.
8. Economic value added is an important concept useful in financial management practices.

Answers: 1. (F), 2. (F), 3. (T), 4. (T), 5. (T), 6. (T), 7. (T), 8. (T)

THEORETICAL QUESTIONS

1. What are the three important decisions that a financial manager has to take for maximizing the value of the shareholders?
2. Discuss the objectives of financial management in the modern day usage.
3. Financial management is more than a procurement of funds. What do you think are the functions of the financial manager?
4. "Wealth maximization is only a decision criteria and not a goal." Comment.
5. "Wealth maximization is superior criteria compare to profit maximization." Discuss.
6. Write notes on the following (*a*) scope of financial management, (*b*) functions of financial management (*c*) organization of finance function (*d*) difference between accounting and financial management.
7. "The financial manager has the role of balancing conflicting goals." Discuss.
8. What is the financial environment within which the financial manager has to function?
9. Discuss the principles of financial management.
10. "A financial manager does not have any role to play in a software company." Discuss.
11. "The concept of finance function has changed and keeps changing along with the evaluation of the content of finance as a business management activity." Elucidate.

12. "Financial management is concerned with solutions of three major decisions a firm must make: investment decisions, the financing decisions and dividend decisions." Explain this statement highlighting the inter-relationship among these decisions.
13. "Investment, financing and dividend decisions are all interrelated." Comment.
14. "Growth is a realistic objective of a joint stock company for financial decision making." Comment.
15. Explain the concept of 'profit maximization' and 'wealth maximization'. Which of these is better operational guide for finance manager?

❑❑❑

2 Time Value of Money

LEARNING OBJECTIVES

2.1 Concept and Relevance of Time Value of Money
2.2 Compounding Techniques
2.3 Compound Value
2.4 Present Value Discount Approach
2.5 Practical Applications of Time Value of Money

This chapter discusses one of the important principles of financial management. The previous chapter introduced the concepts of financial management and how it is applicable in different decision-making areas like investment, financing and dividends. A financial manager has to continuously take a decision on purchases and re-placement of assets. He has to make a comparison of different proposals to find out that which is most useful in the firm in which he is operating. To take these decisions he has to analyse inflows and outflows of cash. These are not comparable because the timing of their occurrences is different. When analysing a project the financial manager may find that some projects give a good return in the beginning while others may be giving a better return on a later date. These cash flows can be made comparable through the use of time value of money.

2.1 CONCEPT OF TIME VALUE OF MONEY

Time value of money covers a wide range of applications. It can be used to take personal and corporate decisions. It provides an insight to questions of savings. It provides answers to taking decisions relating to bank deposits, purchasing a car or house, retirement plans, interest earned, interest paid on loans, dividends earned, price appreciation, depletion of investments value and replacement of assets. Time value can be said to be an explanation on the value of money as it is today and what can be earned after a few years. Time value of money is analysed because the value of money keeps on changing. Most people think that money has a much greater value today than the amount of money that is received at a later date. If the money received at a later date is compensated by receiving a higher amount at the end of the period than it is today. The investor will be indifferent to the amount that he receives today or at a later date. For example, if a person has Rs. 1,00,000 now and if he receives Rs. 1,00,000 after one year he would prefer to posses the money now. If however, Rs. 1,00,000 now brings about the opportunity of Rs. 1,10,000 after one year he will begin to think how much he gains or loses by postponing the receipt of money today. This additional amount of Rs. 10,000 is due to the presence of interest or the time preference rate of money. The juggling of funds to earn a rate of interest, which an individual requires, is called the ***mathematics of finance.*** The time preference of money is usually because of a rate of interest. The individual will try to receive a compensation for the postponement of his receipt of money. He will also have some risk attached to postponement. His required rate of return is called ***the opportunity cost of capital*** and has the components of risk free rate plus risk premium. The importance of time value of money is to make calculations to adjust cash flows received in the future and those received at present by comparing amounts received at different times at a common date. This is called ***future value (FV) and present value (PV)*** comparison.

Time value of money is based on three important aspects. These are: (*i*) compensation for uncertainty (*ii*) preference for present consumption (*iii*) the re-investment opportunity.

(*i*) ***Compensation for Uncertainty:*** An individual is keen to possess money in the present date because he is certain that the money with him is liquid. The future is full of uncertainties. The person who takes the money may not return it in time or a creditor becomes insolvent or inflation may reduce the value of money. For these reasons money is preferred at a current date.

(*ii*) ***Preference for Present Consumption:*** Many people feel that money received today can provide the acquisition of goods and services that they require for their needs. At a future date they may not be able to purchase goods because of risk in the market or due to inflation.

(*iii*) ***The Re-investment Opportunity:*** The relevance of possessing money currently is a justification for investing funds whenever he can earn a higher amount. If an individual has an availability of cash he can determine alternative opportunities to re-invest his funds in those available outlets, which provide a good rate of interest. This is explained through the time value of money. The concept of future value (FV) and present value (PV) is explained next.

2.2 FUTURE VALUE AND PRESENT VALUE

It has been explained earlier that all cash flows concerning future values (FV) and present values (PV) can be adjusted to a common date when money received is compared at different periods of time. A common denominator must be arrived at to compare them. To explain time value of money a common example is taken of cash sales and credit sales. The price, which is received for cash sales, is usually lower than that on credit sales. The person who pays cash usually gets a discount because money received today has a higher value than that which is received in future. The money received today is at the beginning of the period and is called present value or money received in time period (0) zero. The amount received in credit sales is after a gap and may be called future value or time period (1) one. An example may be given of a Honda City Car. If it is purchased in cash it would be Rs. 6,50,000 if it is purchased on credit then the seller would expect an interest rate of a minimum of 10 per cent. Again it depends on whether the money will be received at the end of year 1, 2, 3 or 5 years. This is the future value and the seller has to see what his required rate of return is. He will obviously not like to sell the car at the original price, which he has offered, to the purchaser if he was to pay immediately. The question as to what would be the present value of the future cash flow will be answered through the present value analysis. In case the seller wants to find out the amount of money that he will receive in the future it will be called the 'future value analysis'. The future value (FV) is called the 'compounding technique' and the present value (PV) is the discounting technique of time value.

2.3 COMPOUND VALUE

Compound value of money is analysed by:

(*i*) Annual compounding

(*ii*) Multi-period compounding

(*iii*) Compound value of an annuity

(*iv*) Compound/Future value of annuity due

(*v*) Compound value annuity for sinking funds

(*i*) Annual Compounding

The compound value is the future value (FV) of money. This is calculated for a single cash flow or for a series of cash flows. The future value (FV) consists of the present value (PV), the rate of interest and the number of years for which it is invested. The formula for future value is as follows:

$$FV = PV(1 + i)^n$$

Where,

FV = Future value

PV = Present value

i = rate of interest

n = number of years

Example 2.1 Most decisions involve more than one period. Assume that the required rate of an investor is 10%. In this case an investor would like to receive a minimum of 10% increase in his investments. He is indifferent to Rs. 100 now or Rs. 110 at the end of year (1) one. This investor may want to find out his investment return if he was to keep it for 2 years instead of 1 at 10% return value. This would be Rs. 121 after 2 years. The following will be the formula for year 1, 2 and 3.

Solution

Ist Method

$$FV = PV\,(1 + i)^n$$

$$FV = 100\,(1 + 0.10)^1 = \text{Rs. } 110$$

And for year 2 it will be = $FV = 100\,(1 + 0.10)^2 = \text{Rs. } 121$

IInd Method

This can also be depicted through the following chart.

			Rs.
0 Period (PV)	:	Principal amount in the beginning	100
		Interest for the year (Rs. 100 × 0.10)	10
Year 1		Principal at the end	110
Year 2	:	Principal amount in the beginning	110
		Interest for the year (Rs. 110 × 0.10)	11
		Principal at the end	121
Year 3	:	Principal amount in the beginning	121
		Interest for the year (Rs. 121 × 0.10)	12.10
		Principal at the end	133.10

Therefore, compound value of Rs. 100 deposited today and interest compounded annually for a period of 3 years would be as follows.

> ***Note*:** Calculations through the compound value table become easy for an investor, as he would like to compute for longer periods of time. Manual calculations as shown in the above chart will take a long time to calculate.

Example 2.2 If an investor deposited Rs. 10,00,000 @ 8% rate of interest for 5 years. Calculate the amount he would receive at the end of the period.

Solution

Table A-1 shows the factor @ 8% interest for 5 years to be 1.469.

The future value will be

$$FV = 10{,}00{,}000 \times 1.469 = \text{Rs. } 14{,}69{,}000$$

It can be calculated through compound value table (A-1) in the Appendix.

The compound value factor is 1.110 for 1 year = 100 × 1.110 = Rs. 111

The compound value factor is 1.210 for 2 years = 100 × 1.210 = Rs. 121

The compound value factor is 1.331 for 3 years = 100 × 1.331 = Rs. 133.10

(*ii*) Multi-period Compound Value

Compound value can be calculated for more than one period in a year. It can be calculated semi-annually as well as quarterly. This means that the rate of return will become higher if it is compounded quarterly or semi-annually if the nominal interest rate is 12% per annum. But it is compounded semi-annually so that the effective rate of interest would become higher as the interest will be calculated after every 6 months.

For example if you make a deposit of Rs. 10,000 for 10% rate of return compounded semi-annually the amount of return would be:

Interest = Rs. 10,000 × 10% × ½ = Rs. 50

Now for the next 6 months it will accumulate to Rs. 10,500 × 10% × ½ = Rs. 525

= 10,500 + 525 = 11,025

The effective rate of return will be (500 + 525)/10,000

= 10.25%.

Example 2.3 Multi-period compounding can be done through Table A-1. This is done by multiplying the number of times that has to be compounded with. For example if a company pays an interest of 10% compounded semi-annually on 5 year deposit on Rs. 10,000; then what will be the total amount compounded after 5 years?

Solution

$$\text{Future Value (FV)} = \text{Rs. } 10{,}000 \left(1+\frac{0.10}{2}\right)^{5\times 2}$$

= Rs. 10,000 $(1.5)^{10}$ compounding factor of 1.5 for 10 years @ 10% rate of interest = 2.594 (factor from Table A-1)

= Rs. 25,940

Thus the formula that can be used for computing the compounded value of a sum of money in case of multi-period compounding is the following:

Future value $$\text{FV} = \text{PV}\left(1+\frac{i}{m}\right)^{nm}$$

Where,

FV = Future value

PV = Present value

i = Interest rate

n = Number of years

m = Number of compounding per year

Compound value can be found when funds are deposited and the accumulated value is required. This is called compound value of an annuity. Table A-2 in the Appendix is provided for calculating the amount of an annuity.

(*iii*) Compound Value of an Annuity

Investors deposit single amounts and require an accumulated value at the end of the period. This is called 'compound value calculations'. Some investors may desire to put small amounts periodically and require an accumulated sum of money after a certain period. To calculate cash flows deposited at different periods of time annuity tables are useful. The compound value of an annuity can be calculated if certain conditions are satisfied. When the same amount is deposited with the same interval at the end of the period compound value or future value (FV) of an annuity can be found out. To illustrate we go through an example (Example 2.4).

Example 2.4 Mr. X invests Rs. 1,00,000 every year and with an interval of 12 months regularly at the end of each year. The cash flows are equal and the intervals are regular. The interest that he expects is 10% and the number of years of deposit is 5 years. Find out the accumulated value at the end of the period.

Solution

Graphically it can be shown in the following way:

Compound Value of an Annuity at 10% Interest for 4 Years

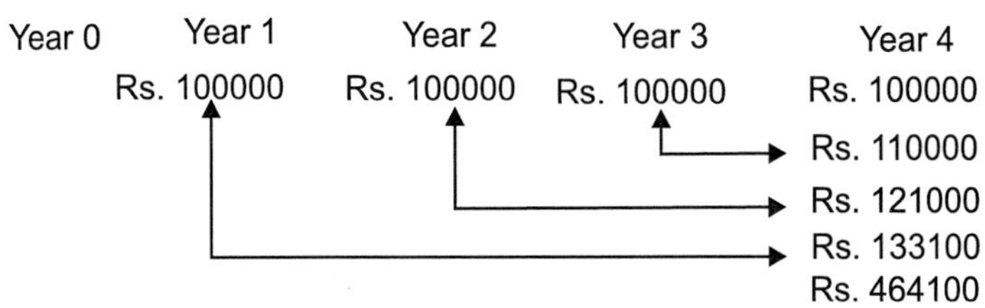

This table is compounded manually to find out its future value. The value of the annuity would be Rs. 4,64,100 at the end of 4 years if Rs. 1,00,000 is deposited every year at the same interval.

This can also be calculated through the short cut method by using Table A-2 (Appendix) showing compound value annuity tables for different years at different periods of time. The formula will be as follows:

	FV	= Annuity amount × $CVAF_{ni}$
Where,	FV	= Future value
	Annuity amount	= Rs. 1,00,000
	CVAF	= Compound value annuity factor (Table A-2)
	n	= Number of years
	i	= Rate of interest

As per Table A-2, the compound value annuity factor is 4.641 at 10% rate of interest for 4 years.

Therefore, future value (FV) Rs. 1,00,000 × 4.641 = Rs. 4,64,100

> ***Note*:** Sometimes the manual calculation may differ with short-cut method found out through Table A-2. For example, if the 5th year calculation was made it would differ by Rs. 10 between manual method and short-cut method. Through manual method it will show Rs. 6,10,510 but by short cut method it would be 6.105 (factor) × Rs. 1,00,000 = Rs. 6,10,500. The use of tables is acceptable.

Annuities are of two kinds. When equal amounts, at equal intervals are deposited at the beginning of the year instead of at the end of the year, it is called an annuity due.

(*iv*) Compound/Future Value of Annuity Due

Compound value of annuity is a series of payments deposited at the end of the period. Compound value of an annuity due is deposited in the beginning of the year. When an amount is deposited in the beginning of the year the formula will be the following:

$$\text{Future value (FV)} = A \times CVAF_{ni}\,(1 + i)$$

$$\begin{aligned} \text{Where, FV} &= \text{Future value} \\ A &= \text{Annuity amount} \\ CVAF &= \text{Compound value annuity factor} \\ n &= \text{Number of years} \\ i &= \text{Rate of interest} \end{aligned}$$

Example 2.5 Mr. X deposits Rs. 1,00,000 at the beginning of each year and desires to know the accumulated value of his amount at the end of 4 years @ 10% rate of interest. Calculate the amount.

Solution

This is the calculation for the annuity due. Table A-2 shows the annuity factor to be 4.641, it will be calculated in the following way.

Since the deposits have been made in the beginning of the year logically at the end of the year the accumulation would be more than it is in the case of deposits made every year at the end of each year. Therefore in annuity due the interest for 1 more year is multiplied by $(1 + i)$:

$$\begin{aligned} FV &= A \times CVAF_{ni}\,(1 + i) \\ FV &= 1{,}00{,}000 \times 4.641\,(1 + 0.10) \\ &= \text{Rs. } 5{,}10{,}510 \end{aligned}$$

> ***Note*:** Example 2.4 showed the annuity value at Rs. 4,64,100 but the annuity due shows Rs. 5,10,510 because interest for 1 year is more than in annuity. The difference in approach in the two cases may be noted.

(*v*) Compound Value Annuity for Sinking Fund

Compound values annuity can be used for calculating instalments to be paid for accumulation of ***sinking funds***. This is explained in the Example 2.6.

Example 2.6 A company wants to create a sinking fund for terminating bonds after 10 years. It wants to accumulate Rs. 90,00,000 what amount should be deposited every year @ 10% rate of return?

Solution

$$FV = \text{Annuity amount} \times CVAF_{ni}$$

$$\text{Or, Annuity amount} = FV / CVAF_{ni}$$

The factor from Table A-2, for 10 years @ 10% rate of interest = 15.937

$$= \frac{90,00,000}{15.937} = \textbf{Rs. 564723.60} \text{ (approx.)}$$

> **Note:** The factor $1/CVAF_{ni}$ is called the sinking fund value factor. It is the reciprocal of the compound value of an annuity.

This amount should be deposited every year to get Rs. 90,00,000 after 10 years.

Time value of money can be applied to decisions relating to present value as well. The concept of present value is discussed ahead.

2.4 PRESENT VALUE (DISCOUNTING APPROACH)

Present value (PV) means finding out the value of money as it is today. The future value/compound value is the accumulated amount on a future date. The value of the amount was multiplied with the rate of interest on a future date. The present value is the reverse of compounding. To find out the present value the discounting approach is used. The present value is that amount of money, which is held at hand and can be used for earning and amount. The present value will be lower than the future value. The present value is useful in the following conditions:

- Present value (Annual discounting)
- Present value (Semi-Annual/Quarterly/Monthly) cash flows
- Present value of uneven cash flows
- Present value of an annuity
- Present value of an annuity due
- Present value for loan instalments
- Present value of perpetuity
- Present value of growing perpetuity
- Present value of a growing annuity

The compounding formula was FV = PV $(1 + i)^n$. The present value formula will be:

$$PV = \frac{FV}{(1+i)^n}$$

Where, PV = Present value

FV = Future value

i = Interest

n = Number of years

This is calculated through the present value tables for different rates of interest and time periods given in Appendix as Table A-3. To illustrate let us take an example (Example 2.7).

Example 2.7 Mr. X expects to receive Rs. 2,00,000 at the end of 3 years. What would be the present value if the rate of discount is 10%.

Solution

In Table A-3, the present value factor for 3 years at 10% is 0.751.

Rs. 2,00,000 × 0.751 = Rs. 1,50,200

This example very clearly shows that the present value of an amount is Rs. 1,50,200. If the person's expectation is 10% he will receive the amount of Rs. 2,00,000 if he invests it for 3 years. The present value will thus always be lower than the future value.

(*i*) Present Value of Uneven Cash Flows

While calculating present value an investor will find that cash flows are not always equal. Cash flows can be for an uneven series, for example the following illustration will explain an uneven series of cash flows.

Example 2.8 Mr. Priyanshu will receive Rs. 7,00,000 after 1 year; Rs. 6,00,000 in year 2; Rs. 8,00,000 in year 3 and Rs. 10,00,000 in year 4. What would be his present value at 8% rate of return?

Solution

This is a question of uneven cash flow stream. It will be depicted in the following manner:

Year	Amount (Rs.)	Factor @ 8% (Table A-3)	Present Value (Rs.)
1	7, 00,000	0.926	6, 48,200
2	6, 00,000	0.857	5, 14,200
3	8, 00,000	0.794	6, 35,200
4	10, 00,000	0.735	7, 35,000
			ΣPV = 25,32,600

This example can also be used to calculate simple things. For example, Mr. Inder wants to borrow Rs. 27,00,000 and pay Mr. Priyanshu Rs. 7,00,000; Rs. 6,00,000; Rs. 8,00,000 and Rs. 10,00,000 in the next 4 years. Mr. Priyanshu should not give the amount of loan if his expectation is 8% rate of return. If he calculates the uneven cash flows which Mr. Inder will return every year it will not fit in to Mr. Priyanshu's calculation because it is below the rate of interest that he expects to receive although the amount returned by Mr. Inder in 4 years is Rs. 31,00,000 against his borrowing of only Rs. 27,00,000 thus present values help in making decisions.

(*ii*) Present Value (Semi Annual/Quarterly/Monthly) Cash Flows

Present values can be calculated for shorter discounting periods. This means that decisions may have to be taken for periods of less than one year. Just like in the case of compounding in the discounting technique the number of time period increases and the discount rate decreases. To illustrate we go through an example (Example 2.9).

Example 2.9 Sanjay will receive Rs. 10,00,000 at the end of 4 years. Find the present value of this cash flow if the discount rate is 12% and discounting is done quarterly.

Solution

The formula for discounting for shorter periods is:

$$\text{Present Value (PV)} = \text{FV} = \left(\frac{1}{(1 + i/m)}\right)^{mn}$$

Where PV = Present Value

FV = Future Value

m = Number of times discounting is done per year

i = Discount rate

This is also calculated as PV = Rs. 10,00,000 × PVF_{nm} the present value factor can be found out from Table A-3.

When $i = 12\%$ and discounting is done quarterly it will become 16 times and at 3% rate of return. The Present Value (PV) factor from Table A-3 for 16 years at 3% rate of return is 0.623.

Therefore, Rs.10,00,000 × 0.623 = Rs. 6,23,000 is the present value if quarterly compounding is done.

(*iii*) Present Value Annuity

Present value can be calculated for annuities just like in the case of future value annuities. In order to find out the present value of an annuity, Table A-4 will be used to find out the factor. Present value annuities consider three important variables these are: annuity amount, rate of interest and the time period of the annuity. The present value of an annuity has an important role in applications. It can be used to determine annual cash flows to be earned to recover an investment. It is widely used in practical situation especially in capital recovery cases. To find out present value of an annuity the formula used is derived from the following equation:

$$PV = \left(\frac{1 - \dfrac{1}{(1-i)^n}}{i} \right)$$

PV = Annuity amount × $PVAF_{ni}$

(Present value annuity factor can be found from Table A-4 in the Appendix)

Where, PV = Present value

PVAF = Present value factor

n = Number of years

i = Rate of interest

This may be explained through Example 2.10.

Example 2.10 Mr. Asif deposits Rs. 70,000 annually for 5 years. He deposits the money at the end of each year. What is the present value of the annuity if the discount rate is 10%?

Solution

Value of this annuity is the sum of the present values of all the cash flows of this annuity.

$$PV = \text{Rs. } 70{,}000\left(\frac{1}{1.10}\right)^1 + \text{Rs. } 70{,}000\left(\frac{1}{1.10}\right)^2$$

$$+ \text{Rs. } 70{,}000\left(\frac{1}{1.10}\right)^3 + \text{Rs. } 70{,}000\left(\frac{1}{1.10}\right)^4 + \text{Rs. } 70{,}000\left(\frac{1}{1.10}\right)^5$$

Solution

On simplifying PV = A × $PVAF_{ni}$ (taking the factor from Table A-4 for 5 years @ 10% rate of return = 3.791)

Therefore, PV = 70,000 × 3.791

= Rs. 2,65,370

(*iv*) Present Value Annuity Due

Present value annuity due is when an amount is deposited in the beginning of each year instead of at the end of the year at equal intervals and equal amount of money. It will be dealt within the same manner as in the case of the compound value annuity dues but the answer will be multiplied with $(1 + i)$.

Example 2.11 If Asif was to deposit Rs. 70,000 every year in the beginning of each year for 5 years @ 10% rate of return, the same formula will be used as in the case of the present value of annuity except with a minor adjustment because the amount has been deposited in the beginning of the year for this year interest will be paid to Mr. Asif. Therefore the answer will be multiplied with $(1 + i)$.

Solution

This is explained as follows:

PV = A × $PVAF_{ni}$ $(1 + i)$

= Rs. 70,000 × 3.791 (1 + 0.10)

= 2,65,370 × 1.10

= Rs. 2,91,907

Since it is a question of annuity due, Mr. Asif's present value will be higher than in an annuity. This is because he receives 1 more year's interest by depositing the amount in the beginning of the year.

(*v*) Present Value for Loan Recovery Instalments

The present value of an annuity is useful when a loan is taken and to repay the loan a specified instalment is to be calculated. This is called ***amortization or capital recovery.***

Example 2.12 Mr. Ali borrowed an amount of Rs. 10,00,000 which he has to return @ 14% rate of interest. What would be the amount of instalment that he would pay, if it were repaid in 10 equal instalments?

Solution

For this take Table A-4 or present value of an annuity factor. The factor is 5.216.

The annual amount = total amount to be repay/$PVAF_{ni}$

Annual amount = 10,00,000/5.216 = Rs. 191717.80 (approx.)

Note: 1/$PVAF_{ni}$ is called *capital recovery factor.*

(*vi*) Present Value of Perpetuity

Perpetuities calculate the value of a fixed income for each year continuously the annual rate of return on perpetuity is calculated in the following manner:

$$\text{Return} = \frac{\text{Cash Flow}}{\text{Present Value (PV)}}$$

Or, $$PV = \frac{CF}{i}$$

Where,
PV = Present value
CF = Cash flows
i = Rate of interest

This can be explained through a practical application.

Example 2.13 A person wants to plan for his retirement. If the rate of interest in a deposit is 8% and if he wants to receive Rs. 1,00,000 a year perpetually what would be the sum that he should deposit with the bank today?

The annual rate of return on perpetuity is equal to the annual payment divided by the present value.

Therefore, $$PV = \frac{\text{Cash Flow}}{\text{Interest}}$$

Or, $$PV = \frac{1,00,000}{0.08} = \text{Rs. } 12,50,000$$

(*vii*) Present Value of Growing Perpetuity

In a growing perpetuity a series of cash flows at periodic intervals, consisting of different amounts and for an infinite period continue to take place. The relationship of cash flows is drawn from the fact that there is a specific growth in each period of time. For example, cash flows of year 2 will be higher than year 1. This is possible when we assume that the rate of return is greater than the growth rate. The simple formula for calculating this is as follows:

$$PV = \frac{\text{Cash Flow}}{(i - g)}$$

This can be seen in the Example 2.14.

Example 2.14 A company is planning to declare a dividend of Rs. 3 at the end of the first year. If the rate of interest is 12% and it is expected to grow @ 10%, find out the present value of the growing perpetuity.

Solution

$$\begin{aligned} PV &= \text{Cash Flow}/\ (i - g) \\ &= \text{Rs. } 3/(0.12 - 0.10) \\ &= 3/0.02 = \text{Rs. } 150 \end{aligned}$$

(*viii*) Present Value of a Growing Annuity

A finite series of equal cash flows at equal intervals that grow at a constant rate in every period is called a growing annuity. When rate of interest equals growth then the present value of the growing annuity will be calculated through the following formula:

Solution

$$PV = \frac{CF_1 \times n}{(1+i)}$$

$$\begin{aligned} PV &= \text{Present value} \\ CF_1 &= \text{Cash flows at the end of period 1} \\ n &= \text{Life of annuity} \end{aligned}$$

> **Note:** This is calculated only when the rate of return is equal to the growth or $i = g$

Example 2.15 Mr. X wants to deposit Rs. 10,000 for the first year and every year the amount will increase by 8%. If the rate of interest is 8% this deposit will continue for 10 years, then what would be the present value of this annuity?

Solution

$$PV = CF_1 \frac{n}{(1+i)}$$

$$= \text{Rs. } 10{,}000 \times \frac{10}{(1 + 0.08)}$$

$$PV = \text{Rs. } 92592.59$$

> **Note:** Calculation for growing perpetuities in this manner is not possible when rate of return is not equal to growth. In this case the following formula will be used:
>
> $$PV = \frac{CF_1}{1-g}\left[1-\left(\frac{1+g}{1+i}\right)^n\right]$$

Example 2.16 An investor has to take a decision on a scheme offered by a bank. The scheme is for 5 years. He would be required to deposit Rs. 5,000 at the end of year 1 and in subsequent years at a growth rate of 10%. Find out the present value if the rate of interest is 15%.

PV = Present value

CF_1 = Cash flows at the end of period 1

n = Life of annuity

Rs. 5,000/(0.15 – 0.10)[1 – $(1.10/1.15)^5$]

= 5,000/0.05 [0.1993]

= 1, 00,000 × 0.1993

= Rs. 19,930

> **Note:** Table 2.1 provides the formulae for compound values and present values. It presents in a nutshell all the formulae that have been explained in the previous examples.

TABLE 2.1: Compounding and Discounting Formulae at a Glance

Purpose	Given	Calculate	Formula
Compound value of a lump sum	PV	FV	$FV = PV(1 + i)^n$
Compound value of an annuity	A	FV	$FV = A\left[\frac{(1+i)^n - 1}{i}\right]$
Sinking fund	FV	A	$A = FV\left[\frac{i}{(1+i)^n - 1}\right]$
Present value of a lump sum	FV	PV	$PV = \left(\frac{1}{(1+i)^n}\right)$
Present value of an annuity	A	PV	$PV = A\left(\frac{(1+I)^n - 1}{i(1+i)^n}\right)$

Contd...

Contd...

Capital recovery	PV	A	$A = PV\left(\frac{i(1+i)^n}{(1+i)^n - 1}\right)$
Present value of a perpetuity	A	PV	$PV = \frac{A}{i}$
Compound value of an annuity due	A	FV	$FV = A\left(\frac{(1+i)^n - 1}{i}\right)(1+i)$
Present value of an annuity due	A	PV	$PV = A\left(\frac{(1+i)^n - 1}{i(1+i)^n}\right)(1+i)$

2.5 PRACTICAL APPLICATIONS OF TIME VALUE OF MONEY

A financial manager can use time value of money for taking decisions in different situations. He has to understand how to use the compounding and discounting techniques. He also has to remember the difference between simple interest and compound interest. Decisions of the financial manager can be in many situations but the common type of decisions are to provide sinking funds, capital recovery decisions, deferred payments, annuities, projecting implicit rate of interest and ascertaining the growth of an amount in different periods of time. Some examples are discussed ahead to provide the use of time value of money:

(*i*) Implicit Rate of Return

It is important to calculate the rate of return that would actually be received by an investor. A finance company may offer a certain return.

Example 2.17 If a person invests Rs. 10,00,000; he will receive Rs. 1,00,000 for the next 15 years. The investor would like to know the rate of interest that he is receiving.

Solution

The following formula will be used to find out the rate of interest:

$$PV = \text{Annuity amount} \times PVAF_{ni}$$

Step 1:

$$10{,}00{,}000 = 1{,}00{,}000 \times PVAF_{ni}$$

$$PVAF_{ni} = 10{,}00{,}000/1{,}00{,}000 = 10$$

Step 2: See present value annuity from Table A-4; closes to interest corresponding to 10. The interest rate is approximately 5% for 15 years (Value shows 10.380).

Therefore the investor should take this scheme only if 5% rate of interest is acceptable to him.

Example 2.18 Implicit rate of return technique can be applied in the case of an amount to be received in future. Mr. Raju pays Rs. 10,000 on a bond, which will mature after 6 years. The amount received at the end of the period would be Rs. 40,000. What would be his implicit rate of return?

Solution

$$\text{FV} = \text{PV} \times (1 + i)^6$$

$$\text{FV} = \text{PV} \times \text{CVAF}_{ni}$$

$$40{,}000 = 10{,}000 \times \text{CVAF}_{ni}$$

$$40{,}000/10{,}000 = 4$$

Use Table A-2 for CVAF. The value 4 may be found for 6-year period at 26%. Therefore the implicit rate of interest works out to 26%.

(*ii*) Determination of Number of Periods

The future value can be used to find out how much a sum of money will grow at a given rate of interest.

Example 2.19 An investor deposit Rs. 50,000 and expects to receive Rs. 1,00,000. The deposit that he is interested in provides a 10% interest compounded annually. How many years should the amount be deposited to arrive at Rs. 1,00,000?

Solution

$$\text{FV} = \text{PV}\ (1 + \text{I})^n$$

$$1{,}00{,}000 = (1 + 0.10)^n$$

$$1{,}00{,}000/50{,}000 = (1 + 0.10)^n$$

$$2 = 1.10^n$$

In Table A-1 look for the value closest to 2 at 10% rate of interest. The values closes to 2 are between 7 years and 8 years. At 7 years, he will receive 1.949 × 50,000 = 97,450 for eight years he will receive 2.144 × 50,000 = Rs. 1,07,200. Hence the investor should aim at depositing the money for 8 years.

(*iii*) Deferred Payments

In some cases loans are given with interest but it is expected that the first repayment start after a few years.

Example 2.20 Mr. X takes a loan of Rs. 5,00,000 at 10% interest. He has to return the loan, which begins 5 years from now. What should be the annual payment if the return of the loan with interest is to be paid in eight equal instalments?

Solution

This is the question of deferred payments. The payment amount begins 5 years from today.

Step 1: Find out the amount due at the end of 4 years or in the beginning of the 5th year from now.

$$FV = PV\,(1 + i)^{n}$$

$$FV = 5{,}00{,}000(1 + 0.10)^{5}$$

$$FV = 5{,}00{,}000\,(1.10)^{5}$$

$$FV = \text{Rs. } 8{,}05{,}255$$

For calculating the annual instalments the amount of loan would be Rs. 8,05,255.

Step 2: From Table A-4 find the factor @ 10% for 8 years. The value is 5.335.

Therefore, the amount to be paid in eight equal instalments is 8,05,255/5.335 = Rs. 150938.14

(*iv*) Sinking Fund

An example of sinking funds has been explained in this chapter. Another example is given for more clarification, as this is an important application in corporate decision making.

Example 2.21 A manager wants to retire bonds of Rs. 50,00,000 at the end of 5 years. What is the amount that he should deposit every year at 10% rate of interest to receive Rs. 50,00,000 after 5 years.

Solution

$$FV = \text{Annuity amount} \times CVAF_{ni}$$

Or, $\text{Annuity amount} = FV/CVAF_{ni}$

Table A-2 shows the value of $CVAF_{ni} = 6.105$

$$\text{Annuity amount} = \frac{50{,}00{,}000}{6.105} = \text{Rs. } 819000.82$$

This amount should be accumulated every year to get a sum of Rs. 50,00,000 @ 10% rate of interest.

(*v*) Capital Recovery

This application as explained helps to find out the annual amount of instalment that a person would have to pay to redeem his amount of loan with interest.

Example 2.22 Amrita borrowed Rs. 8,00,000 to be repaid after 5 years @ 10% per annum. Find out the instalment amount.

Solution

$$PV = \text{Annuity amount} \times PVAF_{ni}$$

From Table A-4 find the value of PVAF for 5 years at 10% rate of interest.

$$\text{Annuity amount} = PV/PVAF_{ni}$$

The PVAF factor from Table A-4 = 3.791

Annuity Amount = 8,00,000/3.791 = Rs. 211026.11. This is the instalment to be paid every year for 5 years for recovery of loan.

This chapter has discussed time value of money and its applications on practical situations. The next chapter will discuss Risk and Return, and Basic Concepts of Valuation of Securities.

POINTS TO REMEMBER

- Time value of money is an important principle of financial management.
- Time preference for money is due to uncertainties or mismatching of cash inflows and outflows.
- Individuals prefer cash ***now***, rather than at future ***period*** money has a time value, rupee today is more valuable than a rupee received later.
- The two most important techniques in time value of money are compounding and discounting. The compounding technique shows future value and can be calculated by the use of FV = PV $(1 + i)^n$. The discounting technique shows present value which can be calculated through PV = FV $(1+ i)^n$
- Time value of money is used for practical applications to find out solutions to annuities, capital recovery, sinking funds, deferred payments, instalments and EMIs and all future and present values.

OBJECTIVE TYPE QUESTIONS

State whether the following statements are true (T) or false (F).

1. Money has a time value.
2. Compounding technique shows present values.
3. The mathematics of finance consists of rate of interest and number of years.
4. Investors have a preference for present money.
5. An infinite series of periodic cash flows growing at a constant rate is an annuity.
6. A growing annuity is a finite series of equal and periodic cash flows growing at a constant rate in every period.
7. Equal instalment at equal intervals will result in an annuity.
8. Cash flows of different years are comparable in absolute terms.
9. Sinking fund is a reciprocal of $CVAF_{ni}$.
10. The effective rate of interest in multiple period compounding is lower than annual compounding.

Answers: 1. (T), 2. (F), 3. (T), 4. (T), 5. (F), 6. (T), 7. (T), 8. (T), 9. (T), 10. (F)

THEORETICAL QUESTIONS

1. "Cash flows at different points of time are not comparable." Comment on this statement.
2. "Time Value of money is an important principle of financial management." Discuss.
3. Why is consideration of time important in financial decision making? How can time be adjusted? **(B.Com Hons, Delhi University, 2000)**
4. Discuss the relevance of time value of money in financial decision making.
5. Write notes on:

   (*a*) Annuity

   (*b*) Effective rate of interest

   (*c*) Applications of time value techniques

   (*d*) Perpetuity

   (*e*) Implicit rate of interest
6. How can time value of money help a financial manager to take decisions?

7. Distinguish between:

   (*a*) Compounding and discounting techniques

   (*b*) Annuity and annuity due

   (*c*) Effective and nominal rate of interest

   (*d*) Present value and future value

ILLUSTRATIVE PROBLEMS

Illustration 2.1 Determine the future value of Rs. 1,00,000 if you invest in a bank for 5 years at 6% rate of interest.

Solution

Since the question pertains to compound value, the future value will be computed from Table A-1.The factor at 6% for 5 years is 1.338.

$$FV = 1,00,000 \times 1.338 = \text{Rs. } 1,33,800$$

Illustration 2.2 Calculate the present value of Rs.6,000. (*i*) Received at the end of five years (*ii*) Received at the end of 15 years (*iii*) Received one year from now. Assume a 7% time preference rate.

Solution

Present value will be computed from Table A-3 (Appendix)

(*i*) The factor at 7% at the end of 5 years is 0.713.

Therefore present value of Rs. 6,000 × 0.713 = 4,278

(*ii*) The factor at 7% at the end of 15 years is 0.362 = 2,172

(*iii*) The factor at 7 % at the end of year 1 is 0.935. Present value of Rs. 6,000 will be 6,000 × 0.935 = Rs. 5,610

Illustration 2.3 Mr. X deposits Rs. 5,00,000 for a period of 10 years at 10% rate of interest. What would the value of his sum be after 10 years?

Solution

The compound value factor can be taken from Table A-1. The factor at 10% and 10 years is 2.594.

The future value will be 5,00,000 × 2.594 = Rs. 12,97,000.

Illustration 2.4 A person invests Rs. 1,00,000. The bank provides an interest of 12% quarterly compounding is done. How much will the investment be after 5 years?

Solution

Since compounding is quarterly, it would be 3% interest per quarter. The number of periods for which it is compounded will be (5 years × 4) quarterly compounding = 20 (see Table A-1 for compound value factor).

$$\text{Therefore, Future value (FV)} = \text{Rs. } 1{,}00{,}000 \times [1 + (0.12/4)]^{5 \times 4}$$
$$= 1{,}00{,}000 \times (1.03)^{20}$$
$$= 3\% \text{ interest for 20 periods} = 1.806 \text{ (CV Factor)}$$
$$= 1{,}00{,}000 \times 1.80611$$
$$\text{FV} = \text{Rs. } 1{,}80{,}611$$

Illustration 2.5 Mr. X deposits Rs. 1,00,000 at the end of each year for 10 years. Calculate the value of his money at the end of 10 years at (*i*) 9% (*ii*) 10% and (*iii*) 12%.

Solution

This is the question of compound value of an annuity.

$$\text{FV} = \text{Annuity amount (A)} \times \text{CVAF}_{(ni)}$$

Where,
FV = Future value
A = Annuity amount
CVAF = Compound value annuity factor
i = Rate of interest
n = Number of years

See Table A-2 to find the factor of future value annuity.

(*i*) Factor at 9% and 10 years is 15.193
FV = 1,00,000 × 15.193 = Rs. 15,19,300

(*ii*) Factor at 10% and 10 years is 15.937
FV = 1,00,000 × 15.937 = Rs. 15,93,700

(*iii*) Factor at 12% and 10 years is 17.549
FV = 1,00,000 × 17.549 = Rs. 17,54,900

Illustration 2.6 A person deposits Rs. 1,00,000 at the beginning of each year for 10 years. What will be the value of his money at the end of 10 years at (*i*) 9% rate of return (*ii*) 11% return.

Solution

This is the question of compound value of annuity due. Find the factor form the Table A-2 (Appendix). Value is multiplied by (1 + *i*) to get the amount at the end of the year

(*i*) 1,00,000 × 15.193 = 15,19,300 (1 + *i*)
= 15,19,300 (1 + 0.09) = Rs. 16,56,037

(*ii*) 1,00,000 × 16.722 = 16,72,200 (1.11) = Rs. 18,56,142

Illustration 2.7 Find out the present value of the following cash flows discounted at 10% rate of return.

Year	Amount (Rs.)
1	15,000
2	25,000
3	50,000
4	1,00,000
5	1,00,000

These mixed streams of cash flows are calculated from Table A-3.

Year	Cash Flows	Present Value Factor @ 10%	Present Value
1	15,000	0.909	13,635
2	25,000	0.826	20,650
3	50,000	0.751	37,550
4	1,00,000	0.683	68,300
5	5,00,000	0.621	3,10,500
			ΣPV = 4,50,635

∴ PV of cash flows = 4,50,635

Illustration 2.8 Find out the present value (PV) of an annuity of Rs. 2,00,000 paid at the end of every year for 5 years @ 8% rate of return.

Solution

Find out the factor from Table A-4 @ 8% return for 5 years.

$$PVAF_{ni} = 3.993$$
$$= A \times PVAF_{ni}$$
$$= 2,00,000 \times 3.993$$
$$= \text{Rs. } 7,98,600$$

Illustration 2.9 Mr. Prabhat pays equal instalments of Rs. 1,50,000 in the beginning of each year for 5 years @ 10% rate of return. What would be present value?

Solution

This is a question of present value (PV) of due. Find the factor from Table A-4 for 5 years @ 10%. The factor is 3.791.

$$PV = \text{Amount} \times PVAF_{ni} (1 + i)$$
$$= 1{,}50{,}000 \times 3.791\ (1.10)$$
$$= 1{,}50{,}000 \times 4.1701$$
$$PV = \text{Rs. } 6{,}25{,}515$$

Since it is a question of annuity due interest is earned for one more year. Hence it is multiplied with interest for one year.

Illustration 2.10 Company wants to clear of its debt by paying off the bondholders Rs. 5,70,00,000 at the end 10 years. It is planning a sinking fund to retire the bond. The sinking fund would be created at 10% rate of interest. What instalment amount should it deposit to accumulate the amount?

Solution

This is a question of compound value. Sinking fund is the reciprocal of the annuity. See Table A-2, the formula would be:

$$FV = \frac{5{,}70{,}00{,}00}{CVAF_{ni}}$$

$$= \frac{5{,}70{,}00{,}000}{15.937} \quad (1/CVAF_{ni} \text{ is the sinking fund value factor})$$

$$= \text{Rs. } 3576582.80$$

Illustration 2.11 If Rs. 5,70,00,000 is borrowed by a company and has to be repaid in 5 instalments @ 12% interest. What would be the annuity amount?

Solution

$$PV = \text{Annuity amount} \times PVAF_{ni}$$

Or,
$$\text{Annuity amount} = \frac{5{,}70{,}00{,}000}{15.937} \quad (\text{factor from Table A-4})$$

$$= \text{Rs. } 15811373.09$$

Illustration 2.12 Ten years from today Brij will begin to receive a pension of Rs. 2,40,000 a year. The pension will continue till the 25th year. What is the worth of the pension today if the rate of interest is 10%?

Solution

Brij will receive the first payment of his pension at the end of the 10th year. This means that he will have 16 years of pension. To explain, the first pension that is received is in the 10th year. If this year becomes the first year of pension then calculate till the end of the 25th year. This means that there are 16 instalments and not 15. Birj will not receive any pension for 9 years. This question will be done in two steps.

Step 1:

Find out the annuity factor for 16 years and 10% rate of interest from present value annuity table. The factor is 7.824.

Therefore, Rs. 2,40,000 × 7.824 = Rs. 18,77,760

Step 2:

Now calculate the present value for 9 years since the value from the 10th year is already calculated above.

Present value factor at 10% rate of interest and 9 year period from present value table. The factor is 0.424.

Therefore, Rs. 18,77,760 × 0.424 = Rs. 796170.24.

Illustration 2.13 My father promised to give me Rs. 10,00,000 on my 21st birthday. Today is my 12th birthday. (*a*) He decides to make the annual payment to a fund after one year. How much should he pay if the fund gives 10%? (*b*) If my father decide to invest a lump-sum in my bank account after one year and allows it to compound annually how much lump-sum should be deposit at the bank rate of 6% per annum? (*c*) If my father decides to invest the sum of money in the beginning of the year instead of the end of the year what would be the amount?

Solution

(*a*) Rs. 10,00,000 = A ($CVAF_{ni}$)

Find factor for 9 years and 10% rate of interest from compound value annuity table since it is compounded after one year. Factor is 5.759.

$$A = \frac{10,00,000}{5.759} = 173641.25$$

(*b*) Rs. 10,00,000 compounded after one year will be A (CVF_{ni}).

Find compound value factor for 9 years at 6% rate of interest since it is compounded after one year. Factor is 1.689.

$$A = \frac{10,00,000}{1.689} = 592066.31$$

(*c*) This is a question of annuity due. Therefore, the factor 1.689 will be multiplied by 1.06.

$$A = \frac{10,00,000}{1.790} = 558659.21$$

Illustration 2.14 A bank has offered an annuity of Rs. 3,00,000 for 12 years. If I invest Rs. 18,00,000 now, what is the rate of return that I will earn from the bank?

Solution

$$18,00,000 = 3,00,000\ (PVAF_{12i})$$

$$(PVAF_{12i}) = \frac{18,00,000}{3,00,000} = 6.$$

Now look at Table IV the present value factor of an annuity equal to 6 is between 12% and 13% which is 6.1944 and 5.9176, by interpolation it will be the following:

$$\text{Rate of return} = 12\% + \frac{6.1944 - 6}{6.1944 - 5.9176} = 12\% + \frac{0.1944}{0.2768} = 12.7\%$$

PROBLEMS FOR PRACTICE

Problem 2.1 Pooja deposited Rs. 2,00,000 today. What would be the value of her money after 5 years when interest rate is (*i*) 6%, (*ii*) 8%, (*iii*) 10% and (*iv*) 12%?

[**Answers:** (*i*) Rs. 2,67,600 (*ii*) Rs. 2,93,800 (*iii*) Rs. 3,22,200 (*iv*) Rs. 2,24,000]

Problem 2.2 Find out present values of the following:

(*a*) Rs. 1,00,000 receivable after 7 years at a discount rate of 10%.

(*b*) An annuity of Rs. 5,000 starting after 1 year for 6 years at 10% rate of interest.

(*c*) An annuity Rs. 50,000 starting immediately and lasting for 10 years at discount of 12%.

(*d*) A perpetuity of Rs. 4,000 starting in year 5 at 15% discount rate.

(*e*) An annuity of Rs. 20,000 starting in year 5 time and lasting for 7 years at a discount rate of 10%.

[**Answers:** (*a*) Rs. 51,300 (*b*) Rs. 5,500 (*c*) Rs. 2,82,500 (*d*) Rs. 46,640 (*e*) Rs. 6618.73]

Problem 2.3 A company issues bonds of Rs. 80,00,000 to be repaid after 7 years. How much should the company invest in sinking fund earning 15% to repay the bonds?

[**Answer:** Rs. 722869.79]

Problem 2.4 A machine costs Rs. 5,00,000 and its effective life is estimated to be 12 years. Its scrap value is Rs. 15,000. What should be retained out of the profits every year to accumulate into a fund to purchase a new machine after 12 years? The compound interest rate would be 8%.

[**Answer:** Rs. 25557.25]

Problem 2.5 Mr. Saxena deposits Rs. 10,00,000 and he receives Rs. 1,00,000 every year for the next 20 years. Find out the rate of interest being offered to the investor.

[**Answer:** Approx 7.6%]

Problem 2.6 A firm takes a loan of Rs. 25,00,000. If the compounding rate of interest is 12%, find out the amount of each instalment if it is repaid in 5 equal instalments.

[**Answer:** Rs. 693481.28]

Problem 2.7 Mr. X has deposited Rs. 5,00,000 @ 20% rate of interest will receive an amount after 5 years from the date of deposit. What is the annual amount that he will receive he has asked for the repayment in 6 equal instalments.

[**Answer:** Rs. 287497.11]

Problems 2.8 Ten years from now Priya's celebrate her 21st birthday. She will start receiving Rs. 10,000 a year for 16 years. How much is the money worth today if the interest rate is 10%.

[**Answer:** Rs. 24418.16]

Problems 2.9 Mala deposits Rs. 50,00,000 in a bank account, which pays 10% rate of interest. How much can she withdraw for 15 years? The instalment would be for the same amount continuously.

[**Answer:** Rs. 6,57,375]

Problems 2.10 What is the future value of Rs. 5,00,000 @ 9% rate of interest after (*i*) 25 years (*ii*) 50 years?

[**Answers:** (*i*) Rs. 43,11,500; (*ii*) Rs. 3,71,77,000]

❑❑❑

3 Valuation of Securities

LEARNING OBJECTIVES

3.1 The Concept of Valuation

3.2 Key Inputs in Valuation

- Cash, Time and Required Rate of Return/Discount Rate

3.3 The Basic Valuation Model

- Bond Valuation—Annual and Semi-annual Interest
- Yield to Maturity
- Valuation of Convertible Debentures
- Valuation of Deep Discount Bonds

3.4 Bond Valuation Features

3.5 Valuation of Preference Share

3.6 Valuation of Equity Shares

- Valuation based on Accounting Information
- Valuation based on Dividends
- Valuation based on Earnings

3.7 Valuation of Equity Shares Based on Accounting Information

3.8 Valuation of Equity Shares Based on Dividends

3.9 Valuation of Shares Based on Earnings

3.10 Share Valuation—Risk and Return

3.1 THE CONCEPT OF VALUATION

Time value of money has many applications. As we have seen in the last chapter it provides compounding techniques to give future values and discounting techniques to give present values of money. In this chapter time value of money is applied for valuation of securities. Securities provide returns in the form of dividends or interests and it also provides a return at the time of sale. These securities have to be valued at different points of time. The returns at the time that it is required to be valued are calculated by discounting the returns at an appropriate discount rate, which depends upon the individual's own perception of risk. The value of an asset therefore varies according to the risk perception and estimation of each individual. It can be said that ***the value of a financial asset is a sum of its future cash flows, which are discounted over specific period of time by using a discount rate.*** The valuation of financial asset is usually for bonds and debenture, preference shares and equity shares. The key inputs that are used for the valuation process are cash flows, time and discount rate. These are described in the following sections.

3.2 KEY INPUTS

(*i*) Cash Flows

As described earlier, a financial asset provides continuous cash flows. These cash flows can be constant, fluctuating or growing. Cash flows may some times be at the time when a financial asset is being redeemed, while there are no cash flows during the lifetime of the asset. These have to be discounted to provide value to the asset to find out whether the asset should be purchased or not.

(*ii*) Time Period

In order to discount the cash flows to the present time or find out the value of future cash flows the number of years for which it is invested has to be stated. A cash flow will have no meaning until some specific time for it is invested has been stated. Only then can the rate of discount be applied to it to find its true value.

(*iii*) Discount Rate

The discount rate is also called ***the required rate or return***. The discount rate would show the risk of the cash flows. It would also help to determine the value the asset. The higher the discount rate greater will be the risk level. If the discount rate is not given it is difficult to bring the values of financial assets to a particular time. The discount rate is thus associated with cash flows and time period of investment. Discount rate consists of the risk free rate of securities and the risk premium. To find out the discount rate the application will be as follows:

$$k = I_f + R_p$$

Where,

I_f = Risk free rate

r_p = Risk premium

k = Required rate of return

I_f or the risk free rate remains the same even though risk increases or decreases. The risk premium increases when risks increase. ***The required rate of return*** comprises the risk free rate, the risk perception and risk premium that is the compensation for taking a risk. This chapter discusses valuation models and its applications to bonds, debenture, preference shares and equity shares. The value of a financial asset is thus explained through a basic model.

3.3 BASIC VALUATION MODEL

The value of a financial asset can be explained by discounting the expected cash flows to the present value at a discount rate, which is appropriate to the risk and return of an investor. The time value of money is applied to find out the value of the financial asset. This is expressed in the following manner:

$$V_0 = \frac{C_1}{(1+k)^1} + \frac{C_2}{(1+k)^2} + \ldots\ldots\ldots\ldots + \frac{C_n}{(1+k)^n}$$

Or,

$$V_0 = \sum_{i=1}^{n} \frac{CF_1}{(1+k)^i}$$

Where,

V_0 = Present value of security

CF_1 = Cash flows expected at the end of year 1

k = Appropriate discount rate

n = Expected life of asset

Valuation has certain concepts, which are used while determining the value of the assets. These concepts are ***book value, market value, going concern, liquidating value and capitalized value*** of financial assets. These concepts are important to understand the value of the financial assets. These concepts are described as follows:

(*i*) **Book Value:** The book value of an equity share can be found out by dividing the net worth of a firm by the number of equity shares issued by the company. The book value of bonds is the value, which is given in the balance sheet. Normally this is the face value of the bond. Book value of an asset is given in the balance sheet of a firm/company and it is based on the historical data. It is an accounting concept. It shows the cost of the asset minus the depreciation accumulated on it. It is equal to the total assets minus the liabilities and preference capital shown on the balance sheet.

(*ii*) **Market Value:** Market value is considered to be more relevant than book value of a financial asset because it depicts the price of the financial asset if it were to be sold. In the case of securities market value can be ascertained of those securities, which are listed on the stock exchange. If it is not listed then it is difficult to get the market price of the share. Time value of money applies security valuation in a way to determine the financial assets ***intrinsic value***. The intrinsic value provides the actual worth of the asset. This is the present value of the cash flows discounted at a required rate of return for the risk that is determined.

(iii) **Going Concern Value:** The value of a business, which is performing and continuing its business operations, is called a running or ***going concern.*** This is an important concept because it is the value that a buyer may consider for buying the business. This value may be more or less than the market value or book value because the value of such a unit depends on its profitability and ability to generate future sales.

(iv) **Liquidating Value:** This value shows the amount, which would be realized if the assets of the company were sold. It is the realizable value of the entire assets minus the external liabilities. The realizable value is the owner's share when a company/firm is dissolved.

(v) **Capitalized Value:** The capitalized value is the intrinsic value of the financial assets. ***It is the present value of cash flows discounted at the required rate of return.*** The capitalized value is the most appropriate concept for valuation of financial assets. It is also useful for evaluation of physical assets. The concept of capitalized value is widely used by financial managers in capital budgeting techniques to determine the valuation of assets. The required rate of return or discount rate is calculated through the capitalized value or intrinsic value of an asset. It comprises the equation $k = I_f + R_p$.

Required Rate of Return: To recapitulate the required rate of return is the discount rate which consists of the risk free rate of return and the risk premium and is denoted by the equation $k = I_f + R_p$.

It can be shown graphically, as in Fig. 3.1.

X-axis shows level of risk and Y-axis depicts the rate of return. O is point of origin and up to I_f is the risk free zone.

The slope after the risk free rate slopes upward. This is the risk premium for compensation—higher the risk the greater the return.

After a basic understanding of the concepts of valuation and using the basic valuation model discussed earlier:

$$V_0 = \sum_{i=1}^{n} \frac{CF_1}{(1 + k)^i}$$

Let us now understand bond valuation models.

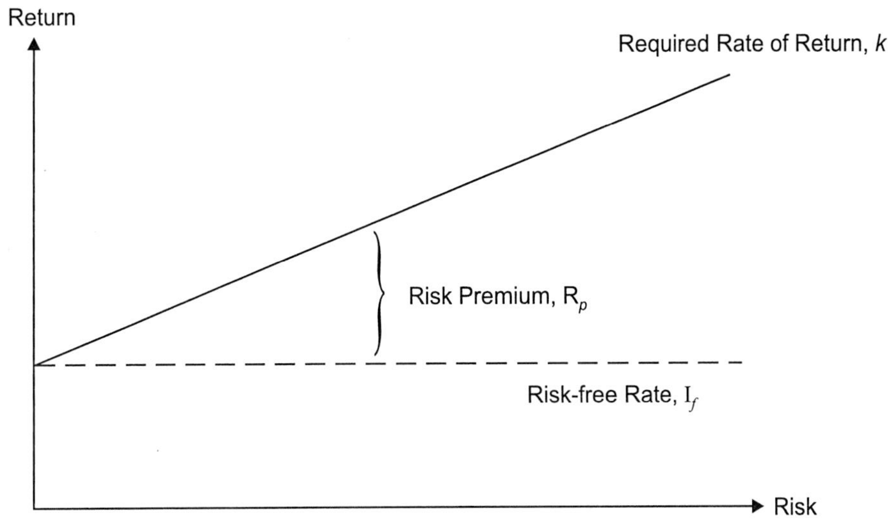

Fig. 3.1 The required rate of return

3.4 BOND VALUATION FEATURES

A bond can be defined as a long-term contract where the borrower agrees to pay interest and the principal sum on a specific date to the holder of the bond. For example, if ABC Co. borrowed Rs. 50,00,000 from Mr. X it would promise that in exchange it would give an annual interest @ 6% and repay the bond on a specified maturity date. Bonds can be corporate bonds, state and local government bonds and foreign bonds. Although it is stated that bonds do not have risk but equity shares are associated with risk, no bond can be said to be completely risk free. Corporate and foreign bonds have a high default risk but government bonds have very low risks. The return depends on the risk of the bond and government bonds give a very low rate of interest. There are certain characteristics of bonds: these are par value, coupon interest rate and maturity date. Bonds can also have the provision of ***call*** or return before the due date. Bonds can have the feature of convertibility or sinking fund provision.

Some of the important characteristics are discussed to explain the background or important features for bond valuation.

(*i*) Par Value

The face value of the bond is called the par value. A bond may be of the value of Rs. 100; Rs. 1,000; Rs. 5,000 or Rs. 10,000. This value shows the amount of money that has been borrowed. This is the principal sum to be returned on the date of maturity. The price at which the bond has been issued can be either more or less than the par value. The amount that is redeemed can also be at a discount or a premium.

(*ii*) Coupon Interest Rate

When the interest is divided by the bond par value it is called the 'coupon interest rate'. For example if a company issued a bond with the face value of Rs. 1,000 and it pays an interest of Rs. 100 every year, the coupon interest rate is 100/1,000 = 10%. The amount, which is fixed at the time that the bond is issued, will continue till the lifetime of the bond. This interest can be paid annually, semi-annually or monthly. Sometimes the bonds, coupon interest varies. Such bonds are called ***floating rate bonds***. Some bonds like ***zero coupon bonds*** do not pay any interest but issue bonds below the par value and offer a good discount and capital appreciation.

(*iii*) Maturity

The date on which a bond redeemed or the expiry date is called the maturity date. For example a company issues bonds on 1 January 2000 to mature on 31 December 2006. This bond has a maturity of 5 years. Some bonds may have the provision of ***call***. This gives the right to a company to redeem the bonds before the redemption date. To redeem before the due date the company usually pays a premium. Some bonds may offer the feature of ***convertibility*** into equity shares on maturity. Other bonds may carry the feature of a ***sinking fund***. If the company does not put a regular amount in the sinking fund, it can be penalized for default. Through this feature the company is required to put an annual sum to be able to redeem the bonds on maturity.

The Value of a Bond is the Present Values of the Cash Flows: The cash flows depends on the bonds contractual features. A usual bond consists of cash flows of interest payment during the lifetime of the bond plus the principal sum on the date of maturity. The discount rate is used to calculate the present value of the bonds cash flows.

> **Note:** k_d is the discount rate to calculate present value of bonds cash flows. k_d is not equal to the coupon rate except when the bonds market rate is at par.

(*iv*) Bond Valuation—Annual Interest

The value of the bond is calculated by the sum of the present value of the future payments plus the present value of the maturity amount through an appropriate discount rate. The value of the bond can be determined through the following equation:

$$B_0 = \sum_{i=1}^{n} \frac{1_i}{(1 + k_d)^i} + \frac{RV}{(1 + k_d)^n}$$

Or,

$$B_0 = I\ (PVAF_{ni}) + RV\ (PVF_{ni})$$

B_0 = Bond value

1_i = Annual interest payment

RV = Redemption amount

k_d = Appropriate discount rate

$PVAF_{ni}$ = Present value annuity factor at the number of years n and rate of interest i

PVF_{ni} = Present value factor at the number of years n and rate of interest i

Example 3.1 The face value of the bond is Rs. 1,000. It is redeemable after 5 years. The bond is currently selling for Rs. 1,100 and the coupon rate is 10%. Two investors Inder and Sanjay want to buy this bond. Inder's required rate of return is 11% and Sanjay's is 12%. What should be the value of the bond according to these investors?

Solution

Value of Inder's Bond

Year	Interest/Redemption of Principal	Discount factor @ 11%	Present Value of Interest/Principal
1 to 5	100	3.696	369.60
5th year	1,000	0.593	593
Value of the bond	–	–	962.60

Value of Sanjay's Bond

Year	Interest/Redemption of Principal	Discount factor @ 12%	Present Value of Interest/Principal
1 to 5	100	3.605	360.50
5th year	1,000	0.567	567
Value of the bond			927.50

Note: The value of the bond for both the investors is different because it is valued according to the investors own risk profile and his personal expected return. The value of the bond is higher with the lower discount rate.

Example 3.1 is shown according to the formula:

$$B_0 = I\,(PVAF_{ni}) + RV\,(PVF_{ni})$$

$$B_0 = 100\,(3.696) + 1{,}000\,(0.593) = 962.60$$

$$B_0 = 100\,(3.605) + 1{,}000\,(0.567) = 927.50$$

(*i*) Required Rate of Return and Coupon Rate

When the required rate of return is different from the coupon rate the bond value differs from the par value.

> **Note:**
>
> (*i*) If required rate of return > Coupon rate, Bond Value < par value.
>
> *(ii) If required rate of return < Coupon rate, Bond Value > par value.*

(*ii*) Required Rate of Return and Maturity

Time of maturity affects the value of the bond when required rate of return is different to the coupon rate.

(*i*) If required rate of return = Coupon rate, bond value is at par till maturity.

(*ii*) If required rate of return changes, the longer the maturity of the bond, the greater its value.

Example 3.2 A bond of Rs. 1,000 is redeemable after 10 years. The coupon rate of the bond is 12%. Find out the value of the bond if the investors required rate of return is 13% and the maturity is either 8 years or 12 years.

Solution

$$B_0 = I\,(PVAF_{ni}) + RV\,(PVF_{ni})$$

When maturity period is 8 years $B_0 = 120\,(4.799) + 1{,}000\,(0.376)$

$= 575.88 + 376 = \mathbf{951.88}$

When maturity period is 12 years $B_0 = 120\,(5.918) + 1{,}000\,(0.231)$

$= 710.16 + 231 = \mathbf{941.16}$

The value of the bond differs according to maturity period.

(*iii*) Bond Value and Semi-annual Interest

Interest on bonds is usually paid annually. Sometimes bonds carry interest semi-annually. In this case the formula will be:

$$B_0 = \sum_{i=1}^{n} \frac{1/2}{(1 + k_d/2)^i} + \frac{RV}{(1 + k_d/2)^{2n}}$$

Where,

(*a*) Half yearly amount is found by dividing the annual interest by 2.

(*b*) The number of years to maturity is multiplied by 2 to get the half yearly periods until maturity.

(*c*) Divide the required rate of return by 2 to convert the half yearly-required rate of return.

Example 3.3 A bond of Rs. 1,000 that has a coupon rate of 10% per annum (*a*) is payable half yearly. Find the value of the bond if it is redeemed in 7 years and the investors required rate of return is 12%. (*b*) Also find out the value if interest is payable annually.

Solution

(*a*) Semi-annual discounting

Coupon rate = 10/2 = 5%

Maturity period = 7 × 2 = 14

Discount rate = 12/2 = 6%

$$\text{Value of the bond} = \text{I}(\text{PVAF}_{14,\ 6\%}) + \text{RV}(\text{PVF}_{14,\ 6\%})$$

$$= 50\ (9.295) + 1{,}000\ (0.442)$$

$$= 464.75 + 442$$

$$= \text{Rs. } 906.75$$

(*b*) Annual discounting

Coupon rate = 10%

Maturity period 7 years

Discount rate = 12%

$$\text{Value of the bond} = \text{I}(\text{PVAF}_{7,\ 12\%}) + \text{RV}(\text{PVF}_{7,\ 12\%})$$

$$=100\ (4.564) + 1{,}000\ (0.452)$$

$$= 456.40 + 452$$

$$= \text{Rs. } 908.40$$

Bond Value is less when interest is paid semi-annually. In the Example 3.3 the value of the bond is 906.75, whereas when it is paid annually it is 908.40. This is the relationship of required rate of return and coupon rate.

Note:

(*i*) When required rate of return > coupon rate, value of semi-annual bond will be lower than the annual interest payment bond.

(*ii*) When required rate of return < coupon rate, the value of semi-annual bond will be higher than value of annual interest payment bond.

(*v*) Yield to Maturity

The rate of return or k_d that makes the discounted values of cash flows equal to the bonds market value is callėd the yield to maturity of a bond. Cash flows consist of regular interest payments and redemption amount. The yield to maturity would be the internal rate of return at a given level of risk. The internal rate of return is thus the value of k_d and an investor who wants to take a decision on purchasing a bond can find out its value through the yield to maturity. Thus yield to maturity is the rate of return, which an investor expects, from a bond if he was to hold it until maturity.

Example 3.4 A bond that carries a 9% coupon rate and matures after 7 years has the market value of Rs. 960. The par value of the bond is Rs. 1,000. What would be the rate of return of the investor if he buys this bond and holds it till maturity?

To find out the value of k_d two methods can be applied:

(*a*) k_d can be found out by trial and error method.

(*b*) k_d can be found out by an approximate method.

Solution

Both methods are explained here but since trial and error method involves tedious calculations, YTM can be calculated by approximate method.

(*a*) Trial and error method

$$B_0 = I\ (PVAI_{ni}) + RV\ (PVF_{ni})$$

$$B_0 = I\ (PVAF_{7,9\%}) + RV\ (PVF_{7,9\%})$$

$$= 90\ (5.033) + 1{,}000\ (0.547)$$

$$= 452.97 + 547$$

= Rs. 999.97 since the value is greater than 700 we have to try a higher value for k_d let us try k_d at 10%

$$= 90\ (4.868) + 1{,}000\ (0.513)$$

$$= 438.12 + 513$$

$$= 951.12$$

$$\text{By interpolation } k_d = 9\% + \frac{(999.97 - 960)}{(999.97 - 951.12)} \times 1$$

$$= 9\% + \frac{39.97}{48.85} \times 1$$

$$= 9\% + 0.818 = 9.8\%$$

(*b*) Approximate Method

$$\text{YTM} = \frac{\text{I} + (\text{RV} - \text{B}_0)/n}{(\text{RV} + \text{B}_0)/2}$$

$$\text{YTM} = \frac{90 + (1{,}000 - 960)/7}{(1{,}000 + 960)/2}$$

$$= \frac{(90 + 5.71)}{980} = 0.09766 = 9.8\%$$

(*vi*) Convertible Debentures

In a convertible debenture the face value is fully or partially converted into equity shares. An example is given to show the valuation of convertible debentures.

$$\text{D}_0 = \sum_{i=1}^{n} \frac{\text{I}}{(1 + k_d)^i} + \frac{\text{RV}}{(1 + k_d)^n}$$

Where, D_0 = Value of Debenture.

RV = Redeemable value of bond call price if surrendered on call-maturity value if redeemed. Conversion value if converted.

I = Interest received yearly.

n = Number of years of holding the debenture.

k_d = Discount rate.

Example 3.5 A convertible bond of Rs. 100 value has a maturity period of 8 years. It has an annual coupon interest of 10%. It has a conversion price of Rs. 50 per share and current share price of Rs. 30. The market price of the convertible on that date was Rs. 95. The convertible bonds were yielding 15% on that date. Determine conversion value, conversion ratio, and security value and conversion premium.

Solution

$$\text{Conversion ratio} = \frac{100}{50} = 2 \text{ shares}$$

$$\text{Conversion value} = 2 \text{ shares} \times 30 = 60$$

$$\text{Security value} = \sum_{t=1}^{10} \frac{\text{Rs. } 10}{(1+0.15)^1} + \frac{\text{Rs. } 100}{(1+0.18)^{10}}$$

$$= \text{Rs. } 10\ (5.019) + 100\ (0.247)$$

$$= \text{Rs. } 50.19 + 24.7 = \text{Rs. } 74.89$$

$$\text{Conversion premium} = 95 - 60 = \text{Rs. } 35$$

The present value of equity share and the present value of interest and principal payment as on 1 July 2005 is Rs. 1501.326.

Convertible debentures can be fully converted or partially converted. When they are partially converted the residual portion earns interest in the remaining period after which it is redeemed. There is also a difference between compulsory convertible debentures (CCD) and optionally convertible debentures (OCD). In CCD the part or full value is converted into specific number of equity shares. In OCD the debenture holder have the option to decide to convert their debentures into equity shares. Logically, he will opt for conversion only when the value of the debenture will give him a higher return than the value before conversion.

(*vii*) Deep Discount Bonds

Deep discount bonds (DDB) are those kinds of bonds, which do not pay any interest to the holder of the bond until maturity. It is attractive because it is sold at a very low price. In India financial institutions have issued DDB's and they have been over subscribed. IDBI issued DDB's for Rs. 2,700 each. They had a par value of Rs. 1,00,000 and would be mature after 25 years.

$$\text{DDB} = \text{Par value}/(1 + k_d)^n$$

$$\text{DDB} = \text{Deep discount bond value}$$

$$k_d = \text{Required rate of return}$$

$$n = \text{Number of years}$$

The valuation of DDB is explained in Example 3.6.

Example 3.6 A DDB is issued for Rs. 1,00,000 (Face Value) and the maturity period is 7 years. Find out the value of the DDB if the required rate of return is 12%.

Solution

$$\begin{aligned} \text{DDB} &= \text{Rs. } 1{,}00{,}000/\,(1.12)^7 \\ &= \text{Rs. } 1{,}00{,}000 \times \text{PVF}_{7,\ 12\%} \\ &= 1{,}00{,}000 \times 0.452 \\ &= \text{Rs. } 45{,}200 \text{ is the value of the bond.} \end{aligned}$$

3.5 VALUATION OF PREFERENCE SHARES

Preference shares differ from equity shares and bonds. They resemble bonds because there is a fixed return on preference shares. This return is however called dividend and not interest. Therefore preference shares like equity shares receive a dividend. These shares can be called hybrid securities or a mixture of equity and bond/debentures. A preference share provides a fixed dividend and a preferential dealing at the time of liquidation of a company/firm. Preference shares can be redeemable or irredeemable. In India, irredeemable shares cannot be issued by companies. There are different kinds of features provided in preference shares. The share may have the feature of cumulative dividend or non-cumulative dividend. In the case of cumulative dividend, the preference shareholder enjoys the right of carry forward of his dividend from the year of loss to the year of profits of the company. He then receives the dividends of loss year and profitable year together. An equity shareholder in comparison to the preference shareholder does not enjoy this right. At the time of liquidation a preference shareholder receives the capital amount paid by him to the company. The equity shareholder can only receive his money after the rights of the preference shareholders has been satisfied. Despite the advantages of greater security, the preference shares are not as popular as the equity shares because the capital appreciation is low in these shares. The reason for the popularity of equity shares is that profits can vary in some years and trading is done continuously in these shares. The assumption is that the equity shareholder has the advantage of high price when he sells his share in the stock market. This may not be true because the equity shares can also suffer losses. The shareholder has to choose from his risk appetite and background whether to buy a preference share or an equity share.

The redeemable preference shares can be valued just like the valuation of a redeemable bond. The formula is:

$$P_0 = \sum_{i=1}^{n} \frac{D}{(1 + k_d)^i} + \frac{RV}{(1 + k_d)^n}$$

Or,

$$P_0 = D\,(\text{PVAF}_{ni}) + RV\,(\text{PVF}_{ni})$$

$$P_0 = \text{Value of preference share}$$

D = Dividend (fixed)

RV = Redemption amount

k_p = Required rate of return of preference shareholder

$PVAF_{ni}$ = Present value annuity factor at the number of years *n* and rate of interest *i*

PVF_{ni} = Present value factor at the number of years n and rate of interest *i*.

Preference share can also be valued when they are issued as irredeemable preference capital. This is valued like perpetuity where fixed dividends are given continuously for the lifetime of the company. The formula would thus change to $P_0 = D/k_p$.

Note:

(*i*) Dividends on preference shares are fixed and paid annually each year. A preference shareholder will receive a dividend after the annual general meeting is held.

(*ii*) The first dividend would be after one year from the date of purchase or issue of the share.

(*iii*) There is no change in dividends. Therefore a company can plan with certainty the amount that has to be kept apart by it to satisfy the claims of preference shareholders annual dividends.

(*iv*) The preference shareholders will receive the stream of future dividends at a fixed rate of dividend.

(*v*) The redeemable preference shareholders will receive the maturity amount at the time of redemption.

(*vi*) The future cash flows ate discounted at an appropriate rate of return, suitable to the preference shareholder.

3.6 VALUATION OF EQUITY SHARES

The equity shareholders are the owners of the company. The financial manager has to maximize the wealth of the equity shareholders because they represent the real ownership interest of a company. The company's image is formed with the value of the equity share in the market. Equity shares are traded in stock markets and are very popular. They have a face value or par value. The market price of the share is normally not the face value. The market price has a premium or discount attached with the face value of the share. The equity shareholders have the rights of the owners of a company. They receive profits of the company only after the debt holders and preference shareholders have been paid their dues. If a company goes into liquidation they have the last right on the company's residual amount. The equity shareholders may receive a very high profit in one year and the very next year there could be a loss in the company and the equity shareholders do not get any dividends. This feature of equity shares makes them very risky shares. Equity shareholders look towards capital appreciation or the premium that they would receive if the company was profitable and they sold their shares and got a capital gain on their shares. The features of the equity shares can be summed up in the following way:

- Equity shares have a face value.
- Equity shares do not have a fixed dividend.
- They receive dividends only when a company is profitable. In the year of loss, they are not entitled to any dividends.
- Equity shares can be traded and sold in a stock market but they have no redemption value.
- Equity shares are risky since dividends are not guaranteed.
- The first dividend is received after one year of purchase.

Since equity shares have varying dividends they are the most difficult to calculate. There are different approaches for valuation of equity shares.

The different approaches are:

- Accounting concept of valuation
- Valuation of equity shares based on dividends
- Valuation of equity shares based on earnings

These methods of equity valuation are now discussed.

3.7 VALUATION OF EQUITY SHARES BASED ON ACCOUNTING INFORMATION

The financial statements provide a lot of information about shares. The balance sheet of a company can be used to find out the value of its shares.

(*i*) **Book Value:** Book value of a share can be ascertained from the balance sheet of a company. The book value of a share is the net worth of a company divided by the number of outstanding shares of a company. It is paid up capital plus reserves and surplus minus accumulated losses divided by the number of equity shares. If a company has Rs. 80,00,000 as its net worth and it has 2 lakh shares then the book value of the share will be 80,00,000/2,00,000 equal to Rs. 40. Book value is an accounting tool and the balance sheet represents historical data which is quite different from the current data. It is subjective and arbitrary and does not provide the real investment value of an equity share.

(*ii*) **Liquidation Value:** The ***liquidation*** value is based on the fact that a company would realize an amount after liquidating its assets and making a payment to the creditors and preference shareholders in settlement of their claims. For example, if ABC Company was to liquidate assets it would realize Rs. 90,00,000 and pay Rs. 22,00,000 to its creditors and preference shareholders. If it has 2,00,000 shareholders, then the value per share will be (90,00,000 – 22,00,000)/2,00,000 is equal to Rs. 34. Liquidity value is more realistic than book value because it gives current realizable values instead of historical values but it does not reflect the earning capacity and it is very difficult to estimate the amount realized from liquidation of various assets.

The methods of book value and liquidation value do not give the value of the share with objectivity. It provides some knowledge about the value of the share but he is not able to find out the return that he would be able to receive on his investment. There are other methods like valuation models based on dividends and earnings. These are now analysed.

3.8 VALUATION OF EQUITY SHARES BASED ON DIVIDENDS

Valuation of equity shares is based on the fact that there would be an expectation of future dividends. Therefore the value of the equity shares is equal to the present value of dividends expected by the shareholders plus the present value of the sale price of the share when the equity share is sold. It has two parts:

(*i*) A stream of future dividends.

(*ii*) Resale price of equity share when the investor sells the share.

The dividend approach assumes:

- Dividends are paid annually.
- The first dividend is received one year from the date of purchase or acquisition of the share.
- The sale of equity shares is at the end of the year.

The valuation of the equity share can be made through the following equation:

$$P_0 = \frac{D_1}{(1 + k_e)^1} + \frac{D_2}{(1 + k_e)^2} + \dots\dots\dots + \frac{D_\infty}{(1 + k_e)^\infty}$$

If an investor expects to hold the share for two years and sell it the formula will be:

$$P_0 = \frac{D_1}{(1 + k_e)^1} + \frac{D_2}{(1 + k_e)^2} + \frac{P_2}{(1 + k_e)^2}$$

Where,
P_0 = Current price of equity share
D_1 = Expected dividend
k_e = Required rate of return of equity share
P_2 = Price of share at year 2

The valuation of equity shares through dividends can be:

(*i*) Constant dividends or zero growth in dividends

(*ii*) Constant growth in dividends

(*iii*) Variable growth in dividends

(*i*) Constant Dividends or Zero Growth in Dividends

The dividend remains constant over the years. Zero growth in dividends is like perpetuity. This means that the dividend would be the same over the years *i.e.*, $D_1 = D_2 = D_3 = D_4 = D_\infty$. The value of equity shares under this model is depicted through the rate of return of equity and the yearly dividend received. The rate of return of the equity holders would be:

$$P_0 = D/k_e$$

$$P_0 = \text{Value of equity share}$$

$$D = \text{Annual dividend}$$

$$k_e = \text{Required rate of return}$$

Example 3.7 A company declared a dividend of Rs. 4. Find the value of the share if the expected rate of return of the investor is 8% and dividend is expected to remain the same every year.

Solution

$$P_0 = D/k_e$$

$$P_0 = 4/.08 = \text{Rs. } 50$$

Value of the share is Rs. 50.

(*ii*) Constant Growth in Dividends

When dividends grow constantly at a rate *g* every year. If a firm pays dividend of D_0 then dividend at the end of year 2 will be:

$$D_2 = D_0(1 + g)^2.$$

The valuation of the equity share under the constant growth model can be found out with the equation:

$$P_0 = \frac{D_0(1+g)^1}{(1 + k_e)^1} + \frac{D_0(1+g)^2}{(1 + k_e)^2} + \frac{D_0(1+g)^\infty}{(1 + k_e)^\infty}$$

Or,

$$P_0 = \sum_{i=1}^{\infty} \frac{D_0(1+g)^i}{(1+k_e)^i}$$

This simplifies to $P_0 = D_0 (1 + g)/(k_e - g)$ and

Since $D_1 = D_0 (1 + g)$

So, $P_0 = (D_1/k_e - g)$

This valuation model is simple P_0 = Current market price

D_1 = Expected dividend per share

k_e = Cost of equity or return expected by shareholder

g = Growth rate

D_0 = Dividend declared last year

Example 3.8 A share having a face value of Re.1 is expected to pay a dividend of 15% at the end of year 1. Its growth rate in dividends is estimated to be 5%. If the investor has a required rate of return of 16%, what would be the value of the equity share?

Solution

$$P_0 = D_1/(k_e - g)$$

$$P_0 = 0.15/(0.16 - 0.05) = 0.15/0.11$$

$$P_0 = \text{Rs. } 1.36$$

> **Note:** Equity share is
> (*i*) Positively co-related with growth rate.
> (*ii*) It is negatively co-related with required rate of return.

The limitations of the constant growth model arise because no firm can continue to have a constant growth in dividends. When profitability increases dividend increases. When profitability falls dividend will decrease. Since the growth in dividends keeps on changing the variable growth in dividends model is used to find out the value of the share. Variable growth in dividends means that for the first few years the dividend growth may be different to the next few years. For example growth rate in dividends may be 2% for 3 years and then 5% for 4 years. It may again fall to 4% for the next 3 years. This kind of problem can be solved through 4 steps:

Step 1: First find out the value of dividend at the end of each year.

Step 2: Find out the present value of the dividends by discounting at the required rate of return.

Step 3: Find out the value of the equity share at the end of the varying growth period.

Step 4: Add present value of the dividends to the present value of the share to get the value of the equity share.

Example 3.9 Miss. Indu bought a share of a company the firm paid a dividend of Rs. 4 per share. Indu's expected rate of return is 8%. Find out the value of a share if the growth rate from year 1 to 3 years is 5%, 4th and 5th year it is 8% and in the 6th year it is 9% thereafter.

Solution

Discounted value of dividends

Step 1:

Year	Expected Dividend	Discount Rate @ 8%	Present Value of Dividends
1	4.20	0.926	3.89
2	4.41	0.857	3.78
3	4.63	0.794	3.68
4	5.00	0.735	3.67
5	5.40	0.681	3.68
		Present value of dividends	**18.70**

Step 2:

Price of the share at the end of year 5 $D_6 = 5.40\ (1 + 0.09) = 5.886$

Step 3:

$$
\begin{aligned}
P_5 &= D_6/(k_e - g)\\
&= 5.886/(0.08 - 0.09)\\
&= \text{Rs. } -588.60
\end{aligned}
$$

Present value of the share $= -588.60 \times 0.681 = \text{Rs. } -400.83$

Step 4: Price of the share $= -400.83 + 18.70 = \text{Rs. } -382.13$

(*iii*) Valuation of Share not Paying Any Dividends

Sometimes a firm does not pay a dividend for a few years because of losses or insufficient profit but once the profitability begins the company provides a dividend. This is depicted in Example 3.10.

Example 3.10 A firm does not pay any dividend for the first 4 years and thereafter it will pay a dividend of Rs. 5 at the growth rate of 10%. The required rate of return is 12%.

Solution

Step 1:

$$
\begin{aligned}
P_4 &= D_5/(k_e - g)\\
&= 5/(0.12 - 0.10) = 5/0.02\\
&= \text{Rs. } 250
\end{aligned}
$$

This is the value of the share at the end of year 4.

Step 2: This value is discounted at 12% to find out the present value.

$$P_4 \times PVF_{4,\ 12\%} = 250 \times 0.636 = \text{Rs. } 159$$

Value of the share is Rs. 159.

3.9 VALUATION OF SHARES BASED ON EARNINGS

The valuation of shares based on earnings is measured through the price-earning ratio. The value of the share as per P/E ratio is expressed as value = Earnings per share (EPS) × Price earning ratio (P/E).

The EPS is calculated by taking profit after tax minus preference dividend divided by number of equity shares.

$$\text{EPS} = (\text{PAT} - \text{Pref. Div.})/\text{No. of Equity Shares}$$

Companies to show the value of their share use the P/E ratio for valuation of shares. They indicate the ability of the firm to pay future dividends.

Example 3.11 Following is the capital structure of a company:

Equity share capital = Rs. 50,00,000
Share premium = Rs. 20,00,000
Reserves = Rs. 5,00,000
Net worth = Rs. 75,00,000

The profit after tax is Rs. 60,00,000 and the face value of the share is Rs. 2. Find out the price earnings ratio.

Solution

EPS = 60,00,000/25,00,000 = Rs. 2.4
No. of equity share = 50,00,000/2 = Rs. 25,00,000 = P/E ratio is 2.4.
Value of the share = 25,00,000 × 2.4 = Rs. 60,00,000

The P/E ratio is used by company to find out the value of the share. Although it has many limitations, it is used because the share price on a particular date provides the investors expectations of the performance of a firm. When P/E ratio is high, investors believe, that the company is projecting a higher return in future. High P/E ratio does not always reflect that the future earnings will be better than what the current earnings project. However, companies use P/E ratios because it projects the ability of a firm to pay dividends in future. A prospective investor can forecast the price of the share by using the P/E ratio for valuation of shares based on earnings of the company.

3.10 SHARE VALUATION—RISK AND RETURN

The equity valuation model based on accounting information, dividends and earnings models have been discussed earlier. The variables of dividends, growth and required rate of return have been analysed. The financial manager also requires information about the market risk to take decisions relating to investments. Since risk and return are important parameters for financial decision making these are briefly discussed.

(*i*) Risk

Financial decision making is usually undertaken in a way that the risk and return are optimized. As discussed in Chapter 1 when return is high, risk is expected to be high. Decisions have to be taken according to the risk capacity and appetite of the investors. The major factors in share valuation consist of dividends, growth and return. Equity shares are highly risky. Their return is uncertain. The return can be very high or very low. The risk has to be adjusted in the valuation process through the required rate of return. The market rate of risk or risk premium depends on β (Beta) thus the market model is used for adjustment of risk. It consists of the general model and the CAPM model as follows:

$$k_e = I_f + r_p \text{ (General model)}$$
$$k_e = I_f + \beta(k_m - I_f) \text{ (CAPM Model)}$$

Where I_f is risk free rate

$$k_m = \text{Market rate of return}$$
$$\beta = \text{Beta}$$
$$r_p = \text{Risk premium}$$
$$k_e = \text{Required rate of return}$$

I_f which is the risk free rate and k_m which is the market rate of return, are both, constant in the above models. The required rate of return or k_e depends on the risk premium that is represented by r_p and β in the above models. When the market risk increases then the required rate of return will also increase.

Example 3.12 A firm pays a dividend of Rs. 3 with a 10% growth rate the risk free rate is 8% and market rate of return is 13%. The firm has a β factor of 1.25. (*a*) What would be the value of the share? (*b*) If β increases to 1.5 what would be the value of the share?

Solution:

$$k_e = I_f + \beta\,(k_m - I_f)$$
$$k = 0.08 + 1.25\,(0.13 - 0.08)$$
$$= 0.08 + 0.0625 = 0.142 \text{ or } 14.2\%$$

And the value of the share using the constant growth model is

$$P_0 = D_1/(k_e - g) = 3/(0.14 - 0.10)$$
$$P_0 = \text{Rs. } 75$$

(*b*) If beta factor increases to 1.5 then

$$k_e = I_f + \beta(k_m - I_f)$$
$$k_e = 0.08 + 1.5\ (0.13 - 0.08)$$
$$= 0.08 + 0.075$$
$$= 0.155 \text{ or } 15.5\%$$

Value of the share is $P_0 = D_1/(k_e - g)$

$$= 3/(0.155 - 0.10)$$
$$= \text{Rs. } 54.54$$

Value of the share, decreases, when beta increases.

(*ii*) Return

The value of the share must be analysed with risk and return. Taking into consideration the return value of the share makes all financial decisions. The return will affect the price of the share.

Example 3.13 A firm pays a dividend of Rs. 2 with a growth rate of 10%. The required rate of return is 15%. (*a*) Find out the value of the share. (*b*) If dividend increases to 11% what would be the value of the share. (*c*) If required rate of return increases from 15% to 16% and growth rate increases from 10% to 11% ?

Solution

(*a*) When D_1= Rs. 2, g = 10%, k_e = 15%,

$$P_0 = D_1/(k_e - g)$$
$$= 2/(0.15 - 0.10)$$
$$= \text{Rs. 40 value of the share.}$$

(*b*) When g increases to 11% value of the share

$$P_0 = D_1/(k_e - g)$$
$$= 2/(0.15 - 0.11)$$
$$= \text{Rs. } 50$$

When growth increases without any corresponding changes the value of the share will increase.

(*c*) When required rate of return increases to 16% and growth rate is 11%

$$P_0 = D_1/(k_e - g)$$
$$= 2/(0.16 - 0.11)$$
$$= \text{Rs. } 40$$

Growth rate has a positive correlation with value of the share. The required rate of return has to be considered while calculating the value of the share. If required rate of return increases, the value of the share will fall if there is no increase in growth rate. In the example, the value of the share was

Rs. 40. When growth rate increased the value of the share also increased as in (*b*) the value of the share was Rs. 50 but when there is no further increase in growth but the investor desires to change his required rate of return by increasing it as in (*c*) above to 16% the value of the share fell to its previous level of Rs. 40.

Risk and return are important dimensions in financial decision making. They have an effect on valuation of shares. The financial manager should analyse their effect before taking decisions.

Table 3.1 Valuation Models—At a Glance

1. Basic Valuation Model

$$V_0 = \frac{C_1}{(1+k_d)^1} + \frac{C_2}{(1+k_d)^2} + \ldots\ldots\ldots + \frac{C_n}{(1+k_d)^n}$$

Or,

$$V_0 = \sum_{i=1}^{n} \frac{CF_1}{(1+k)^i}$$

2. Value of the Bond

$$B_0 = \sum_{i=1}^{n} \frac{I_i}{(1+k_d)^i} + \frac{RV}{(1+k_d)^n}$$

Or,

$$B_0 = I\,(PVAF_{ni}) + RV(PVF_{ni})$$

3. Bond Value with semi-annual interest

$$B_0 = \sum_{i=1}^{2n} \frac{1/2\ (\text{int})}{(1+k_d/2)^i} + \frac{RV}{(1+k_d/2)^{2n}}$$

4. Yield to Maturity

$$\text{Yield} = \frac{1 + \dfrac{RV - B_0}{n}}{\dfrac{(RV + B_0)}{2}}$$

[Contd...]

5. Valuation of compulsory convertible debenture (CCD)

$$B_0\ (\text{OCD}) = \sum_{i=1}^{n} \frac{I_i}{(1+k_d)^1} + \frac{m\,P_1}{(1+k_e)^t} + \frac{RV}{(1+k_d)}$$

6. Valuation of optionally convertible debenture (OCD)

B_o (OCD) = Debenture value or value of CCD whichever is higher + Value of option 'n'

7. Valuation of deep discount bonds

$$B_{0\ (\text{DDB})} = \frac{FV}{(1+i)^n}$$

VALUATION OF PREFERENCE SHARE

8. Valuation of irredeemable preference shares

$$P_0 = \frac{D}{k_p}$$

9. Valuation of redeemable preference shares

$$P_0 = \frac{D_1}{(1+k_p)^1} + \frac{D_2}{(1+k_p)^2} + \frac{D_n}{(1+k_p)^i} + \frac{RV}{(1+k_p)^n}$$

$$P_0 = \sum_{i=1}^{n} \frac{D_1}{(1+k_p)^1} + \frac{RV}{(1+k_p)^n}$$

VALUATION OF EQUITY SHARES

10. Valuation of equity shares based on dividends

$$\text{Constant dividends } P_0 = \frac{D_1}{(1+k_e)^1} + \frac{D_1}{(1+k_e)^2} + \frac{D_\infty}{(1+k_e)^\infty}$$

[Contd...]

11. Constant growth in dividends

$$P_0 = \frac{D_1}{k_e - g}$$

Or,

$$P_0 = \sum_{i=1}^{\infty} \frac{D_0(1+g)^n}{(1+k_e)_n}$$

12. Valuation of shares based on earnings

$$\text{Value} = \text{EPS} \times \text{P/E ratio}$$

$$\text{EPS} = \frac{\text{Profits after tax} - \text{Preference dividend}}{\text{No. of equity shares}}$$

Notations

V_0 = Value of the asset at time period 0 (zero).

C_1 = Cash flow expected at end of year.

k = Discount rate applicable to the cash flows.

n = Life of the asset.

B_0 = Value of the bond at present.

I_i = Annual interest payment.

RV = Redemption value at year n.

k_d = Discount rate.

D_1 = Dividends in year 1.

FV = Future value.

POINTS TO REMEMBER

- Valuation of shares is an application of time value of money. All decisions of valuation are taken with the combined effect of risk and return on securities.
- The present value of expected future cash flows at a relevant period of time with an appropriate discount factor provides the value of securities.
- The value of a bond is the present value of future interest flows and its redemption value.
- The terms that are important in valuation of bonds are its face value, rate of interest, maturity period and its redemption value.
- The bonds have been analysed in case annual interest, semi-annual interest, yields to maturity.
- Convertible bonds may be CCD or OCD. In convertible debentures the value is present value of the future cash flow in terms of interest, redemption value and market price of the share on the date of convertibility.
- Preference shares are hybrid securities as they have the features of both bonds and equity shares. Preference shares may be redeemable or irredeemable. In India only redeemable preferences are issued.
- The value of redeemable preference shares may be defined as the present value of the future cash flows in terms of dividends and maturity payment at the time of redemption at an appropriate discount rate.
- Equity shares are the most popular. They can be traded in a stock market. They have a face value, dividend is uncertain, it is dependent on profitability.
- Equity shares can be valued according to accounting information through balance sheet of a company. They can also be valued on the basis of dividends and earnings.
- Dividends on equity shares can have the features of zero growth or constant dividends, constant growth in dividends, and variable growth in dividends. They may be shares, which are not paying any dividend due to lack of profitability.
- Valuation of shares can be done through earnings model whereby the earnings per share and P/E ratio help to price the shares.
- Risk and return are important dimensions in financial decision making. CAPM model, also called the market model, take into consideration both risk and return to value shares.

OBJECTIVE TYPE QUESTIONS

State whether the following statements are true (T) or false (F).

1. The value of a bond is the present value of future interest flows discounted at an appropriate discount rate.
2. The required rate of return is the same thing as par value of a bond.
3. Bonds do not have a maturity date.
4. A bonds yield to maturity may be defined as the internal rate of return (IRR) for a given level of risk.
5. Deep discount bonds provide a good coupon rate of return.
6. An equity share has a face value a fixed dividend and no redemption date or value.
7. Valuation of equity shares can be based according to information, dividends or earnings.
8. Valuation of equity shares in the constant dividend model is $P_0 = D/k_e$
9. Valuation of securities should be made within the risk and return criterion.
10. Valuation of securities is an application of the value of money.

Answers: 1. (T), 2. (F), 3. (F), 4. (T), 5. (F), 6. (F), 7. (T), 8. (T), 9. (T), 10. (T)

THEORETICAL QUESTIONS

1. Explain the concept of valuation of securities. How is it useful to a financial manager for taking decisions?
2. 'Valuation of securities is the direct application of time value of money'. Elaborate this statement.
3. Discuss the different approaches for valuation of equity shares.
4. What are the similarities in valuing bonds and preference shares?
5. What is the relevance of valuation of securities in financial management?
6. Discuss the important features of a bond. How is a redeemable bonds valued?
7. How do growth factors affect the value of equity shares? Explain constant growth, varying growth and no dividends concept.
8. What is the relevance of dividends in valuing equity shares? If no dividends are given how would you value the share?
9. How do earnings of a company affect the value of an equity share?

10. Write notes on:
    (*a*) Yield to maturity
    (*b*) Risk and return and financial decision making
    (*c*) Valuation of convertible bonds
    (*d*) Varying growth in dividends

ILLUSTRATIVE PROBLEMS

Illustration 3.1 A bond of Rs. 1,000 matures at the end of 20 years. Its coupon rate is 8%. The required rate of return is 10%. What would be the value of Mr. Behl's bonds if he has 10 such bonds?

Solution

The annual interest of this bond is Rs. 80. At the end of 20 years he would receive the principal of Rs. 1,000 and Rs. 80 as interest.

The PV of interest is found out by the present value annuity factor for 10% and at year (Appendix Table A-4). The factor is 8.514.

$$PV = \text{Interest} \times PVAF_{ni}$$
$$= 80 \times 8.514 = 681.12$$

The present value of Rs. 1,000 principal will be found from Table A-3 or present value tables.

$$PV = \text{Principal} \times PVAF_{ni}$$
$$= 1{,}000 \times 0.149 = \text{Rs. } 149$$

The value of the bond is Rs. 681.12 + Rs. 149 = Rs. 830.12

> **Note:** Since discount rate is higher than coupon rate the intrinsic value of the bond is less than par value.

If Mr. Behl has 10 such bonds the value of his bonds will be

$$830.12 \times 10 = \text{Rs. } 8301.20$$

Illustration 3.2 A bond of Rs. 10,000, has a coupon rate of 10% and mature in 10 years. It is currently selling at 95% of its value. Should an investor purchase this bond if his required rate of return is 12%?

Solution

The present value of the bond is $PVAF_{ni}$ for 10 years @ 12% (Table A-4)

Step 1

$$PV = \text{Interest} \times PVAF_{ni}$$
$$= 1000 \times 5.650 = 5{,}650$$

Step 2

PV of the principal sum. See Table A-3 @ 12% for 10 years.

$$= 10{,}000 \times 0.322 = 3{,}220$$

$$= 5{,}650 + 3{,}220 = 8{,}870$$

Step 3

$$\text{Current price} = 10{,}000 \times 95\% = 9{,}500$$

Since current price is higher than the value of returns the investor should not buy it.

Illustration 3.3 ABC Co. Ltd. is planning to issue debentures. The followings details are given:

Face value = Rs. 100

Maturity period = 10 years

Coupon rate of interest:

Year 1 – 2 = 7% per annum

3 – 4 = 12% per annum

5 – 7 = 15% per annum

8 – 10 = 16% per annum

The current market price of similar debentures issued in the market is 16% per annum. The company has a required rate of return of 18% that it proposes to give to its investors. What should be the issue price of the company? The company would provide redemption at 5% premium.

Solution

Interest payments and present value of debentures.

Year	Interest (Rs.)	Present Value @ 18% (Table A-3)	Present Values
1	7	0.847	5.929
2	7	0.718	5.026
3	12	0.609	7.308
4	12	0.516	6.192
5	15	0.437	6.555
6	15	0.370	5.550
7	15	0.314	4.71
8	16	0.266	4.256
9	16	0.225	3.600
10	16	0.191	3.056
			ΣPV = 52.182

Present value redemption amount would be at 18% which is required rate of return of the investor.

$$\text{Rs. } 105 \times 0.191 = \text{Rs. } 20.055$$

PV of the debenture is Rs. 52.182 + 20.055 = Rs. 72.237

The company should issue the debenture at Rs. 72.237 to the debenture holder to yield a return of 18% and premium of 5% at redemption.

Illustration 3.4 XYZ Co. declared an annual dividend of Rs. 15 per share. (*a*) Since it wants to expand its operation, it expects that they will not be any possibility of providing a dividend for the next 3 years. After 3 years it will pay a dividend of Rs. 10 per share and then it expects to provide 11% per annum growth to its shareholders. (*b*) If the board of directors does not come to a consensus for expansion then they propose a dividend for the next 2 years at a growth rate of 8% p.a.

The firms costs of equity is 20% (the return expectations of the equity investors) this will be unaffected by expansion proposal by the company. Calculate the value of the firms share in (*a*) and (*b*) situations given above.

Solution

Situation (*a*)

$$\text{Share price at } P_0 = D_0(1 + g)/(k_e - g)$$
$$= 15\ (1.08)/(0.20 - 0.08)$$
$$= 16.2/0.12 = \text{Rs. } 135$$

Situation (*b*)

(*i*)
$$P_2 = D_3/(k_e - g)$$
$$= 10/(0.20 - 0.11)$$
$$= 10/0.09 = \text{Rs. } 111.11$$

(*ii*) PV of the price is 111.11 × 0.694 = Rs. 77.11 (20% for 2 years Table A-3 = 0.694)

Therefore the price of the firm is better if it expands rather than the current value.

Illustration 3.5 A company paid a dividend of Rs. 5 last year. Its estimated growth is 6% per annum. (*a*) Find out the market price of the equity (*b*) If growth rate of dividends rises to 7% what would be the market price? (*c*) If growth rate declines to 4% give the price of the share. The required rate of return of the shareholders is 16%.

Solution

(*a*)
$$D_0 = \text{Rs. } 5,\ D_1 \text{ will be Rs. } 5.3$$
$$\text{Share price or } P_0 = D_1/(k_e - g)$$
$$= 5.3/(0.16 - 0.06) = \text{Rs. } 53$$

(*b*) If growth rate rises to 7%

$$P_0 = D_1/(k_e - g)$$
$$= 5.35/(0.16 - 0.07) = \text{Rs. } 59.44$$

(*c*) If growth rate falls to 4%

$$P_0 = D_1/(k_e - g)$$
$$= 5.02/(0.16 - 0.04) = \text{Rs. } 41.83$$

Illustration 3.6 Find out the value of an equity share from the following date:

Particulars	Amount (Rs.)
Equity share capital (Rs. 2 each)	80,00,000
Reserves and surplus	50,00,000
10% secured loans	45,00,000
Fixed assets	70,00,000
Investments	25,00,000
Operating profit	95,00,000

Tax rate = 40%

P/E ratio = 15

Solution

Value of the share = EPS × P/E ratio

EPS

Operating profit	95,00,000
Less interest on 10% secured loans	4,50,000
PBT	90,50,000
Tax @ 40%	36,20,000
PAT	54,30,000

No. of equity shares is 80,00,000/2 = 40,00,000 shares

EPS = 54,30,000/40,00,000 = 1.36

Value of the share = EPS × P/E ratio

P/E ratio is given to be 15 = 1.36 × 15 = Rs. 20.40

The share of the face value of Rs. 2 is valued at Rs. 20.40

Illustration 3.7 Mr. Rohatgi has invested in a share whose dividend is expected to grow at 15% for 5 years and thereafter at 5% till the life of the company. Find out the value of the share, if current dividend is Rs. 2 and the investors required rate of return is 6%.

Solution

The dividends of the company are expected to grow at 15% p.a. for 5 years.

Step 1

Calculate present value of dividends at 15% for 5 years

Year	Dividend $g = 15\%$	PVF@ 6%	Present Value
1	2.30	0.943	2.1689
2	2.645	0.890	2.3541
3	3.0417	0.840	2.5550
4	3.4980	0.792	2.7704
5	4.0227	0.747	3.0049
	Total = 15.5074		ΣPV = 12.8533

Total dividends of Rs.15.50 are expected in the next 5 years. Its present value at 6% is 12.85.

The value of the equity share at the end of the 5th year (D_6) k_e and g

$$D_6 = D_5(1 + g) = 4.626$$
$$= 4.0227\ (1.05) = 4.223$$

The share price is $P_5 = D_6/(k_e - g)$ = 4.223/(0.06 – 0.05) = 422.3

Present value of this amount at 6% = 0.747 × 422.3 = 315.458

Value of the share = Present value of dividends + Present value of expected price

= 12.85 + 315.458 = Rs. 328.31

Illustration 3.8 The capital structure of a company consists of equity share capital of Rs. 40,00,000 of Re. 1 each. The reserves and surplus are Rs. 20,00,000. The net worth is estimated at 60,00,000. Reena bought 200 shares of this company on 1 April 2002 at the market price of Rs. 5.50 and sold these shares on 31 March 2006 at Rs. 10 each. She had to pay a dividend tax at 20% and 15% on capital gains.

The company has been consistently paying a dividend at 25%. Do you think Reena has earned her required rate of return of 12%.

Solution

Step 1: Present value of dividend income

Date	Dividend @ 25%	Dividend after Tax	PV Factor	PV
31-03-2003	275	220	0.800	176.0
31-03-2004	275	220	0.640	140.8
31-03-2005	275	220	0.512	112.64
				Total PV = 429.44

Step 2: Selling price of shares at Rs. 10 = Rs. 2,000
Less total cost of shares = Rs. 1,100
Net gain = Rs. 900
Capital gains tax at 15% = Rs. 135
= Rs. 765

Step 3: Total cash inflow
Sale = Rs. 2,000
Capital gains tax = Rs. 135
This amount is receivable after 4 years of purchase of share = Rs. 1865
Present value factor at 12% for 4 years = Rs. 0.636
Present value of 1865 × 0.636 = Rs. 1186.14
Step 4: Present value of dividends = Rs. 429.44
Add PV of cash inflow = Rs. 1186.14
= Rs. 1615.58
Less cost of purchase of share = Rs. 1,100
= Rs. 515.58

Since the investment shows a positive net gain, Reena has achieved her required rate of return at 12%.

Illustration 3.9 A company's dividend has been growing at 20% p.a. The growth rate is expected to continue for 5 years after that the growth rate will fall to 15% for next 3 years. Then the growth rate will grow continuously at 8% p.a. If the last dividend was Rs. 5 per share and the investor's expectation is a required rate of return at 15%, what should be the intrinsic value of the share?

Solution

This is a question of varying growth in dividends.

Step 1:

Present value of dividends at varying growth

Dividends	Dividend Growth (Rs.)	Present Value Factor @ 15%	Present Value
D_1 @ 20%	6	0.870	5.22
D_2	7.2	0.756	5.44
D_3	8.64	0.658	5.685
D_4	10.368	0.572	5.930
D_5	12.442	0.497	6.184
D_6 @ 15%	14.308	0.432	6.181
D_7	16.4545	0.376	6.186
D_8	18.9227	0.327	6.187
			Total PV = 46.995

Step 2: Present value of the dividends = price of the share at the end of 8 years

$P_8 = D_9/(k_e - g) = 20.4/(0.12 - 0.08) =$ Rs. 510

Present value of Rs. 510 at 15% or P_0 = Rs. 166.77

Step 3: P_0 = Rs. 46.995 + Rs. 166.77 = 213.765

Illustration 3.10 A share has a current market price of Rs. 45. The face value of the share is Re. 1. This share is due for a bonus issue in year 2 in a ratio of 1 : 5. Miss Nalini wants to sell this share only at the end of 6 years. She expects the share to be Rs. 400 by that time. Her expense on the purchase of this share was 5% of the market price. At the time of sale of share also she expects to spend the same amount. The required rate of return of the shareholder is 10%. She is not required to pay dividend tax or capital gains tax. The current dividend of this share is Rs. 10. Would you advise the shareholder to buy more shares of this company?

Solution

(*i*) Nalini can buy the share if the present worth of dividend stream is greater than net cost.

(*ii*) Sale proceed is greater than cost paid today.

Present Value of Dividends

Year	Dividend	$PVF_{10\%, 6\ years}$	PV
1	10	0.909	9.09
2	12	0.826	9.912
3	12	0.751	9.012
4	12	0.683	8.196
5	12	0.621	7.452
6	12	0.564	6.768
			Total PV = 50.43

6 (400 – 20) sale Rs. 380	0.564	214.32
		264.75
Less cost of share Rs. 45 + Rs. 2.25		= Rs. 47.75
Net Benefit		217.00

Miss Nalini should buy more shares, as she will profit by it. She will get good cash inflow if she sells at the end of the 6th year.

Note: Rs. 20 and Rs. 2.25 are 5% expenses on purchase and sale of share.

Illustration 3.11 A 10 year bond of Rs. 1,000 has an annual rate of interest of 10%. The interest paid half yearly. If the required rate of return is 14% what is the value of the bond?

Solution

$$B_0 = \sum_{i=1}^{2n} \frac{1/2\,(\text{int})}{(1 + k_d/2)^i} + \frac{RV}{(1 + k_d/2)^{2n}}$$

$$= 50 \times 10.594 + 1{,}000 \times 0.358 = 529.7 + 358 = 887.7$$

The value of the bond is Rs. 887.7.

Illustration 3.12 A company is paying a dividend of Rs. 5 per share. The dividend is expected to grow at a 15% annual rate for 3 years and at 10% rate for the next 3 years. Then it is expected to grow at 7% forever. (*a*) What is the present value of this share if the capitalization rate is 9%? (*b*) If the share is held for 3 years what will be it present value?

Solution

(*a*) Present value during growth period

Year	Dividend	PVF at 9%	PVF x Dividend
1	5 (1.15) = 5.750	0.917	5.273
2	5.750 (1.15) = 6.612	0.842	5.567
3	6.612 (1.15) = 7.604	0.772	5.870
4	7.604 (1.15) = 8.745	0.708	6.191
5	8.745 (1.15) = 10.05	0.650	6.532
6	10.05 (1.15) = 11.56	0.596	6.889
			Total = 36.322

Present value of the end of year 6 = D_6 (1.07) / (k_e – g) = 618.45

Present value of Rs. 618.45 today at 9% discount rate (0.596) = 368.59

Present value of the share today = 36.322 + 368.596 = 404.918

(*b*) Present value during at the end of three years

P_3 = 6.191 + 6.532 + 6.889 = 19.612 + 368.59 = 388.20

Present value of dividend expected at the end of years 1, 2 and 3 is 5.273 + 5.567 + 5.870 = 16.71

The present value of share today that is P_0 = 388.20 + 16.71 = 404.91

Thus the value is the same if the share is held for the three years instead of indefinitely forever.

PROBLEMS FOR PRACTICE

Problem 3.1 A company has issued bonds of the face value of Rs. 1,000. These bonds have 5 years to maturity. They have a coupon rate of 10%. Find the value of the bond of the required rate of return of the investor is 14%. What would be the value of the bond?

[**Answer:** Value of the bond = Rs. 862.30]

Problem 3.2 XYZ Company Ltd. issued a bond of the face value of Rs. 1,000. The coupon rate is 13%. If Ms. Pam is an investor whose expectation of the rate of return is 13%, what would be sale value of the bond? Should the bond be brought for Rs. 900? The bond will mature in 5 years.

[**Answer:** Bond should be purchased for Rs. 900. Value of the bond = Rs. 996.21.]

Problem 3.3 Calculate value of equity share from the following data:

Equity share capital (Rs. 2 each)	90,00,000
Reserves and Surplus	15,00,000
10% secured loans	10,00,000
10% unsecured loans	10,00,000
Fixed assets	35,00,000
Investments	8,00,000
Operating profits 60,00,000	
Tax rate	40%
P/E ratio	8.5

[**Answer:** Value of share = Rs. 6.5]

Problem 3.4 A company issued Rs. 1,000 for 14% perpetual debentures 10 years ago. Interest rate have fallen since then Debentures of this company are now selling at 12% yield.

(*i*) Determine the expected market price of the debentures. Would you buy the debenture for Rs. 750?

(*ii*) If the debentures of the company are sold for Rs. 800 and have 7 years to maturity. Find out the yield of the investor.

[**Answers:** (*i*) Bonds M.P. is Rs. 1,250 (investor should buy @ Rs. 750
(*ii*) at 800 yield is 19.50% investor should buy.]

Problem 3.5 The current price of a share is Rs. 42. The company is expected to pay a dividend of Rs. 6 per share with an annual growth of 5%. If the investors required rate of return is 9% should be buy the share?

[**Answer:** As the investors required rate of return of the investor is 9% and the return on the share is 19%. The investor should buy the share.]

Problem 3.6 A company's earnings and dividends are decreasing at the rate of 7% per annum. If the previous years dividend was Rs. 9 and required rate of return is 10%, what is the current price of the equity share of the company? [**Answer:** Rs. 49.23]

Problem 3.7 A company is issuing a debenture with the face value of Rs. 100. Terms of maturity is 5 years.

Year	Coupon rate
1–2	8%
3–4	10%
5	15%

The current market rate of interest on similar debenture is 15% per annum. The company provides to give a yield of 16% per annum to investors. What is the price of issue? Debentures are redeemed at a premium of 10%.

[**Answer:** The issue price should be Rs. 84.27 to give a yield of 16% to the investor]

Problem 3.8 (*i*) A company paid a dividend of Rs. 15 per share. It does not intend to pay any dividend for next 2 years as it requires funds for its expansion programme. In the 3rd year it will pay a dividend of Rs. 12 and after which it will give dividends at a growth rate of 13% p.a. (*ii*) If the company does not go for expansion, dividend will be paid in the next 2 years and the expected growth will continue at 5% p.a. The firms cost of equity is 20% and it is unaffected by expansion programmes. Calculate the value of the share in both the situations.

[**Answers:** (*i*) Rs. 112 (*ii*) Rs. 118.95]

Problem 3.9 An investor has a share whose dividend is expected to grow at 20% for 5 years and 8% thereafter. What is the value of the share if the current dividend per share is Rs. 2 and the required rate of return is 9%? [**Answer:** Rs. 176.21]

Problem 3.10 The current price of a share is Rs. 135. The company is expected to pay a dividend of Rs. 35 per share with an annual growth of 6%. The investors required rate of return is 15%. Should he buy the share?

[**Answer:** The investor should buy the share as he will get 31.9% return and his required rate of return is 15%.]

❑❑❑

PART II

Financial Analysis and Planning

Statement of Changes in Financial Position

4

LEARNING OBJECTIVES

4.1 What is Statement of Changes in Financial Position?
4.2 Importance of Fund Flow and Cash Flow Statements
4.3 Nature of Changes in the Financial Position (Working Capital Basis)
4.4 Sources and Uses of Working Capital
4.5 Cash Flow Statement Analysis
4.6 Preparation of Cash Flow Statement
4.7 Statement of Changes in Financial Position – Total Resources Basis

4.1 WHAT IS STATEMENT OF CHANGES IN FINANCIAL POSITION?

The Statement of Changes in Financial Position is prepared to identify all changes that take place in a company between two periods of time. The Balance Sheet is prepared on a particular date to show the financial position of a company. This statement is prepared between the two Balance Sheet dates. It consists of two important aspects. These are ***funds flow and cash flow analysis***. ***The Fund Flow Statement*** depicts the sources and uses of funds and how their changes affect the working capital position of a company. ***The cash flow statement*** supports the fund flow statement by finding out the changes in the flow of cash in a company. The two statements are therefore prepared to complement each other.

4.2 IMPORTANCE OF FUND FLOW AND CASH FLOW STATEMENTS

The traditional financial statements of a company are its Profit and Loss Account and Balance Sheet. These are very important sources of data but they have a basic shortcoming that they do not show changes in financial position of a company.

A Statement of Changes in Financial Position is prepared to overcome this limitation. This statement helps in providing answers to some of the following aspects:

(*i*) To find out the causes of changes in assets and liabilities between two periods of time.

(*ii*) To understand the liquidity position of a company.

(*iii*) To find out the projection for future dividends and the reasons for past deviations in payment of dividends.

(*iv*) To find out the reasons for changes in financial resources of a company either due to new investment brought in by the entrepreneur or due to changes in assets and liabilities of a company.

(*v*) To find out the requirements of long-term funds for purchasing fixed assets.

(*vi*) To see that the company does not suffer from lack of working capital and has adequate working capital.

(*vii*) To prepare a statement when loans are required by bankers, portfolio managers, venture capitalist and merchant bankers.

(*viii*) To find out the proper value of the assets in case of mergers, acquisitions, reconstruction and amalgamation.

4.3 NATURE OF CHANGES IN THE FINANCIAL POSITION (WORKING CAPITAL BASIS)

Working capital analysis is important for running a business. Once a firm/company has invested its capital in the venture, it is important that it is run successfully. Therefore day-to-day planning is necessary for the business operations to runs smoothly.

The net working capital of a firm is calculated by the current assets and current liabilities. Working capital is required for acquiring non-current assets/fixed assets and for payment of non-current liabilities/long term liabilities. Such transactions have the effect of increasing or decreasing working capital. When transaction has the effect of increasing working capital it is a ***source*** of working capital. Similarly when there are transactions which show a decrease in working capital, it is an ***application*** of working capital. It is not necessary that there will always be a change in working capital. Sometimes transactions change the form of working capital but they are neither a ***source*** nor an ***application*** of working capital. The basic working capital equation is:

$$\mathbf{WC = CA - CL}$$

Where, CA = Current Assets

CL = Current Liabilities

WC = Working Capital

The transactions which affect the working capital:

(*i*) When current assets ***increase*** without a corresponding increase/decrease in current liabilities, the working capital ***increases.***

(*ii*) When current assets ***decrease*** without a corresponding increase/decrease in current liabilities, the working capital ***decreases***.

(*iii*) When current liabilities ***increase*** without a corresponding increase/decrease in current assets, the working capital ***decreases***.

(*iv*) When current liabilities ***decrease*** without a corresponding increase/decrease in current assets, the working capital ***increases***.

Certain transactions do not affect working capital of a firm/company. These are given below:

(*i*) When current assets and current liabilities ***increase***, simultaneously the working capital is not affected.

(*ii*) When current assets and current liabilities ***decrease***, simultaneously there is no effect on working capital.

(*iii*) When non-current assets and non-current liabilities increase/decrease, simultaneously there is no effect on working capital.

These aspects can be explained by giving examples.

Examples

(*a*) When a company makes a new issue of equity shares, it has surplus cash which increases the current assets. It also increases the non-current liability of a company's working capital.

(*b*) When a company takes the decision of purchasing non-current assets it will have the immediate effect of decreasing the cash resources of the company. This will increase its non-current assets.

(*c*) Depreciation is a non-current asset. It reduces fixed assets of a company but it has no effect on working capital.

(*d*) When a company purchases a non-current asset like heavy machinery, it has the effect of decreasing working capital.

(*e*) Cash received from debtors will not affect the working capital. Cash is a current asset. It increases cash but there is a decrease of debtors. Since both are current asset accounts it does not bring any change in working capital but the composition of working capital is affected.

(*f*) When a company makes two transactions from non-current assets, there will be no effect on the working capital. An example can be sited of a company which buys a factory building by issuing new shares of a company.

Fund Flow Statement

The Fund Flow Statement is a statement of changes in working capital. It determines the sources and uses of working capital between two balance sheet dates. Working capital depicts the liquidity position of a firm/company. We have already noted that working capital is the difference between current assets and current liabilities. The Fund Flow Statement will provide an estimate of the liquidity of a company by preparing working capital flows.

4.4 SOURCES AND USES OF WORKING CAPITAL

Sources of a company provide information to an increase in working capital resources and applications depicts the reasons for a decrease in working capital. Adjustments have to be made to items depicted in the profit and loss account of a company to find out the funds from business operations. Depreciation, dividends, interest, gain and loss from sale of non-current assets are some items which have to be carefully analysis and adjusted. Similarly, the net loss will also have to be adjusted. The Fund Flow Statement is prepared in two parts. (A) The first part gives the sources and uses of funds and (B) part two depicts the schedule of changes in working capital.

(A) The sources of working capital are the following as represented in Table 4.1.

Table 4.1 Fund flow statement part – I

Sources of Funds
(*i*) Funds from business operations (adjusted net income) (*ii*) Sale of non-current assets (*a*) Fixed assets – Land, building, machinery and equipment. (*b*) Sale of long-term investments – Equity shares, preference shares, bonds, debentures. (*c*) Sale of intangible assets – Patents, copyrights, goodwill. (*iii*) Long-term borrowings: (*a*) Loans, bonds, debentures. (*b*) Issue of new/additional equity shares and preference shares. (*iv*) Short-term finances: (a) Borrowing from banks.
Uses of Funds
(*i*) Adjusted net loss from business operations. (*ii*) Purchase of non-current assets. (*a*) Fixed assets – Land, building, machinery and equipment. (*b*) Long-term investments – Equity shares, preferences shares, bonds, debentures. (*c*) Intangible fixed assets – Patents, copyright, goodwill. (*iii*) Redemption of long-term debt – Debentures, bonds, short-term bank borrowings. (*iv*) Redemption of redeemable preference shares. (*v*) Dividends paid to shareholders.

The second part consists of preparing a schedule of changes in the working capital. It represents the changes to be depicted in current assets and current liabilities between two balance sheet dates. Each item of the current assets and the current liabilities is depicted and the increase or decrease in them is given. The final result represents increase or decrease of working capital by:

Current Assets – Current Liabilities = Working Capital increase/decrease

A proforma of a schedule of changes in working capital is given below in Table 4.2 to show how it is worked out.

Table 4.2: Proforma Showing Schedule Of Changes in Working Capital – Part II

Particulars	31 March 2008	31 March 2009	Increase	Decrease
A. Current Assets				
(*i*) Cash				
(*ii*) Debtors				
(*iii*) Inventory				
Total				
B. Current Liabilities				
(*i*) Bills payable				
(*ii*) Creditors				
(*iii*) Other current liabilities				
Total				
C. Networking Capital				
CA – CL				
Increase/Decrease in working capital				

In Table 4.1, there is an item called 'funds from business operations'. This can be calculated by two methods. These are called 'direct method' and 'indirect method'. The funds from business operations through the direct method are calculated in the following manner and is depicted in Table 4.3. The profit and loss account will have to be re-casted. Through this method the expenses on current items will be deducted from revenue from sales.

Table 4.3 Funds from business operations

Recasted Profit and Loss Account (Direct Method)
I. Revenue from sales
II. Less working capital expenses
(*i*) Use of raw materials (cost)
(*ii*) Manufacturing cost (excluding depreciation)
(*iii*) Office expenses
(*iv*) Selling expenses
(*v*) Expenses on insurance
(*vi*) Expenses on advertising
(*vii*) Interest expense
(*viii*) Income tax
I – II = Funds from business operations

The second method which can be used for calculating funds from business operations is called the 'indirect method'. Through this method, adjustments have to be made to profits of the firm/company. It may be stated that any one of the methods may be used to calculate the funds from business operations. In the indirect method:

(*a*) All expenses which do not have an effect on reducing working capital are added back. An example is of depreciation.

(*b*) Income which has not occurred due to business operations are deducted. An example is of dividends received or interest received and does not have a relevance to business operations.

(*c*) All items that do not contribute to working capital but have been added to revenue are deducted. Example may be cited of price appreciation of a building.

Table 4.4 depicts alternate indirect method for calculating funds from business operations. In this method, the net income or loss are depicted by the adjusted profit and loss account. Certain items must be carefully analysed.

Depreciation: The value of an asset decreases due to its use or obsolescence. Depreciation is provided to protect the integrity of capital. Depreciation is the accrual loss of value of an asset from the time it is purchased until its scrap value at the end of its useful life. It is not a valuation but it is an allocation of the cost of an asset in its useful life until it reaches its scrap value. Therefore this is added to net income to calculate funds from business operations.

Redemption of Debentures: When a firm redeems its debentures it has to pay cash. It becomes a *use* of its funds.

Issue of Shares: This brings about income for a company and hence it is used as a *source* of working capital.

Gain on Sale of a Fixed Asset: When a firm sells an asset and there is a gain on it this becomes a source of funds, but if there is a loss it decreases the funds of a company.

Table 4.4 Funds from business operations

(Alternate Indirect Method)
I. Net Income/Loss in profit and loss account
II. Add
(*i*) Depreciation.
(*ii*) Loss on sale of non-current assets.
(*iii*) Amortization of intangible assets, for example, goodwill.
(*iv*) Amortization of expenses on issue of shares.
(*v*) Amortization of discount given on issue of debentures.
(*vi*) Amortization of extraordinary losses in previous years.
III. Less
(*i*) Income from dividends/interest on investments.
(*ii*) Income through revaluation of non-current assets.
(*iii*) Income on sale of equipment.
(*iv*) Amortization of premium amount received from debentures.
I + II – III = Funds from business operations

Example 4.1 From the following income statement for the year ended 31 March 2009 of ABC Company Ltd. Determine business from operations by direct and indirect methods.

Income Statement of ABC Company Ltd.

Particulars	Amount (Rs.)	Amount (Rs.)
Sales Revenue		75,00,000
Less cost of goods sold	20,00,000	
Cash Expenses	4,00,000	
Depreciation	3,00,000	
Amortization of		
(*i*) Patents	8,00,000	
(*ii*) Preliminary Expenses	2,00,000	
Loss on sale of old equipment	4,00,000	41,00,000

[Contd...]

Particulars	Amount (Rs.)	Amount (Rs.)
Operating income		34,00,000
Less Income Tax @ 40%		13,60,000
		20,40,000
Other Income	10,00,000	
Gain on redemption of debentures	2,00,000	
Dividend from received	3,00,000	15,00,000
Net Income		**35,40,000**

Funds From Business Operations – Direct Method I

Particulars	Amount (Rs.)	Amount (Rs.)
Sales Revenue		75,00,000
Less Expenses using working capital	20,00,000	
Cost of goods sold	4,00,000	
Cash expenses	13,60,000	
Income tax	**37,60,000**	
Funds from business operations		**37,40,000**

Funds From Business Operations – Indirect Method II

Particulars	Amount (Rs.)	Amount (Rs.)
Net Income		35,40,000
Add Expenses not involving working capital		
Depreciation	3,00,000	
Amortization of		
(*i*) Patent	8,00,000	
(*ii*) Expenses	2,00,000	
Loss on sale of equipment	4,00,000	17,00,000
		52,40,000
Less Income not part of working capital		
Dividends received	3,00,000	
Income from sale of land (gain)	10,00,000	
Gain from redemption of debentures	2,00,000	15,00,000
Funds from business operations		**37,40,000**

Example 4.2 From the following comparative Balance Sheets of ABC company Ltd prepare (*i*) a statement of sources and uses of funds and (*ii*) schedule of changes of working capital.

Balance Sheet as on 31 March of 2008 & 2009

Particulars	Year 2008 (Rs.)	Year 2009 (Rs.)
Assets		
Cash	5,00,000	7,00,000
Marketable securities	2,00,000	4,50,000
Debtors	5,00,000	6,50,000
Stock	4,00,000	2,80,000
Long-term investments	3,00,000	4,00,000
Machinery	13,00,000	15,00,000
Buildings	30,00,000	36,00,000
Liabilities & Equity		
Accumulated depreciation	2,00,000	2,60,000
Creditors	3,00,000	4,00,800
Bills Payable	1,00,000	2,00,000
Share Capital	35,00,000	35,00,000
Reserves & Surplus	10,00,000	12,00,000
Long-term Loans	5,00,000	6,00,000
P & L A/c	6,00,000	14,20,000
Total	**62,00,000**	**75,80,000**

Additional Information

During the year a machine was sold by the company for Rs. 9,00,000 and dividends of Rs. 5,00,000 to shareholders was paid purchase of shed for storage Rs. 1,70,000.

Solution

Statement of sources and uses of working capital

(Funds Flow Statement)

Sources	Amount (Rs.)
Funds from business operations (Profit increased)	10,20,000
Sale of machine	9,00,000
Long-term loans	1,00,000
Cash	2,00,000
	22,20,000

[Contd...]

Uses	Amount (Rs.)
Dividends paid to shareholders	5,00,000
Long-term investments	1,00,000
Machinery	2,00,000
Building	6,00,000
Marketable securities	2,50,000
Stock	1,20,000
Purchase of shed	1,70,000
Increase in working capital	2,80,000
	22,20,000

The current assets and current liabilities show the increase or decrease in working capital. Therefore, a comparison is made between two balance sheets given in this example and the increase of working capital is reflected in the sources and uses statement prepared.

Schedule of changes in working capital

Particulars	Increase (Rs.)	Decrease (Rs.)
Current Assets	2,00,000	
Marketable securities	2,50,000	
Debtors	1,50,000	
Stock Rs. 6,00,000 – 1,20,000 =	4,80,000	1,20,000
Current Liabilities		
Creditors	1,00,000	
Bills payable	1,00,000	
	2,00,000	

$$\text{Working capital} = CA - CL$$

Working Capital increase = 4,80,000 – 2,00,000 = Rs. 2,80,000.

Funds from business operations	Amount (Rs.)
Increase in Profits	8,20,000
Add reserves increase	2,00,000
	10,20,000

This is shown as a source in the Fund Flow Statement given earlier.

4.5 CASH FLOW STATEMENT ANALYSIS

Cash management is very important for an organisation's day-to-day planning of resources. To find out the availability of cash a firm has to make projections of their cash inflows and outflows. The analysis of past cash flows is useful to provide an analysis for future requirements. The cash flow statement is in other words a ***Statement of Changes in Financial Position*** on cash basis and it depicts the cash position between two balance sheet dates. This statement focuses on **cash** while the fund flow statement provides information on **working capital** funds. This statement is depicted in Table 4.5.

4.6 PREPARATION OF CASH FLOW STATEMENTS

A cash flow statement is prepared on cash basis. The direct method of preparing a statement showing cash flow is to record all inflows of cash as well as outflows of cash. The cash received minus the cash payments accounts for the cash balance of the period. This can be compared to the previous year's cash and the balance would show whether there is an increase or decrease any cash. However, there are many items for which cash has been paid during the year. Adjustments have to be made to non-cash items to arrive at cash from business operations.

Cash from Business Operations: In the cash flow statements cash basis is acceptable. Cash sales are a source of cash and cash purchases are a use of cash. Although credit sales and credit purchases are a part of working capital, they cannot be acceptable on cash basis. Similarly all expenses and incomes in a cash statement will involve only cash items and not on credit.

Table 4.5 Cash flow statement

Sources
Profit from business operations
Decrease in assets (excluding cash)
Increase in liabilities
Issue of equity shares
Issue of preference shares
Uses
Loss from business operations
Increase in assets (excluding cash)
Decrease in liabilities
Redemption of redeemable preference shares
Cash Dividend

Therefore ***prepaid expenses*** or ***outstanding incomes*** do not have any meaning in a cash flow statement. When net changes have to be made from income statements and comparative balance sheets adjustments for non-cash items have to be made. Cash from operations have to be made in a similar manner as in the case of fund flow analysis.

Current assets increase/decrease: The increases or decreases in current assets have an effect on the cash flow of the company. The following may be observed as a general rule:

(*i*) When current assets in a year show an increase it means that cash has reduced from the cash flow of the company.

(*ii*) When current assets decrease in a year it depicts an increase in cash flows.

Examples

(*a*) ***Increase in debtors decreases cash***

(*b*) ***Decrease in debtors increases cash***

(*c*) ***Increase in inventory decreases cash***

(*d*) ***Decrease in inventory increases cash***

(*e*) ***Increase in prepaid expenses means that cash out flow is high***

A cash flow statement can be made either by direct method or by indirect method. In the direct method the cash receipts and cash payments are depicted and in the indirect method the net profit or loss is adjusted for depicting the effect on transactions that are of the nature of non-cash items.

Table 4.6 Direct Method: Cash flow from operating activity

Cash receipts	---------
Less: Payments made to suppliers of material	---------
Less: Expenses of administration paid by cash	---------
Cash from operations	---------
Less: Taxes paid	
Receipts/Payments on extraordinary items	---------
Net cash from operating activities	---------

A format in Table 4.6 depicts the direct method of preparing a cash flow statement.

Indirect method is depicted below in Table 4.7. This is calculated by adjusting the net profit or loss. It depicts changes in receivables and payments it also depicts the non-cash items like depreciation and deferred expenses.

Table 4.7 Indirect method: Cash flow from business operations

Cash flows from operating activities	------------
Net profit	------------
Add: Depreciation	------------
Add: Non-cash expenses	------------

[Contd...]

Add: Loss on sale of assets	------------
Less: Increase in debtors	------------
Less: Interest income	------------
Dividend income	------------
Less: Profit on sale of assets	------------
Operating profit before working capital changes	------------
Add: Decrease in working capital	------------
Decrease in current assets other than cash	------------
Increase in current liabilities	------------
Less: Increase in working capital	------------
Increase in current assets other than cash	------------
Less: Decrease in current liabilities	------------
Cash generated from operations	------------
Adjustment for extraordinary items	------------
Cash flow from business operations	------------

Example 4.3 Prepare a cash flow statement from the following data. The summarized Balance Sheets of XYZ Company Ltd. are given for 2008 & 2009 and the income statements is given for 2008.

Balance Sheets of XYZ Company Ltd. for the year 2008-09

Particulars	Year 2008 (Rs.)	Year 2009 (Rs.)
Assets		
Machinery	20,00,000	25,00,000
Less: depreciation	4,00,000	7,50,000
	16,00,000	17,50,000
Cash	17,00,000	20,00,000
Stock	13,00,000	16,00,000
Debtors	8,00,000	12,00,000
Discount on debentures	2,00,000	1,50,000
	56,00,000	**67,00,000**
Liabilities		
Equity share capital	15,00,000	25,00,000
Profit & Loss A/c	12,00,000	15,00,000
Debentures	20,00,000	20,00,000
Creditors	9,00,000	7,00,000
	56,00,000	**67,00,000**

Income Statement of XYZ Company Ltd. for the year 2009

Particulars	Amount (Rs.)	Amount (Rs.)
Sales Revenue		90,00,000
Less		
Cost of goods sold	50,00,000	
Depreciation	4,00,000	
Interest cost	4,00,000	
Office expenses	21,00,000	
	79,00,000	
Net Profit		**11,00,000**

Solution

Cash Flow Statement

Particulars	Amount (Rs.)	Amount (Rs.)
I. Cash from business operations		
Net profit		11,00,000
Add: Accumulated depreciation		3,50,000
Add: Depreciation		4,00,000
Add: Discount on debentures		50,000
Operating profit		19,00,000
Less: Increase in debtors	4,00,000	
Less: Increase in stock	3,00,000	
Less: Decrease in creditors	2,00,000	
	9,00,000	
		10,00,000
II. Cash from investment activity		
Less: Payment of Fixed Assets	5,00,000	
III. Cash flow from financing activities		
(*i*) Add: Issue of share capital		10,00,000
(*ii*) Less: Interest paid	4,00,000	
(*iii*) Less: dividend paid	8,00,000	
		17,00,000
II + III		
Add: Cash in the beginning		3,00,000
Cash balance at the end		20,00,000

Working Notes:

	Amount (Rs.)
(*i*) Profit & loss A/c	12,00,000
Add Net profit of current year	11,00,000
	23,00,000
Less closing balance	15,00,000
Dividend paid	8,00,000

(*ii*) Discount on debentures has decreased by Rs. 50,000 it is the amount written off during the year.

4.7 STATEMENT OF CHANGES IN FINANCIAL POSITION – TOTAL RESOURCES BASIS

Funds flow statement and cash flow statement are used for analysing the past data and for planning and decision making for the future. The statements highlight the changes in the working capital position and the direction of change and the reasons for such a change between two Balance Sheet Periods. The fund flow statements show the *sources* of funds and their *application* in a company. The cash flow analysis shows the increase and decrease in cash. Items which do not affect cash are excluded. It is useful for short-term planning. Cash flow statement like the funds flow statement can be made by direct method and by indirect method.

The statements showing changes in financial position omit major financial and investment activities as they do not affect working capital or cash of the company. However, they are significant financing and investment activities of a firm. Therefore, statements are prepared on the total resources position of the firm to get an overall view of the financial position. Both fund flow statement and cash flow statement have to be re-casted for preparing them into statements on total financial resources basis. It discloses those items which have a significant effect on the financial position of a firm but do not increase or decrease working capital. When a firm converts its debentures into equity shares, it has a major impact on the company's debt equity position. Even bonus share have the effect of increasing paid up capital of a company. These can be shown through a statement of financial changes on total resource basis. The format for the fund flow statement on total resource position is depicted in Table 4.8.

Table 4.8 Fund flow statement on total resource basis

Particulars	Amount (Rs.)
Sources	
Financial resources from operations	----------
Sale of plant	----------
Loans	----------
Issue of equity shares for cash	----------

[Contd...]

Particulars	Amount (Rs.)
Financial resources not affecting working capital	----------
Issue of equity shares to convert debentures	----------
Issue of equity shares as bonus shares	----------
Financial Resources Provided	----------
Uses	
Purchase of land and building	----------
Purchase of plant and machinery	----------
Payment of cash dividend	----------
Financial resources not affecting working capital	
Payment of debentures through conversion into equity	----------
Payment: Bonus shares	----------
Financial Resources Applied	----------
Increase in working capital	

The cash flow statement can also be re-casted to show a statement on total resource position. Table 4.9 depicts a cash flow statement on total financial resource position.

Table 4.9 Cash flow statement on total resource basis

Particulars	Amount (Rs.)
Sources	
Cash from operations	----------
Sale of plant and machinery	----------
Additional institutional loan	----------
Issue of equity shares	----------
Financial resources not affecting cash	
Issue of equity shares to convert debentures	----------
Issue of equity shares as bonus shares	----------
Financial Resources Provided	
Uses	
Purchase of land and building	----------
Purchase of plant and machinery	----------
Payment of cash dividend	----------
Financial resources not affecting cash	
Payment of debentures through conversion debentures	----------
Payment of bonus shares	----------
Financial Resources Applied	
Increase in Cash	

Thus a fund flow statement is prepared to depict short-term solvency and to include items that show a change in the balance of the working capital. Cash flow statement is prepared to record cash receipts and payments of a firm. It depicts the liquidity position of a firm. All the changes relating to cash between two balance sheet dates are recorded in it.

POINTS TO REMEMBER

- The statements of changes in financial position are prepared to show the flow of funds and cash in an organization.
- The fund flow statement depicts the increase and decrease in current assets and current liabilities between two balance sheet dates. It analyses the changes in working capital of a company.
- The cash flow statements depicts the liquidity of the firm an records all cash receipts and cash payments.
- A fund flow statement is prepared by direct and indirect method and on the basis of total financial position.
- A cash flow statement is also prepared by direct and indirect methods and by re-casting the cash flow statement and showing it according to the total financial position.
- A schedule of changes in working capital is prepared to show increase and decrease in working capital of a firm.
- A schedule of changes in cash flow is prepared to show the increase and decrease in the cash position of a firm.
- The word fund is used in fund flow analysis to mean the difference between current assets and current liabilities. The word fund is also used in a cash flow statement to be cash.
- A fund flow statement helps in finding out the liquidity position and expenditures of a firm.
- A cash flow statement helps in finding out the cash receipts and cash payments of a firm.

OBJECTIVE TYPE QUESTIONS

State whether the following statements are true (T) or false (F).

1. Statement of changes in working capital indicates current assets as a change to total assets.
2. Depreciation is not a source of funds.
3. Sale of intangible fixed assets like goodwill patents or copyright are sources of working capital.
4. Fund flow statement is a summary of the sources and uses of working capital.
5. Cash flow statement depicts uses of capital in the current year.
6. Fund means retention of earnings.
7. Losses are sources of cash.
8. Increase in current liabilities increases cash flow from operations.
9. A statement of changes in financial position is important for short-term planning of resources.
10. Cash flow statement is important for long-term planning.

Answers: 1. (F), 2. (T), 3. (T), 4. (T), 5. (F), 6. (F), 7. (F), 8. (T), 9. (F), 10. (F)

THEORETICAL QUESTIONS

1. What is a statement of changes in financial position? What is its importance and limitations?
2. Distinguish between cash flow statement and fund flow statement. How would you convert them into a statement of changes in financial position on all financial sources basis?
3. What are the sources and uses of working capital? What is the position of depreciation in preparing a statement of changes in financial position?
4. Prepare a statement of sources and uses of each by direct and indirect methods.
5. What is a fund flow statement? Prepare a statement showing sources and uses of funds by direct and indirect method.

ILLUSTRATIVE PROBLEMS

Illustration 4.1 The following is the condensed Balance Sheet of a company at the beginning and end of the year 2009.

Balance Sheets

Particulars	As on 1.1.2009 (Rs.)	As on 31.12.2009 (Rs.)
Assets		
Cash	50,000	40,000
Sundry debentures	77,000	73,000
Short- term investments	1,10,000	84,000
Prepaid Expenses	1,000	2,000
Stock in trade	92,000	1,06,000
Freehold land and sheds	1,00,000	1,00,000
Plant and machinery	72,000	80,000
	5,02,000	4,85,000
Liabilities and Capital		
Sundry creditors	1,03,000	96,000
Outstanding expenses	13,000	22,000
5% debentures	90,000	70,000
Depreciation fund	40,000	44,000
Reserves for contingencies	60,000	50,000
Profit and Loss A/c	16,000	23,000
Share capital	1,80,000	1,80,000
	5,02,000	4,85,000

The following addition information is available:

(*a*) Dividend was paid @ 10%.

(*b*) New machinery of Rs. 20,000 was purchased during the year and old machinery costing Rs. 12,000 was sold for Rs. 4,000 on which accumulated depreciation was Rs. 6,00,000 the factory shares are fully depreciated.

(*c*) 5% debentures of face value of Rs. 100 each worth Rs. 20,000 were redeemed by purchasing them in the open market at Rs. 96 each.

(*d*) Rs. 10,000 was debited to the contingency reserve for settlement of previous tax liability.

(*e*) Investments worth Rs. 26,000 were sold at book value.

You are required to prepare a schedule of changes in working capital and a statement showing sources and application of funds.

Solution

Particulars	Amount (Rs.)
Increase in Profit and Loss A/c	7,000
Add dividend paid	18,000
Depreciation on machinery	10,000
Less on sale of machinery	2,000
Profit on redemption of 5% debentures	37,000
Less:	800
Funds from business operation	**36,200**

Machinery A/c

Particulars	(Rs.)	Particulars	(Rs.)
To balance b/d	72,000	By cash A/c	4,000
To cash purchases	20,000	By Accumulated depreciation A/c	6,000
		By P&L A/c	2,000
		By Balance c/d	80,000
	92,000		92,000

Depreciation A/c

Particulars	(Rs.)	Particulars	(Rs.)
Depreciation on machinery sold	6,000	By balance b/d	40,000
To balance c/d	44,000	By P&L A/c	10,000
	50,000		50,000

Statement of Changes in Working Capital

Particulars	1-1-09 (Rs.)	31-12-09 (Rs.)	Decrease (Rs.)	Increase (Rs.)
Current Assets				
Cash & Bank Balance	50,000	40,000	–	10,000
Sundry Debtors	77,000	73,000	–	4,000
Temporary Investments	1,10,000	84,000	–	26,000
Prepaid Expenses	1,000	2,000	1,000	
Stock	92,000	1,06,000	14,000	
(i)	3,30,000	3,05,000		

[Contd...]

Particulars	1-1-09 (Rs.)	31-12-09 (Rs.)	Decrease (Rs.)	Increase (Rs.)
Current Liabilities				
Sundry creditors	1,03,000	96,000	7,000	
Outstanding liability	13,000	22,000	9,000	
(ii)	1,16,000	1,18,000		
Working capital (i) – (ii)	2,14,000	1,87,000		
Decrease in working capital		27,000	27,000	
	2,14,000	2,14,000	49,000	49,000

Statement showing sources and application of funds for the year ended 31.12.2010

Particulars	(Rs.)	(Rs.)
Sources of Funds		
Funds from operations operating profit	26,200	
Add depreciation	10,000	36,200
Decrease in working capital		27,000
Sale of machinery		4,000
		67,200
Application of Funds		20,000
Repayment of 5% debentures		19,200
Dividend paid		18,000
Tax paid		70,000
		67,200

Illustration 4.2 From the following details relating to the Accounts of Grow More Ltd. prepare Cash Flow Statement.

Particulars	31.03.2001 (Rs.)	31.03.2002 (Rs.)
Liabilities		
Share Capital	10,00,000	8,00,000
Reserve	2,00,000	1,50,000
Profit and Loss Account	1,00,000	60,000
Debentures	2,00,000	
Provision of taxation	1,00,000	70,000
Proposed dividend	2,00,000	1,00,000
Sundry Creditors	7,00,000	8,20,000
	25,00,000	20,00,000

[Contd...]

	31.03.2001 (Rs.)	31.03.2002 (Rs.)
Assets		
Plant and Machinery	7,00,000	5,00,000
Land and Building	6,00,000	4,00,000
Investment	1,00,000	
Sundry Debtors	5,00,000	7,00,000
Stock	4,00,000	2,00,000
Cash on hand/Bank	2,00,000	2,00,000
	25,00,000	20,00,000

(*i*) Depreciation @ 25% was charged on the opening value of Plant and Machinery.

(*ii*) During the year one old machine costing 50,000 (WDV 20,000) was sold for Rs. 35,000.

(*iii*) Rs. 50,000 was paid towards Income tax during the year.

(*iv*) Building under construction was not subject to any depreciation.

Prepare Cash flow Statement. **(CA 2002)**

Solution

Cash flow statement of Grow More Ltd. for the year ended 31 March 2002

	Amount (Rs.)	Amount (Rs.)
Cash Flow from Operating Activities		
Net Profit	40,000	
Proposed Dividends	2,00,000	
Provision for taxation	80,000	
Transfer to General Reserve	50,000	
Depreciation	1,25,000	
Profit on sale of Plant and Machinery	15,000	
Operating Profit before Working Capital changes	4,80,000	
Increase in stock	2,00,000	
Decrease in debtors	2,00,000	
Decrease in creditors	1,20,000	
Cash generated from operations	3,60,000	
Income tax paid	50,000	
Net cash from operating activities		3,10,000

[Contd...]

	Amount (Rs.)	Amount (Rs.)
Cash Flow from Investing Activities		
Purchase of fixed assets	3,45,000	
Expenses on building	2,00,000	
Increase in investments	1,00,000	
Sale of old machine	35,000	
Net Cash used investing activities		6,10,000
Cash Flow from Financing Activities		
Proceeds from issue of shares	2,00,000	
Proceeds from issue of debentures	2,00,000	
Dividend paid	1,00,000	
Net cash used in financing activities		3,00,000
Net increase in cash or cash equivalents		NIL
Cash and Cash equivalents at the beginning of the year		2,00,000
Cash and Cash equivalents at the end of the year		2,00,000

Working Notes:

Provision for taxation account

Particulars	(Rs.)	Particulars	(Rs.)
To cash (Paid)	50,000	By Balance b/d	70,000
To Balance c/d	1,00,000	By Profit and Loss A/c (Bal. figure)	80,000
	1,50,000		1,50,000

Plant and machinery account

Particulars	(Rs.)	Particulars	(Rs.)
To Balance b/d	5,00,000	By Depreciation	1,25,000
To Cash (Balancing figure)	3,45,000	By Cash (sale of machine)	20,000
		(Balancing figure)	7,00,000
	8,45,000		8,45,000

Illustration 4.3 The following are the Balance Sheets of Gama Limited for the year ending 31 March 2004 and 31March 2005:

Balance Sheet as on 31 March 2005

Particulars	2004 (Rs.)	2005 (Rs.)
Capital and Liabilities		
Share Capital	6,75,000	7,87,500
General Reserves	2,25,000	2,81,250
Capital Reserve (Profit on Sale of investment)	–	11,250
Profit & Loss Account	1,12,500	2,25,000
15% Debentures	3,37,500	2,25,000
Accrued Expenses	11,250	13,500
Creditors	1,80,000	2,81,250
Provision for Dividends	33,750	38,250
Provision of Taxation	78,750	85,500
	16,53,750	19,48,500
Assets		
Fixed Assets	11,25,000	13,50,000
Less: Accumulated depreciation	2,25,000	2,81,250
Net fixed assets	9,00,000	10,68,750
Long-term Investments (at cost)	2,02,500	2,02,500
Stock (at cost)	2,25,000	3,03,750
Debtors (net of provision for doubtful debts of Rs. 45,000 and Rs. 56,250 respectively for 2004 and 2005 respectively)	2,53,125	2,75,625
Bills receivables	45,000	73,125
Prepaid expenses	11,250	13,500
Miscellaneous Expenditure	16,875	11,250
	16,53,750	19,48,500

Additional Information

(*i*) During the year 2004–05, fixed assets with a net book value of Rs.11,250 (accumulated depreciation, Rs. 33,750) was sold for Rs. 9,000.

(*ii*) During the year 2004–05, Investment costing Rs. 90,000 were sold, and also investment costing Rs. 90,000 was purchased.

(*iii*) Debentures were retired at a Premium of 10%.

(*iv*) Tax of Rs. 61,875 was paid for 2003–04.

(*v*) During the year 2004–05, bad debts of Rs. 15,750 were written off against the provision for Doubtful Debt account.

(*vi*) The proposed dividend for 2003–04 was paid in 2004–05.

Prepare a Fund Flow Statement (Statement of changes in Financial Position on working capital basis) for the year ended 31 March 2005. **(CA 2005)**

Solution

Computation of Funds from Operation

Particulars	Amount (Rs.)
Profit and Loss balance on 31 March 2005	2,25,000
Add: Depreciation	90,000
Loss on sale of assets	2,250
Misc. Expenditure written off	5,625
Transfer on Reserves	56,250
Premium on Redemption of debentures	11,250
Provision for Dividend	38,250
Provision for Taxation	68,625
	4,97,250
Less: P/L balance on 31 March 2004	1,12,500
Funds from operations	3,84,750

Accumulated Depreciation A/c

Particulars	(Rs.)	Particulars	(Rs.)
To Fixed Assets A/c	33,750	By Bal. b/d	2,25,000
		By P/L A/c	90,000
To Balance c/d	2,81,250	(Prov. For dep.) (Bal. fig.)	
	3,15,000		3,15,000

Fixed Assets A/c

Particulars	(Rs.)	Particulars	(Rs.)
To Balance C/d	11,25,000	By Accumulated Depreciation A/c	33,750
To Bank (purchase of Fixed Assets) (Bal. fig.)	2,70,000	By Cash	9,000
		By P/L (loss on sale)	2,250
		By Bal. c/d	13,50,000
	13,95,000		13,95,000

Provision for Tax A/c

Particulars	(Rs.)	Particulars	(Rs.)
To Cash (tax paid)	61,875	By Bal. b/d	78,750
To Bal. C/d	85,500	By P/L A/c (Prov.) (Bal. Figure)	68,625
	1,47,375		1,47,375

Statement of Changes in Working Capital

Particulars	31 March 2004	31 March 2005	Changes in W/C(+)	(–)
Current Assets				
Stock	2,25,000	3,03,750	78,750	
Debtors	2,53,125	2,75,625	22,500	
Bills Receivables	45,000	73,125	28,125	
Prepaid expenses	11,250	13,500	2,250	
	5,34,375	6,66,000	1,31,625	—
Less: Current liabilities				
Accrued Expenses	11,250	13,500	—	2,250
Creditors	1,80,000	2,81,250	—	1,01,250
	1,91,250	2,94,750	1,31,750	1,03,500
Working Capital	3,43,125	3,71,250	—	—
Increase in Working Capital			—	28,125
			1,31,625	1,31,625

Funds Flow Statement for the year ended 31 March 2005

Particulars	Amount (Rs.)
Sources of Funds	
Working Capital from Operations	3,84,750
Sale of Fixed Assets	9,000
Sale of Investments	1,01,250
Share Capital issued	1,12,500
Total Funds Provided (A)	6,07,500
Application of Funds	**Amount (Rs.)**
Purchase of Fixed Assets	2,70,000
Purchase of Investments	90,000
Payment of Debentures (at a premium at 10%)	1,23,750
Payment of Dividends	33,750
Payment of Taxes	61,875
Total Funds Applied (B)	5,79,375
Increase in Working Capital (A – B)	28,125

Illustration 4.4 The following are Balance Sheets of Tamil Nadu Industrial Corporation Ltd.:

Balance Sheet

Particulars	Previous Year (Rs.)	Current Year (Rs.)
Assets		
Fixed Assets		
Property	1,11,375	1,08,187
Machinery	84,713	94,650
Goodwill	—	7,500
Current Assets		
Stock	82,500	69,000
Trade debtors	64,620	52,073
Cash and bank	1,125	8,250
Pre-payments	2,527	750
	3,46,860	3,40,410
Liabilities		
Shareholders' Funds		
Paid-up capital	1,65,000	2,02,500
Reserves	22,500	30,000
Profit and Loss account	29,768	30,915

[Contd...]

Particulars	Previous Year (Rs.)	Current Year (Rs.)
Current Liabilities		
Creditors	29,250	31,245
Bills payable	25,342	8,250
Bank overdraft	45,000	—
Provision for taxation	30,000	37,500
	3,46,860	3,40,410

During the current year ended 31st March, a dividend of Rs. 19,500 was paid and the assets of another company were purchased for Rs. 37,500 payable in fully paid-up shares. Such assets purchased were:

Stock – Rs. 16,230 Machinery – Rs. 13,770 Goodwill – Rs. 7,500

In addition, plant at a cost of Rs. 4,237 was purchased during the year.

The following depreciation was written off during the year on Property – Rs. 3,187 and on Machinery – Rs. 8,070.

Income tax during the year amounting to Rs. 21,578 was changed to provision for taxation. Net profit for the year before tax was Rs. 57,225.

(*a*) Prepare statement of changes in financial position on total resources basis.

(*b*) Prepare a schedule of changes in the working capital.

Solution

Calculation of Funds from Operations

Particulars	Amount (Rs.)	Amount (Rs.)
Profit and Loss A/c balance at the end		30,915
Add: (1) Depreciation: Property	3,188	
Machinery	8,070	11,258
(2) Provision for dividend		19,500
(3) Transfer to reserve		7,500
		69,173
Less: Profit and Loss A/c balance at the beginning		29,768
Funds from Operations		39,405
Sources		
Fund From Business operations		39,405

[Contd...]

Particulars	Amount (Rs.)	Amount (Rs.)
Issue of Long-term Liabilities		
Issue of equity share (for the purchase of assets of another company)		37,500
(i)		76,905
Applications		
Purchase of non-current assets		4,237
Plant for cash		13,770
Machinery (in exchange for equity shares)		7,500
Dividends paid		19,500
(ii)		45,007
Increase in Working Capital (i) – (ii)		31,898

Schedule of Changes in the Working Capital

Particulars	Year		Working Capital (Rs.)	
	Previous	Current	Increase (+)	Decrease (–)
Current Assets				
Stock	82,500	69,000	—	13,500
Trade debtors	64,620	52,073	—	12,547
Cash and bank	1,125	8,250	7,125	—
Pre-payments	2,527	750	—	1,777
(a)	1,50,772	1,30,073		
Current Liabilities				
Creditors	29,250	31,245	—	1,995
Bills payable	25,342	8,250	17,092	—
Bank overdraft	45,000	—	45,000	—
Provisions for taxation	30,000	37,500	—	7,500
(b)	1,29,592	76,995	—	—
Net Working Capital **(a) – (b)**	21,180	53,078	—	—
Increase in Net Working Capital	31,898	—	—	31,898
	53,078	53,078	69,217	69,217

Illustration 4.5 The Balance Sheet of New Light Ltd. for the years ended 31 March 2001 and 2002 are as follows:

Liabilities	31 March 2001 (Rs.)	31 March 2002 (Rs.)	Assets	31 March 2001 (Rs.)	31 March 2002 (Rs.)
Equity share capital	12,00,000	16,00,000	Fixed Assets	32,00,000	38,00,000
10% preference			*Less*: Depreciation	9,20,000	11,60,000
Share capital	4,00,000	2,80,000		22,80,000	26,40,000
Capital reserve	—	40,000	Investment	4,00,000	3,20,000
General reserve	6,80,000	8,00,000	Cash	10,000	10,000
Profit and Loss A/c	2,40,000	3,00,000	Other current assets	11,10,000	13,10,000
9% Debentures	4,00,000	2,80,000	Preliminary expenses	80,000	40,000
Current liabilities	4,80,000	5,20,000			
Proposed dividend	1,20,000	1,44,000			
Provision for Tax	3,60,000	3,40,000			
Unpaid dividend	—	16,000			
	38,80,000	43,20,000		38,80,000	43,20,000

Additional Information

(*i*) The company sold one fixed asset for Rs. 1,00,000; the cost of which was Rs. 2,00,000 and the depreciation provided on it was Rs. 80,000.

(*ii*) The company also decided to write off another fixed asset costing Rs. 56,000 on which depreciation amounting to Rs. 40,000 has been provided.

(*iii*) Depreciation on fixed assets provide Rs. 3,60,000.

(*iv*) Company sold some investment at a profit of Rs. 40,000; which was credited to capital reserve.

(*v*) Debentures and preference share capital redeemed at 5% premium.

(*vi*) Company decided to value stock at cost, whereas previously the practice was to value stock at cost less 10%. The stock according to books on 31.3.2001 was Rs. 2,16,000. The stock on 31.3.2002 was correctly valued at Rs. 3,00,000.

Prepare Cash Flow Statement as per revised Accounting Standard 3 by indirect method.

(CA 2003)

Solution

Particulars	Amount (Rs.)	Amount (Rs.)
Cash flow from operating activities		
Increase in profit and loss A/c after inventory adjustment		
[Rs. 3,00,000 – Rs. 2,40,000 – Rs. 24,000]	36,000	
Transfer to general reserve	1,20,000	
Proposed dividend	1,44,000	
Provision for tax	3,40,000	
Net profit before taxation and extraordinary item	6,40,000	
Adjustment for		
Preliminary Expenses written off	40,000	
Depreciation	3,60,000	
Loss on sale of fixed assets	20,000	
Decrease in value of fixed assets	16,000	
Premium on redemption of preference share capital	6,000	
Premium on redemption of debentures	6,000	
Operating profit before working capital changes	10,88,000	
Increase in current liabilities		
(Rs. 5,20,000 – Rs. 4,80,000)	40,000	
Increase in other current assets		
[Rs. 13,10,000 – (Rs. 11,10,000 + Rs. 24,0000)]	1,76,000	
Cash generated from operations	9,52,200	
Income taxes paid	3,60,000	
Net cash from operating activities		5,92,000
Cash flow from investing activities		
Purchase of fixed Assets	8,56,000	
Proceeds from sale of fixed assets	1,00,000	
Proceeds from sale of investments	1,20,000	
Net cash used in investing activities		6,36,000
Cash flow from financing activities		
Proceeds from issue of share capital	4,00,000	
Redemption of preference shares	1,26,000	
Dividends paid	1,04,000	
Redemption of debentures (Rs. 1,20,000 + Rs. 6,000)	1,26,000	
Net cash used in financing activities		44,000
Net changed in cash and cash equivalents during the year		Nil
Cash and cash equivalents at the beginning of the year		10,000
Cash and cash equivalents at the end of the year		10,000

Working Notes:

1. Revaluation of stock will increase opening stock by Rs. 24,000

$$\frac{2,16,000}{90} \times 10 = \text{Rs. } 24,000$$

Therefore, opening balance of other current assets would be as follows:

Rs. 11,10,000 + Rs. 24,000 = Rs. 11,34,000

Due to under valuation of stock, the opening balance of profit and loss account be increased by 24,000. The opening balance of profit and loss account after revaluation of stock will be Rs. 2,40,000 + Rs. 24,000 = Rs. 2,64,000.

2. Investment Account

Particulars	(Rs.)	Particulars	(Rs.)
To balance b/d	4,00,000	By Bank A/c	1,20,000
To Capital Reserve A/c		(Balancing figure being investment sold)	
(Profit on sale of investment)	40,000	By Balance c/d	3,20,000
	4,40,000		4,40,000

3. Fixed Assets Account

Particulars	(Rs.)	Particulars		(Rs.)
To Balance b/d	32,00,000	By Bank A/c		
To Bank A/c	8,56,000	(Sale of assets)	1,00,000	
(balancing figure being		By Accumulated dep. A/c	80,000	
assets purchased)		By Profit & Loss A/c	20,000	
		(Loss on Sale of Assets)		2,00,000
		By Accumulated dep. A/c	40,000	
		By Profit and loss A/c	16,000	
		(Assets Written off)		56,000
		By Balance c/d		38,00,000
	40,56,000			40,56,000

4. Accumulated Depreciation Account

Particulars	(Rs.)	Particulars	(Rs.)
To Fixed assets A/c	80,000	By Balance b/d	9,20,000
To Fixed assets A/c	40,000	By Profit and Loss A/c	
To Balance c/d	11,60,000	(Depreciation for the period)	3,60,000
	12,80,000		12,80,000

5. Unpaid dividend is taken as non-current item and dividend paid is shown at Rs. 1,04,000 (Rs. 1,20,000 – 16,000).

Note: Alternatively, unpaid dividend can be assumed as current liability and hence, dividend paid can be shown at Rs. 1,20,000. Due to this assumption cash flow from operating activities would be affected. The cash flow operating activities will increase by Rs. 16,000 to Rs. 6,08,000 and cash flow from financing activities will get reduced by Rs. 16,000 to Rs. 28,000.

PROBLEMS FOR PRACTICE

Problem 4.1 ABC Ltd. gives you the following information. You are required to prepare Cash Flow Statement by using indirect methods as per as 3 for the year ended 31.03.2004:

Balance Sheet

Liabilities	31 March 2003 (Rs.)	31 March 2004 (Rs.)	Assets	31 March 2003 (Rs.)	31 March 2004 (Rs.)
Capital	50,00,000	50,00,000	Plant & Machinery	27,30,000	40,70,000
Retained Earnings	26,50,000	36,90,000	Less: Depreciation	6,10,000	7,90,000
Debentures	—	9,00,000		21,20,000	32,80,000
Current liabilities			Current Assets		
Creditors	8,80,000	8,20,000	Debtors	23,90,000	28,30,000
Bank loan	1,50,000	3,00,000	Less: Provision	1,50,000	1,90,000
Liability for expenses	3,30,000	2,70,000		22,40,000	26,40,000
Dividend payable	1,50,000	3,00,000	Cash	15,20,000	18,20,000
			Marketable securities	11,80,000	15,00,000
			Inventories	20,10,000	19,20,000
				90,000	1,20,000
	91,60,000	1,12,80,000	Prepaid expenses	91,60,000	1,12,80,000

Additional Information

(*i*) Net profit for the year ended 31 March 2004, after charging depreciation Rs. 1,80,000 is Rs. 22,40,000.

(*ii*) Debtors of Rs. 2,30,000 were determined to be worthless and were written off against the previous for doubtful debts account during the year.

(*iii*) ABC Ltd. declared dividend of Rs. 12,00,000 for the year 2003–2004.

(CA 2004)

Problem 4.2 The balance sheets of Hari Ltd. as on 31 December 1993 and 1994 are:

Balance Sheets of Hari Ltd.

Liabilities	31.12.93 (Rs.)	31.12.94 (Rs.)	Assets	31.12.93 (Rs.)	31.12.94 (Rs.)
Share capital	6,00,000	8,00,000	Fixed Assets	16,00,000	19,00,000
Capital reserve	—	20,000	Less: Depreciation	4,60,000	5,80,000
General reserve	3,40,000	4,00,000		11,40,000	13,20,000
Profit & Loss A/c	1,20,000	1,50,000	Investment	2,00,000	1,60,000
Debentures	4,00,000	2,80,000	Current assets	5,60,000	6,60,000
Current liabilities	2,40,000	2,60,000	Preliminary Exp.	40,000	20,000
Proposed dividend	60,000	72,000			
Provision for tax	1,80,000	1,70,000			
Unpaid dividends	—	8,000			
	19,40,000	21,60,000		19,40,000	21,60,000

Additional Information

During the year 1994, the Company:

(*i*) Sold one machine for Rs. 50,000; the cost of which was Rs. 1,00,000 and the depreciation provided on it was Rs. 40,000.

(*ii*) Provided Rs. 1,80,000 as depreciation.

(*iii*) Sold some investments at a profit of Rs. 20,000; which was credited to Capital Reserve.

(*iv*) Redeemed 30% of the Debentures @ 105.

(*v*) Decided to value stock at cost, whereas previously the practice was to value stock at cost less 10%. The stock according to books on 31.12.1993 was Rs. 1,08,000. The stock on 31.12.94 was correctly valued at Rs. 1,50,000 and decided to write off fixed assets costing Rs. 28,000 on which depreciation amounting to Rs. 20,000 has been provided.

Prepare the Funds flow statement for the year 1994.

(CA Final 1995)

Problem 4.3 You have been given the following statement of a company as at 31 December 1995 and 31 December 1996:

Particulars	31-12-1995 (Rs.)	31-12-1996 (Rs.)
Assets		
Fixed assets – Depreciation	7,20,000	12,00,000
Investments	22,500	20,000
Stock in trade	2,85,000	3,92,000
Sundry debtors	1,81,400	2,80,000
Cash at bank	2,60,000	90,000
Prepaid expenses	28,000	42,000
Liabilities		
Share capital	3,94,000	4,60,000
Reserve and surplus	2,96,000	6,24,000
Secured loan from bank	1,74,000	—
Provision for taxation	1,30,000	3,44,000
Sundry creditors	5,02,000	5,96,000
	14,96,900	20,24,000

The following further information is available from the records.

(*a*) The position ion respect of reserves and surplus is as under

Particulars	Amount (Rs.)
Balance as on 1 January 2006	2,96,000
Net Profit for the year	3,97,000
	6,93,000
Less: Dividend	69,000
	6,24,000

(*b*) On 31 December 1996 the accumulated depreciation on fixed assets was Rs. 4,00,000 and on 31 December 1995 was Rs. 3,60,000. Machinery costing Rs. 40,000; which was one-half depreciated, was discarded and written off in 1996. Depreciation for the ear amounted to Rs. 60,000.

(*c*) Investments costing Rs. 10,000 were sold during the year 1996 for Rs. 9,600 and government securities of the face value of Rs. 8,000 were purchased during the year for Rs. 7,500.

You are required to prepare statement of sources and application of funds.

(CS Final 1997)

Problem 4.4 Following information is available from the books of Standard Company Ltd.

Particulars	1994 (Rs.)	1995 (Rs.)
Profit made during the year		2,50,000
Income received in advance	500	600
Prepaid expenses	1,600	1,400
Debtors	80,000	95,000
Bills receivable	25,000	20,000
Creditors	45,000	40,000
Bills payable	13,000	15,000
Outstanding expenses	2,500	2,000
Accrued income	1,500	1,200

Calculate cash flow from operations.

(CS 1996)

Problem 4.5 From the following prepare a Cash Flow Statement for XYZ Ltd. for the year 1996.

XYZ Ltd.

Balance Sheet as on 31 March 1995

Liability & Equity	(Rs.)	Assets	(Rs.)	(Rs.)
Paid-up capital	50	Gross Fixed Assets	1,000	
Retained earnings	350	Less: Accrued Depreciation	100	900
Long-term debt	500	Inventory		110
Notes payable	80	Accounts receivables		50
Accounts payable	80	Cash		10
	1,060			1,060

Balance Sheet as on 31 March 1996

Liability & Equity	(Rs.)	Assets	(Rs.)	(Rs.)
Paid-up capital	50	Gross Fixed Assets	1,125	
Retained earnings	415	Less: Accrued Depreciation	175	950
Long-term debt	550	Inventory		110
Notes payable	100	Accounts receivables		60
Accounts payable	90	Cash		85
	1,205			1,205

Income Statement, 31 March 1996

Particulars		Amount (Rs.)
Sales		1,200
(–) Cost of goods sold		800
Gross Profit		400
(–) Selling, general, and administration expenses		150
EBIT		250
(–) Interest expenses		50
EBT		200
(–) Taxes (50%)		100
Net Income		100
Additional Information		
Dividend paid		35
Additions to retained earnings	65	
Depreciation	75	

(ICWA 1998)

❑❑❑

Financial Statements Analysis (Ratio Analysis) 5

LEARNING OBJECTIVES

5.1 What is Ratio Analysis?
5.2 Advantages of Ratio Analysis
5.3 Significance of Ratio Analysis to Users of Financial Data
5.4 Types of Ratios—Liquidity, Leverage, Coverage Profitability
5.5 Du-pont Analysis Chart
5.6 Ratio Analysis and Standards of Comparison
5.7 Limitation of Ratio Analysis

5.1 WHAT IS RATIO ANALYSIS?

Ratio analysis is a tool of financial analysis. It is described as a relationship between two or more things to evaluate the performance of a company. Traditional financial statements provide absolute accounting figures that do not provide the financial position and performance of a company. In Chapter 4 we discussed statement of changes in financial position. In this chapter ratio analysis is explained. It is used to remove the limitations of traditional financial statements. Ratio analysis helps investors, creditors, management and general public to evaluate the financial position of a company. It is a numerical relationship between two variables. It depicts a quantified index for qualitative judgments to be made about the company's performance.

Ratio analysis helps in comparing related information. Instead of absolute figures it depicts data in relative figures. The figures can be expressed as a percentage or as ratios. It becomes a yardstick for evaluating the financial data of a company. A ratio can be analysed by following a (*a*) trend, (*b*) by inter-firm comparison, (*c*) by comparing figures at a single point of time and (*d*) by comparison with certain standards.

5.2 ADVANTAGES OF RATIO ANALYSIS

Ratio analysis is very useful for financial statement analysis. The following advantages are there to a company for analysing its statements with the help of ratios.

(*i*) ***Simple:*** Ratios are calculated by dividing one number by another. It is easy to calculate and also easy to understand. Most of the ratios do not require any specialized training and are understood by everybody because the formulae used are simple. Everyone understands the formula in the same way. There are no discrepancies (except for some formulas, example formula related to return on capital employed in a company which is perceived differently by different people).

(*ii*) ***Trend Analysis:*** Ratios help in evaluating a firm's performance by measuring the current ratios with those of the past. This depicts facts like improvements in the financial position of a company or a fall or change in direction. After the trend is established by finding out the ratios, the analyst should understand and explain the reasons of change if any in ratios.

(*iii*) ***Forecasting:*** Ratio analysis helps in making an assessment of the future. It determines the past trends from financial statements and establishes future figures by forecasting based on the past experiences of the firm.

(*iv*) ***Inter-firm Comparison:*** Ratios are used for comparing the performance of one firm/company with another. It can also be used for comparison with industry averages. These comparisons will help a company to focus on its policies relating to liquidity, efficiency, solvency and profitability of a company.

(*v*) ***Assessment of Liquidity Position:*** A company has to continuously analyse whether its liquidity position is satisfactory. Ratio analysis is a technique through which a company can be successful in finding out its ability to meet it short-term liabilities. If it continuously meets its deadlines for making payments it will have a good reputation.

(*vi*) ***Determining Efficiency of a Company:*** Ratio analysis assesses the operational efficiency of a company and is able to detect the areas which require more attention. This helps the company to take remedial steps in removing problems to make it efficient.

(*vii*) ***Determining Profitability of the Company:*** Commercial organizations have the objective of running an enterprise successfully. If a company makes a profit it is successful, but if is making losses continuously it either requires to close down or to take remedial measures to make the firm profitable. Ratio analysis finds out the profitability position of the company and analyses them through different cost relationships indicating reasons for gains and losses.

(*viii*) ***Following Standards:*** Ratio analysis follows internal and external standards. Internal standards are made by comparing the firm own past performance and relating it to current and future planning. The external standards are made when a company's performance is compared with similar data of other companies or industry.

Therefore ratio analysis helps in planning the future course of business by determining ratios in a simple manner through trend analysis, inter-firm comparison, assessment of liquidity position of a company, determining efficiency and profitability of the company and calculating ratios through certain internal and external standards.

5.3 SIGNIFICANCE OF RATIO ANALYSIS TO USERS OF FINANCIAL DATA

Ratios have a great significance for different kinds of people. They are used by management, investors, creditors, shareholders and debenture holders, employees, government and general public to assess the performance of a company.

(*i*) ***Investors:*** When people invest money in a firm/company they expect that they have minimum risk and maximum profitability. To them, ratio analysis helps in finding out their earnings per share. Ratio analysis is a means of finding out the stability of a company and its future earning potential. Therefore, investors relay on analysing financial statements through ratio analysis.

(*ii*) ***Managers:*** The most important people in policy making of a firm are its managers in senior positions. They make the future policies of a company. In order to perform well they must analyse the past data of the firm by finding out relationships of different costs with the profitability of the company, its operational efficiency, its liquidity and solvency position and its overall financial position. Ratio analysis is one of the important indications of a firm's health and soundness of business.

(*iii*) ***Creditors:*** Ratio analysis is useful for creditors from whom the company is seeking short-term and long-term loans. Banks and financial institutions find ratios significant in deciding whether the company should be given a loan. People whose sales are on credit to the company have to consistently judge the soundness of a company's credit worthiness. These different kinds of creditors assess a company by its past records and make their own calculations through ratios before giving credit. Ratio analysis is one of the valuable tools for creditors in evaluating a firm.

(*iv*) ***Debenture Holders:*** Ratio analysis helps debenture holders form a specific group of people who have a long-term interest in the firm. They are interested in receiving their interest continuously till the time of liquidity. They analyse a company's financial statements through ratio analysis to judge the soundness of the affairs of the company.

(*v*) ***Government:*** A large factual amount of data pertaining to industry is useful for policy makers of the country. Government requires data and comparisons through ratio analysis to take certain decisions relating to prices of products and future policies for development in different sectors of the economy.

(*vi*) ***Employees:*** The employees of a company have a major interest in their place of work. They are interested in getting their salaries and thus calculate the profitability and operational efficiency of a company as they have a long standing interest in it. Further, they would like to give information to the general public about the performance of their company. The simple way of expressing the direction of their company's profitability and efficiency is through ratio analysis.

(*vii*) ***General Public:*** People are interested in finding out how an industry is faring. They make trends and analysis of development within their own country by making inter-firm comparisons in an industry. People dealing with Software Company's would like to know its demand and direction of flow of funds. Other people would be interested in steel prices and profitability. Yet, another group of people may be interested in finding out about oil and petroleum companies position and direction and flow of costs, prices and profitability. Ratio analysis is very useful for such comparisons and data analysis.

5.4 TYPES OF RATIOS

Ratios can be classified according to the function or financial activity that is required to be evaluated. We have seen above that ratio analysis is significant for different kinds of people in different ways but the main interest is safety of funds and profitability with minimum risk. There are different kinds of ratios which measure liquidity of a firm, long-term financial position of a firm, efficiency of a firm and its profitability. Ratios are therefore analysed according to the following:

(*i*) Liquidity ratios

(*ii*) Leverage ratios

(*iii*) Coverage ratios

(*iv*) Activity ratios

(*v*) Profitability ratios

(*i*) Liquidity Ratios

Liquidity ratios analyses the short-term solvency of a company/firm. The reason for calculating liquidity ratios is to find out if a firm has adequate funds to pay their current requirements whenever they are due. If a firm is able to meet its short-term obligations, it depicts its financial strength and solvency. Creditors that supply short-term loans are keen to know the company's liquidity position. The liquidity ratio is required for an understanding in preparing cash budgets and cash flow statements of a company. In order that a company is efficient there should be no wastage of funds. The funds should be used to gain maximum utility for the company. Thus, there should not be either excess or shortage of funds. Most companies find it difficult to cope with balancing of the right quantity of current assets.

The important ratios for finding out liquidity of a company are (*a*) current ratios and (*b*) quick ratios. Other ratios that can be used to find out liquidity of a company are cash ratios, interval measures and net working capital ratios.

(*a*) ***Current Ratio:*** Current ratios are a measure to find out the liquidity of the business of a company. It is calculated in the following way:

$$\text{Current ratio} = \frac{\text{Current assets}}{\text{Current liabilities}}$$

A current asset consists of cash as well as the assets which can be converted into cash within a year. The current assets that are included are marketable securities, debtors and inventory. If there are any prepaid expenses they will be included as a part of current assets as they are payments that the firm has already paid without any future liabilities in them.

Current liabilities consist of bills payable, creditors, short-term bank loans, income tax liabilities, accrued expenses and long-term debt that is maturing in the current year. All obligations that mature within a year are considered as current liabilities.

The current ratio is used to measure the short-term solvency of a firm. It indicates the number of current assets in comparison with current liabilities. If the current asset ratio is greater than 1, it indicates that the firm has a higher amount of current assets compare to the current liabilities.

Interpretation: A current ratio that is **2 : 1** is considered to be satisfactory. From Example 5.1 the current ratio of ABC Ltd. is the following:

$$\text{Current ratio} = \frac{\text{Current assets}}{\text{Current liabilities}}$$

(*i*) $$\text{Year 2007} = \frac{34,20,000}{11,50,000} = \mathbf{2.97 : 1}$$

(*ii*) $$\text{Year 2008} = \frac{37,25,000}{8,81,000} = \mathbf{4.22 : 1}$$

The current ratio of ABC Ltd. show that it is more than **2 : 1.** The current ratio is an indication that there is a margin of safety for the creditors of the company. The above example indicates that the current ratio is high and hence there is a high degree of safety for creditors of the company.

The current ratio must be assessed carefully as it is test of quantity and not quality. It is an arbitrary standard. The creditors should not completely rely on this standard because the value of current assets can decrease. If a company has a high cost of carrying inventories or it does not have a good and strict receivables policy it will have a slow intake of receipts from debtors. This will reduce its ability to pay and its solvency will decline. Further, the company has to pay its liabilities as they are not liable to change. The creditors of the company have to be paid in time. The current ratio will not provide a quality assessment of payments and receipts of the company. However, it is a simple and easy measure to test the liquidity of a company.

(*b*) ***Quick Ratio:*** The quick ratio is useful to depict liquid current assets as a ratio of current liabilities. It takes into account only those current assets which can be immediately converted into cash without any loss in value. For this ratio cash, debtors, bill receivables and marketable securities are considered. Inventory is considered to be difficult to convert immediately into cash, it is not included in this ratio.

Interpretation: Quick ratio should be **1 : 1** to indicate a satisfactory healthy financial condition of a company. This test is considered to be better than the current ratio because it is able to assess the liquidity of a company since it includes only quick conversion assets. However, this ratio should also be used very carefully because it may be recalled that if a company has certain debts which cannot be immediately converted into cash, then assessment will not be correct. The importance of inventory is also not considered. Some of the raw material and stock in a company can be immediately sold in cash.

A company which has a higher quick ratio can still have the problem of shortage of funds if its receivables and other debtors are slow and long outstanding in making their payments to the company. The company must have a good and tight receivables policy for quick receipt of funds. Similarly, it should also have a good inventory policy so that the inventories are purchased according to the requirements of the company and there is no slow moving inventory in the company. If inventories are kept stored in the company there will be inefficiency in its usage. A company has to continuously make a schedule of inventories. A quick turnover of inventories with a low quick ratio will be a necessary requirement for a firm's liquidity.

Quick ratio can be calculated in the following way:

$$\text{Quick ratio} = \frac{\text{Current assets} - \text{Inventories}}{\text{Current liabilities}}$$

(*i*)

$$\text{Year 2008} = \frac{34,20,000 - 32,20,000}{11,50,000}$$

$$= \frac{2,00,000}{11,50,000} = \mathbf{0.17 : 1}$$

(*ii*)

$$\text{Year 2009} = \frac{37,25,000 - 35,00,000}{8,81,000}$$

$$= \frac{2,25,000}{8,81,000} = \mathbf{0.25 : 1}$$

The results of quick ratio calculated from Example 5.1 indicate that current assets are low in comparison to the current liabilities. The company does not have a good quick ratio. The company may find it a problem to meet its obligations because its quick assets are very low. In 2008, it is **0.17 : 1**; in 2009 also it is not in a good position as it is only **0.25 : 1.**

(*c*) ***Cash Ratio:*** Another test of liquidity in a company is through its cash ratio. Cash and marketable securities are measured with the current liabilities. It is measure in the following manner:

$$\text{Cash Ratio} = \frac{\text{Cash + Marketable Securities}}{\text{Current Liabilities}}$$

Interpretation: This ratio is considered to be a measure of absolute liquidity. It takes into consideration cash in hand and cash at bank. However, in this ratio some experts are of the view that bank overdrafts should not be taken in current liabilities. Cash ratio is usually not calculated. It is taken into consideration when a company is in a financial problem and is unable to meet its obligations. In a cash ratio the acceptable norm is **1 : 2.** This means that when liquid assets are worth Rs. 100 they are sufficient for Rs. 200 of current liabilities.

Since large cash balance is a drain on a company's resources and it does not offer any return therefore companies try to keep their cash balance low and just enough to discharge their current liabilities.

(*d*) ***Cash Interval Ratio:*** This ratio is also called ***Defensive Interval Ratio***. This explains the liquidity position of a company in relation to its daily cash requirements. The daily expenses are calculated as the cost of goods sold plus the expenses on administration selling and general expenses and deducted by depreciation. If the yearly expenses are given, its must be deducted by 360 (no. of days in year) to get the daily expenses.

$$\text{Cash Interval Measure} = \frac{\text{Current assets} - \text{Inventory}}{\text{Average daily expenses}}$$

(*i*) $$\text{Year 2008} = \frac{\text{Rs. } 34,20,000 - \text{Rs. } 32,20,000}{\text{Rs. } 20,000}$$

$$= \frac{2,00,000}{20,000} = \textbf{10 days}$$

(*ii*) $$\text{Year 2009} = \frac{\text{Rs. } 37,25,000 - \text{Rs. } 35,00,000}{\text{Rs. } 30,000}$$

$$= \frac{2,25,000}{30,000} = \textbf{7.5 days}$$

This result indicates that ABC Company had only 10 days reserve of cash in 2008 and in 2009 it has a reserve of 7.5 days. This means that the company has to constantly try and get its debtors to pay the company immediately otherwise it will be low on cash. The company must have a good receivables and inventory policy.

(*e*) ***Net Working Capital Ratio:*** This ratio measures liquidity of the company by calculating current assets minus the current liabilities. It excludes short-term borrowings. The net working capital is divided by the net assets. A company that has a higher net working capital can meet its current obligations successfully. However, this is not always the case because net working capital is not considered to be a satisfactory measure of liquidity of a firm in inter-firm comparisons or in trend analysis because it has certain limitations of comparison. The net working capital ratio can be calculated in the following way from Example 5.1.

$$\text{Net Working Capital Ratio} = \frac{\text{Net Working Capital}}{\text{Net Assets}}$$

$$(i) \qquad \text{Year 2008} = \frac{\text{Rs. } 22{,}70{,}000}{71{,}00{,}000} = \mathbf{0.31 : 1}$$

$$(ii) \qquad \text{Year 2009} = \frac{\text{Rs. } 28{,}44{,}000}{72{,}81{,}000} = \mathbf{0.39 : 1}$$

Example 5.1 A company ABC Ltd. gives the following information for years 2008 and 2009 through its balance sheet. The daily expenses of the company are Rs. 20,000 and Rs. 30,000 in 2009. Inventory as on 31 March 2007 was valued at Rs. 31,00,000. The market value of the share of this company was Rs. 30 in 2008 and Rs. 42 in 2009.

Balance Sheet for the year end (2008 and 2009)

Particulars	2008 (Rs.)	2009 (Rs.)
Liabilities		
Equity stock (Rs. 10 per share)	30,00,000	30,00,000
Free Reserves	19,50,000	24,00,000
12 % Debentures	10,00,000	10,00,000
Bills payable	7,50,000	2,81,000
Taxes (Outstanding)	4,00,000	6,00,000
	71,00,000	72,81,000

[Contd...]

Particulars	2008 (Rs.)	2009 (Rs.)
Assets		
Land & Building	10,00,000	12,00,000
Less: Depreciation	1,20,000	1,44,000
	8,80,000	10,56,000
Plant & machinery	33,60,000	30,00,000
Depreciation	5,60,000	5,00,000
	28,00,000	25,00,000
Inventory	32,20,000	35,00,000
Receivables	2,00,000	2,25,000
	71,00,000	72,81,000

Profit & Loss Account for the year end (2008 & 2009) of ABC Co. Ltd.

Particulars	2008 (Rs.)	2009 (Rs.)
Net Sales 50% on credit	60,00,000	70,00,000
Less: Cost of goods sold	20,00,000	22,00,000
Gross profit	40,00,000	48,00,000
Less: Selling & administrative expenses	2,00,000	2,00,000
Operating Income	38,00,000	46,00,000
Add: other Income	5,00,000	7,00,000
Earnings before interest & taxes	43,00,000	53,00,000
Less: Interest	1,50,000	2,00,000
Profit before tax	41,50,000	51,00,000
Taxes @ 50%	20,75,000	25,50,000
Profit after tax (Reserves in the beginning of the year)	20,75,000	25,50,000
Payment of Cash dividend	1,25,000	1,50,000
Free reserves at the end of the year	19,50,000	24,00,000

(*ii*) Leverage Ratios

Leverage ratios indicate the debt paying ability of a company/firm. There are two types of debts in a company. These are short-term and long-term debts. Leverage ratios calculate the proportion of debt in total financing of a company. It is useful for bankers and creditors to find out the paying capacity of the company. It is also useful for shareholders to find out the debt position of the company and the return on their total capital employed in the company. Leverage ratios examine the ***long-term solvency*** of the company. These ratios are useful for both the shareholders who are the owners of the firm and the outsiders who are the creditors of the firm. Debenture holders and financial institutions also check the solvency position of a company before participating in its financial aspects. The leverage ratio measures the financial risk of the company.

Debt is risky but a company survives with a combination of debt and equity funds. The creditors such as debenture holders, banks and financial institution have to be paid interest regularly and there can be no default in such payments whether the company makes a profit or not but shareholders need not be given dividends if there is no profit. However, if a company takes a debt it is useful for the shareholders because their earnings become magnified by taking debt and they have the benefit of ***financial leverage/trading on equity.*** The shareholders have to constantly assess how much debt should be employed by a company through that they are receiving the benefits of financial leverage.

If the debt in the company is too high, the shareholders will not be able to gain because interest will have to be paid to the lenders. Similarly, it will affect the lenders also because they have to be sure of the company's financial position and its ability to return funds both in the form of interest and capital repayments. Therefore, the company should not be overburdened with debt.

The balance sheet of a company is examined to calculate the proportion of debt to total financing in a company. The most important ratios under leverage are debt equity ratio, debt ratio and capital employed to net worth.

(a) Debt Equity Ratio: This ratio is a measure of long-term financial solvency of a company. It shows the relationship between owners' capital and borrowed capital. It depicts the proportion of debt to equity financing in the assets of the company. From Example 5.1 the debt equity ratio for the years 2008 and 2009 are computed as:

$$\text{Debt Equity Ratio} = \frac{\text{Total debt}}{\text{Net Worth}}$$

(i) $$\text{Year 2008} = \frac{\text{Rs. 10,00,000}}{\text{Rs. 49,50,000}} = \mathbf{0.202 : 1}$$

(ii) $$\text{Year 2009} = \frac{\text{Rs. 10,00,000}}{\text{Rs. 54,00,000}} = \mathbf{0.185 : 1}$$

To calculate the debt equity ratio the shareholders funds comprise all owners contributions like equity shares, preference share capital and reserves and surplus.

The funds provided by outsiders to the company consists of long-term secured and unsecured loans, debentures and bonds from banks, financial institutions and general public.

Interpretation: The desirable norm in a debt equity ratio is **2 : 1** which means that there is a good coverage of funds. The shareholders gain by borrowed funds and the debt holders do not strain the company's financial resources. A high ratio is not favourable to the shareholders as they do not get a good return. Most of the funds are required for interest and capital repayment.

Similarly, the creditors are not sure of the company's financial position and hesitate to give further loans as they are afraid of the financial position of the company and are not sure of the return of their funds. Long-term creditors would look for a low debt equity ratio.

However, the ratio depends on the type of industry the company belongs to. Some companies do not require a very low debt equity ratio.

In this example, the debt equity ratio is highly safe. The company can take more debt in order to give the advantage of financial leverage to the shareholders.

(*b*) ***Total Debt Ratio:*** The total debt ratio can be calculated in different ways. One method is to calculate the total debt divided by the total debt plus net worth of the shareholders. It depicts the lenders' contribution for each rupee of the owners' contribution. The total ratio is depicted as:

$$\text{Total debt ratio} = \frac{\text{Total debt}}{\text{Total debt + Net worth}}.$$

(*i*) $$\text{Year 2008} = \frac{\text{Rs. 10,00,000}}{\text{Rs. 59,50,000}} = \mathbf{0.168 : 1}$$

(*ii*) $$\text{Year 2009} = \frac{\text{Rs. 10,00,000}}{\text{Rs. 64,00,000}} = \mathbf{0.156 : 1}$$

Interpretation: The calculation above show that those who are supplying long-term funds to the firm are in a sound position because debt is very low in comparison to the debt and equity. The desirable norm for this ratio is **2 : 3**. In the above example both in the year 2008 and year 2009 it faults far below this norm.

An alternate way to calculate the total debt ratio is total debt divided by capital employed.

$$\text{Total debt ratio} = \frac{\text{Total debt}}{\text{Capital employed}}$$

(*c*) ***Capital Employed to Net Worth Ratio:*** The debt ratios can also be calculated by comparing capital employed with net worth. This is depicted as:

$$\text{Capital Employed to Net Worth} = \frac{\text{Capital employed}}{\text{Net worth}}$$

(i) $$\text{Year 2008} = \frac{\text{Rs. } 59{,}50{,}000}{\text{Rs. } 49{,}50{,}000} = \textbf{Rs. 1.2021}$$

(ii) $$\text{Year 2009} = \frac{\text{Rs. } 64{,}00{,}000}{\text{Rs. } 54{,}00{,}000} = \textbf{Rs. 1.18}$$

Interpretation: This ratio indicates the contribution of the lenders and owners' it can also be calculated by net assets divided by net worth.

Note: **Treatment of Preference Capital**
Preference capital should also be treated as it is a source of financing for a firm. One question that arises is whether it should be computed in the firm of debt or equity. It must be remembered that the treatment of preference capital depends on its uses. (*i*) When the firms risk for long-term solvency is to be calculated, ***preference capital should be calculated with equity capital***. (*ii*) When debt equity ratio has to indicate the effect of fixed interest or dividend as a source of funds in earnings for shareholders, ***preference capital should be calculated with debt.***

(*iii*) Coverage Ratios

Coverage ratios test the debt servicing capacity of a company. This is part of leverage ratios and the information regarding these ratios is taken from the profit and loss account. These ratios indicate the ability of a firm to meet its interest obligations. The ratios under this category are interest coverage and fixed coverage charges.

(*a*) ***Interest Coverage Ratios:*** This ratio measures the number of times the interest charges are covered by the funds of a company. It is calculated before taking the tax into consideration. Depreciation being a non-cash item is also a part of the available funds for paying interest charges. The interest coverage ratios can also be calculated before depreciation interest and taxes. This ratio is also called ***time interest earned ratio.*** It indicates the safety levels on long-term debt.

$$\text{Interest Coverage Ratio} = \frac{\text{EBIT}}{\text{Interest}}$$

(i) $$\text{Year 2008} = \frac{\text{Rs. } 43{,}00{,}000}{\text{Rs. } 1{,}50{,}000} = \textbf{28.6}$$

(ii) $$\text{Year 2009} = \frac{\text{Rs. } 53{,}00{,}000}{\text{Rs. } 2{,}00{,}000} = \textbf{26.5}$$

Interpretation: In both the years the interest coverage ratio is very high. Although the safety level is high and the lenders are sure that their interest amount will be paid, the company is not using its loan ability to the maximum. It implies that there is unused debt capacity.

Interest coverage ratio can also be calculated with another formula by including depreciation in it.

$$\text{Interest coverage} = \frac{\text{EBIT}}{\text{Interest}}$$

The limitation of the interest coverage ratio is that it does not consider the repayment of loans that the company has to make to its lenders. Therefore, the fixed charges coverage ratio is used in order to find out the loan repayment before tax earnings.

(*b*) ***Fixed Charges Coverage Ratio:*** This ratio adds detail to the interest coverage ratio. It takes into consideration the loan repayment as well. Non-cash charges and depreciation are included and this ratio is calculated with earnings before interest depreciation and tax. It is calculated in the following manner:

$$\text{Fixed charges coverage ratio} = \frac{\text{EBDIT}}{\text{Interest} + \dfrac{\text{Loan repayment}}{1 - \text{Tax rate}}}$$

Interpretation: Coverage ratio can also be found out for preference shareholders and long-term debt. We now discuss some activity ratios.

(*iv*) Activity Ratios

The efficient management of assets helps in generating a good volume of sales. This provides a good return to the owners and the creditors of a company. In ratio analysis, turnover ratios are used to evaluate the efficiency of the use of assets. These turnover ratios are called 'activity ratios'. They indicate the relationship between sales and assets in a company. From these ratios a person can find out how quickly the firm is able to convert its assets into sales. The activity ratios are calculated through sales or cost of sales and the result is expressed either in percentages or number of times to depict the result. A higher turnover ratio will indicate that the resources are utilized efficiently. The following activity ratios are commonly used to find out the utility of the resources.

(*a*) ***Inventory Turnover Ratio:*** This ratio depicts the efficiency of the sales of a firm. It indicates the liquidity of inventory in a firm. It measures the number of times on an average an inventory is sold by the company during the period. To calculate the inventory turn over ratio the cost of goods sold are divided by average inventory.

Interpretation: This ratio indicates the speed of the movement of inventory. If inventory moves fast, it indicates that the company has invested a small amount of cash in inventory.

This would indicate efficiency of a firm. If the ratio is a low it means that a firm is not using its stock resources efficiently. However, inventory turnover depends on the product of sale. A bread factory will have a fast inventory turnover where as an aircraft manufacturing company will have slow movement of inventory. However, care must be taken by firms not to overstock material in the firm.

The average inventory in a firm is calculated by the average of the opening and closing balance of inventory.

$$\text{Inventory turnover ratio} = \frac{\text{Cost of good sold}}{\text{Average inventory}}$$

From Example 5.1

$$(i) \qquad \text{Year 2008} = \frac{\text{Rs. } 20{,}00{,}000}{\left(\dfrac{\text{Rs. } 31{,}00{,}000 + \text{Rs. } 32{,}20{,}000}{2}\right)} = \mathbf{0.6\ times}$$

$$(ii) \qquad \text{Year 2009} = \frac{\text{Rs. } 22{,}00{,}000}{\left(\dfrac{\text{Rs. } 32{,}20{,}000 + \text{Rs. } 35{,}00{,}000}{2}\right)} = \mathbf{0.65\ times}$$

Interpretation: This turnover ratio is very low which means that it is not using its assets inventory efficiently.

Inventory Turnover Ratio Reciprocal: The inventory turnover reciprocal is used to give the number of days of inventory holding by a firm. This is depicted as:

$$\text{Inventory turnover ratio reciprocal} = \frac{\text{Average inventory}}{\text{Cost of good sold}} \times 360$$

$$(i) \qquad \text{Year 2008} = \frac{\text{Rs. } 31{,}00{,}000}{\text{Rs. } 20{,}00{,}000} \times 360 = \mathbf{558\ days}$$

$$(ii) \qquad \text{Year 2009} = \frac{\text{Rs. } 33{,}60{,}000}{\text{Rs. } 22{,}00{,}000} \times 360 = \mathbf{549\ days}$$

(*b*) ***Inventory Turnover Ratio by Sales:*** This ratio indicates that the firm has tied up its inventory for a long period of time and hence cannot be called 'efficient'. Inventory turnover can also be calculated from sales.

$$\text{Inventory turnover} = \frac{\text{Sales}}{\text{Inventory}}$$

(*i*) $$\text{Year 2008} = \frac{\text{Rs. } 60{,}00{,}000}{\text{Rs. } 32{,}20{,}000} = \mathbf{1.86}$$

(*ii*) $$\text{Year 2009} = \frac{\text{Rs. } 70{,}00{,}000}{\text{Rs. } 35{,}00{,}000} = \mathbf{2}$$

Its reciprocal can be used to find out the number of days.

$$\text{Inventory turnover reciprocal} = \frac{\text{Inventory}}{\text{Sales}} \times 360$$

(*i*) $$\text{Year 2008} = \frac{\text{Rs. } 32{,}20{,}000}{\text{Rs. } 60{,}00{,}000} \times 360 = \mathbf{193\ days}$$

(*ii*) $$\text{Year 2009} = \frac{\text{Rs. } 35{,}00{,}000}{\text{Rs. } 70{,}00{,}000} \times 360 = \mathbf{180\ days}$$

***Note*:**

(*i*) Inventory turnover ratio can be calculated by cost of goods sold as well as by sales.

(*ii*) It would be better to calculate by cost of goods sold method because both the inventory and cost of goods sold are taken on original cost figures.

(*iii*) The sales figures that are given are the selling price in the market, whereas the inventory is valued at cost. The figures are not comparable.

(*iv*) A higher inventory turnover is an indication of efficiency in the management of inventory.

(*v*) A low inventory turnover ratio indicates high inventory level with the firm, in other words, there are obsolete inventories lying unused with the firm. It requires good inventory management.

(*c*) ***Debtors Turnover Ratio:*** A firm has to extend its sales by selling goods on credit to customers. Cash sales are very good for a company/firm but sales are limited because customers want some time interval to make their payments. To enhance the sales of a company there have to be sales made on credit. A company has to be careful in selecting customers to whom credit can be extended. For selecting good customers a proper policy for debtors has to be prepared. The debtors have to be rated according to their credit worthiness and past dealings with the company. A debtors list has to be prepared and the time period has to be gauged to find out the extended number of days made by debtors for their payments. A company has to select a balanced policy whereby debtors would be given a credit period which will enhance sales and at the same time collection of payment will not be delayed. Some ratios are used to indicate the liquidity position of the company. These are debtors' turnover ratios.

$$\text{Debtors turnover ratio} = \frac{\text{Credit sales}}{\text{Average debtors}}$$

Credit sales are a good measure of finding out the debtors' turnover ratio because debtors are due to sales made on credit by a company to enhance its sales. A high debtors turnover ratio indicates efficiency of a firm in credit management.

Credit sales are difficult to evaluate as complete data is not available. To calculate average debtors is also not possible. To make it simple the debtors turnover ratio is calculated by total sales position of the company. Thus a more popular ratio of debtors turnover is the following:

$$\text{Debtors turnover ratio} = \frac{\text{Sales}}{\text{Debtors}}$$

(*i*) $$\text{Year 2008} = \frac{\text{Rs. 60,00,000}}{\text{Rs. 2,00,000}} = \mathbf{30}$$

(*ii*) $$\text{Year 2009} = \frac{\text{Rs. 70,00,000}}{\text{Rs. 2,25,000}} = \mathbf{31.11}$$

Interpretation: Therefore the debtor ratio of this company is high and hence the company's credit sales are quickly converted into cash and it is efficient in managing its debtors.

(*d*) ***Collection Period Ratio:*** This ratio measures the efficiency of collecting the payments by the company. The firm should have a good but firm credit policy. If it grants 15 days credit policy it should be able to collect its funds from the debtors after the interval date. If the date keeps on extending further, it means that the company does not have an efficient collection policy.

$$\text{Collection period ratio} = \frac{360}{\text{Debtors turnover}}$$

(*i*) $$\text{Year 2008} = \frac{360}{30} = \mathbf{12\ days}$$

(*ii*) $$\text{Year 2009} = \frac{360}{31.11} = \mathbf{11.57\ days}$$

Interpretation: The collection period of the company shows that the company is efficient in collection of its credit sales. It was able to collect its funds in a gap of 12 days in the year 2008, and 2009 it has reduced to 11.57 days. The firm can increase its collection period and make its credit policy a little more liberal.

Note*: *Ageing Schedule
While calculating debtors ratios to find out the efficiency of the company in collection of debts an ageing schedule should be prepared. The ageing schedule will indicate the length of time for which the debts of the company remain unpaid. It will help the company to streamline its receivables policy.

An example of the ageing schedule is as follows:

Example 5.2 XYZ Company Ltd. has the following debtors as on 30 June 2009.

I. 1 June 2009 Outstanding receivables from company A Rs. 2,00,000.

II. 31 May Outstanding from company B Rs. 3,50,000.

III. 15 April Rs. 5,00,000 receivables from Company C.

IV. 1 April Company D has to pay Rs. 1,00,000.

V. 1 March Outstanding Amount from Company E Rs. 3,00,000.

Solution

Ageing Schedule as on 30 June 2009

Date	Outstanding Period (Days)	Outstanding Debt (Rs.)	% of Outstanding Debts
15 June	1–15	Nil	Nil
1 June	16–30	2,00,000	13.79
31 May	30–45	3,50,000	24.13
1 May	45–60	Nil	Nil
15 April	60–75	Nil	Nil
1 April	75–90	5,00,000	34.48
15 March	90–105	1,00,000	6.89
1 March	105–120	3,00,000	20.6
	Total Debt		14,50,000

This company is grossly negligent in collecting its own money from its debtors. There are outstanding debts between 105–120 days. The total debt is 14,50,000 and 20.6% of this amount is outstanding for a long time. Rs. 5,00,000 outstanding for more than 75 days and amounting to 34.48% is outstanding for a long time which means that the company is following a liberal credit policy. Too liberal a policy will make it difficult for a company to show profitability. A very strict policy will make it difficult for the company to sustain itself in a competitive market. There has to be a balance between cash sales and credit sales. Efficient debtors' management helps in bringing about productivity as well as profitability. Along with the debtors turnover ratio and collection period an ageing schedule should be prepared for an in-depth analysis of the company's efficiency. The next types of ratios that are discussed are called 'assets turnover ratios'.

Assets Turnover Ratios

The activity ratios involve inventory as well as assets of the company. The reason is that efficiently managed assets can increase the sales of the company and bring about greater profitability in the company. Asset turnover is discussed next because it shows the relationship between the sales and assets of a company.

(*a*) ***Net Assets Turnover Ratio:*** This ratio shows the relationship of sales with net assets. It indicates whether a company is utilizing the capacity of its assets. This is required because there are investment costs involved and therefore performance of an asset should be at maximum level in a firm.

$$\text{Net asset turnover ratio} = \frac{\text{Sales}}{\text{Net Assets}}$$

From Example 5.1 of ABC Company Ltd.

(*i*) $\text{Year 2008} = \frac{\text{Rs. 60,00,000}}{\text{Rs. 59,50,000}} = \mathbf{1.0084\ times}$

(*ii*) $\text{Year 2009} = \frac{\text{Rs. 70,00,000}}{\text{Rs. 64,00,000}} = \mathbf{1.0938\ times}$

> ***Note:***
>
> Total Assets = Fixed assets – Depreciation + Current assets – Current liabilities
>
> There is a controversy that intangible assets should not be included in net assets turnover ratio. Fictitious assets, accumulated, losses and deferred expenditures are also not included in calculating net assets turnover ratio.

Net assets turnover ratio explains that ABC Company Ltd. is able to give sales 1.0084 times the capital employed in 2008 and 1.0938 times in 2009.

(*b*) ***Total Assets Turnover Ratio:*** The total assets ratio is calculated to get a view of the turnover of all the assets resources in a company. The following formula is used to compute the ratio.

$$\text{Total assets turnover ratio} = \frac{\text{Sales}}{\text{Total Assets}}$$

From Example 5.1 of ABC Company Ltd.

(*i*) $$\text{Year 2008} = \frac{\text{Rs. 60,00,000}}{\text{Rs. 71,00,000}} = \mathbf{0.845}$$

(*ii*) $$\text{Year 2009} = \frac{\text{Rs. 70,00,000}}{\text{Rs. 72,81,000}} = \mathbf{0.961}$$

***Note*:**

Total assets = Fixed assets – Depreciation + Current assets

The results show that in 2008 and in 2009 the assets were under utilized as the investment was getting only 0.845 as return. It increased slightly to 0.961 in 2009. The assets should be utilized get efficiency.

(*c*) ***Fixed Assets Turnover Ratio:*** This is calculated through the following formula:

$$\text{Fixed assets turnover ratio} = \frac{\text{Sales}}{\text{Net fixed assets}}$$

(*i*) $$\text{Year 2008} = \frac{\text{Rs. 60,00,000}}{\text{Rs. 36,80,000}} = \mathbf{1.630\ times}$$

(*ii*) $$\text{Year 2009} = \frac{\text{Rs. 70,00,000}}{\text{Rs. 35,56,000}} = \mathbf{1.968\ times}$$

Interpretation: This ratio exclusively indicates the turnover of sales from net fixed assets. Another turnover ratio between sales and current assets can also be calculated.

***Note*:** Net fixed assets = (Fixed Assets – Depreciation)

(*d*) ***Current Assets Turnover Ratio:*** This ratio calculates the efficiency of current assets in comparison with sales of a company.

$$\text{Current assets turnover ratio} = \frac{\text{Sales}}{\text{Current Assets}}$$

(*i*) $$\text{Year 2008} = \frac{\text{Rs. } 60{,}00{,}000}{\text{Rs. } 34{,}20{,}000} = \textbf{1.75 times}$$

(*ii*) $$\text{Year 2009} = \frac{\text{Rs. } 70{,}00{,}000}{\text{Rs. } 37{,}25{,}000} = \textbf{1.879 times}$$

Interpretation: This example shows that ABC Company Ltd. is more efficient in its turnover of current assets compared to its fixed assets. If we compare the years 2008 and 2009, both fixed assets and current assets turnover are more efficient in 2009 compared to 2008. The company can improve its efficiency in turnover ratios in both current assets and fixed assets in future.

(*e*) ***Working Capital Turnover Ratio:*** This ratio measures the turnover of sales with working capital.

$$\text{Working capital turnover ratio} = \frac{\text{Sales}}{\text{Current Assets} - \text{Current Liabilities}}$$

(*i*) $$\text{Year 2008} = \frac{\text{Rs. } 60{,}00{,}000}{\text{Rs. } 22{,}70{,}000} = \textbf{2.64 times}$$

(*ii*) $$\text{Year 2009} = \frac{\text{Rs. } 70{,}00{,}000}{\text{Rs. } 28{,}44{,}000} = \textbf{2.46 times}$$

Interpretation: The higher the working capital ratio the more efficient is the utilization of working capital in a company. The profitability of the company is high. However, a very high ratio is not useful because it indicates over trading but a very low ratio indicates that working capital is not used efficiently.

The next part of this chapter discusses the profitability ratios of a company.

(*v*) Profitability Ratios

Profitability ratios indicate the operating efficiency of a company by measuring the revenues of a company. Profitability in a company is essential because a commercial enterprise must sustain itself. However, social obligations, employee's satisfaction, shareholders, debtors and creditors interest have to be kept in mind while working towards profit. To measure profitability the ratios can be calculated in relation to sales or investment. The following ratios are used to calculate profitability of a company.

(*a*) ***Net Profit Margin Ratio:*** Gross profit is measured by deducting the cost of good sold from the sales of a company. However, in India gross profit is defined differently by organizations depending on their interest. Profits can be calculated before tax or after taxes. The investors' interest is in measuring operating profit which means earning before interest or taxes. If non-operating income exists, an after tax basis is to be considered. The net profit is a good indicator of profitability as it takes into consideration all these expenses including interest and taxes. Therefore, the following ratio which is most commonly used is discussed.

$$\text{Net Profit Margin Ratio} = \frac{\text{Profit after tax}}{\text{Sales}}$$

From Example 5.1,

(*i*) $$\text{Year 2008} = \frac{\text{Rs. } 20,75,000}{\text{Rs. } 60,00,000} = \mathbf{0.3458 \text{ or } 34.58\%}$$

(*ii*) $$\text{Year 2009} = \frac{\text{Rs. } 25,50,000}{\text{Rs. } 70,00,000} = \mathbf{0.3642 \text{ or } 36.42\%}$$

(*b*) ***Net Profit Margin after Tax:*** This ratio is calculated before tax because tax is not controllable. This ratio is also called 'modified net profit ratio' as it is calculated before tax figures. A high net profit margin indicates that there is adequate return for the shareholders as well as for the creditors of the company. Similarly a low net profit margin would give the signal of having adequate ability in to carry on good business and this would bring down the reputation of the company.

$$\text{Net profit margin after tax} = \frac{\text{EBIT } (1 - \text{T})}{\text{Sales}}$$

(*i*) $$\text{Year 2008} = \frac{\text{Rs. } 43,00,000\ (1 - 0.5)}{\text{Rs. } 60,00,000} = \mathbf{0.3584 \text{ or } 35.84\%}$$

(*ii*) $$\text{Year 2009} = \frac{\text{Rs.} 53,00,000\ (1 - 0.5)}{\text{Rs. } 70,00,000} = \mathbf{0.3786 \text{ or } 37.86\%}$$

Interpretation: ABC Company Ltd. has a good profitability ratio in 2008 and 2009 indicating a profitable trend in both the years.

(*c*) ***Operating Profitability Ratio:*** This ratio indicates the profitability before interest and taxes divided by the sales.

$$\text{Operating profitability ratio} = \frac{\text{EBIT}}{\text{Sales}}$$

$$(i) \qquad \text{Year 2008} = \frac{\text{Rs. } 43{,}00{,}000}{\text{Rs. } 60{,}00{,}000} = \mathbf{0.7166 \text{ or } 71.66\%}$$

$$(ii) \qquad \text{Year 2009} = \frac{\text{Rs. } 53{,}00{,}000}{\text{Rs. } 70{,}00{,}000} = \mathbf{0.7571 \text{ or } 75.71\%}$$

This ratio is also a net profit margin ratio. It measures the relationship of net profits and sales. It indicates that a company is being run at a comfortable margin to do business. The ABC Company Ltd. has a very high net profit margin measured in terms of operating profit.

(*d*) ***Gross Profit Margin Ratio:*** Gross profit margin is a relationship between prices, sales volume and cost.

$$\text{Gross profit margin ratio} = \frac{\text{Gross Profit}}{\text{Sales}} \times 100$$

$$= (\text{Sales} - \text{Cost of goods sold})$$

$$(i) \qquad \text{Year 2008} = \frac{\text{Rs. } 40{,}00{,}000}{\text{Rs. } 60{,}00{,}000} = \mathbf{0.6666 \text{ or } 66.66\%}$$

$$(ii) \qquad \text{Year 2009} = \frac{\text{Rs. } 48{,}00{,}000}{\text{Rs. } 70{,}00{,}000} = \mathbf{0.6857 \text{ or } 68.75\%}$$

Interpretation: The profit margin of ABC Ltd. is satisfactory.

(*e*) ***Operating Expenses Ratio:*** This ratio is a relationship of expenses in a firm measured by its sales. It explains the expenses as a percentage of the sales in the firm. In this ratio the cost of goods sold is added with selling expenses and administrative and general expenses but excludes interest.

$$\text{Operating expenses ratio} = \frac{\text{Operating Expenses}}{\text{Sales}}$$

$$(i) \qquad \text{Year 2008} = \frac{\text{Rs. } 2{,}00{,}000}{\text{Rs. } 60{,}00{,}000} = \mathbf{0.0334 \text{ or } 3.34\%}$$

$$(ii) \qquad \text{Year 2009} = \frac{\text{Rs. } 2{,}00{,}000}{\text{Rs. } 70{,}00{,}000} = \mathbf{0.0286 \text{ or } 2.86\%}$$

Interpretation: This indicates that the costs of the company are low. Therefore, the interest of the shareholders and creditors is well covered. The expenses ratio can also be taken to indicate separate costs and its relationship can be found out by the sales of the company. In this respect the following ratio will calculate the cost of goods sold in relation to sales.

(*f*) ***Cost of Goods Sold Ratio:*** This ratio is calculated in the following way:

$$\text{Cost of goods sold ratio} = \frac{\text{Cost of goods sold}}{\text{Sales}}$$

$$(i) \qquad \text{Year 2008} = \frac{\text{Rs. } 20,00,000}{\text{Rs. } 60,00,000} = \mathbf{0.334 \text{ or } 33.34\%}$$

$$(ii) \qquad \text{Year 2009} = \frac{\text{Rs. } 22,00,000}{\text{Rs. } 70,00,000} = \mathbf{0.3143 \text{ or } 31.43\%}$$

Interpretation: This ratio indicates that the goods are costing one third of the total sales. Similarly, relationships of other costs like administration cost, cost of sales can also be calculated in relation to sales.

(*g*) ***Return on Investments (Total assets) Ratio:*** Returns to shareholders can also be calculated through investments made in a company. The following ratios will indicate the returns to the shareholders by assets.

$$\text{Return on investments (Total assets)} = \frac{\text{EBIT } (1 - \text{T})}{\text{Total Assets}}$$

$$(i) \qquad \text{Year 2008} = \frac{\text{Rs. } 43,00,000\ (1 - 0.5)}{\text{Rs. } 71,00,000} = \mathbf{0.3029 \text{ or } 30.29\%}$$

$$(ii) \qquad \text{Year 2009} = \frac{\text{Rs. } 53,00,000(1 - 0.5)}{72,81,000} = \mathbf{0.3639 \text{ or } 36.4\%}$$

Interpretation: This ratio indicates the efficiency of assets in a company. ABC Company Ltd. in Example 5.1 indicates that the firm has efficient utilization of its total assets.

(*h*) ***Return on Investments (Net Assets Ratio):*** The before tax net asset ratio is calculated as the earnings before interest and taxes divided by the net assets. Both the before tax and after tax return on investment ratios can be calculated by either total assets or net assets.

$$\text{Return on Investments (Net assets)} = \frac{\text{EBIT } (1 - \text{T})}{\text{Net assets}}$$

(*i*) Year 2008 $= \dfrac{\text{Rs. } 43{,}00{,}000\ (1 - 0.5)}{\text{Rs. } 59{,}50{,}000}$ = **0.3614 or 36.14%**

(*ii*) Year 2009 $= \dfrac{\text{Rs. } 53{,}00{,}000(1 - 0.5)}{\text{Rs. } 64{,}00{,}000}$ = **0.4141 or 41.41%**

Interpretation: This indicates that ABC Company Ltd. has efficiency utilized its return on investments by the net assets.

> ***Note*:** Net asset = Fixed assets + (Current assets – Current liabilities)

(*i*) ***Return on Investment before Tax:*** The variant of the above ratio is to find out the return on investments before taxation. Therefore EBIT is divided by total assets. Alternatively, it can also be divided by net assets to judge the efficiency of the utilization of the asset.

$$\text{Return on investment before Tax} = \frac{\text{EBIT}}{\text{Total assets}}$$

(*i*) Year 2008 $= \dfrac{\text{Rs. } 43{,}00{,}000}{\text{Rs. } 71{,}00{,}000}$ = **0.6057 or 60.57%**

(*ii*) Year 2009 $= \dfrac{\text{Rs. } 53{,}00{,}000}{\text{Rs. } 72{,}81{,}000}$ = **0.7279 or 72.79%**

Interpretation: The return on investment of ABC Company Ltd. is very satisfactory.

(*j*) ***Return on Equity Ratio:*** This ratio measures the return that the shareholders will get from this company. The shareholders net worth is equal to their paid up share capital, share premiums and reserves and surpluses. The accumulated losses are deducted. Therefore, net worth can also be calculated by total assets – total liabilities. There is a controversy of the terminology of net worth of shareholders. The market value of shareholders is considered as their net worth. However, the Balance Sheet records it at book value.

This return on equity is calculated through the following formula:

$$\text{Return on equity ratio} = \frac{\text{Profit after taxes}}{\text{Net worth}}$$

$$(i) \qquad \text{Year 2008} = \frac{\text{Rs. } 22,75,000}{\text{Rs. } 49,50,000} = \mathbf{0.4595 \text{ or } 45.95\%}$$

$$(ii) \qquad \text{Year 2009} = \frac{\text{Rs. } 25,50,000}{\text{Rs. } 54,00,000} = \mathbf{0.4723 \text{ or } 47.23\%}$$

Interpretation: The shareholders a good return in 2008. It further increased to 47.23% in 2009.

(*k*) ***Earnings Per Share Ratio:*** This ratio provides an insight into the earnings of shareholders in a company.

$$\text{Earnings per share ratio} = \frac{\text{Profit after tax}}{\text{No. of equity shares}}$$

$$(i) \qquad \text{Year 2008} = \frac{\text{Rs. } 20,75,000}{\text{Rs. } 3,00,000} = \mathbf{Rs.\ 6.9}$$

$$(ii) \qquad \text{Year 2009} = \frac{\text{Rs. } 25,50,000}{\text{Rs. } 3,00,000} = \mathbf{Rs.\ 8.5}$$

Interpretation: Company ABC Ltd. has a share of Rs. 10 each. Out of which the shareholders earnings are Rs. 6.9 in 2008 and Rs. 8.5 in 2009. This indicates that a company can satisfy its shareholders depending on its policy to give a good return to the shareholder in the form of dividends.

(*l*) ***Dividend Per Share Ratio:*** The earnings of this company are high. Dividends are calculated to find out what proportion of the earnings is given to the shareholders. This is calculated by earnings paid to shareholders divided by the number of shares in the company. Therefore, the following formula is used to find out dividend per share:

$$\text{Dividends per share} = \frac{\text{Earnings paid to shareholder}}{\text{No. of shares}}$$

$$(i) \qquad \text{Year 2008} = \frac{\text{Rs. } 1,25,000}{\text{Rs. } 3,00,000} = \mathbf{Rs.\ 0.4167}$$

$$(ii) \qquad \text{Year 2009} = \frac{\text{Rs. } 1,50,000}{\text{Rs. } 3,00,000} = \mathbf{Rs.\ 0.50}$$

Therefore the company had paid a very low dividend to the shareholders.

(m) ***Dividend Payout Ratio:*** This ratio indicates the amount of money paid to a shareholder out of the earnings of the company.

$$\text{Dividend payout ratio} = \frac{\text{Dividend per share}}{\text{Earnings per share}}$$

(i) $$\text{Year 2008} = \frac{\text{Rs. } 0.4167}{\text{Rs. } 6.9} = \mathbf{0.0603 \text{ or } 6.03\%}$$

(ii) $$\text{Year 2009} = \frac{\text{Rs. } 0.50}{\text{Rs. } 8.50} = \mathbf{0.0588 \text{ or } 5.88\%}$$

Interpretation: Company ABC Ltd. had a low payout ratio between 2008 and 2009. There had been a decline in the payout ratio.

> ***Note:***
>
> Growth in Equity can be measured with the retention ratio and return on equity. The retention ratio is calculated as: 1 – Payout ratio
>
> Therefore, Growth in equity = Retention ratio × Return on equity
>
> Year 2008 the growth in equity = (1 – 6.03) × 0.4192 = **0.3939 or 39.39%**
>
> Year 2009 the growth in equity = (1 – 0.0588) × .4723 = **0.4445 or 44.45%**

Interpretation: This ratio indicates that Company ABC Ltd. has a high growth both in year 2008 and in the year 2009.

(n) ***Earnings Yield Ratio:*** The earnings and dividend yield are both used by shareholders to find out their return in terms of the market value of a share.

$$\text{Therefore Earnings yield} = \frac{\text{Earnings per share}}{\text{Market value per share}}$$

Company ABC Ltd. has 6.9 as its earnings per shares in 2008 and Rs. 30 is its market price. Therefore its earnings yield is the following:

(i) $$\text{Year 2008} = \frac{\text{Rs. } 6.39}{\text{Rs. } 30} = \mathbf{0.23 \text{ or } 23\%}$$

(ii) $$\text{Year 2009} = \frac{\text{Rs. } 8.5}{\text{Rs. } 42} = \mathbf{0.2024 \text{ or } 20.24\%}$$

Interpretation: The earnings yield rate of the company is very high.

(*o*) ***Dividend Yield Ratio:*** A company may have a high earnings yield ratio but its dividend yield may or may not be high. To test dividend yield per share the market value of the share is used, the formula being:

$$\text{Dividend yield} = \frac{\text{Dividend per share}}{\text{Market value per share}}$$

(*i*) $\text{Year 2008} = \frac{\text{Rs. } 0.4167}{\text{Rs. } 30} = \mathbf{0.0139 \text{ or } 1.39\%}$

(*ii*) $\text{Year 2009} = \frac{\text{Rs. } 0.50}{\text{Rs. } 42} = \mathbf{0.0119 \text{ or } 1.19\%}$

Interpretation: Although ABC Ltd. has a high earnings yield its dividend yield is very low. In 2008 it was 1.39% and in 2009 it was even lower at 1.19%.

(*p*) ***Price Earning Ratio:*** The price earning ratio is the reciprocal of the earnings yield. It is used to find out the value of the performance of the firm according to the expectation of the investors. It evaluates the performance of the company in the market. This ratio helps to find out the growth in the earnings of company. It is calculated in the following way:

$$\text{Price earning ratio} = \frac{\text{Market value per share}}{\text{Earnings per share}}$$

(*i*) $\text{Year 2008} = \frac{\text{Rs. } 30}{\text{Rs. } 6.9} = \mathbf{4.34 \text{ times}}$

(*ii*) $\text{Year 2009} = \frac{\text{Rs. } 42}{\text{Rs. } 8.5} = \mathbf{4.94 \text{ times}}$

Interpretation: The Company is earning well and its performance has increased from 4.34 times in 2008 to 4.94 times in 2009.

(*q*) ***Market value to Book Value Ratio:*** This ratio measures the relationship between the market value and the book value of a share. Those company which have low market to book value ratio have higher returns than those which have a high ratio. It is also called 'price to book value ratio'.

$$\text{Market value to book value} = \frac{\text{Market value per share}}{\text{Book value}}$$

(*i*) $$\text{Year 2008} = \frac{\text{Rs. 30}}{\text{Rs. 10}} = \mathbf{3}$$

(*ii*) $$\text{Year 2009} = \frac{\text{Rs. 42}}{\text{Rs. 10}} = \mathbf{4.2}$$

Interpretation: ABC Company Ltd. increased in its market value to book value ratio in 2009 which means that the company's performance in the market is falling.

5.5 DU-PONT ANALYSIS CHART

Du-Pont Company of the US prepared a financial statement analysis system through charts. It made a chart showing return on capital invested and return on total assets and return on net worth. These charts are been used for drawing inter-relationships on the basis of the information from financial statements. The Du-Pont charts indicate many variables. These variables affect the company's performance when changes are seen in them. Return on investment depends on sales, expenses, cost of good sold, working capital, fixed assets. These are all projected in the chart. These indicate that if cost of good sold increase with a corresponding increase in sales, there may not be a change. However if cost of goods sold changes but sales do not, they will be a decrease in the company's profitability. These are reflected through the following charts.

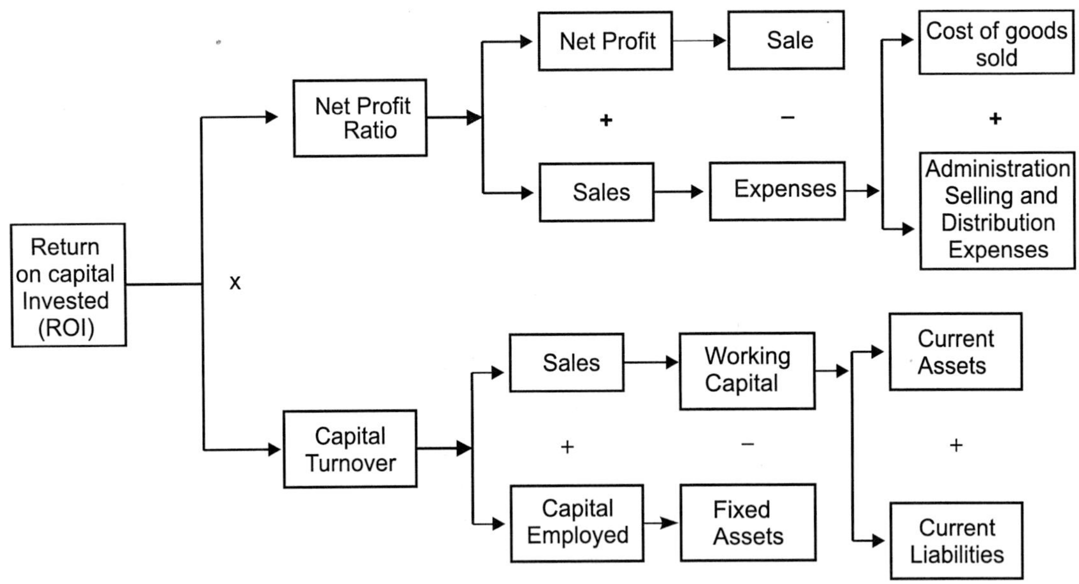

Fig. 5.1 Du-Pont Control Chart: Return on Investments

Figure 5.1 depicts Du-Pont's return on investment chart. It has variables of net profit sale cost of good sold, expenses, capital turnover, sales, working capital, fixed assets, current assets and current liabilities. These are analysed with the return on capital invested. Figure 5.2 is another Du-Pont chart. It analyses return on total assets in terms of profit margin and total assets of the company. Figure 5.3 is another Du-Pont chart in which the return on net worth variables are given. These charts can be used by any company to analyse their financial statements.

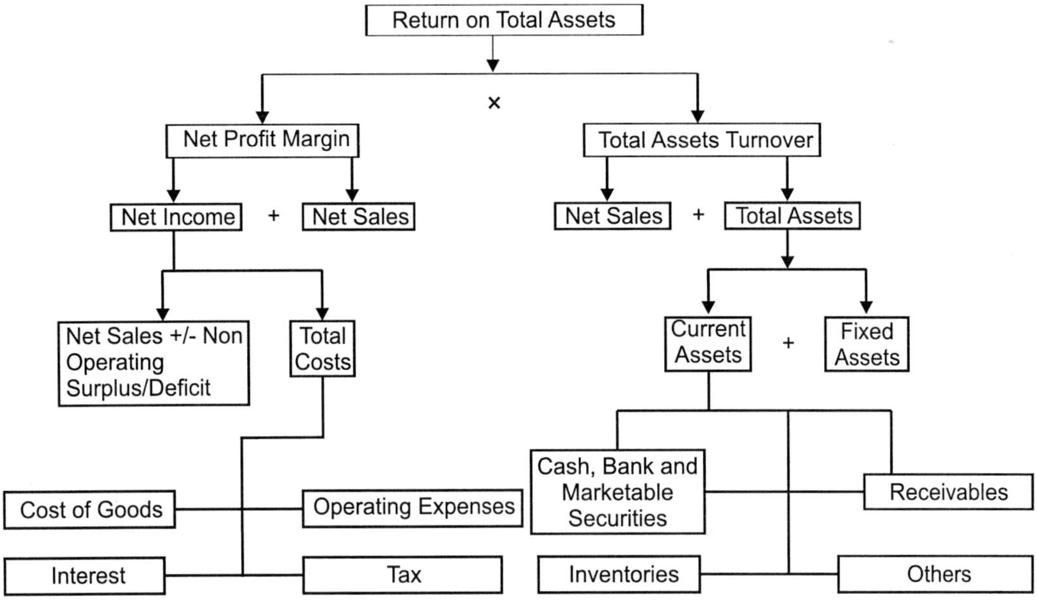

Fig. 5.2 Du-Pont Control Chart: Return on Total Assets

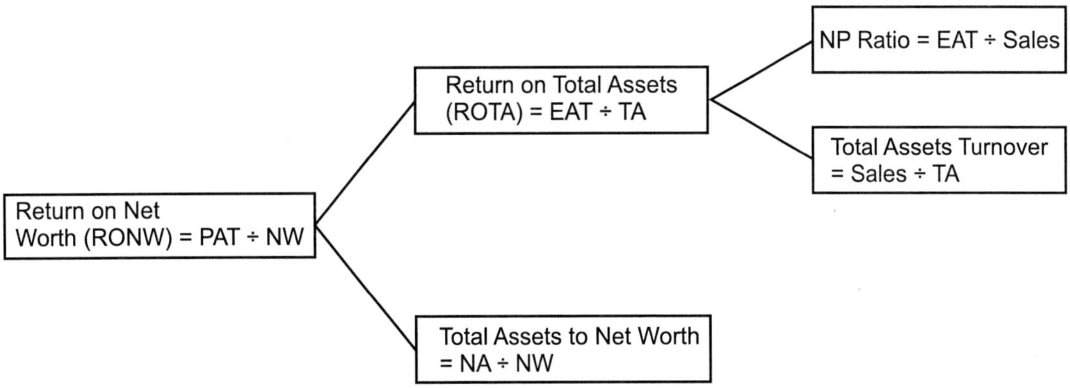

Fig. 5.3 Du-Pont Control Chart: Return on Net

Additional efforts was made by Robert Altman to develop Z scores in the US to calculate the performance of companies to show that they do not fall below the expected standards of shareholders and creditors. He used several formulae and did research on those companies which had gone into liquidation. Therefore, research is continuing in ratio analysis because it is a useful tool and it can be made effective by the use of additional techniques.

5.6 RATIO ANALYSIS AND STANDARDS OF COMPARISON

In order to have a meaningful ratio analysis, it should be calculated by comparing it with some standards. A ratio that is found out for a single event is not meaningful. Some of the standards of comparisons that can be used are discussed here.

(*i*) Trend Analysis

A company's performance can be evaluated through ratio analysis over a period of time. The company's performance can be tested between two years or two time periods or a number of previous years. For example, a trend analysis to find out the profitability of selling sun glasses by a retailer is possible if he compares the profitability over a period of five years. He calculates ratios from balance sheets and profit and loss account statements from 2004 to 2009. Thus he will get ratios of Gross profit/Sales or Net profit/Sales for five years. From these ratios it can establish whether it is profitable for him to continue this business. For example, if the resulting answer of last five years between net profit and sales is 5%, 10%, 12%, 15% and 20%, it means that there has been a continuous increase in profits and it is a profitable business. Supposing the last five years showed the following ratios 10%, 10%, 10%, 10%, 10%. This analysis depicts stability in profits of the company but no improvement in the past 5 years which means that if there are conditions like inflation or change in the business cycle, the sales may go down. Similarly, look at this result the ratio analysis of profitability shows 10%, 20%, 8%, 2% and 25%, what does this trend look like? This indicates a high degree of instability in the business because profitability is changing and reversing trends every two years. This also means that the firm has a potential market for increasing it profits but it is making some mistakes in its selling or administration or internal purchasing policies. These aspects would require attention.

Trend analysis of this kind can also be called 'time series analysis'. This explains the changes in performance level of companies and then explanations can be arrived at to see why such changes have occurred and what requires to be done to make changes fruitful and useful for improving performance of a company.

(*ii*) Industry Analysis

Ratios of a firm/company should be compared with the average ratios of the industry to which it belongs. Each industry has its own characteristics and is different from other types of industries. The calculation of ratios to compare with industry average indicates the financial and operational strength of the firm in comparison to other firms.

There are many problems in calculating industry averages because it is difficult to find out the data of all the companies. The method of accounting used by one company may differ from another. Moreover it is difficult to segregate the accounts of financially weak companies from financially strong companies. How to categorize whether the company whose ratio is calculated is weak or strong? The range of the companies is so wide in an industry that it is difficult to make a good analysis. Another problem that may occur is that some companies may be multinationals, others may be regional, and some of the companies in this category may be government companies. To get a standard ratio from industry analysis would be very difficult.

(*iii*) Cross-sectional Analysis

Ratio analysis can be done of a few selected firms on a particular date. Some companies calculate ratios with their competing companies. This kind of analysis helps a company to assess its position in comparison with similar companies. It provides a cross-sectional analysis and on this basis it can try to improve its performance or reduce any irregularities in its operations.

(*iv*) Proforma Analysis

Proforma financial statements are used for comparing the current ratios with the past ratios or projected future ratios. This provides an insight to a company to look into its operations professionally. It also tries to project its figures on the basis of past operational experience. On the basis of the past ratios the future ratios may be compared.

Although ratio analysis is widely used in Indian industries, it has certain limitations. The analyst should be careful that data is compared after taking into consideration the limitations.

5.7 LIMITATIONS OF RATIO ANALYSIS

Ratio analysis is a useful tool in business. However, there are some problems in using it in the following situations.

(*i*) Differences in Standards of Comparison

A ratio becomes meaningful when it is compared with some standards. However, these standards become problematic due to the following reasons:

(*a*) Standards of comparison are difficult due to differences on the basis of valuation of inventory of each company. Some companies value their inventory according to first in first out method. Other companies may use the evaluation of average cost.

(*b*) Depreciation methods are often different. Some companies prefer straight line method of depreciation because of its simple technique. Other companies use written down value method. In India, it is getting standardized towards written down value method. If depreciation method is same the comparison will become meaningful.

(*c*) There are differences in technique of amortization of intangible assets like patents and goodwill. This will bring a difference in results.

(*d*) Deferred revenue expenditures have to be carefully analysed because every company has a different kind of procedure adopted particularly in conditions of items like discount on issue of shares or preliminary expenses.

(*ii*) Inflation

Traditional financial statements are based on historical cost. The assets of a company are purchased during different periods of time and they are indicated at original cost less depreciation. However when there is inflation, the replacement value or the current value of the assets is different. Interest rates also become high during inflation. These rates are not adjusted during price level changes. Due to these problems the ratio cannot be compared during inflation.

Inventory is greatly affected during price level changes. The reason is that for each time inventory purchased, the costs will be different. These costs will affect the company and the changes will not be reflected.

Inflation affects the profits of a company due to changes in interest levels. The borrowing rate affects the company. The profits of a company do not take into account the borrowing rate and the amount during expression.

(*iii*) Window Dressing

Some companies make their accounts look attractive by presenting them better than their actual position. If these facts are concealed, the ratio analysis will not present a true picture of comparison between different firms. If cross-sectional analysis is made the standard of comparison will differ due to window dressing.

(*iv*) Limiting Picture of a Company

Ratios present some comparison but do not state the circumstances which lead to the result. Those who are finding out about a company should analyse the performance and then make a research study to find out the reason why such projections are being depicted because ratio analysis is meaningless without further analysis. Why an event occurred? Or what steps should be taken to remove a certain style of working? These questions are required to be taken up after the findings of ratio analysis. Thus ratio analysis is an important tool but it cannot be fully relied on. Further investigation has to be carried out for taking corrective action in a company.

Table 5.1 Ratios at a Glance

Liquidity Ratios	
• Current ratio	$= \dfrac{\text{Current assets}}{\text{Current liabilities}}$
• Quick ratio	$= \dfrac{\text{Current assets} - \text{Inventory}}{\text{Current liabilities}}$
• Interval measure	$= \dfrac{\text{Current assets} - \text{Inventory}}{\text{Average daily cash operating expenses}}$
Leverage Ratios	
• Total debt ratio	$= \dfrac{\text{Total debt}}{\text{Capital employed}}$
• Debt-equity ratio	$= \dfrac{\text{Net worth}}{\text{Total debt}}$
• Capital equity ratio	$= \dfrac{\text{Capital employed or net assets}}{\text{Net worth}}$
• Interest coverage	$= \dfrac{\text{EBIT}}{\text{Interest}}$
Activity Ratios	
• Inventory turnover	$= \dfrac{\text{Cost of goods sold or sales}}{\text{Inventory}}$
• No. of days, inventory	$= \dfrac{360}{\text{Inventory turnover}}$
• Debtors turnover	$= \dfrac{\text{Credit sales or sales}}{\text{Debtors}}$
• Collection period	$= \dfrac{360}{\text{Debtor turnover}}$
• Assets turnover	$= \dfrac{\text{Sales}}{\text{Net assets or Capital employed}}$
• Working capital turnover	$= \dfrac{\text{Sales}}{\text{Net working capital}}$

[Contd...]

Profitability Ratios	
• Gross margin	$= \frac{\text{Gross profit}}{\text{Sales}}$
• Net margin	$= \frac{\text{Profit after tax}}{\text{Sales}}$
• Net margin	$= \frac{\text{EBIT}}{\text{Sales}}$
• Net margin	$= \frac{\text{EBIT (1 – T)}}{\text{Sales}}$
• PAT to EBIT ratio	$= \frac{\text{PAT}}{\text{EBIT}}$
• Return on investment (ROI)	$= \frac{\text{EBIT}}{\text{Net assets or Capital employed}}$
• Return on investment (ROI)	$= \frac{\text{EBIT (1 – Tax rate)}}{\text{Net assets or Capital employed}}$
• Return on equity (ROE)	$= \frac{\text{Profit after tax}}{\text{Net worth}}$
• ROE	$= \frac{\text{Sales}}{\text{Net assets}} \times \frac{\text{EBIT}}{\text{Sales}} \times \frac{\text{PAT}}{\text{EBIT}} \times \frac{\text{Net assets}}{\text{Net worth}}$
• Earning Per Share (EPS)	$= \frac{\text{PAT}}{\text{No. of shares}}$
• Dividends Per Share (DPS)	$= \frac{\text{Profit distributed}}{\text{No. of shares}}$
• Dividend Payout Ratio (DPR)	$= \frac{\text{DPS}}{\text{EPS}}$
• Price-earnings ratio (PE)	$= \frac{\text{Market value of share}}{\text{EPS}}$
Market value-book value ratio	$= \frac{\text{Market value of the share}}{\text{Book value of the share}}$

POINTS TO REMEMBER

- A ratio is a comparison between two variables. It is a useful tool to draw conclusions and make interpretations from financial statements of a company.
- Ratios are expressed when one figure is divided by another. It is a numerical expression. It can be expressed as a percentage, a rate or a proportion.
- An absolute figure does not convey any meaning but when it is related with other figures it provides an understanding of a situation in a company.
- Ratios are of various kinds. These are liquidity ratios, leverage ratios, activity ratios and profitability ratios.
- Ratios are useful for investors, debtors, creditors, government, employees and the management itself.
- Liquidity ratios provide a relationship between the current assets and current liabilities to find out the ability of a company to meet its current obligations.
- Leverage ratios establish a relationship between borrowed capital and equity capital.
- To find out the efficiency of a firm activity ratios are used for calculating the proportion of sales to assets.
- The coverage ratios depict the relationship of sales with inventory or interest with earning before interest and taxes.
- The profitability ratios measure the profits of a firm in relation to sales and assets.
- The liquidity ratios are current ratio, quick ratio, cash ratio, cash interval ratio and networking capital ratio.
- Leverage ratios are debt equity ratio, total debt ratio, capital employed to net worth ratio.
- Coverage ratios include interest coverage, fixed charge coverage ratio.
- Activity ratios comprise inventory turnover by cost of goods sold, average inventory and sales. Debtors turnover is calculated by drawing relationship with credits sales and sales. Assets turnover is compared with sales and current assets, fixed assets and total assets.
- An ageing schedule projects the length of time for which a debt has not been recovered by the company. This indicates whether the policy of the company is liberal or stringent. It also indicates that a company's policy is efficient or not in collection of receivables.
- The profitability ratios include gross profit margin, net profit margin ratio, before and after tax ratio, expenses ratio, return on equity ratio, return on investment ratio, earnings per share ratio, dividend per share ratio, earnings yield ratio, dividends yield, price earning ratio and market value to book value ratios.

[Contd...]

- Ratio analysis has certain standards of comparison. Data can be compared intra firm, inter firm, and with industry averages. Trend analysis and cross sectional analysis are quite popular in India.
- Du-Pont charts are depicted to analyse the ratios through charts. The ratio analysis are analysed by using the pictorial chart.
- There are limitations of ratio analysis. It cannot be analyse if accounting procedures are different between two companies. It has difficulty of measurement during inflation as costs are incorporated historically in financial statements and do not reflect change in prices.
- Ratio analysis is a very useful tool. It raises many relevant questions on important managerial issues. A user must be careful as caution needs to be applied while interpreting ratios as they are calculated from accounting numbers. Accounting numbers suffer from limitations of accounting allocation, procedures and inflation.

OBJECTIVE TYPE QUESTIONS

State whether the following statements are true (T) or false (F).

1. Liquidity ratios indicate the financial soundness of a company.
2. Ratios are relative amounts and they depict the relationship between two variables.
3. Profitability ratios can be based on sales or total investments.
4. The activity ratios are also called efficiency or turnover ratio.
5. Turnover ratios indicate the earning strength a firm or company.
6. Profit is the difference between revenue and liabilities of a company.
7. The average collection period indicates the quality of debtors by the speed of collection of funds.
8. The net profit margin is the profit after tax divided by sales.
9. The investor measures the return that he receives from the company through the debt equity ratio.
10. The earning power of a firm is portrayed through a Du-Pont control chart.

Answers: 1. (F), 2. (T), 3. (T), 4. (T), 5. (F), 6. (F), 7. (T), 8. (T), 9. (F), 10. (T).

THEORETICAL QUESTIONS

1. What is the importance of financial statement analysis to (*a*) investors, (*b*) creditors and (*c*) management of the company?
2. Explain the different types of rates to assess the liquidity of a firm or company.

3. What is the significant of ratio analysis to an investor? What are the limitations of such an analysis?
4. Discuss the standards of comparison used for interpretation of financial statements.
5. What is the objective of calculating profitability ratios? Discuss some of the profitability ratios used in analysis of date.
6. What is the use of financial statement analysis? Discuss the relevance of an operating expense ratio.
7. What ratios do shareholders evaluate to judge the returns they are recurring from a company?
8. What are the leverage ratios? What is the limitation of debt equity ratio as a measure of the company's solvency?

ILLUSTRATIVE PROBLEMS

Illustration 5.1 Calculate the P/E ratio from the following:

Particulars	Amount (Rs.)
Equity share capital (Rs. 20 each)	50,00,000
Reverse and surplus	5,00,000
Secured loans at 15%	25,00,000
Unsecured loans at 12.5%	10,00,000
Fixed assets	30,00,000
Investments	5,00,000
Operating profit	25,00,000

Income tax rate—50%. Market Price/Share— Rs. 50.

(CA Final 1995)

Solution

Particulars	Amount (Rs.)	Amount (Rs.)
Operating Profit		25,00,000
Less: Interest on secured loans @ 15%	3,75,000	
Unsecured loans @ 12.5%	1,25,000	5,00,000
Profit before tax (PBT)		20,00,000
Less: Income-tax @ 50%		10,00,000
Profit after tax (PAT)		10,00,000
No. of Equity shares		2,50,000

$$\text{EPS} = \frac{\text{Profit after tax}}{\text{No. Equity of shares}}$$

$$= \frac{\text{Rs. } 10,00,000}{\text{Rs. } 2,50,000} = \text{Rs. } 4$$

$$\text{Market Price per share} = \text{Rs. } 50$$

$$\text{P/E ratio} = \text{Market price per share/EPS}$$

$$= \text{Rs. } 50/\ \text{Rs. } 4$$

$$= 12.50$$

Illustration 5.2 The Net sales of Apex Co. are Rs. 15 crore. The EBIT of the company as a percentage of sales is 12%. The capital employed of the company comprises Rs. 5 crores of equity, Re. 1 crore of 13% preference shares and Rs. 3 crores of 15% debt capital. The company's profit is subject to tax at 40%. Calculate the Return on Equity (ROE) for the company.

(ICWA Final, 1997)

Solution

Particulars	Amount (Rs.)
EBIT	1,80,00,000
Less: Interest	45,00,000
Profit before tax	1,35,00,000
Less: Tax @ 40 %	54,00,000
Profit before tax	81,00,000
Less: Pref. Dividend	13,00,000
Returns for equity	68,00,000

$$\text{Return on Equity} = \frac{\text{PAT} - \text{Pref. Div.}}{\text{Equity}} \times 100$$

$$= \frac{\text{Rs. } 68,00,000}{\text{Rs. } 5,00,00,000} \times 100 = \mathbf{13.6\%}$$

Illustration 5.3 The Profit and Loss Account and Balance Sheet of XYZ Ltd. are as under:

Profit and Loss Account for the year ended 31 December 2006

Particulars	Amount (Rs.)	Amount (Rs.)
Net Sales		3,00,000
Less: Cost of production		2,58,000
		42,000
Less: Operating expenses		
Selling	2,200	
General administration	4,000	
Rent of office	2,800	9,000
Gross operating profit		33,000
Less: Depreciation		10,000
Net-operating profit		23,000
Other income (interest on Government securities)		1,500
Gross income (before tax)		24,500
Less: Other expenses:		
Interest on bank overdraft	300	
Interest on debentures	4,200	4,500
Net income (before tax)		20,000
Tax 50% on net income		10,000
Net income (after tax)		10,000

Balance Sheet as on 31 December 2006

Particulars	Amount (Rs.)	Amount (Rs.)
Liabilities		
Equity share capital		50,000
7% Preference share capital		10,000
Reserves and surplus		40,000
6% Mortgage debentures		70,000
Creditors		6,000
Bills payable		10,000
Outstanding expenses		1,000
Provision for taxation		13,000
		2,00,000

[Contd...]

Particulars	Amount (Rs.)	Amount (Rs.)
Assets		
Fixed assets	1,80,000	
Less: Depreciation	50,000	1,30,000
Investment in Government securities		15,000
Debtors		20,000
Stock		30,000
Cash		5,000
		2,00,000

You are required to calculate the following ratio: (*a*) Return on investment, (*b*) Net profit ratio, (*c*) Current ratio, (*d*) Net worth to capital employed, and (*e*) Cost of production of capital employed.

(CS Inter 1999)

Solution

(*a*) Return on Investment

$$\text{Return on Investment} = \frac{\text{Net profit before interst and tax}}{\text{Capital employed}} \times 100$$

$$= \frac{\text{Rs. } 24{,}200}{\text{Rs. } 1{,}70{,}000} \times 100 = 14.24\%$$

Here net profit includes income from interest on Government securities (less interest on bank overdrafts) and capital employed covers investment in Government securities also.

(*b*) Net Profit Ratio

$$= \frac{\text{Net profit after tax}}{\text{Net sales}} \times 100$$

$$= \frac{\text{Rs. } 10{,}000}{\text{Rs. } 3{,}00{,}000} \times 100 = 3.33\%$$

(*c*) Current Ratio

$$= \frac{\text{Current assets}}{\text{Current liabilities}}$$

$$= \frac{\text{Rs. } 70{,}000}{\text{Rs. } 30{,}000} = 2.33 : 1$$

(**Note:** Current assets inclusive of investment in Government securities).

(*d*) Net Worth of Capital Employed

$$= \frac{\text{Net worth}}{\text{Capital employed}}$$

$$= \frac{\text{Rs. } 1,00,000}{\text{Rs. } 1,70,000} \times 100 = 58.82\%$$

(*e*) Cost of Production to Capital Employed

$$= \frac{\text{Cost of production}}{\text{Capital employed}} \times 100$$

$$= \frac{\text{Rs. } 2,58,000}{\text{Rs. } 1,70,000} \times 100 = 151.76\%$$

Illustration 5.4 JB Ltd. has the following Profit and Loss A/c for the year ended 31 March 1998 and the balance Sheet as on that date.

Profit & Loss Account for the year ended 31 March 1998

Particulars	Amount (Rs.)	Particulars	Amount (Rs.)
To Opening Stock	1,75,000	By Sales credit	12,00,000
Add: Manufacturing cost	10,75,000	Cash sales	3,00,000
	12,50,000		
Less: closing stock	1,50,000		
Cost of goods sold	11,00,000		
Gross profit	4,00,000		
	15,00,000		15,00,000
Administrative Expenses	35,000	By Loss & Profit	4,00,000
Selling Expenses	25,000	Other income	9,000
Depreciation	50,000		
Interest	47,000		
Income tax	1,26,000		
Net Profit	1,26,000		
	4,09,000		4,09,000

Balance Sheet as on 31 March 1998

Particulars	(Rs.)	Particulars	(Rs.)
Liquidities			
Equity share	3,50,000	Plant & Machinery (Net)	7,50,000
10% Preference shares	2,00,000	Goodwill	1,40,000
Reserves & Surplus	2,00,000	Stock	1,50,000
Long-term loan (12%)	1,00,000	Debtors	1,00,000
Debentures (14%)	2,50,000	Prepaid expenses	25,000
Creditors	60,000	Marketable securities	75,000
Bills payable	20,000	Cash	25,000
Accrued expenses	20,000		
Provision for tax	65,000		
	12,65,000		12,65,000

The market pick of the share of JB Ltd on 31 March 1998 is Rs. 45 and Reserve position is:

Particulars	(Rs.)
Reserves in the beginning	1,46,500
Net profit during the year	1,26,000
	2,72,500
Less: Preference Dividends	20,000
Less: Equity Dividends	52,000
Provision for tax	2,00,000

Calculate the following ratios:

(*i*) Current ratio (*ii*) Quick ratio (*iii*) Debt equity ratio (*iv*) Interest coverage (*v*) Fixed charge coverage (*vi*) Stock turnover, (*vii*) Debtors turnover, (*viii*) Average collection period, (*ix*) Gross profit margin, (*x*) Net profit margin, (*xi*) Operating ratio, (*xii*) Return on capital employed (ROCE), (*xiii*) Return on shareholders equity, (*xiv*) Earning per share, (*xv*) P/E ratio, and (*xvi*) Earning yield.

(CS Final 1998)

Solution

(*i*) Current ratio	$= \dfrac{\text{Current assets}}{\text{Current liabilities}}$
	$= \dfrac{\text{Rs. 3,75,000}}{\text{Rs. 1,65,000}} = \mathbf{2.27 : 1}$
(*ii*) Quick ratio	$= \dfrac{\text{Current assets} - \text{Inventories}}{\text{Current liabilities} - \text{Bank overdraft}}$
	$= \dfrac{\text{Rs.2,00,000}}{\text{Rs.1,65,000}} = \mathbf{1.21 : 1}$
(*iii*) Debt Equity ratio	$= \dfrac{\text{Long-term debt}}{\text{Shareholders funds}}$
	$= \dfrac{\text{Rs. 3,50,000}}{\text{Rs. 7,50,000}} = \mathbf{0.467 : 1}$
(*iv*) Interest coverage	$= \dfrac{\text{Profit before interest depreciation and tax}}{\text{Interest}}$
	$= \dfrac{\text{Rs. (1,26,000 + 47,000 + 1,26,000)}}{\text{Rs. 47,000}}$
	$= \dfrac{\text{Rs. 2,99,000}}{\text{Rs. 47,000}} = \textbf{6.36 times}$
(*v*) Fixed charge coverage	$= \dfrac{\text{Profit before interest depreciation and tax}}{\text{Interest + Preference dividend}}$
	$= \dfrac{\text{Rs. 2,99,000}}{\text{Rs. 47,000 + Rs. 20,000}}$
	$= \dfrac{\text{Rs. 2,99,000}}{\text{Rs. 67,000}} = \textbf{4.46 times}$
(*vi*) Stock turnover	$= \dfrac{\text{Cost of goods sold}}{\text{Average inventory}}$

[Contd...]

	$= \dfrac{\text{Rs. } 11{,}00{,}000}{(\text{Rs. } 1{,}75{,}000 + \text{Rs. } 1{,}50{,}000)/2}$
	$= \dfrac{\text{Rs. } 11{,}00{,}000}{\text{Rs. } 1{,}62{,}500} = \mathbf{6.769 \text{ or } 6.8 \text{ times}}$
(*vii*) Debtors turnover	$= \dfrac{\text{Credit sales}}{\text{Debtors}}$
	$= \dfrac{\text{Rs. } 12{,}00{,}000}{\text{Rs. } 1{,}00{,}000} = 12$
(*viii*) Average collection period	$= \dfrac{360 \text{ days}}{\text{Debtors turnover}} = \dfrac{360}{12} = 30 \text{ days}$
(*ix*) Gross profit margin	$= \dfrac{\text{Sales} - \text{Cost of goods sold}}{\text{Sales}} \times 100$
	$= \dfrac{\text{Rs. } 15{,}00{,}000 - \text{Rs. } 11{,}00{,}000}{\text{Rs. } 15{,}00{,}000} \times 100$
	$= \dfrac{\text{Rs. } 4{,}00{,}000}{\text{Rs. } 15{,}00{,}000} \times 100 = \mathbf{26.67\%}$
(*x*) Net profit margin	$= \dfrac{\text{Net profit}}{\text{Sales}} \times 100$
	$= \dfrac{\text{Rs. } 1{,}26{,}000}{\text{Rs. } 15{,}00{,}000} \times 100 = \mathbf{8.4\%}$
(*xi*) Operating ratio	$= \dfrac{\text{Operating expenses}}{\text{Sales}} \times 100$
	$= \dfrac{\text{Rs. } 11{,}00{,}000 + \text{Rs. } 35{,}000 + \text{Rs. } 25{,}000 + \text{Rs. } 50{,}000}{\text{Rs. } 15{,}00{,}000} \times 100$
	$= \dfrac{12{,}10{,}000}{15{,}00{,}000} \times 100 = \mathbf{80.67\%}$

[Contd...]

(*xii*) Return on capital employed (ROCE)	
Capital Employed	
Equity share Capital	Rs. 3,50,000
Preference Capital	Rs. 2,00,000
Reserves and Surplus	Rs. 2,00,000
Long-term loans 12%	Rs. 1,00,000
Debentures 14%	Rs. 2,50,000
Total	**= Rs. 11,00,000**
ROCE	$= \frac{\text{Net Profit before interest and tax}}{\text{Capital employed}} \times 100$
	$= \frac{\text{Rs. } 2{,}99{,}000}{\text{Rs. } 11{,}00{,}000} \times 100 = \mathbf{21.18\%}$
(*xiii*) Return on Shareholders' equity	$= \frac{\text{Net profit}}{\text{Shareholders funds}} \times 100$
	$= \frac{1{,}26{,}800}{7{,}50{,}000} \times 100 = \mathbf{16.8\%}$
(*xiv*) Earnings per share (EPS)	$= \frac{\text{Net Profit} - \text{Preference dividend}}{\text{No. of equity shares}} \times 100$
	$= \frac{\text{Rs. } 1{,}26{,}000 - \text{Rs. } 20{,}000}{\text{Rs. } 35{,}000}$
	$= \frac{1{,}06{,}000}{35{,}000} = \mathbf{3.03\%}$
(*xv*) Price/Earning (P/E) ratio	$= \frac{\text{Market price}}{\text{EPS}}$
	$= \frac{\text{Rs. } 45}{\text{Rs. } 3.03} = \textbf{Rs. 14.85 times}$
(*xvi*) Earning yield	$= \frac{\text{EPS}}{\text{Market price}} \times 100$
	$= \frac{\text{Rs. } 3.03}{45} \times 100 = \mathbf{6.73\%}$

Illustration 5.5 Delhi Ltd, a large professionally managed consumer durable manufacturer, is seeking a medium-term loan of Rs. 500 lakh essentially to finance part of its working capital requirements, following its decision to significantly improve credit terms to its customers, with a view to substantially increasing the demand for its products. The following are the company's summarized financial data, compiled from published accounts.

Particulars	Year 2002 (Rs. lakh)	Year 2003 (Rs. lakh)
Gross fixed assets at cost	2,200	2,000
Accumulated depreciation	(1,600)	(1,500)
Trade investments	100	100
Inventories	480	390
Receivables	590	400
Trade creditors	(170)	(90)
Tax and other provisions	(400)	(400)
Net assets employed	1,200	900
Financed by:		
Equity capital	300	300
Reserves	250	200
Long-term loans	400	200
Overdraft and short-term facilities	250	200
	1,200	900
Sales income	1,800	1,600
Profit before interest and tax	280	280
Interest	100	16
Tax	100	120
Dividends	30	30
Retentions	50	70

The company's fully paid-up equity shares having face value of Rs. 10 per share are quoted at Rs. 15 per share in the stock market. It is known that the plant utilization of the company's facilities is around 60% of its capacity, and there are adequate technical and marketing skills the company to handle a much higher volume of business.

Making such other assumptions, as you consider necessary, prepare a brief note on key indicators having bearing on the company's financial position and its credit and liquidity status from prospective lenders' viewpoint for use at an exploratory meeting scheduled with the company.

(CS Final 2003)

Solution

Working Notes:

Calculation of Capital Employed

Particulars		2003 (Rs. lakh)	2002 (Rs. lakh)
Gross fixed assets		2,200	2,000
Less: Accumulated Depreciation		1,600	1,500
Net Fixed Assets	(*a*)	600	500
Trading Investments	(*b*)	100	100
Current Assets			
Inventories + Receivables		1,000	790
Less: Current liabilities		820	690
(Trade creditors, provisions and overheads)			
	(*c*)	250	100
Capital Employed	(*a*) + (*b*) + (*c*)	950	700

Calculation Ratios	2003	2004
(*a*) Return on capital employed		
$\frac{\text{PBT}}{\text{Capital employed}} \times 100$	$\frac{280}{950} \times 100 = 29.47\%$	$\frac{280}{700} \times 100 = 40\%$
(*b*) Sales margin		
$\frac{\text{PBIT}}{\text{Sales}} \times 100$	$\frac{280}{1,800} \times 100 = 15.56\%$	$\frac{280}{1,600} \times 100 = 17.5\%$
(*c*) Sales to capital employed		
$\frac{\text{Sales}}{\text{Capital employed}}$	$\frac{1,800}{950} = 1.89$	$\frac{1,600}{700} = 2.29$
(*d*) Debt equity ratio		
$\frac{\text{Long-term debt}}{\text{Shareholder equity}}$	$\frac{400}{550} = 0.73$	$\frac{200}{500} = 0.40$
(*e*) Current ratio		
$\frac{\text{Current assets}}{\text{Current liabilites}}$	$\frac{1,070}{820} = 1.30$	$\frac{790}{690} = 1.14$

[Contd...]

(*f*) Quick ratio		
$\frac{\text{Current assets – stock}}{\text{Current liabilities – O.D.}}$	$\frac{590}{570} = 1.04$	$\frac{400}{490} = 0.82$
(*g*) Inventory turnover		
$\frac{\text{Sales}}{\text{Inventories}}$	$\frac{1,800}{480} = 3.75$	$\frac{1,600}{390} = 4.10$
(*h*) Receivables turnover		
$\frac{\text{Sales}}{\text{Receivables}}$	$\frac{1,880}{590} = 3.05$	$\frac{1,600}{400} = 4$
(*i*) Interest cover		
$\frac{\text{PBT}}{\text{Interest}}$	$\frac{280}{100} = 2.80$	$\frac{280}{60} = 4.67$
(*j*) Dividend cover		
$\frac{\text{PAT}}{\text{Dividend}}$	$\frac{80}{30} = 2.67$	$\frac{100}{30} = 3.33$
(*k*) Dividend yield		
$\frac{\text{Dividend}}{\text{Market value of equity}} \times 100$	$\frac{30}{450} \times 100 = 6.67\%$	$\frac{30}{450} \times 100 = 6.67\%$
(*l*) Return on equity		
$\frac{\text{PAT}}{\text{Shareholder's funds}} \times 100$	$\frac{80}{550} \times 100 = 14.55\%$	$\frac{80}{500} \times 100 = 20\%$

Analysis

- The return on capital employed is reduced from 40% of 29.47% and sales margin is reduced from 17.5% to 15.36%.
- There is an increase in capital employed from Rs. 700 lakh to Rs. 950 lakh. It has resulted in decrease of investment turnover from 2.29 to 1.89 times.
- The long-term debt component is doubled in one year and the debt-equity ratio shows a sharp increase from 0.40 to 0.73. The ideal debt-equity ratio is 2 : 1. The current debt position is within the manageable level with least financial risk.
- The working capital position and short-term liquidity position have improved during the last financial year i.e., 2005–06.
- The inventory turnover and receivables turnover shows excessive investment in stock and receivables over the requirement of increase sales.

- The interest service coverage ratio has fallen from 4.67 times to 2.80 times and the dividend cover has shown decline from 3.33 times to 2.67 times.
- The return on equity has fallen from 20% to 14.55%. However, the dividend yield remains unchanged.

Illustration 5.6 JKL Limited has the following Balance Sheets as on 31 March 2006 and 31 March 2005 (Rs. in Lakh).

Balance Sheet

Particulars	31 March 2006	31 March 2005
Source of Fun		
Shareholders' Funds	2,377	1,472
Loan Funds	3,570	3,083
	5,947	4,555
Applications of Funds	3,466	2,900
Fixed Assets	489	470
Cash and bank	1,495	1,168
Debtors	2,867	2,407
Stock	1,567	1,404
Other Current Assets	3,937	3,794
Less: Current Liabilities	5,947	4,555

The Income Statement of the JKL Ltd. for the year ended is as follows:

Income Statement	31 March 2006 (Rs. in Lakh)	31 March 2005 (Rs. in Lakh)
Sales	22,165	13,882
Less: Cost of Goods sold	20,860	12,544
Gross Profit	1,305	1,338
Less: Selling, General and Administrative expenses	1,135	752
Earnings before Interest and Tax (EBIT)	170	586
Interest Expenses	113	105
Profit before Tax	57	481
Tax	23	192
Profit after Tax	34	289

Calculate for the year 2005–06:

(*a*) Inventory turnover ratio

(*b*) Financial Leverage

(*c*) Return on Investment (ROI)

(*d*) Return on Equity (ROE)

(*e*) Average Collection Period

(CAPE II May 2006)

Solution

(*a*) Inventory turnover ratio

$$= \frac{\text{Cost of goods sold}}{\text{Average stock}}$$

$$= \frac{\text{Rs. 20,860 lakh}}{\dfrac{\text{Rs. 2,867 lakh + Rs. 2,407 lakh}}{2}}$$

$$= \frac{20{,}860}{2{,}637} = 7.91 \text{ times}$$

(*b*) Financial leverage

$$= \frac{\text{EBIT}}{\text{PBT}} = \frac{\text{Rs. 170 lakh}}{\text{Rs. 57 lakh}} = 2.98$$

(*c*) Return on investment (ROI)

$$= \frac{\text{EBIT}}{\text{Average capital employed}} \times 100$$

$$= \frac{\text{Rs. 170 lakh}}{\dfrac{\text{Rs. 5,947 lakh + Rs. 4,555 lakh}}{2}} \times 100$$

$$= \frac{\text{Rs.170 lakh}}{\text{Rs.5,251 lakh}} \times 100 = 3.24\%$$

(*d*) Return on equity (ROE)

$$= \frac{\text{PAT}}{\text{Average shareholders funds}} \times 100$$

$$= \frac{\text{Rs. 34 lakh}}{\dfrac{\text{Rs.2,377 lakh + Rs. 1,472 lakh}}{2}} \times 100$$

$$= \frac{\text{Rs. 34 lakh}}{\text{Rs.1,924 lakh}} \times 100 = 1.77\%$$

(*e*) Average collection period $= \dfrac{\text{Average debtors}}{\text{Net credit sales}} \times 365$

$$= \frac{\dfrac{\text{Rs.1,495 lakh + Rs. 1,168 lakh}}{2}}{\text{Rs. 22,165 lakh}} \times 365$$

$$= \frac{\text{Rs.1,331.5 lakh}}{\text{Rs. 22,165 lakh}} \times 365 = 21.93 \text{days}$$

PROBLEMS FOR PRACTICE

Problem 5.1 XYZ Ltd. Company has to prepare a plan for its next year. It is estimated that the company will employ assets of Rs. 10,00,000; 50% of the assets will be purchased by borrowing capital from the market at an interest cost of 10% per annum. Direct costs of the year are estimated at Rs. 4,40,000 and other expenses are estimated at Rs. 60,000 goods that will be sold at 150% of direct costs to customers tax rate is 40%.

Calculate (*i*) net profit ratio (*ii*) returns on assets (*iii*) turnover on assets (*iv*) return on owner's equity.

The Net profit is calculated as follows:

Particulars	Amount (Rs.)
Sales (105% of Rs. 4,40,000)	6,60,000
Direct Costs	4,40,000
Direct Costs	2,20,000
Less: Operating expenses	60,000
	1,60,000
Less: Interest changes 10% of 5,00,000	50,000
Profit before tax	1,10,000
Taxes @ 40%	44,000
Net Profit after tax	66,000

[**Answers:** (*i*) 0.1 or 10% (*ii*) 0.1455 or 14.55%, (*iii*) 0.66 times, and (*iv*) 0.13 or 13.2%.]

Problem 5.2 The Capital of Growfast Co. Ltd. is as follows:

Particulars	Amount (Rs.)
10% Preference shares of Rs. 10 each	50,00,000
Equity shares of Rs. 100 each	70,00,000
	1,20,000
Additional information	
Profit after tax (at 50%)	15,00,000
Depreciation	6,00,000
Equity dividend paid	10%
Market price per equity share	200
Calculate the following:	

(*i*) Cover for the preference and equity dividends
(*ii*) Earnings per share
(*iii*) Price earnings ratio
(*iv*) Net funds flow

(CS Final 1997)

[**Answers:** (*i*) 1.25 times, (*ii*) Rs. 14.29, (*iii*) 14 times, and (*iv*) 21,00,000.]

Problem 5.3 The following information of 3 times is given find the comparative positions of XY and Z company Ltd. Calculate Inventory turnover rates and average collection period. Assume 360 days make a year.

Particular	Firm X	Firm Y	Firm Z
Average Inventory	15,00,000	20,00,000	25,00,000
Credit sales	85,00,000	90,00,000	1,25,00,000
Cost of goods sold	75,00,000	80,00,000	85,00,000
Operating expenses	7,00,000	10,00,000	12,00,000
Average receivables	25,00,000	37,00,000	38,00,000

Answers: (*i*) Inventory turnover ratio X = 5, Y = 4 and Z = 3.4.
(*ii*) Average collection period X = 105.88 days, Z = 109.44 days.

Problem 5.4 The following data is supplied to you by PQR company for the year ending 31 March 2008:

Particulars	Amount (Rs.)
Current assets	6,50,000
Current liabilities	3,00,00
Cost of goods sold	12,00,000

[Contd...]

Particulars	Amount (Rs.)
Operating expenses	4,00,000
Inventory on 1.4.2007	3,00,000
Inventory on 31.3.2008	1,50,000
Fixed assets	8,00,000
Net profit	4,50,000
Net sales	20,00,000

Calculate (*i*) Current ratio (*ii*) Return on capital employed ratio (*iii*) Stock turnover ratio and (*iv*) turnover of fixed assets, and (*v*) Operating ratio.

[**Answers:** (*i*) 2.16 :1, (*ii*) 39.13 %. (*iii*) 5.3, (*iv*) 1.5 and (*v*) 80%.]

Problem 5.5 The following extracts of financial information relate to Curious Ltd.

Bank Sheet as on 31 December

	Year 2007 (Rs. lakhs)	Year 2008 (Rs. lakhs)
Share capital	10	10
Reserves and surplus	30	10
Loan funds	60	70
	100	90
Fixed asset (net)	30	30
Current assets:		
Stocks	30	20
Debtors	30	30
Cash and bank balances	10	20
Other current assets	30	10
	100	80
Less: Current liabilities	30	20
Net	70	60
Total	100	90
Sales	270	300

(*i*) Calculate, for the two years (*a*) Debt-equity ratio, (*b*) Quick ratio, and (*c*) Working capital turnover ratio.

(*ii*) Find the sales volume that should have been generated in 2006 if the company were to maintain its working capital turnover ratio.

(CA Adapted)

[**Answers:** (*i*) (*a*) 1.5 : 1 & 3.5 : 1 , (*b*) 1.33 : 1 & 2.5 : 1, (*c*) 3.86 times and 5 times. (*ii*) Rs. 3,50,00,000.]

❑❑❑

6 Sources of Finance

LEARNING OBJECTIVES

6.1 Introduction
6.2 Analysis of Factors for Sourcing Funds
6.3 Sources and Uses of Short-term, Medium-term and Long-term Funds Equity Shares
6.4 Security Financing
6.5 Loan Financing
6.6 Project Financing
6.7 Loan Syndication
6.8 New Financial Institutions, Services and Instruments
6.9 Factoring
6.10 Venture Capital
6.11 Commercial Papers
6.12 Certificate of Deposit
6.13 International Depository Receipts

6.1 INTRODUCTION

Sources of finance required by a company may be classified into long-term, medium-term and short-term funds. Long-term sources of finance are important for acquiring fixed assets for long-term use in the company. Long-term finance usually ranges from 5 to 25 years and has an effect on the organization's planning and finances for many years. The external sources of long-term finance are from equity capital, debentures, bonds, preference shares, term loans and innovative instruments. The short-term requirements are usually due to the non-synchronization of cash inflows with outflows and are useful for investment in current assets. Such requirements range from a period of one day to a maximum of one year. The sources of short-term financing are trade credit, factoring and forfeiting, bill discounting, overdrafts and cash credits from banks and borrowings against receivables. The firm can also get short-term funds from customers as advance on purchases, and through the use of credit cards.

A company also requires medium-term or intermediate finance for a period that ranges between 1 to 5 years. Medium-term finance is needed by a company to make permanent additions to their working capital or to buy fixed assets. Repayment of loan taken by the company for such an intermediate period is done by liquidating the assets that are financed or through profits or cash flow it generates from its operations. The sources of medium-term finance are leasing and hire purchase as well as fixed deposits from general public and directors of the company, and medium-term loans from banks.

The classification of sources of funds as explained above is given in Fig. 6.1.

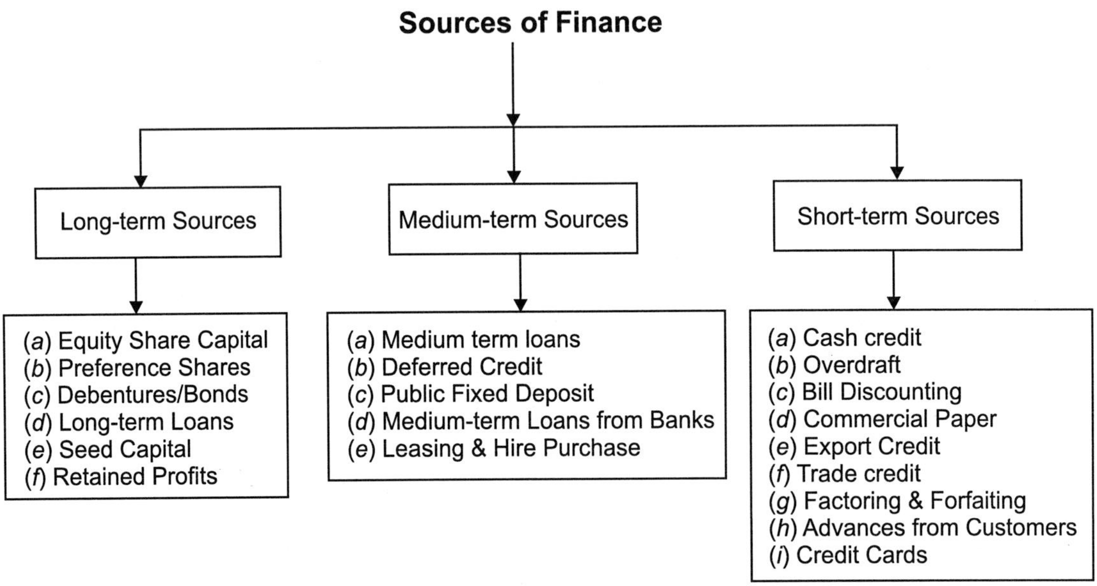

Fig. 6.1 Classification of Souces of Funds

Distinction between Long-, Medium-, Short-term Sources of Funds

Companies borrow funds due to the following reasons:

- To meet the requirements of a company for maintaining business.
- To borrow funds for earning a higher return.
- To expand business units.

Funds are necessary for running and expanding a business unit. They are also useful for improving returns but they also have risks attached to them. When comparing risks between short-term and long-term sources of funds it is expected that short-term sources of funds have comparatively lower risks than long-term funds. However, sources of funding do not comprise short-term fund alone. Different types of funds are required for maintaining a business unit. Long-term funds are required by a company for investing in a new project or planning expansion of existing activities. When long-term funds have been sourced they should be utilized through planned priorities of the organization. They cannot be liquidated immediately as it would only bring heavy losses to a company for their utilization in the long run will result in profitability to a company. If they are immediately liquidated, another company may not be able to use the same assets and hence they would only buy the business at its scrap value. Thus, it is important that before taking loans that the needs are analysed carefully.

Short-term and medium-term funds are required for immediate needs of the company. A high funding would make it difficult for a company to service its debts unless a desirable profit can be attained out of investing such funds in profitable avenues. A company requires borrowed funds as it has limited resources of its own. If funds are not sourced at the right time, shortage of funds will reduce the ability of the company to continue its business. Therefore for reasons of stability, funds will have to be accessed. The short-term funds should be acquired at the right time for the requirements of the firm and easily liquidated when the need arises. Also when a firm has an excess of short-term funds it should immediately invest to take advantage of interest. Techniques of financial management should be constantly applied for sourcing short-term funds and for their uses. The distinction between short-medium and long-term funds is given in Table 6.1.

Table 6.1 Distinction between Short-term, Medium-term and Long-term Finance

Particulars	Short-term Finance	Medium-term Finance	Long-term Finance
Period of finance required	Minimum requirement of one day to a maximum of one year.	Finance is required for a period ranging between one to five years.	Requirement between five to 25 years.
Sources of finance	Trade credit, factoring, forfeiting advances from customers, overdrafts credit cards.	Fixed deposits from public, bank loan, venture capital, leasing and hire purchase.	Reserves, issue of equity shares, bonds, debenture, term loans, reserves of the company.
Uses of funds	Financing seasonal fluctuations and working capital.	Financing purchase of stock and debtors of the company.	Financing long-term assets.
Volume of Funds	Volume of funds is small.	Volume of funds is higher than short-term funds.	Volume of funds is high.
Security	Security through debtors and stocks and reputation of the company in the market.	Security in the form of property and other assets.	Security in the form of property and high value assets.

To summarize:

- Short-term funds are required for working capital requirements for short-term period of time averaging one day to 12 months. Factoring, forfaiting, trade credit, over drafts are some sources for such funds.
- Medium-term funds are utilized between one and five years. Leasing, hire purchase, venture capital and bank loans are sources from which it can be accessed.

- Long-term funds are usually required in large volume. Issue of equity shares and debentures bring in long-term funds. Internal reserves can be used and loans from financial institutions and banks can be taken. The funds have to be planned carefully because they affect an organization for a long-term period up to 25 years.

6.2 FACTORS FOR SOURCING FUNDS

The factors to be considered while borrowing funds for a company's requirements are risk to the shareholders for borrowing funds. The return expected for borrowing funds, cost of financing and the dilution of control of shareholders within the company if funds are borrowed.

(*i*) Risk

The objective of financial management is to maximize the wealth of the shareholders. To fulfil this objective the financial manager should consider the risk and return of all the loans taken on behalf of the company for short-term, medium-term and long-term requirements. Every source of funding is a loan, be it short or long, and has the various kinds of risks attached to it. If the company requires a higher return it has to be prepared for higher risks. Higher risks may temporarily bring about a good return but in the long run it is a potential threat to the shareholders and to the existence of a company so the risks and return trade-off must be considered. Market risk is not controllable as it depends on factors external to the company. Internal risks can be controlled through good management policies. To emphasize, risk and return dimension cannot be ignored, the amount of funding required should be carefully analysed before the company actually decides on taking it.

(*ii*) Return on Funds

When funds are sourced from the market, the financial manager must remember his obligations towards the shareholders. He should assess the level of expectation of return of the shareholders. He must see the effect of new finance in the company with respect to the expected profitability of the company. Interest will have to be paid on the borrowed capital. This may have the effect of increasing or decreasing profitability. Only when the financial manager feels that the return brought about will be good from taking a loan he should take it.

(*iii*) Cost of Financing

There are several costs attached to funding an enterprise. The cost of servicing the finance through interest payments is a major cost and needs analysis before committing the company to it. There is a cost of excess funding as well if the funds are less than the firm's requirements. The cost of illiquidity in the event of not using the funds, increases the cost to the company. If a company does not use the funds that it has sourced and cannot return it, the funds becomes illiquid.

(*iv*) Dilution of Control of Shareholders

Types of funds must be analysed carefully to see that the control of the shareholders is not diluted by taking loans. The increase in the numbers of creditors will reduced the power of the shareholders as they have to return the money to their creditors in addition to paying them interest. The capital structure of the company should be balanced and there should not be a very high level of debt on it. A ratio 2 : 1 of is acceptable as debt reduces costs because of deduction in taxation.

6.3 SOURCES AND USES OF SHORT-, MEDIUM- AND LONG-TERM FUNDS

The funds obtained for financing a company have different kinds of usage. Short term funds have different sources because they are required for the purpose of meeting seasonal fluctuations and trade credit as well as working capital requirements. The need and purpose of medium-term funds is for longer periods of time to achieve the needs of financing working capital and fixed assets through leasing and hiring equipment for a company. The long-term resources of a company are from the issue of new shares or redeemable bonds/debentures/preference shares. The sources and uses of funds is depicted in Table 6.2.

Table 6.2 Sources and Uses of Funds

Types of Capital	Sources	Uses
Long-term	Share capital Retained profit Redeemable preference shares Long-term loans	Broaden borrowing base Financing major fixed assets Financing takeover or merger
Medium-term	Hire purchase Leasing Cash credit Bill discounting	Financing fixed assets Financing working capital
Short-term	Cash credit Bill discounting Export credit	Financing seasonal fluctuations Financing working capital

With this background of sources and uses of funds individual financing sources are discussed ahead.

6.4 SECURITY FINANCING

Security financing is a method of getting external source of financing for the company. The important securities which help in raising funds for a company are the following:

(*i*) **Equity Shares**

(*a*) Bonus share

(*b*) Rights issue

(*c*) Sweat equity share

(ii) Preference Shares

(*a*) Redeemable and irredeemable
(*b*) Cumulative and non-cumulative
(*c*) Participating and non-participating
(*d*) Convertible and non-convertible

(iii) Debentures/Bonds

(*a*) Redeemable and irredeemable
(*b*) Secured and unsecured debentures/bonds
(*c*) Financial engineering securities
(*d*) Tax-free bonds
(*e*) Zero coupon bonds
(*f*) Deep discount bonds
(*g*) Participating debentures
(*h*) Convertible bonds/debentures
(*i*) Convertible debentures redeemable at premium
(*j*) Floating rate bonds
(*k*) Regular income bonds
(*l*) Retirement bonds
(*m*) Double option bonds
(*n*) Inflation bonds
(*o*) Warrants

(*i*) Equity Shares

Equity shares are called 'ownership shares' because the holder of the shares participates in earnings of the company by receiving dividends from it. The ownership rights are exercised through voting in important decision-making areas of the company. Equity shares are called 'high-risk securities' because its return varies with the profitability of a company. Dividend is declared by the company only when there is a profit. The company is legally allowed to declare dividends only after making a provision for reserves, depreciation and taxation. However, equity shares have the benefit of being traded in a secondary market if its shares are listed on the stock markets. While trading a shareholder can make gains or losses. If the company was to go in for liquidation the equity shareholders would have the last rights after satisfying the debentures/bonds holders and preference shareholders. They can only claim residual amount after the claims of all the creditors of the company have been paid off. Equity shares have a face value. This is also called the 'par value'. They can be issued by the company at a par value or at a premium or discount. In the share market where trading takes place, the expectation of the shareholders is to trade at a higher price than the par value. New equity shares are issued in the New Issue Market. Subsequently, the company applies for trading of the shares by listing them in the Stock Market. Once the shares are listed they can be actively traded, the New Issue Market and Stock Market do not have any physical appearance, trading is done electronically through the depository system. In the New Issue Market, pricing of the share is arrived at through demand of the public by bidding through the book building method. The company however decides a price band within which the public decides about the price of the share.

(a) Bonus Share

Bonus shares are issued by a company cost free to its existing equity shareholders. These shares are issued out of reserves or retained profits or share premium. The residual reserve after paying bonus dividend should be 40% of the increased paid up capital. The reason for issuing bonus shares is that the company issues its undistributed profits and uses the same for expansion of business activities. Bonus shares do not have an effect on the volume of shareholders funds. After the bonus issue equity is increased and in the same proportion reserves are decreased. Bonus shares are issued on pro-rata basis, to the existing shareholders and do not affect their voting rights. Bonus shares can only be issued if the articles of association of a company permit it to do so. It increases the confidence level of the shareholders in the company.

Bonus issues increase a number of shares for a company. It has the advantage of allotting higher number of shares than the shareholders owns. It is not taxable for the shareholder. In the year of issue the dividends are reduced because of increase in number of shares, but in the future he will receive a higher dividend with greater number of shares that he owns due to bonus issue. Thus it earns goodwill for the company.

(b) Rights Issue

Right Issue is made to give a prior advantage to existing shareholders to subscribe to new equity shares of the company. The right issue price of the share is usually lower than the market value. This provides confidence to the shareholders. The company sends a letter of offer to its existing shareholders to purchase shares of the company to be issued on pro-rata basis. The letter of offer has two parts. The second part allows the shareholder the right of renunciation of the shares by selling off this rights to someone else in the share market.

(c) Sweat Equity Share

Sweat equity means equity shares issued by a company to its employees or directors at a discount for consideration other than cash for providing services or adding value to the companies work. Sweat equity shares are authorized when a special resolution is passed in the annual general meeting of the company. The resolution must specify the number of shares, their current market price and consideration for which the equity shares were issued. Sweat equity shares can be issued both when the shares of the company are listed or unlisted. In listed securities, the issue is regulated by Securities Exchange Board of India (SEBI). In unlisted securities, the company can issue the sweat equity shares according to the prescribed guidelines.

Rights of Equity Shareholder

Equity shareholders have the following rights:

(*i*) Right to share in the profits of the company in the form of dividends and bonus issues.

(*ii*) Right to control the management of the company. Their control is indirect by approving decisions in the annual general meeting by passing resolutions.

(*iii*) Right to vote at the annual general meeting of the company.

(*iv*) Right to receive a copy of annual accounts and report of the company.

(*v*) Right to claim the residual amount after repaying the claims of the creditors of the company.

(*vi*) Right to call an extraordinary general meeting if required by the company.

(*vii*) Right to trade and sell the shares in stock market.

(*viii*) Right to limited liability to the extent of the value of their shares.

Evaluation of Equity Shares as a Source of Financing for the Company

The advantages of issuing shares as a source of finance are:

(*i*) It is a permanent source of funds.

(*ii*) It does not have any repayment liability.

(*iii*) The company does not have to pay any dividends if it is not making a profit.

The disadvantages of issuing equity capital as a source of financing from the company's viewpoint are:

(*i*) The cost of funds is high because the expected return of shareholders has to be satisfied for the compensation of high risk, by giving high returns.

(*ii*) The company has to pay dividends after paying tax on profits. There are no tax deductible advantages for the company.

(*iii*) The floatation cost of issuing equity capital is high. The company has to pay merchant bankers fees, portfolio manager's fees, brokerage, underwriting costs, cost of advertising etc.

To sum up, equity shares are high-return and high-risk shares with the features of limited liability. They have an indirect control over management and have right to receive dividends.

(*ii*) Preference Shares

Preference shares have ownership rights in the company. They have a right to receive dividends of the company. They have a preferential right to receive dividends before the equity shareholders of the company. Preference shares do not have voting shares but have fixed dividends. Although preference shares resemble equity shares, they have certain special features. They can be issued as cumulative or non-cumulative shares, redeemable or irredeemable, participating and non-participating, convertible and non-convertible shares.

(*a*) *Redeemable and Irredeemable Shares*

Preference shares are usually redeemable. They have a specified number of years with a fixed maturity date and after which the principal sum has to be returned. Sometimes, companies issue irredeemable preference shares. These are not popular.

(*b*) *Cumulative and Non-Cumulative Preference Shares*

Cumulative preference shares have a right to receive dividends even if the company does not make a profit. When the company is at a loss they do not receive dividends but in the year of making profits the dividend is calculated and they receive the dividends even for the years of loss.

In a non-cumulative preference share, the preference shareholder receives dividends only in the year of profit.

(*c*) *Participating and Non-Participating Shares*

Participating preference shares are entitled to receive an extra dividend after payment of equity shareholders dues. It is also entitled to receive an amount in the residual assets of the company at the time of liquidation. Non-participating preference shares do not have these rights but they have a right to a fixed dividend.

(*d*) *Convertible and Non-convertible Shares*

Convertible preference shares can at the time of maturity be issued into equity shares or debentures of a company. Non-convertible shares have to be redeemed at the time of maturity on a specified date.

Evaluation of Preference Shares as a Source of Financing for the Company

The advantages of issuing preference shares as a source of financing are:

(*i*) Irredeemable preference shares do not have a date of maturity. They can be used by the company continuously as a source of financing and they do not have to pay dividends in the years of loss.

(*ii*) Preference shares do not create a charge on the assets of the company. The assets are freely available for the company for raising additional funds from other sources.

(*iii*) Preference shares do not have an effect on the control pattern of the company as they are not entitled to vote except in the matters pertaining to their own interest.

(*iv*) Preference shares are cheaper in financing compared to equity shares.

The disadvantages of issuing preference shares as a source of financing are:

(*i*) Preference shares are not tax deductible hence it affects the profits of the company.

(*ii*) Preference share are more expensive than issuing debentures. In fact, their cost becomes double because cumulative preference shares have to be paid in the year of profit even for the year of loss.

(*iii*) Preference shares have a claim over the equity shareholders on the assets of the company so their control is diluted.

To sum up, preference share is a hybrid security. It resembles both equity shares and debentures through its features. It has a fixed rate of dividend, limited voting rights and it is not tax deductible.

(*iii*) Debentures/Bonds

Debentures and bonds are debt securities and they have the same features. They have a specified rate of interest and a date of maturity. They are a form of sourcing finance for long-term purposes.

Debentures/Bonds have the following distinguishing features:

(*a*) **Form:** The form is like a certificate which states that the company is indebted to the holder to return the money on a particular date. It also states the interest rate that will be paid to the holder of the security.

(*b*) **Interest:** The rate of interest is specified in the debenture/bond form. This is called the *coupon rate* of interest. This may be paid annually, semi-annually or quarterly. The company is legally bound to pay the rate of interest specified on the form.

(*c*) **Redemption:** Debenture/Bond securities have the feature of maturity after a specified number of years. The date may be fixed for 5/10/15/20 years. On that specified date the company returns the principal sum to the holder. To redeem the security a company creates a sinking fund to eliminate financial problems for returning the amount on the due date.

(*d*) **Debenture/Bond Indenture:** A bond indenture is a special document. It is a trust deed between the company that is issuing the security and the trustees that represent the security holders. The trustees have the responsibility of protecting the interest of the security holder. It has the duty to see that the company issuing the debt securities pays interest to the holders on the specified date to fulfil its contractual obligations. This document specifies the terms of agreement between the company and the debenture/bond holders. It describes the rights of the security holders. It also gives the features of the security, its maturity date and any other benefits on it like convertible clause, other redemption and issue benefits like premium or discount on issue or at the maturity date of the security. If the debenture/bond is secured, this document specifies the kind of asset secured against it. If it is a convertible debenture/bond the terms must be written clearly on the document. To create a bond indenture trustees have to be appointed. These trustees can be attorneys/financial institutions/insurance companies.

(*e*) **Call and Put Option:** A company can issue debentures/bonds with the provision of '*called*' or '*buyback*' of the security at a specified price. The call price is usually at a premium offered by the company to attract the holders to redeem the security before the specified time. The put option provides a right to the holder of the security to redeem the security on specified date at a predetermined price.

(*f*) **Credit Rating:** Debentures/Bonds in India have to get themselves rated by a credit rating agency. This is compulsory in India. These credit rating agencies give symbols of rating of securities to ensure the credit worthiness of the issue. However, it is a matter of opinion of the rating agency and the buyer of the security must use his own analysis for assessment before he selects the security.

Types of Bonds/Debentures

There are many types of bonds/debentures. The most traditional security is a redeemable debenture whereby a company uses funds for a particular number of years after which when its requirements are over it releases it. There are lots of developments in debt securities and a large number of innovative securities are now issued in the market with many features to attract the investor so that it benefits both the company that requires funds and the investor who expects a return on his investment. A brief description of the different types of debentures/bonds is as follows:

(*a*) ***Redeemable and Irredeemable Debentures/Bonds***

Debentures/Bonds can be issued with the features of being redeemable or irredeemable. Irredeemable debentures continue till the lifetime of the company. Once they are issued, the holders continue to get a fixed interest called 'coupon rate of interest' until the lifetime of the company. If the company goes in for liquidation the debenture/bond holders have a prior right over the preference and equity shareholders on the assets of the company.

Redeemable debentures/bonds are issued by a company to meet its requirements of funds for long-term purposes. It does not intend to use the debt beyond a specified time. It is usually to purchase a long-term asset. Like the irredeemable bond it has a par value and a specified fixed coupon rate of interest with a fixed maturity date.

(*b*) ***Secured and Secured Bonds/Debentures***

Secured bonds/debentures are issued by a company through a security in the form of a physical asset. It is a lien on the company's specific assets. If the company does not pay interest on the due date and continues to make a default on its payments, the trustees can takeover the specific assets on behalf of the holders of the bonds/debentures holders. Secured debentures have a charge on the present as well as future immovable assets of the company in India.

Unsecured bonds/debentures are not attractive options for investors as they are not protected by any property or assets of the company. Such debentures/bonds are termed as 'naked security'. The company issues such securities based on its reputation and credit worthiness in the market.

(*c*) ***Financial Engineering Securities***

These are new type of securities which combine different features in one security. They are called innovative instruments. Many companies have tried to innovate to give a choice to the investors. The financial institutions and development banks in India have also issued such securities.

(*d*) ***Tax-free Bonds***

Tax-free bonds are issued by public sector financial institutions, Reserve Bank of India, banks and other public enterprises. These bonds are issued for raising funds for projects that are of national interest and importance. Rate of interest on such bonds is lower than the market rate but it is attractive because there is no tax on it and the investor benefits by this feature.

(*e*) ***Zero Coupon Bonds***

These bonds sell at a discount and on the maturity date the face value is paid to the investor. The investor gains by the difference between the purchase price and face value of the bond. There is no coupon rate of interest on this bond. However the purchase price of the bond is so derived that its protects the loss in terms of interest to the investor. The company issuing this bond does not have to pay interest and the project for which this bond was issued gets completed and the bonds are repaid on maturity to the holder of the bond. The implicit rate of return on these bonds works out to Acquisition price = Maturity value/$(1 = i)^n$ where i is the rate of interest and n is the period till maturity.

(*f*) ***Deep Discount Bonds***

Deep Discount Bonds have a long-term maturity period between 20 to 25 years. They carry the feature of *'call'* which means that the company can call back the bond after 5 or 10 years. It is sold at a discount but has no interest. For example, a 25-year bond is issued at Rs. 10,000 but is redeemed at Rs. 1,00,000. The discount makes-up for not receiving any interest during the waiting period.

Deep discount bonds are like the zero interest bonds. The bonds are sold at a discount and there is no interest on them. On the date of maturity, the face value is returned to the bond holder. The difference between the issue price and the maturity value is the return on the investment. Deep discount bonds have long maturity periods. In India, IDBI in 1992 was the first development bank to offer Deep Discount Bonds with the option of different maturity periods for a maximum period of 25 years. The investor has the option to withdraw after the specific number of years. The number of years specified was 5 years. Therefore after every

5 years it could be withdrawn if the investor did not want to continue. So, it had the feature of liquidity. It also had the call feature. IDBI could call back the bond if it could not continue with the scheme. It called back the bond as it was unable to complete the 25-year term due to change in interest rates. These bonds are tradable and the investor can make a capital gain on sale of the bonds. These bonds are issued for a longer period in comparison to zero interest bonds.

(*g*) ***Participating Debentures***

Participating debentures have been issued by companies. The investors are given a part of the excess profits that it has earned after giving a dividend to equity shareholders.

(*h*) ***Convertible Bonds/Debentures***

Convertible bonds and debentures are issued by a company with a promise that on the date of maturity they would be converted into equity shares. Such securities have a lower rate of interest because they are providing the additional feature of convertibility into an equity share. The debentures are converted into equity shares based on the formula of conversion ratio. The conversion ratio is the number of shares for each convertible debenture/bond. It is the par value divided by the conversion price. The conversion price is the price paid by the security holder at the time of conversion. The conversion time is the period from the date of allotment of convertible share after which the option for conversion can be exercised. A conversion period beyond 36 months has a call and put option. The investor can redeem his bonds/debentures before the maturity date. In India, convertible bonds are of 3 types. Those that are compulsorily converted within 18 months. Optionally convertible securities within 36 months and those convertible after 36 months with call and put features. In India, the securities with call and put option are not popular.

There are zero interest fully convertible debentures that do not carry any interest but are compulsorily converted into equity shares after a certain number of specified years at a price that is predetermined. In this security, no interest is paid by the company and when it is converted into shares the investor can get a capital gain.

(*i*) ***Convertible Debentures Redeemable at Premium***

These securities are issued by a company at the par value but the holders have a '*put option*'. This enables the holders to sell the security at a premium.

Zero Interest Fully Convertible Debentures (FCD's): These debentures do not carry any interest but on the specified date they are converted into shares.

(*j*) ***Floating Rate Bonds (FRB's)***

These bonds are issued by financial institutions by linking the interest on the bond to a benchmark interest rate. Floating rate bonds do not have a specified rate of interest. The interest rate changes on the basis of the benchmark rate of interest on treasury bills, bank rate and rate of term deposits. The rate of interest is higher than the benchmark rate. The investors have the advantage of being protected from the effects of inflation. The floating rate bonds are a hedge against volatility of interest rates.

(k) *Regular Income Bonds*

These bonds have '*call*' and '*put*' options. They are for a fixed period of time and they pay interest after every 6 months. The interest can also be monthly and the bond can be called 'monthly income bonds'. It also carries a front end discount.

(l) *Retirement Bonds*

These bonds are useful for investors who are in the retirement stage. They are issued at a discount with the option of monthly income and for a specified fix term period. On the exit time of the bond the investor gets a lump sum amount.

(m) *Double Option Bonds*

Double option bonds are made into two parts. One for the principal sum and the other for the interest with the redemption premium. Both these certificates are listed with the stock exchange. These can be traded by the investor. IDBI has issued these securities. It has a face value of Rs. 5,000 and an interest of 15%. The maturity period is 10 years and the redemption amount with premium is Rs. 16,500.

(n) *Inflation Bonds*

These bonds are issued by adjusting the interest rate against the inflation rate. The investor is protected from inflation. If the interest rate on such bonds is 10% and the rate of inflation is 5%, the investor will receive 15% thus taking care of inflation.

(o) *Warrant Bonds*

A Warrant is an attractive feature offered to a bond/debenture holder. These warrants are bearer documents of title or coupons to buy a specified number of equity shares at a specified price. Warrants can be exercised over different years as they have a long-term life period. Such bonds have a low rate of interest but they become attractive as the conversion into equity shares gives the investors capital appreciation value.

Warrants are detachable coupons and can be sold as they are traded in the stock market. The warrant bond holder is entitled to the benefits of such a bond only after it is converted into equity shares. Warrants are converted through an exercise price that is always higher than the current market price of the specified equity share. The company can sell detachable warrants. Some warrants have the option of selling back the security to the company on the maturity date. These warrants can be naked or secured and can be offered with the option of conversion into equity shares or bonds. Warrants are thus like derivatives with the '*put*' and '*call*' option.

Evaluation of Debentures/Bonds as a Source of Financing for the Company

The advantages of issuing debentures/bonds as a source of financing are:

(*i*) Debentures are a source of long-term funds with stable rate of return. The coupon rate of return is known to the company and offered by it in the terms suitable to it for returning it on maturity.

(*ii*) The cost of debentures/bonds is low due to the feature of tax deduction of interest payments.

(*iii*) Debentures/Bonds do not create any dilution of control as the holders do not have voting rights.

(*iv*) A company creates a sinking fund in which an amount is deposited every year to enable it to return the funds without any shortage of funds on the date of maturity.

The disadvantages of issuing debentures/bonds as a source of financing are:

(*i*) Debentures/Bonds create an obligation for the company to give an interest continuously to the holders of the security creating a financial burden on the company.

(*ii*) The funds sourced out of debentures/bonds should be used judicially for the right uses for which it is sourced, otherwise the company will have a high financial risk.

(*iii*) Debentures suit only those companies which have a stable return. In case a company has fluctuations in its earnings, it will have an effect on the dividends of the shareholders as they can only receive dividends after the interest payments have been made to debenture/bonds holders.

(*iv*) If a company fails and goes into liquidation, the debentures holders have a right to a charge on the property and assets of the company.

6.5 LOAN FINANCING

Long-term loans are taken by industrial organization at the time of starting a new business for expanding their business activities. These loans are of periods between 5 years and 10 years. In India such loans were being disbursed to industry by financial institutions like Industrial Development Bank of India (IDBI), Industrial Credit and Investment Corporation of India (ICICI) and Industrial Financial Corporation of India (IFCI). These institutions were specially set up to provide financial support and facility to industry for development. Commercial banks since 1991 after India's new economic reforms have emerged into institutions providing long-term loans in addition to their services to provide loans only for working capital requirements to industries.

Special Features of Loans

The special features of loans are the following:

(*i*) **Security:** Term loans are fully secured. The assets that are financed through term loans become the primary security. The company also provides collateral security on its immovable property as a first equitable mortgage or a floating charge or its current assets. The movable properties are hypothecated in favour of banks as an additional security.

(*ii*) **Interest Rate:** The long-term loans have a fixed rate of interest. The rate of interest depends on the prevailing rate in the market but in India since long-term loans were given for development by government financial institutions, the rate of interest is low.

(*iii*) **Repayment of Loan/Loan Amortization:** The borrowers have to return the loan in instalments. The instalment is calculated according to the equated periodical payments which means that instalments are smaller initially and increase in later years. The common practice in India was to give a payment holiday, called the moratorium period, in the first few years of development. Every instalment consists of a part of the return of the principal amount and a part of the return of interest payable on the loan amount. The borrower is expected to pay a commitment charge on the unutilized amount of loan. The debt of the borrower declines with repayments of loan. The interest burden is higher in the beginning and declines over time but the principal amount is constant.

(*iv*) **Restrictive Provisions/Covenants:** Covenants are clauses or provisions which are restrictions placed on the borrower. The borrower has to furnish periodical financial statements, maintain a minimum working capital, create sinking fund for redemption of debts and maintain its net worth.

In addition covenants or restrictions can be imposed by the lender whereby the borrower is prohibited to take further loans without the knowledge of the lender. It cannot create a charge on its previously mortgaged property with the lender. It is not permitted to sell its fixed assets without the approval of the lender of funds. It also cannot reduce its debt equity ratio. The lender can insist that the borrower should maintain its working capital according to a minimum current ratio.

The borrower may have restrictions to expand or start new projects without the lenders permission. It can also be restrained to give dividends to shareholders or to take additional funds on loans. The lender may have further control provisions like ceilings on the salaries and perks of managerial staff. It can also interfere in the company's selection of important professionals like directors, consultants or other important managerial staff.

***Types of Covenants*:** The different kinds of covenants are:

(*a*) ***Asset related covenants:*** These are the ones in which the borrowers are restricted to have an additional charge on the security provided to the lender against the loan obtained from them. The borrowers have to maintain their assets base.

(*b*) ***Liability related covenants:*** These are the ones in which the borrowing firm is restricted from incurring additional debts without repaying the existing loan. The firm also has to maintain its debt-equity ratio according to the limitations placed by the lenders.

(*c*) ***Cash flow related covenants:*** These are the ones in which the company is restrained from paying dividends or spending on capital expenses in the company without the lenders permission.

(*d*) ***Control related covenants:*** These are the ones in which the lenders interfere in the management of the company to protect their own rights. The lenders may appoint their own nominee director to look into the operations of the company.

Evaluation of Loan Finance as a Source of Financing for the Company

The advantages of loan as a source of financing are:

(*i*) Term loans taken by industry from financial institutions are attractive because they have a low rate of interest and have a low financial burden on the resources of the company.

(*ii*) It has the advantage of a moratorium period, thereby the company does not have to pay in the initial years of taking a loan. This helps the company to set up its organization and develop it before the loan return instalments begin.

(*iii*) Interest charges are tax deductible.

The disadvantages of loan as a source of financing are:

(*i*) Term loans have restrictions on the working of the company.

(*ii*) Some covenants are negative and the functioning of the company becomes difficult because permission has to be taken from the lender for every small change it wants to incorporate.

(*iii*) Flexibility in working is reduced and the company has to work according to the rules and regulations framed by the lender until the loan is returned.

To sum up, term loans have a low rate of interest and does not affect the control position of the shareholders directly. But the lender places restrictions on the freedom and flexibility on the working of the operations of the company.

6.6 PROJECT FINANCING

Project financing refers to managing and financing the economic activities of large infrastructural projects. High cost with large volume of funds such as power stations, fertilizer plants, satellites, oil, gas and hotel projects are some infrastructure related project. Special techniques are required to manage its finances. The financial techniques which had been applied to oil and gas are now being used for financing other large projects. The two most important aspects in project financing of these industries are risk and cash flow analysis.

Project finance is a series of techniques for assessing risks and calculations of cash flows generated by a project. It is a method of risk sharing by the owners or sponsors and lenders of the company. Project finance is risk management and risk sharing approach so that the owner or sponsors exposure is limited. Banks and equity investors can get a greater spread over their cost of funds or returns, enhancing their overall yield on portfolios. In this manner developing countries can develop many projects. If government and private players become partners, the government can use funds belonging to other than their own for developing projects with limited liability for any shortfalls of cash required for payments of debt and equity holders.

Project financing involves three important concepts. These are the following:

(*i*) **Cash Generating Assets:** A new special purpose company is formed in which all cash generating assets are transferred. The reason for this is that usually lenders give finance against future cash flows of the company and not according to the market value of the collateral which is pledged for receiving obligations. The reason for this is that in case of restructure and sale of the project, it becomes simple to make the evaluation.

(*ii*) **Special Project Account:** A special project account will be opened in which mortgages of properties, assignment of cash flows, insurance and other interests in assets will be accounted for.

(*iii*) **Recourse:** This means that the sponsors and other guarantors support the project through contracts or commitment of additional funds or guarantees of revenues. Recourse can be full recourse or limited recourse. In full recourse, the lenders gets full supports from the sponsors. In limited recourse, the degree of support has to be defined and in non-recourse the lenders do not have any support from the sponsors. Projects have full recourse in the beginning at the start of stage because of high risk but once they are operational they shift to limited recourse or non-recourse.

Project Financing Methodology

Project financing can be done through the traditional method of balance sheet financing or modern technique of project financing. Figure 6.2 depicts both form of financing.

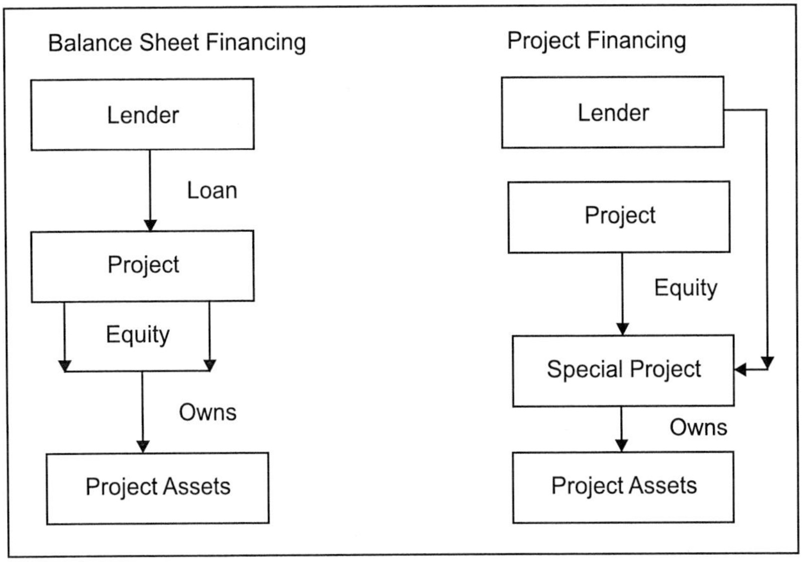

Fig. 6.2 Project Financing

Balance Sheet Financing

In this form of financing the lenders to the project view the cash flows and assets of the whole company to service debt and provide security.

Project Financing

(*a*) A separate entity is created (as explained) which receives equity from sponsors and loans from lenders.

(*b*) It is highly leveraged financing as debt is very high.

(*c*) All cash flows on this project will be transferred to the special project entity which will be different to the company itself.

(*d*) The assets of the project will be used as collateral for paying the loans.

Evaluation of Projet Finance as a Source of Financing for the Company

The advantages of project financing are:

(*i*) It provides the company's owners to finance large projects beyond the financial ability of the company.

(*ii*) The sponsor's accounts do not have the impact of the project finance because it is a separate entity.

(*iii*) The high leverage used by project financing benefits the equity holders.

(*iv*) Sponsors, customers, suppliers and government share the risk of the project and therefore projects of large magnitude can be started for the development of the country.

The disadvantages of project financing are:

(*i*) The projects consist of a large volume of funds and are subject to risks such as market risks, foreign exchange risks, currency depreciations, risk of supplies and project completion risk. These add to the cost of the project and are subject to losses. The company can make a high profit but can also make heavy losses. Therefore, it has to be prepared to take such high risk.

(*ii*) Project finance requires good management from the lenders and the sponsors. It requires risk management and cash flow analysis. It also requires a technical advantage. All these are high cost activities.

(*iii*) Project financing requires many expenses like government guarantees, paying royalties, and raising debt.

(*iv*) Project financing requires surrender of all or part of the interest to another company in exchange for finance and reduced net profits and interest of these sponsors.

6.7 LOAN SYNDICATION

Loan syndication is a service provided by merchant bankers for financing a project or for working capital requirements of a company. The financial institutions like IFCI, IDBI, ICICI, Life Insurance Corporation of India, Unit Trust of India, and General Insurance Companies and state financial institutions like SFC's and SDC's are suppliers of finance for loan syndication. The merchant bankers undertake the service of loan procurement and raising of loans from India and abroad. They prepare the loan application forms and follow up the loan procedure with financial institutions and banks.

The steps involved in loan syndication are:

(*i*) Merchant bankers prepare a detailed project report and make an estimate of the capital that would be required for the project.

(*ii*) This is a fees based activity and merchant bankers do this service for their clients. They have a list of prospective lenders. They identify the lenders, who according to them would be interested in giving a loan for the kind of project under consideration.

(*iii*) When merchant bankers have identified the lending sources, they begin to hold meetings and discussions and negotiate with the lenders on the loan amount, rate of interest and other terms regarding the loans.

(*iv*) When the preliminary discussions have taken place, the next step is to prepare a loan application.

(*v*) The merchant bankers submit the completed application forms to the financial institution from whom the loan is desired. They assist the institution in appraising the project.

(*vi*) When the lenders are satisfied, the merchant banker obtains a letter of intent and a letter with the sanction obtained from the lending institution.

(*vii*) Negotiations regarding the security offered on loans are made with financial institutions. The different kinds of covenants and clauses attached to the disbursement of the loan are discussed. Covenants are useful for the protection of the lenders but since they are sometimes too restrictive and make it difficult to function, the merchant bankers must see that they are fair and just and not negative to the functioning of the organization.

(*viii*) When the loan document is complete in all respects, the merchant banker assists the financial institution to disburse the loan to the borrower.

Evaluation of Loan Finance as a Source of Financing for the Company

The advantages of loan syndication as a source of financing are:

(*i*) **Identification of Finance:** The company does not have to identify potential sources of finance for taking loans; merchant bankers take up the work for a fee.

(*ii*) **Best Price:** Merchant bankers have preliminary discussions with the financial institutions for the benefit of both the parties. The company can rely on their trusted merchant bankers to get them the best deals.

(*iii*) **Disbursal of Loan:** Merchant bankers draw up the loan deed and also get the amount disbursed quickly. The company does not have to spend endless hours on getting the loan amount passed or in making contacts with the financial institutions.

The disadvantage of loan syndication as a source of financing are:

(*i*) **Payment of Fees:** Merchant bankers provide services that are fee based. This is an additional burden on the resources of the company besides the interest charges that they have to pay to the financial institutions and banks.

To sum up, loan syndication by merchant bankers makes it less time consuming for the company when they take the decision to take loans. Merchant bankers prepare project reports and have contacts with financial institutions. They are able to get sanctions of loans at a short time and take care that the loan disbursement is done without any delay.

6.8 NEW FINANCIAL INSTITUTIONS, SERVICES AND INSTRUMENTS

In India, several reforms were made to strengthen the financial system after 1991. The financial sector encompasses the financial institutions, markets, instruments and services. Financial reforms were intended to move from a controlled economy to a free economy with a liberal environment with the following objectives:

(*i*) To develop financial sector infrastructure in order to upgrade existing facilities, services and technologies for modernization.

(*ii*) To bring about financial supervision for investor protection and flow of fund in the right direction through discipline.

(*iii*) Financial liberalization for moving from a controlled economy to an efficient market economy.

(*iv*) To bring about improvement in quality of services through new financial services for the investors and to bring in confidence among the savers for encouraging savings in the economy.

(*v*) To introduce new financial instruments for giving options to the investor to invest his money.

(*vi*) To emphasize the requirement of protection of investors from fraudulent bills.

Types of Financial Services

The different kind of services in India after 1991 can be categorized as the following:

(*a*) **Security Related:** Securities related financial services are with respect to mutual fund services, underwriting services, security trading, clearance, placement, lending and settlement services.

(*b*) **Commercial Services:** Commercial services are mainly bank based services of advisory and custodian nature for providing finance for trade, letter of credits, transaction services and credit cards.

(*c*) **Fee Based:** Fee based services have been developed for corporate counselling, issue management, loan syndication, portfolio management services, foreign collaboration, mergers and acquisitions, and capital restructuring.

(*d*) **Fund Based:** There are also fund based services which help with equipment leasing, hire purchase financing, venture capital, factoring, bills discounting, loans and investments.

Contributors to the Financial System

The new institutions, instruments and services are directed towards five important contributors towards the development of the financial system. These are:

(*a*) **Household sector:** These are the supplier of funds because they save from current consumption and make investments.

(*b*) **Firms:** These are engaged in commercial activities and require various kinds of funds for carrying on business activities. They require new forms of financing and new services for developing the industrial centre.

(*c*) **Government:** It has an important role to regulate the market through policies and regulations and gives it direction. Therefore, government regulators have adopted the role of bringing the financial markets, institutions, instruments and services together conducive towards development.

(*d*) **Financial institutions:** They have to provide the role of giving funds and putting the savers and investors together. Therefore, there are insurance companies, mutual funds, merchant bankers, portfolio managers, underwriters, hire purchase and consumer finance institutions, venture capitalists, depositories with the intention of developing the market.

(*e*) **Financial instruments:** These are required for different kinds of needs of the borrowers. The instruments are financial assets that have claims on themselves and are used for facilitating transfer of money within a country and internationally.

Long-term financial sources have already been discussed earlier. The next part of the discussion deals with some new instruments and institutions like depositories, factoring, venture capital, credit rating, commercial papers, certificate of deposit, stock invest, global depository receipts that are being used now for developing large projects.

6.9 FACTORING

Factoring is a financial service for financing credit sales in which the receivables are sold by a company to a specialized financial intermediary called '*factor*'. The factor provides several services to the company that draws up an agreement, for managing its receivables. These services pertain specially to protection of the company from credit risks. In addition, the factor also manages the finances of the company, maintains its accounts, and collects its debts. For this service, the factor charges a fee or a commission for taking the responsibility of realizing the receivables from the customers.

While factoring is a financial intermediary for credit sales within the country, forfaiting* is *financing of receivables that arise out of international trade. Banks and financial institutions purchase trade bills or promissory notes through discounting and cover the risk of non-payment at the time of collection of dues. The *forfaiter/purchaser* becomes responsible for the risk. He pays cash to the seller on discounting of the bills.

Parties to Factoring

There are three parties involved in the factoring contract. These are the seller, the buyer and the factor. Each one has a definite service to perform. It must be clearly stated that the factor perform the service on behalf of the seller of goods. Their services are explained as:

(*a*) **The seller:** The seller prepares a memorandum of understanding with the buyer and sells goods on credit to him. He gives him the delivery invoice and instructs the buyer to pay the amount due on credit sales to his ***agent or factor.*** The factor deducts his service charges and pays 80% of the amount on receivables.

(*b*) **The buyer:** The buyer makes an agreement with the seller after negotiating his terms and signing a memorandum of understanding. Then he receives the delivery of the goods and the instructions from the seller regarding mode and date of payment to his agent/factor. The buyer then makes a payment to the factor on the due date. If he cannot keep his commitment on the due date he can ask for an extension of time from the factor. The factor may agree to extend the time through the same conditions or ask for a higher charge. He also has the right to go for legal settlement.

(*c*) **The factor:** The factor is a financial intermediary between the buyer and the seller. He is an agent of the seller as he makes an agreement with him for looking after all his credit sales. The seller sends the sale documents to the factor. The factor pays 80% of the price in advance and receives the payment from the buyer on the due date. He then remits the balance to the seller after deducting his commission.

The sale deed should clearly state the name of the factor and the agreement made with him to enable him to recover the money on credit sales from the buyer on the due date.

Functions of the Factor

The factor has a very important role to play. He maintains the sales ledger, collects the accounts receivable, and provides financing facility and takes care of the credit risks.

(*a*) **Sales ledger***:* The factor administers the sales ledger. When he receives the sales invoice his work on opening the ledger begins. He writes the entries of receipts from the customer and sends periodic reports to the seller. He keeps the seller informed of his account with the buyer of goods. On the due date when he receives the full payment, he sends the final account to the seller on whose behalf he is the factor.

(*b*) **Collection of receivables***:* The factor keeps a record of the collection that he has to make on behalf of his client. He sends notices to the debtor reminding him of the due date. For collection of the receivables the factor maintains a trained staff. The staff should be courteous while making demands on customers but they also have to be firm so that the debt is collected on the desired date.

(*c*) **Financing:** A factor purchases the book debts from the seller in his own favour. He makes advance payments to the seller for assigning the debts to him. On factoring ***without recourse to debt*** the factor becomes responsible if the buyer does not make a payment because the seller will not refund the payment to the factor. On factoring ***with recourse*** the factor is refunded by the seller in case of defaults by the buyer. This is the unique financing function of the factor.

(*d*) **Credit risks***:* Factoring service is usually ***without recourse to debt***. The factor takes up the entire risk of collection of debt and protects the seller in the event of default by the buyer. This service helps the seller to spend his time in fruitful business ventures and leave the collection work to the factor. The factor does the service of assessing the customers. It makes a report on the buyers' background and earlier business dealings and gives it to the seller before entering into a sale deed. Further, he keeps in constant touch with the buyer and updates him on due dates. Thus the seller can concentrate on other important work in business transactions and the factor takes care of all the credit risk.

The factor thus becomes a close associate of the seller/client. He gives information to his clients about emerging trends in the market. He also gives advice on banking, leasing, merchant banking and other services if required to do so.

Types of Factoring

Factoring is the function of collection of receivables and all formalities attached to it. There are many types of factoring but the two common types that are normally used in business are with recourse and without recourse factoring.

(*a*) **With recourse factoring:** In with recourse factoring, the factor does not take any credit risk which is associated with receivables. The factor still has the right to receive his commissions and his expenses for maintaining a sales ledger and for any expenses that occur for collection of dues.

(*b*) **Without recourse factoring:** Without recourse factoring means that the factor has to bear all losses that arise out of irrecoverable receivables. For this service he charges a higher commission which is a premium for the higher risk and it is called ***del-credere commission***. In this type of factoring the factor takes a great interest in the business matters of the client. He makes a summary of the purchaser's credibility and background and makes a rating before giving him goods on credit. This precaution is taken by the factor because in case the purchaser does not pay the dues, the factor has the bear the loss as he does not have the right of recourse.

There are certain legal formalities of a factoring contract. These must be considered before entering into a contract.

Legal Formalities of Factoring

Factoring is a service that was recommended by the Kalyansundaram Committee which was set up by RBI in 1989. The first factoring company in India was SBI Factors and Commercial Limited (SBI FACS). The first service in the private sector was started in 1992 by Fair Growth Factor Limited. Some of the following legal implications to be considered are:

(*a*) **Approval:** Factoring as a business activity can be started in India only with the approval of the Reserve Bank of India. Banks can undertake indirect participation of factoring services with the approval of RBI by investing in shares of other factoring companies. Banks can open subsidiaries for carrying out factoring business individually or jointly with other banks if they get approval from RBI for this business.

(*b*) **Genuine transactions:** The factoring contract can arise only out of genuine business transactions between the buyer and the seller.

(*c*) **Fees/Commission:** The factor receives commission/fees as compensation for his services. He also has the right to receive all expenses in connection with the factoring work that he undertakes.

(*d*) **Agreement:** It is a sale purchase agreement governed by the law of contracts. The time framework and mode of termination are provided in the agreement.

(*e*) **Payment:** The factoring agreement must have full details about the mode, amount and date of payment that the factor has to take from the purchasers of goods on credit. The legal status of the factor is that of an assignee to his client. The buyer has the obligation of making the payment to the factor that has to receive the payment and then remit the same to his client.

6.10 VENTURE CAPITAL

Venture capital finance is a private equity investment fund through which funds are borrowed by investors who have the technical know-how. The venture capitalists make an agreement whereby they support the project and fund it, in return for monetary gains, shareholding and acquisition rights in the business financed by them. This service has the advantage of merging of technical ability with financial strength with part ownership of an enterprise coupled with capital gains.

The first venture capital fund in India was established by Industrial Finance Corporation of India (IFCI) in 1975. It was called the Risk Capital Foundation (RCF) Venture capital funds in India are of four different types. These are the sponsored venture capital funds by development financial institutions, the state level sponsored development financial institutions, funds promoted by public sector banks and private venture capital funds.

Features of Venture Capital

The features of venture capital relating to the type of finance offered, period of finance given, and involvement in business are described as:

(*a*) **Finance:** Venture capital is based on equity contributions made in ***new small and medium sized companies***. It is usually in the form of equity investment, but it can also be in the form of convertible debt and loan finance.

(*b*) **Period:** Venture capital covers long-term period of investment in small or medium firms which are growth oriented.

(*c*) **Capital appreciation:** Venture capitalists invest in companies to get a capital appreciation on their contribution.

(*d*) **Involvement:** Venture capitalists provide funds and business skills to companies in which they invest their funds. They participate in developing the firm, and they take an active interest in its working.

(*e*) **Controlling interest:** Venture capitalists do not interfere with the management of the firm. They do not have a controlling interest in the company in which they invest. Their prime interest is to earn a capital gain at the time of exit from the company.

(*f*) **High risk:** Venture capital is given to entrepreneurs for an idea and skill that is not yet tested. It is provided to new companies that may have lot of competition and market risk. The risk in these companies is very high because they may develop and give profits or losses may occur. It is only after its development that its capital appreciation can be received. Hence venture capital is highly risky.

(*g*) **High return:** Venture capital is given with the objective of receiving a high return on the investment made by them. The return is expected only after the firm is well developed. The return is assumed to be in the form of capital appreciation.

(*h*) **Idea based:** Venture capital is based on certain ***new ideas***. Its concept is growth oriented. It is not based on high technology or for established companies. Its focus is on new companies.

(*i*) **Exit:** The venture capitalist exit by buying the shares of the company and then selling it again at an initial public offering. They can also make an exit by sale of shares to employees, by sale to another company, by liquidation and by selling to new investors. The transfer of management control is through a ***management buyout or a management buy in***. A management ***buyout*** *i*s the part or full acquisition of a company or it shares in that company from the existing owners by the internal operating management. A management ***buy in*** is when an external group of managers buy a running company. Management ***buyouts*** are more popular than management ***buy-ins***.

Valuation of the Proposal

The venture capitalists provide finance by following certain steps. The process requires the exploration and decision of investment opportunities, analysis of the investment proposal, and valuation of the proposal, price, monitoring and exit. Venture capitalist analyse specific proposals by making an appraisal of the entrepreneurs requiring the funds, the nature of the projects, the stage of financing required and the method of financing. They also look into the economic and financial position of the firm and its management. The capitalist also tries to find out the future exit mechanism and the profitability at that time from the firm.

Proposals are valued through the conventional valuation method, First Chicago Method and the Revenue Multiplier Method.

(*a*) **Conventional Valuation Method:** It takes into account the starting time of the venture and the exit time. The venture capitalist calculate the revenue at the beginning period and at the liquidating period and compound it by the expected annual growth rate for the period that they decide to hold the investment in the firm. They calculate the expected earnings levels which is equal to future earnings level multiplied by after tax margin percentage on liquidation. After this they compute the future market valuation by multiplying the expected P/E ratio with the earnings level. Then they value the investment of the company by using a discount factor. If the present value of the venture capital undertaking is Rs. 100 lakh and the entrepreneur is interested in Rs. 50 lakh, the venture capitalist ownership will be 50%. This method ignores the losses and concentrates on exit. To explain, this method calculates ***annual revenue, expected earnings levels, future market valuation, and present value of venture capital and minimum percentage of ownership.***

(*b*) **First Chicago Method:** This method takes the complete earning stream from the starting point to the exit. To calculate through this method, three alternative routes are calculated. These are success, sideways survival and failure rate. They are then given a probability rating. The venture capital undertaking is then discounted to its present value with a discount rate higher than the risk. The discounted present value is multiplied by the probabilities assigned. The expected present value of the venture capitalist is equal to the three alternate situations. If the present value of the undertaking is Rs. 20 crore and the fund requirement is Rs. 10 crore, the minimum ownership requirement is 50%.

(*c*) **Revenue Multiplier Method:** The Revenue Multiplier method is used in the early stage of venture capital investments when the earnings based on after tax profit is low or negative. The venture capital investment is calculated by multiplying annual revenue of the company with estimated revenue multiplier.

Venture Capital Funds in India

There are many venture capital funds in India. Some of these are:

(*i*) IDBI Venture Capital Fund

(*ii*) ICICI Venture Funds Management Company Limited

(*iii*) Small Industries Bank of India Venture Capital Finance

(*iv*) IFCI Venture Capital Funds Limited

(*v*) Can Bank Venture Capital Fund

(*vi*) Gujarat Venture Capital Finance Limited

Some of the other known funds are: South Asian Regional Apex Fund, Auto Ancillary Fund, Indus Venture Management Limited, Marigold Capital Management Limited and HSBC Private Equity Management Limited, and Walden Nikko India Management Company Limited.

Thus the venture capital concept is new to India but there are a large number of funds operating in India. The major interest of these funds is to provide finance and to make an exit at the right time to earn profits. Such funds are also of advantage to the entrepreneurs as they are able to get finance at the right time and the right amount which they are not able to arrange from their own means

6.11 COMMERCIAL PAPER (CP)

A commercial paper is an unsecured, short-term negotiable instrument with a fixed maturity. It is used for raising short-term debt. It is an obligation of the issuer. It is an unsecured promissory note. It does not have any collateral and it is issued for a period between seven days and three months. In India commercial papers are popularly used between 91–180 days. It is a promise by the borrowing company to return the loan on the specified date of payment.

Commercial paper no doubt is a very important alternate source to bank financing for short-term requirements. It is not tied to any specific trade transaction and very little paper work is involved. A corporate organization can directly issue commercial papers to investors. This direct dealing between a company and an investor is called a '***direct paper***'. The commercial paper can be indirectly issued through a bank or through a dealer. This is called '***dealer paper***'. The dealer buys at a lower price and sells at a higher price and gets a commission In India this is a relatively new instrument it was introduced in 1990 with the objective of providing short-term borrowings. A company is allowed to issue commercial papers. Individuals, non-resident Indians, banks, companies and registered organizations can invest in commercial papers. Non-resident Indians cannot transfer or repatriate the commercial papers issued to them. They are issued at a discount on the face value and their rate is determined through the interplay of market process of demand and supply. Reserve Bank of India regulates the commercial papers in India.

Advantages of a Commercial Paper

A commercial paper has the following advantages:

(*a*) **Security:** The commercial paper is made without pledging any assets. It is a promise based on reputation of the company.

(*b*) **Guarantee:** The guarantee in the agreement is based on credit worthiness, earning capacity and liquidity of the company.

(*c*) **Documentation:** A commercial paper is a very useful instrument for short-term requirements as no documentation is required.

(*d*) **Flexible:** The commercial paper can be designed between the issuer and the acceptor and according to their needs the maturity period can be fixed.

(*e*) **Transaction:** It is not necessary to have any trading transaction between the parties entering into an agreement and making a commercial paper.

Disadvantages of a Commercial Paper

A commercial paper has some disadvantages which are as follows:

(*a*) **Issue:** Commercial paper does not have any collateral; it depends on the credit worthiness of the company. Only large well-known companies can make use of this instrument. Small companies are unable to use this instrument for their short-term requirements.

(*b*) **Reliability:** Commercial paper is not as reliable a source as a bank. A buyer of a commercial paper has no obligation towards anyone. He uses the opportunity for a short-term gain with a minimum risk.

(*c*) **Redemption:** Commercial paper has the disadvantage that it cannot be liquidated before the maturity date. A firm cannot repay the amount before maturity even though it has received payment from some other source and would like to return the funds. Interest will have to be paid until the maturity date of the instrument.

(*d*) **Extension:** There is no flexibility after the commercial paper has been designed and signed. The maturity date is fixed and it cannot be extended after the due date.

6.12 CERTIFICATE OF DEPOSIT (CDS)

A certificate of deposit is a securitized short-term deposit issued by banks at high interest rates during period of low liquidity. The liquidity gap is met by banks by issuing CDs for short-term periods of time. Since the interest rate is attractive CDs are kept till maturity. Since CDs are becoming popular, there has been a reduction on their stamp duty, withdrawal of tax deduction at source, opportunity for trading in the stock market and requirement of closure of deposits only at maturity. In India, CDs are being issued by banks either directly or through dealers. A CD is negotiable short-term instrument in bearer form. They are a part of bank deposits and are issued for 90 days but the maturity period can vary according to the requirements of corporate organizations. The minimum issue of CDs to single investor is Rs. 10 lakh and can be further issued in multiple of Rs. 5 lakh. They can issue at a discount on the face value and they are transferable after a lock in period of 30 days from the time of issue. The CDs market is larger than the CPs market. The rate of CDs is determined by the market. They are used for interim requirements and for financing current transactions.

Advantages of Certificate of Deposit

Certificate of deposit has the following advantages:

(*a*) **Reliable:** Certificate of deposit is financed by banks. It is a formal financing method and it has a structured form which is filled in by the bank. It is very reliable as a source of funding.

(*b*) **Liquidity:** It provides liquidity through funding to small, medium and large companies during a period when finance is difficult to get from other market sources.

(*c*) **Flexible:** The maturity date of the instrument can be designed for a particular investor depending on his requirement for funds. This gives flexibility to the instrument.

(*d*) **Trading:** CDs have the facility of being traded in the stock exchange.

Disadvantages of Certificate of Deposit

Certificate of deposit has the following disadvantages:

(*a*) **Cost:** Certificate of Deposit is a high cost of financing as banks charge a high rate of interest.

(*b*) **Expenses:** Certificate of Deposit is an expensive instrument as they have stamp duties levied on it.

6.13 INTERNATIONAL DEPOSITORY RECEIPTS

The most popular negotiable certificates adopted in the international equity markets are the American Depository Receipts (ADRs) in the US, European Depository Receipts (EDRs) in Europe and Global Depository Receipts (GDRs) internationally and in the US.

(*i*) American Depository Receipts

The American depository receipts are a method of raising funds in the US stock markets. The first American Depository Receipt was issued in 1920 to invest in overseas markets and to provide a base to the non-US companies to invest in the stock market in the US.

The ADRs could be traded only in the US and EDRs in Europe in Euros. The increasing popularity and volume of trade in 1990 brought about a change in policies to make the receipts ***'fungible'*** which mean that they could be traded settled and cleared with one receipt.

ADRs have to be issued and registered according to the provisions of the Securities Exchange Commission (SEC).

ADRs can be sponsored or non-sponsored. Sponsored ADRs can be used for raising additional capital in the US. New un-sponsored ADRs are similar to stock exchange trading transfers and transactions with fixed outstanding equity.

(*ii*) European Depository Receipts

The EDRs are issued in Europe and denominated in European currency. They resemble the ADRs but are not attractive instruments. EDRs have a very small market. They are not well developed like the ADRs and GDRs.

(*iii*) Global Depository Receipts

GDRs are an instrument for raising equity capital by organizations which are in Asian countries. They are placed in the US, Europe and Asia. They have a low cost and help in bringing liquidity. A company usually raises capital simultaneously from two countries. For example, the GDR may be issued in India and simultaneously placed in the US and Europe through one security. The issuer deals with a single depository bank which facilitates the secondary and inter-market trading among investors situated in different counties. It is a fungible instrument and the issuer does not have any exchange risk. He can freely use the foreign exchange collected from this issue. Government of India allowed Indian companies to mobilize funds from foreign markets through Euro issues of global depository receipts and foreign currency convertible bonds. Companies with a good track record can issue GDRs for developing infrastructure projects in power, telecommunications, and petroleum and in construction and development of roads, airports and ports in India.

Features of Global Depository Receipts

Some of the features of Global Depository Receipts are:

(*a*) **Financial instrument:** It is a financial instrument in the form of a depository receipt. It has been created by a depository bank outside the Indian boundary. It deals with a fixed number of equity shares of a company.

(*b*) **Trading:** It is listed and traded in a foreign market.

(*c*) **Custodian bank:** The shares are issued in Indian currency in the Indian market with an Indian bank as its custodian.

(*d*) **Price:** The price of the Global depository receipts are quoted in the US dollars.

(*e*) **Voting rights:** The Global depository receipts do not have any voting rights in the issuing company.

(*f*) **Conversion:** The instrument gives the right of conversion to the holder from GDRs to equity shares of the company. It also has the right and option to convert the equity shares into GDRs.

(*g*) **Shareholder:** The issuing company has to deal with the depository bank which is its only customer. It does not have to deal with multiple shareholders.

(*iv*) Indian Depository Receipts (IDRs)

Indian Depository Receipts are like the American Depository Receipts and Global Depository Receipts. This is a new instrument as a source of raising finance. This instrument provides global companies to have an entry in the Indian capital market. Global companies can issue IDRs and raise money from India. Although this instrument has been accepted as an international financial instrument for raising funds the legal formalities are still being worked out by the Department of Company Affairs.

POINTS TO REMEMBER

- The different sources of finance required by a company are classified into long-term, medium-term and short-term funds.
- The sources of long-term finance are from equity capital, debentures, bonds, preference shares, term loans and innovative instruments. Internal resources can also be used for long-term finance.
- The sources of medium-term finance are leasing and hire purchase, fixed deposits from general public and directors of the company, and medium-term loans from banks.
- The sources of short-term financing are trade credit, factoring and forfaiting, bill discounting, overdraft and cash credit from banks and borrowings against receivables.
- Short term funds are required for seasonal fluctuations and working capital requirements. Medium-term funds are used by a company for financing purchase of stock and debtors and long-term funds for financing long-term assets and projects of the company.
- The period of finance required for short-term funds is for a period ranging between one day to a maximum of one year, medium-term funds requirement can be classified as a period between one year to five years and long-term funds between five and 25 years.

[Contd...]

- The factors to be analysed for taking funds from different sources are risk, return on funds, cost of financing and degree of control.
- Equity shares are high risk ownership securities. They are entitled to dividends out of the profits of the company. Shares can be traded in the stock market. They can get capital appreciation or loss.
- Bonus shares are given to equity shareholders out of reserves or retained profit or share premium. It increases the number of shares and paid up capital of the company and decreases its reserves.
- Rights issue is a subscription to new equity shares given as a prior advantage to existing equity shareholders.
- Sweat equity are equity shares of the company given to employees or directors at a discount for consideration other than cash for providing services to the company.
- Preference shares have different features. They are hybrid securities resembling equity and preference shares. They can be issued as cumulative, non-cumulative, redeemable-irredeemable, participating, non-participating, convertible and non-convertible.
- Bonds are debt securities with a specified rate of interest and date of maturity. Bonds may be redeemable, secured, with warrants, tax saving, zero coupon bonds, deep discount bonds, participating, convertible, floating rate bonds, regular income, double option and inflation bonds.
- Loan financing can be done by a company from financial institutions and banks. The security interest rate, repayment and restrictive provisions of governance must be valued.
- Project financing is done by forming a special purpose company in which the project account is opened and financing is done by different agencies. This is for large projects.
- Loan syndication is a service provided by merchant bankers for financing a project or for working capital requirements.
- Many new types of financial instruments and institutions have started in India after the new economic reforms in 1991.
- Factoring is a financial service for financing credit sales. Venture capital is a private equity investment through which funds are borrowed by an agreement for a share in the company's profits and acquisition of shareholders rights.
- New instruments like commercial papers and certificate of deposits and unsecured short-term instruments have become very popular.
- International financial instruments are being widely used. These are global depository receipts under which there are American Depository Receipts, European Depository Receipts and Indian Depository Receipts.

OBJECTIVE TYPE QUESTIONS

State whether the following statements are true (T) or false (F). Give justification for your answer.

1. Global Depository Receipts are registered in America but trade takes place in Singapore.
2. Certificate of Deposit is an instrument used for long-term finance.
3. Venture capital finance is high risk and high return form of business.
4. Reserve Bank of India is responsible for a factor's risks.
5. Dematerialized shares have distinction numbers and they are given to shareholders.
6. Trading of shares is through re-materialization of shares.
7. Book building offers shares to the public based on pricing through bids.
8. Project financing a large project by fund raising from lenders and sponsors.
9. Loan syndication is a financial service given by merchant bankers.

Answers: 1. (F), 2. (F), 3. (T), 4. (F), 5. (F), 6. (F), 7. (F), 8. (T), 9. (T).

THEORITICAL QUESTIONS

1. Distinguish between the following:
   (*a*) Long-term, medium-term and short-term finance.
   (*b*) Project financing and loan syndication.
   (*c*) Tax saving bond and warrant bonds.
   (*d*) Venture capital and factor financing.
   (*e*) Commercial Paper and certificate of deposit.
2. Classify the different kinds of sources of finance and the purpose for which they are required by a company.
3. What is 'project financing'? What are its distinguish features? What kind of companies should take funds under project finance?
4. What are 'financial engineering securities'? Discuss some of these securities.
5. What is a 'floating rate bond'? How is it different from warrant bonds?
6. Evaluate equity shares as a form of financing for a company.
7. What are the factors to be considered while taking a loan-term loan as a financial measure?
8. What is a 'covenant'? How do they restrict a company from borrowing funds?
9. What is the meaning of 'loan syndication'? Discuss the steps for taking such a loan.

10. How would you evaluate project financing as a source of finance for a company?
11. What are the different types of financial services developed in India?
12. Write notes on:
    (*a*) Global depository receipts
    (*b*) Indian depository receipts
    (*c*) Factoring
    (*d*) Commercial papers
    (*e*) Certificate of deposits
13. What is the role of the three parties involved in factoring as a means of financing?
14. What is 'venture capital'? How does valuation take place of a proposal?
15. Discuss the following international financial instruments:
    (*a*) American depository receipts
    (*b*) European depository receipts
    (*c*) Global depository receipts
    (*d*) Indian depository receipts

❑❑❑

PART III

Long-term Capital Decisions

7 Capital Budgeting

LEARNING OBJECTIVES

- 7.1 Introduction to Capital Budgeting
- 7.2 Relevance of Capital Budgeting Decisions
- 7.3 Process of Capital Budgeting
- 7.4 Problems in Capital Budgeting
- 7.5 Kinds of Capital Budgeting Decisions
- 7.6 Capital Budgeting Decisions – Assumptions
- 7.7 Principles of Capital Budgeting
- 7.8 Accounting Profit and Cash Flow Analysis
- 7.9 Pattern of Cash Flows
- 7.10 Incremental Cash Flows
- 7.11 Techniques – Traditional and Modern/Discounting Techniques
- 7.12 Techniques of Evaluation
- 7.13 Traditional Techniques
- 7.14 Discount Cash Flow Techniques

7.1 INTRODUCTION TO CAPITAL BUDGETING

Capital budgeting techniques are used in financial management for planning long-term funds. Since these funds are high in volume, they have long-term implications. They also affect the profitability of the company/firm. Capital budgeting decisions pertain to the purchase of assets like land, building, plant and machinery and development programmes of a product. Such decisions are also taken at the time of diversification or expansion of product line or introduction of new products. Research and development, and promotional expenses form part of long-term decision-making process.

Capital budgeting is a process, which is a continuous activity in an organization. Work within the firm is dynamic in nature and may require expansion, diversification or replacement of assets.

Capital budgeting can thus we defined as an important decision to invest in long-term assets with a view to get the benefit of cash inflows over many years. The long-term assets are usually those assets, which would affect a firms operation that extend beyond a one-year period. The focus of capital budgeting decisions is on acquisition, modernization, expansion and replacement of assets. These decisions have a direct impact on the value of the firm and in maximizing the wealth of the shareholders. If the investments are profitable, it will add value to the firm. If cash inflows are higher than the opportunity cost of capital, it will provide an increase to the wealth of the shareholder.

The financial manager is expected to analyse each proposal and after evaluating alternative proposal, he should select that proposal which contributes to enhancing the wealth of the shareholders over a long-term period of time.

7.2 RELEVANCE OF CAPITAL BUDGETING DECISIONS

Capital budgeting decisions are significant because of the involvement of a huge reservoir funds that have implications on the growth of a company. A decision, which brings about positive cash inflows, will help to maximize the wealth of the shareholders. If the cash inflows are negative, it means that the decision is incorrect. This will affect the firm's value and its reputation will fall. The following reasons show how capital budgeting decisions will affect the firm:

(i) **High Commitment of Funds:** In capital budgeting decisions the commitment of funds is very high. The long-term nature of commitment of funds makes the investment risky. A company expects a good return but it has to be careful of the risk associated with the return. The company can have high capital gains as well as high capital losses. The presence of large volume of funds for making investments makes capital budgeting decisions very significant.

(ii) **Long-term Decisions:** Capital budgeting decisions extend for long periods. They make an assessment of future requirement of a firm. Since the decisions influence a period of more than one year, the decisions are very complex in nature. The decisions to invest funds cover internal risks as well as external risks caused by uncontrollable factors like market risks, economic risks and political risks.

(iii) **Irreversible Decisions:** Capital budgeting decisions cannot be reversed because a huge outlay of funds is invested. It is not possible to abandon the project once the funds have been invested in it. If the company plans to scrap the assets without using them, the loss will be very high. Capital budgeting decisions should be taken only after a careful analysis of the project. The projects should be such that it will help in expanding revenues of a company or reduce its costs.

Capital budgeting decisions should follow a certain process for taking wise decisions. The process can be analysed in six different steps. These are discussed in the next section.

7.3 PROCESS OF CAPITAL BUDGETING

Capital budgeting decisions should be taken by formulating a certain procedure. This will help in analysing and evaluating the projects. The process will provide an answer to taking wise decisions to avoid potential losses and to earn good revenue.

Step 1: Identification of Investment Opportunities: A financial manager should identify investment opportunities and prepare a document by formulating the advantages and disadvantages of the investment proposal. He should try to assess the costs and benefits of the project. He may study the political, social and cultural factors that will affect the project. He must be aware of the background of the project. This is the introductory phase and he must ensure all the environmental pressures on the project.

Step 2: Coordinating Investment Proposals: The financial manager must take the views of the different departments in the company about project proposals. He should form a committee to decide whether the proposal will be useful for the company's requirements at this stage. The project should be classified to find out whether the investment will be (*i*) to purchase a new asset, (*ii*) to replace an asset, (*iii*) to expand an existing investment, and (*iv*) to find out if the investment is for providing social welfare.

Step 3: Analysis of Investment Proposals: Proposals are analysed by estimating the (*i*) capital amount or cost of the investment, (*ii*) estimation of future cash inflows, (*iii*) applying capital budgeting techniques like average rate of return, payback, such as and discounted cash flow techniques like net present values, profitability index and internal rate of return to judge the applicability of the investment to the needs of the firm.

Step 4: Preparing a Capital Budget Programme: The financial manager has to take a decision on the right project through the application of the techniques. When a decision is taken the financial manager has to prepare the methodology of conducting the programme. He has to decide on the different timing of beginning a project, continuing it and monitoring the amount spent on investment.

Step 5: Implementation of the Investment Proposal: The project has to be implemented in an efficient manner. To bring about efficiency in a project, a financial manager has to provide guidelines to the different departments emphasizing on time management, cost limits and cost control. Delays bring about losses. The project has to be controlled by installing evaluation review techniques.

Step 6: Review and Feedback of Performance: The financial manager has to continuously compare the actual performance with the projected performance. This will be useful in providing a review of the performance. If he is not satisfied with the performance, the financial manager must change the manner in which the work is being done. While implementing the project many problems and difficulties may arise. Some of these problems are discussed in the next section.

7.4 PROBLEMS IN CAPITAL BUDGETING

Capital budgeting decisions are complex in nature. These decisions are confronted with different kinds of problems. They are affected by internal and external environmental factors. The problems arise due to the following reasons:

(*i*) **Long-term Implications:** One of the major problems in capital budgeting relates to comparison of outflows and inflows of cash. The outflow of cash is immediate as the cost of the project is incurred in the beginning of the project but the inflow begins in the future. The recovery of the funds is in the future period. The problem that arises is to compare the cost and benefits of the project. The longer the time period, the greater is the problem of comparison. In order to compare cash inflows and cash outflows, the time value of money is used to make the adjustments.

(*ii*) **Risk and Uncertainty:** In the process of capital budgeting, a project is analysed, evaluated and coordinated. There is also a review and feedback of the project. There is cost control and programme evaluation technique to measure the performance of the project. However, the time period involved in the project is long and the decisions cannot undertake complete guarantee of returns due to change in demand, future competition, political changes, tax laws and legal procedures.

(*iii*) **Measurement:** The measurement of capital budgeting decisions is extremely difficult in quantitative terms. The assessment of costs and benefits are difficult as the incidences of cash flows are at different timings. Sometimes there may be an accounting profit and a cash flow. Accounting profits consider non-cash items like depreciation but cash flow do not consider such items. In such matters, measurement in quantitative terms is very difficult.

7.5 KINDS OF CAPITAL BUDGETING DECISIONS

Capital budgeting decisions have to be taken by identifying certain background features. The decisions depend on the (*i*) ***Type of firm/company*** for which decisions have to be taken and for (*ii*) ***different situations.*** These are classified as follows:

(i) Type of Firm/Company

Capital budgeting decisions depend on the nature of a firm. A firm may be a new firm or an existing firm.

New Firm: A new firm would be interested in purchasing new assets for the use of the company. When it is at the start-up stage, there would be a large requirement for the purchase of new equipment and begin new projects. The financial manager will have to analyse and evaluate the requirement of purchases for long-term use. He must use capital budgeting techniques for taking the right decision.

Existing Firm: When it is an existing company it would require capital budgeting decisions in three different situations:

(*a*) **Expansion of the Market Share:** In this case capital budgeting decisions have to be analysed to find out the future costs and benefits. The purchase of new assets should be made only when the benefits exceeds the costs. The utility of the asset should be for a long-term period of time.

(*b*) **Replacing and Modernizing Plant and Machinery:** A replacement decision is to be taken when the asset has completed its lifetime productivity and a new one is required to increase the efficiency of the plant. Sometimes the economic life of the machine is not completed but technological modernization is important to bring about reduction in cost and improvement in efficiency.

(*c*) **Diversifying into New Products:** Capital budgeting decisions have to be taken with the intention of increasing the revenue of the company. It is important to make cash flow analysis to look into the usefulness of the product. Time value of money and incremental analysis help in establishing the need for diversification and capital budgeting decisions thereof.

The kinds of capital budgeting decisions to be taken in the case of a new firm and an existing firm may be summarized as:

- Capital budgeting decision for acquisition of new assets in a new firm.
- Decision to purchase new asset in an existing firm for expansion.
- Decision to purchase new asset for replacement and modernization.
- Decision to purchase new asset for diversification to increase revenue of the firm.

(*ii*) Capital Budgeting Decisions in Different Situations

Capital budgeting decisions are classified on the basis of whether it is a new firm or an existing firm. It takes decisions from the point of view of different situations like taking a decision on a *single independent proposal, mutually exclusive project, contingent decision and capital rationing projects.*

(*a*) **Single Independent Proposal:** Each project should be evaluated on its own merit when there are single independent proposals. This means that the proposal has to be of some merit to be accepted or else it should be rejected. This is called ***accept-reject decision.*** Such projects are analysed and evaluated by taking into consideration their costs and benefits by making cash flows, using time value techniques and also applying capital budgeting techniques. These projects do not affect any other proposals. Many proposals may be evaluated without bias on their own competitive strength to find out their usefulness for the company.

(*b*) **Mutually Exclusive:** If one investment is undertaken, it follows that other similar ones will have to be rejected as they are all of the same type. The best suited should be selected. When two proposals are equally competitive and useful for the work of the company, only one of them is selected. This means that when there are two alternatives, the company should be able to select only one and reject the other. For example, one machine has to be purchased and the company evaluates two proposals of equal costs. Machine ‘A’ is manufactured in Germany and machine ‘B’ is manufactured in Korea. Having similar costs and similar features, the Indian company will have to decide which is better suited to its environment in India. If it decides on machine ‘A’, machine ‘B’ will be rejected.

(*c*) **Contingent Decisions:** Dependant or Contingent decisions mean that to fit a requirement of a company, there has to be a change in installation of other machines to fit with the new machine. If a project begins for *e.g.*, shoe project with showroom, leather treatment, uppers etc., all of it is treated like one investment. Thus the new shoe project cannot begin working unless other conditions are also fulfilled.

(*d*) **Capital Rationing Decisions:** When a firm has a very large investment and it has a limited amount of funds at its disposal, then may either take up one project at a time or it may decide to do all the projects together. But it has to extend the budget in such a manner that it is able to cover the minimum costs of all the projects that it wants to cover. In no case can it exceed its budget. Such decisions are called ‘capital rationing’. ***Capital budgeting decisions are assumed to be taken by firms, which do not have the pressure of capital rationing.*** Projects are selected and when they are completed, new projects are undertaken with enough resources to work to make the projects successful.

7.6 CAPITAL BUDGETING DECISIONS – ASSUMPTIONS

Capital budgeting decisions have implications over a long-term period of time. In order to analyse projects, which constitute capital proposal some assumptions, have to be taken. These are as follows:

(*i*) **Profit Motive:** Capital budgeting decisions assume that the motive for making a large investment is enhancing the profitability of the firm/company.

(*ii*) **Costs and Benefits:** It is assumed that while evaluating projects, the estimation of costs and benefits can be done for the complete period of the project. Capital budgeting decisions involve huge outlay of funds and cover more than one year. It may extend to period of 5 years, 10 years, 15 years or even 20 years. The assumption is that there is an accurate estimation of future costs and benefits for the entire life of the project.

(*iii*) **Availability of Capital:** One important assumption is that capital is sufficient and does not need to be rationed for other uses. Projects are selected according to need and usefulness and that the decision is made with the view that the capital can be arranged and used when the project demands it in the course of its operations.

Capital budgeting decisions can be put into action after certain important principles of decision making are considered. The three important decision-making aspects are considered. These are: (*a*) estimating costs and benefits of a proposal, (*b*) finding the required rate of return, and (*c*) selecting the technique. These principles are discussed separately in the next section.

7.7 PRINCIPLES OF CAPITAL BUDGETING

The capital budgeting decisions assume that there is a correct estimation of future costs and benefits. It also assumes that there will be profitability through the use of new additional assets. Its focus is on the wealth of the shareholder and it assumes that there is the availability of funds to cover the costs of these new projects. Such capital budgeting decisions will begin to work through some principles. The main principles are: (*i*) estimation of costs and benefits of the proposal, (*ii*) finding the cost of capital through required rate of return, and (*iii*) selection of the right technique for profitability.

(*i*) **Estimation of Costs and Benefits:** The costs of a proposal refer to the cash outflow or amount required to start a project. The benefits are associated with the change in revenues and costs. The revenues are expected to increase and costs in terms of labour and overheads are expected to decrease to bring about profitability. It is important to know the difference between accounting profit and cash flow analysis. In capital budgeting proposals in finance ***cash flow analysis is used and not the accounting profits.***

(*ii*) **Required Rate of Return:** The cost of capital is referred to as the 'required rate of return'. It is that rate of return, which is required to find out the future cost and benefits of a proposal. The rate of return is useful in adjusting the different costs to a certain time framework. It is the application of the time value techniques. It is also called ***the minimum rate of return or the discount rate or the cut off rate.*** In other words it can be called ***the opportunity cost of investment of funds*** [Cost of capital techniques are discussed in Chapter 8].

(*iii*) **Selection of Appropriate Technique:** There are different types of capital budgeting techniques. There are traditional techniques and non-traditional techniques for application in capital budgeting. These techniques are both traditional and modern. They have to be applied according to the size of a company/firm, number of transactions, number of employees, work process and requirement of the business. The techniques refer to average rate of return and payback techniques, which are traditional in nature, and discounted cash flow techniques like the net present value, profitability index and internal rate of return. The discounted techniques require a rate of return, which is necessary to adjust the time value of money. One of these techniques must be used to select the right project. These techniques will help the organization to take decisions on the selection of the project, as they are useful in evaluating a project's future costs and benefits.

(*iv*) **Incremental Cash Flows:** One of the important aspects of capital budgeting is that it is measured in incremental cash flows. These cash flows are relevant to a particular proposal, which is adopted. It means that the cash will appear only when the project will be undertaken.

(*v*) **Taxation:** Capital budgeting decisions are made after tax has been deducted. The expenses or costs are to be considered as ***incremental after tax cash flows.***

7.8 ACCOUNTING PROFIT AND CASH FLOW ANALYSIS

Costs and benefits of proposals have to be estimated. The two methods, which can be applied, are the accounting profit and the cash flow analysis methods. In capital budgeting, cash flow analysis is used. The reason for analysis through cash flow analysis and not through accounting profits is explained ahead.

Cash Flow Analysis

The cash flows refer to the outflows of expenditure and inflows of revenues in a firm with the initiation of a project. Cash flow analysis considers (*a*) time value of money, (*b*) costs and benefits are measured in actual flows of cash, (*c*) considers only cash items, and (*d*) incremental cash flows.

(*a*) **Time Value of Money:** Cash flow analysis makes an adjustment of cash flows through a required rate of return which considers all the cash flows with a common denominator. It takes into consideration all the cash flows and discounts it through present values. This makes the cash outflows at zero periods comparable with future cash inflows.

(*b*) **Measurement in Actual Cash Flows:** Cash flows provide measurement of economic value of the assets. This approach recognizes inflows of cash as revenue, which is received by the firm. It also records actual expenditures.

(*c*) **Consideration Cash Items Only:** In capital budgeting, decisions have to be taken to measure economic value and not book entries. Cash flows do not consider non-cash items like depreciation allocation of indirect costs and inventory valuation. Cash flows satisfy this condition as they consider only those entries that actually take place in the firm.

(*d*) **Incremental Cash Flows:** All cash additions and deductions pertaining to new projects are called 'incremental cash flow analysis'. If a project is accepted, it is a new investment project. It is likely to have some effect on the costs and benefits of the existing project. In capital budgeting incremental analysis is considered as relevant for calculating the costs and benefits of the projects. If a new project is started only relevant costs are added. Fixed costs remain the same whether a new project is taken up or not. Since fixed costs do not increase, they are not considered unless fixed costs increase takes place due to the introduction of a new project.

Accounting Profit

Accounting profits also measures costs and benefits of a proposal. It is a good estimate for judging profits but it does not satisfy all the requirements of capital budgeting proposals. Accounting profit is described to show the distinction between cash flows analysis and accounting profit to provide the reasons for favouring the use of cash flow analysis and not accounting profit.

(*a*) **Profit based on Accrual Method:** Accounting profit recognizes the inflow of cash immediately when there is a promise of receiving a cash flow. It also takes the effect of future expenditures. In capital budgeting, it is useful to consider the cash flow approach of receipts and payments, that have actually been incurred. Since accounting profits are based on both actual and accruals, the procedure and the approach are different.

(*b*) **Adjustment through Different Techniques:** Accounting profits can be adjusted through the techniques of different inventory valuation methods, depreciation methods and amortization of expenses. The profits become different when different methodologies are used.

(*c*) **Time Value of Money:** Accounting profit does not have any discounting rate through which the time value of money can be measured. This does not provide a good economic value to judge the efficiency of a new project. It does not measure or compare two mutually exclusive proposals or funds received at different periods of time because it does not use discounting techniques.

(*d*) **Consider Cash and Non-cash Items:** The accounting profit is a good measure for finding out the profitability of a firm. In terms of estimating the value or benefits of a proposal, it does not give a true measure as it considers non-cash items like depreciation, writing off past losses, and inventory valuation. An example may be cited between accounting and cash flow items:

Example 7.1 A firm has a revenue of Rs. 5,00,000. It has to provide for depreciation @ 10% on straight-line basis. It has cash expenses of Rs. 1,00,000. The taxes are @ 50%. Show the net earnings on the basis of accounting approach and cash flow basis.

Solution

Cash Flows *vs* Accounting Profit

Particulars	Cash Flow Approach (Rs.)	Accounting Approach (Rs.)
Revenue	5,00,000	5,00,000
Less		
Cash expenses	1,00,000	1,00,000
Depreciation		50,000
Earnings	4,00,000	3,50,000
Before tax		1,75,000
Taxes at 50%	1,75,000	1,75,000
Net Earning after		
Taxes/Cash flow	2,25,000	1,75,000

(*i*) Presence of non-cash items like depreciation in accounting profits approach.

(*ii*) Cash flow takes into account time value of money as it records transactions when they actually take place with exchange of cash payments and receipts and not verbal recording.

(*iii*) Cash flow approach shows inflows and outflows of cash of a project incremental analysis as very important.

(*iv*) Effect of taxes is considered.

(*v*) Effect on other projects is also considered through incremental changes.

It can be summarized by showing the distinctions between the cash flow analysis and accounting profit in Table 7.1.

Table 7.1 Cash Flow Analysis *vs* Accounting Profit

Cash Flow Analysis	Accounting Profit
It considers time value of money through a required discounting rate of return.	It ignores time value of money as it does not have any common required rate of return or cost of capital.
Cash flow measures economic value through actual cash inflows and outflows.	Accounting profit considers book entries value of an asset.
Cash flows consider only cash items. It does not consider items like depreciation thus creating economic value of the assets.	Accounting profit considers non-cash items like depreciation for evaluating the worth of an asset.
Cash flows have a uniform method of calculation. They follow the same methodology in valuing an asset.	Accounting profit uses different techniques of inventory valuation, depreciation, amortization of expenses.
Cash flows evaluate projects through incremental analysis. They consider the costs, which are attributable to new investment opportunities.	Accounting profit considers the profits of a firm in one complete unit and not as a separate new entity. Thus the economic value cannot be measured correctly.

Due to the above differences in cash flow analysis and accounting profit, the cash flow analysis is considered to be superior to the accounting profit method. Capital budgeting techniques therefore use the cash flow method for calculating costs and benefits of a project.

7.9 PATTERN OF CASH FLOWS

Inflows and outflows of cash are associated with investment costs and revenues. Costs are determined through cash *outflows* and benefits are incurred through cash *inflows*. The decisions are complex, long-term in nature and usually irreversible. The commitment in terms of funds is of a large amount. Decisions have to be taken for new business expansion of existing business and replacement and modernization. This improves operating efficiency and reduces costs. There are revenue expansion investments and cost reduction investments. Replacement decisions involving modernization and technological improvements expand revenue and reduce costs. Cash inflows and outflows may be classified as conventional cash flows and non-conventional cash flows.

(*i*) **Conventional Cash Flows:** The cash flows whereby initial outflow of funds is followed by cash inflows till the lifetime of the asset. For example, a firm invests Rs. 10,00,000 at time period zero and this is followed by annual revenue of Rs. 2,00,000 during the lifetime of the asset, which is 8 years (Fig. 7.1).

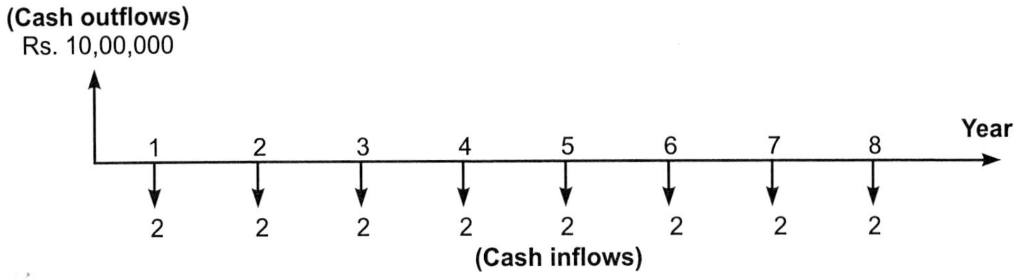

Fig. 7.1 Conventional Cash Flows (Rs. Lakh)

(*ii*) **Non-Conventional Cash Flows:** In non-conventional cash flow pattern a firm makes an outflow of funds at zero periods as well as subsequently whenever the need arises. There are both cash inflows and outflows. This kind of cash flow is most commonly observed in modern day manufacturing units. An investment is made with the expectation of future generation of cash inflows. However, repairs and technological modernization can enhance efficiency and life of an asset. There would be many outflows in different years bringing about changes in cash inflows. For example, Fig 7.2 shows non-conventional cash flows. The example is of a firm, that makes an investment of Rs. 10,00,000. It receives a return of Rs. 2,00,000 till the 3rd year. In the 4th year, it has cash outflow of Rs. 3,00,000 to modernize the machine. This enhances the life of the asset from 8 to 10 years. It also increases inflows to Rs. 3,00,000 every year. This uneven cash inflows and outflows is called 'non-conventional cash flow analysis'.

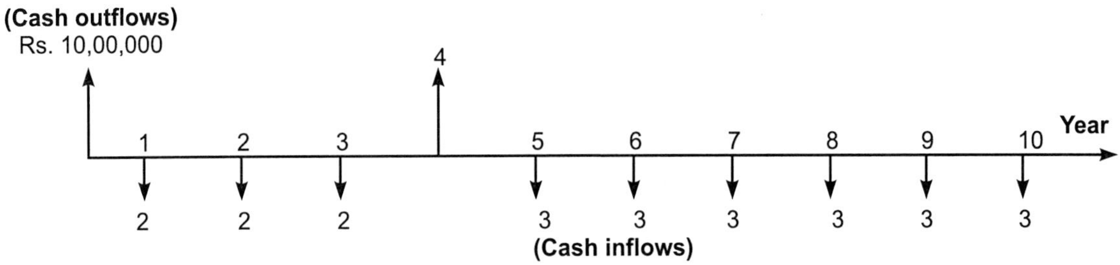

Fig. 7.2 Non-conventional Cash Flows (Rs. Lakh)

Thus cash inflows and outflows have certain patterns that follow during the lifetime of the asset. The cash flows for single project and mutually exclusive projects, which follow expansion and replacement, will be explained in detail. The discussion further explains initial cash outflows, subsequent inflows and outflows and terminal cash flows. It also shows the effect of taxation, depreciation, financial cash flows, effect of indirect expenses and working capital. This will explain the process of capital budgeting. It will show whether the project should be accepted or not accepted. The relevant cash flows are discussed in the next section.

7.10 IDENTIFICATION OF CASH FLOWS

Cash flows can be identified into (*i*) initial cash flow, and (*ii*) subsequent cash flows, and (*iii*) terminal cash flow. In order to take capital budgeting decisions a study of the different cash flows is useful. These are as follows:

(*i*) **Initial Cash Outflows:** The initial cash outflows are important because it involves a huge outflow of funds. It can be termed as the cost of purchase of assets from which the future cash inflows can be expected. The following cash flows will be required in the beginning of the project.

(*a*) **Initial Investment:** This is the investment required for beginning a new project. This investment will be large and refers to the cost of the new asset.

(*b*) **Installation Cost:** The initial cost includes the cost of bringing an asset into working condition. The transportation and installation of the asset is part of the initial cost.

(*c*) **Additional Working Capital:** A new project requires additional working capital to function and become operational. Since the working capital changes due to the requirement of the new project it will form part of initial investment. An additional investment is considered to be a new investment in purchasing assets like building, plant, machinery and furniture, and it will be added to initial cost.

Working capital will be required throughout the life of the project. In the last year of the project the working capital which is invested is expected to be released. An adjustment will have to be made in the last year. If it is not released at the end of the project, the cash flows of the project will be overestimated.

(*ii*) **Subsequent Cash Flows:** A project has an initial investment and it is expected that it will generate a series of cash inflows every year during the lifetime of the project. The cash inflows may be conventional cash flows or non-conventional cash flows. These cash flows are called ***operational or operating cash flows.*** The important rule to remember in subsequent cash flows is that they have to be adjusted according to the time value of money. All subsequent cash flows must be calculated in capital budgeting decisions. If certain amounts are spent during the lifetime of the asset, it should be considered as an outflow of funds. If revenue is generated it will be called an inflow of that year.

(*iii*) **Terminal Cash Flows:** The cash inflows of the last year are called the 'terminal cash flows'. In this year, there is revenue generating annual cash inflow. Added to this inflow, there will be a scrap value if it can be sold for some amount at the end of its economic life. The working capital that was invested in the beginning will be released, as it is no longer used in the project. The market value of land, if it is used, will also become part of terminal cash inflow.

7.11 ADDITIONAL ASPECTS OF INCREMENTAL CASH FLOW ANALYSIS

Cash flows in capital budgeting are measured according to incremental analysis. This means that only those cash flows will be considered which occur on the new project. Certain overhead costs may actually pertain to the whole business. The changes in the cash flows, which are relevant to the proposed project, must be considered. Incremental analysis considers all costs that are directly attributable to the proposed proposal. These costs occur because the new project was accepted. Thus incidental effect is a very important part of incremental analysis: (*i*) sunk costs, (*ii*) opportunity costs, (*iii*) incidental costs, and (*iv*) allocation of overhead costs are important in incremental analysis.

(*i*) **Sunk Cost:** Sunk costs are irrelevant in capital budgeting decisions. A sunk cost means that the cost of a particular asset has already incurred. It is like a fixed cost, which will not increase if a new project has started. Similarly if a machine has already been purchased and was not being used but now and its utility has been realized and the firm wants to use it, the sunk cost becomes irrelevant. However if a sum of Rs. 2,00,000 is spent for technological advancement to make the machine useful for the new project, this amount would be a relevant cost and it would be a part of initial investment. **Sunk costs are irrelevant and must be ignored**. However it must be remembered that the firm must recover sunk cost in order to remain profitable.

(*ii*) **Opportunity Cost:** The opportunity cost is an important aspect of the cost of a proposal. When some resources are being used which could be used for other purposes, the opportunity cost will arise. This cost should be included as part of the initial cost of a project. Suppose a company has one room available within the company, which it decides to transfer to the project. Since no cash is spent ideally the project should not be charged with this cost. However, since alternate investment using the room for this project loses opportunity, the project can charge a market value rental as opportunity cost for the use of this area. Opportunity costs are difficult to compute so it is calculated according to the market value if the asset can be sold in the market.

(*iii*) **Incidental Effects:** Incremental analysis considers incidental effects. Incidental effects may be complementary or it may actually create a problem in the existing project. If the starting of a new activity generates high revenue in the new proposal but because of this proposal the existing proposal incurs a loss, it becomes an incidental effect of the new project. This is called a 'negative deal' and the cost on the lost cash flows will be charged to the new project.

(*iv*) **Allocated Overheads:** Overheads will be incurred whether the new project is undertaken or not started. These allocated overheads will be ignored in net cash flow of the investment. However if overheads increase because the new project has been undertaken, overheads will be charged which are relevant to the new project. Sometimes certain overheads like rent, employees' welfare, supervision may not bring about any change in the new project immediately but it may increase as a cumulative effect. This kind of increase is difficult to calculate. The organization has to identify overheads on the new project through some rational basis. In other words, it can be said that ***incremental overhead cost*** will be considered as a cost and will be cash outflow.

(*v*) **Product Cannibalization:** When a new product reduces the productivity and sales of the old product it is called ***Product Cannibalization.*** An example may be given of product 'A' and 'B'. If B is a new product introduced by a company XYZ. The sales of B do well beyond the expectation of other companies, it reduces the sale of product 'A'. The incremental effect is said to be negative and the lost cash flows from product 'A' would be a cost and the decision would have to be taken to include the cost of lost sales. If a cash inflow or outflow can be directly attributed to product 'B', only then the cost can be charged to product B. Any cash inflow or outflow, which is as a result of product 'B' should be considered.

(*vi*) **Cash Flows Depending on Coexistence of Proposal:** If there are two projects and one of them requires an annual maintenance while the other project requires technological improvement, then that project on which there has been a cash outflow will be charged to it. For example, project 'A' requires annual maintenance and 'B' requires technological improvement. If XYZ Company decides to go in for technological improvement, the expenses will be charged to project 'B'.

Incremental costs may be summarized with the following guidelines:

(*a*) All incidental effects should be considered.

(*b*) The sunk costs must be ignored.

(*c*) The opportunity costs should be charged to the project.

(*d*) Allocated overhead costs like administrative expenses, managerial salary, legal expenses, rent paid has to be allocated according to the project use. Only those costs will be charged which have increased as part of the new activities.

(*e*) Incremental costs are also called ***relevant costs.***

Depreciation and Cash Flows in Capital Budgeting: Depreciation being a non-cash item is not a concept of financial management, as it does not directly affect the firm in terms of a cash resource. Depreciation has the effect of reducing the profits of a company. ***It is deductible in determining the taxable income.*** Depreciation has the effect of reducing the taxable income and also the tax liability. Depreciation in capital budgeting is deducted to calculate the profit and it is added back to the profit after tax to calculate cash inflows. Depreciation has an accounting treatment and an income tax treatment.

Accounting Treatment: Every asset will be depreciated. In accounting terminology depreciation can be deducted according to different methods. The usual methods are the straight-line method and the written down value method. Every year an annual charge is made on an asset and when the life of the asset is completed it is usually scrapped. It is called the 'written down value of the asset'. If it can be sold then it is called the 'salvage value'. The difference between the written down values will be a capital gain or a loss. If the written down value is less than the salvage value, it will be a capital gain but when written down value is more than the salvage value it is called a 'capital loss'. This value is adjusted in the year in which the asset is discarded. The procedure of calculation is as follows:

Example 7.2 A firm purchases a machine for Rs. 10,00,000. It has an operating profit of Rs. 3,00,000 for 4 years and depreciation is at 20% of written down value and tax @ 40%. After 4 years the asset will be sold at Rs. 1,50,000. Find out the cash flows for different years.

Solution

Initial outflow = Rs. 10,00,000

Subsequent Annual Cash Inflows

Year (1)	Written down value (2)	Depreciation (3)	PBD (4)	PBT (5 = 4 – 3)	Tax @ 40%(6)	PAT (7 = 5 – 6)	CF (8 = 7 + 3)
1.	10,00,000	2,00,000	3,00,000	1,00,000	40,000	60,000	2,60,000
2.	8,00,000	1,60,000	3,00,000	1,40,000	56,000	84,000	2,44,000
3.	6,40,000	1,28,000	3,00,000	1,72,000	68,800	1,03,200	2,31,000
4.	5,12,000	1,02,400	3,00,000	1,97,600	79,040	1,18,560	2,20,960

Terminal cash flows	
Scrap value of the asset	Rs. 1,50,000
Profit on sale	Rs. 1,50,000
Written down value Rs. 5,12,000 – Rs. 1,02,400	= 4,09,600
Loss	Rs. 2,59,600

There is no tax liability, as the scrapped asset is sold at a price lower than its written down value.

Treatment under Income Tax Act: Depreciation is calculated in the Income Tax Act 1961 in a manner which is different to the accounting calculation the income tax act provides the concept of block of assets. Block of assets consists of a group of assets in which the rate of depreciation will be the same. For example, assets like building machinery or furniture under the same block will have the same rate of taxation. A block of assets can comprise either one asset or a number of assets.

Block of One Asset: If there is only one asset in the block the following two guidelines will apply:

(*i*) In the terminal year no depreciation will be allowed when the asset is scrapped or sold.

(*ii*) The scrap value will be compared with the written down value. If the written down value is greater than the scrap value, it will be a loss. If the written down value is less than the scrap value, it will be a gain. The gain or loss is treated as short-term capital gain/loss. It will be treated as an ordinary income or loss.

Block of Many Assets: When there is more than one asset in a block, the following guidelines will apply:

(*i*) Find out the value of the block on the first day of the financial year. If a new asset is added to this block, the cost of the new asset is added to the written down value of this block and depreciation is charged on the total value of the asset for the year.

(*ii*) When an asset is sold from the block, the sale value is to be subtracted from the written down value. The depreciation will be charged to the net value of the block, for example, if the written down block is Rs. 20,00,000 and assets of Rs. 10,00,000 are added to the block, depreciation will be provided on the block of Rs. 30,00,000. But if an asset is sold for Rs. 5,00,000, depreciation will be charged only on Rs. 25,00,000 available in the block.

(*iii*) The capital flows will not indicate any capital gain or loss unless the full block of asset is scrapped. In this case, the written down value minus the scrap value will be treated as short-term capital gain/loss. For example in Example 7.2, if the block is of one asset only then the depreciation would be Rs. 2,00,000; Rs. 1,60,000; Rs. 1,28,000 and Rs. 1,02,400 for years 1 to 4 respectively. The written down value in the beginning of year 4 would be Rs. 5,12,000 and short-term capital loss will be Rs. 5,12,000–1,50,000 or Rs. 3,62,000.

(*iv*) If the entire block of assets have been sold out, there would be either short-term capital loss or short-term capital gain. If the resultant value is positive, depreciation will be charged on the prescribed rate.

Example 7.3 Another example may be cited. Suppose a firm has the following assets in the year 2005–06.

Asset	Rate of Depreciation %	Written Down Value of Assets on 01.04.2008 (Rs.)
P	20	1,50,000
Q	15	2,50,000
R	20	1,20,000
S	20	1,35,000
T	30	1,80,000

Further information: (*i*) Asset Z is purchased for Rs. 1,20,000 at the depreciation rate of 20% in the year 2008–2009 and asset P is sold for Rs. 1,75,000.

(*ii*) The firm purchased an asset X at 15% depreciation rate at the cost of Rs. 1,20,000 and asset Y of 10% depreciation at Rs. 1,80,000.

(*iii*) Asset T is sold for Rs. 2,00,000 or for Rs. 1,50,000. Calculate depreciation (for both the cases).

Solution

Depreciation According to Income Tax Method

Step 1: Let us first calculate depreciation for the block of 20% rate of depreciation

Particulars	Amount (Rs.)
Value of block as on 01.04.2008	4,05,000
Add cost of new assets purchased during the year (asset Z)	1,20,000
Less sale of asset	1,75,000
Value of the block on 31.03.2009	3,50,000
Depreciation for the year 2008–2009 at 20%	70,000
Value of the block as on 01.04.2009	2,80,000
Depreciation for this block is Rs. 70,000	

Step 2: Calculation showing depreciation for the block of 15%

Particulars	Amount (Rs.)
Value of block as on 01.04.2008	2,50,000
Add cost of new assets purchased during the year (asset X)	1,20,000
Less sale of asset	Nil
Value of the block on 31.03.2009	3,70,000
Depreciation for the year 2008–2009 at 15%	55,500
Value of the block as on 01.04.2009	3,14,500
Depreciation for this block is Rs. 55,500	

Step 3: Calculation showing depreciation at 10%

Particulars	Amount (Rs.)
Value of block as on 01.04.2009	Nil
Add cost of new assets purchased during the year (asset Y)	1,80,000
Less sale of asset	Nil
Value of the block on 31.03.2009	1,80,000
Depreciation for the year 2008–2009 at 10%	18,000
Value of the block as on 01.04.2009	1,62,000
Depreciation for this block is Rs. 18,000	

Step 4: Calculation showing depreciation at 30%

Particulars	Asset Sold (Rs.)	Asset Sold (Rs.)
Value of block as on 01.04.2008	1,80,000	1,80,000
Add cost of new assets purchased during the year (asset)	Nil	Nil
Less sale of asset	2,00,000	1,50,000
Value of the block on 31.03.2009	20,000 (short-term capital gain)	30,000(short-term capital loss)
Depreciation for the year 2008–2009	Depreciation will not be levied as the block of asset ceases to exist on the last day of the financial year.	Depreciation will not be levied as the block of asset ceases to exist on the last day of the financial year.

The above examples show that there is a difference in computation of depreciation according to the accounting method and income tax method.

> *Note:* While calculating capital budgeting proposals depreciation should be correctly calculated. In practice, depreciation has to be calculated according to Income Tax Act. For a theoretical understanding of the subject, accounting treatment is considered to show the effect of tax deductions of depreciation on cash flows.

Interest Exclusion Principle: The incremental cash flow analysis states that interest on debt should not be considered. If interest on debt is deducted in the process of cash flow analysis, the cost of debt will be counted twice and this will be an error. Therefore interest exclusion principle means that ***interest on long-term debt is ignored while computing profits and taxes. Dividends are also ignored for cash flow analysis.***

Interest and dividend will be ignored because they are not treated as relevant cash flows. In capital budgeting, only operating cash flow should be considered. The reason for excluding interest and dividend from cash flow analysis is that it will be calculated separately in the weighted average cost of capital. Investment decisions and financing decisions should be considered separately.

Effect of Working Capital: Working capital is the difference between the current asset and current liabilities. When a new project is started the requirement of cash, inventory and the liabilities of creditors may arise. The increase in current assets will not exactly match the current liabilities. The increase in working capital is added as an initial cost. The effect of increase in working capital has a positive effect on the future cash inflows. Working capital has to be adjusted in the beginning as a cash outflow. Another adjustment has to be made only at the end of the project. Although as cash inflows keep on coming in after an initial investment, working capital will be released, but for the sake of simplicity it is released only at the end of the project. Therefore ***adjustment in working capital will be at the beginning of the period and at the end of the period, but not in subsequent cash flow.***

Determination of Relevant Cash Flows: Cash flows can be summed up into relevant and irrelevant cash flows. These are shown in Table 7.2.

Table 7.2 Relevant and Irrelevant Cash Flows

Relevant	Irrelevant
Costs of new projects	Sunk costs
Installation cost	Allocated overheads
Working capital requirements	Interest
Scrapped value of old asset	Dividend
Amount on cost saving	
Tax benefits of depreciation	
Revenue from new proposal	

The incremental cash flows can be summarized in Table 7.3.

Table 7.3 Cash Flow Analysis

Initial Cash Outflow	Subsequent/Operational Cash Inflows	Terminal Cash Flows
Costs of new plant	Annual cash inflows	Annual cash inflow
Installation cost	Profit after tax	Add working capital released
Additional working capital	Add depreciation	Add scrap value
Less tax benefits on capital loss (Sale of old asset)	Deduct repairs	
Scrap/Salvage value of old asset	Deduct capital expenditure	
Add tax liability, capital gain (sale of old asset)		

To illustrate cash flows of a single project:

Cash Flows at 0 Period when Purchasing An Asset

> Cost of New Project + Installation Cost + WC requirements
> – Tax benefit due to investment allowance for eligible assets.

Determination of Subsequent Cash Inflows of Single Project

Sales – Cash operating costs = Cash inflows before taxes (CFBT) – Depreciation = Taxable income – Tax = Earning after taxes + Depreciation = Cash flow after taxes (CFAT) + Salvage value in n^{th} year + Recovery of working capital in n^{th} year

Nominal cash flows at nominal rate

Real cash flows at real rate

Cash flows of single projects and replacement projects are depicted in the following example:

Example 7.4 Shows cash flows of a new project.

New Project: A company is considering a new proposal. The following information is provided.

(*i*) The project will require the purchase of a machine at Rs. 60,00,000 and the working capital required for this project is Rs. 20,00,000. Installation charges are Rs. 50,000.

(*ii*) Life of the project is 5 years and the scrap value of the asset is Rs. 5,00,000. Book value of the asset is Rs. 5,50,000.

(*iii*) The project will bring about an inflow of cash of Rs. 80,00,000 per year and the cash expenses on the project will be Rs. 20,00,000.

(*iv*) The tax rate is 40% and depreciation will be at 30% p.a. through written down method.

(*v*) Calculate cash outflows and inflows.

Solution

Step 1:

Initial cash flows	Amount (Rs.)
Purchase price	Rs. 60,00,000
+ Installation cost	Rs. 50,000
+ Working capital increase/required	Rs. 20,00,000
	Rs. 80,50,000

Step 2: Subsequent/Operational Cash Flows (annual) (amount in Rs.)

New Machine	Year 1	Year 2	Year 3	Year 4	Year 5
Annual revenue	80,00,000	80,00,000	80,00,000	80,00,000	80,00,000
Cash expenses	20,00,000	20,00,000	20,00,000	20,00,000	20,00,000
Profit before depreciation	60,00,000	60,00,000	60,00,000	60,00,000	60,00,000
– Depreciation 30%	18,15,000	12,70,500	8,89,350	6,22,545	435781.5
Profit before tax	41,85,000	47,29,500	51,10,650	53,77,455	5564218.5
– Tax @ 40%	16,74,000	29,08,200	27,55,740	26,49,018	2574312.6
Profit after tax	25,11,000	43,62,300	41,33610	39,73,527	3861468.9
Depreciation added back	18,15,000	12,70,500	8,89,350	6,22,545	435781.5
Annual cash flow	43,26,000	56,32,800	50,22,960	45,96,072	4297250.4

Step 3:

Particulars	Amount (Rs.)
Terminal cash flows	
Scrap value	5,00,000
– Book value	5,50,000
Short-term capital loss on sale	50,000
Net cash inflow	45,96,072
+ Working capital released	20,00,000
	65,96,072
+ Scrap value	5,00,000
Incremental cash inflow	70,96,072

Note: (*i*) Depreciation has been calculated at 30% of the written down value.

In Year 1, Rs. 60,00,000 + 50,000 installation charges = 60,50,000 × 30% = 18,15,000

Year 2 = 60,50,000 – 18,15,000 = 42,35,000 × 30% = 12,70,500

Year 3 = 42,35,000 – 12,70,500 = 29,64,500 × 30% = 8,89,350

Year 4 = 29,64,500 – 8,89,350 = 20,75,150 × 30% = 6,22,545

Year 5 = 2075150 – 622545 = 14,52,605 × 30% = 435781.25

Replacement Project: The next illustration will show the calculation of cash flows in a replacement situation.

Example 7.5 A company proposes to replace a machine, which has completed its life. The purchase price of the new machine is expected to be Rs. 16,00,000. The new machine has a life of 5 years and it will bring an annual return of Rs. 12,00,000 as its revenue. It has cash expenses every year of Rs. 2,00,000. The salvage value of the new machine is expected to be nil. The existing machine has a scrap value of Rs. 2,00,000. It has a life of 5 years in which it can generate annual cash flows of Rs. 10,00,000 with cash expenses of Rs. 2,40,000 every year. The company pays a tax @ 50% and can write off depreciation @ 25% on written down value of new machine. Old machine is depreciated at Rs. 1,25,000 every year. Compute incremental cash flows of the replacement decision.

Solution

Step 1:

Initial cash flows	Amount (Rs.)
Cost of the new machine	16,00,000
Less cash from sale of existing machine	2,00,000
Net cash outlay	14,00,000

Step 2: Subsequent/Operational Cash Flows (annual) (amount in Rs.)

New Machine	Year 1	Year 2	Year 3	Year 4	Year 5
Annual revenue	12,00,000	12,00,000	12,00,000	12,00,000	12,00,000
Cash expenses	2,00,000	2,00,000	2,00,000	2,00,000	2,00,000
Profit before depreciation	10,00,000	10,00,000	10,00,000	10,00,000	10,00,000
– Depreciation	2,50,000	1,87,500	1,40,625	105468.75	79101.56
Profit before tax	7,50,000	8,12,500	8,59,375	894531.25	920898.44
– Tax @ 50%	3,75,000	4,06,250	429687.50	447265.63	460449.22
Profit after tax	3,75,000	4,06,250	429687.50	447265.63	460449.22
Depreciation added back	2,50,000	1,87,500	1,40,625	105468.75	79101.56
Annual cash flow	6,25,000	5,93,750	570312.50	552734.38	539550.78
– Cash flow of old asset	4,42,500	4,42,500	4,42,500	4,42,500	4,42,500
Incremental cash flows	1,82,500	1,51,250	127812.50	110,234.38	97050.78

Step 3: Annual cash flows of old machine

Particulars	Amount (Rs.)
Annual Cash Flows	10,00,000
– Cash expenses	2,40,000
	7,60,000
– Depreciation	1,25,000
PBT	6,35,000
– Tax @ 50%	3,17,500
Profit after tax	3,17,500
Add back depreciation	1,25,000
Net cash inflows	4,42,500

Note: The net cash inflow of Rs. 4,42,500 from old machine will be deducted from cash inflow of new machine to get incremental cash inflows.

Cash flows can be summarized in the following manner:

(*i*) Relevant cash flows are to be considered for cash flow analysis.

(*ii*) Cash flows should be considered on incremental basis.

(*iii*) Cash flows ignore sunk cost, interest and dividends.

(*iv*) Additional working capital is an outflow in the initial investment and an inflow in the year when the asset has completed its life.

(*v*) If taxes are saved it brings cash inflows.

(*vi*) Opportunity cost must be considered.

(*vii*) Cash flows should be considered only after tax.

(*viii*) Outflows are assumed to occur in the beginning of the period.

(*ix*) Inflows occur only at the end of the period.

To conclude cash flows help in estimating costs and benefits of a proposal. Further, it is important to evaluate different proposals through techniques of evaluation. These techniques are classified into traditional non-discounting techniques and modern discounting techniques. These techniques are now being explained in detail.

7.12 TECHNIQUES OF EVALUATION

Evaluation of different proposals has to be done in order to take a decision about the economic worth of an investment. The essential requirement of a technique for evaluation is that it should maximize the shareholders wealth. The following are some of the important considerations for a good evaluation technique:

(*i*) The technique should be able to determine the true profitability of an investment proposal. All cash flows of the proposal should be considered.

(*ii*) The technique should aim at ranking of the projects to assist in identifying the most profitable project.

(*iii*) The technique should help to choose projects, which are mutually exclusive.

(*iv*) It should be able to recognize early cash flows from the later ones as cash flows at an earlier date are preferable.

(*v*) The technique should be able to incorporate time value of money, as cash flows will be received in different periods of time.

(*vi*) It should be an objective method for identifying the right project, which will focus on maximization of shareholders wealth.

The techniques of capital budgeting may be classified into traditional techniques and modern/discounted cash flow techniques:

(*i*) Traditional Techniques

(*a*) Average Rate of Return (ARR)

(*b*) Payback Method (PB)

(*ii*) Discounted Cash flow Techniques

(*a*) Net Present Value Method (NPV)

(*b*) Internal Rate of Return (IRR)

(*c*) Profitability Index (PI)

7.13 TRADITIONAL TECHNIQUES

The traditional techniques of *average rate of return* (*ARR*) and *payback* (*PB*) methods are simple and non-discounted techniques of evaluation. Though these are traditional, they are simple techniques and contribute to the evaluation of proposals. The following discussion provides a detailed analysis of these techniques.

(*i*) Average Rate of Return (ARR)

The average rate of return method is also called 'accounting rate of return'. It is a return on investment by using accounting information to measure profitability of a proposal. Its information can be identified from the financial statement of a firm. It is a very simple method of evaluation and it can be found out by the following formula:

$$\text{ARR} = \frac{\text{Average Profits (After Tax)}}{\text{Average Investment}} \times 100$$

The decision rule to be applied while accepting or rejecting a proposal is:

Accept project when ARR > minimum rate

Reject project when ARR< minimum rate

The method to find out average investment:

Average Investment = + ½ (Initial Cost of Machine – Salvage Value) + Additional Working Capital + Salvage Value

In order to find out the **average investment** while computing the ARR method, the original cost of an investment plus the installation cost will be considered. The salvage value will be deducted and it is divided by the number of the years of the economic life of the machine.

The **accept/reject** decision will be taken when the predetermined cut off rate has been calculated. If the ARR is higher than the minimum acceptable rate, only then can the project be accepted. For example, if the minimum cut of rate is 22% and the ARR is 20% the proposal will be rejected. However, if ARR is 24%, it is greater than the minimum cut off rate at 22% and the proposal is likely to be accepted.

Working Capital: When working capital is required it will be added to find out the average investment.

Depreciation: This method to find out the ARR is called the 'short cut method'. It can be used when depreciation is calculated on straight-line method (SLM).

Salvage Value: The salvage value is first deducted and later added back. The salvage value is added to find out annual depreciation. Since this value is released at the end of its economic life. It is added back to find out the average investment.

Average Investment: Average investment can be calculated by another method also. For example it can be calculated through the book value method. A company buys a small machine of Rs. 1,80,000. It has an expected life of 5 years and the salvage value is Rs. 30,000. The average investment of the proposal can be calculated by two methods:

Method 1

Year	Opening Book Value (Rs.)	Closing Book Value (Rs.)	Average Book Value (Rs.)
1	1,80,000	1,50,000	1,65,000
2	1,50,000	1,20,000	1,35,000
3	1,20,000	90,000	1,05,000
4	90,000	60,000	75,000
5	60,000	30,000	45,000
		Total	**5,25,000**

Average investment = Rs. 5,25,000/5 = Rs. 1,05,000

Method 2

Average investment = ½ (1,80,000 – 30,000) + 30,000 = Rs. 1,05,000

Let us take an example showing calculation of ARR method.

Example 7.6

Purchase Price of a Small Office Printer	Rs. 22,000
Salvage Value	Rs. 2,000
Working Capital	Rs. 4,000
Service Life	5 Years

Straight Line Method of Depreciation is adopted. If average income is Rs. 32,000 and Company's Cut-off rate is 80% state whether project is acceptable.

Solution

Average Investment = Networking Capital + Salvage Value + ½ (Initial cost of Machine – Salvage Value)

Average Investment = 4,000 + 2000 + ½ (22,000 – 2,000) = 6,000 + 10,000 = 16,000

$$\therefore \quad ARR = \frac{\text{Average Annual Income}}{\text{Average Investment}} = \frac{32,000}{16,000} \times 100 = 200\%$$

Accept/Reject Decision: Since the cut off rate of the company is 80% a project would be accepted when its average rate of return is greater than 80%, otherwise it would be rejected. In this case the ARR is 200%. The machine should be accepted.

Example 7.7 Another example may be taken to take a decision on the purchase of machine A and machine B details of which are as follows:

Determine ARR from the data for two machines A and B.

Particulars	Machine A (Rs.)	Machine B (Rs.)
Cost	1,00,000	1,00,000
Income after depreciation + taxes		
Year 1	7,000	15,000
Year 2	9,000	13,000
Year 3	11,000	11,000
Year 4	13,000	9,000
Year 5	15,000	7,000
	55,000	55,000
Estimated life	5 Years	5 Years
Salvage value	5,000	5,000
Income tax rate	50%	50%

The firm will accept the proposal if the minimum cut off rate is 18%.

Solution

Machine (A)

Method 1:

$$\text{ARR} = \frac{\text{Average Income}}{\text{Average Investment}} \times 100$$

$$\text{Average Income} = \frac{55{,}000}{5} = 11{,}000$$

$$\begin{aligned}\text{Average Investment} &= \text{NWC} + \text{Salvage Value} + \tfrac{1}{2}(\text{Initial Cost} - \text{Salvage Value})\\ &= 5{,}000 + \tfrac{1}{2}(1{,}00{,}000 - 5{,}000)\\ &= 5{,}000 + \tfrac{1}{2}(95{,}000)\\ &= 5{,}000 + 47{,}500\\ &= 52{,}500\end{aligned}$$

$$\therefore \text{ARR} = \frac{11{,}000 \times 100}{52{,}500} = 20.9\%$$

ARR method has more than one formula. Instead of $\frac{\text{Average Annual Profits}}{\text{Average Investments}} \times 100$

Method 2:

Alternatively ARR can be found out by original cost

The formula for original cost method is $\frac{\text{Average Annual Profits}}{\text{Original Cost}} \times 100$

$$\therefore \text{By original cost method, ARR} = \frac{11{,}000}{1{,}00{,}000} \times 100 = 11\%$$

Machine (B)

Method 1:

$$\text{ARR} = \frac{\text{Average Income}}{\text{Average Investment}} \times 100$$

$$\text{Average Income} = \frac{55{,}000}{5} = 11{,}000$$

Average Investment = NWC + Salvage Value + ½ (Initial Cost – Salvage Value)

$$= 5{,}000 + \tfrac{1}{2}(1{,}00{,}000 - 5{,}000)$$

$$= 5{,}000 + \tfrac{1}{2}(95{,}000)$$

$$= 5{,}000 + 47{,}500$$

$$= 52{,}500$$

$$\therefore \text{ ARR} = \frac{11{,}000}{52{,}000} \times 100 = 20.9\%$$

ARR method has more than one formula. Instead of $\frac{\text{Average Annual Profits}}{\text{Original Cost}} \times 100$, we can use

$$\frac{\text{Average Annual Profits}}{\text{Average Investments}} \times 100$$

Alternatively ARR can be found out by original cost

The formula for original cost method is $\frac{\text{Average Annual Profits}}{\text{Original Cost}} \times 100$

Method 2:

$$\therefore \text{ By original cost method, AAR} = \frac{11{,}000}{22{,}000} \times 100 = 50\%$$

Accept/Reject Decision: If the minimum cut off rate acceptable by the firm is 18%, then by the average investment method, the proposal should be accepted because ARR is 20.9%. However by the original cost method, it is only 11% and this is not acceptable as it falls below the minimum cut off rate of the firm.

In this problem the two machines have the same cost. The results are exactly the same because the ARR method does not consider time value of money. Machine A has a progressively increasing cash flow and machine B has a decreasing cash flow, but ARR method puts both the machines in the same slot.

Another example of ARR method is given in Example 7.8.

Example 7.8 A computer machine will cost Rs. 40,000. Its earnings before depreciation, interest and taxes (EBIT) during its 5 year lifetime is expected to be 10,000; 12,000; 14,000; 16,000 and 20,000. Assume a 50% tax rate and depreciation in SLM Method. The minimum cut-off rate acceptable is 15%.

Solution

Items	Average Rate of Return (ARR) (Amount in Rs.)					
	year 1	year 2	year 3	year 4	year 5	Average
EBIT + Depreciation	10,000	12,000	14,000	16,000	20,000	14,400
Depreciation	8,000	8,000	8,000	8,000	8,000	8,000
EBIT	2,000	4,000	6,000	8,000	12,000	6,400
Taxes at 50%	1,000	2,000	3,000	4,000	6,000	3,200
Earnings before PAT	1,000	2,000	3,000	4,000	6,000	3,200

Average Investment = NWC + Salvage Value + ½ (Initial Cost – Salvage Value)

Average Investment = ½ Initial Cost = Rs. 20,000

$$\text{ARR} = \frac{3,200 \times 100}{20,000} = 16\%$$

Alternatively ARR can be found out by original cost

The formula for original cost method is $\frac{\text{Average Annual Profits}}{\text{Original Cost}} \times 100$

ARR by alternate method will be $\text{ARR} = \frac{3,200 \times 100}{40,000} = 8\%$

Accept/Reject Decision: In this example, the firm can accept the proposal by average investment method but not by original cost method.

Evaluation of ARR Method: The ARR method is very simple and can be easily applied to any organization. It helps to provide the economic utility of an investment in terms of a percentage return. If ARR is higher than the minimum cut-off rate acceptable by a company, the proposal can be accepted. The ARR method considers all the cash flows throughout the economic life of the project. It has many limitations, it does not take time value of money, and it also does not project cash flows because it is based on the accounting rate of return. The merits and demerits of ARR techniques can be summarized in the following way:

Merits of ARR method are:

(*a*) ARR method is simple to calculate and it is easily understandable. This makes the use of this method very practical.

(*b*) It is based on accounting information and most people in business are familiar with the information provided in financial statements. The information can be obtained easily.

(*c*) It considers all the benefits received during the life of the project.

Limitations of ARR method are:

(*a*) It does not provide time value of money.

(*b*) It can be calculated through different methods. The results are very different through different methods. The identification of the right method to compare with the cut-off rate is difficult to apply.

(*c*) Its main limitation is that it is based on accounting principle and not cash flow analysis.

(*d*) It does not consider benefits of earlier years and later years. The two cash flows are different because earlier returns are considered to be better and cannot be valued at par.

Though ARR method has some merits, it cannot be called an 'efficient evaluation technique'.

(*ii*) Payback Method of Evaluation

The payback method indicates the length of time, which is required to recover the initial costs of the project. It can be defined as the time required for its cash inflows to be equal to its cash outflows. The payback period can be calculated in two situations.

(*a*) When the cash flows are in the form of an annuity. This is in a situation when equal cash inflows are generated every year. The formula will be:

$$\text{Payback Period} = \frac{\text{Initial Investment}}{\text{Annual Cash Inflow}}$$

(*b*) When the annual cash flows are a mixed stream. The formula will be payback period = n^{th} year + original cumulative cash flows after tax for n^{th} year/CFAT for the (n + 1 year).

Accept/Reject Decision:

Accept PB < Standard Payback

Reject PB > Standard Payback

An example is given to explain situation 1.

Example 7.9 If a machine has an initial investment of Rs. 50,00,000 and it generates an annual cash inflow of Rs. 10,00,000 for 5 years, what will be the payback period? What would be the cut-off rate of the company?

Solution

$$\text{Payback Period} = \frac{\text{Initial Investment}}{\text{Annual Cash Inflow}}$$

$$= \frac{50,00,000}{10,00,000} = 5 \text{ years}$$

$$\text{Percentage of Initial Investment} = \frac{\text{Annual Return}}{\text{Investment}} \times 100$$

$$= \frac{10,00,000}{50,00,000} \times 100$$

$$= 20\% \text{ rate of return}$$

Company's cut off rate is 20%.

Example 7.10 A machine costs Rs. 10,00,000; how long will it take to recover it?

The following uneven cash inflows have been received. Find out the payback period.

Year	Cash Inflows after Taxes (Rs.)
1	5,00,000
2	7,00,000
3	4,00,000
4	4,00,000
5	4,00,000

Solution

Year	Cash Inflows (Rs.)	Cumulative Cash Inflows (Rs.)
1	5,00,000	5,00,000
2	7,00,000	12,00,000
3	4,00,000	16,00,000
4	4,00,000	20,00,000
5	4,00,000	24,00,000

> ***Note:*** In the above table the payback period shows that it is able to recover its investment between the first and second year. If first year is taken as n^{th} year, the value of the payback period will be payback period = n^{th} year + original cumulative cash flows after tax for n^{th} year/CFAT for the (n + 1 year).

Cost has been recovered between 1st + 2nd year

Payback period = 1 + (10,00,000 – 5,00,000)/7,00,000 = 1+ 0.71 = 1.71 years

Note that the payback period is between 1st year and 2nd year. The difference between the two is Rs. 7,00,000. The investment is Rs. 10,00,000. The cash inflow in the first year is Rs. 5,00,000. Therefore the initial investment minus the 1st year divided by cash inflows of 2nd year minus first year provides the period between 1st and 2nd year. The amount is recovered after the 1st year but before the 2nd year.

Evaluation of Payback Method: The payback method is simple and easy to apply in business situations. It is better than the ARR approach because it is based on cash flow analysis. It has several merits but still cannot be called the best method of evaluation. As a ranking method, the shortest payback period is given the highest ranking. This means that when two mutually exclusive projects are appraised the project with the shorter payback would be selected. However one of its serious limitations is that it does not consider the cash inflows, which are earned after the payback period. Example 7.10 depicted that the payback period was 1 year and 7 months after which the cash flows are not considered at all. Take another example of two machines that have to be ranked according to payback method.

Example 7.11 Show that two mutually exclusive machines of Rs. 10,00,000 each will be generating the following cash flows in the 6-year life of the machine. Machine A will give cash inflows (after tax) in 1st year Rs. 4,00,000; 2nd year Rs. 6,00,000; 3rd year Rs. 3,00,000 and in 4th, 5th and 6th year, cash inflows are nil. Machine B generates 1st year Rs. 5,00,000; 2nd year Rs. 5,00,000; 3rd year Rs. 4,00,000; and 4th year Rs. 4,00,000; for 5th and 6th year Rs. 3,00,000 each.

Solution

Particulars	Machine A (Rs.)	Machine B (Rs.)
Costs of the machine (0 period)	10,00,000	10,00,000
Year 1 (inflows)	4,00,000	5,00,000
Year 2	6,00,000	5,00,000
Year 3	3,00,000	4,00,000
Year 4	Nil	4,00,000
Year 5	Nil	3,00,000
Year 6	Nil	3,00,000
Payback period	2 years	2 years

This example shows that two proposals machine A and machine B have the same investment of Rs. 10,00,000. Both have exactly the same payback period of two years. According to the payback method both the proposals would be given equal ranking, but this is not a correct measure of choice because it does not consider the total benefits which accrue from the proposal. It also does not consider projects in terms of timing or magnitude of cash flows. The payback method only considers the recovery period. It ignores time value of money. It also does not indicate the cash inflows generated by machine B in 4th, 5th and 6th years. Even though machine 'A' had a nil return both A and B are taken in the same bracket.

Evaluation of Packback Period

Merits of payback period are:

(*a*) It is easy to understand and even inexperienced people can use the method to find out when their investment will be recovered.

(*b*) It uses cash flow information, which is part of the principles of financial management.

(*c*) It is a good indicator of liquidity. If an entrepreneur wants to have greater liquidity he can choose the proposal, which will provide early cash inflows.

(*d*) It is also useful in evaluating projects from the point of view of risk. The shorter recovery of the investment would mean that the project is less risky.

(*e*) The payback method is useful for a small firm, which has limited manpower because of its simplicity in application to business situations.

Limitations of the payback method are:

(*a*) It ignores time value of money, which is an important principle of financial management.

(*b*) It ignores cash flow after payback period and so it is not a good measure of profitability. It gives misleading results.

(*c*) It ignores the magnitude and timing of cash flows.

(*d*) It is only useful as a measure of capital recovery and not as a measure of profitability. It covers only large conventional projects but not those projects, which do not have any initial investment and are spread over a long period of time.

(*e*) It does not give any importance to salvage value. It does not consider the full economic life of a proposal.

A solution to improve the payback method is by determining the payback period of discounted cash flows.

Discounted Payback Period: The number of periods taken to recover the investment on the present value basis will provide the discounted payback period. The present value of cash inflows are compared to the present values of the outflows to find out the recovery period. However even after calculating the discounted payback period, the method still has a flaw because it does not consider cash flows, which occur after the payback period.

The above discussion made an evaluation of traditional or non-discounted methods of evaluation of proposals. The following discussion is on discounted cash flow techniques, which adhere to the principles of time value of money. Table 7.4 gives the formulae and accept/reject decision at a glance of the different techniques of evaluation.

Table 7.4 Techniques of Capital Budgeting

Non-discounted Cash Flow Techniques	
1. Accounting/Average Rate of Return Method (ARR) $ARR = \frac{\text{Average Profit}}{\text{Average Investment}}$	• Accept project when ARR > minimum rate • Reject project when ARR < minimum rate
2. Payback Method (PB) $PB = \frac{\text{Initial Investment}}{\text{Annual Cash Inflow}}$	• Accept Project when PB < Standard Payback • Reject Project when PB > Standard Payback
Discounted Cash Flow Techniques	
3. Net Present Value (NPV) $NPV = \sum_{i=1}^{n} \frac{CF_i}{(1+k)^i} - C_0$	• Accept Project when NPV > 0 (Positive)

[Contd...]

$NPV = \frac{CF_0}{(1+k)^0} + \frac{CF_1}{(1+k)^1} + \ldots + \frac{CF_n}{(1+k)^n}$ $= \sum_{i=0}^{n} \frac{CF_i}{(1+k)^i}$	• Reject Project when NPV < 0 (Negative) • Indifferent when NPV = 0
4. Profitability Index (PI) $PI = \sum_{i=1}^{n} \frac{CF_i}{(1+k)^i} \div C_0$	• Accept Project when PI > 1 • Reject Project when PI < 1 • Indifferent when PI = 1
5. Internal Rate of Return (IRR) $CO_0 = \frac{CF_0}{(1+r)^0} + \frac{CF_1}{(1+r)^1} + \frac{CF_2}{(1+r)^2} + \frac{CF_n}{(1+r)^n} + \frac{SV + WC}{(1+r)^n}$ $CO_0 = \sum_{i=1}^{n} \frac{CF_1}{(1+r)^1} + \frac{S+W}{(1+r)^n}$ Or, $O = \sum_{i=1}^{n} \frac{CF_1}{(1+r)^1} + \frac{S+W}{(1+r)^n} - CO_0$	• Accept Project when IRR > k • Reject Project when IRR < k • Indifferent when IRR = k

7.14 DISCOUNTED CASH FLOWS TECHNIQUES

The discounted cash flow techniques are also called 'modern techniques'. They consider time value of money and are also called 'time adjusted cash flow techniques'. They are based on cash flows and the techniques follow the principles of financial management. The cash flows that occur first are given preference to those which occur later. The net present value method, profitability index and the internal rate of return are discounted cash flow techniques. They are based on the discounting procedure through a required rate of return. The cash flows are discounted to the present date.

The common discounting procedure works through a required rate of return. This rate of return is called the 'cost of capital' (dealt in detail in Chapter 9) discusses it in detail. The discount rate is thus the minimum rate of return, which a firm wants to earn on the investment in a capital budgeting project.

The discounted cash flow techniques, directly apply the time value of money concept. In order to discount the cash flows, the present value tables in Table A-3 are used. The following Example 7.12 shows the methodology of finding out the present values.

Example 7.12 A company wants to find out the present value of the amount that is invested. The cash flows are from the present time period to 5 years, which is the life of the asset. The cash outflow for purchasing the machine was Rs. 10,00,000. The cash inflows from year 1 to year 5 are Rs. 5,00,000 in 1st, 2nd and 3rd year and Rs. 4,00,000 in the 4th and 5th year. The discount rate is 10%. The working capital increase was of Rs. 1,00,000 which will be released after 5 years. The salvage value of the machine is Rs. 1,00,000.

Solution

This will be calculated by the following method:

Time Period	Cash Flows (Rs.)	PV Factor @ 10%	Present Values (Rs.)
0 (Cash outflow)	10,00,000	1.00	10,00,000
1 (Cash inflow)	5,00,000	0.909	4,54,500
2 (Cash inflow)	5,00,000	0.826	4,13,000
3 (Cash inflow)	5,00,000	0.751	3,75,500
4 (Cash inflow)	4,00,000	0.683	2,73,200
5 (Cash inflow)	4,00,000	0.621	2,48,400
Cash inflows > cash outflow of Rs. 10,00,000	In the 5th year two more inflows of working capital and salvage value are given.		7,64,600
5 (Working capital)	1,00,000	0.621	62,100
5 (Salvage value)	1,00,000	0.621	62,100

(*i*) Net Present Value (NPV)

The NPV technique is considered to be the best capital budgeting technique. In this approach the cash outflow is deducted from the sum of the present values of cash inflows. This can be calculated both in conventional cash flows and non-cash flows. In other words, it is the excess of present value of inflows over present value of outflows. It can be calculated through the following formula:

$$\text{NPV} = \sum_{i=1}^{n} \frac{\text{CF}_i}{(1+k)^i} - \text{C}_0$$

Where C_0 is the initial cost of the proposal

CF_i = Cash flows at different periods of time ...0, 1, 2, 3, 4 . . . *n*

k = Discount rate

n = Life of the project

This equation can be used in conventional cash flows when the cost of the project is incurred only in the beginning of the period.

In case of non-conventional cash flows, NPV is calculated in the following way:

$$\text{NPV} = \frac{\text{CF}_0}{(1+k)^0} + \frac{\text{CF}_1}{(1+k)^1} + \ldots + \frac{\text{CF}_n}{(1+k)^n}$$

$$= \sum_{i=1}^{n} \frac{\text{CF}_i}{(1 + k)^i}$$

The criteria for accepting or rejecting proposals are when:

(*a*) NPV > 0: Accept the proposal

(*b*) NPV = 0: The proposal may be accepted by the firm, it may not accept it. This is called an 'indifferent condition'.

But when NPV < 0: The proposal should be rejected.

Positive NPV will result only if project would generate cash inflows at a rate higher than the opportunity cost of capital.

Total present value of cash inflows – cash outflows = NPV.

Following is an example to show how net present value is calculated and whether it should be accepted or rejected.

NPV can be calculated when the inflows are continuously of the same value every year as well as for proposals, which have different, cash inflows. When cash inflows are the same every year, it is treated like an annuity and the present value factor will be same from (Table A-4) and when the cash inflows are uneven then (Table A-3) will be used to find out present values. Examples 7.13 and 7.14 clearly explain these facts. The NPV can be calculated for:

- An Annuity, when cash inflows are equal every year till the lifetime of the asset.
- When cash flows are not equal or uneven during the life of the project.

When Cash Inflows are Equal

Example 7.13 Calculate NPV of an initial investment of Rs. 2,00,000 which periods a net cash inflow of Rs. 60,000 every year for 6 years. Assume cost of funds to be 8%. There is no scrap value.

Net present value of a project is equal to the sum of the present value of all the cash flows associated with the project.

Particulars	PV of Cash Flows (Rs.)
60,000 × 4.63 ($\text{PVAF}_{6,8\%}$ Table A-4)	2,77,380
Less: cash outflows (Investment)	2,00,000
NPV	77,380

Since inflows of Rs. 2,77,380 are higher than the outflows, the proposal should be accepted.

The discount value '*k*' @ 10% represents cost of capital.

When Cash Inflows are Uneven

Example 7.14 Calculate NPV initial investment 10,00,000. Machine life is 5 years. Is it feasible to buy this project? The cash flows and the years are given below. The cost of capital is 10%. Analyse the following machine.

Year	Cash Outflows/Inflows (Rs.)
0 (outflow)	–10,00,000
1 (inflows)	2,00,000
2 (inflows)	2,00,000
3 (inflows)	3,00,000
4 (inflows)	3,00,000
5 (inflows)	3,50,000

Solution

Year (1)	Cash Flow (2)	PV Factor @ 10%	Value(2) × (3)
0	–10,00,000		– 10,00,000
1	2,00,000	0.909	1,81,800
2	2,00,000	0.826	1,65,200
3	3,00,000	0.751	2,25,300
4	3,00,000	0.683	2,04,900
5	3,50,000	0.621	2,17,350
			Σ = 9,94,550

Outflow Rs.10,00,000 – Inflow Rs. 9,94,550 = –5450.00. The proposal should be rejected, as outflow is more than the sum of inflows of cash.

Evaluation of NPV

The Net Present Value method can be used in conventional and non-conventional cash flow series. It can be used to evaluate single proposal or two or more proposals. It is useful to evaluate an independent proposal and a mutually exclusive proposal. NPV is calculated by the direct application of time value of money. The cash flows, which occur at different time, are made comparable by using the discount rate.

NPV considers all cash inflows and it is not like the payback method, which only considers cash flows till the recovery of the investment. It is based on cash flows and not accounting profit. The discount rate is applied to find out if the minimum required rate of return has been achieved.

NPV method has many merits but it is difficult as it involves a lot of calculations. It requires training of the staff to predetermine the required rate of return. It is based on absolute numbers and it ignores the difference in the initial cash outflows and the side of the different proposal when mutually exclusive projects have to be evaluated. The net present value technique can be summarized in the following way:

Merits of NPV are:

(*a*) It takes into account time value of money.

(*b*) It considers cash flow stream in its entirety.

(*c*) It is suitable for evaluation of independent proposals as well as mutually exclusive projects.

(*d*) It considers the objective of wealth maximization concept for the shareholders.

Limitations of NPV method are:

(*a*) It requires skill for calculation.

(*b*) The calculations of these methods are tedious.

(*c*) The cost of capital or the discount rate k is difficult to ascertain and errors may occur.

(*d*) It provides the results of evaluation in absolute terms. Two projects would be comparable only if the cash outflow of the proposal is similar.

The NPV technique, it can be concluded is a superior method of evaluation. It is the best method for taking decisions as it adheres with the principles of financial management. It provides maximization of shareholders wealth.

Terminal Value (TV)

The net present value can be extended to a new technique, which is called the 'terminal value technique'. In this technique the future cash values are discounted to make them comparable. It is based on the assumption that future cash inflows are reinvested at a prevailing rate of interest till the end of the economic life of the investment. The future cash flows are first compounded at the expected rate of interest till the end of the economic life. They are then discounted at an appropriate rate to find out the present values. The present values are then compared with the cash outflows. If cash inflows are higher than cash outflows, the proposal will be accepted. To give an example of the terminal value approach the following Example 7.15.

Example 7.15 A firm has an investment proposal of Rs. 3,20,000. The machine has a four-year life and the firms expect to generate cash inflows of Rs. 80,000 p.a. If it expects a rate of return of 10% and can invest cash inflows at the rate of 8%. Calculate the terminal value.

Solution

Step 1: Calculate Compound Values From Compound Value (Table A-1)

Year	Cash Inflows (Rs.)	Remaining Years	CVF @ 8%	Compound Values (Rs.)
1	80,000	3	1.260	1,00,800
2	80,000	2	1.166	93,280
3	80,000	1	1.080	86,400
4	80,000	0	1.000	80,000
			Total Compounded Value = 3,60,480	

Alternate Method: Since this is an annuity of Rs. 80,000 instead of compound value tables, compound value of annuity table A-2 can be used @ 8% for 4 years. The value is 4.506 therefore the compound value will be Rs. 80,000 × 4.506 = Rs. 3,60,480.

Step 2: Take the discount factor of 10%. Now Rs. 3,60,480 will be discounted from the present value factor at 10% for 8 years. The factor is 0.683 the present value, *i.e.*, of Rs. 3,60,480 × 0.683 = Rs. 246207.84

Step 3: Compare present value with cash outflow Rs. (246207.84 – 3,20,000) = Rs. –73792.16

The present value is Rs. –73792.16.

Accept/ Reject Decision

Independent Proposal: Proposal is accepted if compounded value of cash inflows is greater than present value of cash outflows.

Proposal is rejected if compounded value of cash inflows is less than the present value of cash outflows.

Mutually Exclusive Projects: Select project with highest priority.

The TV method is an extension of the net present value technique. It has most of the advantages of the net present value method. Its main drawback is that the compound values of future cash inflows are required. Therefore it has to be an estimation of the future rate of interest at which the inflows have to be compounded.

(*ii*) Profitability Index Method (PI)

The profitability index method is also called the 'benefits cost ratio'. It is the ratio of the present value of cash inflows, at the required rate of return, to the initial cash outflows of an investment. It measures the present value of the returns, which have been invested. It is based on net present value method. Net present value method is an absolute method and was not considered to be reliable for evaluating those projects, which require different initial investment. The PI method solves this problem, as it is the relative measure, which can be calculated by dividing the present value of cash inflows by cash outflows.

Profitability Index Measures PV of returns per rupee that is invested in a project as:

$$PI = \frac{\text{Present Value of Cash Inflows}}{\text{Present Value of Cash Outflows}}$$

Accept/Reject Rule

When PI >1 Accept the project.

When PI < 1 Reject the project.

When PI = 1 it is indifferent. The proposal may or may not be accepted.

In mutually acceptable proposals, the proposal with a higher positive PI will be selected. Example 7.16 shows the calculation of PI index and how it is to be interpreted.

Example 7.16 Computer A costs Rs. 56,000 and computer B costs Rs. 60,000. The following are the cash inflows, calculate NPV and PI index. The cost of capital is 10% discount.

Solution

Computer A

(1) Year	(2) CFAT (Rs.)	(3) PV Factor (Table A–3)	(2 x 3x 4) PV (Rs.)
1	14,000	0.909	12,726
2	16,000	0.826	13,216
3	18,000	0.751	13,518
4	20,000	0.683	13,660
5	25,000	0.621	15,525
			ΣPV = 68,645

Computer B

(1) Year	(2) CFAT (Rs.)	(3) PV Factor (Table A–3)	(4) PV (Rs.)
1	22,000	0.909	19,998
2	20,000	0.826	16,520
3	18,000	0.751	13,518
4	16,000	0.683	10,928
5	17,000	0.621	10,557
			ΣPV = 71,521

$$\text{PI Machine A} = \frac{68{,}645}{56{,}000} = 1.225$$

$$\text{B} = \frac{71{,}521}{60{,}000} = 1.192$$

Both the machines are positive and are acceptable by PI method.

According to NPV method, Computer A will be acceptable. The cost was Rs. 56,000 and the present value of inflows is Rs. 68,645; the difference being Rs. 12,645; and computer B is also acceptable because the inflows are greater than the outflow of Rs. 60,000 at Rs. 11,521. Both the computers give positive results.

The PI method however shows the relative ranking and in this case also Computer A would be better than Computer B.

Evaluation of PI Method

PI is called an extension of NPV. It is a discounted cash flow technique. It is in accordance with the principles of financial management. It considers the elements of capital budgeting and reflects time value of money. It is useful in evaluating projects of capital rationing. It considers all the cash flows of the project and provides maximization of wealth to the shareholders. It is thus a sound method of appraising proposals. However when cash outflows occur beyond the current period, the PI method is not suitable for selection of a proposal. It is also not useful in conditions where many small projects have to be aggregated and compared with the large project. It ranks projects correctly when capital budget is limited to the current period and in most conditions it accepts and rejects the same proposals as that of the net present value.

Merits of PI technique are:

(*a*) It is very simple and easy to understand.

(*b*) It conceptualizes time value of money.

(*c*) It considers all cash flows during the life of the project.

(*d*) It is in accordance with the principles of financial management.

(*e*) It emphasizes wealth maximization.

Demerits of PI technique are:

(*a*) The cost of capital which is used to discount cash flows may create errors in calculation.

(*b*) It is not useful when small projects are to be compared with a large project.

(*c*) It presumes that intermediate cash flows can be reinvestment at the discount rate. This presumption is not practical in use in business application.

NPV and PI

There are many similarities and differences between NPV and PI. The similarities and differences between NPV and PI can be summarized as follows:

(*a*) NPV and PI give the same accept/reject decision.

(*b*) PI provides greater than one for positive projects of NPV. PI provides equal to one for NPV = 0, when PI < 1, NPV will be less than zero.

(*c*) NPV and PI have conflicting results, sometimes while evaluating mutually exclusive proposals.

(*d*) The PI technique is able to give a relative measure of two projects, whereas NPV provides the proposals to be either positive or negative. The NPV technique is thus an absolute form of evaluation.

(*e*) NPV and PI may also give different evaluation results when initial costs and the monetary benefits are different.

(*f*) In times of capital rationing, PI decisions give superior results.

(*g*) In all conditions except in capital rationing, the NPV technique is superior and is preferred.

The NPV technique and the PI technique, both satisfy the principles of time value of money. They are both discounted cash flows techniques. However, NPV technique would be considered superior to the PI technique, except in mutually exclusive projects.

(*iii*) Internal Rate of Return (IRR)

The internal rate of return is an important discounted cash flow technique. It is also called marginal efficiency of capital, yield on investment and marginal productivity of capital. It is a rate of return. It can be defined as the rate at which the present value of cash outflows is equal to the present value of cash inflows. IRR is the value at which the net present value of the project becomes zero. In IRR technique, the proposal would be accepted only if the IRR is greater than or equal to a predetermined cut off rate. The proposal is rejected when it is less than the cut off rate which is the minimum required rate of return of a firm.

$$\text{IRR CO}_0 = \frac{\text{CF}_0}{(1+r)^0} + \frac{\text{CF}_1}{(1+r)^1} + \frac{\text{CF}_2}{(1+r)^2} + \frac{\text{CF}_n}{(1+r)^n} + \frac{\text{SV + WC}}{(1+r)^n}$$

CO_0 = Cash outflow at 0 (zero) period.

CF_1 = Cash inflow at different periods.

n = Life of the project.

r = Rate of discount.

SV and WC = Salvage value and working capital respectively at the end of 'n' years.

$$CO_0 = \sum_{i=1}^{n} \frac{CF_n}{(1+r)^1} + \frac{S+W}{(1+r)^n}$$

Or,

$$0 = \sum_{i=1}^{n} \frac{CF_1}{(1+r)^i} + \frac{S+W}{(1+r)^n} - CO_0$$

Calculation for IRR: IRR can be calculated when:

(*a*) When cash flows are equal.

(*b*) When cash flows are unequal.

(*a*) **When cash flows are equal:** In a conventional cash flow analysis, when the proposal has an outflow of cash, it is followed by equal cash inflows. The cash flows in this case will be equal till the life of the proposal. When equal cash inflows are to be calculated, it is in the form of an annuity. The calculation in case of an annuity is done in the following way:

Step 1: Calculate payback (PB) period of the project.

Step 2: Find out PVAF from (Table A-4) according to the number of years of the project.

Step 3: Note down two values—one greater than and one less than the payback period. But closest to it. Also note down the interest rates corresponding to them.

Step 4: The smaller value will be called L and the interest rate against it will be called I_L and the higher value will be called H and the interest rate against it will be called I_H.

Step 5: Now use the formula:

$$IRR = I_L + \frac{(L - PB)}{(L - H)} \times (I_H - I_L)$$

Where, PB = Payback period

I_L = Lower rate of interest

I_H = Higher rate of interest

L = Discount factor at lower rate

H = Discount factor at higher rate

This can be understood by Example 7.17.

Example 7.17 A firm is evaluating a proposal. The project cost is Rs. 20,00,000 and has equal cash inflows of Rs. 5,00,000 at the end of each of next 6 years. There is no salvage value. Cut off rate is 12%. Find out the IRR.

Solution

$$\text{The payback period is } = \frac{20,00,000}{5,00,000} = 4\text{ years}$$

Find value nearest to 4 in Present Value is for 6 years. See Table A–4 under year 6. Closest to 4 will be 12% and 13%.

$$I_L = 12\%$$

$$I_L + \frac{(L - PB)}{(L - H)} \times (I_H - I_L)$$

$$= 12 + \frac{(4.111 - 4.000)}{(4.111 - 3.998)} \times (13 - 12)$$

$$= 12 + 0.98 = 12.98\%$$

This same formula can be used with 13% or higher rate of interest but there will be a slight change in the formula. The example with higher rate is shown next:

With higher rate of interest the formula will be

$$IRR = I_H - \frac{(PB - H)}{(L - H)} \times (I_H - I_L)$$

$$\text{With 13\% rate of interest, IRR} = 13 - \frac{(4 - 3.998)}{(4.111 - 3.998)}$$

$$= 13 - \frac{0.002}{0.113}$$

$$= 13 - .0176 = 12.98\%$$

Thus IRR can be calculated either by the lower interest or higher interest rate, the result will be the same as 12.98%.

> ***Note:*** Interpolation method is an approximation of IRR. The interpolation should be made between two closest discount rates having a positive and a negative NPV.

Alternate Method:

Step 1: Make a rough estimate with reference to payback period. The payback period calculated to be 4 years.

$$\text{NPV} = (\text{Cash inflows} \times \text{PVAF}_{ni}) - \text{Investment}$$

$$\text{At 12\% NPV} = (5{,}00{,}000 \times 4.111) - 20{,}00{,}000$$

$$= 20{,}55{,}500 - 20{,}00{,}000$$

$$\therefore \quad \text{NPV} = \text{Rs. } 55{,}500$$

$$\text{At 13\% NPV} = (5{,}00{,}000 \times 3.9980) - 20{,}00{,}000$$

$$= 19{,}99{,}000 - 20{,}00{,}000$$

$$\text{NPV} = \text{Rs. } -1{,}000$$

Interpolate between 12% and 13%.

IRR is the rate of discount in which NPV is 0,

$$\text{At 12\% NPV} = 55{,}500$$

$$\text{At 13\% NPV} = -1{,}000$$

∴ Rate at which NPV = 0 will be higher than 12 but less than 13% by interpolation difference of 1%

i.e., $55{,}500 - (-1{,}000)_{\text{LNVP}} = 56{,}500$ cost of project.

$$\text{IRR} = 12\% + \frac{20{,}55{,}500 - 20{,}00{,}000}{20{,}55{,}500 - 19{,}99{,}000}$$

$$= 12\% + \frac{55{,}500}{56{,}500}$$

$$= 12 + .98\%$$

$$\therefore \quad \text{IRR} = 12.98\%$$

IRR can also be ascertained by 13%, as:

$$\text{IRR} = 13\% - \frac{(20{,}00{,}000 - 19{,}99{,}000)}{(20{,}55{,}500 - 19{,}99{,}000)}$$

$$= 13\% - \frac{1{,}000}{56{,}500}$$

$$= 13\% - 0.0176 = 12.99\%$$

Where, L = Lower Net Present Value

H = Higher Net Present Value

If IRR > cut off rate, accept.

IRR is greater than cut off rate so the project should be accepted. IRR is 12.98% or 12.99% by alternate methods which is higher than the cut off rate of 12%. Therefore, the proposal should be accepted.

(*b*) **When future cash inflows are unequal:** When cash flows are not equal they are called 'mixed stream of cash inflows'. The method of calculation in this uneven stream of cash flows is different. The following steps will be used for calculations when the cash flows are non-conventional in nature.

Step 1: Calculate the weighted average cash flow after tax. The weights should be given in reverse order to give maximum weight to year 1 where the earliest cash inflow is expected.

Step 2: Find out the fake payback period of the project. (In this example weights have been given to find out payback period).

Step 3: Look into Table A-4 and find out PVAF factor of two values—one greater than and one less than the payback period as close as possible to the value.

Step 4: Interpolate and find IRR.

When cash inflows are not equal

Example 7.18 A proposal costs Rs. 3,20,000 and generates cash inflows of Rs. 80,000 ; Rs. 1,20,000; Rs. 1,00,000; Rs. 1,00,000 and Rs. 80,000. There is no salvage value. Find IRR.

Solution

IRR can be found out in the following way:

Step 1: Find weighted average of cash flows.

Year	Cash Inflows (CF)	Weight (W)	CF × W
1	80,000	5	4,00,000
2	1,20,000	4	4,80,000
3	1,00,000	3	3,00,000
4	1,00,000	2	2,00,000
5	80,000	1	80,000
		15	14,60,000

Weighted Average $\frac{14,60,000}{15} = 97333.33$

Weights are used in reverse order. This is to give maximum weight to early returns.

Step 2: Consider weighted average as the annuities of cash inflows and find out the payback period.

3,20,000/97333.33 = 3.28767 is the payback period.

Step 3: Now find out value closest to 3.288.

Step 4: Take present value annuity tables.

Find value closest to 3.288 in 5 years.

IRR is between 15% and 16% = 3.352 and 3.274

Step 5: IRR by interpolation is between IRR = 15% and 16%.

Now find NPV.

Year	Cash flow (Rs.)	PVF @ 16%	PVF @ 15%	PV @ 16%	PV @ 15%
1	80,000	0.862	0.870	68,960	69,600
2	1,20,000	0.743	0.756	89,160	90,720
3	1,00,000	0.641	0.658	64,100	65,800
4	1,00,000	0.552	0.572	55,200	57,200
5	80,000	0.476	0.497	38,080	39,760
				3,15,500	3,23,080

At 15% NPV = 3,15,500 – 3,20,000

Cash inflows are = –4,500 less than cash outflows.

At 15% NPV = 3,23,080 – 3,20,000

= + 3,080

The rates of NPV at 15% NPV is +3,080 and 16% NPV is –4,500. Therefore rate of NPV is 0 will be less more than 15% and less than 16% by interpolating difference of 1 % *i.e.*, 16% – 15%.

Over NPV difference, + 3080 – (– 4500) = 7,580

$$\text{IRR} = 15\% + \frac{(3,23,080\ -\ 3,20,000)}{(3,23,080\ -\ 3,15,500)} \times 1$$

$$\text{IRR} = 15 + \frac{3,080}{7580} = 15.40\%$$

IRR can also be ascertained through 16% as:

$$\text{IRR} = 16\%\ -\ \frac{(\text{Cost}\ -\ \text{HPV})}{(\text{LPV}\ -\text{HPV})}$$

$$IRR = 16\% - \frac{3,20,000 - 3,15,500}{3,23,080 - 3,15,500} \times 1$$

$$= 16\% - \frac{4,500}{7,580} = 15.40\%$$

HPV = Higher Present Value

LPV = Lower Present Value

In a mutually exclusive project proposal with highest IRR is given top priority, and project with lowest IRR is given the lowest priority.

Rule: NPV of the project is 0 if its cash flows are discounted at the minimum required rate i.e., k. IRR r of the proposal is internal to the project while the minimum required rate k, is external to the project.

Evaluation of IRR Technique

IRR technique is a discounted cash flow method and considers time value of money. It selects all the proposals, which are expected to earn more than the cut off rate. Since it is expressed as a percentage, it can be compared with the cut off rate. It also considers all the cash flows, which occur during the lifetime of the asset. It also considers the salvage value of an asset and the working capital, which is increase in the beginning of the project and decrease in the end of the project.

The IRR also has some flaws. It is difficult to calculate and one has to make a trial and error evaluation. It assumes that future cash inflows will be reinvested at the same rate as the IRR. It is also projects favourably towards larger projects, which yield a much higher percentage than smaller projects. IRR suffers from the problems of complex calculations which is not understandable by untrained people.

However, the IRR satisfies the wealth maximization criteria and hence it is considered to be a sound evaluation technique.

Merits of IRR are:

(*a*) It is an important technique takes all cash flows.

(*b*) It takes time value of money into account.

(*c*) It selects projects more than minimum rate of return.

(*d*) It compares with cut off ratio and is based on cash flows rather than accounting rate.

(*e*) It is expressed as a percentage rate.

(*f*) It provides all the advantages for wealth maximization.

Demerits of IRR are:

(*a*) The IRR calculations are very complex and the staff must be properly trained before applying them to business situations.

(*b*) The calculations are tedious and time consuming.

(*c*) IRR is biased towards small projects and gives importance to larger projects.

Table 7.5 Merits and Demerits of Capital Budgeting Techniques

Merits	Demerits
Average Rate of Return	
• Simple method and easy to calculate. • Does not cost to institute this technique. • Useful for small business.	• Ignores time value of money • Does not use cash flow method. • An approx. method. It is not objective or exact.
Payback Method	
• Simple and easy to understand. • Emphasis is on liquidity. • Uses cash flow information. — —	• Ignores time value of money. • Ignores cash flows after the payback period. • Does not measure profitability. • Not an objective method for calculating standard payback. • Does not work in accordance with the principle of financial management.
Net Present Value (NPV)	
• Based on time value of money. • Considers all the cash flows. • Measures profitability. • Consistent with the principle of wealth maximization. • Best technique as in accordance with the principles of financial management.	• Calculations are difficult in this method. • Requires computation through discount rates creating practical problems. — — —
Profitability Index (PI)	
• Recognizes time value of money. • Considers all the cash flows.	• Difficult to calculate, as the calculations are teddies and long. • At times does not indicate the right choice between mutually exclusive projects.

[Contd...]

Merits	Demerits
• Relative measure of profitability.	——
• Consistent with wealth maximization principle of financial management.	——
• In agreement with NPV results.	——
Internal Rate of Return (IRR)	
• Considers all cash flows.	• The most difficult technique for calculations.
• Based on time value of money.	• At times does not give correct choice between mutually exclusive projects.
• Good measure of profitability.	• Yields multiple rates.
• In accordance with wealth maximization principle.	• Trial and error methods takes long for calculations.
——	• Requires special training to use this method.
——	• Applicable mainly in large business.

7.15 COMPARISON BETWEEN NPV AND IRR TECHNIQUES

The different evaluation techniques in capital budgeting help a firm to take decisions regarding the choice of the asset, that is useful to increase the profitability of a company. It also provides a measure to create and maximize the wealth of the shareholders. The decisions that have to be taken by a firm involve different situations such as:

(*a*) Acceptance or rejection of independent proposals.

(*b*) Decisions relating to use of existing asset or replacement of the asset.

(*c*) Selection of one asset also called mutually exclusive decisions.

(*d*) Decisions under conventional and non-conventional cash flows.

NPV and IRR: The NPV and IRR are used to take important decisions. There are certain similarities and differences in the results that would occur while evaluating the proposals with the two methods. Generally the NPV and IRR would give similar results. To judge a sound project, both the methods should be used as they would accept the proposal if it is good and reject it when it is not sound. Those proposals, which have to be appraised independently without affecting the cash inflows and outflows of other projects, are simple to evaluate.

(*i*) **Independent Project: The accept/reject decision** when ***independent projects*** are appraised in the case of ***NPV technique*** is the following: Accept the proposal when it is greater than or equal to zero and rejected when it is negative. In the case of ***IRR technique,*** the proposal should be accepted if the IRR is greater than or equal to a predetermined cut off rate which is the minimum required rate of return and reject the proposal when the IRR is less than the cut off rate.

(*ii*) **Project Replacement Decisions:** In the case of a ***replacement decision,*** the NPV technique would be accepted after calculating the NPV of the incremental differences between cash outflows and inflows of the asset. The proposal would be accepted only if it is positive and rejected when it is negative. In the case of IRR, the incremental cash flows would be computed and proposals would be accepted for replacement only when IRR is greater than the cut off rate. In cases IRR is less than the cut off rate, it would not be accepted and the existing asset would be continued. This would amount to rejection of the proposal of replacing a new asset.

When mutually exclusive projects have to be evaluated and only one of the projects can be selected, it would be called a 'mutually exclusive decision'. Since only one of them would be selected a choice would be made after ranking the proposal. The proposal with the highest ranking would be selected and the other would be rejected. One condition which is necessary in evaluating these proposals is that the life of all the projects under evaluation is similar. Accept or reject decision of different proposals in ***NPV technique*** would be to select the project which has the highest positive NPV while ranking them. In the ***IRR technique*** the proposal with the highest IRR, which is more than the cut off rate, should be selected. This can be summarized in the following manner:

- NPV and IRR give identical results in conventional cash flows.
- NPV and IRR give identical results in independent proposals.
- The condition of identical results is when similar economic life of the proposals is compared.
- The IRR should be greater than or equal to cut off rate to be selected.
- The highest NPV and IRR are given priority for selection of the project.

Conflicting Results Between NPV and IRR

NPV and IRR do not always give identical results. Sometimes they are conflicting in nature. The differences arise in case of these problems when:

(*i*) The proposals evaluated have a size disparity.

(*ii*) The proposals that are being evaluated have the disparity in terms of time.

(*iii*) Proposals, which have unequal lives.

Let us take examples for each of these **conflicting cases**.

(*i*) **Size Disparity:** When two proposals are being evaluated and the **cost** of the two proposals is different, the ranking of both the proposals will be different. This is because NPV technique provides the **absolute** net benefits and IRR gives **relative** net benefits. The NPV is affected by the size of the proposals as it would give priority to those proposals where inflows are greater than the outflows. IRR ignores the size of the proposal.

Example 7.19 Cost of proposal A is Rs. 10,00,000; cash inflows are Rs. 5,00,000; Rs. 6,00,000 and Rs. 4,00,000.

Cost of proposal B is Rs. 20,00,000; cash inflows are Rs. 10,00,000; Rs. 12,00,000 and Rs. 8,00,000. Discount rate is 10%.

NPV

Proposal A

Year	Cash Inflow (CF)	PVF_{ni}	CF × PVF
0	10,00,000		10,00,000
1	5,00,000	0.909	4,54,500
2	6,00,000	0.826	4,95,600
3	4,00,000	0.751	3,00,400
			2,50,500

Proposal B

Year	Cash inflow (CF)	PVF_{ni}	CF × PVF
0	20,00,000		20,00,000
1	10,00,000	0.909	9,09,000
2	12,00,000	0.826	9,91,200
3	8,00,000	0.751	6,00,800
			5,01,000

IRR

$$\text{Average cash inflow} = \frac{15,00,000}{3} = \text{Rs. } 5,00,000$$

$$\text{Fake payback period} = \frac{\text{Cash outflow}}{\text{Average annual cash inflow}} = \frac{10,00,000}{5,00,000} = 2 \text{ years}$$

$$\text{Average cash inflow} = \frac{20,00,000}{3} = 666666.66$$

$$\text{Fake payback period} = \frac{\text{Cash outflow}}{\text{Average annual cash inflow}}$$

$$= \frac{20,00,000}{666666.66} = 3 \text{ years}$$

Proposal A will be between 23% and 24% and Proposal B will be between 0% to 1%.

Therefore according to IRR proposal A is better. Hence size disparity can show different result by NPV and IRR.

(*ii*) **Time Disparity:** NPV and IRR will also give a difference in results when there is the problem of time disparity. In the case of mutually exclusive proposals. The NPV results would be considered superior to IRR. In this condition two mutually exclusive proposals would give conflicting results because of the timing of receipts of cash inflows from different project. The proposal which gives higher cash inflows in the earlier years would be preferred to the higher cash inflows in later years. Take Example 7.20.

Example 7.20 The following two projects are being evaluated at 10% discount rate.

Cash Flow Period	Project P	Project Q
0	12,25,000	12,25,000
1	1,00,000	10,00,000
2	5,00,000	5,00,000
3	10,00,000	1,00,000

The NPV when calculated shows that it is Rs. 29,900 in project P and Rs. 1,72,100 in project Q. Therefore project Q should be accepted because it gives a higher early return. Q gives a cash inflow of 10,00,000 in year one whereas P gives only Rs. 1,00,000. But the internal rate of return indicates that Project P and Project Q have the same IRR at 14.82%. Hence project Q is better because NPV is more realistic. The conflict arises in the two methods mainly due to the fact that NPV assumes that the inflows will be reinvested at the given cost of capital at 10%, whereas IRR assumes the reinvestment rate at the internal rate of return expected. The NPV is therefore superior as it is more realistic.

(*iii*) **Unequal Lives:** When two proposals with unequal lives are evaluated, the conflict will arise between NPV and IRR. When the required rate of return of two proposal is same but one proposal is completed in one year, whereas the other is completed in more than one year the results will not be similar. An example may be given.

Example 7.21 There are two projects X and Z. The initial cash outlay of the projects is Rs. 2,00,000 each. Project X has a 1-year life span in which it generates Rs. 2,40,000 whereas Z generates Rs. 4,02,000. The lifespan of Z is expected to be 5 years. If the required rate of return is 10%, the proposal shows on calculation that while the IRR will give a return of approximately 20% in X and it would be only 15% in Z. In the case of project X the NPV is Rs. 1,81,600 and for project Z it is Rs. 4,90,000. Which of these should be accepted?

Solution

Logically the answers according to both the methods are different. The NPV prefers project Z and IRR prefers project X. This is a conflict situation. To resolve such a case a modification is applied the modification is through two approaches. These are: (*a*) common time horizon approach and (*b*) equivalent annual value approach.

(*a*) **Common Time Horizon Approach:** It suggest that to provide a good comparison the two projects would be comparable at the same period of time. If one project has a life of 2 years and the other project of 5 years, the comparison would be made for a period of 10 years, with the replacements of the projects. The assumption of this approach is that the investment, which is replaced because its time period is completed, will be able to produce cash flows of the same amount as it had done before the replacement. This approach has some problems because the replacement of the asset would have to be of the previous technology and earlier price, but this becomes very difficult. Another method, which can be applied to remove this problem, is called the equivalent annual value/cost approach.

(*b*) **Equivalent Annual Value Approach:** In this method, the NPV of the project is divided by the annuity factor corresponding to the life of the project at an appropriate cost. This method is useful in revenue expanding and cost reduction proposals. In revenue expanding projects, the project with the maximum equivalent annual value will be selected and when cost reduction proposals are evaluated the proposal, which has minimum equivalent annual value, would be selected.

In mutually exclusive proposals, the NPV and IRR would give different ranking to proposals when cash inflows of the proposals are different, when the size of the proposals is different, and when they have unequal lives of the projects. The implicit reinvestment rate will be different depending on the cash flow pattern of investment proposals. Thus conflicts will arise. Such conflicts will be higher in non-conventional cash flows rather than conventional cash flows.

NPV is a superior method and the result should be selected according to the NPV technique.

The above discussion can be summarized by stating that NPV should be preferred to IRR despite conflicting results because:

(*a*) NPV provides an absolute amount of net addition to the shareholders wealth.

(*b*) NPV accepts projects, which have a reinvestment rate higher than, cost of capital, whereas IRR accepts only the rate of return, which is more or equal to implied reinvestment rate.

(*c*) NPV always ranks mutually exclusive proposals correctly, whereas IRR may not be able to give correct ranking.

Hence NPV is a superior technique and is considered better than IRR.

Projects under capital rationing: The projects in a firm have to sometimes be finalized when there is a constrained of funds. The combination of projects would have to be selected. The selection would be by calculating net present value of the combined projects. The selection of proposals when capital rationing occurs is done in two steps. The first step involves the identification of all the proposals suitable for the firm. These are grouped into acceptable and non-acceptable projects. The acceptable projects are then kept for selection and in step 2 the combination of projects are selected through IRR method or through PI. This selection is dependent on whether a proposal can be accepted or rejected completely because it is indivisible or if it has many parts and some divisible parts can be accepted/rejected.

7.16 SELECTION OF EVALUATION TECHNIQUES

In this chapter the average rate of return, payback method, net present value method, profitability index and internal rate of return have been analysed.

The *ARR technique* uses profit maximization and not wealth maximization. It also ignores cash generation through the taxable benefits in depreciation. However, it is useful in small firms where the return of an investment through profitability is required.

The *payback technique* is another traditional technique. It helps a firm to find out the proposal, which will yield cash flows and the time period when the initial investment can be recovered. Its main drawback is that it does not consider cash flows after the payback period. It also does not provide time value to money.

Net present value technique considers all the cash flows, provides time value to money, has a discount rate and is able to select individual and mutually exclusive project. It totally relates with the objective of providing wealth maximization to the shareholders.

The *PI technique* supports the NPV technique and can be used with it to make selections. The NPV provides the analysis in absolute terms and the PI gives the relative performance of the proposals.

The *IRR technique* uses a predetermined cut off rate to evaluate proposals. It is a sound technique and gives value to proposals in terms of time value and wealth maximization. But it is a little tedious in terms of calculations.

In most situations, NPV, PI and IRR will be in agreement for selection of a proposal. Sometimes, conflicts do arise in mutually exclusive proposals. These techniques are need based depending on the size of the business, training level of staff members, size and life of proposals and many practical situations. Each method has its own merits and demerits but the NPV method is the most suitable and it is often called the best technique.

POINTS TO REMEMBER

- Capital budgeting is concerned with long-term decision making. It consists of selection of a proposal according to the requirements of a company.
- Capital budgeting decisions have long-term effects. Decisions once taken are irreversible. They should be taken very carefully.
- Capital budgeting decisions are related to the selection on independent proposals and mutually exclusive proposals. They may be taken for replacement, expansion or diversification.
- The capital budgeting process covers three distinct steps. These are estimation of costs and benefits, finding out the required rate of return and using an appropriate technique for selection of a proposal.
- There are three steps involved in finding out the costs and benefits of a proposal. These are initial cash flows, subsequent cash flows and terminal cash flows.
- Capital budgeting is based on only relevant cash flows. Sunk costs, allocated overheads and those costs, that do not pertain directly to the proposal, are not calculated for finding out costs and benefits.
- The different techniques of capital budgeting are based on traditional methods and discounted cash flow methods.
- The traditional techniques are average rate of return and payback period method.
- Discounted cash flows are better techniques as they use time value of money and cost of capital through a discount rate. There are three techniques: NPV, PI and IRR.
- NPV method is considered to be the most superior method. It is consistent with the objectives of wealth maximization of the shareholders.
- In mutually exclusive proposals, there can be differences in ranking of the proposal but the NPV technique is to be preferred.

OBJECTIVE TYPE QUESTIONS

State whether the following statements are true (T) or false (F).

1. Capital budgeting decisions can be easily reversed.
2. Sunk cost is a relevant cost in capital budgeting.
3. Allocated overhead costs are not relevant unless actually appropriated on the new project.
4. In independent project, firm can select all feasible projects.

5. In mutually exclusive projects only one project can be selected.
6. Incremental cash flow analysis is known as relevant cash flows.
7. Opportunity cost in considered in capital budgeting.
8. Payback technique is based on discounting technique.
9. In Net Present Value technique only cash inflows are discounted. Cash outflows are ignored.
10. NPV technique is the best evaluation technique.
11. NPV and IRR give identical decisions.
12. Cash inflows are compounded for calculating Net Present Value.
13. Traditional techniques of capital budgeting use time value of money.

Answers: 1. (F), 2. (F), 3. (T), 4. (T), 5. (T), 6. (T), 7. (T), 8. (F), 9. (F), 10. (T), 11. (F), 12. (F), 13. (F), 14. (T).

THEORETICAL QUESTIONS

1. What are incremental cash flows? Briefly explain the effects of sunk costs, incidental costs, allocated costs and opportunity costs.
2. How should depreciation be traded in capital budgeting? Discuss the Accounting and Income Tax treatment of depreciation.
3. Explain conventional and non-conventional cash flows. Why are cash flows important in investment decision making?
4. What is capital budgeting? Discuss its main features.
5. "Cash flow approach is considered to be superior to according profit approach." Comment.
6. Examine the effects of depreciation policy on the cash flows of a firm.
7. What adjustments would you make in cash flows relating to working capital, taxation and depreciation?
8. Write notes on:

   (*a*) Reinvestment rate

   (*b*) Discounted cash flows method

   (*c*) Incremental cash flows

   (*d*) Traditional capital budgeting techniques.
9. "While selecting NPV and IRR methods give identical results in conventional cash flows." Explain.

10. Why do NPV and IRR give conflicting results? Discuss.
11. What is the Net Present Value technique? Do you think it can be called the best technique?
12. Discuss the similarities and differences between NPV and IRR. Which of the two methods is considered to be superior?
13. What is Profitability Index? Which is superior in ranking—NPV or PI?
14. What is accounting rate of return? How is it calculated? What are its limitations?
15. "The payback period is more a method of liquidity rather than profitability." Examine.
16. How is payback period calculated? How is it used in determining Internal Rate of Return (IRR)?
17. How is time value of money applied in capital budgeting techniques?
18. Compare IRR and NPV techniques. Why do these techniques have a conflict in ranking of projects?
19. Explain how NPV and IRR have identical decisions in ranking independent projects.
20. How does payback method before from profitability index?

ILLUSTRATIVE PROBLEMS

Illustration 7.1 A company is considering an investment proposal. The following information is provided. Prepare cash flow analysis.

Particulars	Amount (Rs.)
Purchase Price of an asset	80,00,000
Installation costs	2,00,000
Increase in working capital with purchase of new machine	5,00,000
Annual cash inflows of new machine	35,00,000
Annual cash expenses of the new machine	5,00,000
Scrap value of the new machine	4,00,000
Life of new machine	4 years
Book value of old asset	4,00,000
Scrap value of old asset	5,00,000
Annual cash inflow from old asset	30,00,000
Annual cash expenses of old asset	8,00,000
Depreciation of new asset in the ratio 7 : 8 : 5	90% for 4 years
Depreciation of old asset at the rate of	Rs. 1,50,000 p.a.
Tax rate	40%

Solution

Step 1: Initial cash flows

Particulars	Amount (Rs.)
Purchase price	80,00,000
Add installation cost	2,00,000
Add increase in working capital	5,00,000
	87,00,000
– Scrap value of old asset	5,00,000
	82,00,000
– Tax on gain on sale of old asset	40,000
Net cash outflows	81,60,000

Step 2: Subsequent/Operational cash flows of new machine

Particulars	Year 1	Year 2	Year 3	Year 4
Annual cash inflow	35,00,000	35,00,000	35,00,000	35,00,000
Cash Expenses	5,00,000	5,00,000	5,00,000	5,00,000
Profit before depreciation	30,00,000	30,00,000	30,00,000	30,00,000
– Depreciation	20,66,000	23,61,600	14,76,000	14,76,000
Profit before tax	9,34,000	6,38,400	15,24,000	15,24,000
– Tax @ 40%	3,73,600	2,55,360	6,09,600	6,09,600
Profit after tax	5,60,400	3,83,040	9,14,400	9,14,400
Depreciation added back	20,66,000	23,61,600	14,76,000	14,76,000
Cash flows	26,26,400	27,44,640	23,90,400	23,90,400
– Cash flows of old asset	13,40,000	13,40,000	13,40,000	13,40,000
Incremental cash flow	12,86,400	14,04,640	10,50,400	10,50,400

Step 3: Subsequent cash flows of old machine

Particulars	Amount (Rs.)
Annual cash inflows	30,00,000
– Cash Expenses	8,00,000
	22,00,000
Depreciation	1,50,000
Profit before tax	20,50,000
– Tax @ 40%	8,60,000
Profit after tax	11,90,000
Depreciation added back	1,50,000
Annual cash inflows	13,40,000

Note: Calculation for depreciation of new machine.

Particulars	Amount (Rs.)
Purchase	80,00,000
+ Installation	2,00,000
82,00,000 × 90% =	73,80,000
73,80,000 in the ratio of 7 : 8 : 5	
Year 1	20,66,400
Year 2	23,61,600
Year 3	14,76,000
Year 4	14,76,000

Step 4: Terminal cash flows

Particulars	Amount (Rs.)
Scrap value	4,00,000
– Book value (10% of 82 lakh)	8,20,000
Loss on sale	4,20,000
+ Scrap value	4,00,000
+ Working capital released	5,00,000
	9,00,000
+ Cash inflow of year 4	9,50,400
Total cash inflows	18,50,400

Illustration 7.2 A company plans to replace a machine, which costs Rs. 10,00,000. It has a written down value of Rs. 3,00,000. The machine has another 5 years of its remaining life. After 5 years its salvage value will be nil. If the machine is sold today its salvage value will be Rs. 2,00,000. The company for its technological superiority is evaluating a new machine. The new machine will provide annual revenue of Rs. 6,00,000 and will cost Rs. 18,00,000. Its life will be 5 years and its scrap value will be Rs. 3,00,000. The tax rate of the firm is 40%. Find out the cash flows. Capital gain is subject to 20% tax rate. Depreciation is at SLM methods.

Solution

Step 1: Initial cash flow

Particulars	Amount (Rs.)
Cost of new machine	18,00,000
– Scrap value of old machine	2,00,000
	16,00,000

Step 2: Subsequent cash flow

Particulars	Amount (Rs.)
Annual cash flow	6,00,000
– Incremental depreciation	2,80,000
Profit before tax	3,20,000
– Tax @ 40%	1,28,000
Profit after tax	1,92,000
Annual cash inflow + Depreciation added back	2,80,000
	4,72,000

Step 3: Terminal cash flow

Particulars	Amount (Rs.)
Scrap value of new machine	3,00,000
+ Net cash inflow	4,72,000
Total inflows	7,72,000

Note: Calculation of depreciation

Depreciation of new machine = Rs. (3,00,000 – 2,00,000)/5 20,000

Incremental depreciation 2,80,000

Illustration 7.3 A company is planning to replace 6-year-old equipment. It has to incur an expenditure of Rs. 12,00,000 if it wants to modernize and continue to use it. The equipment has a nil written down value. If modernized the equipment can be used for 5 more years. The salvage value after 5 years would be Rs. 2,00,000. The company may opt to buy new equipment instead of modernization. The new equipment will cost Rs. 20,00,000 with an economic life of 5 years. It would have a salvage value of Rs. 5,00,000. The following added information is provided.

The expenses of the factor in the existing equipment was Rs. 8,00,000 but with modernization it would fall to Rs. 2,00,000; but if a new machine was purchased the cost would further reduce to Rs. 4,50,000.

The tax rate of the company is 50%. Depreciation is changed on straight-line basis. Should the company modernize its equipment or buy new equipment? Give an indication by calculating net cash inflows. If cost of capital is 10%.

Solution

Incremental cash flows

Particulars	Modernization Amount (Rs.)	New Machine Amount (Rs.)	Difference Amount (Rs.)
Savings in expenses	6,00,000	7,50,000	1,50,000
Less Depreciation	2,00,000	3,00,000	1,00,000
Profit Before Tax	4,00,000	4,50,000	50,000
Tax @ 50%	2,00,000	2,25,000	25,000
Profit After Tax (PAT)	2,00,000	2,25,000	25,000
Add back depreciation	2,00,000	3,00,000	1,00,000
Net Cash flow	4,00,000	5,25,000	1,25,000

If cost of capital is 10%

Modernization = – 12,00,000 + (4,00,000 × 3.791) + (2,00,000 × 0.621)
= – 12,00,000 + 15,16,400 + 1,24,200
= Rs. 4,40,600

Note: Depreciation is calculated at (Cost – Salvage)/No. of years.

Modernization (12,00,000 – 2,00,000)/5 = Rs. 2,00,000
New machine (20,00,000 – 5,00,000)/5 = Rs. 3,00,000

New machine – 20,00,000 + (5,25,000 × 3.791) + (5,00,000 × 0.621)
= – 20,00,000 + 19,90,275 + 3,10,500
= Rs. 3,00,775

Hence the company should modernize its equipment but not purchase a new one, as NPV is higher Rs. 4,40,600 when modernization takes place.

Illustration 7.4 A firm purchased a machine for Rs. 80,00,000 in 2004 has a worked well for 2 years. It has a remaining life of 5 years and a book value of Rs. 5,00,000.

The firm is planning to purchase a new machine for Rs. 1,60,00,000. The cost of installation will be Rs. 80,000. The increase in working capital required is Rs. 2,00,000. The expected cash flows of existing and new machine are given below:

Expected cash flow

Year	Existing Machine (Rs.)	New Machine (Rs.)
1	60,00,000	80,00,000
2	60,00,000	90,00,000
3	60,00,000	1,00,00,000
4	60,00,000	1,10,00,000
5	60,00,000	1,20,00,000

The firm depreciates its assets according to straight-line method. The tax on income and capital gain is 40%.

Calculate incremental cash flows when the scrap value of existing machine is (*i*) Rs. 8,00,000 and (*ii*) Rs. 3,00,000.

Solution

Step 1: Incremental initial cash flows

When scrap values are different

Particulars	(i)	(ii)
Scrap Value	8,00,000	3,00,000
Cost of new machine	1,60,00,000	1,60,00,000
+ Installation cost	80,000	80,000
	1,60,80,000	1,60,80,000
+ Addition WC	2,00,000	2,00,000
	1,62,80,000	1,62,80,000
– Scrap value	8,00,000	3,00,000
	1,54,80,000	1,59,80,000
Tax liability/saving	1,20,000	– 80,000
Cash outflow	1,56,00,000	1,59,00,000

Note: Calculation of Tax Paid/Saved

Particulars	Amount (Rs.)	Amount (Rs.)
Book value of old plant	5,00,000	5,00,000
– Scrap value	8,00,000	3,00,000
Profit/Loss	3,00,000	2,00,000
Tax @ 40% on capital gain/loss	1,20,000	–80,000

Step 2: Subsequent (Annual) Cash Flows

Particulars	Year 1 (Rs.)	Year 2 (Rs.)	Year 3 (Rs.)	Year 4 (Rs.)	Year 5 (Rs.)
Annual cash inflow	80,00,000	90,00,000	1,00,00,000	1,10,00,000	1,20,00,000
New machine – Old Machine	60,00,000	60,00,000	60,00,000	60,00,000	60,00,000
Incremental cash inflows	20,00,000	30,00,000	40,00,000	50,00,000	60,00,000
Depreciation	32,00,000	32,00,000	32,00,000	32,00,000	32,00,000
Profit before tax	–12,00,000	–2,00,000	8,00,000	18,00,000	28,00,000
– Tax @ 40%	—	—	3,20,000	7,20,000	11,20,000
Profit after tax	–12,00,000	–2,00,000	4,80,000	10,80,000	16,80,000
Depreciation added back	32,00,000	32,00,000	32,00,000	32,00,000	32,00,000
Net cash inflows	20,00,000	30,00,000	36,80,000	42,80,000	48,80,000

Note: Depreciation is calculated in the following way:

(*i*) Depreciation on new machine

∵ Purchase price; 1,60,00,000 + Installation cost; 80,000

∴ Depreciation = 2,40,00,000/5 = Rs. 48,00,000

(*ii*) Depreciation of old machine

= Purchase price 80,00,000/5 years = Rs. 16,00,000

(*iii*) Incremental depreciation

= 48,00,000 – 16,00,000 = Rs. 32,00,000

There will be a further inflow of Rs. 2,00,000 as release of working capital in the 5th year.

Illustration 7.5 A company purchased a machine last year for Rs. 12,00,000. The machine was estimated to have a useful life of 12 years with no salvage value. The annual cash operating cost is Rs. 2,00,000. A new machine can be purchased as a cost reducing machine is Rs. 20,00,000. It has an estimated life of 12 years with zero salvage value. If straight-line depreciation is used and the company's income tax is 40%, compute the incremental cash flows after taxes.

Solution

Step 1: Calculation of incremental cash flows

Initial outflow = Cost of new machine	20,00,000 – 10,00,000
– Sale of old machine	= 10,00,000

Step 2: Subsequent annual inflows

Particulars	**Amount (Rs.)**	**Amount (Rs.)**
Cash operating costs of old machine	2,00,000	—
– Cash operating costs of new machine	1,20,000	—
Savings in cash operating costs	80,000	80,000
Depreciation of old machine	12,00,000/12	= 1,00,000
Depreciation of new machine	20,00,000/12	=1,66,666
Increase in depreciation		= 66,666
Net increase in profit	13,334	13,334
Tax @ 40%		5333.60

Incremental cash flow

Particulars	Amount (Rs.)
Savings in cash operating costs	66,666.00
– Increase in tax liability	5333.60
Net cash inflow	61332.40
Terminal inflows	Nil

Illustration 7.6

(*a*) Find Payback time of the two machines A and B. Suggest which is better given that:

(*i*) Machine A costs Rs. 50,000 and generates a cash flow of Rs. 18,000 for 4 years.

(*ii*) Machine B costs Rs. 75,000 and generates Rs. 20,000 for 6 years.

(*b*) A project requires an investment of 5 lakh and yields an annual cash flow of 6 lakh for 10 years. What is the payback period of the project?

Solution

(*a*) Payback

$$\text{Machine A} = \frac{50{,}000}{18{,}000} = 2.78 \text{ years}$$

$$\text{Machine B} = \frac{75{,}000}{20{,}000} = 3.75 \text{ years}$$

In this example, machine A recovers its investment in 2 years and 7 months and machine B recovers the investment in 3.75 years.

(*b*) Payback (PB) period of the project

$$\text{PB} = \frac{5{,}00{,}000}{6{,}00{,}000} = 0.83 \text{ years}$$

Illustration 7.7 Prepare Ranking chart between NPV and PI Index when the initial investment on a proposal of purchase of a machine is Rs. 1,00,000. The cash inflows for year 1 to 4 are Rs. 25,000; Rs. 40,000; Rs. 40,000; and Rs. 50,000 respectively. Find out if the machine is acceptable by NPV and PI technique. The cost of capital is 12%.

Solution

A firm has a cost of capital of 12%

Initial Investment = 1,00,000

Year	Cash Inflows (Rs.)	PVF	PV (Rs.)
1	25,000	0.893	22,325
2	40,000	0.797	31,880
3	40,000	0.712	28,480
4	50,000	0.636	31,800
			ΣPV =1,14,485

$\therefore$ PI >1 Accept the proposal as $\dfrac{1,14,485}{1,00,000} = 1.145$ by PI method

NPV > 0, Accept the proposal cash inflows of Rs. 1,14,485 – Rs. 1,00,000 = Rs. 14,485

The proposal can be accepted by both NPV and PI method.

Illustration 7.8 A company is considering the following investment projects.

Project	Initial Investment		Cash Flow	
	C_0	C_1	C_2	C_3
A	10,00,000	+ 10,00,000	Nil	Nil
B	10,00,000	+ 7,50,000	+ 7,50,000	Nil
C	10,00,000	+ 2,00,000	+ 4,00,000	+ 12,00,000
D	10,00,000	+ 10,00,000	+ 3,00,000	+ 3,00,000

Rank the projects according to (*i*) payback, (*ii*) ARR and (*iii*) NPV assuming discount rates at 10% and 30%.

Solution

(*i*) Payback Method

Project A 10,00,000/10,00,000 = 1 year

Project B 10,00,000 / 7,50,000 = $1\frac{1}{3}$ years

Project C 2 years + $\dfrac{10,00,000 - 6,00,000}{12,00,000} = \dfrac{7}{3}$ = 2.33 years

Project D 1 year

(ii) ARR Method

$$\textbf{ARR} = \frac{\text{Average Profit}}{\text{Average Investment}}$$

Average Investment = NWC + Salvage Value + (½ Initial Cost – Salvage Value)

Project A $\frac{10,00,000}{3} = \frac{33,3333.332}{5,00,000} = .66 = 66.66\%$

Project B $\frac{15,00,000}{3} = \frac{5,00,000}{5,00,000} = 1 = 100\%$

Project C $\frac{18,00,000}{3} = \frac{6,00,000}{5,00,000} = 1.2 = 120\%$

Project D $\frac{7,00,000}{3} = \frac{2,33,333}{5,00,000} = 0.46 = 46.6\%$

(iii) (a) NPV Method at 10% discount

NPV

Project A at 10% – 10,00,000 + (10,00,000 × 0.909) = – 91000 **Reject**

Project B at 10% – 10,00,000 + (7,50,000 × .909 + 7,50,000 × .826) = +3,01,250 **Accept**

Project C at 10% – 10,00,000 + (2,00,000 × 0.909 + 4,00,000 × 0.826
+ 12,00,000 × 0.751) = (+ 4,13,400) **Accept**

Project D at 10% – 10,00,000 + (10,00,000 × 0.909 + 3,00,000 × 0.826 + 0.751)
= (+1,56,800.751) **Accept**

(b) NPV at 30% Discount

Reject Project A 30% – 10,00,000 + (10,00,000 × 0.769) = – 2,31,000 **Reject**

Project B 30% – 1 0,00,000 + (7,50,000 × 0.769 + 7,50,000 × 0.592) = + 20,750 **Accept**

Project C 30% – 10,00,000 + (2,00,000 × 0.769 + 4,00,000 × 0.592
+ 12,00,000 × 0.455) = – 63,400 **Reject**

Project D 30% – 10,00,000 + (10,00,000 × 0.769 + 3,00,000 × 0.592
+ 3,00,000 × 0.4555) = + 83,250 **Accept**

Project ranked as follows:

Project	PB	ARR	NPV at 10%	NPV at 30%
A	1	4	4	4
B	2	2	3	2
C	3	1	1	3
D	1	3	2	1

Illustration 7.9 Calculate IRR. A Project costs Rs. 36 lakh and generates Rs. 11,20,000 every year for 5 years.

Solution

$$\text{IRR} = I_L + \frac{(L - PB)}{(L - H)} \times (I_H - I_L)$$

Where, PB = Payback period

I_L = Lower rate of interest

I_H = Higher rate of interest

L = Discount factor lower rate

H = Discount factor at higher rate

The payback period is 3.214 for 5 years. Cut off rate 16.5%

According to Table A-4 discount factor closest to 3.214 for 5 years are 3.274 (16% rate of interest) and 3.199 (17%) rate of interest

$$\text{Payback Period is } \frac{36,00,000}{11,20,000} = 3.214$$

The actual value of IRR lies between 16% and 17%

i.e.,
$$\text{IRR} = 16 + \frac{(3.274 - 3.214)}{(3.274 - 3.199)}$$

$$= 16 + \frac{0.060}{0.075} = 16 + 0.8$$

$$= 16.8\%$$

Alternatively starting with higher rate of Payback

$$IRR = 17 - \frac{(3.214 - 3.199)}{(3.274 - 3.199)}$$

$$= 17 - \frac{0.015}{0.075} = 17 - 0.2 = 16.8\%$$

Illustration 7.10 A company wants to buy a machine so that it can produce 1,00,000 staplers. Advise whether machine A or B should be selected.

Particulars	Machine (A)	Machine (B)
Cost of the machine	Rs. 10,00,000	Rs. 15,00,000
Life of the machine	5 years	5 years
Salvage value	Rs. 20,000	Rs. 40,000

Depreciation is by straight-line method. They are mutually exclusive machines. If A is selected, B will not be selected and vice versa.

The staplers can be sold for Rs. 40 each but the cost of production is Rs. 10 in A and Rs. 8 in B. The company is in tax bracket of 50% and cost of capital is 12%.

Solution

Method 1

Calculate NPV of both machines and select the one with a higher net present value.

Machine A

Step 1: Cash outflows

Cost of machine Rs. 10,00,000

Step 2: Cash inflows

Earnings = (SP – Cost of production per unit) × Number of units sold

Earnings = (40 – 10) × 1,00,000 = 30 × 1,00,000 = Rs. 30,00,000

Depreciation = (Cost of machine – Salvage value)/Life of machine

Depreciation = (10,00,000 – 20,000)/5 = 980,000/5 = Rs. 1,96,000

Year 1–5	Amount (Rs.)
Earnings	30,00,000
– Depreciation	1,96,000
Earnings after depreciation	28,04,000
Tax @ 50%	14,02,000

[Contd...]

Year 1–5	Amount (Rs.)
Earnings after tax	14,02,000
Add back depreciation	1,96,000
CFAT	15,98,000
Discount factor @ 12%	= 3.605
Present Value (PV) of CFAT	57,60,790
Salvage value × Discount factor (20,000 × 0.567)	= 11,340
	57,72,130
Less: Cash Outflow	10,00,000
	47,72,130

Machine B

Step 1: Calculation of cash outflow

Cost of machine = Rs. 15,00,000

Step 2: Calculation of cash inflow.

Earnings = (SP per unit – Cost of Production) × No. of units

Earnings = (40 – 8) × 1,00,000 = 32 × 1,00,000

= Rs. 32,00,000

Depreciation = (Cost of machine – Salvage value)/Life of machine

Depreciation = (15,00,000 – 40,000)/5

= Rs. 2,92,000

Cash Inflows for 5 years	Amount (Rs.)
Earnings	32,00,000
Less depreciation	2,92,000
Earnings after depreciation	29,08,000
Tax @ 50%	14,54,000
Earnings after tax	14,54,000
Add back depreciation	2,92,000
Cash flow after taxes	17,46,000
Discount factor @ 12%	3.605
	62,94,330
Salvage value PV (40,000 × 0.567)	22,680
	63,17,010
Less: outflows	15,00,000
	48,17,010

Machine B should be preferred to machine A, as inflow is higher in machine B. The difference is Rs. 44,880.

Alternative Method

Instead of working out NPVs separately we can compare incremental costs and benefits of both the machines.

Step 1: Differential cost = Cash outflows of machine B – Cash outflow of machine A

= 15,00,000 – 10,00,000

= Rs. 5,00,000

Differential earnings = 32,00,000 – 30,00,000

= Rs. 2,00,000

Step 2: Cash inflows

Year 1–5	Amount (Rs.)
Earnings	2,00,000
– Depreciation	96,000
EAD	1,04,000
Tax @ 50%	52,000
EAT	52,222
Add back depreciation	96,000
CFAT	1,48,222

Step 3:

Particulars	Amount (Rs.)
CFAT	1,48,000
Discount factor @ 12%	3.605
NPV	5,33,540
Salvage Value	3,11,340
20,000 × 0.567	8,44,880
Less: Cash outflows	5,00,000
	3,44,880

Since NPV is positive the machine can be replaced.

Illustration 7.11 Find NPV if project A + B are evaluated. Which of these should be accepted?

An Equipment A costs Rs. 75,000 and brings a net cash flow of Rs. 20,000 per year for 6 years. A substitute equipment B would cost Rs. 50,000 and generate net cash flow of Rs. 15,000 per year for 6 years. The required rate of return of both the equipment is 11%. Calculate NPV which equipment should be accepted?

Solution

NPV Equipment A = (20,000 × 4.231) – 75,000

= 84,620 – 75,000 = Rs. 9,620 **Accept**.

NPV Equipment B = (14,000 × 4.231) – 50,000

= 59,234 – 50,000 = Rs. 9,234

If mutually exclusive, equipment 'A' should be chosen otherwise both A and B have positive NPV and are acceptable.

Illustration 7.12 A firm is formed to undertake an investment project. The project will cost Rs. 1,00,000 and will provide a revenue of Rs. 80,000 a year.

Cash expenses are Rs. 30,000 a year. Depreciation is by SL Method. Salvage Value is 0 after 4 years and tax rate is 50%. The company plans to finance the projects by 50% debt and 50% equity. Assume shareholders require 19% dividend and lenders expect 14%. The company will repay the debt after 4 years. Add WC required Rs. 30,000; depreciation = Rs. 25,000. Find cash flows.

Solution

Particulars	Amount (Rs.)
Revenue	80,000
Expenses	30,000
Depreciation	25,000
EBIT	25,000
Interest $\frac{14}{100} \times 50{,}000$	7,000
PBT	18,000
Tax	9,000
PAT	9,000
Add Back depreciation	25,000
Net Cash Flows	34,000
– Dividends $\frac{19\%}{100} \times 50{,}000$	9,500
	24,500

[Contd...]

Particulars	Amount (Rs.)
4th year	24,500
Debt	50,000
Add release of W.C	25,500 30,000
Net Cash in Flow	**55,500**

Illustration 7.13 A company is considering an investment proposal.

Particulars	Amount (Rs.)
Purchase Price of asset	80,00,000 (1) New
Installation costs	3,00,000 (2) New
Add working capital	3,00,000 (3) New
Scrap value after useful life of 4 years of new asset	9,00,000
Cash expenditure on new asset annual	10,00,000
Revenues annual	45,00,000
Current book value of (old asset)	5,00,000
Scrap value of old asset	6,00,000 (old asset)
Rev. from old asset annual	20,00,000
Cash Exp. of old asset	12,00,000
Book value at the end of 4 years	8,00,000
Planning period 4 years	
Depr. on new asset SLM	
Existing asset is depreciation At SLM method	
Tax rate existing 40%	

Solution

Particulars	Amount (Rs.)
Purchase Price	80,00,000 New (1)
+ Inst. Cost	3,00,000 New (2)
	83,00,000
+ Add working capital	3,00,000 New (3)
	86,00,000
– Scrap value of old asset	6,00,000 Old Asset
	80,00,000

[Contd...]

Particulars	Amount (Rs.)
+ Tax on gain on rate of old asset	40,000
40% Excess of book value	80,40,000
Sale value	6,00,000
Book value	5,00,000
Gain	1,00,000

Incremental Cash Flow:

Subsequent annual cash flows

New Machine	Year 1	Year 2	Year 3	Year 4
Annual Revenue	45,00,000	45,00,000	45,00,000	45,00,000
– Expenses	10,00,000	10,00,000	10,00,000	10,00,000
	35,00,000	35,00,000	35,00,000	35,00,000
Profit before Depreciation	20,75,000	20,75,000	20,75,000	20,75,000

PBT	14,25,000
Tax @ 40%	– 5,70,000
PAT	8,55,000

$$\frac{\text{Cost of machine + Installation cost}}{\text{No. of years}} = \frac{83,00,000}{4 \text{ years}}$$

Depreciation	20,75,000
	29,30,000
Annual cash flow	6,80,000
	22,50,000

Illustration 7.14 A company buys a machine for 55,00,000 and expects operating profits before depreciation at 20% WDV and tax at 50% per annum for the useful life of 4 years. The scrap value is expected to be Rs. 2,00,000. Cost of the asset is Rs. 55,00,000 and the company has only one asset.

Year	WDV (Rs.)	Depreciation (Rs.)
1	55,00,000	11,00,000
2	44,00,000	8,80,000
3	35,20,000	7,04,000
4	28,16,000	5,64,000

Solution

In this example, if Block is consisting of one asset only, the depreciation would be Rs. 11,00,000; Rs. 8,80,000; Rs. 7,00,000 and Nil for 1–4 years respectively. WRV in the beginning of 4th year will be Rs. 28,20,000 and capital loss will be (28,20,000 – 2,00,000) = Rs. 26,20,000

55,00,000	44,00,000	35,20,000
– 11,00,000	– 8,80,000	– 7,04,000
44,00,000	35,20,000	28,16,000

PBT (1)	WDV (2)	Depreciation (3)	4 (1 – 3)
27,50,000	55,00,000	11,00,000	16,50,000
27,50,000	44,00,000	8,80,000	18,70,000
27,50,000	35,20,000	7,04,000	20,46,000
27,50,000	28,16,000	5,63,200	21,86,800

Tax @ 50%	PAT	Add Back	Add Back Depreciation
8,25,000	8,25,000	11,00,000	19,25,000
9,35,000	9,35,000	8,00,000	18,15,000
10,23,000	10,23,000	7,04,000	17,27,000
10,93,400	10,93,400	5,63,200	16,57,000

Terminal Cash Flow

Scrap Value of the asset	Rs. 1,37,500
Sale Value	Rs. 2,00,000
WDV	Rs. 2,00,00,000
Net Cash inflow	= 28,16,000 – 5,63,200 = Rs. 22,52,800
	= Rs. 2,00,000 (loss)

Short-term capital loss

Opening Value of asset in the 4th year.

Loss	= 28,16,000 – 2,00,000
	= Rs. 26,16,000

Accounting Treatment

First find capital gain or capital loss when salvage value is more than WDV it is capital gain.

Taxation of Block of Assets

Building, machinery, Furniture.

(*a*) If there is only one asset compare it with WDV. Difference is treated as short-term capital gain or loss and is treated as ordinary income or loss.

(*b*) Block consisting of more than 1 asset. Then to the WDV add the cost of the new asset. Individual treatment cannot be made.

The entire block will have to be scrapped.

Sale proceeds of the asset (scrap value) are reduced from WDV of the block if the assets falls in a block.

Capital gain/loss will arise.

(*i*) When sale proceeds or scrap exceeds WDV of the whole block.

(*ii*) When entire block is sold.

(*iii*) When there are 100% depreciable assets.

(*iv*) Terminal loss is spread over a number if year up to 8 years.

If it is a block of assets

$$28{,}20{,}000 - 5{,}64{,}000 \ = \text{Rs. } 22{,}56{,}000$$

IRR is that discount rate which equates the present value of cash inflows with PV of cash outflows.

Financial BEP = Fixed Change + Preference/(1 – t)

ABC is considering purchase of a machine to replace existing machine of a book value of Rs. 24,000 and can be sold for Rs. 12,000. Salvage value of old machine in 4 years is 0 and depreciated on a straight-line basis. The proposed machine will perform the same function the old machine is performing. Improvement in technology will bring in Rs. 56,000 cash benefits (before depreciation and taxes) in material, labour and overhead. The new machine has a 4-year life costs Rs. 1,12,000 and can be sold for Rs. 16,000 at the end of the 4th year assuming straight-line depreciation and 40% tax rate. Compute cash flows.

Solution

Cash Outflow	Amount (Rs.)
Cost of new machine	1,12,000
Salvage value	12,000
	1,00,000
Tax saving on loss on sale 40%	4,800
	(24,000 – 12,000)
	95,200

Cash Inflows	Amount (Rs.)
Saving in Exp.	56,000
– Depreciation (Increase)	18,000
	(24,000 – 6,000)
	38,000
– Tax 40%	15,200
	22,800
Add back depreciation	18,000
Cash flow	40,800

From the sale of the new machine, there will be a terminal cash inflow of Rs. 16,000 at the end of 4th year.

Illustration 7.15 XYZ Ltd. is considering purchase of a machine in replacement of an old one. Two models viz, 'MOLIN' and 'SKODA' are offered at prices of Rs. 22.50 lakh and Rs. 30 lakhs respectively. Further particulars regarding these models are given below:

Particulars		Molin	Skoda
Economic life (years)		5	6
Scrap value at the end of the economic life		2	2.50
After tax annual cash inflows:	Year		
	1	5.00	6.00
	2	7.50	8.00
	3	10.00	10.00
	4	9.00	12.00
	5	8.50	10.50
	6	–	9.50

Present value factors at 12% per annum are as follows:

Year	1	2	3	4	5	6
P.V. factors (1)	0.893	0.797	0.712	0.636	0.567	0.507

Evaluate the two proposals under: (*a*) Payback period, and (*b*) Net present value method. Which model would you recommend and why? **(I.C.W.A. Inter June 2000)**

Solution

(*a*) Computation of Payback Period

Year	MOLIN (Rs. Lakh)		SKODA (Rs. Lakh)	
	Cash inflow	Cumulative Cash inflow	Cash inflow	Cumulative Cash inflow
1	5.00	5.00	6.00	6.00
2	7.50	12.50	8.00	14.00
3	10.00	22.50	10.00	24.00
			12.00	36.00
Payback Period		3 years		3 ½ years

(*b*) Computation of Net Present Value

End of Year	MOLIN			SKODA	
	Discount Factor	Cash inflow	Cumulative Cash inflow	Cash inflow	Cumulative Cash inflow
1	0.893	4.465	5.00	6.00	5.358
2	0.797	5.977	7.50	8.00	6.376
3	0.712	7.120	10.00	10.00	7.120
4	0.636	5.724	9.00	12.00	7.632
5	0.567	5.954	8.50 + 2.00	10.50	5.953
6	0.507	—	—	9.50 + 2.50	6.084
Total PV of Cash Inflow			29.240		38.523
Less: Initial Investment			22.500		30.000
Net Present Value			6.740		8.523

As net present value is more for 'SKODA', it should be preferred.

Illustration 7.16 The following is the information of two proposals. If A is selected then X will be rejected evaluate and rank the proposals by NPV and IRR techniques. The minimum required rate of return is 10%. The life of the projects is 3 years and the cash flows are as follows:

Year	Cash Flows for A (Rs.)	Cash Flows for X (Rs.)
0	–10,00,000	–20,00,000
1	5,00,000	10,00,000
2	6,00,000	15,00,000
3	4,00,000	10,00,000

Solution

(*i*) NPV technique at 10%

Particulars	Cash Flows for A (Rs.)	Cash Flows for X (Rs.)
Cash outflows	10,00,000	20,00,000
PV = 0.909 (Year 1)	4,54,500	9,09,000
= 0.826 (Year 2)	4,95,600	12,39,000
= 0.751 (Year 3)	3,00,400	7,51,000
	12,50,500	28,99,000
	–10,00,000	–20,00,000
	2,50,500	8,99,000

NPV indicates that machine X is better than machine A because its net benefits of Rs. 8,99,000 is better than Rs. 2,50,500.

(*ii*) IRR Technique

(*a*) **Step I:** Find out weighted average on cash inflows

Machine A:

Year	Cash Flows	Weight	CF × W
1	5,00,000	3	15,00,000
2	6,00,000	2	12,00,000
3	4,00,000	1	4,00,000
Total		6	31,00,000

$$\text{Weighted Average} = \frac{31,00,000}{6} = 516666.66$$

Note: Weights are taken in reverse order. Higher weight for year 1 as early cash inflow has greater value.

Machine X:

Year	Cash Flows	Weight	CF × W
1	10,00,000	3	30,00,000
2	15,00,000	2	30,00,000
3	10,00,000	1	10,00,000
Total		6	70,00,000

$$\text{Weighted Average} = \frac{70,00,000}{6} = 1166666.66$$

Step II: The weighted average should be considered as the annuity of cash inflows and payback period is thus found out.

$$\text{For the above it will be} = \frac{\text{Cost of the project}}{\text{Weighted average}}$$

$$\text{For Project A} = \frac{\text{Cost of the project}}{\text{Weighted average}} = \frac{10,00,000}{516666.66} = 1.93$$

$$\text{For Project X} = \frac{\text{Cost of the project}}{\text{Weighted average}} = \frac{20,00,000}{1166666.66} = 1.714$$

Step III: (*i*) Project A: Look at the value nearest to 1.93 for three years in PVAF table for the project. The closest to it 25% and 26%, it lies between 1.952 and 1.923.

(*ii*) Project X: It lies between 34% and 35%, between 1.719 and 1.696.

Project A

Year	Cash inflow	$PVF_{24\%}$	$PVF_{25\%}$	$PV_{24\%}$	$PV_{25\%}$
1	5,00,000	0.806	0.800	4,03,000	4,00,000
2	6,00,000	0.650	0.640	3,90,000	3,84,000
3	4,00,000	0.524	0.512	2,09,600	2,04,800
Total				10,02,600	9,88,800

By trial and error it was found that it does not lie between 25% and 26% but between 24% and 25%.

Project X

Year	Cash inflow	$PVF_{34\%}$	$PVF_{33\%}$	$PV_{34\%}$	$PV_{33\%}$
1	10,00,000	0.746	0.752	7,46,000	7,52,000
2	15,00,000	0.557	0.565	8,35,000	8,47,500
3	10,00,000	0.416	0.425	4,16,000	4,25,000
Total				19,97,500	20,24,500

By trial and error it was found that it does not lie between 35% and 34% but between 34% and 33%.

Step V:

Project A

$$\text{IRR} = \text{L} + \frac{\text{L} - \text{C}}{\text{L} - \text{H}} \times i$$

$$= 24\% + \frac{10,02,600 - 10,00,000}{10,02,600 - 9,88,800} \times 1$$

$$= 24\% + \frac{2,600}{13,800} \times 1 = 24.18\%$$

Project X

$$\text{IRR} = \text{L} + \frac{\text{L} - \text{C}}{\text{L} - \text{H}} \times i$$

$$= 33\% + \frac{20,24,500 - 20,00,000}{20,24,500 - 19,97,500} \times 1$$

$$= 33\% + \frac{24,500}{27,000} \times 1 = 33.90\%$$

Proposal X is better than A. Thus while evaluating through NPV and IRR in the case of NPV proposal X is good according to IRR also proposal X is better. In terms of maximization of shareholders wealth proposal X should be selected.

Illustration 7.17 A company is evaluating to proposals of machine A and machine B. Machine A gives a return of Rs. 5,00,000 every year for four years. It has a cost of 10 lakh. Machine B costs Rs. 12,00,000 and as a return of Rs. 4,00,000 every year for four years. Rank these proposal according to NPV and IRR. Minimum discount rate is 10%.

Solution

Proposal A : NPV

Year	Cash Flows (Rs.)	$PVF_{10\%}$	CF × PVF
0	– 10,00,000	—	– 10,00,000
1	5,00,000	0.909	4,54,500
2	5,00,000	0.826	4,13,000
3	5,00,000	0.751	3,75,500
4	5,00,000	0.683	3,41,500
			5,84,500

Proposal B : NPV

Year	Cash Flows (Rs.)	$PVF_{10\%}$	CF × PVF
0	–12,00,000	—	– 12,00,000
1	4,00,000	0.909	3,63,600
2	4,00,000	0.826	3,30,400
3	4,00,000	0.751	3,00,400
4	4,00,000	0.683	2,73,200
			67,600

Proposal A is better than Proposal B.

Step I:

(*ii*) IRR

Proposal A

The payback period is $= \dfrac{\text{Cost of the machine}}{\text{Annual cash inflow}} = \dfrac{10,00,000}{5,00,000} = 2$ years.

It lies between 34% and 35%.

$$I_L + \frac{L - PB}{L - H} \times (I_H - I_L)$$

$$= 34 + \frac{2.029 - 2}{2.029 - 1.997} \times 1 = 34 + \frac{0.029}{0.032} \times 1$$

$$= 34 + 0.90 = 34.90\%$$

Proposal B

$$\text{The payback period is} = \frac{\text{Cost of the machine}}{\text{Annual cash inflow}} = \frac{12,00,000}{4,00,000} = 3 \text{ years.}$$

$$I_L + \frac{L - PB}{L - H} \times (I_H - I_L)$$

$$= 12 + \frac{3.037 - 3}{3.037 - 2.974} \times 1$$

$$= 12 + \frac{0.037}{0.063} \times 1$$

$$= 12 + 0.58 = 12.58\%$$

It lies between 12% and 13%.

Select Project A.

Illustration 7.18 The following are two mutually exclusive proposals P and Q for 3 years. Proposal P cost is Rs. 10,00,000 and proposal Q cost is Rs. 30,00,000. The cash inflows are as follows: Proposal P gives Rs. 5,00,000 every year and proposal Q gives Rs. 20,00,000 every year. The discount rate is 10%.

NPV

Proposal P = 5,00,000 × $PVAF_{ni}$ = 5,00,000 × 2.487 = 12,43,500 – 10,00,000 = Rs. 2,43,500.

Proposal Q = 20,00,000 × $PVAF_{ni}$ = 20,00,000 × 2.487 = 49,74,000 – 30,00,000 = Rs. 19,74,000.

IRR

$$\textbf{Proposal P = Payback period} = \frac{10,00,000}{5,00,000} = 2$$

It lies between 34% and 35%.

$$I_L + \frac{L - PB}{L - H} \times (I_H - I_L)$$

$$= 34 + \frac{2.029 - 2}{2.029 - 1.997} \times 1$$

$$= 34 + \frac{0.029}{0.032} \times 1 = 34 + 0.90 = 34.90\%$$

$$\text{Proposal Q} = \text{Payback period} = \frac{30,00,000}{20,00,000} = 1.5$$

$$I_L + \frac{L - PB}{L - H} \times (I_H - I_L)$$

$$= 39 + \frac{1.609 - 1.5}{1.609 - 1.589} \times 1$$

$$= 39 + \frac{0.109}{0.02} \times 1 = 44.45\%$$

It lies between 39% and 40%.

Select Project Q.

PROBLEMS FOR PRACTICE

Problem 7.1 Chandra Ltd. purchased a special machine one year ago at a cost of Rs. 12,000. At that time the machine was estimated to have a useful life of 6 years and no salvage value. The annual cash operating cost is approximately Rs. 20,000. A new machine has just come to the market, which will do the same job, but with an annual cash operating cost of only Rs. 17,000. The new machine costs Rs. 21,000 and has an estimated life of 5 years with zero salvage value. The old machine can be sold for Rs. 10,000 to a scrap dealer. Straight-line depreciation is used and the company's income tax rate is 40%. Assume a cost of capital of 8%, compute the incremental cash flows after taxes.

[**Answer:** Cash outflows is Rs. 11,000 savings, cash operating costs is Rs. 3,000. Incremental cash in flow isRs. 2,680, and terminal inflow nil.]

Problem 7.2 A small part of a machine costs Rs. 25,000 and generates cash inflows of Rs. 9000, Rs. 8000, Rs. 7000, Rs. 6000, and Rs. 5000 in years 1 to 5. Opportunity cost of capital is at 10%.

[**Answer:** 224.9 accept the machine.]

Problem 7.3 On the basis of the following data calculate (*i*) ARR on projects A and B (*ii*) Payback period for A and B.

Depreciation is to be charged on straight-line basis. Life of the projects is 5 years. Cost of the projects is Rs. 56,125.

Cash flows after depreciation and taxes

Year	Project A (Rs.)	Project B (Rs.)
1	3,375	11,375
2	5,375	9,375
3	7,375	7,375
4	9,375	5,375
5	11,375	3,375

[**Answer:** (*i*) 26.28% Project A and 26.28% Project B

(*ii*) Payback period Project A = 3.307 years and Project B = 2.695 years]

Problem 7.4 A company has a machine whose book value is Rs. 240,000. The salvage value is Rs. 1,10,000. In the next 4 years salvage value will be zero. The company is planning to purchase a new machine for Rs. 11,20,000. The new machine will last for 4 years and have a salvage value of Rs. 4,50,000. The company has a tax rate of Rs. 5,60,000 every year. Both machines will be depreciated on straight-line method. Should the new machine be purchased if the cost of capital is 12%?

[**Answer:** NPV = Rs. 2,63,088; machine should be purchased as it is profitable.]

Problem 7.5 A company buys a machine for Rs. 55,00,000 and expects operating profits before depreciation at 20% written down value and tax at 50% per annum for the useful life of 4 years. The scrap value is expected to be Rs. 2,00,000. Cost of the asset is Rs. 55,00,000 and the company has only one asset. The cash inflows per annum is Rs. 27,50,000. Prepare cash flow analysis.

[**Answer:** Rs. 26,16,000]

Problem 7.6 ABC is considering purchase of a machine to replace existing machine of a book value of Rs. 24,000 and can be sold for Rs. 12,000. Salvage value of old machine in 4 years is 0 and depreciated on a straight-line basis. The proposed machine will perform the same function the old machine is performing. Improvement in technology will bring in Rs. 56,000 cash benefits (before depreciation and taxes) in material, labour and overhead. The new machine has for a 4-year life and costs 1,12,000, can be sold for Rs. 16,000 at the end of the 4th year. Assuming straight-line depreciation and 40% tax rate, compute cash flows.

[**Answer:** 56,800]

Problem 7.7 A company is considering a project whose cost price is Rs. 10,00,000. The firm has a required rate of return of 12%. The expected cash inflows for 6 years life are the following. Scrap value = 0.

Year	Cash inflows (Rs.)
1	20,00,000
2	20,00,000
3	20,00,000
4	10,00,000
5	10,00,000
6	10,00,000

Is the project valuable by IRR technique?

[**Answer:** 12.84%]

Problem 7.8 A company plans to purchase a machine of Rs. 12,00,000. The future cash inflows are expected to be Rs. 5,00,000; Rs. 4,00,000 and Rs. 6,00,000. (*i*) Calculate NPV and PI when minimum cost of capital is 10% and the life of the machine is 3 years. (*ii*) Would you still purchase the machine if the cost of capital is 12%?

Answers: (*i*) NPV @ 10% 35,500 positive PI = 1.029

(*ii*) NPV @ 12% 12% – 8600 negative PI = 0.992

Accept in 1, Reject in 2.

Problem 7.9 A machine costs Rs. 75,00,000. It generates cash flows Rs. 20,00,000 for each year for 6 years. Machine B costs Rs. 50,00,000 and generates Rs. 14,00,000. Required rate of return is 11%. Calculate IRR and NPV. Which one should be acceptable?

[**Answers:** Machine A NPV = Rs. 9,62,000, IRR = 15.34%.

Machine B NPV = Rs. 9,23,400; IRR = 17.192%.

Both the machines are acceptable but accept machine A because NPV is higher.]

Problem 7.10 ABC company is planning to evaluate proposals to take a replacement decision. There are two machines, which are mutually exclusive. If P is purchased, Q will be automatically excluded. The life of both the machines is 5 years. Calculate (*i*) Payback period (*ii*) Net Present Value and (*iii*) Profitability Index and then provide the decision. The following cash flows and details are given:

Year	Machine P (Rs.)	Machine Q (Rs.)
1	--	10,00,000
2	5,00,000	14,00,000
3	20,00,000	16,00,000
4	14,00,000	17,00,000
5	6,00,000	8,00,000

The cost of capital is 16% and machine P can be purchased for Rs. 25,00,000. Machine Q is priced at Rs. 4,00,000.

[**Answers:** (*i*) Payback period for P and Q machines = 3 years.(*ii*) Net present value (P) = Rs. 2,11,900 and (Q) = Rs. 2, 47,000 (*iii*) PI Index for P = 1.085 and Q = 1.062 (*iv*) Conflict between NPV and PI, select Q due to higher NPV).]

Problem 7.11 Analyse the following two proposals. Each of them has a lifespan of 4 years and cost of capital is 10%. The proposal is mutually exclusive. Which one will you select by NPV and IRR method? The initial investment of project K is Rs. 80,00,000 and L is Rs. 24,00,000. The cash inflows of the proposals are Rs. 28,00,000 per annum for proposal K, and Rs. 9,80,000 per annum for L.

[**Answers:** (*i*) NPV of K = Rs. 8,73,200 and NPV of L = Rs. 7,05,600 (*ii*) IRR of K = 15% and L = 23%.]

Select K due to high NPV.

Problem 7.12 Calculate Payback period, net present value, IRR and PI for Project A and Project B. Which would you, choose? k =12%

Year	A	B
0	20,00,000	30,00,000
1	4,00,000	4,00,000
2	4,00,000	4,00,000
3	4,00,000	4,00,000
4	4,00,000	4,00,000
5	4,00,000	4,00,000
6	4,00,000	3,00,000
7	4,00,000	3,00,000
8	4,00,000	2,00,000
9	4,00,000	2,00,000
10	4,00,000	2,00,000

[**Answers:** Project A, payback 5 years, NPV Rs. 2,60,000, PI = 1.13 Project B, payback 9 years, NPV – 10,52,900, PI = 0.649. Select A]

❑❑❑

8 Risk Analysis in Capital Budgeting

LEARNING OBJECTIVES

8.1 Introduction

8.2 Classification of Risks

8.3 Assumptions of risks in Capital Budgeting

- Techniques of Risk Analysis–Payback Period
- Risk Adjusted Discount Rate (RADR)
- Certainty Equivalent Approach (CE)
- Sensitivity Analysis
- Probability Distribution Approach
- Decision Tree Approach

8.1 INTRODUCTION

The last chapter discussed the methodology of capital budgeting and the application of financial management techniques associated with it. Since future estimates are exposed to different kinds of risk, forecasts cannot be made with certainty. Risk arises in investment evaluation because it is difficult to anticipate the future events with certainty. Cash flows depend on future events and these are likely to change. A project may be evaluated because it has a very high demand in the present. But this would be different if there are shifts in the future demand of a product due to economic and political changes or customers preferences.

Risk and profitability are closely associated. A profitable project may also be very risky. A financial manager has to manage a trade-off between risk and return. A number of techniques have been developed to handle risk in capital budgeting. These techniques consist of the conventional techniques such as:

(*i*) Payback technique

(*ii*) Risk adjusted discount rate

(*iii*) Certainty equivalent approach

(*iv*) Sensitivity analysis

Statistical techniques include:

(*i*) Probability distribution approach

(*ii*) Decision tree approach

8.2 CLASSIFICATION OF RISKS

The events that influence risk can be classified as broad spectrum risks (market risks), industry specific risks, unique risks of the individual company and international risks.

(*i*) **Broad Spectrum Risks:** These risks are the risks associated with the business activities within a country. They are affected by economic policies, government and monetary policies, fiscal policies and social changes. These kind of risk are called ***market risk.*** Risks in the market are due to demand and supply conditions, inflation, interest rate changes. These risks affect the cash inflows of a project. The changes in cash inflows will also bring about change in the profitability of a proposal.

(*ii*) **Industry Specific Risks:** An industry faces a risk, which can have common parameters for the entire industry. An example may be taken of the cement industry, which is particularly affected by the policies of the government regarding subsidies, pricing of the product and taxation. Similarly, an industry dealing with television manufacture may be faced with the problem of technology change.

(*iii*) **Unique Risks of the Individual Company:** A company may face the risk of competition from similar products, for example a hair colouring company may be faced with competitive colours from other companies by introducing new colours. The sales of one company will fall in favour of the other company. Another example may be of certain disputes between management and the staff. Such problems will only affect the specific company.

(*iv*) **International Risks:** Economic policies of different countries are related, business is global, trade takes place between different countries and networking contracts are made. Consequently there are exchange rate risks and also political and economic risks involved in contracts. Risks have to be diversified or reduced in such a manner that profitability continues to take place.

The different methods, useful in reducing the problem of risks, are discussed in the next section.

8.3 ASSUMPTIONS OF RISKS IN CAPITAL BUDGETING

Before discussing the techniques of risk analysis let us give the assumptions of capital budgeting risks:

(*i*) A firm is risk averse. A proposal will not be evaluated if risk can be detected or identified. Additional risk is acceptable only when the increase in positive returns is expected to be very high.

(*ii*) When two proposals are evaluated, the proposal with the lower risk will be preferred.

(*iii*) When two proposals of the same risk class have been identified, the proposal with the greater positive return will be preferred.

(*iv*) A firm does not have a shortage of funds and accepts all profitable projects and rejects non-profitable risky projects.

(*v*) The firm does not have the problem of capital rationing.

(*vi*) The net investment of a proposal can be evaluated with certainty.

(*vii*) The required rate of return indicates the risk and return of a proposal.

(*viii*) The required rate of return of a firm is predetermined.

Payback Period

The payback period is used mainly for finding out the time period when the investment is recovered by the firm. If the payback period is less than the standard expected payback period, the proposal is selected. The payback period as discussed earlier is a very simple method and is quite popular with business firms because they prefer short recovery periods of their investments. The payback period method provides an indication whether the projects have a short or long recovery period.

The payback period focuses on recovery of the investment. As a technique of risk analysis it is useful in assessing the risks of time nature, and it ignores the time value of money. For example if there are two projects with a 5-year payback and project A recovers its capital with even cash flows every year, it will be preferred to project B which recovers its capital in the last year. Project B will be considered more risky.

The payback method fails to measure a risk, which differs in degree in different kinds of projects. It also does not consider the cash flows after the payback period. The payback period method can be used after the risk has been identified by:

(*i*) Adjusting the discount rate

(*ii*) Using a risk less rate of discount

Risk Adjusted Discount Rate

This method has a simple approach. The amount of risk in the project is inbuilt in the discount rate to make the present value calculations. The discount rate would be high when the risk is high. For example, a 10% discount rate may be considered useful to calculate the cash inflows of a project. In order to incorporate risk the discount rate can be increased. If it is low risk it can be increased to 11%, and if it is high risk the discount rate can be increased to a higher rate. In the above case as the risk goes on increasing the discount rate could be 12% or 13% or even 15% if the risk is very high. The difference between a proposal, which is at a risk-less rate, and a risky one is called the 'risk premium' or the 'risk adjusted discount rate'.

The risk adjusted discount rate considers both time and risk factors. This risk can be measured by using statistical measures like standard deviation and coefficient of variation. It can also be used through the net present value method. The NPV formula is given as:

$$NPV = \sum_{t=1}^{n} \frac{CF_t}{(1+k)^t} - C_0$$

Where, CF = Expected cash flows

k = Adjusted discount rate

C_0 = Initial cash outflow

Evaluation of Risk Adjusted Discount Rate (RADR)

It has been derived from the NPV technique of capital budgeting. The rate of discount is higher than that of the NPV to make adjustments for the risk.

Merits of risk adjusted discount rate method are:

(*a*) It is a simple technique and is compatible with both NPV and IRR.

(*b*) It helps to find out the expected future profits, generated by a risky project.

Demerits of risk adjusted discount rate method are:

(*a*) The assumption of the RADR is that investors are risk averse. However people do assumed risks and are also willing to pay a premium to take risk. Thus incorporating risk is a subjective measure. One individual would consider a risk of 12% as appropriate, whereas another person would find that 14% is a better discount rate.

(*b*) The RADR does not adjust the future cash flows, which are also uncertain.

(*c*) The risk premium, which is added to the discount rate, has the limitation of the effect of compounding of risks. The financial management principles states that discounting is important for taking time value and not risk conditions.

(*d*) RADR is useful only when risk increases with time. If risk does not increase, the proposal cannot calculate correctly.

The **accept/reject** decision through the RADR technique can be used both in NPV and IRR calculations. If NPV is used, the cash inflows should be higher than the cash outflows, at the risk adjusted discount rate, to be accepted as a good capital budget proposal. In the case of IRR, the internal rate of return should exceed the risk adjusted rate of return.

The following example explains how the RADR method can be used in evaluating a proposal.

Example 8.1 The proposal has a cash outlay of Rs. 5,00,000. It is expected to generate cash flows of Rs. 2,50,000; Rs. 2,00,000; Rs. 1,00,000 and Rs. 1,00,000 respectively from year 1–year 4. It had a risk free discount rate of 8% and a lifetime of 4 years. However due to increase in risk, the risk adjusted discounted rate of 10% is applied. Find out if the proposal should be accepted.

Solution

Year	Cash inflows	PVF @ 10%	NPV
1	2,50,000	0.909	2,27,250
2	2,00,000	0.826	1,65,200
3	1,00,000	0.751	75,100
4	1,00,000	0.683	68,300
			ΣNPV = 5,35,850

Since NPV of cash inflows is higher than the cash outflows (Rs. 535,850 – Rs. 5,00,000).

The proposal at the higher risk rate of 10% will be acceptable.

Certainty Equivalent Approach (CE)

This approach is considered to be an alternate method to the RADR approach. It considers the adjustments of cash inflows and not the discount rate. This is based on the fact that the future returns are uncertain and there is a risk in receiving future cash inflows. The method of applying this technique is to identify the cash inflows and then to incorporate risk into it.

Example 8.2 A firm estimates an inflow of cash of Rs. 15,00,000 per annum, but this has a risk. The expectation is that the cash inflows of Rs. 10,00,000 will be certain. Find out the certainty equivalent (CE) coefficient.

Solution

The CE coefficient would be the relationship between risk-less and risky cash flows or risk-less cash flows/risky cash flows or Rs. 10,00,000/15,00,000 = 0.6 × (*i.e.*, Risky cash inflow) × Rs. 15,00,000 = Rs. 9,00,000 (Certainty cash flow)

The coefficient can assume a value between zero and one and can be used by both NPV and IRR techniques.

Merits of the CE approach are:

(*a*) It incorporates risks associated with cash inflows, which are uncertain.

(*b*) It is superior to the RADR because it does not compound the future risk.

Demerits of the CE technique are:

(*i*) It is a subjective approach because the risk expected from cash flows may vary and the correct discount rate is difficult to apply.

(*ii*) It does not use statistical method for adjusting risk.

We have discussed the risk adjusted methods in capital budgeting. There are certain statistical methods also which enable the firms to take decisions under risky conditions. Let us now give an introduction to statistical techniques, which are used to incorporate risk in capital budgeting decisions.

Sensitivity Analysis

This approach helps to take decisions of accepting or rejecting a project through the estimation of Net Present Value. If three situations are given when cash flow estimates are provided, the Net Present Value (NPV) will decide which of the projects should be selected. Sensitivity analysis are also evaluated in conditions of finding out about a project when there is a change in one of the variables by analysing after tax cash flows of combined forecast of the variables. The sensitivity analysis can be used through NPV or IRR.

Merits of sensitivity analysis are:

(*a*) It is a simple method and can be followed without any specific attention to train the personnel.

(*b*) Since NPV approach is used, it provides an objective judgment on the proposals under evaluation.

Demerits of sensitivity analysis are:

(*a*) The probabilities, which are assigned, are prepared in a subjective manner. Each individual provides his own estimate and the basis of assigning probabilities varies from person to person.

(*b*) It does not give clear results because it does not focus on the interrelationships between variables.

The steps for analysing sensitivity analysis are:

(*a*) Identify the variables, which have an influence on the NPV or IRR of a proposal.

(*b*) The mathematical relationship of the variables should be defined.

(*c*) An analysis of change in the variables is made through the NPV.

(*d*) On the basis of the results the proposal may be accepted or rejected.

The following example will indicate how sensitivity analysis is calculated.

Example 8.3 There are two proposals. The following details pertain to them. Which one should be selected?

Proposal	Cash Flows (Rs.)		
	Pessimistic	Likely	Optimistic
1	8,00,000	10,00,000	16,00,000
2	2,00,000	10,00,000	20,00,000

The cost of capital is 14% and cash flow annuity estimates are of 10 years. The cost of the proposals is Rs. 50,00,000 lakh. Calculate NPV.

Solution

Proposal 1

Situation	CFAT	Annuity @ 14%	PV	Cost	NPV
Pessimistic	8,00,000	5.216	41,72,800	50,00,000	–8,27,200
Likely	10,00,000	5.216	52,16,000	50,00,000	2,16,000
Optimistic	16,00,000	5.216	83,45,600	50,00,000	33,45,600

Proposal 2

Situation	CFAT	Annuity @ 14%	PV	Cost	NPV
Pessimistic	2,00,000	5.216	10,42,200	50,00,000	–39,57,800
Likely	10,00,000	5.216	52,16,000	50,00,000	2,16,000
Optimistic	20,00,000	5.216	1,04,32,000	50,00,000	54,32,000

Proposal 2 is riskier than Proposal 1 because it has a higher negative value in pessimistic situation. Choose Proposal 1 as per sensitivity analysis.

Probability Distribution Approach

Capital budgeting decisions are made by forecasting future cash flows. There are uncertainties in assigning these cash flows. Where cash flows are independent in nature and the cash flows receipt in the current year do not have any relationship with the next year, probabilities can be assigned to the cash flows. Probability is a measure, which is related to the likelihood of the occurrence of an event. If a probability certainly occur it is said that there is the probability of one, but when it is not certain the probability of occurring of the event is zero. Thus probabilities lie between 0 and 1. A probability distribution consists of many estimates but usually firms/companies have three or four estimates. For example, a probability distribution can be classified as—optimistic, likely and pessimistic. Similarly it can be classified into high risk, medium risk and low risk. The annual cash flow from a project can be classified into Rs. 3,50,000 as optimistic; Rs. 2,00,000 as likely and Rs. 1,00,000 as pessimistic estimate of future cash flow. To these estimates probability of the occurrences will be assigned to make it more accurate. In the Example 8.1, Rs. 2,00,000 which is believed to be most likely could be assigned as probability of 60% and 20% each to optimistic and pessimistic. The cash flows described above can be shown in the Example 8.3.

Table 8.3 Depicting Situation Cash Flows and Probabilities

Situation	Cash flows (Rs.)	Probability
Optimistic	3,50,000	0.20
Likely	2,00,000	0.60
Pessimistic	1,00,000	0.20

After assigning probabilities the expected net present value will be calculated. The net present value is found out by multiplying the monetary values of the cash flows with their probability. The total of the net present value is calculated with the formula:

$$\text{NPV} = \sum_{t=1}^{n} \frac{\text{CF}_t}{(1+k)^t} - \text{C}_0$$

Risk is incorporated in capital budgeting decisions through the calculation of the sum of the net present values. With the net present value technique, the **standard deviation** is combined to measure the dispersion or difference in the possible cash flows, which are estimated. When two proposals are compared, standard deviation will indicate which one of the projects is more risky in absolute terms. This sometimes creates a problem in choice of a project because a project may be profitable but it may also be more risky. In such a case, **coefficient of variation** is used as it is a relative measure of risk.

$$\sigma_{(\text{NPV})} = \sqrt{\sum_{t=1}^{n} \frac{\sigma_t^{\,2}}{(1+i)^{2t}}}$$

Calculation of Standard deviation or about NPV

$$\sigma_{(\text{NPV})} = \sqrt{\frac{(\sigma_1)^2}{(1+i)^2} + \frac{(\sigma_2)^2}{(1+i)^4} + \frac{(\sigma_3)^2}{(1+i)^6}}$$

Calculation of Probability of the NPV being zero or less

$$\text{Normal Variety (Z)} = \frac{\text{X} - \overline{\text{X}}}{\sigma}$$

This can be depicted through an example (Example 8.4).

Example 8.4 A project has a cash outlay of Rs. 6,00,000. It is expected to generate the following cash flows with probabilities in next 3 years.

Period 1		Period 2		Period 3	
CFAT	**Probability**	**CFAT**	**Probability**	**CFAT**	**Probability**
3,50,000	0.1	3,00,000	0.3	3,00,000	0.2
2,00,000	0.2	2,75,000	0.2	2,00,000	0.2
4,00,000	0.3	3,50,000	0.2	3,00,000	0.3
3,00,000	0.4	3,00,000	0.3	2,00,000	0.3

Firm's cost of capital is 10%. Risk free rate is 5%. Determine the expected value of NPV and standard deviation about the expected value.

Solution

Step 1: Determination of Expected NPV

Period 1			Period 2			Period 3		
CFAT	**Probability**	**Cash Flow**	**CFAT**	**Probability**	**Cash Flow**	**CFAT**	**Probability**	**Cash Flow**
3,50,000	0.1	35,000	3,00,000	0.3	90,000	3,00,000	0.2	60,000
2,00,000	0.2	40,000	2,75,000	0.2	55,000	2,00,000	0.2	40,000
4,00,000	0.3	1,20,000	3,50,000	0.2	70,000	3,00,000	0.3	90,000
3,00,000	0.4	1,20,000	3,00,000	0.3	90,000	2,00,000	0.3	60,000
	Mean CF 1	**3,15,000**		**Mean CF**	**23,05,000**		**Mean CF**	**32,50,000**

Step 2: Determination of expected NPV of period 1, 2, 3

Mean CF	**PVF @ 5%**	**PV**
3,15,000	0.952	2,99,880
3,05,000	0.907	2,76,635
2,50,000	0.864	2,16,000
		ΣPV = 7,92,515
Less: cash outflows		6,00,000
Expected NPV		1,92,515

Step 3: Determination of standard deviation

Period 1

Mean CF			**3,15,000**
$CF_N - CF_1$	**$(CF_N - CF_1)^2$**	**Probability**	**$(CF_N - CF_1)^2 \times$ Probability**
35,000	1,22,50,00,000	0.1	12,25,00,000
−1,15,000	13,22,50,00,000	0.2	2,64,50,00,000
85,000	7,22,50,00,000	0.3	2,16,75,00,000
−15,000	22,50,00,000	0.4	9,00,00,000
			5,02,50,00,000

Standard deviation $\sigma = \sqrt{5,02,50,00,000} = 70,887.2$

Period 2:

Mean CF			**3,05,000**
$CF_N - CF_1$	**$(CF_N - CF_1)^2$**	**Probability**	**$(CF_N - CF_1)^2 \times$ Probability**
−5,000	2,50,00,000	0.3	75,00,000
−30,000	90,00,00,000	0.2	18,00,00,000
45,000	2,02,50,00,000	0.2	40,50,00,000
−5,000	2,50,00,000	0.3	75,00,000
			60,00,00,000

Standard deviation $\sigma = \sqrt{60,00,00,000} = 24,494,89$

Period 3:

Mean CF			**3,50,000**
$CF_N - CF_1$	**$(CF_N - CF_1)^2$**	**Probability**	**$(CF_N - CF_1)^2 \times$ Probability**
50,000	2,500,000,000	0.2	50,00,00,000
−50,000	2,500,000,000	0.2	50,00,00,000
50,000	2,500,000,000	0.3	75,00,00,000
−50,000	2,500,000,000	0.3	75,00,00,000
			2,50,00,00,000

Standard Deviation $\sigma = \sqrt{2,50,00,00,000} = 50,000$

Step 4: Determination of standard deviation of the probability distribution of NPV

$$\sigma_{(NPV)} = \sqrt{\sum_{t=1}^{n} \frac{\sigma_t^2}{(1+i)^{2t}}}$$

$$\sigma_{(NPV)} = \sqrt{\frac{(\sigma_1)^2}{(1+i)^2} + \frac{(\sigma_2)^2}{(1+i)^4} + \frac{(\sigma_3)^2}{(1+i)^6}}$$

$$\sigma_{(NPV)} = \sqrt{\frac{(7088.72)^2}{(1.10)} + \frac{(24494.89)^2}{(1.216)} + \frac{(50,000)^2}{(1.34)}}$$

$$= \sqrt{45681773.85 + 493420753.38 + 1865671641.79}$$

$$= \sqrt{2404774169.02}$$

$$= 49038.5$$

Step 5: Calculation of probability of NPV being zero or less

$$\text{Normal Variate (Z)} = \frac{X - \overline{X}}{\sigma}(Z)$$

$$Z = (0 - 1,92,515 \text{ from Step 2})/49038.39 = -3.925$$

Now use Table A-5 (Appendix) for Z values.

– 3.925 is under the required area of 0.5000 therefore probability of being less than zero is 50%.

Decision Tree Approach

In the previous technique, we have discussed the probability distribution approach. In that technique, evaluation was useful, when cash flows from one year to the next were independent of each other. ***The decision tree approach*** is useful when the cash flows of the project are dependent in nature. In this method, cash flows are assigned probabilities. Every future possibility in terms of cash flow is evaluated after giving them weights in probability terms. It takes the impact of all potential cash flows. Decision tree approach evaluates risky investments. It can also evaluate a sequential part to take decisions. It is a representation of cash flows like a picture. It is called a decision tree because it has a structure, which looks like a tree with branches.

The methodology of preparing a decision tree can be explained with an example (Example 8.5).

Example 8.5 A company is considering a new machine. The net cash flows have been estimated as follows:

Year 1 (CFAT)	Probability	Year 2 (CFAT)	Probability
1,00,000	0.4	80,000	0.5
1,20,000	0.6	1,20,000	0.5
		1,60,000	0.4

The cost of the machine is Rs. 2,00,000 with an estimated life of 2 years and the cost of capital of the firm is 12%. Use the decision tree approach to recommend whether the equipment should be purchased or not?

Solution

The decision tree is presented in the following manner:

Year 0	Year 1 0.5	Year 2	NPV (Rs.)	Joint Probability	Expected NPV (Rs.)
0.4	0.5 1,00,000	80,000	–46,940	0.20	–9,390
–2,00,000	0.4	1,20,000	–15,060	0.20	–3,010
0.6	0.6 1,20,000	1,60,000	34,680	0.24	8,320
		2,00,000	66,560	0.36	23,960
				1.00	19,880

The decision tree has depicted the timing of the cash flow, the CFAT outcome every year and the probability associated with the outcome. This decision tree makes the management aware when NPV is positive and when it is negative. The expected NPV is calculated through the following formula:

$$\overline{NPV} = \sum_{j=1}^{m} P_j NPV_j$$

Where, P_j = Probability of the jth

And , NPV_j = NPV of the jth path

The decision tree thus states that the proposal should be accepted when NPV is positive and rejected when it is negative.

POINTS TO REMEMBER

- There are different methods for evaluating risk and capital decisions. These are discounted payback method, RADR method, CE method, sensitivity analysis, probability distribution and decision tree.
- Risk is the variability of return of a project. If it is not evaluated or estimated, the estimation of future cash flows will not give the soundness of the project.
- In the RADR approach adjusting the discount rate incorporates risk. The risky projects have a higher discount rate than the projects with lower risk.
- The CE approach shows the relationship between risky and risk-less cash flows.
- The discounted cash flow method provides discount rate to the payback period.
- The probability distribution approach is able to analyse risk through probabilities. The computation of standard deviation of expected cash flow is prepared; probabilities of the different values of NPV are based on Z values given in Table A-5 in the Appendix.
- The decision tree approach estimates potential outcomes. It also takes into account the impact of probable estimates.

OBJECTIVE TYPE QUESTIONS

State whether the following statements are true (T) or false (F).

1. Probability distribution approach is used when cash flows are dependent in nature.
2. Decision tree can be used when cash flows are independent and dependent in nature.
3. Certainty equivalent approach overcomes the limitations of the risk adjusted discount rate approach.
4. Sensitivity analysis is very objective as the probabilities are assigned objectively.
5. Risk adjusted approach incorporates risk by increasing the discount rate on the basis of the expected risk.
6. Decision tree has the structure of a tree with branches.

Answers: 1.(F), 2.(F), 3.(T), 4.(F), 5.(T), 6.(T)

THEORETICAL QUESTIONS

1. Discuss the advantages of risk adjusted discount rate. What is the problem in using this approach?
2. 'Certainty equivalent approach is theoretically superior to the risk adjusted discount rate'. Do you agree? Give reasons.
3. What are the limitations of the payback method to handle risk?

4. What is Decision Tree? How is it different from the Probability Distribution Method?
5. How is risk handled by using the Probability Distribution Method? What are the merits and limitations of this method?
6. Write notes on: (*i*) Certainty Equivalent method (*ii*) Probability Distribution method (*iii*) Sensitivity Analysis (*iv*) Decision Tree.

ILLUSTRATIVE PROBLEMS

Illustration 8.1 The following two proposals are being evaluated. Suggest their viability? Which one of them should be accepted? The firm's cost of capital is 12% and risk free rate is 6%.

Year	Proposal Y	CE	Proposal Z	CE
0	2,50,000	1	2,50,000	1
1	1,50,000	0.8	1,00,000	0.9
2	1,50,000	0.7	1,50,000	0.8
3	1,50,000	0.6	2,00,000	0.7

Solution

Proposal Y

Year	CFAT	CE	Adjusted CFAT	PVF @ 6%	PV–Cost
0	2,50,000	1	2,50,000	1	
1	1,50,000	0.8	1,20,000	0.943	1,13,160
2	1,50,000	0.7	1,05,000	0.890	93,450
3	1,50,000	0.6	90,000	0.840	75,600
				NPV =	2,82,210
				2,82,210 – 2,50,000 =	32,210

Proposal Z

Year	CFAT	CE	Adjusted CFAT	PVF @ 6%	PV–Cost
0	2,50,000	1	2,50,000	1	
1	1,00,000	0.9	90,000	0.943	84,870
2	1,50,000	0.8	1,20,000	0.890	1,06,800
3	2,00,000	0.7	1,40,000	0.840	1,17,600
				NPV =	3,09,270
				3,09,270 – 2,50,000 =	59,270

Proposal Z should be accepted.

Illustration 8.2 Which of the following two proposals is more risky? Calculate and give your opinion using sensitivity analysis for selecting one of the proposals.

	Machine X	Machine Y
Cost	50,00,000	50,00,000
Pessimist	8,00,000	1,00,000
Most likely	10,00,000	5,00,000
Optimistic	12,00,000	25,00,000

Cash flows annuity is to be estimated for 10 years and the cost of capital is 14%.

Solution

Machine X

	CFAT	Annuity	PVAF of CFAT	NPVPV – Cost
Pessimist	8,00,000	5.216	41,72,800	–8,27,200
Most likely	10,00,000	5.216	52,16,000	+2,16,000
Optimistic	12,00,000	5.216	62,59,200	+12,59,200

Machine Y

	CFAT	Annuity	PVAF of CFAT	NPVPV – Cost
Pessimist	1,00,000	5.216	5,21,600	–44,78,400
Most likely	5,00,000	5.216	26,08,000	–23,92,000
Optimistic	25,00,000	5.216	130,40,000	+80,40,000

Both machine X and Y can be accepted but machine Y is more risky than machine X and in mutually exclusive conditions proposal X should be accepted. In the pessimist condition machine Y is negative. It is also negative in most likely conditions and only in optimistic conditions they machine Y shows a high positive return. Therefore if the person undertaking the business can take high risk, he can think of project Y. Project X is also negative during the pessimistic time but in most likely an optimistic conditions it is positive. On the whole both projects should be improved during pessimistic conditions.

Illustration 8.3 A company is planning to purchase a machine which has the following cash flows:

Year 1 (CFAT)	Probability	Year 2 (CFAT)	Probability
9,00,000	0.5	9,00,000	0.5
9,00,000	0.5	15,00,000	0.5
13,00,000	0.5	18,00,000	0.6
13,00,000	0.5	15,00,000	0.4

The machine costs Rs. 12,00,000 with an estimated life of 2 years. The cost of capital of the firm is 12%. Make your recommendation through the decision tree method.

Solution

Step1:

Year 1 (CFAT)	PVF @ 12%	Col 1 × Col 2	Year 2 (CFAT)	PVF @ 12%	Col 4 × Col 5	Col 3 × Col 6
9,00,000	0.893	8,03,700	9,00,000	0.797	7,17,300	15,21,000
9,00,000	0.893	8,03,700	15,00,000	0.797	11,95,500	19,99,200
13,00,000	0.893	11,60,900	18,00,000	0.797	14,34,600	25,95,500
13,00,000	0.893	11,60,900	15,00,000	0.797	11,95,500	23,56,400

Step 2:

PV	Probability Year 1	Probability Year 2	Joint Probability	PV × Joint Probability
15,21,000	0.5	0.5	0.25	3,80,250
19,99,200	0.5	0.5	0.25	4,99,800
25,95,500	0.5	0.6	0.30	7,78,650
23,56,400	0.5	0.4	0.20	4,71,280
			PV =	21,29,980
			–Cash outflow	12,00,000
			NPV	9,29,980

The project is positive and viable according to decision tree method. It can be accepted.

Illustration 8.4 Which of the following products would you select? The following information regarding the products with the probability distributions is given.

Units Sold	Product 1	Product 2
50	0.1	0.2
75,000	0.2	0.3
1,00,000	0.3	0.2
1,25,000	0.3	0.1
1,50,000	0.1	0.1
2,25,000	0	0.1

(ICWA Final, Dec 1989)

Solution

Expected Sale of the Products

Product 1			Product 2		
Units	**Probability**	**Total (Rs.)**	**Units**	**Probability**	**Total (Rs.)**
50,000	0.1	5,000	50,000	0.2	10,000
75,000	0.2	15,000	75,000	0.3	22,500
1,00,000	0.3	30,000	1,00,000	0.2	20,000
1,25,000	0.3	37,500	1,25,000	0.1	12,500
1,50,000	0.1	15,000	1,50,000	0.1	15,000
2,25,000	0	---	2,25,000	0.1	22,500
		1,02,500			1,02,500

Analysis: Both the products have the same expected sales of Rs. 1,02,500 and same break-even points at 1,00,000 units. It has an expected profit of Rs. 10,000 in product 1. Product 2 appears to be of a greater risk, since the probability of sales is 0.2 in product 2 compare to product 1 which is 0.3. In case of 1,00,000 units. Product 2 is likely to have less sales compared to product 1. Product 2 has a greater variation in sales so the likelihood of loss in sales is higher in product 2. Accept product 1 and not product 2.

Illustration 8.5 A company is considering two projects, Project P and Q. As a financial manager which of the projects would you recommend on the basis of coefficient of variation? The following information is provided.

Particulars	Project P	Project Q
Expected NPV	6,60,000	5,50,000
Standard deviation	4,00,000	2,20,000

Solution

On the basis of standard deviation proposal Q has a lower standard deviation compared to proposal P. For P it is 4,00,000 and for Q it is 2,20,000. Therefore Q should be accepted. Now let us evaluate the proposals according to coefficient of variation.

Project P, CV = σ/Expected NPV = 4,00,000/6,60,000 = 0.606

Project Q, CV = σ/Expected NPV = 5,50,000/2,20,000 = 2.5

Analysis proposal P has a coefficient of variation of 0.606 and for project Q is 2.5. Select Project P as it has lower risk.

Illustration 8.6 A company has determined the following probabilities for net cash flow generated by a project.

Year 1	Year 1	Year 2	Year 2	Year 3	Year 3
Cash flow	**Probability**	**Cash flow**	**Probability**	**Cash flow**	**Probability**
2,000	0.10	2,000	0.20	2,000	0.30
4,000	0.20	4,000	0.30	4,000	0.40
6,000	0.30	6,000	0.40	6,000	0.20
8,000	0.40	8,000	0.10	8,000	0.10

Calculate the expected net cash flows also calculate the present value of the expected cash flows at 12% discount rate.

Solution

Year 1			Year 2			Year 3		
Cash flow	**Proba-bility**	**Expected Value**	**Cash flow**	**Proba-bility**	**Expected Value**	**Cash flow**	**Proba-bility**	**Expected Value**
2,000	0.1	200	2,000	0.2	400	2,000	0.3	600
4,000	0.2	800	4,000	0.3	1200	4,000	0.4	1600
6,000	0.3	1800	6,000	0.4	2400	6,000	0.2	1200
8,000	0.4	3200	8,000	0.1	800	8,000	0.1	800
		6000			**4800**			**4200**

Present value of the expected value of cash flow at 12% discount rate is as follows:

$$\text{Present value} = 6{,}000 \times 0.893 + 4{,}800 \times 0.797 + 4{,}200 \times 0.712 = 5538 + 3825.6 + 2990.4$$

$$= \text{Rs. } 12{,}354$$

Illustration 8.7 A company is considering projects X and Z with the following information:

Particulars	Project X	Project Z
Expected NPV	5,00,000	8,00,000
Standard Deviation	30,000	40,000

Which project will you recommend? If you use coefficient of variation as a measure of risk, what will be your answer?

Solution

Project Z has a higher standard deviation therefore it is more risky than Project X. On the basis of standard deviation Project X will be accepted.

Coefficient of variation of Project X and Project Z are as follows:

$$\text{For Project X, CV} = \frac{30{,}000}{5{,}00{,}000} = 0.06$$

$$\text{For Project Z, CV} = \frac{40{,}000}{8{,}00{,}000} = 0.05$$

Project Z is better than Project X because it has a higher NPV and lower coefficient of variation. Therefore Project Z should be selected.

Illustration 8.8 A company is considering two mutually exclusive projects. The company uses a certainty equivalent approach. The estimated cash flow and certainty equivalent for each project is follows:

Year	Project 1 Cash Flow	Project 1 Certainty Equiv.	Project 2 Cash Flow	Project 2 Certainty Equiv.
0	–1,00,000	1.00	–2,00,000	1.00
1	50,000	0.90	80,000	0.90
2	50,000	0.85	60,000	0.80
3	30,000	0.80	40,000	0.70
4	30,000	0.75	30,000	0.60

Which project should be accepted if the risk free discount rate is 5%?

Solution

Project 1

$$= \text{NPV} = 1.00\ (-1{,}00{,}000) + \frac{0.90\ (50{,}000)}{1.05} + \frac{0.85\ (50{,}000)}{(1.05)^2} + \frac{0.80\ (30{,}000)}{(1.05)^3} + \frac{0.75\ (30{,}000)}{(1.05)^4}$$

$$= \ -1{,}00{,}000 + 42857.14 + 38548.75 + 20732.10 + 18510.80 = 20648.79$$

Project 2

$$= \text{NPV} = 1.00\ (-2{,}00{,}000) + \frac{0.90\ (80{,}000)}{1.05} + \frac{0.80\ (60{,}000)}{(1.05)^2} + \frac{0.70\ (40{,}000)}{(1.05)^3} + \frac{0.60\ (30{,}000)}{(1.05)^4}$$

$$= -2{,}00{,}000 + 68{,}571.42 + 43{,}537.41 + 24{,}187.45 + 14{,}808.64 = -\ 48{,}895.07$$

Project 1 should be accepted as it has a positive NPV.

Illustration 8.9 A company is considering to mutually exclusive Project X and Project Z. The initial cost of both projects is Rs. 10,00,000 each and both have life of 4 years. The three possible economic states of the economy are good normal and bad. Their annual cash flows and associate probabilities are as follows:

Economic State	Probability	Project X Cash Flow (CF) (Rs. in lakh)	Project Z Cash Flow (CF) (Rs. in lakh)
Good	0.3	12	11
Normal	0.4	8	8
Bad	0.3	4	5

If the discount rate is 10%, which project should the company accept?

Solution

Project X

Economic State	Prob.	CF	CF × Prob.	Deviation	Prob. x (Deviation)^2
Good	0.3	12	3.6	$(12 - 8)^2 = 16$	$16 \times 0.3 = 4.8$
Normal	0.4	8	3.2	$(8 - 8)^2 = 0$	$0 \times 0.4 = 0$
Bad	0.3	4	1.2	$(4 - 8)^2 = 16$	$16 \times 0.3 = 4.8$
			8.0		9.6

$$\sigma = \sqrt{9.6} = 3.09$$

$$\text{ENPV} = -10 + (8 \times \text{PVAF}_{0.10,5}) = -10 + (8 \times 3.791) = 20.32$$

Project Z

Economic State	Prob.	CF	CF × Prob.	Deviaton	Prob. x (Deviation)^2
Good	0.3	11	3.3	$(11 - 8)^2 = 9$	$9 \times 0.3 = 2.7$
Normal	0.4	8	3.2	$(8 - 8)^2 = 0$	$0 \times 0.4 = 0$
Bad	0.3	5	1.5	$(5 - 8)^2 = 9$	$9 \times 0.5 = 4.5$
		24	8.0		7.2

$$\sigma = \sqrt{7.2} = 2.68$$

$$\text{Mean} = \frac{24}{3} = 8$$

$$\text{ENPV} = -10 + (8 \times \text{PVAF}_{0.10,5}) = -10 + (8 \times 3.791) = 20.32$$

The expected net present value of both projects X and Z are Rs. 20.32 lakh but their standard deviations are different. Since the standard deviation is lower in project Z. Therefore, Project Z should be selected as risk is lower in this case.

Illustration 8.10 A company is considering new machine. The expected life of the machine of 2 years. The net cash flows of the machine have been estimated as follows:

	Year 1 (Rs. in lakh)	Probability	Year 2 (Rs. in lakh)	Probability
Net Cash Flow	15	0.4	12	0.5
			16	0.5
Net Cash Flow	16	0.6	18	0.4
			20	0.6

The cost of the machine is Rs. 20,00,000 and the company's cost of capital is 12%. Show whether the decision tree should the machine be purchased or not?

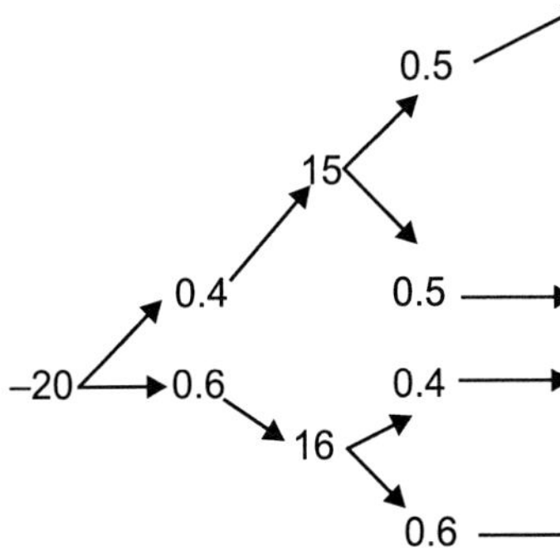

(i)	(ii)	(iii)	(iv)	(v)	(vi)
0	1	2	NPV	Joint Probability	Expected NPV
		12	2.959	0.20	0.5918
		16	6.147	0.20	1.2294
		18	8.634	0.24	2.07216
		20	10.228	0.36	3.6820
				1.00	7.57544

NPV of each path in the decision tree is calculated by discounting net cash flow at 12% discount rate.

$$-20 + (15 \times 0.893) + (12 \times 0.797) = 2.959$$

$$-20 + (15 \times 0.893) + (16 \times 0.797) = 6.147$$

$$-20 + (16 \times 0.893) + (18 \times 0.797) = 8.634$$

$$-20 + (16 \times 0.893) + (20 \times 0.797) = 10.228$$

PROBLEMS FOR PRACTICE

Problem 8.1 The following proposals are being evaluated. The firm's cost of capital is 12% and risk free rate is 7%. Advise using certainty equivalent approach whether proposal P is better or Q. Further information about the two proposals is as follows:

Year	Proposal P		Proposal Q	
	CFAT	CE	CFAT	CE
0	2,50,000	1	3,50,000	1
1	2,00,000	0.7	1,00,000	0.9
2	1,50,000	0.6	1,60,000	0.8
3	1,50,000	0.5	2,00,000	0.4

[**Answer:** Select proposal P (Q is negative)]

Problem 8.2 Which of the two proposals is more risky? Which of the two is more acceptable? Evaluate the proposals.

	Machine D	Machine E
Cost	2,50,000	2,50,000
Cash flow	Estimates annuity for 10 years	
Pessimist	0	50,000
Most likely	80,000	60,000
Optimistic	1,60,000	1,00,000

[**Answer:** Machine D is riskier as in pessimistic conditions the answer is showing negative NPV. Machine E has positive NPV in all three conditions. Select machine E.]

Problem 8.3 The following table presents the proposed cash flows for proposals M and N with their probabilities. Which of the two should be preferred?

Possibilities	Proposal M		Proposal N	
	Cash flow	Probability	Probability	Cash flow
1	7,000	0.10	12,000	0.10
2	8,000	0.20	8,000	0.10
3	9,000	0.30	6,000	0.10
4	10,000	0.20	4,000	0.20
5	11,000	0.20	2,000	0.50

(ICWA Final, Dec. 2001)

[**Answer:** The expected monetary value of proposal M is higher than proposal N. Prefer proposal M.]

Problem 8.4 PQR Ltd. is considering introduction of a new product. The anticipated demand probability of demand and profits for each product are given below. Which of the products would you choose 'X' or 'Y'?

Product X			Product Y		
Product Demand (Units)	Prob. of Demand (%)	Profit (%)	Product Demand (Units)	Prob. of Demand (%)	Profit (Rs.)
50,000	20	–8,000	30,000	15	–12,000
60,000	10	–5,000	40,000	15	–10,000
70,000	30	11,000	50,000	40	+14,000
80,000	20	14,000	60,000	20	+16,000
90,000	20	17,000	70,000	10	+18,000
	100			100	

ICWA June 1988

[**Answer:** Product X = 7,400 and Product Y = 7,300. Product X will be selected.]

Problem 8.5 A company is interested in the purchase of a new machine. Two proposals are to be evaluated. Proposal A and B. The cost of each machine is Rs. 95,00,000. The cash inflows are as follows:

Year	Cash inflows (Machine A)	Cash inflows (Machine B)
1	30,00,000	40,00,000
2	30,00,000	30,00,000
3	20,00,000	20,00,000
4	10,00,000	10,00,000
5	5,00,000	10,00,000

The cost of capital is 2%. Risk premium is 20% for A and 7% for B. Which investment should be purchased?

[**Answer:** Machine A –20,87,500, Machine B + 3,31,000, select Machine B.]

❑❑❑

Cost of Capital 9

LEARNING OBJECTIVES

9.1 INTRODUCTION TO COST OF CAPITAL

Cost of Capital refers to the minimum required rate of return of a proposal that a company must earn to cover the cost of investment. Funds can be procured from different sources such as equity or preference shareholders, debt holders and depositors. All those who have invested in the company, would require a return on their investment. Return to the stakeholders will be paid out of the revenue earnings of the firm. To satisfy the expectations of the stakeholders, the projects of the firm must be able to attain a minimum cut off rate. Capital raised from different sources is called the 'components of cost of capital'. Each of these sources has a cost. This is a specific cost and it must be calculated to give the correct cost of capital. When specific costs are combined the weighted cost of capital can be calculated. For example, a specific cost would be cost of equity, but combined cost would be the overall cost of capital or the weighted cost of equity, preference capital and cost of debt combined.

Cost of capital is represented by the symbol 'k' and it is the minimum rate of return, which must be earned by a company to maintain its share value. This is to achieve the objective of bringing about maximization of wealth for the shareholders. It is also called the hurdle rate for taking investment decision of a firm.

Cost of capital is affected by three important factors. These are the risk free interest rate, the business risk premium and financial risk premium. It can be presented in the form of an equation:

$$k = r_0 + b + f$$

Where, k = Cost of Capital

r_0 = Return at 0 level of risk

b = Premium for business risk

f = Premium for financial risk

9.2 FACTORS AFFECTING COST OF CAPITAL

The cost of capital is the rate, which has to be achieved by the firm to break even. The minimum rate of return can be achieved by the consideration of risk and the required rate of return of the firm. Risk is of different types. It may be the risk that is perceived by the investors of the firm or the firm's own expectation of risk. The three different types of risk are risk free interest rate, business risk and financial risk. Let us discuss these risk factors that affect the cost of capital of a firm.

(*i*) **Risk Free Interest Rate:** The interest, which has no default risk in the payment of a promised fixed periodic amount, is called the 'risk free interest rate'. Usually government securities are risk free because they pay a fixed promised interest rate periodically and repay the principal sum of money at the time of maturity. The risk free rate is dependent on the demand and supply of funds in the market. When the demand is high and supply of funds is low, a higher interest rate will be provided. Similarly when supply of funds is high and the demand is low because of the general economic condition in the market the rates of interest will fall. The interest free rate of return consists of the real interest rate and the premium paid for purchasing power risk. The real interest rate is the rate of interest prevailing in the market with the interaction of demand and supply. The purchasing power risk consists of the risk of inflation and it is usually above the real interest rate.

Thus risk free interest rate consists of:

(*a*) Determination of interest free rate through the interaction of the ***demand and supply*** for money in the market for funds.

(*b*) ***The real interest*** rate or the rate prevailing at which the buyers and lenders are ready to lend and to demand for funds.

(*c*) The premium paid for ***inflation*** or purchasing power risk in the economy.

(*ii*) **Business Risk:** The risk in business is dependent on the changes in the earnings of a firm. If the profit is high, it is because of an accelerated demand of a product. If the profits are low, it means that the sales could not take-off because the competitor brand was better than the product or the market itself was at a downswing or government policies changed during the course of business. Whatever the reasons of profit or loss, a firm would be more concerned when it is making a loss. In the situation of a loss it will not be able to meet its obligations or expectations of shareholders and the public at large. The creditors would also pressurize the firm for its funds. If the company is unable to meet its costs it will lose its reputation. This will increase the cost of capital of the company. It will further affect the earnings of the company. Every new project that a firm undertakes will have some effect on the risk complexion of the firm. ***Business risk in terms of cost of capital is analysed as a risk, which is due to internal reasons and not external market conditions.***

In financial management terms, if risk in business is due to internal reasons and not external factors, cost of capital would be affected with every new proposal and it must be analysed and evaluated before it can be accepted. A new proposal would be accepted only if it adds to the revenue of the company, without increasing the risk factor because it will be added to the cost of capital. A business risk premium is added to every proposal to calculate the cost of capital. Therefore, in addition to the interest free rate of risk, the premium for business risk is incorporated and added to the cost of capital.

(*iii*) **Financial Risk:** The source from which capital is raised affects the cost of capital of a company. The most common sources of capital consist of equity capital, preference capital and debt. These sources form the capital structure of a company. The ability of a firm to meet its obligations to these suppliers of funds is the financial risk of the company. The higher the number of equity shares, the greater would be the responsibility of the company to meet their expectations. The debt policy of the firm also affects its cost of capital. Debt is cheaper than ownership capital because it is tax deductible, but creditors have to be paid in time and the company should be able to earn enough revenue to pay its interest in time. Premium for financial risk consists of debt equity mix, the more debt content the higher will be the risk, because the firm requires higher operating profit to cover periodic interest payments and repayments of principal at the time of maturity.

All these factors have to be considered because the composition of the debt and equity will affect the overall cost of capital. The mixing of debt and equity with a proper evaluation can minimize the cost of capital. As a compensation for an expected financial risk, the firm adds a financial risk premium to the risk free interest rate. The rate of interest is now composed of ***risk free rate of interest, business risk and financial risk. Both business risk and financial risk pertain to internal risk of a firm whereas risk free rate is due to external reasons.***

(*iv*) **Other Considerations:** Another consideration is the liquidity of an investment. If an investment is easily marketable, an investor will not be interested in demanding a premium on the investment. If however, investment is not marketable the investor will require a premium on the rate of return.

The cost of capital is thus defined through the equation $k = r_0 + b + f$.

The cost of capital is thus the rate of return, which is calculated through a discount rate to calculate the net present value of a project. It is also called cut off rate, hurdle rate, and the minimum required rate of return. The discount rate is the opportunity cost of capital. It is the rate of return for the compensation of risk and time for the use of capital. Each proposal will have its own risk. ***Hence cost of capital is measured through a discount rate, which comprises a risk free rate of interest and compensation for business and financial risk.***

9.3 IMPORTANCE AND SIGNIFICANCE OF COST OF CAPITAL

The concept of cost of capital derives its importance from its usefulness in investment management proposals. Cost of capital is used in capital budgeting and capital structure decisions.

(*i*) **Capital Budgeting Decisions:** It is applied in capital budgeting decisions and is important for evaluating or determining business proposals. It uses the required rate of return for discounting cash flows to determine the net present value of a proposal. It evaluates the proposals to see that the minimum cut off rate is achieved. If the minimum rate is achieved the project is accepted otherwise it should be rejected. It measures the financial utility of a proposal. If the NPV is positive and the IRR is above the cut off rate the proposal should be accepted. To maximize the value of the firm, the cost of capital should be as low as possible. Cost of capital is useful in financial appraisal, whether money should be invested or not in a proposal.

(*ii*) **Capital Structure Decisions:** The application of cost of capital techniques optimizes risk and cost factors in different sources of capital. The combination of equity, preference and debt of the right quantity gives the maximum return. Raising debt in the form of loans is good from tax point of view, but is expensive and involves high financial risk. Cost of each source of funds is considered with risk involved in it to take a decision. Cost of capital proposes to find out the cost of capital from each source and then to mix them to get maximum return and minimum risk.

Cost of capital derives its importance from the objective of achieving wealth maximization of shareholders. It is useful in two strategic areas of finance. It takes decisions regarding accept/reject proposals in capital budgeting and in capital structure. Its main objective is to attain maximum return and minimum risk. There are certain assumptions while applying cost of capital techniques. These assumptions should first be clarified before studying the analysis of the cost of capital.

9.4 ASSUMPTIONS IN THE MEASUREMENT OF COST OF CAPITAL

The techniques of cost of capital are applied under some assumptions. These assumptions relate to business risk and financial risk.

(*i*) **Business Risk Assumption:** Capital budgeting decisions determine the business risk of a firm. It is assumed that business risk is not affected by the proposal, which is evaluated under cost of capital. This means that every firm has some risk under which condition it operates. The composition of this risk remains unchanged when a new proposal is accepted. ***The business risk is unchanged and the changes of earnings before interest and taxes to sales revenue remain constant.***

(*ii*) **Financial Risk Assumption:** In the above discussion it has been stated that financial risk is internal. Another aspect that is assumed is that it remains unchanged. Debt financing which in turn affects the capital structure of a firm affects the overall capital of the company. It is assumed that any funds, which are in addition to the existing funds, are constant. This implies that the additional funds will be raised in the same proportion. This is particularly relating to debt financing which is expected to continue in the same degree of financing. Debt is measured on an after tax basis. In capital budgeting cash flows are discounted after tax whether it is calculated by NPV or IRR. ***To keep a consistency in the evaluation process it is assumed that financial risk is unchanged.***

$$k = r_0 + b + f$$

(*iii*) **Concept of Risk and Return:** Thus in the equation on measurement of cost of capital, the business risk and financial risk remain unchanged but the risk-free rate of interest depends on supply and demand of the different types of available funds. The risk free rate of interest is usually the lowest. Government securities do not have any risk but their return is also very low. The rate of return is higher than the government securities if government issues bonds from banks or different departments. In the case of preference shares and bonds and deposits issued by the corporate sector the rate of interest is higher than that of government securities and government bonds. The rate of return is highest in equity shares but it is also high-risk investment. It has the highest risk premium. When the risk is high, the premium will also be very high; this increases the cost of capital and the required rate of return of the investors. The difference in the risk is reflected by the required rate of return. The higher the risk premium the greater the required rate of return of the investors. The risk premium increases with the increase of income in different securities. Fig. 9.1 shows the risk and return relationship of different types of securities.

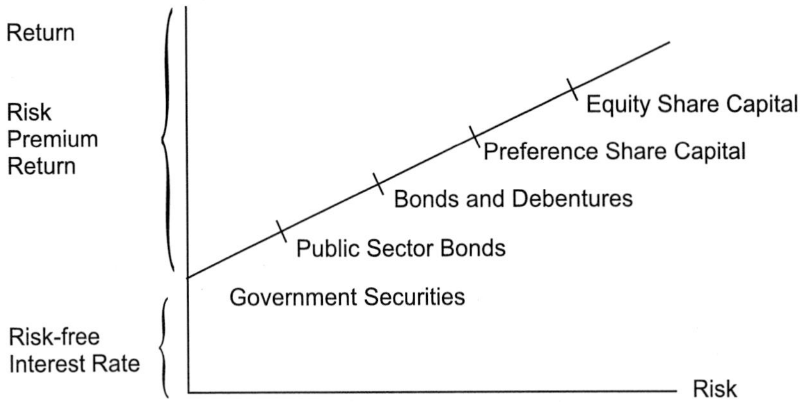

Fig. 9.1 Risk and Return of different types of securities

(*iv*) **Cost of Capital and Taxes:** The concept of cost of capital is useful for taking capital budgeting decisions. The capital budgeting decisions are taken after the taxes have been paid. Since cost of capital is useful for discounting cash flows to their present values to take decisions, they are also evaluated after tax to bring uniformity in the evaluation process. When IRR is used to take decisions, the cut off rate is also used after tax. Taxes affect the cost of capital decisions in the evaluation of debt securities, as the interest is tax deductible. The equity shares and preference shares do not require tax adjustments, as they do not get any advantage of taxes.

9.5 CLASSIFICATION OF COSTS OF CAPITAL

Cost of capital can be classified into explicit costs and implicit costs, specific costs and overall costs of capital, historical costs and future costs, marginal and average cost.

(*i*) **Explicit and Implicit Cost of Capital:** Explicit costs are the discount rate, which equates the present value of cash inflows with cash outflows. If a company raises Rs. 10,00,000 by way of loan at 10% rate of interest. The company will have a cash inflow of Rs. 10,00,000 but every year there will be an outflow of Rs. 1,00,000 in terms of interest. The explicit cost will be that rate of internal return, which equates Rs.10,00,000 the initial cash flow repayable after 12 years. Explicit costs are when funds are raised. Implicit costs are when funds are used. All funds have both explicit and implicit costs. Implicit cost is that return which is foregone by shareholders and company. Explicit costs may be defined as:

$$I_0 = \frac{C_1}{(1+k)^1} + \frac{C_2}{(1+k)^2} + \frac{C_3}{(1+k)^3} - \frac{C_n}{(1+k)^n}$$

Where initial cash inflow received by the firm is equal to the cash outflows at period 1, 2, 3...*n*, which is the cash payment, made to the capital source.

I = Inflows of funds

C = Cash outflows

k = Explicit cost of capital

Implicit costs are the opportunity for investment, which is foregone if the present proposal under evaluation is accepted. ***The retained earnings*** of the company are the implicit costs. It is the income, which the shareholders would have earned if the earnings were distributed and invested by them. There is a controversy, that retained earnings do not attach any costs. The firm does not spend any funds to raise them. If a firm does not declare a dividend and retains the earnings of the shareholders, it has an implied obligation to generate resources to compensate the shareholders for the dividends foregone. ***Retained earnings have implicit costs even if there are no explicit costs of retaining them.***

(ii) **Specific and Overall Cost of Capital:** Cost of capital measures specific costs of debt, preference shares and equity shares. The combined costs of all these categories are called the 'overall cost of capital'. The costs of specific aspects are first measured and then the overall cost of capital is computed. The computation of each specific costs of capital has been explained. The importance of retained earnings are also given.

(iii) **Historical Weights and Future Costs:** Historical weights are based on the proportion of existing sources of capital. It is the proportion of funds, which have already been issued by the company. It is assumed that if a firm makes additional investments they would be raised in the same proportion as the existing capital structure because the capital structure is optimum. A firm would continue to issue new capital in the same pattern as the existing one.

This assumption is not realistic because several times the existing capital structure is not optimum. The firm may not be able to issue new shares in the same proportion as existing shares because of demand and supply conditions or change in political scenario.

Future costs are more important than historical costs because they have still to be incurred. Future costs can be planned by considering the present scenario of different types of costs. Historical costs have already been incurred. They are sunk costs because the opportunity is lost to do another activity. These costs cannot be recovered but their experience can be useful in planning for the future. Therefore, historical costs are less important than future costs but they are valuable for predicting future costs. Their significance cannot be underestimated.

Historical weights can be calculated either through ***book value or market value***.

(iv) **Book Value Weights:** Book value weights are applied by giving weights on the face value of different sources of capital. This value can be taken from the balance sheet of a firm. Book value weights do not take into consideration market value weights and so they cannot be considered as realistic. The minimum rate of return through book values will not reflect the true economic value while calculating overall cost of capital. Hence market value weights are also applied. Both historical and market values have their own advantages and limitations.

(*v*) **Market Value Weights:** The market value weights are the amount of weight of each security dependent on the market price of the security. This is realistic because it provides and estimates of the investors required rate of return in the present scenario. However market value weights also have limitations.

Market value weights have the problem of change in the price of shares from day to day. Thus to get the current weight the price of the share in the market will have to be determined daily. It is also difficult to calculate the proportion between equity shares and retained earnings.

Advantages of market value weights are:

(*a*) They are useful for giving the present estimates to an investor to enable him to calculate his required rate of return.

(*b*) They provide an estimate to a company of an amount that they would required for investing in additional funds from the market.

(*c*) They also provide the current estimate and are consistence with their use in the overall cost of capital.

Limitations of market value weights are:

(*a*) They have to make the current estimate between the equity capital and retained earnings because the value of retained earnings cannot be estimated with precision according to the market rates because they are based on past profits.

(*b*) Market value of securities change depending on the demand and supply conditions what is relevant today will change the next day. External factors influence market value of securities.

(*c*) The weighted average cost of capital according to market value will be higher than the book value because the value of equity capital changes.

(*vi*) **Target Weights:** The target weights are used in preparing the capital structure of a firm. When a firm operates in an optimum capital structure, the historical weights are equal to the target weights. The target weights are more useful in long-term rather than short-term planning. It is useful in finding out the weighted average cost of capital.

(*vii*) **Marginal Weights:** The marginal weight is the proportion in which a firm intends to raise new capital in addition to the existing capital. When additional funds are raised weights are given to the incremental addition to capital. This method is used only when additional funds are required because when new funds are added the sources of funds may be raised in a different proportion depending on the requirement of the firm. In the existing capital structure the equity share may be in a 50% proportion to debt. In additional funds new equity may be only 30% and the rest may be retained earnings, preference capital and debt. Thus the proportion is changed according to the requirement of the firm.

Marginal weights have certain limitations. They ignore the long-term implications of the current financing undertaken by the firm. For example, debt is cheaper than equity and the firm may raise the entire amount of debt even if is not feasible.

9.6 MEASUREMENT OF SPECIFIC COSTS OF CAPITAL

The specific costs may be classified into cost of debentures/bonds, preference shares, equity shares and retained earnings. These are explained in the next section.

9.7 COST OF BONDS AND DEBENTURES

The calculation of bonds and debentures will depict the cost of debt or the borrowed funds used to finance a project. It is important to measure the cost of debt because there is a cost of interest on the firm. However the interest on debt is tax deductible and so it has an advantage as the after tax costs is lower than the cost calculated before tax.

Procedure for Calculation of Bonds and Debentures

Debt securities have certain important considerations. These refer to the (*i*) interest payment, (*ii*) maturity date, (*iii*) tax adjustments, and (*iv*) issue price.

(*i*) **Interest Payment:** All debt securities have an important feature of an annual payment, which is a reward for parting with funds. This is called 'interest'. Interest as we have seen earlier is according to the risk and return considerations. Debt securities have a fixed interest and for convenience firms pay it annually. If a company issues 10% debt securities, of the face value of Rs. 1000 then the interest payment is Rs. 100 annually. Interest is paid on the face value of the debt security. The debt may be sold at a premium or discount but this has no effect on the interest payment. One single rule is applied and that is interest payment is to be made on the face value of the bond.

(*ii*) **Maturity Date:** The maturity date has a great significance in debt repayment because this is the date when the debt plan has its exit date. After this date the firm has no obligation to pay further amounts to debt holders as its responsibility is completed. The debt holder will receive his last interest payment and the principal sum that he had invested on the date of maturity. A debt security can mature at the face value by giving the exit option at par. Debt securities can also mature at a premium or discount. Unlike interest payments, which are according to face value only, exit plans have different options. Besides premium and discount options, there can be the option to convert debt into equity on the date of maturity.

(*iii*) **Tax Adjustments:** As discussed before debt has an adjustment for taxes, as the interest is deductible for tax purposes. Thus the valuation of debt is always cost of capital after tax. The tax savings brings down the cost of debt therefore cost of debt is the cost of capital before taxes multiplied by (1– tax). Tax is deductible on debt securities, in profit making companies. These adjustments cannot be made in non-tax paying companies.

The cost of bonds and debentures can be calculated for both irredeemable and redeemable situations. In the case of irredeemable debt the formula is:

$$k_d = \text{I/NP}$$

Where, I = Interest

NP = Net proceeds or issue price

Since it is tax deductible the firm is free from tax liability, therefore k_d after tax is:

$$k_d = \frac{\text{I}}{\text{NP}}(1 - t)$$

Where, t = Tax rate

(*iv*) **Issue Price:** The cost of bonds and debentures can be calculated if it is issued at par, at a premium or at a discount. The net proceeds will change. For example, if a bond is of the value of Rs. 1,000 and it is sold at Rs. 1,000; the bond is said to be sold at par and the net proceed will be Rs. 1,000. If the same is sold at a 10% discount, then the net proceeds will be Rs. 900. Similarly if it is sold for a premium of 10%, then the net proceeds will be Rs. 1,100.

I. Cost of Inredeemable Debt

Cost of inredeemable debt is calculated as follows.

Example 9.1 A Company issues 10% irredeemable debentures of Rs. 10,00,000. Calculate cost of debt before and after tax. Company is in 50% tax bracket, calculate cost of debt before as well as after tax if debentures are issued (*i*) at par (*ii*) 10% discount and (*iii*) premium before tax cost of debt.

Solution

Cost of debt after taxes $k_d = \frac{\text{I}}{\text{NP}}(1 - t)$

I = Annual interest payment

NP = Net proceeds of debentures

t = Tax rate

$\therefore$ $k_d = \frac{1,00,000}{10,00,000} = 10\%$

(*i*) Issued at par $k_d = \frac{1,00,000}{10,00,000}(1 - 0.50)$

$= 10\% \ (1 - 0.5) = 5\%$

$= \frac{1}{10} \times 0.50 = 0.050 \text{ or } 5\%$

(*ii*) Issued at premium $$k_d = \frac{1,00,000}{11,00,000}(1 - 0.50)$$

$$= \frac{1}{11} \times 0.50 = 0.045 \text{ or } 4.5\%$$

(*c*) Issued at discount $$k_d = \frac{1,00,000}{9,00,000}(1 - 0.50)$$

$$= \frac{1}{9} \times 0.50 = 5.55\%$$

> ***Note:*** It is assumed that there is no change in financial risk and business risk. Benefits of a project are taken on an after tax basis.

II. Cost of Redeemable Debt

Redeemable debt can be calculated by the trial and error method as well as by the shortcut method. The shortcut method saves a lot of time and is usually used for the calculation of redeemable debt. The redeemable debt can also be redeemed at par; premium or discount the following is the formula of redeemable debt (*i*) by trial and error method and (*ii*) by shortcut method.

(*i*) By Trial and Error Method

The following example will explain the trial and error method for calculation of redeemable debt. The following is the equation

$$k_d = \sum_{i=1}^{n} \frac{I(1-t)}{(1+k_d)^1} + \frac{C_0}{(1+k_d)^2} + \frac{C_{0_n}}{(1+k_d)^n}$$

Where I = Interest

t = Tax

C_0 = Cash outflows in different years (1, 2, …n)

k_d = Cost of debt

Example 9.2 A company issues 10% debentures of the face value of Rs. 100 each redeemable after 5 years. Debentures have a floatation cost of 2% and are issued at 5% discount. What is the cost of capital when tax rate is 50%?

Solution

k_d = Rs. 100 – Rs. 5 (discount) – Rs. 2 (floatation cost) = Rs. 93

Interest = 10 (1 – 0.5) = Rs. 5.

Since interest is tax deductible the after tax interest would be Rs. 5.

Putting the values in the above equation,

$$93 = 5\,(\text{PVAF}_{ni}) + 100\,(\text{PVF}_{ni})$$

The value of the equation is to be made equal to Rs. 93

$$\text{By trial and error, } k_d\ 7\% = 5\,(4.100) + 100(0.713)$$

$$= 20.5 + 71.3 = \text{Rs. } 91.8$$

The value of PVAF_{ni} is taken from Table A-4 (Appendix) Present Value Annuity Tables for 5 years at 7% rate of interest and PVF_{ni} or present value is taken from Table A-3, for 5 years at 7% rate of interest. Now find a value, which is more than Rs. 93, try 6% rate of interest for 5 years.

Solution

$$\text{Substituting at } 6\% = 5\,(4.212) + 100\,(0.747)$$

$$= 21.06 + 74.7 = 95.76$$

Now 7% or 91.8 is less than 93 and at 6% 95.76 is greater than 6.7%.

By interpolation,

$$k_d = 6\% + \frac{95.76 - 93}{95.76 - 91.8} \times 1 = 6\% + \frac{2.76}{3.96} = 6\% + 0.696$$

$$k_d = 6.69\%$$

$$\therefore \quad \text{Cost of debt} = 6.69\%$$

Thus by trial and error method and through interpolation, the cost of redeemable debt can be calculated. However we have seen that the trial and error method is difficult. Therefore the shortcut method given below is applied to find out cost of redeemable debt.

***(ii)* By Shortcut Method**

(*a*) Redeemable Debentures

$$k_d = \frac{\text{I}\,(1 - t) + (\text{RV} - \text{NP})/n}{(\text{RV} + \text{NP})/2)}$$

Where,

RV = Redemption value

t = Tax rate

n = Life of debenture

NP = Net proceeds of issue per debenture

Example 9.3 A company issues 10% debentures of Rs. 100 each redeemable at the end of 10 years. The debentures are issued at a discount of 5% and floatation costs are 1%. Find out cost of capital of debentures. Given that the firm tax rate is 50%.

$$k_d = \frac{\text{I}\,(1 - t) + \{((f + d + pr - pi)/n\}}{(\text{RV} + \text{NP})/2)}$$

Where there are floatation costs or discounts on issue of debt or premium on issue of debt or redemption of debt, the floatation costs and discounts or premiums will also have to be taken into account. This example states that the debenture is issued at a discount of Rs. 5 on the redemption value and floatation costs of 1% these must be accounted for. Hence in the calculations the floatation cost works out to Rs. 10 on a Rs. 100 debenture and Rs. 5 for discount on the redemption value as the following example indicates:

$$k_d = \frac{I(1-t) + (f + d + pr - pi)/N}{(RV + \text{Net Proceeds})/2}$$

$$= \frac{[\{10\ (1 - 0.5)\} + \{(10+5)/1\}]}{(100 + 94)/2}$$

$$k_d = \frac{20}{97} = 20.6\%$$

Evaluation of Cost of Debt

Debt is therefore easy to calculate. There is a controversy that debt is cheaper than other sources of capital like equity shares. The shareholders in the case of equity shares will have to be paid a dividend but in the case of debt there is no obligation on behalf of the company to pay to its bondholders any dividend. It is also stated that debt is interest deductible for payment of taxes and it reduces the liability of a firm.

Debt however has certain obligations. A company has to pay interest regularly when the interest becomes due, whether the firm earns any profit or not. If it does not pay interest in time its reputation in the market falls and this will have an effect on the profitability of the company.

Debt also has a maturity value, which has to be paid by a firm at the end of the maturity period. Hence it cannot be said that a firm is not exposed to any risk when it takes a debt.

At the time of liquidation the rights of the debenture holders have to be satisfied only after that can the claims of the shareholders be sorted out.

Finally it can be stated that there is an advantage to a firm for issuing debt but, it has risk and this must be considered in the evaluation process. To summarize:

(*a*) Debt is cheaper than capital because interest is deductible for tax purposes.

(*b*) A firm does not have to pay any dividends or any earnings of the company compulsorily.

(*c*) Debt has a maturity value.

(*d*) Interest has to be paid regularly and the principal sum has to be paid at maturity.

(*e*) At liquidation the debt holders have the first claim to the company's assets.

9.8 PREFERENCE SHARES

Preference shares are called 'hybrid securities'. They are called shares but they have a fixed rate of return like debentures. The return is called a dividend and not interest. In this respect they resemble the equity shares. The preference shareholders have a priority over the equity shareholders. They receive their dividend continuously even for the years in which there is a loss to the company. In this respect they resemble debentures and not equity shares. Equity shareholders do not get any dividends when a company makes a loss. Like the equity shares, they are not tax deductible. Hence, there is no tax advantage to the company in issuing preference shares. Preference shareholders have an edge over the equity shareholders at the time of liquidation. The preference shareholders have a charge on the liquidation of a company after the debt holders have been paid but the equity share holders have the last right on the company's assets. The equity shareholders can make high profits when a company is profitable but preference shareholders will continue to get fixed amount of return. Preference shares can be redeemable and irredeemable. The irredeemable preference shares do not have a date of maturity, whereas redeemable preference share have a maturity date. Irredeemable preference shares will have a continuous fixed dividend till the lifetime of the company. The redeemable preference shares will have a fixed dividend till they reach the maturity date. On the date of maturity, the preference shareholder will receive the principal amount like the redeemable debentures. The cost of capital can be calculated both for irredeemable and redeemable preference shares. The formula for calculating the cost of irredeemable preference shares is the following:

$$k_p = \frac{d}{P_0(I - f)}$$

Whene, k_p = Cost of preference capital

d = Annual dividend payment

P_0 = Expected sale price of preference shares

f = Floatation cost as % of sales price

An example of calculation of cost of capital of irredeemable preference shares is depicted in Example 9.4.

Example 9.4 (*a*) A company issues 13% irredeemable preference shares of the face value of Rs. 100 each. Floatation costs are estimated at 5% of expected sale price. What is the '*k*' if preference shares are issued at (*i*) par value (*ii*) at 10% premium (*iii*) 5% discount.

(*b*) A company issued 11% irredeemable preference shares of the face value of Rs.100 each. Floatation costs are estimated at 3% of expected sale price. What is the cost of preference shares if they are issued at par, 5% premium and 4% discount?

Solution

(*a*)

$$k_p \text{ at par} = \frac{13}{100(1-0.05)}$$

$$= \frac{13}{95} = 0.1368 = 13.68\%$$

$$\text{Premium} = \frac{13}{110\,(1 - 0.05)} = \frac{13}{104.5} = 0.1244 = 12.44\%$$

$$\text{Premium} = \frac{13}{95\,(1 - 0.05)} = \frac{13}{90.25} = 0.1440 = 14.40\%$$

(*b*)

$$k_0 = \frac{11}{100\,(1 - 0.03)} = \frac{11}{97} = 0.113 = 11.3\%$$

$$= \frac{11}{105\,(1 - 0.03)} = \frac{11}{101.85} = 10.8\%$$

$$= \frac{11}{96\,(1 - 0.03)} = \frac{11}{93.12} = 11.81\%$$

Equation for redeemable preference shares:

$$P_0(1 - f) = \sum_{t=1}^{n} \frac{DP_1}{(1 + k_p)^1} + \frac{P_n}{(1 + k_p)^n}$$

P_0 = Sale price of preference share

P_n = Repayment of preference capital

DP = Dividends paid on preference capital amount

f = Floatation cost as percentage of expected sale price

Cost of redeemable preference shares can be calculated through this shortcut formula:

$$k_p = \frac{D + \dfrac{RV - NP}{n}}{\dfrac{RV + NP}{2}}$$

Where, k_p = Cost of preference share capital

D = Preference Dividend

n = Number of years of maturity

RV = Redeemable value

NP = Net proceeds of preference capital

Redeemable preference shares like the redeemable debentures can be calculated by the trial and error method as well as by the shortcut method. Although shortcut method is an approximate method it is widely used because trial and error method is difficult to apply. Let us first take an example of trial and error method and then apply the shortcut method.

Example 9.5 A company issues 10% preference shares of the face value of Rs. 100 each at a flotation cost of 5%. Find out the cost of preference capital if it is redeemable after 7 years at a premium of 10%.

Solution

Rs. 100 – Rs. 5 (Floatation cost) = Rs. 95

$$P_0 = \sum_{i=1}^{7} \frac{10}{(1+k)^1} + \frac{110}{(1+k)^7}$$

$$k_p \text{ at } 13\% = 10(PVAF_{7,13\%}) + 110(PVF_{7,13\%})$$

$$= 10\,(4.423) + 110\,(0.425)$$

$$= 44.23 + 46.75 = 90.98$$

$$k_p \text{ at } 12\% = 10\,(4.564) + 110\,(0.452)$$

$$= 45.64 + 49.72 = 95.36$$

By interpolation,

$$12\% + \frac{(95.36 - 95)}{(95.36 - 90.98)} = 12.08\%$$

Example 9.6 demonstrates the application of shortcut method.

Example 9.6 A company has 15% redeemable of preference shares of Rs.1,00,000 redeemable at the end of the 10th year from the year of their issue. The underwriting costs came to 5%, calculate cost of preference share capital.

Solution

$$k_p = \frac{15,000 + (1,00,000 - 95,000)/10}{(1,00,000 + 95,000)/2}$$

$$= \frac{15,000 + 500}{97,500} = 0.1589$$

$$\therefore \quad k_p = 15.89\%$$

9.9 COST OF EQUITY SHARE CAPITAL

The equity shareholders are in effect the owners of the company to the limit of their shareholding. They provide the capital of the company. In return for their participation, they receive a dividend from the profits of the company.

The equity capital has a cost like other sources of capital. This can be measured but it is difficult because the equity shareholders do not get a fixed rate of dividend like the preference shareholders or the debenture holders. Since the dividends are variable and dependent on the profits of the company, the measurement of cost of capital is not according to a standard format.

The cost of equity can be measured according to different approaches like dividend approach, capital asset pricing model approach, earning price approach. Equity can be measured by the dividend approach when dividends grow at a uniform rate perpetually or when the dividend grows at different rates. The CAPM approach measures the risk of the capital and the earning price approach measures the equity shares in terms of market price of the share.

Equity shares are known to be very risky, yet they are very popular. They are traded in the stock market. The expectation of the shareholders is that they would receive both dividends and capital appreciation. The capital appreciation is due to the market judging the profitability and reputation of the firm. If the firm has a good profit the shares quoted in the market will increase in price. A shareholder estimates a continuous stream of dividends from the capital that he invests in the firm. The dividends that he receives, he discounts it to get the present value of the dividends stream. The rate of discount, which the shareholder applies to his expected dividends to be able to determine the present value, is ***the cost of equity capital***. The equation that applies is based on the fact that the market price of the share is equal to the present value of the future dividends and the sale proceeds received by him when he sells the share. The following equation provides the methodology for measuring cost of capital:

$$P_0 = \frac{D_1}{(1+k_e)^1} + \frac{D_2}{(1+k_e)^2} + ... + \frac{D_n}{(1+k_e)^n} + \frac{P_n}{(1+k_e)^n}$$

P_0 = Current market Price of equity share

D = Dividend in different years (D_1, D_2.....D_n)

k_e = Cost of equity capital

P_n = Market price at the time of sale of share

Let us first calculate the cost of capital according to the dividend approach.

Dividend Approach

Dividends of a firm can grow at a uniform rate perpetually; this is called a 'perpetuity of dividends'. It is calculated in the following manner:

$$k_e = \frac{D_1}{P_0} + g$$

D_1 = Dividend per share

P_0 = Current market price or net proceeds per share

g = Growth in constant dividends

(*i*) Perpetual Growth of Dividends

Example 9.7 If the dividend per share of a firm is expected to be Rs.15 per share next year and is expected to grow at 10% constantly (*i*) determine cost of capital if market price per share is Rs. 50, calculate k_e. (*ii*) Find expected value of a share of the firm at the end of the year 1 and year 2.

Solution

(*i*)
$$k_e = \frac{D_1}{P_0} + g$$

D_1 = Dividend per share

P_0 = Current market price or net proceeds per share

g = Growth in constant dividends

$$= \frac{15}{50} + 10\%$$

$$k_e = 0.3 + 0.10 = 0.4$$

This is called 'perpetual growth' or 'constant growth' in dividends.

(*ii*) The market price of the share for year 1 and 2 can be calculated through the following equation:

$$P_0 = \frac{D_0\,(1+g)}{(k_e - g)}$$

$$\text{MP in year 1} = \frac{16.5}{(0.4 - 0.10)} = \text{Rs. } 55.00$$

$$\text{MP in year 2} = \frac{D_0\,(1+g)}{(k_e - g)}$$

$$= \frac{18.15}{(0.40 - 0.10)} = \text{Rs. } 60.50$$

The assumptions in the above model are the following:

(*a*) $D_0 > 0$ or the present dividend is positive.

(*b*) Dividend payout ratio is constant.

(*c*) $k_e > g$

(*d*) Current market price is a function of future expected dividends of the share.

(*ii*) Varying Growth Rates in Dividends

The cost of equity can be calculated when there are varying growths in dividends. The following equation considers the varying growth rates in dividends:

$$P_0 = \sum_{t=1}^{n} \frac{D_o(1+g_n)^{t-1}}{(1+k_e)^t} + \sum_{t=n+1}^{\alpha} \frac{D_n(1+g_c)^{t-1}}{(1+k_e)^t}$$

g_n = Rate of growth in earlier years

g_c = Constant growth rate in later years

Example 9.8 Dividend paid on the outstanding shares over the past 6 years is as follows:

Year	Dividend per share
1	10.00
2	11.02
3	11.50
4	12.50
5	12.76
6	13.38

(*i*) Calculate growth rate in dividends. (*ii*) Cost of the equity share when current market price is Rs. 150. (*iii*) Cost of new equity share if floatation cost is 2%.

Solution

(*i*) Growth rate in dividends

From the above 13.38 equals 10 $(1 + g)^5$

Therefore, $(1 + g)^5 = 13.38/10 = 1.338$

Using compound values from Table A-1 (Appendix), the growth rate for 5 years closest to 1.338 is 6%.

(*ii*) Cost of the equity share when current market price is Rs. 150.

$$\text{Cost of Equity} = \frac{\text{Expected dividend}}{\text{Current market price}} + g$$

Substituting we get

$$13.38\ (1 + .06) = 14.18$$

$$14.18/150 = 0.094 = 9.4\%$$

(*iii*) Cost of new equity share if floatation cost is 2%.

$$\text{Cost of new equity share} = \frac{\text{Expected dividend}}{\text{Current market price } (1-f)} + g$$

$$k_e = \frac{14.10}{147} + 6\% = 9.59\% + 6\% = 15.59\%$$

(*iii*) Cost of Capital of Newly Issued Equity

A firm may require additional capital for expansion of financing of new projects. The equity capital, which exists in a firm, earns from the project and provides a return in the form of a stream of dividends. When new capital is issued the shareholders would expect to earn the same amount of return on the new issue. The minimum rate of return expected by the shareholders on the new issue of shares is called the 'cost of new equity'.

A company usually has to spend additional amounts of funds for making a new issue. The expenses are for floatation of new issue and underwriting expenses, brokerage and advertisement. The cost of new issue can be estimated in the following method.

Example 9.9 A company is expected to pay dividends of Rs. 5 per share. The present market price of its shares is Rs. 70 and the growth rate is 8% per annum. It plans to raise additional equity capital. It is planning to price its new shares at Rs. 69 and it expects an additional cost of Re. 1 per share as expenses. Find out the cost of equity shares which are existing and the new equity cost if dividend and growth rate are continuing at the same level.

Solution

The following data is provided:

Market price, P_0 = Rs. 70

New equity price = Rs. 69

Floatation cost = Re. 1

Net proceeds = Rs. 68

Growth rate = 8%

Dividend (D_1) = Rs. 5

Step 1: Cost of existing capital

$$k_e = \frac{D_1}{P_0} + g = \frac{5}{70} + 0.08 = 15.14\%$$

Step 2: Cost of new issue

$$k_e = \frac{D_1}{NP} + g$$

$$= \frac{5}{68} + 0.08 = 15.35\%$$

Cost of equity shares can be measured by capital asset pricing model.

(*iv*) Capital Asset Pricing Model (CAPM)

This model considers the risk in a security. There are two kinds of risks. These are systematic and unsystematic risk. Systematic risk is due to a broad spectrum of uncontrollable risk. It covers macro economic environmental factors such as demand, supply, change in government policies and political issues. Such a risk is measured by β which measures change in market value of equity shares relative to change in market index. Unsystematic risk is a unique risk related to the company. The problems relating to management, staff, expenses, losses, strikes and other issues directly affect the company's own operations.

The market price of a share is influenced by systematic and unsystematic risk. If β is high, the company's shares will have high risk. The CAPM model calculates cost of equity through the following equation:

$$k_e = k_f + \beta\,(k_m - k_f)$$

Where

k_e = Cost of equity capital

k_f = Cost of risk free asset

β = Coefficient of systematic risk

k_m = Cost of market portfolio

This can be explained through Example 9.10.

Example 9.10 The risk free rate of return equals 10%. Firm's equals 1.25 and market return on portfolio is 12.25%. Find cost of equity through CAPM method.

Solution

$$k_e = 10\% + 1.25\,(12.25\% - 10\%) = 12.81\%$$

(*v*) Earning Price Approach

Earning price approach takes into consideration dividends and retained earnings. The cost of capital is measured through the equation:

$$k_e = E/NP$$

Where,

E = Earnings per share

NP = Net proceeds

When the cost of existing equity shares is determined the market price is used, but in the case of new issues net proceeds are used to calculate the cost of capital.

9.10 COST OF RETAINED EARNINGS

Retained earnings are the savings or reserves of a company. Retained earnings are used so that a firm has sufficient funds in future for making reinvestments, which are profitable in future. They are considered as the opportunity cost of foregone dividends. Cost of retained earnings ***cannot be called cost free*. *Retained earnings do not have explicit costs. They have implicit costs***. The company does not pay dividends to shareholders to retain these funds. Therefore the shareholders are deprived of dividends. A firm to make it worthwhile for shareholders in some other way should utilize these funds. Hence a firm should generate future profits from utilizing them.

The cost of retained earnings is in this sense considered to be having the same cost as that of equity shares. However in actual practice it is stated that the cost of retained earnings is less than cost of equity capital because there is no expense on brokerage, dividend or tax on it. To calculate the retained earnings the following equation is used:

$$k_r = k_e (1 - t)(1 - b)$$

Where, k_r = Cost of retained earnings

t = Tax

b = Brokerage cost

The discussion on retained earnings as a cost may be summarized in the following manner:

Retained earnings are not a cost:

(*a*) Some experts are of the opinion that there is no cost in having retained earnings in the firm as no dividends are being paid out of such reserves.

(*b*) They are stored within the company so that it has sufficient funds for future profitable reinvestments.

Retained earnings are a cost:

(*a*) They are considered as the opportunity cost of foregone dividends.

(*b*) The shareholders are deprived of dividends since the company does not pay any dividends to them the funds have a carrying cost unless they are utilized in profitable avenues.

(*c*) The utility of these funds should be worthwhile for shareholders.

(*d*) The firm should generate future profits by utilizing retained earnings usefully.

Note: The cost of retained earnings is considered to have the same cost as that of equity shares. However, in practice it is stated that the cost of retained earnings is less than cost of equity capital because there is no expense on brokerage, dividend or tax on it.

9.11 MEASUREMENT OF WEIGHTED AVERAGE COST OF CAPITAL

The specific costs of capital are the equity shares preference shares and debt. After calculating the specific costs the next step is to calculate the ***overall cost of capital***. The overall cost of capital derives its importance from the fact that the rate of discount, which is calculated as the weighted average costs of the specific costs of capital, is used for evaluating capital budgeting proposals. The overall cost of capital is the minimum rate of return or the cut-off rate to be earned by a firm to meet the satisfaction of different categories of investors.

Therefore weighted average cost of capital is the following:

$$\text{WACC} = wk_e + wk_d + wk_p$$

Where, wk_e = Weighted cost of equity

wk_d = Weighted cost of debt

wk_p = Weighted cost of preference shares

There are different kinds of weights these are historical, marginal and target weights. They are also based on book value and market value weights.

An example of the calculation of weighted average cost of capital according to book value and market value is given in the following example.

Example 9.11 Calculate overall cost of capital through Book Value Weights and Market Value Weights.

Source	Book value (Rs.)	Market value (Rs.)
Equity Share Capital (Rs. 10 each share)	60,00,000	90,00,000
Preference share capital	10,00,000	10,00,000
Debentures	30,00,000	30,00,000

The after tax cost of different sources of finance is as follows:

Equity share capital 15%, preference share capital 10%, debentures 5% (After tax).

Solution

Step 1: Calculate the Weighted Average Cost of Capital by Book Value.

The following calculation is done by first finding out the weights. Add equity preference debentures the total is Rs. 1,00,00,000. Now the weight of equity will be 60,00,000/1,00,00,000, which is 0.60. Similarly find weights of preference capital and debentures.

Step 2: Multiply weights with after tax cost to get weighted cost of each specific costs given in column 5.

Step 3: Add weighted costs. The book value weighted average cost of capital is indicated to be 11.2%.

Computation of weighted average cost of capital— Book value weights

Method (1)

(1)	Book value (2)	Weights proportion (3)	After tax (4)	Weighted cost (5) (*i.e.*, 3 × 4)
Equity	60,00,000	0.60	0.15 or 15%	9.0
Preference Capital	10,00,000	0.10	0.10 or 10%	1.0
Debentures	30,00,000	0.30	0.05 or 5%	1.5
	1,00,00,000			11.5

Method (2)

	Book value	After tax cost	Weighted cost
Equity	60,00,000	15%	9,00,000
Pref. Share Capital	10,00,000	10%	1,00,000
Debentures	30,00,000	5%	1,50,000
Total	1,00,00,000		11,50,000

$$\text{Weighted average cost of capital } k_0 = \frac{11{,}50{,}000}{1{,}00{,}00{,}000} \times 100 = 11.5\%$$

MARKET VALUE WEIGHTS

Computation of weighted average cost of capital

Source	Market value	Proportion	After tax	Weighted cost
Equity	90,00,000	0.692	15%	10.380
Preference Share Capital	10,00,000	0.077	10%	0.770
Debentures	30,00,000	0.231	5%	1.155
	1,30,00,000			12.305

∴ Weighted average cost of capital $k_0 = 12.3\%$

The market value weighted average cost of capital is calculated in the same way as the book value weights. This is a simple calculation without any adjustment made for retained earnings. Another example may be given to explain the method of adjustment in retained earnings.

Example 9.12 Calculate weighted average cost of capital through book value and market value weights.

Equity (paid up) share capital	4,50,000
Retained earning (reserve)	1,50,000
Preference share capital	1,00,000
Debentures	3,00,000
Total	10,00,000

The firm's expected after tax component costs for the various sources of finance are as follows:

Source	Cost %
Equity capital	18
Retained earning	18
Preference Capital	11
Debentures	8

Suppose the current market price of equity shares is Rs. 20. Assuming market values of debentures to be Rs. 3,50,000 and preference shares to be Rs. 1,50,000 is same, find weighted average cost of capital by market value.

Solution

Weighted Average Cost of Capital – Book Value Weights

Source	Amount (Rs.)	Proportion	After tax	Weighted cost
Equity Capital	4,50,000	0.45	0.18	0.081
Retained Earning	1,50,000	0.15	0.18	0.027
Preference Capital	1,00,000	0.10	0.11	0.011
Debentures	3,00,000	0.30	0.08	0.024
	10,00,000	1.00		0.143

Weighted average cost of capital = 14.3%

Market value weights will be calculated in two steps.

Step 1: The value of equity shares is found to be (20 × Rs. 4,50,000) = Rs. 90,00,000

Step 2: The proportion of equity and retained earnings will be maintained from the book value weights. The total of equity capital and retained earnings is Rs. 6,00,000. The proportion of equity is 4,50,000/ 6,00,000 = 0.75 and retained earnings is 0.25. In the same proportion calculate equity and retained earnings. Out of Rs. 9,00,000, equity will be Rs. 6,75,000 and retained earnings will be Rs. 2,25,000.

Step 3: The weights is multiplied with after tax costs to get the weighted cost of specific sources. Add the costs. The weighted average cost of capital according to market value weights is given below. It is depicted as 14.7%.

Weighted Average Cost of Capital – Market Value Weights

		Weights	After tax cost (%)	WACC
Equity	90,00,000 × 0.75 = 60,75,000	0.63	18	0.1134
Retained Earnings	29,25,000	0.31	18	0.0558
Preference Capital	1,50,000	0.02	11	0.0022
Debentures	3,50,000	0.04	8	0.0032
Total	95,00,000			0.1746

WACC = 17.46%

9.12 MEASUREMENT OF MARGINAL COST OF CAPITAL

The overall cost of capital or the weighted average cost of capital provides the pattern of financing when it is constant. In cases when additional investment has to be raised from new sources, which may be either through retained earnings or through the issue of new capital, because new projects are taken up then marginal cost of capital must be calculated. The weighted average cost of capital (WACC) is revised in to the weighted marginal cost of capital (WMCC) when more than one source of capital is taken up in the new financing.

Marginal cost of capital is thus used:

(*i*) When there is requirement of additional funds.

(*ii*) When cost of more than one source must be calculated.

(*iii*) Financial risk may be affected with the new composition of funds.

(*iv*) Investors perceive that change in funds may affect business risk.

(*v*) Increase in financial and business risk may have an effect on increasing marginal cost of capital.

To calculate marginal cost of capital there are certain assumptions, which must be clarified before explaining the details:

(*i*) It is assumed that market value weights are used to calculate WMCC.

(*ii*) Since new funds have to be added to existing funds market value weights are rational in calculations.

(*iii*) The specific costs are calculated correctly.

The WMCC can be used in different situations: (*a*) when there is no external financing and only retained earnings are used for financing new projects, (*b*) when external financing is done with the existing sources of cost of capital in the same proportion as the existing one, and (*c*) when different costs of capital are raised and the proportions are also changed.

The simplest form of calculation is when retained earnings finance a new proposal. For example if 80% of the total requirements are financed by the equity shareholders funds and the cost of capital is 15% and 20% is financed by the issue of 10% bonds with an after tax cost of capital of 5% the WACC of the firm will be:

$$\text{WACC} = (0.05 \times 0.2) + (0.8 \times 0.15) = 13\%$$

$$\text{WMCC} = 15\%, \text{ which is the cost of retained earnings}$$

Note :

(*i*) ***No external financing:*** Therefore, when there is no external financing, WMCC will be equal to the specific cost of retained earnings.

(*ii*) ***External financing with existing cost and proportion of capital:*** When a firm raises additional capital in the same proportion, as it exists.

The WMCC and WACC are equal. Supposing a firm has 60% equity at 10% cost of capital 30% preference capital at 8% cost of capital and 10% cost of debt then WACC will be:

WACC = 0.6 (0.10) + 0.3 (0.08) + 0.1 (0.04) = 8.8%. If the firm wants to raise an additional finance and the cost of capital continuous to be the same as the existing one then,

$$\text{WMCC} = 0.6\ (0.10) + 0.3\ (0.08) + 0.1\ (0.04) = 8.8\%.$$

Therefore, WACC = WMCC.

(iii) When cost of capital differs and proportion varies: When the cost of capital is different and the proportion is also different then the WMCC will change.

For example,

Source	Amount (Rs.)	Weight	Specific cost (%)
Equity	50,00,000	0.57	12
Retained Earnings	25,00,000	0.29	12
10% Debentures	12,50,000	0.14	5

Solution

Since tax rate is 50% cost of debt is 5% now,

$$\text{WACC} = (0.57 \times 0.12) + (0.29 \times 0.12) + (0.14 \times 0.05) = 11.02\%$$

Suppose an investment proposal is Rs. 25,00,000 and it expects to generate retained earnings from existing operations. The remaining funds would be raised by equity capital of Rs. 15,00,000 at 13% and Rs. 5,00,000 from 12% bonds.

$$\text{WMCC} = (0.6 \times 0.13) + (0.2 \times 0.12) + (0.2 \times 0.6) = 22.2\%$$

WACC and WMCC are different when proportions and costs of new capital are different.

The WACC of the firm can be calculated in the following manner:

Source	Amount (Rs.)	Weight	Cost of capital	Weight × Cost of capital
Equity	50,00,000	0.444	0.12	5.328
Equity	15,00,000	0.133	0.13	1.729
Retained Earnings	25,00,000	0.222	0.12	2.664
Retained Earnings	5,00,000	0.045	0.12	0.540
Debentures	12,50,000	0.111	0.05	0.555
Debentures	5,00,000	0.045	0.06	0.270
	1,12,50,000	1.000		11.08

WACC has decreased to 10.32% with the influence of WMCC.

When financing amount increases the specific costs of different sources also increases. **The level at which specific cost of capital increases are called 'breaking point'.** WMCC should be measured at each of these breaks. The followings steps are applied:

(*a*) Percentages of new financing are established.

(*b*) A list of each source is made with amount, which has to be raised.

(*c*) To determine breaking points of a source and to calculate WMCC at each breaking point.

$$\text{Breaking point} = \text{MF/W}$$

$$\text{MF} = \text{Maximum finance available}$$

$$\text{W} = \text{Weight}$$

Capital Budgeting Decision and WMCC

(*i*) WMCC can be used in capital budgeting in new investment opportunities. It can be used as a minimum cut-off rate for evaluation of new proposals.

(*ii*) If WMCC is constant it can be evaluated through calculation of NPV. The project, which has the highest NPV, will be selected.

(*iii*) Capital budgeting will not give desired result if a firm continues to increase its investments as the return will decrease. A firm should accept those proposals where WMCC is equal to the marginal return on investment proposals otherwise the returns will not be acceptable because the cost will rise and the return will decrease. This will make the proposal ineffective and non-feasible.

POINTS TO REMEMBER

- Cost of capital is the minimum cut-off rate, which is acceptable to a firm to take an investment decision. It is also called the 'required rate of return' or the 'hurdle rate'.
- It provides the basic data for preparing the capital structure of a company.
- The cost of capital can be explicit or implicit. The explicit cost is the cost of raising the different sources of capital like equity, preference and debt. The implicit cost is the opportunity cost of funds.
- Retained earnings are implicit cost of capital and are important in determining the overall cost of capital.
- Cost of debt is considered to be cheaper than cost of equity because the interest is tax deductible.
- Debt and preference share can be redeemable or irredeemable. Redeemable securities can be calculated either through the trial and error method or shortcut method.
- The equity capital can be calculated by dividend approach, earnings approach and CAPM approach.
- WACC is also called 'overall cost of capital' and it can be calculated by book value or market value weights.
- WMCC can be used for evaluating projects with new capital investment.

OBJECTIVE TYPE QUESTIONS

State whether the following statements are true (T) or false (F).

1. Debt is cheaper than equity.
2. Implicit cost is the cost of using the fund.
3. Retained earnings do not have any cost.
4. The market price of the share determines the current price of the share.
5. Cost of new equity and existing equity is the same.
6. Cost of capital is the hurdle rate, or the required rate of return.
7. Retained earnings are not included in WACC because they do not have any market value.
8. All sources of capital have the same cost.
9. Historical weights are used to calculate WACC.
10. Marginal weights are the proportions in which different sources of funds are raised.
11. Target weights are used for long-term planning of resources.
12. Business risk is internal to the firm.
13. Financial risk is external to the firm.
14. Risk free rate is dependent on demand and supply conditions in the markets.
15. Book value and market value cannot be the same.
16. Dividends to equity shareholders reduce tax liability.
17. Interest on debentures reduces tax liability.
18. Cost of capital is the basic data used for NPV calculations.

Answers: 1. (T), 2. (T), 3. (F), 4. (T), 5. (F), 6. (T), 7. (F), 8. (F), 9. (T), 10. (T), 11. (T), 12. (T), 13. (F), 14. (T), 15. (F), 16. (F), 17. (T), 18. (T).

THEORETICAL QUESTIONS

1. What is the meaning of the term cost of capital?
2. Distinguish between explicit and implicit costs of capital. Do retained earnings have a cost?
3. What are the different approaches for calculating equity? Are retained earnings cost free?
4. What is the value of market value weights in computing weighted average cost of capital?
5. 'Equity shareholders provide risk capital.' Comment on this statement.
6. Explain briefly financial risk and business risk.

7. What is the meaning of cost of capital? What is its significance in financial decision making?
8. What is the risk free rate of interest? How is it different from business and financial risk?
9. What is weighted average cost of capital? Why is it used? Should cost of capital be calculated according to book value or market value weights?
10. 'Debt is cheaper than equity.' Comment on this statement.
11. What are the components of cost of capital? Discuss the steps in computation of weighted average cost of capital.
12. 'New issue capital is more expensive than retained earnings'. Comment.
13. 'Cost of retained earnings is the same as cost of equity.' Comment.
14. Why cost of capital measured on an after tax basis. What effect does it have on specific cost of capital?
15. Cost of preference capital is lower than cost of equity. Give reasons.
16. Write notes on:
    (*i*) Implicit cost of capital
    (*ii*) Explicit cost of capital
    (*iii*) Weighted average cost of capital
    (*iv*) Target weights
    (*v*) Book value and market value weights
17. Comment on:
    (*i*) Retained earnings do not have any costs.
    (*ii*) Market value weights are more important than historical weights.
    (*iii*) Interest free rate of risk considers business and financial risk.
    (*iv*) Debt is cheaper than equity.
    (*v*) New issue of capital is more expansive than retained earnings.
18. Discuss the different approaches to the calculation of cost of equity. Are retained earnings cost free?

ILLUSTRATIVE PROBLEMS

Illustration 9.1 A company issued a 10% perpetual debt for Rs. 15,00,000. The company is in the 40% tax bracket. Find the cost of debt after tax (*i*) at par (*ii*) at a discount of 15% (*iii*) at a 10% premium.

Solution

Cost of irredeemable debt at par:

$$k_d = \frac{I}{NP}(1-t)$$

Where

k_d = Cost of debt

I = Annual interest

t = Taxable rate

NP = Net proceeds

(*i*) Cost of debt after tax $\quad k_d = \frac{1,50,000}{15,00,000}(1 - 0.40) = 0.06 \text{ or } 6\%$

(*ii*) Cost of debt at a discount of 15%

$$k_d = \frac{1,50,000}{12,75,000} \times (1 - 0.40) = 0.07 \text{ or } 7\%$$

(*iii*) Cost of debt at 15% premium

$$k_d = \frac{1,50,000}{17,25,000}(1 - 0.40) = 0.052 \text{ or } 5.2\%$$

Illustration 9.2 Compute the after tax cost of capital in the following cases:

(*i*) A bond sold at par at the coupon rate of 13%.

(*ii*) A preference share sold at par at 14% dividend.

(*iii*) A 10-year redeemable year bond of Rs. 1,000 at 9% rate of interest sold at Rs. 900.

(*iv*) An equity share selling at a market price of Rs. 150 paying a current dividend of Rs. 12 per share which is expected to grow at 8% rate of interest.

The tax rate of the company is 40%. In the above cases, compute after tax costs.

Solution

(*i*) Cost of the bond is

$$k_d = 0.13\ (1 - 0.4) = 0.078 \text{ or } 7.8\%$$

(*ii*) Cost of preference share at 14% dividend

$$k_d = \frac{1}{NP}(1-t) = 0.14\ (1-0.4) = 0.084 \text{ or } 8.4\%$$

(*iii*) Cost of redeemable debt

$$k_d = \frac{\text{Interest}\ (1-t) + (RV - NP)/N}{(RV + NP)/2}$$

$$= \frac{90\ (1-0.4) + (1{,}000 - 900)/10}{(1{,}000 + 900)/2}$$

$$= \frac{(54+10)}{950} = 0.067\% \text{ or } 6.7\%$$

(*iv*) $P_0 = 150\ D_0 = 12,\ g = 0.08$

$D_1 = 12\ (1 + 0.08) = 12.96$

$k_e = D_1/P_0 + g = 12.96\ /\ 150\ + 0.08\ = 0.1664 \text{ or } 16.64\%$

Illustration 9.3 A company issued redeemable debenture of the face value of Rs. 100. It has a coupon rate of 13%, floatation costs of 10% at a tax bracket of 40%. The debentures are redeemed after 5 years at a premium of 10%. Find the after tax cost of debt.

Solution

$$\text{Cost of redeemable debt} = \frac{I\ (1-t) + (f + d + p_r - p_i)/N}{(RV + NP)/2}$$

$$= \frac{13\ (1-0.4) + (10+10)5}{(110+90)/2}$$

$$= 7.8 + 4/100 = 11.8\%$$

Illustration 9.4 A company issued a debenture with a face value of Rs. 100. The coupon rate is 9%. Determine the market price of the debenture if the current yield on the debenture is (*i*) 10% (*ii*) 11% and (*iii*) 9%.

Solution

MP = I/Rate of current yield

(*i*) MP = 9/0.1 = Rs. 90 when current yield is 10%

(*ii*) MP = 9/0.11 = Rs. 81.8 when current yield is 11%

(*iii*) MP = 9/ 0.09 = Rs. 100 when current yield is 9%

Illustration 9.5 A company issued debentures with the face value of Rs. 100. The expected interest payment from the company is based on varying interest rates. From year 1 to 5 the rate of interest is 6%. For 6 to 8 years 8% interest, and from 9th to 10th year the rate of interest is 11%.

The debenture matures after 10 years. Investor's expectation is to receive an effective yield of 13%. What would be the price of the debentures if they are redeemable at (*i*) par (*ii*) premium of 10% (*iii*) discount of 10%.

Solution

(*i*) When debentures are redeemed at par

Year	Interest	PV @ 13% discount factor	PV
1–5	6	3.517	21.102
6	8	0.480	3.84
7	8	0.425	3.40
8	8	0.376	3.008
9	11	0.333	3.663
10	(100 + 11) = 111	0.295	32.745
			MP of debentures = 67.758

(*ii*) Value of debenture redeemable at 10% premium

Year	Interest	PV @ 13% discount factor	PV
1–5	6	3.517	21.102
6	8	0.480	3.84
7	8	0.425	3.40
8	8	0.376	3.008
9	11	0.333	3.663
10	(110 + 11) = 121	0.295	35.695
			MP of debentures = 70.708

(*iii*) Value of debentures at 10% discount

Year	Interest	PV @ 13% discount factor	PV
1–5	6	3.517	21.102
6	8	0.480	3.84
7	8	0.425	3.40
8	8	0.376	3.008
9	11	0.333	3.663
10	(90 + 11) = 101	0.295	29.795
			MP of debentures = 64.808

Illustration 9.6 A company has the following capital structure as on 30 March 2007.

Equity shares 50,00,000 of Rs. 2 each	1,00,00,000
10% Preference shares	40,00,000
15% Debentures	80,00,000
Total	2,20,00,000

The shares of the company have a market price of Rs. 50 each. The company will pay a dividend of Rs. 15 per share and it will grow at 10% continuously. The tax rate of the company is 40%. Compute the weighted average cost of capital.

Solution

Cost of debt after tax

$$k_d = 15\ (1 - 0.4) = 9\%$$

cost of equity share capital

$$k_e = D_1/P_0 + g = 15/50 + 0.10 = 40\%$$

Calculation of WACC

Source	Amount (Rs.)	Weight	Cost of capital	WACC
Equity	1,00,00,000	0.454	0.40	0.1816
10% Preferebce Capital	40,00,000	0.182	0.10	0.0182
15% Debentures	80,00,000	0.364	0.09	0.03276
Total	2,20,00,000			0.23256

The weighted average cost of capital = 23.25%.

Illustration 9.7 A company's market price of a share is Rs. 40. It has paid Rs. 2 per share as dividend and the investor's expectation of the rate of growth is 6% per annum.

(*i*) Compute the company's equity cost of capital

(*ii*) If the cost of capital of the company is 9% and growth is 6%, calculate market price, if dividend of Rs. 2 is to be paid at the end of year 1.

Solution

(*i*) The equity cost of capital is

$$k_e = D_1/P_0 + g$$
$$= 2.12/40 + 0.06 = 11.3\%$$

(*ii*) If $k_e = 9\%$ and $g = 6\%$, D = 2

$$P_0 = D_1/(k_e - g)$$
$$= 2/(0.09 - 0.06) = \text{Rs. } 66.66$$

The market price of the share is Rs. 66.66

Illustration 9.8 A company declared a dividend of Rs. 2 per share last year. The shareholders have a required rate of return of 15%. What would be the market price of the share if the growth rate of the dividend is expected to the growth rate of the dividend is expected to be (*i*) 9% (*ii*) 11% (*iii*) 14% (*iv*) –10%

Solution

(*i*) The market price of a share when growth is 9%

$$MP = \frac{D_1}{(k_e - g)} = \frac{2\,(1\ +0.11)}{(0.15\ -\ 0.11)}$$

$$= \frac{2.22}{0.04} = \text{Rs. } 36.33$$

(*ii*) The market price of the share when growth is 11%

$$MP = \frac{D_1}{(k_e - g)}$$

$$= \frac{2\,(1\ +0.11)}{(0.15\ -\ 0.11)}$$

$$= \frac{2.22}{0.04} = \text{Rs. } 55.5$$

(*iii*) MP of the share when the growth is 15%

$$MP = \frac{D_1}{(k_e - g)}$$

$$= \frac{2(1\ +0.15)}{(0.15\ -\ 0.14)} = \text{Rs. } 230$$

(*iv*) When MP of the share is –10%

$$MP = \frac{D_1}{(k_e - g)} = \frac{2[1\ +(-0.10)]}{[0.15-(-0.10)]}$$

$$= \frac{1.8}{0.25} = \text{Rs } 7.2$$

Illustration 9.9 A company is planning to issue new equity shares. The dividends declared by the company are the last 5 years is as follows:

Year	Amount (Rs.)
1	10.00
2	11.50
3	12.75
4	13.50
5	15.00

The floatation cost is expected to be 2% of the selling price. Compute the cost of (*i*) existing equity shares, and (*ii*) cost of new equity shares.

The current market price of the shares is Rs. 150.

Solution

(*i*) Cost of existing shares

Step 1: Calculation of growth rate of dividends

$$D_5 = D_1 (1 + g)^4$$

$$D_5/D_1 = 1 (1 + g)^4$$

$$= 15/10 = 1.5$$

Refer to Table A-1, and find that compound value closes to 1.5 for 4 years.

The value is approximately 11%.

The expected dividend will be 15 (1 + 0.11) = Rs. 16.65

Step 2:

$$\text{Cost of equity shares} = \frac{\text{Expected dividends}}{\text{Current market price}} + \text{Growth rate}$$

$$= \frac{16.65}{150} + 11\% = 11.1\% + 11\% = 22.1\%$$

$$(ii)\ \text{Cost of equity of new shares} = \frac{\text{Expected dividends}}{P_0 \left(1 - f\right)} + g$$

$$= \frac{16.65}{150\left(1 - 0.02\right)} + 11\%$$

$$= 11.326\% + 11\% = 22.32\%$$

Illustration 9.10 A company declared a dividend of Rs. 3 last year. It is expected to have a growth of 14% in the next 2 year. In the 3rd and 4th year it would be 12% and after that it would be 10%.

At what price should the share be purchased if shareholders expect a return of 16% per annum?

Solution

Step 1: Find the intrinsic value of the share

Intrinsic value of the share will be equal to the present value of the next 4 dividends plus present value of the market price of the share in the 4th year.

Year	Dividends (Rs.)	PV @ 16%	Total PV
0	3	–	–
1	3.42	0.862	2.95
2	3.89	0.743	2.89
3	4.36	0.641	2.79
4	4.89	0.552	2.70
Total			11.33

Price in the 4th year

$$P_4 = D_3/(k_e - g)$$

$$D_5 = \text{Expected dividend } 4.89\ (1.10) = 5.379$$

Price at the end of the 4th year = 5.379/(16% – 10%)

Therefore price at the end of the 4th year = Rs. 89.65

Present value of the market price = 89.65 × 0.552 = Rs. 49.49

Total intrinsic value = 60.81

The shareholders should purchase the share for a price, which is less than Rs. 60.81, which is its intrinsic value.

Illustration 9.11 The equity shares of a company are quoted at Rs. 105. The company plans to declare a dividend of Rs. 10 per share next year. The growth rate of dividends is 5%. The tax rate is 50%. Calculate weighted average cost of capital when the capital structure of the company as on 31 March 2007 shows the following details:

Equity share capital 9,00,000 shares of Re 1 each	9,00,000
10% preference shares	6,00,000
10% debentures	5,00,000
Total capital	20,00,000

Solution

Step 1: Calculate cost of equity

$$\text{Cost of equity} = \frac{\text{Expected dividend}}{\text{Current market price}} + \text{Growth rate}$$

$$= \frac{10}{105} + 5 = 9.5 + 5 = 14.5\%$$

Step 2: Calculate cost of debt

$$k_d = I(1 - t)$$
$$= 0.10\ (1 - 0.5) = 5\%$$

Step 3: Method (1)

Weighted Average Cost of Capital			
	Cost	Amount (Rs.)	Cost × Amount
Equity Preference	14.5%	9,00,000	1,30,50,000
Debenture	10%	6,00,000	60,00,000
(after tax)	5%	5,00,000	25,00,000
		20,00,000	2,15,50,000

Method (2)

Weighted Average Cost of Capital				
	Cost	Capital	Weight	Weight × Cost
Equity	14.5%	9,00,000	0.45	6.525
Preference	10%	6,00,000	0.3	3.000
Debt	5%	5,00,000	0.25	1.250
		20,00,000		10.775

Weighted average cost of capital is 10.775%

Illustration 9.12 A company wants to raise additional capital of Rs. 20 lakh for its new investment plans. It has Rs. 4,20,000 as retained earnings. Further details are as following:

(*i*) Debt equity mix 30% and 70%.

(*ii*) Cost of debt up to Rs. 3,60,000 10% before tax, beyond Rs. 3,60,000 16% before tax.

(*iii*) Earnings per share Rs. 8.

(*iv*) Dividend payout 50% of earnings.

(*v*) Expected growth in dividends 10%.

(*vi*) Current market price per share Rs. 88.

(*vii*) Tax rate 50%.

Compute (*a*) Pattern for raising additional capital

(*b*) The after cost of additional capital

(*c*) The cost of retained earnings and cost of equity

Solution

(*a*) Pattern for raising additional capital

Step 1: Debt 30% of Rs. 20,00,000 = Rs. 6,00,000

Equity 70% of Rs. 10,00,000 = Rs. 14,00,000

Total = Rs. 20,00,000

Step 2: Composition of new investment sources

Sources	Amount (Rs.)
10% debt	3,60,000
16% debt	2,40,000
Total	6,00,000
Retained earnings	4,20,000
Total	10,20,000
Equity 14,00,000 – 4,20,000	9,80,000
	20,00,000

(*b*) The after cost of additional capital

After tax cost of debt

3,60,000 × 10% = 36,000

2,40,000 × 16% = 38,400

Total debt 6,00,000 74,400 (Interest)

Cost of debt = (74,400/6,00,000) × 100 = 12.4%

After tax cost = 12.4 (1 – 0.5) = 6.2%

Cost of retained earnings

$$k_r = k_e(1 - t)\ (1 - b)$$
$$= 14.5\ (1 - 0)\ (1 - 0) = 14.5\%$$

Cost of equity capital

$$k_e = D_1/P_0 + g$$
$$D_0 = 50\% \text{ of Rs. } 8 = \text{Rs. } 4,\ g = 10\%$$
$$D_1 = D_0(1 + g)$$
$$= 4\ (1 + 10\%) = 4.40$$

Illustration 9.13

Source	Amount	Specific cost (%)
Equity share capital		
3,00,000 shares of Rs. 10 each	30,00,000	10
Preferred share capital		
1,00,000 shares of Rs. 10 each	10,00,000	9
Retained earnings	10,00,000	10
10% debentures of Rs. 1,000 each	25,00,000	5

At present debentures are being traded at 90% preferences shares at par and equity share at 20 rupees per share. Find out WACC based on book value weights.

Book value source	BV	Weights	Cost	Weighted capital
Equity	30,00,000	0.4	0.1	0.040
Retained earnings	10,00,000	0.13	0.1	0.013
Preference shares	10,00,000	0.13	0.09	0.011
10% debentures	25,00,000	0.33	0.05	0.016
	75,00,000			0.080
			= 8.0%	

Illustration 9.14 A company has the following capital structure

Source	Book Value (Rs.)	Market Value (Rs.)
Equity share capital	80,00,000	1,20,00,000
Retained earnings	25,00,000	–
Preference share capital	5,00,000	5,50,000
Long-term debt	20,00,000	25,00,000
	1,30,00,000	1,50,50,000

Additional Information

Equity shares have the current market price of Rs. 140 per share. The expectation of dividend at the end of the current year is Rs. 20. The company paid varying dividends in the last 5 years of Rs. 15.45, Rs. 17, Rs. 18.50, Rs. 19 and Rs. 19.50 respectively. The expectation is that new equity shares can be sold at Rs. 138 per share underwriting commission is Rs. 3 per share.

15% **preference shares** can be sold for a premium of 10% and underwriting commission is Rs. 2 per share.

Debentures The company sold 15% debentures with a maturity period of 15 years. They are of Rs. 1,000 each and can sell for Rs. 980. Underwriting commission is 2%.

Calculate (*i*) specific cost of capital and (*ii*) overall cost of capital. Corporate tax is 50%.

Solution

(*i*) Specific cost of capital

Equity share capital

Step 1: Calculate growth rate of equity

The compound value factor of dividend is

$$D_5/D_1 = (1 + g)^4$$
$$= 19.50/15.45 = 1.2621$$

The growth rate is 6% from Table A-1, compound value table for 4 years closest to 1.2621

Step 2: Calculate cost of equity

$$k_e = \frac{D_1}{P_0(1 - f)} + g = \text{Rs. } 20$$

$$= \frac{20}{(138 - 3)} + 0.06 = 20.8\%$$

Step 3: Calculate cost of retained earnings

Cost of retained earnings is the same as equity but there is no underwriting cost on it. Cost of retained earnings will be calculated in the following way:

$$k_r = D_1/P_0 + g = 20/138 + 0.06 = 20.49\%$$

Cost of preference share capital $k_p = \frac{D_1}{P_0(1 - f)} + g = 15/108 = 13.9\%$

The net proceeds of debt is 980 – 20 = 960

Long-term debt $k_d = \frac{I(1 - t) + (RV - NP)/n}{(RV + NP)/2}$

Where, RV = Redemption Value

t = Tax rate

n = Life of debenture

NP = Net proceeds of issue per debenture

$$k_d = \frac{150(1 - 0.5) + (1{,}000 - 960)/15}{(1{,}000 + 960)/2}$$

$$= 77.66/980 = 0.079 \text{ or } 7.9\%$$

(*ii*) Overall cost of capital based on book value and market value weights

Source	Book value (BV)	Market value (MV)	Cost of capital (CC)	BV × CC	MV × CC
Equity	80,00,000	91,20,000	20.8%	16,64,000	18,96,960
Retained earnings	25,00,000	28,80,000	20.5%	5,12,500	5,90,400
Preference capital	5,00,000	5,50,000	13.9%	69,500	76,450
Debt	20,00,000	25,00,000	7.9%	1,58,000	1,97,500
	1,30,00,000	1,50,50,000		24,04,000	27,61,310

Note: MV of equity is Rs. 1,20,00,000. This is divided between equity share capital and retained earnings in the ratio of their book value *i.e.* Rs. 80,00,000 : Rs. 25,00,000 or 0.76 and 0.24 of Rs. 1,20,00,000.

(*a*) Overall cost of capital according to book value weights = 24,04,000/1,30,00,000 = 18.49%.

(*b*) Market value weights 27,61,310/1,50,50,000 = 18.35%.

Illustration 9.15 The following is the capital structure of a company as on 31.12.2009

Sources	Amount (Rs.)
Equity shares 10,00,000 of Re. 1 each	10,00,000
15% preference capital of Rs. 100 each	6,00,000
13% debentures	8,00,000
	24,00,000

The market price of the company's share is Rs. 120 and an expected dividend of Rs. 12 would be declared after one year. The dividend growth rate is 8%.

The company is in the tax bracket of 50%.

(*a*) Compute weighted average cost of capital.

(*b*) Calculate the revised weighted average cost of capital when a company plans to borrow Rs. 14,00,000 at 15% rate of interest. This decision will help to increase dividend from Rs. 12 to Rs. 15 per share. The market price of the share is expected to decrease from Rs. 120 to Rs. 110 per share.

Solution

(*a*) Calculation of weighted average cost of capital

Sources	Amount (Rs.)	Weight	Cost	Weighted cost
Equity shares	10,00,000	0.42	18%	7.56
15% preference Share	6,00,000	0.25	15%	3.75
13% debentures	8,00,000	0.33	6.5%	2.15
	24,00,000		WACC =	13.46%

Note: Cost of equity $= D_1/P_0 + g = 12/120 + 0.08 = 18\%$

Cost of debenture = 13% (1 – 0.5) = 6.5%

(*b*) Calculation of revised weighted average cost of capital

Sources	Amount	Weight	Cost	Weighted cost
Equity shares	10,00,000	0.26	21.6%	5.62
15% pref. Share	6,00,000	0.16	15%	2.40
13% debentures	8,00,000	0.21	6.5%	1.37
15% loan	14,00,000	0.37	7.5%	2.77
	38,00,000		WACC =	12.16%

Note: Cost of equity = 15/110 + 0.08 = 21.6%

Cost of debenture = 13% (1 – 0.5) = 6.5%

Cost of loan = 15% (1 – 0.5) = 7.5%

Illustration 9.16 A company has the following capital structure:

Sources	Amount (Rs.)
Equity shares 35,00,000 of Re. 1 each	35,00,000
11% preference capital	2,00,000
15% debentures	5,00,000
Total	42,00,000

The current market price of the company's equity share is Rs. 30. The expected dividend per share for next year is Rs. 2 with the growth rate of 10%. The company can issue new debentures at 16%. The company's debentures are selling at Rs. 95 per debenture. The company's new preference share can be sold at a price of Rs. 9.15 with the face value of Rs. 10 each.

The tax rate of the company is 50%.

Compute (*i*) After tax cost of new debt, preference share and equity share capital. (*ii*) Weighted marginal cost of capital.

Solution

(*i*) After tax cost of new debt, preference share and equity share capital.

After tax cost of debt

$$k_d = 16/95\ (1 - 0.5) = 0.0842 \text{ or } 8.42\%$$

After tax cost of preference capital

$$k_p = 1.1/9.15 = 0.120 \text{ or } 12.0\%$$

After tax cost of equity share capital

$$k_e = D_1/P_0 + g = 2/30 + 0.10 = 16.66\%$$

(*ii*) Weighted marginal cost of capital.

Source	Weight	Cost of Capital	Weighted cost of capital
Equity	0.83	0.1667	0.1383
11% Preference capital	0.05	0.1200	0.006
16% Debenture	0.12	0.0842	0.0101
		WMCC =	0.1490

Weighted marginal cost of capital = 14.90%

Illustration 9.17 (*i*) The current market price of a share is Rs. 90 and expected dividend at the end of the current year is Rs. 5 with a growth rate of 10%. Calculate cost of capital.

(*ii*) The current market price of share is Rs. 100. The firm needs Rs. 1,00,000 for expansion and new shares can be sold at Rs. 95, expected dividend at the end of current year is Rs. 4.75 with a growth rate of 6%. Also calculate cost of capital of new equity.

Solution

(*i*)
$$k_e = \frac{D_1}{P_0} + g = \frac{5}{90} + 0.10$$

$\therefore$ Cost of capital $= 0.15 = 15\%$

(*ii*)
$$k_e = \frac{D_1}{P_0} + g = \frac{4.75}{100} + 0.06 = 10.75\%$$

New equity cost,

$$k_e = \frac{4.75}{95} + 0.06 = 11\%$$

Illustration 9.18 The equity share capital of a company consists of Rs.1,00,000 equity shares of Rs. 100 each. Its current earnings are Rs. 10,00,000 p.a. The company wants to raise add funds of Rs. 25,00,000 by issuing new shares. The floatation is expected to be 10% of the face value. Find cost of equity capital, given that earnings are expected to remain same for coming years.

The shares of a company are being:

(*i*) Currently sold at Rs. 20 per share. It paid a dividend of Rs. 2 last year. The profits are expected to growth at 10% p.a. and company has a payout ratio of 100%. Determine cost of equity capital of the company.

(*ii*) What should be expected current price of the share if growth rate is 8%?

Solution

Net Proceeds on issue of equity shares are Rs. (100 – 10) = Rs. 90 and earnings per share is Rs.10.

$$\text{Cost of new equity } k_e = \frac{D_1}{P_0} \text{ or } \frac{D_1}{NP} = \frac{10}{90} = 11.1\%$$

$$\text{Current } P_0 = \text{Rs. } 20$$

$$\text{Dividend Paid} = \text{Rs. } 2$$

$$\text{Growth rate } g = 10\%$$

$$D_1 = 2 \times (1 + 0.10) = 2.20$$

$$k_e = \frac{D_1}{P_0} + g$$

$$= \frac{2.20}{20} + 0.1$$

$$= 21\%$$

If growth rate is 8%

$$2\,(1 + 0.8) = 2\,(1.08) = 2.16$$

$$D = 2.16$$

$$P_0 = \frac{D_1}{k_e - g}$$

$$P_0 = \frac{2.16}{0.21 - 0.08}$$

$$= 16.61\%$$

If it is 12% then,

$$2\,(1 + 0.12) = 2\,(1.12) = 2.24$$

$$D_2 = 2.24$$

$$k_e = \frac{D_1}{NP} + g$$

$$= \frac{14.03\,(1.07)}{(125 - 3.75)} + 0.07 \quad = 19.38\%$$

$$\text{Cost of existing equity } \frac{D_1}{P_0} + g = \frac{14.03\,(1.07)}{125} + 0.07 = 19.01\%$$

$$\text{Cost of new equity} = \text{Dividend} \times \text{growth rate of } 7\%$$

$$\left(\frac{15.0121}{121.25} + 0.07\right) = 19.38\%$$

Illustration 9.19 The following information is available relating to risk free interest rate I_f and market rate R_m of a security during last 6 years.

Year	I_f	R_m
1	0.06	0.14
2	0.05	0.03
3	0.07	0.21
4	0.08	0.26
5	0.09	0.03
6	0.07	0.11

On the basis of this information. Find out cost of equity capital on the basis of CAPM given that beta factor is 0.863.

To find out cost of equity as per CAPM. First find average risk free rate and average market rate of security.

$$\text{Average } I_f = \frac{0.06 + 0.05 + 0.07 + 0.08 + 0.09 + 0.07}{6} = 0.07$$

$$\text{Average } R_m = \frac{0.14 + 0.03 + 0.21 + 0.26 + 0.03 + 0.11}{6} = 0.13$$

$$\therefore \quad k_e = I_f + \beta\,(R_m - I_f) = 0.07 + 0.863\,(0.13 - 0.07) = 12.2\%$$

Illustration 9.20 Find out weighted average cost of capital through book value and market value when the following information is provided.

Source of Capital		Book value specific cost (%)	Market value
Debt	10,00,000	7	11,00,000
Preference shares	2,00,000	15	2,50,000
Equity shares	13,00,000	16	30,00,000
	25,00,000		

Solution

(*i*)

Source of Capital	Book Value	Amount (Rs.)
Debt	$10,00,000 \times 7.0$	70,000
Preference Capital	$2,00,000 \times 15$	30,000
Equity shares	$13,00,000 \times 16$	2,08,000
	25,00,000	3,08,000

$$k_0 = \frac{3,08,000}{25,00,000} \times 100 = 12.32\%$$

(*ii*)

Source of Capital	Market Value	After tax costs	Amount (Rs.)
Debt	11,00,000	7%	77,000
Preference Capital	2,50,000	15%	37,500
Equity shares	30,00,000	16%	4,80,000
	43,50,000		5,94,500

$$k_0 = \frac{5,94,500}{43,50,000} \times 100 = 0.136$$

Illustration 9.21 JKL Ltd. has the following book-value capital structure as 31 March 2002.

Particulars	Amount (Rs.)
Equity share capital (2,00,000 shares)	40,00,000
11.5% preference shares	10,00,000
10% debentures	30,00,000
	80,00,000

The equity share of the company sells for Rs. 20. It is expected that the company will pay next year a dividend of Rs. 2 per equity share, which is expected to grow at 5% p.a. forever. Assume a 35% corporate tax rate.

Compute:

(*i*) Weighted average cost of capital (WACC) of the company based on the existing capital structure.

(*ii*) The new WACC, if the company raises an additional Rs. 20 lakh debt by issuing 12% debentures. This would result in increasing the expected equity dividend to Rs. 2.40 and leave the growth rate unchanged, but the price of equity share will fall to Rs. 16 per share.

(C.A. PE-II, May 2003)

Solution

(*i*) WACC based existing capital structure

(*a*) Cost of equity capital

$$k_e = \frac{D_1}{P_0} + g = \frac{2}{20} + 0.05 = 0.15 \text{ or } 15\%$$

(*b*) Cost of preference shares

$$k_p = \frac{D_P}{NP} = \frac{11.5}{100} = 0.115 \text{ or } 11.5\%$$

(*c*) Cost of debentures

$$k_d = I(1 - t) = 10\%\ (1 - 0.35) = 6.5\%$$

WACC (based on book values)

Source of capital	Book values (Rs.)	Weight	Post-tax cost (%)	Weighted cost (%)
Equity share capital	40,00,000	0.500	15.0	7.50
11.5% Preference shares	10,00,000	0.125	11.5	1.44
10% Debentures	30,00,000	0.375	6.5	2.44
	80,00,000	1.000		WACC = 11.38%

(*ii*) WACC (based revised capital structure)

(*a*) Cost of equity capital

$$k_e = \frac{2.40}{16} + 0.05 = 0.20 \text{ or } 20\%$$

(*b*) Cost of preference shares

$$k_p = \frac{D_P}{NP} = \frac{11.5}{100} = 0.115 \text{ or } 11.5\%$$

(*c*) Cost of 10% debentures

$$k_d = \text{I}\,(1 - t) = 10\%\,(1 - 0.35) = 6.5\%$$

(*d*) Cost of 12% debentures

$$k_d = \text{I}\,(1 - t) = 12\%\,(1 - 0.35) = 7.8\%$$

WACC (based on book values, after raising additional finance by issue of 12% debentures)

Source of finance	Book values (Rs.)	Weight	Post-tax cost (%)	Weighted cost (%)
Equity share capital	40,00,000	0.4	20.0	8.00
11.5% Preference shares	10,00,000	0.1	11.5	1.15
10% Debentures	30,00,000	0.3	6.5	1.95
12% Debentures	20,00,000	0.2	7.8	1.56
	1,00,00,000	1.0		WACC = 12.66%

PROBLEMS FOR PRACTICE

Problem 9.1 (A) A company has 15% perpetual debt of Rs.15,00,000 the tax rate is 50%. Determine before tax and after tax assuming debt is issued at (*i*) par (*ii*) 10% premium and (*iii*) 10% discount.

(B) A company has a perpetual debt at 18% of Rs.15 lakh debentures. If company tax rates is at 5% find before and after tax cost of debt at par (*i*) If the debt are sold at a discount of 8%, (*ii*) at a discount12% and (*iii*) at a premium.

[**Answers:** A.(*i*) 7.5%, A.(*ii*) 6.8% A.(*iii*) 8.33%; B.(*i*) 9%, B.(*ii*) 9.78%, B.(*iii*) 8.04%]

Problem 9.2 Compute the after tax cost of capital in the following cases:

(*i*) A perpetual bond at the coupon rate of 13% and sold at par.

(*ii*) A 14% preference share sold at par.

(*iii*) A redeemable bond of 10 years maturity at 10% rate of interest of Rs. 1,000 sold at Rs. 850.

(*iv*) An equity share selling at Rs. 180 paying a dividend of Rs. 20 per share and expected to grow at 10%.

The company is in the tax bracket of 40%.

[**Answers:** (*i*) 7.8% (*ii*) 14% (*iii*) 8.1% and (*iv*) 22.2%]

Problem 9.3 A company issues debentures of the face value of Rs. 1,000. The debentures have a maturity period of 10 years out of which 5 year have been completed. The debentures have a coupon rate of 15%. At what price can a debenture be purchased today if the required rate of return is 12% and

(*i*) The debenture is redeemed at par

(*ii*) Redeemed at a premium of 10%

(*iii*) Redeemed at a 10% discount

[**Answers:** The debentures can be purchased for a market price less than (*i*) 1107.75 (*ii*) 1164.45 (*iii*) 1051.05]

Problem 9.4 Find cost of capital for X Ltd. for existing equity share and new share

(*i*) Each share is Rs. 125 per share

(*ii*) Underwriting cost 3%

(*iii*) Following dividend for last 5 years

(*iv*) The Company has a fixed dividend Payout ratio.

Year	Dividend per share
1997	10.70
1998	11.45
1999	12.25
2000	13.11
2001	14.03

[**Answer:** 15.59]

Problem 9.5 A company has 12% rate of return on equity shares. What would be the market price of shares if the previous dividend (D_0) was Rs. 2 and investors expect dividends to grow at a constant rate of 40%, 11%, 12% and 14%?

[**Answers:** 26,222; Infinity, –114]

Problem 9.6 The following information has been extracted from the balance sheet of Fashions Ltd. as on 31.12.1994.

Particulars	(Rs. in lakh)
Equity	400
12% debentures	400
Term loans (interest 18%)	1200
Total	2,000

(*a*) Determine the weighted average cost of capital. It had been paying dividends at a consistent rate of 20% per annum.

(*b*) What would be the difference if the current market price of Rs. 100 per share is Rs. 160.

(*c*) Determine the effect of income tax on the cost of capital under both conditions.

(ICWA June, 1995)

[**Answers:** (*a*) 17.2% (*b*) 12.5% (*c*) 11.92% and 10.42%]

Problem 9.7 Calculate weighted Average cost of capital

Equity (Paid up) share capital	4,50,000
Retained earning (reserve)	1,50,000
Preference share capital	1,00,000
Debentures	3,00,000
	10,00,000

The firm's expected after tax component costs of the various sources of finance are as follows:

Source	Cost (%)
Equity capital	18
Retained earning	18
Pref. capital	11
Debentures	8

[**Answer:** Weighted Average Cost of Capital = 14.3%]

Problem 9.8 A company issued a bond with a face value of Rs. 1,000 redeemable after 10 years. The expected interest payments from year 1 to year 7 are at the rate of 9%. Year 8 and 9 are 10% and 12% in year 10. Investors effective yield is 14%. What would be the price of the debentures if they are redeemable at (*i*) par (*ii*) premium of 10% and (*iii*) discount of 10%.

[**Answer:**(*i*) Rs. 754.22 (*ii*) 781.22 (*iii*) 727.22]

Problem 9.9 A company has a track record of the following dividend payments.

Year	Dividend (Rs.)
1	12.00
2	13.50
3	15.00
4	16.50
5	18.00

Compute cost of (*i*) existing equity shares and (*ii*) new equity shares if current. Market price is Rs. 160 and floatation cost is 2% of issue price in the issue of new shares.

[**Answer:** Growth rate = 11% (*i*) cost of existing equity shares = 23.48%
(*ii*) cost of new equity shares = 23.62%]

Problem 9.10 A company declared a dividend of Rs. 2 last year. It is expected to have a growth rate of 10% in the next 2 years and 8% in the third and fourth year. After that it would be 6%. Compute the price of the share at which the shareholder should purchase it if his expectation is a growth rate of return of 12%.

[**Answer:** Investor should buy the bond at a price less than Rs. 71.437.]

Problem 9.11 Aries Ltd. wants to raise additional finance for Rs. 10,00,000 for its new investment plans. It has Rs. 2,10,000 as retained earnings, which can be used for investment. The following information is provided:

(*i*) Debt/Equity mix 30/70

(*ii*) Cost of debt up to Rs. 1,80,000 – 10% before tax more than 1,80,000 – 16% before tax.

(*iii*) Earnings per share Rs. 4

(*iv*) Dividend pays out 50% of earnings

(*v*) Expected growth rate in dividend 10%

(*vi*) Current market price per share Rs. 44

(*vii*) Tax rate 50%

You are required to (*a*) determine the pattern for raising the additional finance (*b*) determine after tax average cost of additional debt (*c*) compute cost of equity and retained earnings (*d*) compute overall weighted average after tax cost of additional finance.

(CA, Final May 1993)

[**Answers:** (*a*) Debt Rs. 3,00,000, Equity Rs. 4,90,000, retained earnings Rs. 2,10,000 (*b*) Cost of debt after tax 6.2% (*c*) k_e = 15% (*d*) weighted average cost of capital = 12.36%]

Problem 9.12 A company gives the following information of its balance sheet as on 31 March 2007.

Ordinary shares 33,00,000 shares of Re. 1 each	33,00,000
Share Premium	2,00,000
Retained profits	10,00,000
	45,00,000
12% perpetual debt face value Rs. 100 each	15,00,000
	60,00,000

The ordinary shares are currently valued at Rs. 75 ex-dividend each. The debentures are valued at market price of 110% ex-interest and tax rate of the company is 50%. The company's cost of equity is 15%, calculate weighted average cost of capital based on market value of the company.

[**Answers:** k_e =15%, k_d = 7.5%, WACC = 12%]

❑❑❑

PART IV

Financial Decisions

Financing Decisions: Operating and Financial Leverage

10

LEARNING OBJECTIVES

10.1 Concept of Leverage
10.2 Operating Leverage
10.3 Financial Leverage
10.4 Combined Leverage
10.5 Analysis of EBIT and EPS
10.6 Financial Break-Even Point
10.7 Points of Indifference
10.8 Limitation of EBIT-EPS Analysis

10.1 CONCEPT OF LEVERAGE

In the previous chapters we have discussed the basic concepts of financial management. We have also covered the principles of capital budgeting, concepts of risk and uncertainty in long-term decision making and the different costs of capital and their measurement. This unit is a study of financing decisions of a firm and decisions relating to capital structure and valuation of a firm. This chapter discusses leverages and analysis of earnings per share and ***earnings before interest and taxes (EBIT)***. The two important aspects that are covered are the following:

- Analysis of leverages
- Relationship of EBIT and EPS

What is leverage? Leverage is the employment of sources of funds to get the advantage in running of business favourably. It is a relationship between interrelated variables whereby the percentage change in a variable reflects a percentage change in another variable. Wherever two variables are directly linked with each other then the result show that the percentage change in one variable is equal to the percentage change in another variable. In the case of leverages the percentage change in one variable has the effect of an increase or decrease in the other variable but it is not a directly proportionate change. The reason for this effect is that there are different kinds of costs while financing a firm. The fixed costs in a firm create an impact on the financing decision of a firm. When a firm has to pay a fixed cost, then it must make a choice relating to the mix of the different sources of funds to arrive at a favourable financing pattern.

There are two kinds of leverages. These are called ***operating leverage (OL) and financial leverage (FL)***. Operating leverage draws a relationship between the sales revenue of a firm and its earnings before interest and taxes. Financial leverage is an attempt to analysis the earnings before interest and taxes and the earnings available for the shareholders. When we combine operating leverage and financial leverage it is called ***combined leverage.***

Operating leverage is the percentage change in EBIT divided by the percentage change in sales revenue and financial leverage is the percentage change in earnings per share divided by the percentage change in EBIT.

10.2 OPERATING LEVERAGE

Operating leverage results due to fixed operating cost used by a firm in its requirements. These fixed costs are used to magnify the effect of changes in sales on the pattern of earnings of a firm. The fixed costs are used by a firm when it begins its business. These costs do not change even if the firm expands its business but variable costs change. Thus ***there are two kinds of costs—fixed and variable.*** Variable costs are those which increase with the increase in the number of units manufactured but fixed costs have to be paid irrespective of increase or decrease in business. There are certain variable costs, which are partially fixed and partially variable. These are called semi-variable costs. Such costs remain fixed on the increase of business but up to a certain range only. When business continues to expand they also increase. Thus there are three categories of costs—***fixed costs, variable costs and semi-variable costs.*** When fixed costs are used to increase profitability it is said that there is the use of leverage for financing decision.

$$\text{Therefore, Operating leverage (OL)} = \frac{\%\ \text{Change in EBIT}}{\%\ \text{Change in sales}}$$

The important aspects to take the opportunity of operating leverage for increasing the earnings before interest and taxes is to remember certain important aspects such as:

(*i*) Fixed costs do not vary with sales volume they are a function of time and contractual in nature.

(*ii*) The fixed costs must be paid regardless of revenues available.

(*iii*) Variable costs vary with sales.

(*iv*) Semi-variable costs are partly fixed and partly fixed and partly variable. Costs of a firm can be broken into fixed and variable components.

Operating leverage is the firm's ability to use fixed operating costs to magnify the effect of changes in sales on EBIT. Assets are invested and used having fixed cost with the expectation that revenues will be able to cover all fixed and variable costs. In effect with fixed costs the % change in profits accompanying a change in volume is greater than the % change in volume. This is degree of operating leverage.

$$\text{DOL} = \frac{\text{\% Change in EBIT}}{\text{\% Change in sales}} > 1$$

Greater the degree of operating leverage the higher the operating leverage.

This can be explained through an example.

Example 10.1 A company sells 5000 units @ Rs.100 per unit. Cost of production is Rs. 75 per unit. The whole of the costs is variable in nature.

$$\text{DOL of the firm} = \frac{\text{\% Change in EBIT}}{\text{\% Change in sales}}$$

$$= \frac{\text{Increase in EBIT / EBIT}}{\text{Increase in sales / sales}}$$

The profit of the firm is 5000 × (100 – 75) = Rs. 125,000.

Suppose the firm increases its sales by 50%, the profit of the firm

$$= 7{,}500\ (5{,}000 + 2{,}500 \text{ units})$$

$$= 7{,}500 \times (100 - 75) = \text{Rs. } 1{,}87{,}500$$

$$\therefore \qquad \text{OL} = \frac{62{,}500/1{,}25{,}000}{2{,}500/5{,}000} = \frac{0.5}{0.5} = 1$$

EBIT level increases or decreases in direct proportion to increase or decrease in sales value because there are no fixed costs. Profit level varies with sales level = 1.

Now introduce fixed costs. For every increase or decrease in sales level there will be more than proportionate increase or decrease in the level EBIT.

Fixed costs are Rs. 1,00,000. If fixed costs are not there increases or decreases in EBIT is direct and proportional to increase or decrease in sales level. Operating leverage is always greater than 1 for any firm which has fixed costs. This can be explained through another example.

Example 10.2 A firm has present sales of 500 units. It expects to increase its sales to 700 units. The fixed costs are Rs. 1,00,000. Show the operating leverage in both the cases.

Solution

Sales in Units	Present	Expected
Sales @ Rs. 100 per unit	5,00,000	7,50,000
Variable costs @ Rs. 75 per unit	3,75,000	5,62,500
Contribution	1,25,000	1,87,500
Fixed costs	1,00,000	1,00,000
EBIT	25,000	87,500

$$\text{DOL} = \frac{\%\text{ in EBIT}}{\%\text{in Sales}}$$

$$= \frac{\text{Increase in EBIT / EBIT}}{\text{Increase in sales / sales}}$$

$$= \frac{62{,}500/25{,}000}{2{,}50{,}000/5{,}00{,}000} = \frac{2.5}{0.5} = 5$$

If DOL is greater than 1, operating leverage exists.

The same example given above can also show leverage of the firm by calculating contribution/ EBIT.

$$\text{DOL} = \frac{\text{Contribution}}{\text{EBIT}} = \frac{1{,}25{,}000}{25{,}000}$$

$$= \frac{1{,}87{,}500}{87{,}500} = 2.14$$

DOL decreases with every level of sales increase, if firm is operating at a sales level above BEP. In the above example it has decreased from 5 to 2.14 by increasing the sales level from 5,000 units to 7,500 units.

Positive DOL means that a firm is operating above the BEP level. Financial leverage helps in finding out the break-even point of business. An example can be given to depict the break-even point of business.

Example 10.3 Firm A and B manufacture pencil sharpeners. Selling price is Rs. 8 per unit of product and is equal for both firms. Fixed costs for firm A and B are Rs. 80,000 and Rs. 2,00,000 while variable costs are Rs. 6 and Rs. 4. (*i*) What are BEP of the firms? (*ii*) How much profits are earned by the firms if sales range between 20,000 units and 80,000 units; and (*iii*) calculate the degree of leverage in Firm B when it changes its sales from 70,000 to 80,000 units.

Solution

The BEP for the firms are:

For Firm A, $$\text{BEP} = \frac{80,000}{8-6} = \frac{80,000}{2} = 40,000 \text{ units}$$

Break-even sales in units

$$S = \frac{F}{S-V} = \frac{\text{Fixed cost}}{\text{Contribution}}$$

Sale price – Variable cost

For Firm B, $$\text{BEP} = \frac{2,00,000}{8-4} = \frac{2,00,000}{4} = 50,000 \text{ units}$$

Firm A

Units	Sales	Variable cost	Fixed cost	Total cost	EBIT
20,000	1,60,000	1,20,000	80,000	2,00,000	– 40,000
30,000	2,40,000	1,80,000	80,000	2,60,000	– 20,000
40,000	3,20,000	2,40,000	80,000	3,20,000	0
50,000	4,00,000	3,00,000	80,000	3,80,000	20,000
60,000	4,80,000	3,60,000	80,000	4,40,000	40,000
70,000	5,60,000	4,20,000	80,000	5,00,000	60,000
80,000	6,40,000	4,80,000	80,000	5,60,000	80,000

Firm B

Units	Sales	Variable cost	Fixed cost	Total cost	EBIT
20,000	1,60,000	80,000	2,00,000	2,80,000	–120
30,000	2,40,000	1,20,000	2,00,000	3,20,000	– 80
40,000	3,20,000	1,60,000	2,00,000	3,60,000	– 40
50,000	4,00,000	2,00,000	2,00,000	4,00,000	0
60,000	4,80,000	2,40,000	2,00,000	4,40,000	40
70,000	5,60,000	2,80,000	2,00,000	4,80,000	80
80,000	6,40,000	3,20,000	2,00,000	5,20,000	120

Operating profits and sales for firm A and B have been depicted Figures 10.1 and 10.2. Firm B has higher fixed costs and high operating leverage is more vulnerable to changes in sales. A given change in sales produces a much higher change in B's profits than in A's profits. The increase in sales in a firm with high operating leverage benefits more in terms of an increase in profits. When sales are falling it loses more and thus high operating leverage is not good. A highly capital-intensive industry like an airline will have high fixed costs and profit is sensitive to the number of passengers carried. A retail business generally has high variable costs and negligible fixed costs profit fluctuations occurring due to high fixed costs are referred to as 'operating risks'.

$$\text{DOL} = \frac{\%\text{ Change in operating profit}}{\%\text{ Change in sales}}$$

$$= \frac{\text{Increase in EBIT/EBIT}}{\text{Increase in sales/sales}}$$

For firm B if sales change from 70,000 to 80,000 units;

DOL at 70,000 units,

$$\text{DOL} = \left\{\frac{\left(\dfrac{1,20,000-80,000}{80,000}\right)}{\left(\dfrac{6,40,000-5,60,000}{5,60,000}\right)}\right\} = \frac{0.500}{0.143} = 3.5$$

It indicates that if sales increase by 100 operating profit will increase by 3.50 times for firm 'A' that employs less fixed cost. If sales increase by 100% DOL = 2.33. Firm A's operating profit will increase by only 2.33 times sales are falling it leverage is not good.

Costs and their Effect on Break-even Point	
Fixed operating costs	**Break-even point**
(*i*) Increases	Increases
(*ii*) Decreases	Decreases
Sales price per unit	
(*i*) Increases	Decreases
(*ii*) Decreases	Increases
Variable cost per unit	
Increases	Increases
Decreases	Decreases

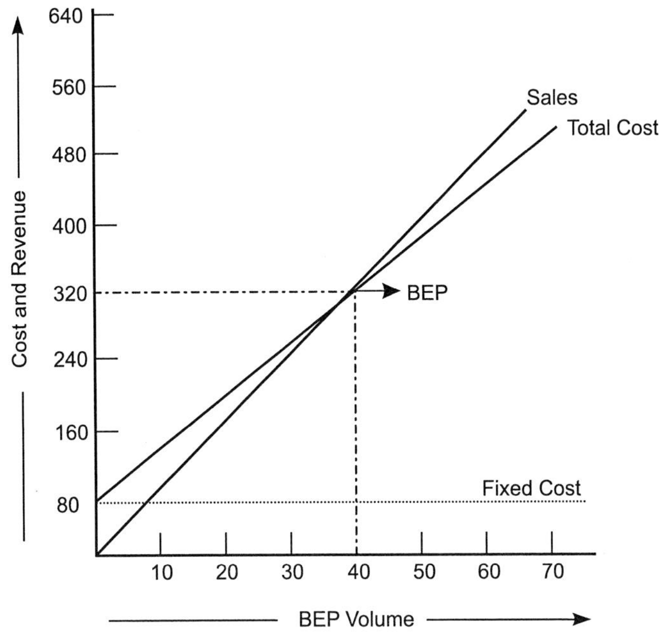

Fig. 10.1 Break-even analysis (Firm A)

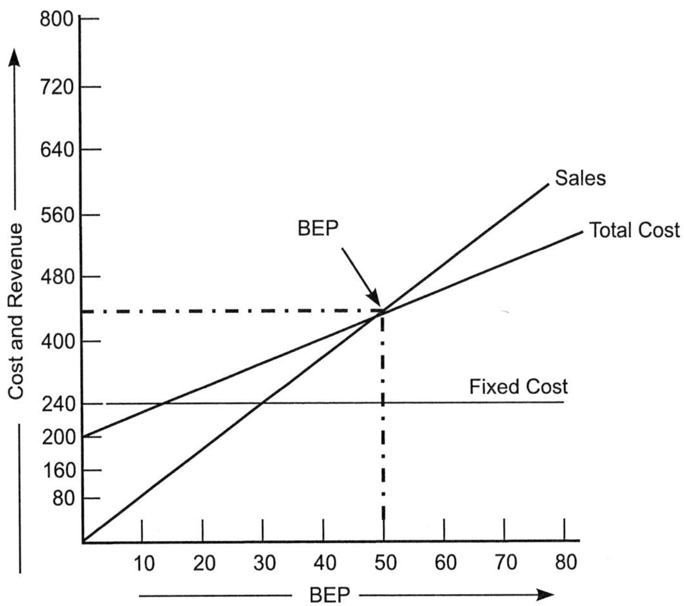

Fig. 10.2 Break-even analysis (Firm B)

Also, $$\text{DOL} = \frac{\text{Contribution}}{\text{EBIT}}$$

$$\text{DOL} = \left(\frac{70{,}000\ (8-4)}{70{,}000\ (8-4) - 2{,}00{,}000}\right)$$

$$= \left(\frac{2{,}80{,}000}{80{,}000}\right) = 3.5$$

Example 10.4 Determine BEP and show the effect of changes in costs on BEP for the following firms:

Particulars	Firms A	Firms B	Firms C
Sales per unit (Rs.)	100	50	30
Variable cost (Rs.)	50	10	5
Fixed operating cost (Rs.)	2,00,000	3,00,000	1,00,000

Solution

$$\text{Break-even point BEP} = \frac{F}{S - V}$$

Break-even point	Units	Amount (Rs.)
(*i*) $\frac{2{,}00{,}000}{100-50}$	4,000 units	4,00,000 (sales)
(*ii*) $\frac{3{,}00{,}000}{50-10}$	7,500 units	3,75,000 (sales)
(*iii*) $\frac{1{,}00{,}000}{30-25}$	4,000 unis	1,20,000 (sales)

In the case of Firm A effect on BEP when costs change

Change in cost		BEP (Units)	BEP (Sales)
(*i*) Fixed cost increase, BEP increase			
If fixed cost increases to	3,00,000/(100 – 50)	6,000	Rs. 6,00,000
If fixed cost decrease to 1,00,000	1,00,000/(100 – 50)	5,000	Rs. 2,00,000
(*ii*) Sale price increases to Rs. 150			
Sale prices increases to Rs. 100	2,00000/(150 – 50)	2,000	Rs. 3,00,000
Sale price decrease to Rs.90	2,00,000/(90 – 50)	5,000	Rs. 4,50,000
Then BEP increases			
EBIT at this point will be 0			
Increase in variable cost per unit increase in BEP			
(iii) When variable cost is Rs. 75 and fixed cost is Rs. 2,00,000			
and sales is Rs. 100			
Variable cost increase to Rs. 75	2,00,000/(100 – 75)	8,000	Rs. 8,00,000
Variable cost decreases to Rs. 20	2,00,000/(100 – 20)	2,500	Rs. 2,50,000

In the case of Firm B effect on BEP when costs change

Change in cost		BEP (Units)	BEP (Sales)
(*i*) Fixed cost			
Increase to 5,00,000	5,00,000/(50 – 10)	12,500	Rs. 6,25,000
Reduces to 2,00,000	2,00,000/(50 – 10)	5,000	Rs. 2,50,000
(*ii*) Sale price per unit			
Increases to Rs. 60	3,00,000/(60 – 10)	6,000	Rs. 3,60,000
Reduces to Rs. 40	3,00,000/(40 – 10)	10,000	Rs. 4,00,000
(*iii*) Variable cost			
Increases to Rs. 20	3,00,000/(50 – 20)	10,000	Rs. 5,00,000
Decreases to Rs. 5	3,00,000/(50 – 5)	7,500	Rs. 37,500

In the case of Firm C effect on BEP when costs change

Change in cost		BEP (Units)	BEP (Sales)
(*i*) When fixed cost			
Increases to 2,00,000	2,00,000/(30 – 5)	8,000	Rs. 2,40,000
Decreases to 50,000	50,000/(30 – 5)	2,000	Rs. 60,000
(*ii*) When sale price per unit			
Increases to Rs. 50	1,00,000/(50 – 5)	2,222	Rs. 1,11,111
Decreases to Rs. 20	1,00,000/(20 – 5)	6,667	Rs. 1,33,340
(*iii*) Variable cost			
Increases to Rs. 10	1,00,000/(30 – 10)	5,000	Rs. 1,50,000
Decreases to Rs. 2	1,00,000/(30 – 2)	3,571	Rs. 1,07,142.85

This shows that the break-even point has different kinds of effects when costs and prices change. The above example proves this point.

Importance of Operating Leverage

Operating leverage helps a financial manager to take decisions relating to increase or decrease in sales for gaining profitability. It also helps to judge the operating risk in a firm. The higher the fixed costs in a firm the greater will be the risk. If a firm is not able to cover its fixed costs then it will ultimately be considered unprofitable and it will not be able to reach the break-even point of revenue and expenses. This means that there is the presence of large fixed costs. However, if a manager can analyse the costs and revenue structure of the company he can use it to the advantage of the firm. By mixing and matching revenues and costs as his ultimate duty is to enhance the wealth of the shareholders.

The financial manager can also analyse risk by understanding the relationship of contribution and EBIT. A change in sales can also improve risk conditions of the firm. Similarly decrease in sales also has an effect on the firm's earning power and risk. A continuous analysis of increase or decrease in sales with the fixed costs in the firm will provide an active and healthy work environment. Thus the financial manager will be able to protect and maximize the wealth of the shareholders.

10.3 FINANCIAL LEVERAGE

Investment acquisition activity is called 'operating leverage' while leverage associated with financing activities is called 'financial leverage'. Operating leverage explains the impact of change in sales on the level of operating profits while financial leverage is the relationship between EBIT and earnings per share (EPS). It is defined by percentage change in earnings per share divided by percentage change in earnings before interest and taxes. Financial leverage arises due to the presence of the fixed financial costs such as cost of interest to the firm. Financial leverage can be indicated in the following way.

$$\text{Financial Leverage} = \frac{\%\text{ Change in earnings per share}}{\%\text{ Change in EBIT}}$$

Or,

$$FL = \frac{\text{Increase in earnings per shares/Earnings per share}}{\text{Increase in EBIT/EBIT}}$$

Or,

$$FL = \text{EBIT/PBT}$$

If return on investment is > interest it is a favourable leverage.

When return of investment = Interest, there is no financial leverage and earnings per share will not be affected.

High operating leverage coupled with high financial leverage will bring about a high risk situation.

An example of financial leverage will clarify the above relationship.

Example 10.5 EBIT of a company is Rs. 25,000. Tax is 50% and there is no debt financing. The number of equity shares in situation (1) is 5,000; and in situation (2) there are 10%; 1,000 debentures of Rs. 100 each and 4,000 equity shares, and in situation (3) there is an increase in debentures from 1,000 to 2,000 of Rs. 100 each and equity shares are 4,000.

Financial leverage

$$\text{Relationship between EBIT and EPS} = \frac{\%\text{ Change in EPS}}{\%\text{Change in EBIT}} = \frac{\text{Increase in EPS/EPS}}{\text{Increasein EBIT/EBIT}}$$

Solution

Situation 1: Without debt EPS

$$\text{EPS} = \frac{(\text{EBIT} - \text{interest}) \times (1-t)}{\text{Numbers of Shares}}$$

$$= \frac{(25{,}000 - 0) \times (1 - 0.5)}{5{,}000}$$

$$= \frac{25{,}000 \times 0.5}{5000} = \frac{12{,}500}{5{,}000} = 2.5$$

Situation 2: With introduction of debt

1,000 debentures of Rs. 10 each @ 10% rate of interest

$$(i)\ \text{EPS} = \frac{(\text{EBIT} - \text{Interest}) \times (1-t)}{\text{Number of Shares}}$$

$$= \frac{(25{,}000 - 1{,}000) \times (1-0.5)}{4{,}000} = \frac{12{,}000}{4{,}000} = 3$$

With the introduction of debt the earnings per share has increased from 2.5 to 3.

Situation 3: Introduction of further debt

If debentures are increased to 2,000 of Rs. 100 each @ 10% rate of interest

$$(ii)\ \frac{(25{,}000 - 2000) \times (1-0.5)}{4{,}000} = \frac{23{,}000 \times 0.5}{4{,}000} = 2.875$$

Trading on Equity

The increase in debentures has further increased the earnings per share of the shareholders. Thus the presence of debt helps in increasing the earnings available to equity shareholders. This is known as trading on equity. Trading on equity is useful when the return on the investment is greater than the rate of interest of borrowed funds. It is of advantage to those companies, which are continuously stable in their earnings. Sometimes a firm extends financial leverage beyond its capacity to earn and this increases the financial risk of a company. Thus leverage has an advantages but it must be applied with caution and care to see that there is an advantage and the company is gaining by it. Thus the financial manager should use financial leverage as a tool for increasing the wealth of the shareholders but it should not use leverage without understanding the implication and the effect on profitability, earnings per share and other basic aspect of financing.

The example that we are taking was financial leverage with the same EBIT level but when EBIT changes then let us see the effect on earnings per share. Let us take an example, Case 1: change in EBIT with no debt financing. When no debt financing is applied then the increase in EBIT has a direct increase on the earnings per share.

Example 10.6 In the following case, the EBIT levels of I and II are respectively Rs. 25,000 and Rs. 40,000. Sales are of Rs. 5,000 of I and Rs. 6,500 of II. There is no debt financing but tax level is 50%. Calculate the effect on EPS when the EBIT level has increased from Rs. 25,000 to Rs. 40,000. The numbers of shares are 5,000.

Solution

Case 1 Change in EBIT no debt financing

	I (Rs.)	II (Rs.)
Sales	5,000	6,500
EBIT	25,000	40,000
Interest	—	—
– Tax @ 50%	12,500	20,000
	12,500	20,000
Number of shares (units)	5,000	5,000
EPS	2.5	4

This case shows that there is no debt financing, when the EBIT level changes the earnings per share will also increase with increase in EBIT level. In this case it has increased from Rs. 2.5 to Rs. 4. The EPS have increased by 60%. This is directly proportionate to the change in EBIT. EBIT has increased from 25,000 to 40,000 *i.e.*, a 60% increase. In this example, Case 2 can be analysed when with the same EBIT level debentures have been financed and the numbers of shares are reduced to 4,000. Debt has been introduced at 10% of which the interest is Rs. 1,000 on the debt. Now let us see the change and the effect on EPS when the EBIT level has increased from Rs. 25,000 to Rs. 40,000 which is a 60% change. Let us analyse the effect of debt on earnings per share.

Case 2 Change in EBIT with debt financing

	I (Rs.)	II (Rs.)
Sales	5,000	6,500
EBIT	25,000	40,000
Interest	1,000	1,000
PBT	24,000	39,000
– Tax @ 50%	12,000	19,500
	12,000	19,500
Number of shares (units)	4,000	4,000
EPS	3	4.875

Compare Case 2 with Case 1

The percentage increased in earnings per share will be higher than the percentage increase in EBIT. EBIT has increased by 60% but the earnings per share have increased by 175 times, this shows that the increase in EPS is higher than the increase in EBIT. The reason for this is the presence of fixed interest charges has brought about an advantage for the equity shareholders. Interest is paid to the debt holders but interest has a tax shield which brings about an advantage for the shareholders.

Now in Case 3 let us see if the advantage continues to the shareholders if the proportion of debt is further increased so that the firm has now increased its sales level to 7500 units and it has to pay an increased interest.

Case 3 When EBIT increases and debt also increases

	I (Rs.)	II (Rs.)
Sales	5,000	6,500
EBIT	25,000	40,000
Interest	2,000	2,000
PBT	23,000	38,000
Tax 50%	11,500	19,000
PAT	11,500	19,000
Number of shares (units)	3,000	3,000
EPS	3.8	6.3

The EPS has increased by 65.7 times. If we see in Case 2, we find that the advantage continues to exist but as interest charges keep on increasing the advantage will ultimately reduce.

Financial leverage exists then when degree of leverage is greater than one. The financial risk is high when the degree of financial leverage is high. As long as the firm is able to earn higher than the capital employed by it it will continue to have an advantage. But this advantage ceases to exist when interest costs are high and there is no advantage. In the above case if the firm operates at an EBIT of 25,000 and it is just equal to its fixed financial charges then it becomes the financial break-even point at which EBIT is equal to the fixed financial charges. In this case there will be no EPS.

Break-even point is that point when $\text{DFL} = \dfrac{\text{EBIT}}{\text{EBIT} - \text{Interest}}$

At this point the shareholders will not get any earnings.

Significance of Financial Leverage

Financial leverage is very useful to a financial manager as it helps him to take decisions regarding borrowings from the market. The financial manager can analyse the financial situation of a company and the earnings available to the shareholders. When the rate of return is higher than the interest on debt, he can raise debt financing. When the rate of return is lower than the cost of debt, he should not borrow funds, as there will not be any surplus generated by the firm. If financial leverage is unfavourable, the function of financial leverage loses its importance. Since financial leverage can be applied when there are fixed financial charges it is necessary that leverage bring about a favourable situation for the shareholders. The duty and responsibility of a financial manager is to maximize the wealth of shareholders. Financial leverages help him to use debt financing carefully and also usefully. The manager should be able to interpret risk as well as advantages through the application of financial leverage. The significance of financial leverage can be summarized as:

(*i*) Financial leverage helps to analyse the advantage to the firm by introducing debt. Debt financing is cheaper than equity due to the advantage of tax deduction on interest paid.

(*ii*) It provides a measure to analyse the risk situation in the firm. A high financial leverage means high risk. Risk should be manageable as the firm should be profitable and not have the risk of bankruptcy.

(*iii*) Financial leverage is as a result of fixed charges on a firm. It is useful as long as ROI > the cost of debt and the earnings per share are enhanced.

10.4 COMBINED LEVERAGE (CL)

In the previous section we have discussed operating leverage and financial leverage. Both OL and FL are interrelated. OL is analysed to find out if increasing sales revenue (through the presence of some fixed costs) which do not change, can increase profitability. Financial leverage explains the advantages to the shareholders on their earnings per share through debt financing while OL has an effect on EBIT, FL shows the effect of EBIT on earnings per share. When OL and FL are combined by multiplying the result with each other it is combined leverage. It helps to explain the risk of the firm. If both OL and FL are high it means that the firm has very high risk, whereas OL is high and FL is low the risk is reduced. Thus risky situation is when high operating leverage is combined with high financial leverage. A normal situation is when OL is high and FL is low or vice versa and the ideal situation is when both operating leverage and financial leverages are low.

$$\text{Therefore combined leverage} = \frac{\text{Contribution}}{\text{EBIT}} \times \frac{\text{EBIT}}{\text{PBT}}$$

$$= \frac{\text{Contribution}}{\text{PBT}}$$

$$\text{Or,} \qquad \text{CL} = \text{OL} \times \text{FL or CL} = \frac{\text{\% Change in EBIT}}{\text{\% Change in sales}} \times \frac{\text{\% Change in EPS}}{\text{\% Change in EBIT}}$$

$$= \frac{\text{\% Change in EPS}}{\text{\% Change in sales}}$$

Example 10.7 shows degree of operating leverage, financial leverage and combined leverage.

Example 10.7 A firm has sales of Rs.10,00,000; variable cost is 20% on sales; fixed costs Rs. 2,50,000; and debentures of Rs. 5,00,000 at 10% rate of interest. Calculate OL, FL and CL.

Solution

Particulars	Amount (Rs.)
Sales	10,00,000
Variable Cost	200,000
Contribution Cost	8,00,000
Fixed cost	2,50,000
Operating Profit or EBIT	5,50,000
Less interest at 10% on 5,00,000	50,000
Profit before tax	5,00,000

$$\text{Operating leverage} = \frac{\text{C}}{\text{OP}} = \frac{8,00,000}{2,50,000} = 3.2$$

$$\text{Financial leverage} = \frac{\text{OP}}{\text{PBT}} = \frac{5,50,000}{5,00,000} = 1.1$$

$$\text{Combined leverage} = (3.2 \times 1.1) = 3.52$$

10.5 ANALYSIS OF EBIT AND EPS

A study of the relationship of EBIT and EPS is explained through alternative method of financing under different assumptions of EBIT. A firm can raise funds for investment proposals from various sources of funds. These sources of funds can be raised in different proportions. They can be raised through the use of equity capital only or through the use of only debt, but the advantage to the firm will be limited unless a proper combination of different funds are used to raise capital at a particular level of EBIT. There will be a different effect on the EPS depending on the kind of sources of funds used for financing the proposals. In the following discussion EBIT and EPS analysis is made when (*i*) EBIT is constant and (*ii*) with varying EBIT and different sources of capital.

(*i*) Constant EBIT and Change in Financing Pattern: In the following example, the EBIT and EPS relationship is analysed through 4 proposals where the firm is planning to raise Rs. 50,00,000 for starting a new project. The different combinations of the sources of funds are used in different proposals to see the advantage of each of them. Plan 1 is an all equity plan. Plan 2 has preference capital along with equity shares but it has no debt. Plan 3 has equity preference and debt and plan 4 also has equity preference and debt but the proportions are different. The effect of such mixing of sources is analysed with respect to the effect on EPS.

Example 10.8 A company XYZ Ltd. is a software Co. has an EBIT of Rs. 60,00,000 on an investment of Rs. 50,00,000. It is in the 50% tax bracket.

The company can raise funds by issuing

(*a*) Equity share capital of Rs. 100 each.

(*b*) 50% equity and 50% of 10% preference shares.

(*c*) 50% equity 25% preference capital and 25% of 10% debentures.

(*d*) 25% equity and share capital 25 % preference shares 50% issue of 10% debentures. Interest is tax deductible.

EPS under the 4 options will be:

Particulars	1 (Rs.)	2 (Rs.)	3 (Rs.)	4 (Rs.)
Equity	50,00,000	25,00,000	25,00,000	12,50,000
10% Preference shares	—	25,00,000	12,50,000	12,50,000
10% Debentures	—	—	12,50,000	25,00,000
Total Funds	50,00,000	50,00,000	50,00,000	50,00,000
EBIT	60,00,000	60,00,000	60,00,000	60,00,000
Interest	—	—	1,25,000	2,50,000
PBT	60,00,000	60,00,000	58,75,000	57,50,000
Tax at 50%	30,00,000	30,00,000	29,37,500	28,75,000
Profit after tax	30,00,000	30,00,000	29,37,500	28,75,000
Preference Dividend	—	2,50,000	1,25,000	1,25,000
Profits for equity shares	30,00,000	27,50,000	28,12,500	27,50,000
No. of Equity shares (units)	50,000	25,000	25,000	12,500
EPS	60	110	112.5	220

The table shows that when the proposal was completely equity financed, the EPS was 60 but in Plan 2 when the presence of fixed charge was introduced through the issue of preference shares the earnings per share increased to 119. The introduction of debt is shown in Plan 3 and Plan 4 in which there is debt in both but Plan 4 is more favourable than Plan 3. The reason for this is that preference capital is not tax deductible. The total of preference and equity in Plan 3 is 37,50,000 : 15,50,000 debt but in plan 4 the proportion is 50% debt and 50% equity and preference capital. With this proportion the advantage to the shareholders has increased considerably from 112.5 to 220. Thus proportion of debt has a great significance on the effect on earnings per share. The change in earnings per share is due to the return on investment. When the return on the investment is higher than the cost of debt, the financial leverage is favourable and the earnings available for shareholders will be high. When return on investment is equal to the cost of debt, it will not affect the earnings of the shareholders. Therefore if the return on investment is less than cost of debt, there will be an unfavourable impact on the earnings per share given that the level of EBIT is constant.

***(ii)* Varying EBIT with Different Patterns:** The example explained the relationship of EBIT and EPS when EBIT was constant and different combinations of sources of funds were employed. But it is usually difficult to assume as EBIT keeps on changing and such an assumption of a constant EBIT is unrealistic. Hence earnings per share are analysed in the following example with different EBIT and 3 financing plans.

Example 10.9 There are 3 firms company 1, 2 and 3. These firms are similar but they have different leverages. Their capital structure is as follows:

Capital Structure of 3 Firms

Particulars	1 (Rs.)	2 (Rs.)	3 (Rs.)
Capital structure	80,00,000	80,00,000	80,00,000
Share capital of Rs. 100 each	80,00,000	40,00,000	60,00,000
10% debentures		40,00,000	20,00,000
Return on investments	10%	12%	20%
Tax is @ 50%	Poor	Normal	Good
Economic conditions			

These 3 firms have to earn a return on investments depending upon the economic conditions in the economy. In poor economic conditions, they must earn a return of 10%. In normal conditions the expectation would be 12% and in optimistic conditions the expectations was 20%. The analysis of EBIT and EPS of the capital structure given above is analysed in the following table:

Particulars	Firm 1		
Total Assets	80,00,000	80,00,000	80,00,000
ROI	10%	12%	20%
EBIT	8,00,000	9,60,000	16,00,000
– Interest	—	—	—
PBT	8,00,000	9,60,000	16,00,000
– Tax @ 50%	4,00,000	4,80,000	8,00,000
Profit after tax	4,00,000	4,80,000	8,00,000
No. of shares	80,000	80,000	80,000
	5	6	10

Particulars	Firm 2		
EBIT	8,00,000	9,60,000	16,00,000
– Interest	4,00,000	4,00,000	4,00,000
PBT	4,00,000	5,60,000	12,00,000
– Tax @ 50%	2,00,000	2,80,000	6,00,000
Profit after tax	2,00,000	2,80,000	6,00,000
No. of shares	40,000	40,000	40,000
	5	7	15

Particulars	Firm 3		
EBIT	8,00,000	9,60,000	16,00,000
– Interest	6,00,000	6,00,000	6,00,000
PBT	2,00,000	3,60,000	10,00,000
– Tax @ 50%	1,00,000	1,80,000	5,00,000
Profit after tax	1,00,000	1,80,000	5,00,000
No. of shares	20,000	20,000	20,000
	5	9	25

On an analysis of the table it shows that Firm 1 is not levered. It does not have any advantage of fixed charges. Therefore it does not have a magnifying effect and EPS increases from 5 in poor conditions to 6 in better conditions and to 10 in good conditions. The increase would be 20% from poor to normal conditions and 66.6% between normal to good conditions. Firm 2 takes the advantage of debt it has Rs. 40,00,000 share capital and Rs. 80,00,000 debt. Its relative increase in earnings per share is higher than in Firm 2, but Firm 3 has the best proportion as in poor conditions its earnings per share is the same as in Firm 1 and 2 but in good conditions its earnings per share increases to 25. Therefore Firm 3 may be considered as the best out of the three firms in good conditions.

10.6 FINANCIAL BREAK-EVEN POINT

If EBIT of a firm covers fixed financial charges only it is called ***Financial Break-Even Point***.

- The financial break-even point is that level where EPS = 0.
- If EBIT is below the fixed charges EPS will be negative.
- If firm has debt but no preference shares. Financial break-even is that level where EBIT = Interest charges.
- When a firm has debt and preference capital financial break-even EBIT = Interest + Preference dividend/$(1 - t)$.

This can be explained with the Example 10.10.

Example 10.10 A firm has to pay an interest of Rs. 30,000 and it has a preference dividend of Rs. 40,000 its tax rate is 50%. Find out financial break-even point.

Solution

$$\text{Financial BEP} = \text{Interest charges} + [\text{Preference Dividend}/(1 - t)]$$
$$= 30{,}000 + [40{,}000/(1 - 0.5)]$$
$$= 30{,}000 + [40{,}000/0.5]$$
$$= 30{,}000 + 80{,}000 = \text{Rs. } 1{,}10{,}000$$

If EBIT is Rs. 1,10,000 interest of Re. 30,000 will be deducted then the resulting amount = Rs. 80,000 and taxes will be 50%. The remaining profit would be Rs. 40,000 just enough to cover preference dividend. There is no profit for equity shareholders and EPS = 0

The indifference level is one where EPS remains the same. A firm may evaluate different plans on the level of EPS for a given level of EBIT. Out of different plans a firm may have 2 or more financial plans, which result in the same level of EPS for a given EBIT. The level of EBIT where 2 or more plans have the same EPS is called the 'indifference point'.

10.7 POINT OF INDIFFERENCE

The level at which earnings before interest and taxes remains the same as the rate of return on capital is the indifference point. At this point the earnings per share remain the same at whatever debt equity mix. This is represented in Fig. 10.3.

Rate of return = Rate of interest on debt. This is also the break-even level of EBIT.

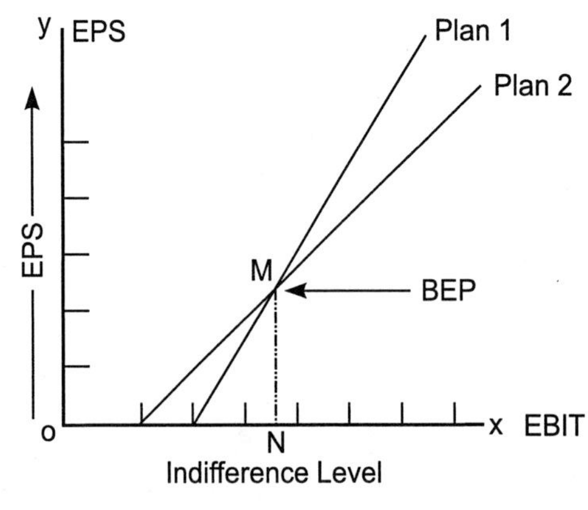

Fig. 10.3 Point of Indifference

The break-even analysis is based on two variables—EPS in two alternative financial plans is an independent variable and EBIT is the dependent variable. At the indifference point, the ROI equals after tax cost of debt. This is explained through the two plans.

$$\frac{(X - I_1)(1-t) - P}{N_1} = \frac{(X - I_2)(1-t) - P}{N_2}$$

X = Point of indifference or BEP or EBIT

I_1 = Interest of 1st alternative

I_2 = Interest of 2nd alternative

t = Tax rate

P = Preference dividend

N_1 = Number of equity shares under 1st alternative.

N_2 = Number of equity shares under 2nd alternative.

Earnings per Share (EPS)

(*i*) Sales

(*ii*) Less: All costs Including Depreciation but excluding Interest on Debt EBIT

(*iii*) Less: Interest on Debt

(*iv*) Profit before tax (PBT)

(*v*) Less: Tax = Profit after tax (PAT)

(*vi*) Less: Preference dividend

(*vii*) Earnings available to equity shareholders

(*viii*) Dividend by number of equity share = EPS

$$EPS = \frac{(EBIT - I)(I-t) - P}{N}$$

P = Preference dividend

t = Tax rate

N = Number of equity shares

Formula

EPS formula for All Equity Plan

$$EPS = \frac{(1-t)\ EBIT}{N_1}$$

$$D = 0$$

Where N_1 is the number of common shares under first plan and there are no debt and no interest charges.

Where Interest Charges Exist

$$\text{EPS} = \frac{(1-t)(\text{EBIT}-\text{I})}{\text{N}_2}$$

$$\frac{(1-t)\ \text{EBIT}}{\text{N}_1} = \frac{(1-t)(\text{EBIT}-\text{I})}{\text{N}_2}$$

The indifference point can be calculated for different situations. (*i*) All equity plan *vs* debt equity mix, (*ii*) Debt equity mix *vs* equity and preference mix, (*iii*) All equity plan *vs* equity, preference and debt mix, and (*iv*) Debt equity mix *vs* debt equity mix.

(*i*) All Equity *vs* Debt Equity Mix

$$\frac{\text{EBIT}\ (1-t)}{\text{N}_1} = \frac{(\text{EBIT}-\text{I})\ (1-t)}{\text{N}_2}$$

(*ii*) Debt Equity Mix *vs* Equity Preference Mix

$$\frac{\text{EBIT}\ (1-t)}{\text{N}_1} = \frac{(\text{EBIT}-\text{I})\ (1-t)}{\text{N}_2}$$

(*iii*) All Equity Plan *vs* Equity Preference and Debt

$$\frac{\text{EBIT}\ (1-t)}{\text{N}_1} = \frac{(\text{EBIT}-\text{I})\ (1-t)}{\text{N}_2}$$

(*iv*) Debt Equity Mix *vs* Debt Equity Mix

$$\frac{(\text{EBIT}-\text{I}_1)\ (1-t)}{\text{N}_1} = \frac{(\text{EBIT}-\text{I}_2)\ (1-t)}{\text{N}_2}$$

The following example depicts the indifference point.

Example 10.11 Corporate Tax 50% equity share of Rs. 10 each. Calculate the level of EBIT at which the indifference point between the alternatives financial will occur.

Solution

(*i*) Equity Share Capital of Rs.10,00,000 of Rs.10 each or 15%, debentures of Rs. 5,00,000 and Equity Capital of Rs. 5,00,000 at Rs. 10 each.

$$\frac{(1-t)\ \text{EBIT}}{\text{N}_1} = \frac{(1-t)(\text{EBIT}-\text{I})}{\text{N}_2}$$

$$\frac{(1-0.5)\text{ EBIT}}{1,00,000} = \frac{(1-0.5)(\text{EBIT}-75,000)}{50,000}$$

$$0.5\text{ EBIT} = \frac{1,00,000}{50,000}(0.5\text{ EBIT} - 37,500)$$

$$0.5\text{ EBIT} = 1.0\text{ EBIT} - 75,000$$

$$\text{EBIT} = (-75,000)/(-0.5) = 1,50,000$$

(*ii*) Equity shares of 1 lakh or 13% Preference Capital of Rs. 5,00,000 and Equity Shares 50,000.

$$\frac{(1-0.5)\text{ EBIT}}{N_1} = \frac{(1-t)(\text{EBIT})-P}{N_2}$$

$$\frac{(1-0.5)\text{ EBIT}}{1,00,000} = \frac{(1-0.5)\ (\text{EBIT})-65,000}{50,000}$$

$$0.5\text{ EBIT} = 2\ (0.5\text{ EBIT} - 65,000)$$

$$0.5\text{ EBIT} = 1\text{ EBIT} - 1,30,000$$

$$\text{EBIT} = (-1,30,000)/(-0.5) = 2,60,000$$

(*iii*) Equity 1 Lakh Shares or Equity Shares 50,000 and 13% Preference Capital of Rs. 2,00,000 and 15% Debentures of Rs. 3,00,000.

$$\frac{(1-t)\text{ EBIT}}{N_1} = \frac{(1-t)(\text{EBIT}-I)-P}{N_2}$$

$$\frac{(1-0.5)\text{ EBIT}}{1,00,000} = \frac{(1-0.5)\ (\text{EBIT}-45,000)-26,000}{50,000}$$

$$0.5\text{ EBIT} = 2\ (0.5\text{ EBIT} - 22,500) - 52,000$$

$$0.5\text{ EBIT} = 1.0\text{ EBIT} - 45,000 - 52,000$$

$$\text{EBIT} = \frac{-97,000}{-0.5} = 1,94,000$$

When EBIT just covers fixed financial charges it is called Financial BEP level or EBIT Indifference Point.

Test for Confirmation

(*a*)

Particulars	Equity plan	Equity + Debt financing
EBIT	1,50,000	1,50,000
Less Interest	—	75,000
Earnings before tax	1,50,000	75,000
– Less taxes	75,000	37,500
Earnings after taxes	75,000	37,500
Earning for Equity Holders	75,000	37,500
EPS	0.75	0.75
No. of equity shares	1,00,000	50,000

(*b*)

Particulars	Equity	Equity + Preference
EBIT	2,60,000	2,60,000
Less taxes	1,30,000	1,30,000
Earning after taxes	1,30,000	1,30,000
Less Preference div		65,000
Earnings for equity share holder		65,000
No. of equity shares	1,00,000	50,000
EPS	1.3	1.3

(*c*)

Particulars	Equity	Equity + Preference + Debt
EBIT	1,94,000	1,94,000
Less Interest	--	45,000
EBT	1,94,000	1,49,000
Less taxes at 50%	97,000	74,500
EAT	97,000	74,500
Less dividend on Preference Share		26,000
Earnings available to equity shareholders		48,500
No of equity shares	1,00,000	50,000
EPS	0.97	0.97

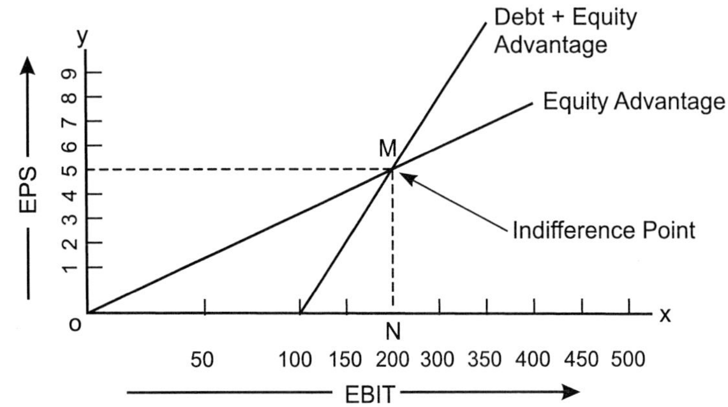

Fig. 10.4 Indifference chart

This chart (Fig. 10.4) is useful in selecting the most suitable capital structure of the firm *i.e.*, debt equity mix. Equity has no fixed cost and debt has a fixed cost of Rs. 1,00,000 which is shown in the BE chart. The debt financing is more advantageous above the indifference point, whereas equity is more advantageous below indifference point.

If the firm's income is anticipated to be higher than the indifference level, debt will be advantageous otherwise raising funds will not be beneficial EPS will decline. Hence the study of indifference analysis is very useful in selecting the most profitable pattern of capitalization.

The main points of indifference point can be summarized as:

- The shareholders earnings will not be affected by level of leverage if return on assets is just equal to interest costs. ROI = Interest costs (no affect on EPS).
- Shareholders will benefit by the use of financial leverage in terms of the increased EPS if return on assets is higher than the interest cost. ROI > Interest costs = Increase in EPS.
- Shareholders will have reduced EPS if earnings on assets are lower than the interest cost. Earnings on assets < interest costs = fall in EPS.

Another example (Fig. 10.5) can be taken of a graphic representation of indifferent point in the Fig, 10.4, the X-axis shows EBIT and Y shows EPS. It depicts EPS at various levels of EBIT. Two sets of EBIT-EPS are presented. 100% equity plan has started from the origin because EPS is zero if EBIT is zero. The point at which the two lines. One with 50% debt and the other with no debt are drawn at the point of intersection is the indifference point.

BEP is also called indifference point. The point of intersection EBIT = EPS indicates indifference point.

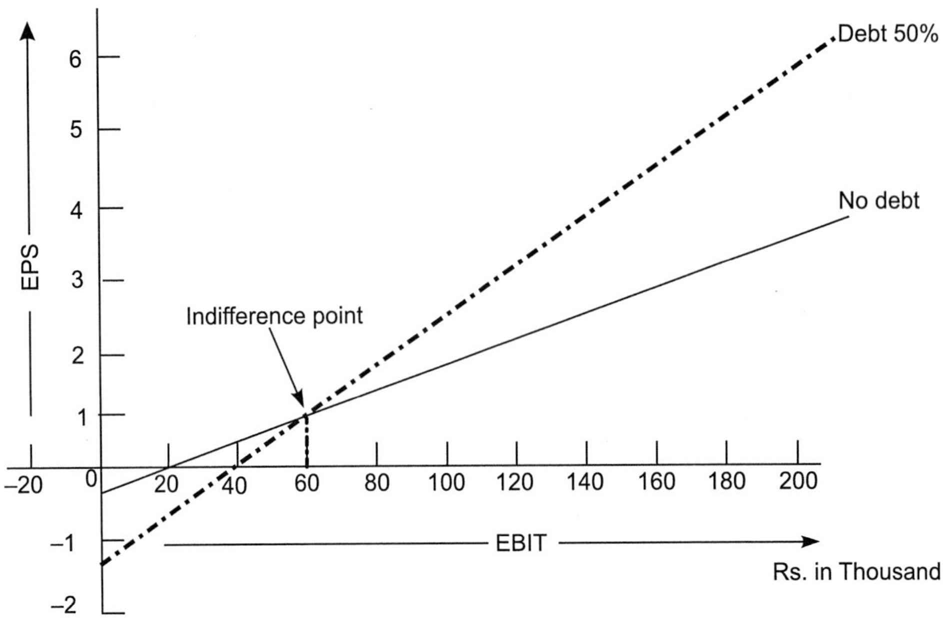

Fig. 10.5 Indifference point

The EPS lines for all equity and 50% debt plans intersect at EBIT Rs. 60,000.

EPS becomes steeper with more debt, and the steeper the line the more the profit potential to the shareholders with increasing EBIT. If EBIT is declining, loss to shareholders will be magnified. The point of intersection of EBIT and EPS is called 'Indifference Point' or Break-even Point.

EPS will be same regardless level of financial leverage. It is same for all financial points. EPS shifts to the right when financial leverage increases.

This chart is useful in selecting the most suitable capital structure of the firm debt.

EBIT higher than indifference point is good. Increase in EBIT will have a magnifying effect on EPS.

10.8 LIMITATIONS OF EBIT-EPS ANALYSIS

The indifference point helps in providing a basis for selection of a capital structure for a company but it has certain limitations. There are two important conditions to be remembered:

(*i*) When indifference point is negative.

(*ii*) When there is no new issue of equity shares in alternative plans.

In both these cases the indifference point is not useful in making a choice for a good capital structure of a firm. The indifference point when plotted on the graph, the lines will be parallel to each other and they will not intersect.

This can be explained with the help of an example.

Example 10.12 A firm having Rs. 60,000 equity shares requires additional funds of Rs. 5,00,000 for which two options are available: (*i*) To issue 10,000 equity shares of Rs. 25 each and to raise Rs. 2,50,000 through the issue of 9% bonds; (*ii*) To issue 65,000 equity shares at Rs. 25 each and to issue 1,250, 12% preference shares of Rs. 100 each when the tax rate is 50%. Calculate indifference level.

Solution

$$\frac{(\text{EBIT} - 22{,}500)(1-0.5)}{60{,}000} = \frac{\text{EBIT}(1-0.5) - 15{,}000}{65{,}000}$$

Or $$\frac{0.5\ \text{EBIT} - 11{,}250}{60} = \frac{0.5\ \text{EBIT} - 15{,}000}{65}$$

Or $$32.5\ \text{EBIT} - 7{,}31{,}250 = 30\ \text{EBIT} - 9{,}00{,}000$$

Or $$2.5\ \text{EBIT} = -1{,}68{,}750$$

Or $$\text{EBIT} = -67{,}500$$

Indifference point is indeterminate.

Example 10.13 When no new equity shares are issued in either of the new plans the indifference point will be negative. This can be explained with the help of the following example.

A firm has an equity capital of 50,000 shares. It raises Rs. 5,00,000 in additional capital. There are two plans available, (*i*) issue of bonds of Rs. 5,00,000 with 10% rate of interest, or (*ii*) by issuing 12% preference shares of Rs. 100 each. Calculate indifference level.

Solution

$$\frac{(\text{EBIT} - 50{,}000)(1-0.5)}{50{,}000} = \frac{\text{EBIT}(1-0.5) - 60{,}000}{50{,}000}$$

$$= -35{,}000$$

Indifference point is negative. Hence no decisions on capital structure can be made.

TYPES OF LEVERAGE AT A GLANCE

(1) ROI Leverage

$$\text{ROI Leverage} = \frac{\text{Sales}}{\text{Total Assets}} \times \frac{\text{EBIT}}{\text{Sales}} = \frac{\text{EBIT}}{\text{Total Assets}}$$

It is an index of operational efficiency.

(2) Assets Leverage

Assets turnover is the ratio of Sales to Total Asset. Sales ÷ Total assets aspect of ROI Leverage is often referred to as 'Assets Leverage'.

(3) Operating Leverage

Degree of Operating Leverage (DOL)

$$= \frac{\text{Contribution}}{\text{Operating Profit}} \text{ or } \frac{\text{Contribution}}{\text{EBIT}}$$

It is related to fixed cost. A high operating leverage indicates high risky situation as it consists of large fixed costs.

Financial Leverage

$$\text{Degree of Financial Leverage (DFL)} = \frac{\text{EBIT}}{\text{PBT}}$$

If return on investment exceeds rate of interest on debt it is favourable financial leverage otherwise it is unfavourable. If ROI is exactly equal to the rate of interest on debt there is no financial leverage and EPS will not be affected. High financial leverage is not good as it indicates the large content of fixed interest charges.

Risky Situation: High operating leverage combined with high financial leverage will constitute risky situation.

Normal Situation: One should be high and another should be low *i.e.*, if company has a low operating leverage financial leverage can be higher and vice versa.

Ideal Situation: Both should be low

$$\text{Combined Leverage} = \text{Operating Leverage} \times \text{Financial Leverage}$$

$$= \frac{\text{Contribution}}{\text{EBIT}} \times \frac{\text{EBIT}}{\text{PBT}} = \frac{\text{Contribution}}{\text{PBT}}$$

POINTS TO REMEMBER

- The most common leverages are the operating leverage, financial leverage and combined leverage.
- Operating leverage is as a result of the presence of fixed charges which are used to gain an advantage in terms of profitability of a firm.
- Financial leverage is due to the presence of debt on the capital structure. It is used to magnify the earnings per share of the shareholders.
- Break-even analysis is a point where the cost are equal to the revenue of the company. When the company has achieved its break-even point, fixed expanses remaining the same it will gain with an increase in the sales of the firm.
- Leverages help to establish relationships between earnings, revenue as well as the earnings per shares of the shareholders.
- Leverages help in designing the capital structure of a firm.
- The financial manager can analyse the different relationships to maximize the wealth of the shareholders.
- The operating leverage shows the effect of sales on EBIT and financial leverage shows the relationship between EBIT and EPS.
- Operating leverage makes an analysis of the break-even point to see the effect on the revenues of the firm whereas the financial break-even point is the point where EBIT and EPS is zero.
- Financial break-even point is also called the 'indifference point'.
- OL and FL show the risk of the firm. A high operating leverage shows high risk in the company. Similarly, high financial leverage also means high risk and the possibility of the fall in profits and earnings per share of the shareholders.
- The result of OL when multiplied with the results of FL gives combined leverage. A high combined leverage means high risk for the firm.
- An ideal situation is when the leverage is low.

OBJECTIVE TYPE QUESTIONS

State whether the following statements are true (T) or false (F).

1. OL provides the relationship between EBIT and EPS.
2. OL is used to enhance the profitability of the company.
3. Risk is associated with high operating leverage.
4. Leverage arises due to presence of fixed costs.
5. Combined leverage shows an ideal relationship when it is high.
6. FL is another name for trading on equity.
7. The benefits of FL accrue always for the shareholders.
8. CL is a relationship of OL and FL.
9. EBIT and operating profit mean the same.
10. EPS is zero when the EBIT is at the level of indifference.

Answers: 1. (F), 2. (T), 3. (T), 4. (T), 5. (F), 6. (T), 7. (F), 8. (F), 9. (T), 10. (T)

THEORETICAL QUESTIONS

1. Differentiate between business risk and financing risk of a firm. How are they measured by leverage?
2. Discuss the concepts of OL, FL and CL. How are they measured? What is their significance in planning a firm?
3. Why does a financial manager keep in mind the degree of financial leverage in evaluating various financial plans? When does FL become favourable?
4. What is the significance of the indifference level?
5. What are the limitations of EBIT-EPS analysis?
6. Explain the algebraic and graphical approach for determining EBIT-EPS relationship.
7. Write notes on OL, FL, CL and indifference point.
8. How does the financial manager use OL and FL for taking financing decisions of a firm?
9. What is the significance of OL and FL? How should they be interpreted for use in financial decision making?

ILLUSTRATIVE PROBLEMS

Illustration 10.1 From the following data calculate degree of operating leverage. Which firm is more risky X or Z?

Particulars	X	Z
Sales	Rs. 50,00,000	Rs. 60,00,000
Variable cost	50% of sales	25% of sales
Fixed cost	Rs. 8,00,000	Rs. 10,00,000

Solution

DOL = Sales – Variable Cost/EBIT

Particulars	X (Rs.)	Z (Rs.)
Sales	50,00,000	60,00,000
Less variable costs	25,00,000	15,00,000
Less fixed costs	8,00,000	10,00,000
EBIT	17,00,000	35,00,000

$$\text{DOL} = (\text{Sales} - \text{Variable Cost})/\text{EBIT}$$
$$X = (50{,}00{,}000 - 25{,}00{,}000)/17{,}00{,}000$$
$$= 1.47$$
$$\text{DOL for } Z = (60{,}00{,}000 - 15{,}00{,}000)/35{,}00{,}000$$
$$= 1.28$$

X is riskier than Z.

Illustration 10.2 Calculate the degree of operating leverage (DOL), degree of financial leverage (DFL) and degree of combined leverage (DCL) for the firm X.

Particulars	Firm X (Rs.)
Output	1,00,000
Fixed costs	Rs. 87,000
Variable costs per unit	Rs. 25
Interest on borrowed funds	Rs. 4,00,000
Selling price per unit	Rs. 500

Solution

Particulars	Firm X (Rs.)
Output	1,00,000
Selling Price per unit	500
Variable cost per unit	25
Contribution	475
Total contribution	4,75,00,000
Less: Fixed cost	87,000
EBIT	4,74,13,000
Less: Interest	4,00,000
Profit before tax	4,70,13,000

Degree of operating leverage

Contribution/EBIT = 4,75,00,000/4,74,13,000 = 1.00

Degree financial leverage EBIT/PBT = 4,74,13,000/4,70,13,000 = 1.008

Degree of combined leverage = Contribution/PBT = 4,75,00,000/4,70,13,000 = 1.01

The risk in this firm is quite low. Hence the proposal can be expected.

Illustration 10.3 From the following data calculate the degree of operating leverage. Which of the two firms have greater risk?

Particulars	Firm X (Rs.)	Firm Z (Rs.)
Sales	10,00,000	20,00,000
Variable costs	20% of sales	20% of sales
Fixed cost	4,00,000	1,00,000

Solution

Particulars	Firm X (Rs.)	Firm Z (Rs.)
Sales	10,00,000	20,00,000
Less: Fixed costs	4,00,000	1,00,000
	6,00,000	19,00,000
Less: Variable costs	2,00,000	4,00,000
EBIT	4,00,000	15,00,000

OL = Contribution/EBIT

X = 8,00,000/4,00,000 = 2

Z = 16,00,000/15,00,000 = 1.06

X is riskier than Z because its OL is higher than Z.

Illustration 10.4 From the following data calculate financial leverage. There are two companies P & Q. Company P has sales of Rs. 15,00,000; variable cost of Rs. 4,50,000 and fixed costs of Rs. 3,00,000 and it pays an interest of Rs. 1,00,000. Company Q has sales of Rs. 20,00,000; variable costs of Rs. 6,00,000; fixed costs of Rs. 3,00,000 and pays an interest of Rs. 1,25,000.

Solution

Particulars	P	Q
Sales	15,00,000	20,00,000
Less: Variable cost	4,50,000	6,00,000
Contribution	10,50,000	14,00,000
Less: Fixed cost	3,00,000	3,00,000
EBIT	7,50,000	11,00,000
Interest	1,00,000	1,25,000
PBT	6,50,000	9,75,000
(*i*) DOL = Contribution/EBIT	$\frac{10,50,000}{7,50,000}$ = 1.4	$\frac{14,00,000}{11,00,000}$ = 1.27
(*ii*) DFL = EBIT/PBT	$\frac{7,50,000}{6,50,000}$ = 1.15	$\frac{11,00,000}{9,75,000}$ = 1.12

Both degree of operating leverage and financial leverage is higher in Q. Hence it has more risk than P.

Illustration 10.5 A firm provides the following information sales Rs. 20,00,000; variable cost at 20% on sales. Fixed costs Rs. 3,00,000 and Rs. 4,00,000; debit @ 12% of interest. What are its operating, financial and combined leverages? If the firm doubles its sales what would be the effect on OL and FL other expends (except variable expenses) remain unchanged.

Solution

Particulars	Amount (Rs.)
Sales	20,00,000
– Variable costs @ 20% on sales	4,00,000
Contribution	16,00,000
– Fixed cost	3,00,000
EBIT	13,00,000
– Interest @ 12% on 4,00,000	48,000
	12,52,000

$$\text{Operating leverage} = \frac{\text{Contribution}}{\text{EBIT}} = \frac{16,00,000}{13,00,000} = 1.23$$

$$\text{Financial leverage} = \frac{\text{EBIT}}{\text{PBT}} = \frac{13,00,000}{12,52,000} = 1.03$$

Combined leverage = 1.23 × 1.03 = 1.267

The sales required to double the EBIT operating leverage explains that increase in sales will have an effect on the operating profit of the firm. Since operating leverage is 1.23 let us see the effect when sales are doubled.

Particulars	Amount (Rs.)
Sales	40,00,000
– Variable costs (20%)	08,00,000
Contribution	32,00,000
– Fixed cost	3,00,000
EBIT	29,00,000
Interest @ 12% on variable cost	96,000
PBT	28,04,000

$$\text{Degree of Operating Leverage} = \frac{\text{Contribution}}{\text{EBIT}} = \frac{32,00,000}{29,00,000} = 1.10$$

$$\text{Degree of Financial Leverage} = \frac{\text{EBIT}}{\text{PBT}} = \frac{29,00,000}{28,05,000} = 1.03$$

Degree of Combined Leverage = 1.10 × 1.03 = 1.13

The increase in sales has brought down the risk level.

Illustration 10.6 The balance sheet of Shaw and Co. is as follows:

Liabilities	Amount (Rs.)	Assets	Amount (Rs.)
Equity share capital	60,000	Fixed assets	1,50,000
Retained earnings	20,000	Current assets	50,000
10% long-term debt	80,000		
Current liabilities	40,000		
	2,00,000		2,00,000

The Co.'s total asset turnover ratio is 3. Its fixed operating costs are Rs. 1,00,000 and the variable operating cost ratio is 40%. The income tax rate is 50%. Calculate for the company the different types of leverages. Given that the face value of the share is Rs. 10.

Solution

Sales level is calculated through total assets turnover ratio.

$$\text{Total assets turnover ratio} = \frac{\text{Sales}}{\text{Total assets}}$$

$$3 = \frac{\text{Sales}}{2{,}00{,}000}$$

Particulars	Amount (Rs.)
Sales	6,00,000
Less variable costs (40%)	2,40,000
Contribution	3,60,000
– Fixed costs	1,00,000
EBIT	2,60,000
– Interest 10% of	8,000
PBT	2,52,000
Tax @ 50%	1,26,000
PAT	1,26,000
No. of shares	6,000
EPS	21

$$\text{Degree of operating leverage} = \frac{\text{Contribution}}{\text{EBIT}}$$

$$= \frac{3{,}60{,}000}{2{,}60{,}000} = 1.38$$

$$\text{Degree of financial leverage} = \frac{\text{EBIT}}{\text{PBT}}$$

$$= \frac{2{,}60{,}000}{2{,}52{,}000} = 1.03$$

$$\text{Degree of combined leverage} = 1.38 \times 1.03 = 1.42$$

Illustration 10.7 From the following information for 4 companies calculate (*i*) EBIT (*ii*) EPS (*iii*) OL (*iv*) FL.

Particulars	P	Q	R	S
Selling price per units	15	20	25	30
Quantity	10	15	20	25
No. of units	20,000	25,000	30,000	40,000
Fixed costs	30,000	40,000	50,000	60,000
Interest	15,000	25,000	35,000	40,000
Tax rate 40%	40	40	40	40
No. of equity shares	5,000	9,000	10,000	12,000

Solution

Calculation of EBIT, EPS, OL, FL.

Particulars	P	Q	R	S
Units	20,000	25,000	30,000	40,000
Sales Revenue	3,00,000	5,00,000	7,50,000	12,00,000
– Variable cost	2,00,000	3,75,000	6,00,000	10,00,000
Contribution	1,00,000	1,25,000	1,50,000	2,00,000
Less fixed costs	30,000	40,000	50,000	60,000
(i) EBIT	70,000	85,000	1,00,000	1,40,000
Less interest	15,000	25,000	35,000	40,000
PBT	55,000	60,000	65,000	1,00,000
Less tax @ 40%	22,000	24,000	26,000	40,000
PAT	33,000	36,000	39,000	60,000
No. of equity shares	5,000	9,000	10,000	12,000
(ii) EPS	6.60	4	3.90	5
(iii) OL = $\frac{\text{Contribution}}{\text{EBIT}}$	$\frac{1,00,000}{70,000}$	$\frac{1,25,000}{85,000}$	$\frac{1,50,000}{1,00,000}$	$\frac{2,00,000}{1,40,000}$
	= 1.43	= 1.47	= 1.50	= 1.43
(iv) FL = $\frac{\text{EBIT}}{\text{PBT}}$	$\frac{70,000}{55,000}$	$\frac{85,000}{60,000}$	$\frac{1,00,000}{65,000}$	$\frac{1,40,000}{1,00,000}$
	= 1.27	1.42	1.54	1.40

Illustration 10.8 A company has the following data:

Total assets	60,000
Total assets turnover based	2
On sales	
Variable cost as % sales	60%
Fixed cost	10,000

The company has the following financing plans.

Particulars	Plan I	Plan II
Equity	30,000	20,000
10% debentures	25,000	40,000
Rate of Interest	10%	10%

Prepare income statement and calculate leverages for both the cases.

Solution

Total assets turnover ratio = Sales/Total assets = 2

Sales of the company can be calculated with the above formula 2 × 60,000 = 1,20,000

Particulars	Plan I	Plan II
Sales	1,20,000	1,20,000
Less variable cost	72,000	72,000
Contribution	48,000	48,000
Less fixed costs	10,000	10,000
EBIT	38,000	38,000
Less interest	2,500	4,000
PBT	35,500	34,000
$DOL = \frac{\text{Contribution}}{\text{EBIT}}$	$\frac{48,000}{38,000}$ = 1.26	$\frac{48,000}{38,000}$ = 1.26
$DFL = \frac{\text{EBIT}}{\text{PBT}}$	$\frac{38,000}{35,500}$ = 1.07	$\frac{38,000}{34,000}$ = 1.11
$DCL = \frac{\text{Contribution}}{\text{PBT}}$	1.3	1.4

Illustration 10.9 A firm sells its products for Rs.1000 per unit and has a variable cost of Rs.500 per unit and fixed operating costs of Rs. 50,00,000 per year. Show the various level of EBIT that would result from the sale of 10,000 units; 20,000 units; 30,000 units; 40,000 units; and 50,000 units.

Solution

Sales in units	10,000	20,000	30,000	40,000	50,000
Sales revenue	1,00,00,000	2,00,00,000	3,00,00,000	4,00,00,000	5,00,00,000
– Variable cost	50,00,000	1,00,00,000	1,50,00,000	2,00,00,000	2,50,00,000
Contribution	50,00,000	1,00,00,000	1,50,00,000	2,00,00,000	2,50,00,000
– Fixed cost	50,00,000	50,00,000	50,00,000	50,00,000	50,00,000
EBIT	Nil	50,00,000	1,00,00,000	1,50,00,000	2,00,00,000
	—	1.00	1.5	1.33	1.25

Illustration 10.10 Calculate DLFL and CL.

Particulars	A	B	C
Output	50,000	25,000	1,00,000
Fixed costs	7,000	14,000	1,500
Variable costs per unit	0.20	1.50	0.10
Interest on borrowed capital	4,000	8,000	Nil
Selling price per unit (Rs.)	1.00	5.00	0.50

Solution

Particulars	A	B	C
Output	50,000	25,000	1,00,000
SP per unit	1.00	5.00	0.50
Variable cost per unit	0.20	1.50	0.10
Contribution	0.80	3.50	0.40
Per unit total contribution	40,000	87,500	40,000
– Fixed cost	7,000	14,000	1,500
EBIT or operating profit	33,000	73,500	38,500
– interest	4,000	8,000	Nil
PBT	29,000	65,500	38,500
$DOL = \frac{\text{Contribution}}{\text{EBIT}}$	$\frac{40,000}{33,000}$	$\frac{87,500}{73,500}$	$\frac{40,000}{38,500}$
	= 1.21	= 1.19	= 1.038

[Contd...]

Particulars	A	B	C
Degree of financial leverage			
$\frac{\text{EBIT}}{\text{PBT}}$	$\frac{33,000}{29,000} = 1.137$	$\frac{73,500}{65,000} = 1.13$	$\frac{38,500}{38,500} = 1$
Degree of combined leverage			
$\frac{\text{Contribution}}{\text{PBT}}$	$\frac{40,000}{29,000} = 1.3$	$\frac{87,500}{65,500} = 1.3$	$\frac{40,000}{38,000} = 1.05$

Illustration 10.11 Calculate OL and CL at different operating levels and financial plans 1, 2, 3.

Installed capacity	1,200 units		
Actual production and sales	800 units		
Selling price per unit	Rs. 15		
Variable cost per unit	Rs. 10		
Fixed situation A	Rs. 3,000		
Cost situation B	Rs. 1,000		
Cost situation C	Rs. 3,500		
Financial plan	I	II	III
Equity	5,000	7,500	2,500
Debt	5,000	2,500	7,500
Cost of debt at 12%	—	—	—

Solution

Operating Leverage

Particulars	Situations		
	A	B	C
Sales 800 units Rs. 15	12,000	12,000	12,000
– Variables cost (800 unit × Rs. 10)	8,000	8,000	8,000
Contribution C = 800 x 5	4,000	4,000	4,000
– Fixed cost (F)	3,000	1,000	3,500
Operating Profit (OP) EBIT	1,000	3,000	500
Operating Leverage = $\frac{\text{C}}{\text{EBIT}}$	$\frac{4,000}{1,000}$	$\frac{4,000}{3,000}$	$\frac{4,000}{500}$
	= 4	= 1.3	= 8.00

Statement of Financial Leverage

Particulars	Financial Plans		
Situation A	I	II	III
Operating profit (EBIT)	1,000	1,000	1,000
– Interest on debt 12%	600	300	900
Profit before tax PBT (EBIT)	400	700	100
Financial Leverage = $\frac{OP}{EBIT}$	0.25	1.42	10
Situation B			
Operating profit	3,000	3,000	3,000
Less: Interest on debt 12%	600	300	900
PBT	2,400	2,700	2,100
Financial leverage	= 1.25	= 1.11	= 1.42
Situation C			
Operating Profit	500	500	500
Less: interest at 12%	600	300	900
PBT	– 100	200	– 400
Financial leverage = $\frac{OP}{EBIT}$	–5	2.5	–1.25

Illustration 10.12 A Company has estimated for a new product its BEP is 2,000 units if the item is sold for Rs. 14 per unit. The costing department has identified variable cost of Rs. 9 per unit. Calculate degree of operating leverage for sales volume of 2,500 units and 3,000 units. What do you infer from the degree of operating leverage at the sales volume of 2,500 units and 3,000 units and their difference, if any?

Solution

Statement of Operating Leverage

Particulars	Per unit	2,000 units	2,500 units	3,000 units
Sales	14	28,000	35,000	42,000
Variable costs	9	18,000	22,500	27,000
Contribution	5	10,000	12,500	15,000
Fixed costs		10,000	10,000	10,000
Operating profit (OP)			5,000	5,000
		Nil	2,500	5,000
Operating Leverage = $\frac{C}{OP}$			$\frac{12500}{2500}$ = 5	$\frac{15000}{5000}$ = 3

At the sale volume of 3,000 units operating profit is Rs. 5000, which is double the operating profit of Rs. 2500, which is at the sales volume of 2,500 units because operating leverage is 5 times the sales volume of 2,500 units. Hence by increase of 20% in sales volume the profit is increased by 100% *i.e.*, 5 times of 20%. At the level of 3,000 units the operating leverage is 3 times.

Illustration 10.13 A company has capital structure exclusively of ordinary shares amounting to Rs. 5,00,000. The Co. desires to raise additional funds of Rs. 5,00,000 for financing its expansion programme. The Co. has 4 alternative financial plans:

A. It can raise the entire amount by equity capital.

B. It can raise 50% as equity and 50% as 5% debentures.

C. It can raise the entire amount as 6% debentures.

D. It can raise 50%as equity and 50% as 6% Preference Capital. The existing EBIT is Rs. 60,000; tax rate 50%; outstanding ordinary shares number 5,000 and market price per share is Rs.100 under all 4 alternatives which financing plan should be selected.

Solution

EPS under 4 Financing Plans

Particulars	A	B	C	D
EBIT (Rs.)	60,000	60,000	60,000	60,000
Less: Interest	—	12,500	30,000	—
	—	(5% debentures)	(6% of 5 lakh)	-
EBIT	60,000	47,500	30,000	30,000
Less: Taxes at 50%	30,000	23,750	15,000	30,000
Earnings After Tax	30,000	23,750	15,000	30,000
Less: Preference dividend	—	—	—	15,000
				(6% of 25,000)
Earnings available to				
ordinary shareholders	30,000	23,750	15,000	15,000
No. of shares	10,000	7,500	5,000	7,500
	(5,000 + 5,000)	(5,000 + 2,500)	(5,000)	(5,000 + 2,500)
EPS (Rs.)	3.00	3.17	3.00	2.00

He should select Plan 2 as the earnings per share is the highest with the combination of 5,000 shares and 2,500 debentures.

Illustration 10.14 There are two plans: Plan 1 has the following capital structure—Equity Rs. 6,00,000 and 15% debentures of Rs. 4,00,000 of Rs.10 Plan two has the following details Equity Rs. 4,00,000 and 13% preference capital of Rs. 2,00,000; 15% debentures of Rs. 400,000. Face value of equity shares is Rs. 10 in Plan 1 and 2. Find their indifference point.

Solution

$$\frac{(1-t)(\text{EBIT} - I_1)}{N_1} = \frac{(1-t)(\text{EBIT} - I_2) - P}{N_2}$$

Plan 1

$$\frac{(1-0.5)(\text{EBIT} - 60{,}000)}{40{,}000}$$

Plan 2

$$\frac{(1-0.5)(\text{EBIT} - 60{,}000) - 26{,}000}{40{,}000}$$

$$0.5 \text{ EBIT} - 30{,}000 = 1.5\ (0.5 \text{ EBIT} - 30{,}000 - 26{,}000)$$

$$0.5 \text{ EBIT} - 30{,}000 = 0.75 \text{ EBIT} - 84{,}000$$

$$0.5 \text{ EBIT} - 0.75 \text{ EBIT} = -84{,}000 + 30{,}000$$

$$\text{EBIT} = (-54{,}000)/(-0.25) = 2{,}16{,}000$$

Illustration 10.15 Find the indifference point between the two alternative financial plans.

(*i*) Equity	Rs. 8,00,000
13% Preference Capital	Rs. 2,00,000
Tax rate	50%
(*ii*) Equity	Rs. 4,00,000
13% Preference Capital	Rs. 2,00,000
15% Debentures	Rs. 4,00,000

Face value of equity shares is Rs. 10 in Plan 1 and 2.

Solution

$$\frac{(1-t)\ \text{EBIT} - P_1}{N_1} = \frac{(1-t)(\text{EBIT} - I) - P_2}{N_2}$$

$$\frac{(1-0.5)\ \text{EBIT} - 26{,}000}{80{,}000} = \frac{(1-0.5)(\text{EBIT} - 60{,}000) - 26{,}000}{40{,}000}$$

$$\Rightarrow \quad 0.5 \text{ EBIT} - 26{,}000 = 2\{(0.5 \text{ EBIT} - 30{,}000) - 26{,}000\}$$

$$\Rightarrow \quad 0.5 \text{ EBIT} - 26{,}000 = (\text{EBIT} - 60{,}000) - 52{,}000$$

$$\Rightarrow \quad 0.5 \text{ EBIT} - 26{,}000 = \text{EBIT} - 60{,}000 - 52{,}000$$

$$\Rightarrow \quad 0.5 \text{ EBIT} - \text{EBIT} = -60{,}000 + 26{,}000 - 52{,}000$$

$\Rightarrow \quad -0.5 \text{ EBIT} = -86{,}000$

$\Rightarrow \quad \text{EBIT} = \dfrac{86{,}000}{0.5}$

$\Rightarrow \quad \text{EBIT} = \text{Rs. } 1{,}72{,}000$

Illustration 10.16 The following figures are made available to you:

Particulars	Amount (Rs.)
Net Profits for the year	18,00,000
– Interest on secured debentures at 15% p.a.	
(Debentures were issued 3 months after the commencement of the year)	1,12,500
	16,87,500
– Income tax at 35% and dividend distribution tax	8,43,750
Profit after tax	8,43,750
Number of Equity shares (Rs. 10 each)	1,00,000
Market quotation of equity share	Rs. 109.7

The company has accumulated revenue reserves of Rs. 12 lakh. The company is examining a project calling for an investment obligation of Rs. 10 lakh; this investments is expected to earn the same rate of return as funds already employed.

You are informed that a debit equity ratio (Debt divided by debt plus equity) higher than 45% will cause the price earning ratio to come down by 25% and the interest rate on additional borrowings will cost company 300 basic points more than on the current borrowal on secured debentures.

You are required to advise the company on the probable price of the equity share, if:

(*a*) The additional investment were to be raised by way of loans.

(*b*) The additional investments were to be raised by way of equity. **[CA 1998]**

Solution

Step 1: Existing rate of return on capital employed

$$\text{ROCE} = \frac{\text{EBIT}}{\text{Capital Employed}} \times 100$$

$$= \frac{18{,}00{,}000}{32{,}00{,}000} \times 100 = 56.25\%$$

Existing Capital Employed = Equity + Debentures + Revenue Reserves

= 10,00,000 + 10,00,000 + 12,00,000 = Rs. 32,00,000

Step 2: Existing P/E Ratio

$$\text{EPS} = \frac{\text{EBIT} - \text{Tax}}{\text{No. of equity shares}}$$

$$= \frac{16{,}87{,}500 - 5{,}90{,}625}{1{,}00{,}000} = 10.97\%$$

$$\text{P/E Ratio} = \frac{\text{Market price}}{\text{EPS}} = \frac{109.70}{10.97} = 10$$

Step 3: Return on New Capital Employed = 56.25% of (Rs. 32,00,000 + Rs. 10,00,000)

= 56.25% of 42,00,000 = 23,62,500.

Step 4: Debt – Equity Ratio in case additional investment is raised by way of debt

$$= \frac{10{,}00{,}000 + 10{,}00{,}000}{42{,}00{,}000} \times 100 = 47.62\%$$

Step 5:

Probable Price of the Equity Share

Particulars	Loan Alternative (Rs.)	Equity Alternative (Rs.)
EBIT	23,62,500	23,62,500
– Interest on 15% Debentures	1,50,000	1,50,000
– Interest on 18% Loan	1,80,000	———
EBT	20,32,500	22,12,500
– Tax @ 35%	7,11,375	7,74,375
EAT	13,21,125	14,38,125
No. of equity shares	1,00,000	1,09,116
EPS	13.21	13.18
P/E ratio	7.5	10
Market price	99.075	131.80

The company is advised to raise additional investment by way of Equity.

Illustration 10.17 A firm has sales of Rs. 40,00,000; variable cost of Rs. 25,00,000; fixed cost of Rs. 6,00,000; 10% debt of Rs. 30,00,000; and equity capital of Rs. 45,00,000. **(CA 2007)**

Solution

Particulars	Amount (Rs.)
Sales	40,00,000
– Variable cost	25,00,000
Contribution	15,00,000
– Fixed cost	6,00,000
EBIT	9,00,000
– Interest	3,00,000
EBT	6,00,000

$$\text{Operating Leverage} = \frac{\text{Contribution}}{\text{EBIT}} = \frac{15,00,000}{9,00,000} = 1.67$$

$$\text{Financial Leverage} = \frac{\text{EBIT}}{\text{EBT}} = \frac{15,00,000}{9,00,000} = 1.50$$

Illustration 10.18 The following data relate to RT Ltd.:

Particulars	Amount (Rs.)
Earnings before interest and tax (EBIT)	10,00,000
Fixed cost	20,00,000
Earnings before tax (EBT)	8,00,000

Calculate Combined Leverage

(CA 2008)

Solution

$$\text{Combined Leverage} = \frac{\text{Contribution}}{\text{EBIT}} \times \frac{\text{EBIT}}{\text{EBT}}$$

$$= \frac{\text{Contribution}}{\text{EBT}} = \frac{\text{EBIT + Fixed cost}}{\text{EBT}}$$

$$= \frac{\text{Rs. } 10,00,000 + \text{Rs. } 20,00,000}{\text{Rs. } 8,00,000} = 3.75$$

Illustration 10.19 Delta Ltd. currently has an equity share capital of Rs. 10,00,000 consisting of 1,00,000; equity shares of Rs. 10 each. The company is going through a major expansion plan requiring to raise funds to the tune of Rs. 6,00,000. To finance the expansion the management has following plans:

Plan I : Issue 60,000 equity shares of Rs. 10 each.

Plan II : Issue 40,000 equity shares of Rs. each and the balance through long-term borrowing at 12% interest p.a.

Plan III : Issue 30,000 equity shares of Rs. 10 each and 3,000 Rs. 100, 9% Debentures.

Plan IV : Issue 30,000 equity shares of Rs. 10 each and the balance through 6% Preference shares.

The EBIT of the company is expected to be Rs. 4,00,000 p.a. assume corporate tax rate of 40%. (*i*) Calculate EPS in each of the above plans. (*ii*) Ascertain the degree of financial leverage in each plan.

(CA 2008)

Solution

Statement Showing the Calculation of EPS and Financial Leverage

Particulars	Plan I (Rs.)	Plan II (Rs.)	Plan III (Rs.)	Plan IV (Rs.)
EBIT	4,00,000	4,00,000	4,00,000	4,00,000
– Interest on 15% Loan	—	24,000	—	—
EBT	—	—	27,000	—
– Tax @ 40%	4,00,000	3,76,000	3,73,000	4,00,000
EAT	1,60,000	1,50,400	1,49,200	1,60,000
– Preference dividends	2,40,000	2,25,600	2,23,800	2,40,000
Earnings for equity shares	—	—	—	18,000
No. of equity shares	2,40,000	2,25,600	2,23,800	2,22,000
EPS (G/H)	1,60,000	1,50,400	1,30,000	1,30,000
Degree of Financial leverage	1.50	1.61	1.72	1.71
$\left(\frac{\text{EBIT}}{\text{EBIT - I}}\right)$ or $\left(\frac{\text{EBIT}}{\text{EBT}}\right)$	1.00	1.06	1.07	1.00

Note: Plan III can be accepted by the management since its EPS and degree of financial leverage both are highest.

Illustration 10.20 Annual sales of a company is Rs. 60,00,000. Sales to variable cost ratio is 150% and fixed cost other than interest is Rs. 5,00,00 per annum. Company has 11% debentures of Rs. 30,00,000. You are required to calculate the Operating, Financial and Combined Leverage of the company.

(CA 2008)

Solution

$$\frac{\text{Sales}}{\text{Variable cost}} = 150\%$$

$$\frac{60{,}00{,}000}{\text{Variable cost}} = 1.5$$

$$\text{Variable cost} = \frac{60{,}00{,}000}{1.5} = \text{Rs. } 40{,}00{,}000$$

Particulars	Amount (Rs.)
Sales	60,00,000
– Variable cost	40,00,000
Contribution	20,00,000
– Fixed cost	5,00,000
EBIT	15,00,000
– Interest	3,30,000
EBT	11,70,000

$$\text{Operating Leverage} = \frac{\text{Contribution}}{\text{EBIT}} = \frac{20{,}00{,}000}{15{,}00{,}000} = 1.33$$

$$\text{Financial Leverage} = \frac{\text{EBIT}}{\text{EBT}} = \frac{15{,}00{,}000}{11{,}70{,}000} = 1.28$$

$$\text{Combined Leverage} = \frac{\text{Contribution}}{\text{EBT}} = \frac{20{,}00{,}000}{11{,}70{,}000} = 1.70$$

PROBLEMS FOR PRACTICE

Problem 10.1 A firm sells products for Rs. 100, Rs. 466.66 and Rs. 300 has variable operating costs of Rs. 60 per unit. It has fixed costs of Rs 60,000 per year show the various levels of EBIT when 500, 1500 and 3,500 units are sold.

[**Answers:** EBIT = 4,10,000; 550,000; 660,000.]

Problem 10.2 X Corporation has estimated that for a new product. Its break-even point is 2,000. Fixed costs Rs. 10,000 units, if the item is sold for Rs. 100 per unit. Variable cost is Rs. 80 per unit. Calculate degree of operating leverage for sales volume of 2,000 units and 3,000 units.

[**Answers:** 1.33, 1.2]

Problem 10.3 (*i*)Find OL from the following data:

Sales	Rs. 50,000
Variable costs	60%
Fixed costs	Rs. 12,000

(*ii*) Find FL from the following data:

Net worth	Rs. 25,00,000
Debt/Equity	3/1
Interest rate	12%
Operating profit	Rs. 20,00,000

(CA Final, May 1995)

[**Answers:** OL = 2.5, FL = 1.82]

Problem 10.4 M. Ltd is considering a major expansion of its production facilities and wants to raise Rs. 50,00,000 for it. The following alternatives are available to raise the required amount.

Sources	Alternatives		
	A	B	C
Equity share capital	50	20	10
15% debentures	––	20	15
16% preference capital	––	10	25

Expected earnings before interest and taxes, is 25% of investment. Corporate tax is 40%. At present the company has no debt which of the alternatives would you choose of the objective of the firm is to maximize the rate of return on equity capital.

[B.Com. (H), DU 2001]

[**Answers:** A = 15%, B = 20.5%, C = 21.5%]

Problem 10.5 X and Y companies have the following information on their financial data.

Particulars	X	Y
Total assets	1,00,000	1,10,000
Total assets turnover based on sales	3	2
Variable cost as % of sales	55%	40%
Fixed cost	25,000	20,000
The following financial plans are given		
Equity	60,000	20,000
10% Debentures	20,000	60,000
Rate of interest	12%	14%

Prepare income statement of the companies and calculate all types of leverages of the company.

[**Answers: X** DOL 1.22, DFL = 1.02, DLC = 1.24; **Y** DOL = 1.17, DFL = 1.08, DCL = 1.26]

Problem 10.6 A firm having 1,00,000 equity shares requires additional funds of Rs. 5,00,000 for which two options are available (*i*) to issue 10,000 equity shares of Rs. 25 each and to raise Rs. 2,50,000 through 9% bonds; (*ii*) to issue 15,000 equity shares of Rs. 25 each and 1,250, 12% preference shares of Rs. 100 each. Tax rate is 50%, calculate indifference point.

[**Answer:** 4,51,500]

Problem 10.7 A new project under consideration requires an additional capital outlay of Rs. 3,00,000. Funds can be raised by issue of equity shares of Rs. 100 each or by equity shares of Rs. 200,00,000 and by issue of 15% loan of Rs. 100,00,000. Find out the indifference level of EBIT. Tax rate is at 50%.

[**Answer:** EBIT = Rs. 45,00,000.]

Problem 10.8 A company has 1,00,000 equity shares of Rs. 10 each. It wants to raise additional 10,00,000 capital. It has two options (*i*) issue of 1,00,000 equity shares (*ii*) issue of 14% debentures. The tax rate of the company is 50%.

What would be the EPS of the two optional plans at the operating level of Rs. 4,00,000?

[**Answer:** EPS = 1 with equity financing and 1.30 with debt financing.]

Problem 10.9 A company is planning to raise Rs. 2,00,000. It has three optional plans to finance it. Plan 1 consists of issue of equity shares of face value of Rs. 10 each at a premium of Rs. 10 per share. Plan 2 consists of 50% equity and 50% debt equity at a premium of Rs. 10 and debt would cost 8%. Plan 3 would be to raise 50% equity of Rs. 10 each at a premium of Rs. 10 and preference shares at 8% dividend. The firm would be operating at an EBIT of Rs. 80,000 and tax rate is 35%.

(*i*) Find earnings per share (*ii*) Indifference point.

[**Answers:** EPS 5.2, 9.36, 8.8; Indifference point Plan1 and 2 = Rs. 16,000;
Plan 2 and 3 is indeterminate and Plan 1 and 3 = Rs. 24,615]

Problem 10.10 The following information of two companies A and B are given. Calculate OL, FL and CL for both the companies. Which of the companies has a greater risk?

Particulars	Company A	Company B
Sales	50,00,000	80,00,000
Variable cost	20,00,000	25,00,000
Fixed cost	12,00,000	15,00,000
Interest	8,00,000	12,00,000

[**Answers:** OL (A) = 1.667, OL (B) = 1.375; FL (A) = 1.8, FL (B) 1.429; CL (A) =3.0, CL (B) 1.964. A has very high leverage so it has high risk.]

❑❑❑

Capital Structure Planning and Value of the Firm

11

LEARNING OBJECTIVES

11.1 Concept of Value of Firm
11.2 Theories of Capital Structure
11.3 Net Income Approach (NI)—Durand
11.4 Net Operating Income Approach (NOI)
11.5 Traditional Theory
11.6 Modigilliani Miller Approach (MM)
11.7 Planning and Designing Capital Structure

11.1 CONCEPT OF VALUE OF FIRM

The objective of financial management is to bring value to a firm to maximize the wealth of the shareholders. In the previous chapter we analysed the profitability of a firm after achieving the break-even point. We also described the earnings per share of the shareholders and how financial leverage helps in assessing risks and the earning potential of the shareholders. In Chapter 9, we explained the cost of capital and the overall cost of capital. In this chapter, the value of the firm is explained with the interrelationships of cost of capital, the earnings before interest and taxes and the overall cost of capital, which determine the value of the firm. Capital structure helps in providing value to the firm and in fulfilling the objective of shareholders wealth maximization.

Value of a firm is based on its investment decisions and its earnings on its investments. Investments have a cost. Depending on the cost benefit analysis a capital structure is designed to get the maximum value of a company. The earnings before interest and taxes of the company are divided among the shareholders, debt holders and the taxes that have to be paid to government. The shareholders get the last share out of the EBIT of the company. The total value of the firm comprises the three aspects—the taxes, the interest paid to the debt holders and the residue amount to be paid to the equity shareholders.

Debt can be used for increasing the value of the firm. It helps to increase the earnings per share of the shareholders. Interest is tax deductible. The increase in EBIT increases the share of the shareholders and consequently the value of the share increases. This is called 'capital gearing'. However debt does not directly increase the value of the firm.

Investment decisions directly increase the value of the firm. It is important to consider the cost of the investments as this helps to mix the kind of sources of capital to enhance the value of the investments. The cost of each source of capital is calculated, the costs are compared to find out the benefits of each source of capital.

Reducing the overall cost of capital would enhance the value of the firm. Debt brings down the cost of capital but it should be used with caution because beyond a point debt will not bring any positive returns to the value of the firm. When interest becomes excessive, the firm begins to lose its value. Optimum capital structure refers to the combination of debt and equity that leads to maximization of the value of the firm. This is called 'optimum capital structure'. Investment decision increases the value of the firm by increasing the size of EBIT. Financial leverage does not affect the total earnings but earnings increase in earnings per share affects the market value. The overall cost of capital should be controlled as lower cost of capital increases the value of the firm. Figure 11.1 illustrates value of the firm.

$$\text{Value of the Firm} = \frac{\text{Earnings Before Interest and Taxes}}{\text{Overall Cost of Capital}}$$

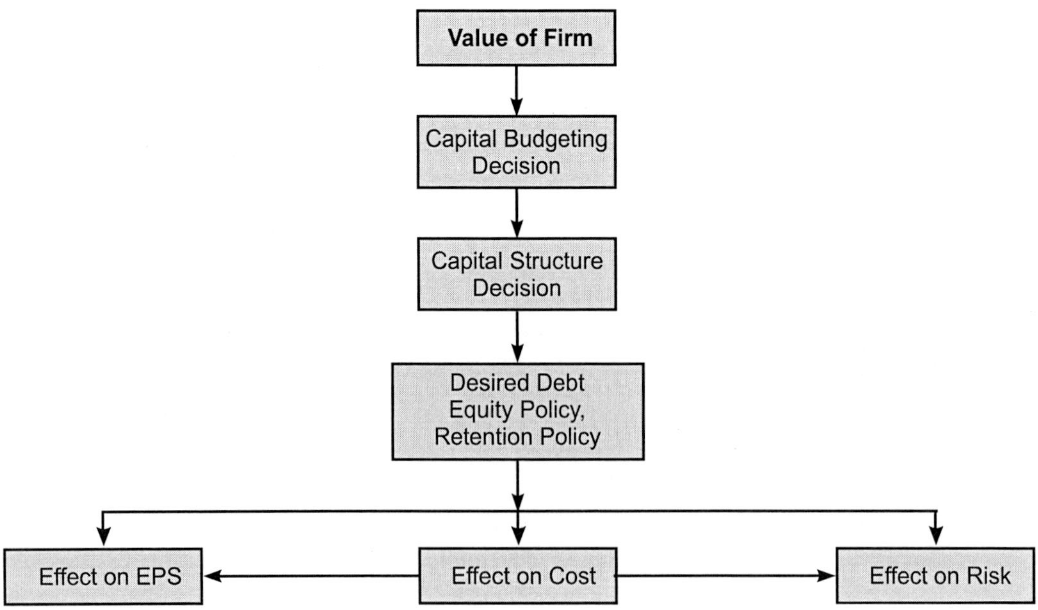

Fig. 11.1 Value of the Firm

There are different theories of capital structure, which shows the relationship of the value of the firm, and its capital structure. These theories have different approaches. The basic aspect of the theories is towards the combination of debt and equity for an appropriate capital structure leading to value maximization of a firm. These theories are discussed in the next section.

11.2 THEORIES OF CAPITAL STRUCTURE

(*i*) Net Income Approach

(*ii*) Net Operating Income

(*iii*) Traditional Approach

(*iv*) Modigliani–Miller Approach

Assumptions of Capital Structure Theories

The capital structure theories have certain assumptions. These are:

(*a*) There are only 2 kinds of funds—Equity Shares and Risk-less Debt.

(*b*) There are no corporate taxes but these assumptions are later removed in one of the theories.

(*c*) Dividend Payout Ratio is 100%, so there is no retention of funds.

(*d*) Firm's assets do not change as investments are constant.

(*e*) Firms financing is constant but the degree of leverage can change by reducing debentures or equity shares or by adding equity.

(*f*) EBIT is given and it is not expected to grow.

(*g*) All investors have same expectation of EBIT of the firm.

(*h*) Business risk is constant and is independent of capital structure and financial risk.

(*i*) Firm has perpetual life.

Three aspects of the Assumptions

- The different theories assume that there are no taxes.
- Debt cost is less than equity.
- The use of debt does not change the investor's perception of the risk of the firm.

Optimum capital structure means combination of debt and equity that lead to maximum value of a firm. The following abbreviations are used to calculate the value of the firm.

E = Total market value of equity

D = Total market value of debt

V = Total market value of fund (E + D)

I = Interest

NI = Net Income Available to Equity shareholder

$$\text{Cost of debt} = \frac{I}{D}$$

$$\text{Value of debt} = D = \frac{I}{k_d}$$

Cost of equity Capital

$$k_e = \frac{D_1}{P_0} + g$$

Where D_1 = Net dividend

P_0 = Current market price of shares

g = Growth rate

k_d = Cost of debt

k_e = Cost of equity

k_0 = Overall cost of capital

11.3 NET INCOME APPROACH (NI)—DURAND

Durand has contributed to the Net Income Approach. According to this approach, capital structure decision is relevant to valuation of firm. A change in capital structure will bring about change in overall cost of capital and value of the firm. If debt to equity is increased the weighted average cost of capital will decline, while value of firm and price of equity share will increase. A decrease in leverage will bring about an increase in overall cost of capital and decline in the value of the firm and the market price of equity share.

The assumptions of this theory are the following:

(*i*) There are no taxes.

(*ii*) Cost of debt is less than equity capitalization rate or cost of equity $k_d < k_e$.

(*iii*) Use of debt does not have an impact on change of risk perception of investors. k_d and k_e remain constant even though there is an increase in financial leverage.

Capital structure decision is relevant to the valuation of the firm as:

(*a*) Increase in leverage reduces cost value of firm and market price of capital equity shares will increase.

(*b*) Decrease in leverage will cause an increase in the overall cost of capital and decline in value of firm plus market price of equity share.

$$k_0 = \frac{\text{EBIT}}{\text{V}}$$

E = Market Value of equity

D = Value of debt

V = (E +D) market value of fund available to shareholders

I = Total interest

NI = Net income

The following example that the use of debt will increase the market value of firm and shareholders earnings will explain Durand's Theory.

Example 11.1 A firm has an expected annual net operating income of Rs. 1,00,000 an equity rate of 10% and Rs. 5,00,000 of 6% debt. The value of the firm according to NI approach.

Solution

Value of the Firm: NI approach

Situation 1	Amount (Rs.)
Net Operating Income (NOI) EBIT	1,00,000
Total cost of debt 5,00,000 × (6/100)	30,000
NI available to shareholder	70,000
Market value of Equity E	7,00,000
Market value of debt D	5,00,000
Market value of firm V = E + D	12,00,000

Cost of debt is 6% Equity 10% overall cost of capital

$$k_0 = \frac{\text{EBIT}}{\text{V}} = \frac{1,00,000}{12,00,000} \text{ or } 0.0833 \text{ or } 8.33\%$$

Alternatively

$$k_0 = k_d \frac{\text{D}}{\text{V}} + k_e \frac{\text{E}}{\text{V}}$$

$$= 0.06 \frac{5,00,000}{12,00,000} + 0.1 \frac{7,00,000}{12,00,000} = 8.34\%$$

Situation 2

If the firm is assumed to employ a debt of Rs.7,00,000 instead of Rs. 5,00,000 the value of the firm under NI approach is shown as:

Particulars	Amount (Rs.)
Net Operating Income	1,00,000
Total cost of debt 7,00,000 × 6%	42,000
NI available to shareholders	58,000
Market value of Equity E 58,000/0.10	5,80,000
Market value of Debt D	7,00,000
Market value of Firm V = E + D	12,80,000
Overall or weighted Average	

Cost of capital

$$k = \frac{\text{NOI}}{\text{V}} = \frac{1,00,000}{12,80,000} = 7.81\%$$

Alternatively

$$k_0 = k_d \frac{\text{D}}{\text{V}} + k_e \frac{\text{E}}{\text{V}} = 0.06 \frac{7,00,000}{12,80,000} + 0.10 \frac{5,80,000}{12,80,000}$$

$$= 0.06\ (0.547) + 0.10\ (0.453)$$

$$= 0.0328 + 0.0453 = 0.0781 \text{ or } 7.81\%$$

Thus by increasing debt the firm is able to increase the value of the firm. In Situation 2, the debt was increased from Rs. 5,00,000 to Rs. 7,00,000. The value of the firm increased from Rs. 12,00,000 to Rs. 12,80,000. The overall cost of capital decreased with the employment of increased debt from 8.33% to 7.81% showing inverse relationship between value of the firm and cost of capital when debt is increased. Suppose in Situation 3 the debt level is reduced to 3,00,000. Let us see the changes in the value of the firm and market value of equity.

Situation 3

If the firm is assumed to employ a debt of Rs. 3,00,000; the value of the firm under NI approach is the following:

Value of the firm	Amount (Rs.)
Net Operating Income (NOI) EBIT	1,00,000
Total cost of debt 3,00,000 × (6/100)	18,000
NI available to shareholder	82,000
Market value of Equity E = 82,000/0.10	820,000
Market value of debt D = 30,000/0.06	3,00,000
Market value of firm V = E + D	11,20,000

Cost of debt is 6% Equity 10% overall cost of capital

$$k_0 = \frac{\text{EBIT}}{\text{V}} = \frac{1,00,000}{11,20,000} \text{ or } 0.0847, \text{ or } 8.47\%$$

$$= 0.6\frac{3,00,000}{11,20,000} + 0.10\frac{8,20,000}{11,20,000} = 8.47\%$$

Alternatively,

In Situation 3, the market value has reduced to Rs. 11,20,000 and the cost of capital has increased to 8.47 with the reduction in the employment of debt. From this we can summarize and state that with an increase in debt the market value of the firm increases and the cost of capital falls.

Limitations of NI Approach

(*i*) The NI approach ignores the fact that market price is related to risk.

(*ii*) It only considers value of the firm with the proportion of the debt.

(*iii*) Since there are no taxes it cannot be a practical approach.

This approach can also be explained graphically (Fig. 11.2).

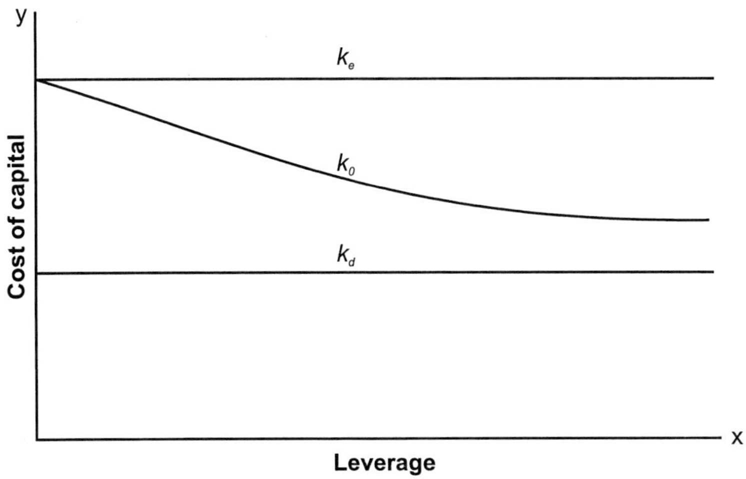

Fig. 11.2 Value of the Firm: Net Income Approach

Figure 11.2 presents the value of the firm by NI approach. It shows k_d, k_0 and k_e. k_d and k_e are constant for all the levels of debt financing. As debt increases k_0 decreases as k_d is less than k_e the value of the firm increases. It shows that as debt increases k_0 moves towards it. However k_d and k_0 will not meet as there is some equity on the capital structure. In a firm which has 100% equity k_0= k_e. The position of k_0 thus depends on k_e and k_d. Thus as k_d increases the overall cost of capital will fall. The minimum cost of capital indicates maximum value of a firm.

Therefore value of the firm by NI approach is value of equity + value of debt.

11.4 NET OPERATING INCOME APPROACH (NOI)

While net income approach concluded that capital structure makes a difference to the value of the firm, the net operating income approach suggests that the value of the firm does not depend upon the overall cost of capital. It is quite opposite to the net income approach according to which the earnings before interest and taxes determined the value of the firm.

In NOI approach firm is not affected by capital structure changes. The market capitalization value of the firm debt and equity split is not important. Although this approach is opposite to the net income approach, this theory is also contributed by Durand.

In this theory the advantage of debt is affected by the increase in equity capitalization rate k_e.

$$V = \frac{\text{EBIT}}{k}$$

$$V = \text{Value of firm}$$

$$k = \text{Overall cost of capital}$$

$$\text{EBIT} = \text{Earnings before interest and taxes.}$$

Therefore, $E = V - D$

The assumptions of this theory are:

(*i*) There are no corporate taxes.

(*ii*) The debt equity mix does not affect the overall cost of capital.

(*iii*) The increase in debt changes the risk perception of the shareholders.

(*iv*) Overall cost of capital is constant. It is dependent on business risk which is also constant.

(*v*) Cost of debt is constant.

Durand explains that when debt increases there is an increase in the interest burden of a company. When interest increases, shareholders begin to expect a higher return from the company. This increases the cost of equity and overall value of the firm does not gain from increase in debt proportion of the firm.

This theory is explained through the following example.

Example 11.2 The net operating income (EBIT) of a firm is Rs. 1,00,000. The overall capitalization rate is 10%. The outstanding debt is Rs. 2,00,000 with 8% as the cost of debt. What is the value of the firm and equity capitalization rate? If debt increases from Rs. 2,00,000 to Rs. 3,00,000 find out the effect on the value of the firm? If debt decreases to Rs. 1,00,000 what would be the value of the firm?

Solution

Situation 1

When outstanding debt of the company is Rs. 2,00,000

Value of firm is unaffected by its capital structure

Value of Firm	Net Operating Income Approach
EBIT 1,00,000	
Overall capitalization rate k_0	0.10
Market Value of Firm (V) = EBIT / k_0	10,00,000
Total value of Debt	2,00,000
Market value of equity E = V – D	8,00,000
Equity capitalization rate k_e	
$= \frac{EBIT - I}{V - D} = \frac{\text{Earnings available to equity holders}}{\text{Total market value of equity shares}}$	
$= \frac{100,000 - 16,000}{8,00,000} = \frac{84,000}{8,00,000} = 0.105 = 10.5\%$	
Alternatively,	
$k_e = k_0 + (k_0 - k_d)\frac{D}{E}$	
$= 0.10 + (0.10 - 0.08)\ \frac{2,00,000}{8,00,000}$	= 10.5%
= 0.10 + 0.02 (0.25)	= 10.5 %
Situation 2	
When Debt of the company is Rs. 3,00,000	
EBIT	1,00,000
Overall capital rate	0.10
MV of firm EBIT/k_0	10,00,000
Total value of debt	3,00,000
Market value of equity = V – D	7,00,000

[Contd...]

Value of Firm	Net Operating Income Approach
$= \frac{EBIT - I}{V - D} = \frac{\text{Earnings available to equity holders}}{\text{Total market value of equity shares}}$	
$= \frac{100{,}000 - 24{,}000}{7{,}00{,}000} = \frac{76{,}000}{7{,}00{,}000} = 0.108$	= 10.8%
Alternatively,	
$k_e = k_0 + (k_0 - k_d)\frac{D}{E}$	
$= 0.10 + (0.10 - 0.08)\ 300{,}000 / 7{,}00{,}000$	
$= 0.10 + 0.02\ (0.428)$	
Situation 3	
When debt of the company is Rs. 1,00,000	
Overall Cost of Capital (k_0)	0.10
Value of firm	10,00,000
Market value debt 1,00,000	1,00,000
$= \frac{EBIT - I}{V - D} = \frac{\text{Earnings available to equity holders}}{\text{Total market value of equity shares}}$	9,00,000
$= \frac{100{,}000 - 8{,}000}{9{,}00{,}000}$	10.2%
Alternatively,	
$k_e = k_0 + (k_0 - k_d)\frac{D}{E}$	
$= 0.10 + (0.10 - 0.08)\ 100{,}000 / 9{,}00{,}000$	
$= 0.10 + 0.02\ (0.428)$	= 10.2%

Analysis

When the debt was Rs. 2,00,000 equity capitalization rate was 10.5%, when cost of debt increased to Rs. 3,00,000 k_e increased to 10.8% and when debt reduced to Rs. 1,00,000. Cost of equity was 10.2%. In all the three situations value of the firm remains the same.

Value of firm remains the same but equity capitalization rate changes with leverage.

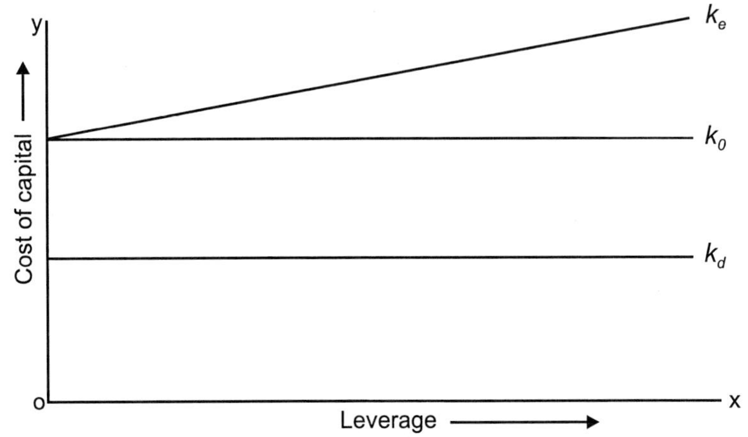

Fig. 11.3 Value of the firm: Net Operating Approach

Figure 11.3 shows the value of the firm and cost of capital. When debt increases shareholders risk also increases. But the overall cost of capital remains the same. ***According to NOI approach there is no optimum capital structure.*** The real cost of debt is equal to the real cost of equity. The capital structure cannot in any way influence the value of the firm.

11.5 TRADITIONAL THEORY

Traditional view is a compromise between NI and Net operating income approaches. Value of firm can be increased or cost of capital can be decreased by a judicious mix of debt and equity.

This approach clearly states that cost of capital decreases within reasonable limit of debt and then increases with leverage. It states that a little debt is good for the firm but when debt increases there is an increased burden on the firm. Hence the advantage of debt does not continue with continuous increase in debt.

The value of firm increases with leverage but not necessarily with higher degrees of leverage. Through a proper use of debt and equity proportions, a firm can increase its total value and thereby reduce its overall cost of capital. Debt is relatively cheaper source of funds, which causes a decline in the cost of capital. If debt continues to increase it becomes financially more risky to the investors and cost of capital increases. Up to a point, leverage is good for a firm but beyond that point the use of debt will adversely affect it. At that level debt equity ratio of capital structure is at the optimum level. There is no one optimum capital structure but it can be at an optimum level in a range.

The traditional view can be explained graphically in the traditional approach the cost of equity is assumed to be higher than the cost of debt. If it is a completely equity financed firm then $k_0 = k_e$ but with the introduction of debt k_e does not increase with leverage. Thus k_e remains constant and the overall cost of capital falls. However this position changes if more debt is infused in the firm. If debt is very high then the risk to the shareholder begins to increase. This also has the effect of increasing the overall cost of capital and consequently reduces the value of the firm. Figure 11.4 (*i*) shows that there is an optimum level of leverage where cost of capital is the lowest. Fig. 11.4 (*ii*) shows that there is a range of optimum capital structure. Beyond this range there is a disadvantage, which begins to occur in the firm. Figure 11 (*i*) & (*ii*), show the positions of k_d, k_0 and k_e. k_0 lies between k_d and k_e beyond the optimal point there is no use of further debt. It only increases the interest burden of the firm and thus increases the risk both for the firm as well as its shareholders. Example 11.3 is given to show the traditional approach.

Example 11.3 A firm is expecting a net operating income of Rs. 1,50,000 on a total investment of Rs.10,00,000 Equity capitalization rate is 10%. If the firm has no debt but it would increase to 10.56% when firm substitutes equity capital by issuing debentures of Rs.Rs. 3,00,000 and to 12.5% when debentures of Rs. 6,00,000 are issued to substitute equity capital assume Rs. 3,00,000 debentures can be raised at 6% rate of interest, whereas Rs. 6,00,000 are raised at the rate of interest at 7%.

Market Value of the Firm

Particulars	Un-levered Firm (Rs.)	Levered Firm (Rs.)	Levered Firm (Rs.)
	No debt	3,00,000 debt	6,00,000 debt
NOI EBIT	1,50,000	1,50,000	1,50,000
Total cost of debt	0	18,000	42,000
Net Income	1,50,000	1,32,000	1,08,000
Cost of Equity k_e	0.10	0.1056	0.125
Market value of share			
$E = (X - \text{int})/k_e$	15,00,000	12,50,000	8,64,000
Market value of Debt	0	3,00,000	6,00,000
Total Value of firm	15,00,000	15,50,000	14,64,000
V = E + D			
Average cost of capital			
$= \frac{\text{EBIT}}{V}$	$\frac{1,50,000}{15,00,000}$	$\frac{1,50,000}{15,50,000}$	$\frac{1,50,000}{14,64,000}$
k_0	0.10	0.097	0.1024

This example states that when the firm has taken debt its market value has increased from Rs. 15,00,000 to Rs. 15,50,000. But the situation changes when the debt is increased further. When the rate of debt increases, it increases burden on the firm. As can be seen above, in the example the value of the firm is reduced to Rs. 14,64,000. Similar changes can be seen in the overall cost of capital, which reduces from 10% in Situation 1 to 9.7%, in Situation 2 to increase to 10.24% in

Situation 3. Therefore a little debt is useful as it is of advantage to a firm. When debt limit is to be increased it should be done carefully after analysing the effects on the overall cost of capital. The traditional view is more balanced than the NI approach or the NOI approach but critics have found a limitation of this approach. According to them this approach has the limitation of finding out the value of the firm as the measure of profitability rather than an attempt to project the debt and equity mix requirements to make a capital structure optimum. The next theory, which is to be discussed, is called the MM Hypothesis. It is considered as an extension of the NOI approach. It is based on the theory of arbitrage.

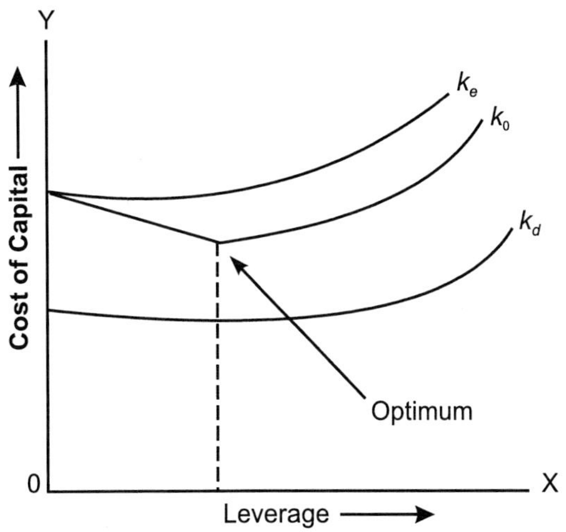

Fig.11.4 (*i*) Degree of Leverage

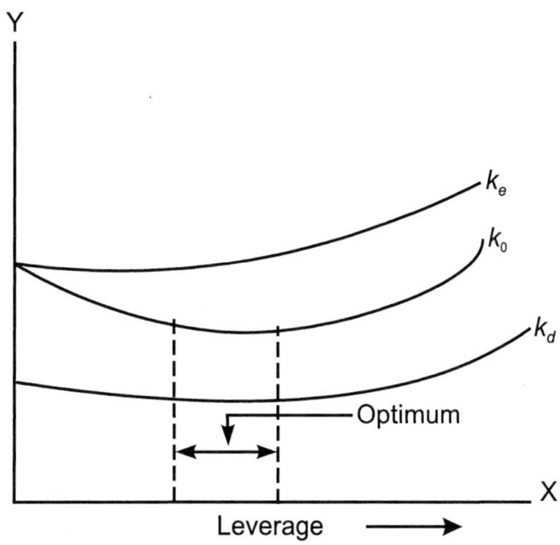

Fig. 11.4 (*ii*) Degree of Leverage

Approaches to Capital Structure	
• Traditional view	Compromise between NI and Net Operating Approach. It follows mid-way approach.
• NI Approach	Use of debt will always affect overall cost of capital and total value of firm.
• NOI Approach	Use of leverage has no effect on capital structure.

11.6 MODIGILLIANI MILLER APPROACH (MM)

MM approach supports NOI approach relating to cost of capital and degree of leverage. They maintain that weighted average cost of capital is not affected with the proportion of debt to equity on the capital structure. They offer behavioural justification for this statement.

There are three basic proposals of MM approach:

(*i*) Overall cost of capital k_0 and V are independent of its capital structure k_0 and V are constant for different degrees of leverage.

(*ii*) k_e increases in a manner to offset the use of sources of funds represented by less expensive means of debt.

(*iii*) The cut off rate is independent of the way in which investment is financed.

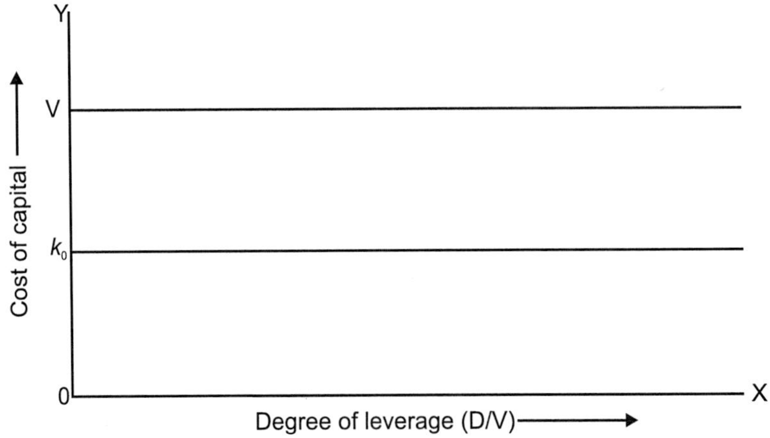

Fig. 11.5 Leverage and valuation of firm

Figure 11.5 shows that the overall cost of capital remains the same even though the proportion of debt and equity is changed. According to MM approach, the NOI approach also considers the independence of the value of the firm from its financial mix, but it does not offer a behavioural significance for it. MM researched and supported the NOI but also offered a justification to it. They stated that the change in the proportion of debt does not affect the cost of capital of a firm. In the long run due to the process of arbitrage, the value of the firm remains the same.

Assumptions

Cost of capital is constant is based on the following assumptions:

(*i*) There are perfect capital markets. This means that investors are free to buy and sell securities.

(*ii*) Investors can borrow money without any restrictions.

(*iii*) Individuals can borrow at the same terms and conditions as firms.

(*iv*) Information is perfect. All investors have the same expectations and awareness to value the firm.

(*v*) There are no transaction costs. Every investor has the freedom to switch from one firm to another without any restrictions or costs of making the change.

(*vi*) Investors have the same expectation of firm's EBIT with which to evaluate the value of any firm. All investors are rational.

(*vii*) Business risk is equal among all firms with similar operating environment.

(*viii*) Dividend Payout Ratio is 100%.

(*ix*) There are no corporate axes.

Total value of the firm must remain the same even with the changes in the debt equity ratio. The cost of capital as well as the market value of the equity shares must be constant despite any financing mix.

Operational justification for MM Hypothesis is the arbitrage process of buying a security at a lower price and selling at a higher price in different markets, bringing about equilibrium in the market price of a security. MM refers to arbitrage process with reference to valuation in terms of two firms one who has used leverage and the other is unlevered. The investors of the firm whose value is higher will sell the shares and instead buy the shares of the firm whose value is lower. Investors will be able to earn the same return at lower capital investment. The investor would without restrictions shift from one firm to another in the proportion of his share in degree of leverage in the firm in which he had an investment to another firm in which we wants to shift.

Example 11.4 There are two firms A and B identical firm A has 10% of Rs. 6,00,000 debenture, B has no debt. EBIT of both firms are equal Rs. 1,50,000. k_e of firm A is 16% B is 13%. Find value of firm.

Total value of firms A and B

Particulars	Amount (Rs.)	
	A	B
EBIT	1,50,000	1,50,000
Less Interest	60,000	–
Earnings available to Equity shareholders	90,000	150,000
Equity capitalization rate	0.16	0.13
k_e = 90,000/16%		
Total market value of equity	5,62,500	11,53,846
Market value of debt	6,00,000	Nil
Market Value of firm	11,62,500	11,53,846
Overall cost of capital, k_0 = EBIT/V	12.9%	13%

Market value of firm employing more debt is more than the value of unlevered firm. According to MM hypothesis this situation cannot continue as ***personal leverage*** will operate and the value of the two firms will be made identical.

An investor holds 10% shares of firm A his holdings are 10% of Rs. 5,62,500 = Rs. 56,250.

His share in the earnings of equity holders would amount to 9000 or 10% of equity shareholders value.

He sell his holdings in firm A and invest in B. since firm B has no debt. The capital structure financial risk of the investor will be less in firm B. The investor will borrow by using personal leverage.

The investor will borrow Rs. 60,000 at 10% rate of interest.

His proportionate holding of 10% in firm B will bring about Rs. 1,15,384.6 as his holding. Out of which he will receive a dividend income of Rs. 15,000. The investor's position will be the following:

Effect of arbitrage

	Amount (Rs.)
(*a*) Mr. X's position in firm A levered firm with 10% holding	
(*i*) Investment outlay	56, 250
(*ii*) Dividend Income	9, 000
(*b*) Mr. X's position in firm B with unlevered firm 10% holding	
(*i*) Total funds available	
Own funds 56,250 + borrowed funds 60,000	1,16,250
(*ii*) Investment outlay	
Own funds 55,384 + borrowed funds 60,000	1,15,384
Mr. X's Shares	
Dividend Income 10% of 1,50,000	15,000
Less: Interest payable on borrowed funds	6,000
	9,000
Mr. X's position in firm B if he invests his total funds available	
(*i*) Investments amount available	1,16,250
(*ii*) He needs to invests only	1,15,384.6
He has a surplus of	865.4

He will get identical income with less investment outlay. He has a surplus on which he can earn more funds or use it for another opportunity.

This process of shifting from one firm to another will continue. Investors will follow Mr. X and the switching process will continue from one firm to another until in the long run the value of the firm will remain the same.

Effect of Reverse Arbitrage

Value of levered firm cannot be more than unlevered firm. After a while two firms are at equilibrium by switching shares from one to the other continuously.

There is neither advantage nor disadvantage to the firms of using leverage.

Benefit of leverage is offset by increased cost of equity. The firm's market value will remain unaffected. Leverage will give more earnings per shareholder but also higher cost of equity.

Just like Mr. X shifted from a levered firm A to unlevered firm B there are many investors who would like to shift from unlevered firm B to levered firm A. This will create an arbitrage process of movement from B to A without any transaction costs and corporate taxes, switching becomes easy. This shift in the opposite direction is called 'reverse arbitrage process'. Investor Y will take out 10% of his share from B to A. Thus he will sell his 10% share of 11,53,846 *i.e.*, 1,15,384.60 in 10% of firm A. He has a much higher amount and he is required to invest only Rs. 56,250. Thus he will have a surplus amount of 59,134.60. He can use this amount to get an additional cash flow. In this manner the prices of shares of A and B will continue to shift until an equilibrium position will be attained.

Arbitrage Process Reverse Direction

Since debt financing does not have any advantage it does not have any disadvantage either. Just as value of levered firm cannot be more than unlevered firm similarly arbitrage can be said to affect in the opposite direction as well. Investors can shift from unlevered to levered firm. An example to explain reverse arbitrage is given below:

Example 11.5 There are two firms X and Z. k_e is 20% in levered firm and unlevered firm is 12%. Firm X and Z have an EBIT of 10,00,000 and Firm X has 10% Rs. 10 lakh debentures.

Solution

Particulars	X	Z
EBIT	10,00,000	10,00,000
– Interest	1,00,000	—
Earnings available to Equity shareholders	9,00,000	10,00,000
k_e	20%	12.5%
Market value of E	45,00,000	80,00,000
Market value of debt	10,00,000	—
Total MV	55,00,000	80,00,000
$k_0 = \frac{\text{EBIT}}{\text{V}}$	18.18	12.5%

Mr. Mohan had 10% shares in firm Z he earns 10% of Rs. 10,00,000 = Rs. 1,00,000. He will sell his securities in Z and invest in undervalued firm X (levered). He will purchase 10% of firm X's debt at a cost of Rs. 1,00,000 and 10% equity at Rs. 4,50,000 debt will give him interest of Rs. 10,000 and it will give him 10% return of Rs. 45,000 from the levered firm.

Effect of Arbitrage

(*a*) Mr. Mohan position in firm Z

Investment cost	8,00,000
Dividend Income	1,00,000

(*b*) Mr. Mohan sells his holding in firm Z and purchases 10% of levered firm's equity and debentures.

Investment Cost

Debt	1,00,000	**Income**
Equity	4,50,000	90,000
	5,50,000	

Mohan would prefer X to Z as he can earn a greater income. He has a surplus amount of Rs. 2,50,000. He invests Rs. 2,50,000 @ 10% rate of interest which is of the same risk group. This amounts to Rs. 25,000 hence his total earnings are Rs. 1,15,000 in firm Z which is higher than what he was earning in firm X.

Limitations of MM Hypothesis

MM Model states that the proportion of equity and debt do not affect the capital structure of a firm. We have seen that the cost of debt is lower than the cost of equity but MM hypothesis states that if there is a benefit of borrowing funds then it is offset by expensive equity and there is an increase in costs of both equity and debt. The value of cost of debt being lower than cost of equity is depicted graphically in Fig. 11.6 shows that cost of debt is lower than cost of equity. However, MM hypothesis implies that the cost of capital is affected by investment decisions and not financing decisions. The behavioural justification of their model is not practical. The limitations are:

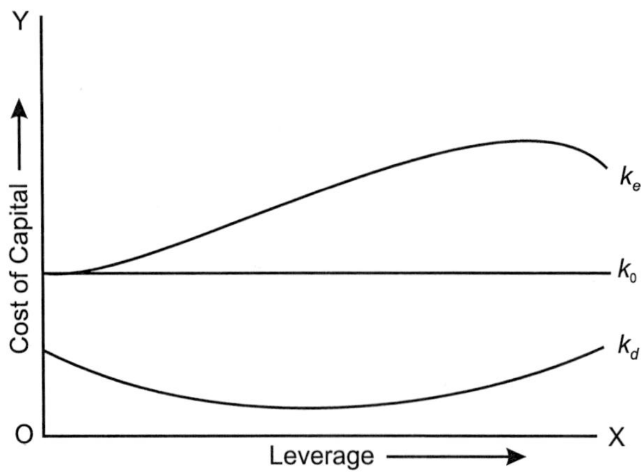

Fig. 11.6 MM Model—Cost of debt, equity and overall cost of capital

(*i*) **Transaction Costs:** MM model has assumed that shifting from levered firm to unlevered firm and in the reverse direction is simple and such movements are taking place all the time, to keep the corporate organization in an equilibrium position. In reality it is not possible that an investor has no transaction costs. There are costs of brokerage and the cost of DEMAT of shares. Investors also have certain costs of travel and movement and so it is not easy to switch companies. When an investor sells shares the net amount that he receives is usually less than the gross amount. The transaction costs are usually small but they must be accounted for.

(*ii*) **Personal Leverage:** MM hypothesis assumes that investors can borrow funds at the same rate as an institution. In practice there are different lending agencies and their lending rates are different. It is difficult for an individual to borrow from the same agency as the company in which he has invested his funds. He will also not get the same rates, as institutional rates are different from individual rates.

(*iii*) **Personal Capital Gearing:** MM hypothesis has confused personal capital gearing with institutional or corporate gearing. If an individual takes a loan in a personal capacity, this gearing cannot be shifted and have the effect of making a firm levered. A firm is levered only when it takes a loan in its own capacity. A firm is responsible for the debt it takes. A shareholder has limited liability. It is limited to the extent of its shareholding and not to the extent of the total debt of the firm. Hence personal leverage cannot be substituted with corporate gearing.

(*iv*) **Problems of Personal Leverage:** MM model states that individual will shift from firm to firm because they can easily take a loan and get a personal leverage. In fact, there are a large number of formalities while taking a loan. An individual will try to avoid taking a loan for small reasons of movement from one firm to another. He will also not get the advantages that the institutions can avail of. Thus personal leverage is highly unpractical.

(*v*) **Influence of Share Prices:** Share prices cannot be influenced by a single individual switching his shares from one firm to another. The prices of shares change with bulk purchases and sales of securities. Large institutions can makes some changes by influencing share prices but individuals cannot influence the companies share prices or value of the firm.

(*vi*) **Information Access:** MM hypothesis expects every investor to have complete information of all the companies. If information is complete, investors can shift from one firm to another. In a realistic situation investors do not have full information of all the companies.

(*vii*) **Corporate Taxes:** The model assumes that there is no tax. In fact, a levered firm has a higher value and it takes the advantage of leverage to give greater earnings per share to the shareholder. This is due to the fact that there is an interest tax shield due to the presence of deduction available on interest paid by the company.

Therefore it can be summarized that there are many limitations of MM model.

Limitations of MM Model

These are:

(*i*) Transaction costs interfere with arbitrage.

(*ii*) Discrepancy in lending and borrowing reduces efficiency in arbitrage.

(*iii*) Personal and homemade leverage cannot be substituted for corporate leverage.

(*iv*) Access to information is not complete and this creates problems in the arbitrage process.

(*v*) The absence of corporate taxes is unrealistic because interest on debt is tax deductible and this gives advantage to a levered firm. Due to corporate taxes value of levered firm is higher than value of unlevered firm.

Modigilliani–Miller (MM) Model: Revised with Introduction of Taxes

Modigillani and Miller revised their hypothesis and later introduced it as their model showing the effect of taxes in two identical firms, one firm that is levered and the other unlevered to find out the advantage of debt.

The revised model shows that the value of the firm will increase and cost of capital will decline with leverage and introduction of taxes because interest is tax deductible. The revised model has depicted that the levered firm will have greater value than the unlevered firm.

Value of levered firm would have greater market value. Value of levered firm would exceed that of unlevered firm by an amount equal to the levered firm's debt multiplied by tax rate.

$$V_L = V_U + D_t$$

V_L = Value of levered firm

V_U = Value of unlevered firm

D = Debt

t = Tax rate

Value of levered firm is more and overall cost of capital will fall. Firm should use debt up to a point.

The value of unlevered firm will be the following:

$$V_U = \frac{\text{EBIT}\ (\text{I} - t)}{k_0}$$

EBIT will be equal to PBT because there will be no interest liability in an unlevered firm.

$$V_L = V_U + \text{PV of interest tax shield}$$

$$V_L = V_U + D_t$$

V_L = Value of levered firm

V_U = Value of unlevered firm

Debt = Debt by levered firm

t = tax rate

Excess cash flow available to investors can be calculated as *interest charged* × *tax rate.* This is the difference between levered firm and unlevered firm. This is also called 'interest tax shield'.

The relevance of capital structure under corporate taxes was accepted in 1963. MM shows value of firm will increase with debt due to debt deductibility of interest and value of levered firm will be higher than unlevered firm.

Example 11.6 Suppose two firms L and U are identical except for use of debt Firm U is equity financed with 10,00,000 equity capital and Firm L employ Rs. 5,00,000 equity and Rs. 5,00,000 debts at 14% rate of interest. Both firms have an expected earning before interest and taxes of Rs. 2,50,000. Pay corporate taxes at 50% and distribute 100% earnings as dividends to shareholders. The after tax earnings is shown.

Solution

Particulars	U (Rs.)	L (Rs.)
EBIT	2,50,000	2,50,000
Less: interest	0	70,000
Earning available to equity share holders	2,50,000	1,80,000
Tax rate 50%	1,25,000	90,000
Profit after tax	1,25,000	90,000
Interest to debt holders	0	70,000
Total income to investors	1,25,000	1,60,000
Interest tax shield	0	35,000

Interest tax shield is Rs. 35,000 therefore, it can be stated that:

- MM model without taxes implies that the capital structure of the firm is irrelevant and the value of the levered firm is equal to the value of the unlevered firm. Cost of equity $k_e = k_0 + (k_0 - k_d)\text{D/E}$
- MM model with taxes implies that the value of the levered firm is equal to the value of the unlevered firm plus the present value of the interest shield.

  $V_L = V_U + D_t$ and $k_e = k_0 + (k_0 - k_d)(\text{D/E}) \times (1 - t)$

Corporate Taxes, Personal Taxes and Other Issues: MM model[1] also considered the complication of personal taxes paid with corporate taxes. If investors and company pay the same rate of tax on debt, then problems will arise in calculation of personal tax rate with the debt and stock returns. There are other problems in addition to taxes. These are: the cost of bankruptcy, difference in home-made leverage and agency costs.

---

[1] Views expressed by Modigliani and Miller in a paper written by them "Taxes and the Cost of Capital: A Correction," *American Economic Review*, vol. 53, June 1963, 433–443.

11.7 PLANNING AND DESIGNING CAPITAL STRUCTURE

The analysis of capital structure has explained the relationship of cost of capital, leverage and value of the firm. Different theories have explained how the debt equity mix leads to an optimum capital structure. The importance of debt in enhancing the value of the firm and increasing the earnings of the shareholders has been amply demonstrated. These aspects explain the background and help in designing an optimum capital structure. The objective of designing a capital structure is to maximize the wealth of the shareholders. Let us analysis the different factors which should be considered while designing the capital structure of a company.

(*i*) **Profitability (EBIT–EPS Analysis):** The objective of an optimum capital structure is to maximize the profitability of the shareholders. Profitability can be enhanced by an analysis of EBIT and EPS. The EBIT of a company explains the earnings before interest and taxes. Fixed financial charges or the use of debt financing can enhance the returns of the shareholders; this is called ***Trading on Equity.*** While analysing the relationship of EBIT and EPS the capital structure should be designed in such a manner that: (*a*) Financial leverage is taken when the return to the firm is greater than the amount of debt taken by the company and the company is in a position to pay interest on debt; (*b*) Financial risk with the use of debt does not create a situation that the benefits do not accrue in the earnings per share of the shareholders. EPS is important for performance but it is not a decision criterion. Yet it cannot be ignored because the management decision should be in the best interest of the shareholders; (*c*) While analysing EBIT and EPS the coverage ratio is an important factor in deciding the amount of debt on the capital structure. An increase in debt increases the financial risk of the shareholders. With every increase in debt financing there is the risk of losing money in the long run. This could bring about ***financial distress***[2] as the use of financial leverage has benefits as well as problems. With an increase in financial leverage, financial distress will increase. These three issues must be considered while considering the issue of profitability in designing the capital structure of a company.

EBIT–EPS analysis determines the effect of different financing alternatives on EPS at different levels of EBIT.

(*a*) When EBIT is greater than the indifference level, debt financing is of advantage.

(*b*) If EBIT less than the indifference point, there is the probability of occurrence of risk.

(*c*) If the probability is high, EBIT is highly risky and in most circumstances it will be below the indifference point.

The financial manager should analyse the financing mix before deciding about the debt equity ratio. If the assets yield greater return than the cost of debt, the earnings per share will increase. Those companies which have a good return in the form of earnings and for whom

---

[2] Solomon E. and J.J. Pringle; *Introduction to Financial Management;* pp. 471; Good Year Publishing Co., Santa Monica; California; 1977.

EBIT level is high, they can use debt for enhancing the earnings per share. The financial manager should consider the effect of different types of financing on EBIT. If debt increases the earnings per share only then should high debt financing be used.

Limitations of EBIT-EPS Analysis

The EBIT–EPS analysis should be very carefully used because of the limitations like:

(*a*) It ignores the effect of leverage on overall risk.

(*b*) It fails to measure the variability of EPS and risk-return trade off.

(*c*) It does not provide perspectives to long-term financial making decision.

(*ii*) **Control:** The difference between equity shareholders and the debt holders is that the control of the company lies with the equity shareholders. A capital structure, which gives power to the equity shareholders, can issue debt, as it does not affect the control of the shareholders. The issuers of debt do not have powers of voting within the company or the right to attend its meetings. It is argued that since debt does not affect the control of the company, the company should take as much debt as possible as this will increase its profitability. However, the risk keeps on increasing with an increase in debt. Hence the capital structure should be designed in such a way that there is a balance between equity and debt. Certain kinds of debt can dilute control, for example, convertible debentures and convertible preference shares will reduce the control of the shareholders at the time of conversion. This must be carefully analysed before issuing such types of securities. Preference shares have a right to vote on the resolutions of a company if their dividends are unpaid for two financial years but they do not form part of decision making. While considering the issue of control, the rights and liabilities of the securities holders should be studied before preparing a capital structure. Hence financing plans can be prepared with different combinations of equity and debt, and the alternative financing plans can be examined to avoid the issue of dilution of control of the equity shareholders.

(*iii*) **Flexibility:** A capital structure should be flexible. This means that it should have the ability to expand and change its debt and equity ratio according to the requirements of the firm. Flexibility of the capital structure should be in obtaining finance and also refunding capital whenever the company requires it. A company may issue a high debt policy when a firm wants to expand but it may find that its operational efficiency is falling because of high debt. In this situation it should have the flexibility of making changes on its capital structure in the best interest of the firm. Flexibility has a cost but if it is in the interest of a firm, it should be exercised. Callable bonds and preference shares can be issued for maintaining flexibility. Such bonds will cost higher than non-callable bonds but they are useful to maintain the requirement of flexibility. The benefits of flexibility and the costs associated with it should be analysed while designing the capital structure of a company.

(*iv*) **Risk:** An important factor to be considered in designing the capital structure of a firm refers to risk. Risk may be business risk or financial risk. Every firm has from both: risk from the market forces and from the internal aspects. The greater the fixed costs of a firm, the higher will be the risk of business. If business risk is high, the capital structure should have less financial leverage. Financial leverage affects EBIT and earnings per share. If debt is high, financial risk will be high. It is best to keep both business risk and financial risk low but this will not give the benefit of profitability. Hence some risk is good for a firm. As long as a firm benefits with the use of debt risk can be taken. Total risk should be kept at a minimum level to be able to service its debt and use it to attain a beneficial position in the firm.

Business risk is influenced by the variability in demand. If the products manufactured by a company have a great variability in demand it will have a high business risk. Risk also increases with variability in prices of products. If there is a high volatility in the prices of products due to continuous changes in demand, the business risk will be high. Similarly if raw materials have quick changes in prices of goods procured, business risk will be high due to variability in input prices of goods. Risk can be kept to a minimum by minimizing fixed costs.

Financial risk increases or decreases due to a high or low proportion of debt on the capital structure.

(*v*) **Financial Distress:** When a firm finds it difficult to honour its commitments to its debtors, it is called a ***financial distress*** situation. Financial distress reduces profitability in a firm. It is a situation, which creates financial problems for an organization. The problems result due to high debt in the capital structure. Financial distress brings about minor liquidity shortages and the firm is unable to meet its commitments. It can lead to major problems of bankruptcy. Financial distress continues to magnify the problems in an organization when there is an increase in the use of financial leverage. It is stated that financial leverage provides a tax shield by providing deduction on interest paid. However there has to be a judicious use of debt otherwise the cost that the company will have to bear on financial distress will be higher than the tax benefit. Therefore there is a high risk in the use of debt and it should be used to create an advantage. Whenever it is not sufficient to cover the debt payments the coverage ratio must be analysed. Interest coverage ratio = EBIT/Fixed interest charges. Thus the proportion of debt on the capital structure must be constantly analysed so that the firm's debt payments are made regularly and the company does not face loss of reputation.

(*vi*) **Liquidity (Cash Flow Analysis):** Cash flow analysis explains how much funds a company require to run its business. It refers to finding out the cash inflows and outflows in a company to meet its obligations. Projected cash flows can be prepared through cash budgets, inventory of financial resources, preparing statements showing changes of cash requirements in the company. The company has to take care of its capital requirement for capital investments. It also has to create resources for financial flows relating to payment of dividends, taxes, interest and other payments, which it has to make.

In a cash flow analysis, it is important that the company does not arrive at a situation of financial distress because this will result in problems of insolvency and the debt capacity will also fall. A distress situation can be avoided if the company uses techniques to determine its debt capacity and employs only that much debt as it is able to service. There is an opinion of some financial experts that cash flow analysis is superior and should be used instead of the EBIT–EPS analysis. Some of the advantages of the cash flow analysis are:

(*a*) It projects the issue of liquidity by making an analysis of the solvency of a firm.

(*b*) It can evaluate the situation of liquidity for a long-term period of time.

(*c*) It considers changes of balance sheet and profit and loss account statements.

(*d*) It can prepare cash flows, which are useful for taking decisions in unfavourable situations.

(*e*) It can take decisions of more than one period. This means that decisions can be taken at different periods of time.

(*f*) Cash flow analysis is able to determine the debt capacity of a firm and in this way avoid financial distress.

The cash flow analysis states that a high debt equity ratio does not increase the risk of the company if it is stable and is able to meet its financial obligations by generating high revenues. Van Horne[3] stated that cash flow analysis indicates the debt equity ratio. This tends to maximize share price and does not indicate the magnitude and stability of cash flows in determining capital structure of a company. Thus cash flow analysis has its limitation. It should not be the only measure to determine a firm's debt policy.

(*vii*) **Nature of Industry:** In designing the capital structure of a company the ratio of debt to equity should be analysed with the background of the kind of industry to which the company belongs. The design of the capital structure will be different for a company, which is highly liquid in the sense that there is no waiting period between cash outflows and cash inflows. Those industries, which have long credit cycles, have to design their capital structure in a way that they are able to meet their requirements in making payments until they receive payments from their own creditors. Firms with long credits periods would require debt more than those, which have shorter cycle of receiving payments. While designing capital structure fluctuations in business cycle have also to be analysed. If sales of a company are subject to fluctuations, the degree of leverage should be low. In such situations there will be high operating leverages, so it should be balanced with low financial leverage. Manufacturing companies should be conservative in employing debt. Firm representing items with high capital intensity will have to be differentiated with that involving low capital intensity to take decisions. Firms in the industry class of large consumer goods like refrigerators, televisions, and machine tools will be analysed differently to items like stationery, calculators, pins and clips. Similarly firms representing services like telephone, electricity and water should have a different type of capital structure.

In preparing the capital structure of a company, nature of industry is useful for predicting the risk in the profits of a company. Risks can be analysed between companies that are stable or those representing style. The stable companies can take a greater proportion of debt compared

---

[3] James Van Horne, *Financial Management and Policy*, Prentice Hall, India, 1985, pp–290.

to those, which represent style. The companies representing style are highly competitive and subject to many changes. Such companies may be those representing garment industry, fashion dark glasses, jewellery; and stable companies may consists of those selling consumer goods like toothpaste, matches, soaps and other useful food items.

The life cycle of the industry should also be analysed before decision regarding the proportion of debt is taken on the capital structure of the company. An industry, which is new, can take more debt and higher risk because it has to begin its work. When the industry is new, it also has the danger of death due to financial distress because it cannot take strain of starting the business. These dangers have to be analysed for constructing a capital structure. A mature business becomes stable and they recognize the problems of debt. At this stage debt is inevitable in running the business, however with a proportion of debt, the capital structure should maintain flexibility of movement from debt whenever it recognizes an alarm in a disadvantageous condition of business situation.

(viii) **Company Profile:** A company within a certain industry may be of the nature of control while carrying out the business. Its controlling share in the sales of its goods may be very high. This would provide it with a good status and having almost a monopoly in the goods that it deals with. Such a company can take higher debt on its capital structure.

A widely held company can take a higher debt to have a greater earning for its shareholders but a closely held company has to be careful that the debt proportion does not affect the capital structure of the company. A closely held company should give importance to a higher degree of flexibility and should be in a safe position as they may find it difficult to service loans with restrictive covenants of banks and lending institutions.

The size of the company is important to determine the quantity of debt on its capital structure. A small company can have serious problems of financial distress if it cannot service its loans in the given period of time. Even if it wants to expand it should only take financial leverage to the extent that it is able to gain out of the debt that it has taken. Small companies should be careful that the capital structure is flexible and they do not have inconvenient terms of loans or covenants. A large company has greater advantages and facilities while taking loans, but they should definitely analyse EBIT–EPS relationships and make a cash flow analysis before taking debt on their capital structure.

(ix) **Timing of Issue:** A public offering depends on the state of the market. In a buoyant market equity and debt can be raised, but when the market is in a depressed condition it is not good to issue debt securities. Government policies keep on changing and this is reflected in the capital market. When the rates of interest are low a firm may resort to the sale of debt securities. It will have to pay a low rate of interest and be able to gain by doing good business. Sometimes when the market is depressed even equity issues do not find favour with the public. However when trading is active even unknown companies are able to raise funds easily from the market. Hence the parameters of the market must be actively analysed before taking a decision on making a public offering of either equity or debt securities.

(*x*) **Tax Planning:** A company must plan its resources according to the taxable laws and benefits derive from taxation. The cost of borrowing is deductible in the year of incurring the expenditure except in the case of pre-commencement of business when it is disallowed. The cost of issue of shares is allowed in India as a deduction in 10 years. Since April 2003 dividends are subject to an excess of 10% under Section 115. Under the Income Tax Act of 1961, interest on borrowed capital is allowed as a deduction thus providing a tax benefit. All these considerations should be taken while designing the capital structure of a company.

(*xi*) **Loan Covenants:** Before designing a capital structure a company must hire an investment consultant to take an opinion from institutional investors, bankers and lenders to find out the issues relating to borrowed funds. Many banks and lenders have their own terms and conditions while providing loans or making investments restraining a company from certain activities through covenants. These covenants are agreements, which put restrictions on distributing dividends, incurring capital expenditure and raising additional finances to maintain working capital balances. These restrictions are with a view of protecting the lenders own interest but it reduces the flexibility of the company which is taking a loan. These costs of debt financing are also called 'agency costs' or 'implied costs of financing'. Every agency, which is part of giving a loan, exerts control over the company by limiting it from entering into new contracts without paying off previous debt. Sometimes such agencies also become directors of the company to enable control over the company indirectly. There is no direct of a financing company over a borrowing company but it exists, indirect controls through directorships, permissions, lien on a company's property as part of agency costs on the company. Hence loan covenants must be carefully examined while designing the capital structure of a company.

(*xii*) **Legal Framework:** While designing the capital structure the legal formalities and restriction should be considered. The guidelines relating to the issue of equity shares should be strictly followed. All approvals, which have to be taken by statute, must be followed. A specific debt equity ratio has to be maintained to get loans from companies for the issue of securities. This also must be followed. Since legal aspects have modifications and changes in rules and regulations, these must be constantly reviewed and followed to build a capital structure and to make changes whenever required.

Thus in designing the capital structure of a firm, many conflicting considerations have to be constantly analysed. The main issue is to create an optimum capital structure. An optimum capital structure for each company will be different and unique depending on their own requirements of debt and equity. The optimum capital structure should be able to create value to the company and enhance the returns of the shareholders. The objective of a good capital structure is to maximize the value of the share of the shareholder. Hence in designing a capital structure of a company the relationship of EBIT and EPS must be analyzed. Other issues of liquidity, flexibility, control, legal framework and timing of an issue are considered while designing a capital structure.

POINTS TO REMEMBER

- Capital structure is the relationship of cost of capital and value of a firm.
- The proportion of debt and equity creates an optimum capital structure.
- There are different theories, which explain the relationship of capital structure and value of the firm. These are (*i*) Net income approach, (*ii*) Net operating income approach (*iii*) Traditional approach and (*iv*) Modigliani and Miller approach.
- The NI approach states that capital structure is relevant for valuation of a firm.
- The NI approach states that as debt increases in a firm the cost of capital decreases and the value of the firm increases.
- The NOI approach is opposite to NI approach. It states that capital structure does not affect its cost of capital and hence the value of the firm becomes irrelevant.
- NOI states that increase in debt in the capital structure, increases the financial risk of the shareholders for which the cost of the equity capital also increases and the advantage of debt is neutralized with the cost of equity.
- The traditional approach is considered to be a balanced approach in between the NI and NOI approaches. It states that little debt is good for the firm but too much debt increases financial risk and beyond a point debt is not good for the firm.
- The MM approach provides a behaviour and operational justification to the irrelevance of debt and equity to value a company.
- MM approach states that the value of two identical firms one with leverage and the other with only equity financing will in the long run be the same due to arbitrage and introduction of home-made personal leverage into corporate leverage.
- MM approach was criticized and its validity was doubted. Hence Modigliani & Miller introduced corporate taxes to show that there is a tax shield and debt is useful in increasing the EBIT level and earnings of shareholders.
- To design an appropriate capital structure the factors that should be analysed are: profitability liquidity control, loan covenants, timing of issue, tax considerations and legal framework for issue of debt and equity.
- The EBIT–EPS relationship is important. The indifference point, break-even analysis and debt equity ratios should be carefully analysed.
- The cash flow analysis provides the liquidity position of the company. Financial distress should be avoided and there should be a high asset coverage ratio.
- In order to retain control in the company, debt is preferred to the issue of equity shares.
- Flexibility must be considered to avoid financial distress.
- The different factors for designing capital structure are often contradictory but they have to be analysed to find out the proportion of debt and equity, which leads to an optimum capital structure, and to avoid financial distress.

OBJECTIVE TYPE QUESTIONS

State whether each of the following is True (T) or False (F).

1. The Net Income Approach states that the increase in proportion of debt maximizes the value of the firm.
2. Net Income Approach and Net Operating Income Approach are both contributed by Durand.
3. The risk perception of the shareholder does not change with increase in debt.
4. Net Operating Income and Net Income Approach both give preference to debt for increasing the value of the firm.
5. The Traditional Approach emphasizes the value of debt but up to a certain stage.
6. At the point of optimum capital structure, the cost of capital is the maximum.
7. The MM Approach states that levered firm is better than unlevered firm, in the absence of corporate taxes.
8. Financial distress is a situation of loss, when there are a large number of unpaid bills and the firm is unable to pay them.
9. MM Approach provided a behavioural justification to the NOI Approach.
10. In MM Model, personal leverage and corporate leverage is considered to be the same.
11. In capital structure analysis, only financial risk is considered and total risk of the firm is ignored.
12. As debt is cheaper than share capital, higher leverage should be taken while designing the capital structure.
13. Preference share capital and debt financing dilute controlling power of management.
14. A financial manager while designing a capital structure should do cash flow analysis.
15. There is an agency cost of debt financing.
16. EBIT–EPS has many limitations. The capital structure should however be designed by analyzing their relationship.

Answers: 1. (T), 2. (T), 3. (T), 4. (F), 5. (T), 6. (F), 7. (F), 8. (T), 9. (T), 10. (T), 11. (F), 12. (F), 13. (T), 14. (T), 15. (T), 16. (T).

THEORETICAL QUESTIONS

1. Discuss the assumptions, theory and limitations of NI Approach.
2. The NOI Approach is similar to MM hypothesis comment.
3. 'Traditional theory is a compromise between NI and NOI Approach.' Comment on the statement.
4. Critically examine the NI and NOI Approach to capital structure decisions.
5. Modigliani and Miller argue that in the absence of taxes a firm's market value and cost of capital remain invariant to the changes in the capital structure. What behavioral justification do they give in their hypothesis?
6. Comment on the utility of the Net Income Approach of capital structure in the practical world.
7. Write notes on:
   (*a*) Optimum capital structure
   (*b*) Home-made leverage
   (*c*) Financial distress
   (*d*) EBIT–EPS relationship
   (*e*) Value of the firm
8. Discuss MM Model of capital structure. How do two firms achieve equilibrium? Discuss.
9. Discuss MM Model without taxes and after incorporating taxes.
10. Write notes on:
    (*a*) NOI Approach in capital structure
    (*b*) Cost of capital and value of the firm
    (*c*) Importance of debt financing
    (*d*) Agency cost of debt financing
    (*e*) Loan covenants
    (*f*) Risk
    (*g*) Profitability

ILLUSTRATIVE PROBLEMS

Illustration 11.1 A company has earnings of Rs. 5,00,000. The capital structure of the company has debt and equity in which debt of Rs. 8,00,000 is borrowed at 10%. The cost of equity capital is currently 12%. Calculate the value of the firm and overall cost of capital through Net Income Approach.

Solution

Value of the firm

Particulars	Amount (Rs.)
EBIT	5,00,000
Less interest 8,00,000 @ 10%	80,000
Earnings for shareholders	4,20,000
k_e = Cost of equity capital	12%
Market value of equity	35,00,000
Market value of debt	8,00,000
Value of the firm	43,00,000

$$\text{Overall cost of capital} = \frac{\text{EBIT}}{\text{V}} = 11.62\%$$

Illustration 11.2 A company has an EBIT of Rs 10,00,000. The capital structure has a debt of Rs. 15,00,000 borrowed at 10%. Its cost of equity is current 12%. Calculate by NI Approach:

Case I Value of the firm and cost of capital.

Case II If debt is increased to Rs. 17,00,000 @ 10%, what would be the cost of capital?

Case III If debt is decreased to Rs. 13,00,000 @ 10% borrowed capital, what would be the cost of capital?

Solution

Value of the Firm

Particulars	Case I	Case II	Case III
Debt	15,00,000	17,00,000	13,00,000
EBIT	10,00,000	10,00,000	10,00,000
Less: interest	1,50,000	1,70,000	1,30,000
Earnings for shareholders	8,50,000	8,30,000	8,70,000
k_e cost of equity capital	12%	12%	12%
MV of equity	70,83,333.33	69,16,666.66	72,50,000
MV of debt	15,00,000.00	17,00,000.00	13,00,000
Value of the firm	85,83,333.33	86,16,666.66	85,50,000
Overall cost of capital $k_0 = \frac{\text{EBIT}}{\text{V}}$	11.65%	11.60%	11.69%

The increase in debt has increased the value of the firm and reduced the overall cost of capital. When debt is decreased the cost of capital increases and value of the firm falls.

Illustration 11.3 A company has an EBIT of Rs. 2,00,000 and overall cost of capital of 13%. It has a debt of 5 lakh borrowed @ 11%.

Case I Find the value of firm using NOI approach.

Case II If debt is increased to Rs. 6 lakhs what is the value of the firm? If decreased to 4 lakhs. Calculate the value of the firm and the costs of equity in each of these cases.

Solution

Value of the firm and Cost of Equity Capital

Particulars	Case I	Case II	Case III
Debt	5,00,000	6,00,000	4,00,000
Cost of debt	11%	11%	11%
EBIT	2,00,000	2,00,000	2,00,000
Overall cost of capital	13%	13%	13%
MV of firm	1538461.50	1538461.5	1538461.5
Less market value of debt	5,00,000	6,00,000	4,00,000
MV of equity	1038461.50	9,38,461.5	11,38,461.5
Interest	55,000	66,000	44,000
	983461.50	872461.5	1094461.5
EBIT – I = Earnings for shareholders	1,45,000	1,34,000	1,56,000
$k_e = \frac{\text{EBIT} - \text{I}}{\text{MV of equity}}$	$\frac{1,45,000}{1038461.50}$	$\frac{1,34,000}{938461.50}$	$\frac{1,56,000}{1138461.50}$
Cost of equity	13.97%	14.27%	13.7%

Illustration 11.4 The following data is given of two companies X and Z. Calculate the value of the firm by NOI approach.

Particulars	Firm X	Firm Z
EBIT	1,50,000	1,50,000
Debt	3,50,000	0
Rate of interest	7%	
Equity capitalization rate		10%
Tax @ 50%		

Firm with no debt

$$\text{Company Z} = \text{EBIT } (1 - t)/k_e$$
$$= 1,50,000\ (1 - 0.5)/0.10 = 7,50,000$$

Firm with debt

$$\text{Company X} = \text{Value of firm Z} + \text{Debt} \times \text{Tax}$$
$$= 7{,}50{,}000 + 3{,}50{,}000 \times 0.50 = 9{,}25{,}000$$

Firm with debt has a higher value.

Illustration 11.5 The following data is given of two firms A and B. Calculate the values of the two firms using NOI approach.

Particulars	Firm A	Firm B
EBIT	1,50,000	1,50,000
Debt	4,00,000	0
Rate of interest	10%	0
Tax	50%	50%
Equity capitalization rate	15%	15%

Solution

Value of firm B without any debt

$$\text{Value of a firm} = \text{EBIT } (1 - t)\ k_e$$
$$\text{Value of firm B} = 1{,}50{,}000\ (1 - 0.5)/0.15$$
$$= 5{,}00{,}000$$
$$\text{Value of firm A} = \text{Value of firm B} + \text{Debt} \times \text{Tax}$$
$$= 5{,}00{,}000 + 4{,}00{,}000 \times 0.50 = 7{,}00{,}000$$

Value of levered firm is higher than unlevered firm.

Illustration 11.6 A company has an EBIT of Rs. 3,00,000. It has a debt of Rs. 5,00,000 at the rate of 10%. Find the value of the firm and overall cost of capital through traditional theory. The equity capitalization rate is 12%.

Solution

Value of the firm by traditional method

Particulars	Amount (Rs.)
EBIT	3,00,000
Less: Interest	50,000
Earnings for the shareholders	2,50,000
Equity capitalization rate	12%
Market value of equity	2083333.33
Market value of debt	5,00,000
Total market value of the firm (V = E + D)	2583333.33

$$k_0 = \frac{\text{EBIT}}{\text{V}} = 11.61\%$$

Illustration 11.7 A company has the following details

$$\text{EBIT} = \text{Rs. } 4{,}00{,}000$$
$$\text{Debt} = \text{Rs. } 6{,}00{,}000$$
$$k_d = 10\%$$
$$k_e = 15\%$$

Calculate value of the firm and overall cost of capital k_0 through the traditional method.

Solution

Value of the firm: Traditional method

EBIT	4,00,000
Less: Interest	60,000
Earnings for the shareholders	3,40,000
Equity capitalization rate k_e	15%
Market value of equity	22,66,666.66
Market value of debt	6,00,000.00
	28,66,666.66
$k_0 = \frac{\text{EBIT}}{\text{V}}$	$\frac{4{,}00{,}000}{28{,}66{,}666.66}$
k_0	13.95%

Illustration 11.8 There are two companies P and Q. The companies are earning 20% on their assets of Rs. 30,00,000. P has a debt of Rs. 10,00,000. Cost of debt being 12%. The tax rate is 14%. Calculate the value of both the firm through NI and NOI approach.

Solution

$$\text{EBIT} = \frac{20}{100} \times 30{,}00{,}000 = \text{Rs. } 6{,}00{,}000$$

(*i*) Calculation of value of firm – NI approach

Particulars	P	Q
EBIT	6,00,000	6,00,000
Less: Interest	1,20,000	0
Earnings before taxes	4,80,000	6,00,000
Less: Taxes @ 50%	2,40,000	3,00,000
Earnings after taxes	2,40,000	3,00,000
k_e	14%	14%
Value of equity	1714285.71	2142857.14
Value of the firm (V = E + D)	2714285.71	2142857.14
Overall cost of capital k_0 = (EBIT/V)	22.10%	28%

Value of levered firm is higher than unleveled firm and overall cost of levered firm is 22.10%, which is lower than unleveled firm, which is 28%.

(*ii*)Value of firm: NOI approach

$$\text{Value of unlevered firm} = \text{EBIT } (1\text{–t})/k_e$$
$$= 6{,}00{,}000\,(1 - 0.5)/0.14$$
$$= 2142857.14$$
$$\text{Value of levered firm} = \text{Value of unlevered firm} + \text{Debt} \times \text{Tax rate}$$
$$= 2142857.14 + (10{,}00{,}000 \times 0.5)$$
$$= 2142857.14 + 5{,}00{,}000$$
$$= 2642857.14$$

Illustration 11.9 Two companies are identical except that A Ltd. has a debt of Rs. 10,00,000 at 10%, whereas B Ltd. does not have debt on its capital structure. The total assts of both the companies is Rs. 20,00,000 on which the companies earn a return of 20%. Find the value of the firm and overall cost of capital by NI and NOI approach. Both companies have an equity capitalization rate of 15%. Taxes are at 50%.

Solution

$$\text{EBIT} = \frac{20}{100} \times 20{,}00{,}000 = \text{Rs. } 4{,}00{,}000$$

Particulars	A Ltd.	B Ltd.
EBIT	4,00,000	4,00,000
Less: Interest	1,00,000	—
EBT	3,00,000	4,00,000
Less: Taxes @ 50%	1,50,000	2,00,000
PAT	1,50,000	2,00,000
k_e	15%	15%
Value of equity	10,00,000	1333333.33
Value of debt	10,00,000	
Value of the firm (V)	20,00,000	13,33,333.33
Overall cost of capital (k_0 = EBIT/V)	4,00,000/20,00,000	4,00,000/1333333.33
k_o	20%	30%

(*i*) Value of the firm – NOI Approach

$$\text{Value of unlevered firm} = \text{EBIT}(1 - t)/k_e$$
$$= 4{,}00{,}000\ (1 - 0.5)/0.15 = \text{Rs. } 1333333.33$$

Value of levered firm $= \text{Value of unlevered firm} + (\text{Debt} \times \text{Tax})$

$$= 1333333.33 + 5,00,000 = 1833333.33$$

To calculate overall cost of capital we use the following formula

$$k_0 = k_d(\text{D/V}) + k_e(\text{E/V})$$

Firm A	Rs.
EBIT	4,00,000
Less: Interest	1,00,000
EBT	3,00,000
Less: Taxes @ 50%	1,50,000
PAT	1,50,000
Value of levered firm	1833333.33
Less: Market value of debt	10,00,000
Market value of equity	833333.33

$$k_e = \text{PAT/E} = 1,50,000/8,33,333 = 18\%$$

$$k_0 = 5\% \,(10,00,000/1833333.33) + 18\% \,(8,33,333/1833333.33)$$

$$= 0.02727 + 0.0818$$

$$= 10.90\%$$

Note: Since taxes are 50% and debt gets an interest tax shield, therefore the cost of debt works out to 5% and not the given 10%.

Illustration 11.10 There are two identical firms. One is levered (P Ltd.) and the other is un-levered (Q Ltd.). Calculate from the data available by the MM Approach the benefit accruing to an investor switching from levered firm to un-levered firm. Mr. X the investor is holding a 10% share of the levered company.

Particulars	Levered firm P Ltd.	Unlevered firm Q Ltd.
EBIT	2,00,000	2,00,000
Debt	10,00,000	0
Rate of interest	12%	–
k_e	20%	16%

Solution

Step 1: Calculation of the value of the firms.

Particulars	P Ltd.	Q Ltd.
EBIT	2,00,000	2,00,000
Less: Interest	1,20,000	0
	80,000	2,00,000
Equity capitalization rate k_e	20%	16%
Market value of equity E	4,00,000	12,50,000
Market value of debt D	10,00,000	0
Market value of firm (V = D + E)	14,00,000	12,50,000

Since one is levered and the other is not, Mr. X would like to switch to the unlevered firm which is less risky. Now arbitrage will take place.

Step 2: Determine X's income in firm P. Mr. X holds 10% of the shares of the company. His earnings would be 10% of the total earnings of the shareholders. 10% would be Rs. 8,000.

Step 3: Mr. X would like to purchase 10% of Q Ltd. Mr. X will sell 10% of market value of equity of firm P = 4,00,000 × 10% = 40,000

Step 4: Mr. X requires 10% of Q Ltd., *i.e.*, 12,50,000 × 10% = 1,25,000

Step 5: Mr. X should have the same financing risk as he had in P Ltd. He will borrow 10% of his share of P which is 1,00,000 @ 12% rate of interest.

Step 6: Mr. X will now have Rs. 40,000 out of the amount he sold as his share in P + 1,00,000 which he has borrowed = 1,40,000. He will have a surplus of 1,40,000 – 1,25,000 = Rs. 15,000

Step 7: His dividend income of 10% of his shares in Q will be

Dividend Income	= Rs.	20,000
Less: Interest on borrowed funds 1,00,000 × 12%	=	12,000
	=	8,000

X has earned 8,000 by investing 1,25,000

Step 8: He can earn an additional income by investing Rs. 15,000 which was his surplus. This will yield 20,000/1,25,000 × 15,000 = Rs. 2,400.

Thus X has earned 10,400 (8,000 + 2,400) and has gained by acquiring shares in unlevered firm Q. Other shareholders will leave levered firm and the demand for Q will increase. This process of switching from one to another will continue until equilibrium.

Illustration 11.11 There are two companies. A Ltd. and B Ltd. both are identical with an EBIT of Rs. 5,00,000. A company is levered with a debt of Rs. 20,00,000 @ 10% rate of interest. A Ltd. has equity capitalization rate of 20% and B Ltd. has a rate of 16% k_e. An investor Mr. Balwant holds shares of levered company A. Show the investor's position if he switched to B Ltd.

Solution

Step 1: Value of the firm

Particulars	Levered Firm A	Un-levered Firm B
EBIT	5,00,000	500000
Less: Interest	200000	0
Earnings available for shareholders	3,00,000	500000
Equity capitalization rate k_e	0.20	0.16
Market value of equity E	15,00,000	31,25,000
Market value of debt D	20,00,000	—
Value of the firm (V = E + D)	35,00,000	31,25,000
Overall capitalization rate k_0 = EBIT/V	5,00,000/35,00,000	5,00,000/31,25,000
k_0	14.28%	16%

Step 2: Mr. Balwant holds 10% shares of levered firm A. His income in A = Dividend Income 10% of Rs. 3,00,000 = Rs. 30,000.

Step 3: Arbitrage process he sells his holding for Rs. 1,50,000 which is 10% of Rs. 15,00,000. Market value of equity of A to acquire 10% holding in B.

Step 4: He requires Rs. 3,12,500 which is 10% of his holding in B. He should borrow Rs. 2,00,000 which is 10% of his share of debt in company A.

Step 5: His position in company B

Dividend income	Rs. 50,000
Less interest paid on load @ 10%	Rs. 20,000
Net income	Rs. 30,000

Rs. 30,000 has been earned on an investment of Rs. 3,12,500.

Therefore Mr. Balwant has excess funds. He made an investment by taking a loan of Rs. 2,00,000 and by selling his share for Rs. 1,50,000 in the previous company. His surplus funds are Rs. 37,500.

Mr. Balwant can earn on the excess funds by investing in equity shares of un-levered firm.

Return on excess funds 50,000/3,12,500 × 37,500 = Rs. 6,000

Hence he has gained by shifting from levered firm to un-levered firm.

Illustration 11.12 Two companies L and U are identical but L has taken a debt of Rs. 3,00,000 @ 12%. L has an equity capitalization rate of 20% whereas U has a capitalization rate of 16%. Both companies have an EBIT of Rs. 3,00,000. Show how an investor will benefit by switching his investment to L Ltd. The investor has 10% shareholding of L Ltd.

Solution

Step 1: Value of the firm.

Particulars	L Ltd.	U Ltd.
EBIT	3,00,000	3,00,000
Less: Interest	30,000	0
Earnings for shareholders	2,70,000	3,00,000
Equity capitalization rate k_e	0.20	0.16
MV of equity E	13,50,000	18,75,000
MV of debt D	3,00,000	—
MV of firm V = D + E	16,50,000	18,75,000

Step 2: Investor has 10% of the earnings which is 10% × 3,00,000 = Rs. 30,000

Step 3: The investor sells 10% of his holding of Rs. 18,75,000 for Rs. 1,87,500 to acquire 10% of L Ltd. 13,50,000 × 10% = 1,35,000. The investor has surplus funds 1,87,500 – 1,35,000 = Rs. 52,500.

To have the same level of risk he will invest the surplus funds 52,500 × 12% = Rs. 6,300.

Dividend income from L Ltd = Rs. 27,000

Total return = Rs. 6,300 + Rs. 27,000 = Rs. 33,300

33,300 – 30,000 = Rs. 3,300 extra earnings. So the investor has benefited by reverse arbitrage from unlevered to levered firm.

Illustration 11.13 The following data is given of two companies P and Q. Both are identical having an EBIT of Rs. 100,000. P has a debt of Rs. 50,000. Rate of debt is 10% and k_e = 20% for P and 15% for Q. The investor holds 10% share of Q. Calculate the value of the firm and show the utility of reverse arbitrage.

Solution

Step 1: Value of the firm

Particulars	Firm P	Firm Q
EBIT	1,00,000	1,00,000
Less: Interest	5,000	—
Earnings for shareholders	95,000	1,00,000
Equity capitalization rate	0.20	0.15
MV of equity E	4,75,000	6,66,666.66
MV of debt D	50,000	—
MV of the firm V = E + D	5,25,000	6,66,666.66

Step 2: Arbitrage process

The investor will sell his holding of 10% from Q = 66666.66 to acquire 10% of P for which he needs 10% of Rs. 4,75,000 which is 47,500. Hence he has a surplus of 66666.66 – 47,500 = Rs. 19166.66. He would invest this at 10% which is at the same risk class of debt. He would earn 1916.66, he would also get a dividend of Rs. 9,500 from P. His total earnings in P are Rs. 9,500 + 1916.66 = Rs. 11416.66. Whereas he was earning Rs. 10,000 from the unlevered firm Q. Thus reverse arbitrage has an advantage.

Illustration 11.14 Two firms X and Y are identical in all respects including risk, except for debt/equity. X issued 10% debentures of Rs. 18,00,000 while Y issued equity. Both firms earn 20% before interest and taxes on their total assets of Rs. 30,00,000. Assuming tax rate of 50% and equity capitalization rate of 15% for an all equity firm. Compute value of companies X and Y using net income approach.

Solution

Valuation of bond X and Y – NI approach

Particulars	Firm X	Firm Y
EBIT 0.20 × 30,00,000	6,00,000	6,00,000
Less interest 0.10 × 18,00,000	1,80,000	—
Taxable income	4,20,000	6,00,000
Less taxes	2,10,000	3,00,000
Earnings for equity shareholders	2,10,000	3,00,000
Equity capitalization rate k_e	0.15	0.15
MV of equity E	14,00,000	20,00,000
MV of debt D	18,00,000	—
Value of the firm (V = E + D)	32,00,000	20,00,000

Illustration 11.15 Following is the income statement of a company XYZ Ltd.

Particulars	Amount (Rs.)
Sales	8,00,00,000
Cost of good sold	2,00,00,000
Selling and administration costs	50,00,000
EBIT	1,50,00,000
Taxes @ 50%	75,00,000
Net Income	75,00,000

The companies cost of capital is 10% and its net assets are worth Rs. 6,00,00,000.

(*i*)What is the return on investment? (*ii*) What is the net addition to the wealth of the shareholders in the current year in terms of Economic Value Added (EVA)?

Solution

$$\text{Return of investment} = \text{Net income/Net assets}$$
$$= 75{,}00{,}000/10{,}00{,}000 = 0.075 \text{ or } 7.5\%$$
$$\text{Economic Value Added} = \text{Net Income} - \text{Cost of capital employed}$$
$$= 75{,}00{,}000 - 6{,}00{,}00{,}000 \times 0.10 = \text{Rs. } 15{,}00{,}000$$

Illustration 11.16 Two companies U and L belong to an equivalent risk class. These two firms are identical in every respect except that U company is unlevered while company has 10% debentures of Rs. 30,00,000. The other relevant information regarding their valuation and capitalization rates are as follows:

Particulars	Firm U	Firm L
Net operating income (EBIT)	7,50,000	7,50,000
Interest on debt (I)	—	3,00,000
Earnings to equity holders (NI)	7,50,000	4,50,000
Equity capitalization rate k_e	0.15	0.20
MV of equity (S)	50,00,000	22,50,000
MV of debt (B)	—	30,00,000
Total value of the firm (V = S + B)	50,00,000	52,50,000
Overall capitalization rate (k_0)	0.15	0.143
Debt equity ratio (B/S)	0	1.33

An investor owns 10% equity shares of company L. show the arbitrage process and the amount by which he could reduce his outlay through the use of leverage.

According to Modigliani and Millar, when will this arbitrage process come to an end?

Solution

Step 1: The investor has dividend income of Rs. 45,000 in firm L. He sells his equity for Rs. 2,25,000 which is 10% of Rs. 22,50,000 to buy 10% of the share of firm U for which Rs. 5,00,000 is required.

Step 2: He takes a loan of Rs. 3,00,000 at 10% rate of interest to have the same level of financial risk. Therefore total funds available with Mr. X are Rs.. 5,25,000.

Step 3: Mr X's position in firm U Ltd.

Dividend income (10% of 7,50,000)	75,000
Less interest paid	30,000
Net income	45,000

Step 4: Mr X has an excess of Rs. 25,000. He has spent Rs. 5,00,000 on investments. X would earn excess through investment in equity shares of U Ltd.

Return on excess funds = Rs. 75,000/5,00,000 × 25,000 = Rs. 3,750

Similarly other investors would shift and the process would continue until equilibrium. In the long run there will be no advantages as the firms will become equal.

PROBLEMS FOR PRACTICE

1. A company's EBIT is Rs. 75,000. It has Rs. 2,50,000 10% debentures. The equity Capitalization rate k_e of the company is 12.5%.(*i*) Find the value of the firm according to NI approach. (*ii*) Suppose the firm decides to raise debentures by another 1,00,000. Calculate value of the firm. (*iii*) If the firm reduces its debentures to 1,50,000. What would be the value of the firm and overall cost of capital in all the three situations? There are no taxes.

   [**Answers:** (*i*) 6,50,000 and k_0=11.53%, (*ii*) 6,70,000 and k_0=11.19%, (*iii*) 6,30,000 and k_0 = 11.9%]

2. *Situation I* A firm has 25% debt and 75% equity on its capital structure. The cost of debt and equity are to be assumed to be 12% and 15% respectively. What is overall cost of capital? *Situation II* The firm increases its debt position to 50%. k_d is 12% and k_e is 17%. What is the cost of capital? *Situation III* k_d =13% and k_e =19%, 70% debt 30% equity. Find out the overall cost of capital in all the three situations according to traditional approach.

   [**Answers:** *Situation I* = 15%, *Situation II* = 14.5%, *Situation III* =14.8%]

3. *Situation I* A firm has an EBIT of Rs. 50,000. It has 10% debentures of 1,00,000 and equity capitalization rate of 17%. *Situation II* The firm increases leverage by adding Rs. 50,000 debentures. If firm increase debt k_e will be 11% and k_e 18%. *Situation III* The firm issues additional debentures and now has a debt of 2,00,000 k_d would rise to 13% and k_e to 20%. Find value of firm and k_0 in all the three situations by traditional approach.

   [**Answers:** *Situation I* 3,35,294.11; k_0 = 14.9%, *Situation II* 3,36,111; k_0 = 14.87% *Situation III* 3,20,000 and k_0 = 15.6%]

4. Two firms U and L unlevered and levered have identical NOI of 10,000 value of levered firm (V_1) is Rs. 1,10,000 and value of equity shares E = 60,000 debt (D_1) = 50,000 and value of unlevered firm V_U is 1,00,000. Firm L has borrowed at the expected rate of return of 6%. Assume further that an investor holds 10% shares in levered firm L. What is the return of his investment in the shares of firm L? If the investor wants to use arbitrage and shift to unlevered firm show his position in the unlevered firm.

   [**Answer:** He will have a surplus of Rs. 1,000 which he can invests at the same risk class of 6% and avail an extra benefit, above the same return as in the levered firm.]

5. *Situation I* Firm's EBIT is Rs. 18,00,000 with 8 lakh debt at 8% and an overall capitalization rate of 10%. *Situation II* If debt is increased from Rs. 8,00,000 to Rs. 18,00,00,000. Find value of equity capital in both situations by net operating income approach.

[**Answers:** *Situation I* Rs. 1,72,00,000 and k_e = 10.1%, *Situation II* Rs. 1,64,00,000; k_e = 10.2%]

6. Following is the data of a Co. Expected Net Operating Income Rs. 6,00,000

(*a*) Debt Rs. 16,00,000 @ 12%

Equity capitalization rate 15%

What will be the effect on the value of the firm and k_0?

(*b*) If the company raises its debt by taking Rs. 8,00,000 lakh further loan at 12% and NOI is expected to increase by Rs. 1,20,000.

(*c*) With increase in leverage equity capitalization rate increases to 18% and debt equity ratio of 1 : 1.

Find value of the firm and k_0 in *a*, *b* and c by traditional approach.

[**Answers:** (*a*) Rs. 43,20,000 and k_0 = 1389%, (*b*) Rs. 52,80,000 and k_0 = 13.64%, (*c*) Rs. 48,00,000 and k_0 = 15%.]

7. Two firms A and B in the same risk class have an NOI of Rs. 5,00,000 each. Firm B has 10,00,000 of 5% bonds and firm A has all equity. Both firms have an equity capitalization rate of 10%. Show Mr. X's position if he has 10% of stock in B. What is the effect of arbitrage according to MM hypothesis explain.

[**Answer:**		
	Total income 10% of 5,00,000	50,000
	***Less* Interest payable**	**5,000**
	Borrowed funds10%	45,000
	Mr. X position in firm A	
	Investment costs	50,000
	Total Income 10% 50,000	5,000]

8. S Ltd. and T Ltd. are in the same risk class and identical in all respects except that company S uses debt while company T does not use debt. The levered firm has Rs. 9,00,000 debentures carrying 10% rate of interest. Both firms earn 20% operating profit on total assets of Rs. 15,00,000. The company is in the tax bracket of 35% and the equity capitalization rate of 15% on all equity shares. You are required to compute the value of S Ltd. and T Ltd. using Net Income Approach.

[**Answers:** Value of the firm S = Rs. 18,10,000 and T = Rs. 13,00,000.]

9. A Co. has 8,00,000 shares of Rs. 10 each and 10% debentures of Rs. 10,00,000. The equity share and debentures at par value. The return on equity shares is 20%. Find equity rate of return applying MM model without taxes.

[**Answer:** k_0 16.6% As per MM Model k_0 of the levered and unlevered firm is same. In the unlevered firm $k_0 = k_e$, so equity return of unlevered firm is 16.6%.]

10. Following is the income statement of a company.

Particulars	Rs.
Sales	10,00,000
Less: Cost of goods (including depreciation)	250,000
Less: Selling and administrative expenses	50,000
EBIT	700000
Taxes@50%	3,50,000
Net Income	3,50,000

The company cost of capital is 12% and net assets are worth Rs. 6,00,000 (*i*) what is the return on investment? (*ii*) What is the net addition to the wealth of the shareholders in the current year in terms economic value added (EVA)?

[**Answers:** ROI = 58.3%, EVA = Rs. 2,78,000]

11. The NOI of a firm is Rs. 3,00,000 and the market value of its 12% debt is Rs. 4,00,000. The equity capitalization rate of an unlevered firm of the same risk class is 16%. Find out the value of the levered firm given that the tax rate is 50% for both the companies.

[**Answers:** Value of unlevered firm Rs. 9,37,500, value of levered firm = Rs. 11,37,500.]

12. A company employed 20% debt of Rs. 20,00,000 in its capital structure. The net operating income of the firm is Rs. 15,00,000 and it has an equity capitalization rate of 16%. Assuming that there is no tax, find value of the firm under NI approach.

[**Answer:** Value of the firm = Rs. 88,75,000]

❑❑❑

PART V

Dividend Decisions

Dividend Decisions and Valuation of the Firm 12

LEARNING OBJECTIVES

12.1 SIGNIFICANCE OF DIVIDENDS

There are three important decisions to be taken by the financial manager for running an enterprise. These are interrelated decisions of investment, financing and dividend decision making. Dividend decisions pertain to the shareholders' share in the profits of the company. Since, the equity shareholders contribute to the capital of the company, they expect some return from the company. One of the measures of return expectations is from a cash dividend which is received annually whenever the company earns a profit. Besides the equity shareholder, there are preference shareholders in a company but they are paid a fixed dividend like an annual interest on their holding. The debt suppliers in the form of bonds, debentures or loans are paid an annual interest on the amount supplied by them. Hence, they do not get any part of the profits of the company as dividends. However, at the time of liquidation they get priority over the shareholders. The dividend decision is taken specifically for the equity shareholders. Dividend is thus that portion of the company's profits which is distributed to the shareholders. The earnings of the company can be divided into two portions.

The portion which is distributed is called dividend and the portion which is retained is called retained earnings.

The financial manager fulfils his role in maximizing the value of the share by taking decisions relating to dividends carefully. One of the most significant decisions regarding dividends is the portion which must be distributed and that which should be retained. Dividends are paid to the shareholders out of the earnings of the company. However, the shareholders can be given a dividend only after making provisions for reserves. Reserves are necessary because there may be certain years when a company does not make any profits. In those years when the earnings are low, business continues to be carried on. In those lean years the company will have to meet its fixed liabilities. One of the most important payments refers to interest payable to creditors or suppliers of funds. The company also has to pay its taxes regularly to government. Thus retained earnings are very important for a company.

Distributions of profits to the shareholders are as important as retaining profits. A shareholder is loyal to a company and if he does not receive a dividend, he is dissatisfied with his holding. The financial manager must take a decision about the amount of dividends to be paid to earn some goodwill from the shareholders.

There are many kinds of dividends. Dividends can be in the form of cash to be paid annually or in the form of interim dividend which is paid more than once during the year. Dividends can also be in the form of bonus issues. One of the issues concerning dividends is the form of dividend which should be selected for making dividends.

A financial manager has to take a decision regarding liquidity of a firm by the provision of a reserve through retained earnings which are ploughed back from the earnings of the company. The financial manager has to maximize the present value of the firm as well as the wealth of the shareholders. These are both very significant decisions in running a firm.

Decisions relating to dividends are important for the following reasons:

(*i*) Maximizing the present value of the firm.

(*ii*) Maximizing the wealth of the shareholders.

(*iii*) Maintaining liquidity for a firm to meet its obligations to government and debt holders.

(*iv*) Providing a return to the shareholders to maintain goodwill with the owners of the company.

(*v*) Distribution of profits annually or in interim periods or to give bonus dividend.

(*vi*) The portion of earnings which should be distributed and that which should be ploughed back as retained earnings.

The valuation of the firm through different dividend models will be discussed in this chapter while the next chapter will take up the issues and considerations relating to dividend policies and how they should be framed to maximize the wealth of the shareholders and also maximize the value of the firm.

12.2 DIVIDEND AND VALUATION OF THE FIRM

There are various models which have explained the value of the firm and the impact on it with the distribution of dividend. It is a well-recognized fact that if dividends are paid there will be an impact on reserves as they will be reduced. On the other hand, if the entire earnings of the company are paid as dividend, liquidity will shrink and the company will be at a risk to make its payments due to the creditors of the company. Hence, there has to be a balance between a retained earnings and dividend distribution.

There is a controversy about whether dividends should be paid or should not be distributed to the shareholders. ***This controversy has arisen because some financial experts are of the opinion that dividends are irrelevant. They do not have any effect on share prices or on investor preferences relating to cash dividends or future rewards in the form of capital appreciation of shares. There are other experts who believe that current cash dividends are relevant in establishing a positive impact on the value of the firm.***

> ***Note*: Dividend Theories: Conflicting Opinions**
>
> **Opinion A**
>
> That dividend affects the value of the firm.
>
> **Opinion B**
>
> The payment of dividends has no effect on the value of the firm.

The important theories on the relevance and irrelevance of dividends are the following:

The proponents of relevance of dividends are:

(*i*) Walter's Model

(*ii*) Gordon's Model

The irrelevance of dividends has been discussed by the following theories:

(*i*) Residuals theory of dividends

(*ii*) Modigliani and Miller Model

In the practical world, shareholders expect returns from their shareholding. One needs to decide whether the shareholders be distributed ***current dividends*** or should they be promised ***future earnings***. An example may be given of two well-known Indian firms. Tata Tisco pays a regular dividend to its shareholders. Bharti Airtel group has never declared a dividend. Both companies are making good profits and their management has highly paid executives. The question that arises is that if management gets a fair share of the profits of the company, why should the shareholders not benefit by the amount that they have invested in the company? Is it fair to the shareholders? These are some questions which are controversial in nature even though relevant for decision making in firms. Investors prefer companies which are profitable and distribute cash dividends. Investors in fact are interested in current dividends as well as in future gains. Let us discuss the different theories and their effects on the value of the firm.

12.3 DIVIDEND MODELS AND VALUE OF THE FIRM

There are different theories which discuss relevance and irrelevance of dividends. Let us first discuss the models which lay an emphasis on relevance of dividends.

(*I*) Water's Model (Relevance of Dividends)

The choice of an appropriate dividend policy influences the value of the firm.[1]

The Model proposes a relationship between the return on the firm's investment or internal rate of return (r) and its cost of capital or the required rate of return (k).

The firm's dividend policy should be optimized according to the relationship of r and k.

(*a*) If $r > k$ the firm should retain its earnings because it can earn well on its investments. In fact, it can provide better returns than single shareholders can manage to do so. Where rate of return is greater than the cost of capital ($r > k$), price per share increases when dividend payout ratio decreases. Where $r > k$ they are called growth firms and the optimum D/P ratio is 0. Such firms should plough back the entire earnings within the firm. The market value of the shares will be maximized.

(*b*) If a firm cannot earn profitably when $r < k$ the shareholders will be able to earn a higher return by using the funds elsewhere. In such a case a d/p ratio of 100% would give optimum dividend policy. When $r < k$ the rate of return is less than cost of capital, the price per share increases as dividend payout ratio increases.

(*c*) If $r = k$, it is a (normal firm). It is a matter of indifference whether earnings are retained or distributed. This is so because for all D/P ratios between 0 to 100 market price of shares will remain constant. Therefore, price per share does not vary with changes in dividend payout ratio.

Assumptions

(*a*) Financing is done through retained earnings external financing is not used.

(*b*) r and k are constant with additional investments business risk does not change.

(*c*) There is no change in the key variables, earnings per share (E) and dividends per share (D)

The firm has a perpetual life.

$$P = \frac{D}{k_e - g}$$

D = Dividend
k_e = Cost of equity capital
g = Expected growth rate of earnings

Earnings retention we have is shown as follows:

[1]Walter J.T., Dividend Policy: Its Influence on the Value of the Enterprise, *Journal of Finance,* 18 May 1963, pp. 280–291.

$$P = \frac{D}{k_e - rb}$$

r = expected rate of return on firm's investments

b = Retention rate (E – D)/E

E = Earnings per share

D = Dividends per share

P = Price of equity share

rb measures the growth rate of dividends

$$k_e = \frac{D}{P} + g \text{ and}$$

Substituting, $$g = \frac{\Delta P}{P}$$

$$P = (r/k_e)(E - D)$$

$$k_e = \frac{D + (r/k_e)\,(E - D)}{P}$$

∴ $$P = \frac{D + \dfrac{r}{k_e}(E - D)}{k_e}$$

Where, P = Prevailing market price of share

D = Dividend per share

E = Earnings per share

r = Rate of return on the firm's investment

Walter's Model

$$P = \frac{D}{k_e - b}$$

b = Retention rate (E – D)/E

r = Expected rate of return

E = Earnings per share

Therefore, *rb* measures growth rate in dividends which is the product of rate of profitability of retained earnings (r) and the earning retention percentage (b).

We know, $$k_e = \frac{D}{P + g}$$

$$g = \frac{\Delta P}{P}$$

We have ΔP = Price Exchange

$$k_e = \frac{D}{P} + \frac{\Delta P}{P}$$

Since $$\Delta P = \frac{r}{k_e\ (E - D)}$$

The value of a share is the present value of all dividends plus the present value of all capital gains.

Substituting Value of ΔP

$$k_e = \frac{D + \frac{r}{k_e}(E - D)}{P}$$

$$P = \frac{D + \frac{r}{k_e}(E - D)}{k_e}$$

An example of Walter's model is depicted in Example 12.1 to show the implications of the value of the share in three different conditions.

Example 12.1 The following information is available. EPS = Rs. 10, k_e = 10%. Assume the rate of return on investment expected by the shareholders (r) = 15%, 10% and 6%. Show the effect of dividend policy on the market price of a share using Walter's Model when payout ratio is 0%, 40%, 80% and 100%.

Solution

Dividend Policy and Value of Share (Walter's Model)

$r > k$	$r = k$	$r < k$
$r = 0.15$ $k_e = 0.10$ E = 10	$r = 0.10$ $k_e = 0.10$ E = 10	$r = 0.06$ $k_e = 0.10$ E = 10
	Payout Ratio 0%	
(*a*) D = Rs. 0 $P = \frac{0 + (0.15/0.10)(10 - 0)}{0.10}$ = Rs. 150	D = Rs. 0 $P = \frac{0 + (0.10/0.10)(10 - 0)}{0.10}$ = Rs. 100	D = Rs. 0 $P = \frac{0 + (0.06/0.10)(10 - 0)}{0.10}$ = Rs. 60
	Payout Ratio 40%	
(*b*) D = Rs. 4 $P = \frac{4 + (0.15/0.10)(10 - 4)}{0.10}$ = Rs. 130	D = Rs. 4 $P = \frac{4 + (0.10/0.10)(10 - 4)}{0.10}$ = Rs. 100	D = Rs. 4 $P = \frac{4 + (0.06/0.10)(10 - 4)}{0.10}$ = Rs. 76
	Payout Ratio 80%	
(*c*) D = Rs. 8 $P = \frac{8 + (0.15/0.10)(10 - 4)}{0.10}$ = Rs. 170	D = Rs. 8 $P = \frac{8 + (0.10/0.10)(10 - 8)}{0.10}$ = Rs. 100	D = Rs. 8 $P = \frac{8 + (0.06/0.10)(10 - 8)}{0.10}$ = Rs. 92
	Payout Ratio 100%	
(*d*) D = Rs. 10 $P = \frac{10 + (0.15/0.10)(10 - 10)}{0.10}$ = Rs. 100	D = Rs. 10 $P = \frac{8 + (0.10/0.10)(10 - 10)}{0.10}$ = Rs. 100	D = Rs. 10 $P = \frac{8 + (0.06/0.10)(10 - 10)}{0.10}$ = Rs. 100

This example shows that

- When $r > k$ the price of the share is maximum when dividend is zero. The price of the share is Rs. 150 when dividend payout ratio is zero. It goes on decreasing and when the payout ratio is 100% the price of the share is the minimum at Rs. 100.
- When $r = k$, the price of the share is Rs. 100 at all levels of payout ratio 0%, 40%, 80%, 100%.

- When $r < k$, the price of the share keeps on increasing with the dividend payout ratio. When dividend payout ratio is zero the price is Rs. 60 it keeps on increasing with the pay out ratio and when dividend payout ratio is 100% the price of the share is maximum *i.e.*, Rs. 100.

Walter's Model therefore, shows the relevance of dividends and price of the share.

Criticism of Walter's Model

(*a*) r is assumed to be constant but this is not realistic because when increased investments are made by the firm r also changes.

(*b*) Financing of the firm is exclusively by retained earnings. The model is not realistic. It is not applicable in present day conditions where external financing becomes necessary to work on large projects and retained financing is not enough to finance it. This model would be applicable only in the case when a firm is an all equity financed firm.

(*c*) By assuming k_e constant Walter's model ignores the effect of risk on the value of the firm.

(*d*) This model does not explain the behaviour of share prices when the rate of return is equal to the cost of equity.

(*ii*) Gordon's Model (Relevance of Dividends)

Gordon's model related the market value of the firm to dividend policy. It is based on the following assumptions:

(*a*) The firm is an all equity firm.

(*b*) No external financing is available. Consequently, retained earnings would be used to finance any expansion. Thus, Gordon's model and Walter's model both discuss that dividend policy is relevant with investment policy.

(*c*) The appropriate discount rate k_e remains constant. Thus, Gordon's model also ignores the effect of change in the firm's risk class and its effect on k.

(*d*) The firm and its stream of earnings are perpetual.

(*e*) Corporate taxes do not exist.

The firm's retention ratio (E – D)/E is constant. Thus, the growth rate $g =\ r$ is constant.

(*f*) $k_e = rb = g$. If this condition is not fulfilled there can be no meaningful analysis.

According to Gordon's model, dividend policy does affect the value of the firm even where $r = k$. This view is based on the fact that under conditions of uncertainty investors would prefer a firm which gives dividend rather than a firm which does not pay dividend. The value of the share of the firm paying dividends would, therefore, be higher than a firm which retains dividends because retention in risky. Investors argue that 'a bird in hand is worth two in a bush.'[2]

---

[2] Krishan J.E., *Principles of Investment*, McGraw Hill, pp.77, 1993.

In two identical firms, a firm paying dividends will have a higher value. Investors would be ready to pay more for a firm paying dividends.

$$P = \frac{E(1-b)}{k_e - br}$$

Where,
P = Price per share
E = Earnings per share
$br = g$ = growth rate
b = Retention ratio
D/P = Ratio = $1 - b$
$1 - b$ = D/P, *i.e.*, percentage of earnings distributed as dividends
k_e = Capitalization rate cost of capital
r = Rate of return on investments

Example 12.2 Illustrates the implications of Gordon's Model

Dividend Policy and Value of the Firm

Growth Firm	Normal Firm	Declining Firm
$r > k$	$r = k$	$r < k$
$r = 0.15$	$r = 0.10$	$r = 0.06$
$k = 0.10$	$k = 0.10$	$k = 0.10$
E = Rs. 10	E = Rs. 10	E = Rs. 10

Solution

Growth firm	Normal firm	Declining firm
D/P Payout Ratio $(1-b)$ = 40%	Retention Ratio (b) = 60%	
$g = br = 0.6 \times 0.15$	$g = br = 0.6 \times 0.10$	$g = br = 0.6 \times 0.06$
$= 0.09$	$= 0.6$	$= 0.36$
$P = \frac{10\ (1-.6)}{0.10-0.09}$	$P = \frac{10\ (1-.6)}{0.10-0.06}$	$P = \frac{10\ (1-.6)}{0.10-0.036}$
$= \frac{4}{0.01}$	$= \frac{4}{0.04}$	$= \frac{4}{0.064}$
= Rs. 400	= Rs. 100	= Rs. 62.5

[Contd...]

Growth firm	Normal firm	Declining firm
D/P Payout Ratio $(1-b) = 60\%$	Retention Ratio $(b) = 40\%$	
$g = br = 0.4 \times 0.15$	$g = br = 0.4 \times .10$	$g = br = 0.4 \times .06$
$= 0.06$	$= 0.04$	$= 0.024$
$P = \frac{10\,(1-.4)}{0.10-0.06}$	$P = \frac{10\,(1-.4)}{0.10-0.04}$	$P = \frac{10\,(1-.4)}{0.10-0.024}$
$= \frac{6}{0.04}$	$= \frac{6}{0.06}$	$= \frac{6}{0.076}$
= Rs. 150	= Rs. 100	= Rs. 78.94

Growth firm	Normal firm	Declining firm
D/P Payout Ratio $(1-b) = 90\%$	Retention Ratio $(b) = 10\%$	
$g = br = 0.10 \times .15$	$g = br = 0.10 \times .10$	$g = br = 0.10 \times .06$
$= 0.015$	$= .01$	$= .006$
$P = \frac{10\,(1-0.1)}{0.01-0.015}$	$P = \frac{10\,(1-0.1)}{0.01-0.01}$	$P = \frac{10\,(1-0.1)}{0.01-0.06}$
$= \frac{9}{0.085}$	$= \frac{9}{0.09}$	$= \frac{9}{0.094}$
= Rs. 106	= Rs. 100	= Rs. 95.74

Gordon states

- When $r > k_e$, price of share is favourably affected with more retentions.
- Retentions do not affect the market price of shares when $r = k$.
- More retention leads to decline in market price when $r < k$.

Under Gordon's model (*i*) market value of the firm P_0 increases with the retention ratio (*b*) for firms with growth opportunities *rk*.

(*ii*) Market value of the share increases with the pay-out ratio $(1 - b)$ for declining firms $(1 - b)$. The market value of the share $r = k$ in Gordon's model is unaffected. Gordon's conclusions are similar to Walter's model.

There is no optimum dividend policy market price of share is not affected by D/P ratio whether firm retains profits or distributes it is indifferent.

Gordon revised his model in which he has stated that when $r = k_e$, the dividend payout ratio is relevant because investors prefer current dividends as they are risk averse. Future dividends are uncertain and investors feel that capital gains are uncertain and should be discounted at a higher capitalization rate. Thus current dividends are certain and should be preferred.

There is another opinion that dividends do not affect the value of the firm.

The argument is that dividend decision is passive decision and is out of the residual value. If the company has investment opportunities, *i.e.*, so long as *r* (rate) is greater than *k* (cost of capital) the firm would keep on investing its funds and the investors would not mind whether dividend is distributed or not. The proposition is that the firm should be able to earn more than its equity capitalization rate. Dividends are irrelevant because investors are indifferent between dividends and capital gains. But if returns on opportune investment are less, then the investors would prefer a dividend. Let us now discuss the second opinion given by MM Hypothesis on the irrelevance of dividends.

(*iii*) MM Hypothesis (Irrelevance of Dividends)

MM Hypothesis explains that dividend policy has no effect on share prices and is, therefore, of no consequence. What matters is the investment policy through which the firm can increase its earnings and thereby the value of the firm.[3] Splitting earnings into retention and dividends is a matter of detail and not of any consequence.

Assumptions

The assumptions of MM Hypothesis are:

(*a*) (*i*) Perfect capital markets; (*ii*) investors are rational; (*iii*) there are no transaction costs; (*iv*) securities are infinitely divisible; (*v*) no investor is large enough to influence market price of securities; (*vi*) there are no floatation costs.

(*b*) There are no taxes. Alternatively, there are no differences in tax rates between capital gains and dividends.

(*c*) A firm has a fixed investment policy which will not change over a period of time. Financing of new investments will not change in the required rate of return.

(*d*) There is perfect certainty by every investor as to future investments and profits of the firm. In other words, investors are able to forecast future prices and dividends with certainty.

According to the MM hypothesis, the crux of the matter is the "arbitrage process" or the switching and balancing operation. It also refers to the simultaneous movement of two transactions which exactly offset each other. The two transaction involved are paying dividends and raising capital through external funds either through the sale of new shares or raising additional funds through loans to finance investment programmes.

---

[3]Miller MH & F Modigliani; Dividends Policy, Growth and Valuation of Shares; *Journal of Business*; XXIV; Oct 1961.

Proposal I

If dividends are distributed, an amount will have to be raised through the sale of new shares. The increased value per share through dividends will be exactly offset by the external raising of shares. The terminal value of shares will decline. Shareholders are indifferent between retention of dividend or payment, but they are interested in the firm's future earnings.

Proposal II

If instead of raising equity shares the firm raises amount in the form of loan, there will be no difference between debt and equity because of leverage, and also the real cost of debt is the same as the real cost of equity.

Therefore, according to the MM hypothesis, the dividend policy is irrelevant. The arbitrage process also implies that the dividend payout ratio between two identical firms should be the same and so also the total value of the firm. The individual shareholder can invest his own earnings as well as the firm would, with dividend being irrelevant. A firm's cost of capital would be independent of the dividend.

Finally, in the arbitrage process the dividend policy would be irrelevant even under uncertainty.

Market price of the firm should also be the same for two identical firms.

Method 1

Step I

The market price of a share at the beginning of the period is equal to the present value of the dividends paid at the end of the period plus the market price of share at the end of the period.

Thus, $$P_0 = \frac{1}{(1+k_e)}(D_1 + P_1)$$

P_0 = Current market price of share

k_e = Cost of equity

D_1 = Expected dividend

P_1 = Market price of the share at the end of the period

Step 2

Assuming no external financing, the total capitalized value of the firm would be the number of shares (n) times the price of each shares P_0.

Thus, $$nP_0 = \frac{1}{(1+k_e)}(nD_1 + nP_1)$$

Step 3

If the firm's internal source of financing falls short, Δn is the number of new share issued at the end of year 1 at price P_1.

Thus, $$nP_0 = \frac{1}{(1+k_e)}(nD_1 + \Delta n)\,P_1 - \Delta n P_1$$

This equation implies that the total value of the firm is the capitalized value of the dividends.

Δn = Change in the number of shares outstanding.

n = Number of shares outstanding for the period to be receiving during the period plus the value of the number of shares outstanding at the end of the period considering any newly issued shares less the value of the newly issued shares.

Step 4

If the firm were to finance all investment proposals, the total amount of new shares issued:

$$\Delta n P_1 = I - (E - nD_1)$$

$$\Delta n P_1 = I - E + nD_1$$

$\Delta n P_1$ = Amount obtained from the sale of new shares to finance capital budget

I = Total amount requirement of capital budget (Investment)

E = Earnings of the firm during the period

ND_1 = Total Dividends paid

$(E - nD_1)$ = Retained earnings

The equation states that whatever investment needs (C) are not financed by retained earnings must be through the sale of additional equity shares.

Step 5

If Step 4 is substituted into Step 3.

$$nP_0 = \frac{1}{1+k_e} nD_1 + (n + \Delta n)\,P_1 - (I - E + nD_1)$$

Solving the equation

$$nP_0 = \frac{nD_1 + (n + \Delta n)\,P_1 - I + E + nD_1}{1 + k_e}$$

There is a positive nD_1, and a negative nD_1. Therefore, nD_1 cancels, we then have

$$nP_0 = \frac{(n + \Delta n)\,P_1 - I + E}{(1 + k_e)}$$

Step 6

Since Dividend D are not found in Step 5, MM Hypothesis concludes that dividends do not count and that the dividend has no effect on the share price.

A company has an equity capitalization rate of 10%. Its currently outstanding shares are Rs. 20,000 selling at Rs. 100 each. The firm is planning to declare dividend of Rs. 5 per share at the end of the current financial year. The company expects to have a net income of Rs. 2,00,000 and proposes to make new investments of Rs. 4,00,000. What will be the value of the firm's share at the end of the year if (*i*) a dividend is not declared, and (*ii*) assuming that the firm pays a dividend how many shares must be issued? Use MM Model to answer these questions:

(*i*) Value of the firm when dividends are paid

(*a*) Price per share at the end of year 1

$$P_0 = \frac{1}{(1+k_e)}(D_1 + P_1)$$

$$100 = \frac{1}{(1+0.10)}(5+P_1)$$

$$110 = \text{Rs. } 5 + P_1$$

$$\text{Rs. } 105 = P_1$$

(*b*) Amount required to be raised from the issue

$$\begin{aligned} \Delta n P_1 &= I - (E - nD_1) \\ &= 4{,}00{,}000 - (2{,}00{,}000 - 1{,}00{,}000) \\ &= 4{,}00{,}000 - 1{,}00{,}000 \\ &= 3{,}00{,}000 \end{aligned}$$

(*c*) Number of additional shares to be issued

$$\Delta n = \frac{3{,}00{,}000}{105} \text{ shares} = 2{,}857 \text{ shares}$$

Existing shares = 20,000 + (new shares) 2,857 = 22,857

(*d*) Value of the firm

$$nP_0 = \frac{(n+\Delta n)P_1 - I + E}{(1+k_e)}$$

Or, Total no. of shares × Market price of the share

$$= 22{,}857 \times 105 = 23{,}99{,}985$$

(*ii*) Value of the firm when dividends are not paid (*a*) Price per share at the end of the year 1

$$P_0 = \frac{1}{(1+k_e)}(D_1 + P_1)$$

$$100 = \frac{P}{1.10}$$

$$\text{Rs. } 110 = P$$

Amount required to be raised from the issue of new shares:

$$\Delta n P_1 = (4{,}00{,}000 - 2{,}00{,}000) = 2{,}00{,}000$$

(*iii*) Number of new shares to be issued in both cases:

$$\Rightarrow \quad \frac{2{,}00{,}000}{110} \Rightarrow = 1818.18$$

$\therefore$ Total no. of shares = 20,000 (existing shares) + new shares 1818 = 21,818

$\therefore$ Value of the firm $= 21{,}818 \times 110 = 23{,}99{,}980 = \text{Rs. } 24{,}00{,}000$

Thus, whether dividends are paid or not paid the value of the firm is the same.

Method II

The same problem can be depicted through a table.

Step 1

Calculating the price of the share at the end of year 1, which is Rs. 110 when dividends are not paid and Rs. 105 when dividends are paid as calculated in Method I.

Step 2

Particulars	When dividends are paid	When dividends are not paid
Net Income	2,00,000	2,00,000
– Dividends paid	1,00,000	0
Retained earnings	1,00,000	2,00,000
Investment	4,00,000	4,00,000
Amount to be raised by new issues	3,00,000	2,00,000
Market price	105	110
No. of new shares	3,00,000/105 = 2857	2,00,000/110 = 1,818
Existing shares	20,000	20,000
New shares	2857	1,818
Total shares	22,857	21,818
Value of the firm	22,857× 105	2,1818 x 110
	= 2399985	= 23,99,980
Rounding off	24,00,000	24,00,000

Therefore it makes no difference whether a firm declares a dividend or does not declare a dividend. The value of the firm remains the same.

Limitations of MM Hypothesis

Modigliani and Miller have argued that it makes no difference to the investors if a firm retains earnings or declares a dividend. According to them retained earnings and external financing balance each other. Their assumptions appear to be unrealistic and unpractical although theoretically it is appealing. Some of the problems of MM approach are due to imperfects markets, transaction costs, floatation costs and uncertainty of future capital gains and the preference for current dividends. These are listed out as:

(*a*) *Perfect Capital Markets:* MM model assumes that there are perfect capital markets. Such perfect markets do not exist in the practical world.

(*b*) *Floatation costs:* MM model assumes that there are no floatation costs and no time gaps are required in raising new equity capital. In the practical world, floatation costs must be incurred and legal formalities must be completed and then issues can be floated in the market.

(*c*) *Transaction Costs*: Although the model assumes that there are no transaction costs in the real world there is an expense leading to commission and brokerage to sell shares. Therefore shareholders do have a preference for current dividends.

(*d*) *Taxes:* The model assumes that there is no tax. This assumption is not realistic as taxes have to be paid when shares are sold and there is a capital gain. Thus investor prefers current dividends.

(*e*) *Uncertainty:* MM model states that a company is able to issue additional equity shares. This model is not valid when there is under pricing or sale of shares at a price which is lower than the current market price. This means that the firm will have to sell more shares if it does not want to give a dividend. In this condition, the firm should be retaining the profits and not pay dividends. Therefore the model is not applicable in uncertain conditions.

(*iv*) Residual Theory of Dividends (Irrelevance of Dividends)

This theory is in agreement with the MM approach and assumes that external theory cannot be used because cost of financing of new investments is high through them. It also believes that external financing is not available when required by the firm. Since external financing is not possible the firm finances its projects through retained profits. The profits that would be distributed as dividends are that amount which is not retained for further use.

A profitable firm which has many new avenues of investments should retain the funds within the firm as it is able to maximize the wealth of the shareholders by retaining the profits and reinvesting them in profitable investment opportunities. In this situation, the firm should decide on how much profit it should retain and not how much dividend should be paid to the shareholder. According to this theory, dividend decision should be a passive decision to be taken after retaining profits for investment opportunities. This theory is called the 'residual theory of dividends'. The market price of the share is taken as the present value of all future dividends. Since residual theory believes in dividend as a passive decision, it states that dividend fluctuations do not change the perception of the shareholders when a company has profitable investment opportunities.

POINTS TO REMEMBER

- Investment decision, financing decision and dividend decision are three interrelated important activities of a financial manager. This chapter deals with different theories regarding relevance and irrelevance of dividend and its effect on share prices.
- There are two conflicting approaches of explaining whether it is important to pay dividends or to retain earnings.
- Walter's model and Gordon's model explain the relevance of dividends in the valuation of shares and the value of the firm. These models show the relevance of dividends as according to them, investors prefer current income to future capital appreciation. Hence current dividends are better than future dividends.
- MM hypothesis and the residual theory state that dividends are irrelevant for the value of the firm. MM model explains the importance of retention of the profits of the firm as they are useful for making new investments. According to MM model, dividends are distributed only when they are not retained as it makes no difference to the firm whether dividends are paid or not.
- MM model explains the irrelevance of dividends through the arbitrage process through which the value of the firm remains unchanged whether dividends are given or not.
- The residual theory believes that dividend decisions do not matter to the shareholders when dividends fluctuate as long as the firm has profitable investment opportunities. The shareholders are compensated for reduced dividend through capital gains.

OBJECTIVE TYPE QUESTIONS

State whether the following statements are true (T) or False (F).

1. An effective dividend policy helps in achieving wealth maximization.
2. MM model states that dividends are relevant to the valuation of a share.
3. Dividend payout ratio is the portion of earnings distributed among shareholders.
4. Walter's model supports the view that dividend is irrelevant for the failure of the firm.
5. Gordon's model supports the view that dividend payment does not affect the market value of the share.

6. The residual theory is the same as Gordon's model.
7. Dividend policy is one of the important interrelated decisions relating to maximization of shareholders wealth.
8. Shareholders prefer current income to future income.

Answers: 1. (T), 2. (F), 3. (T), 4. (F), 5. (F), 6. (F), 7. (T), 8. (T).

THEORETICAL QUESTIONS

1. Discuss the assumptions theory and limitations of Walter's approach to dividend decisions.
2. Discuss in brief the opinions of the theories proposing relevance and irrelevance of dividends.
3. How does Gordon's model differ from Walter's approach to relevance of dividends? What are their similarities?
4. 'The Modiglini and Miller irrelevance approach to dividends is unrealistic.' Explain this statement.
5. Explain the *'bird in hand'* argument explaining that dividends have an impact on share prices.
6. Explain the arbitrage process of MM model in support of irrelevance of dividends.
7. Discuss the controversy relating to relevance and irrelevance of dividends.
8. What is the significance of dividends for a shareholder?
9. 'In a world of no taxes and transaction costs, a firm cannot be made more valuable by manipulating the dividend payout ratio.' Explain this statement.
10. Do you agree that dividends are irrelevant?
11. 'Payment of dividend is an important decision for wealth maximization of shareholders.' Comment on this statement.

ILLUSTRATIVE PROBLEMS

Illustration 12.1 The following information is available about a company.

$$k_e = 15\%, \text{EPS} = 20$$

Assume that the return on investments r = 18%, 15%, 12%.

Show the effect of dividend policy on the market price of shares using Walter's model when D/P ratio is 0%, 25%, 50%, 75%, 100%.

Solution

$$P = \frac{D + \frac{r}{k_e}(E - D)}{k_e}$$

Walter's model

Particulars	R > k_e	$r = k_e$	$r < k_e$
	18% > 15%	15% = 15%	12% < 15%
EPS	**20**		
(*a*) When D/P ratio is 0	$P = \frac{0 + \frac{0.18}{0.15}(20-0)}{0.15}$	$P = \frac{0 + \frac{0.15}{0.15}(20-0)}{0.15}$	$P = \frac{0 + \frac{0.12}{0.15}(20-0)}{0.15}$
D = 0	**P = 160**	**P = 133.33**	**P = 106.66**
(*b*) When D/P ratio is 25%	$P = \frac{5 + \frac{0.18}{0.15}(20-5)}{0.15}$	$P = \frac{5 + \frac{0.15}{0.15}(20-5)}{0.15}$	$P = \frac{5 + \frac{0.12}{0.15}(20-5)}{0.15}$
D = 5	**P = 153.33**	**P = 133.33**	**P = 113.33**
(*c*) When D/P ratio is 50%	$P = \frac{10 + \frac{0.18}{0.15}(20-10)}{0.15}$	$P = \frac{10 + \frac{0.15}{0.15}(20-10)}{0.15}$	$P = \frac{10 + \frac{0.12}{0.15}(20-10)}{0.15}$
D = 10	**P = 146.66**	**P = 133.33**	**P = 120**
(*d*) When D/P ratio is 75%	$P = \frac{15 + \frac{0.18}{0.15}(20-15)}{0.15}$	$P = \frac{15 + \frac{0.15}{0.15}(20-15)}{0.15}$	$P = \frac{15 + \frac{0.12}{0.15}(20-15)}{0.15}$
D = 20	**P = 140**	**P = 133.33**	**P = 126.66**
(*e*) When D/P ratio is 100%	$P = \frac{20 + \frac{0.18}{0.15}(20-20)}{0.15}$	$P = \frac{20 + \frac{0.15}{0.15}(20-20)}{0.15}$	$P = \frac{20 + \frac{0.12}{0.15}(20-20)}{0.15}$
	P = 133.33	**P = 133.33**	**P = 133.33**

Illustration 12.2 From the following information k_e = 120%, EPS = 15

Assume rate on investments 10%, 20%, 12%. Show the effect of dividend policy on the market price of shares using Walter's model when D/P ratio is 0%, 50%, 75%, 100%.

Solution

Walter's model

Particulars	$r < k_e$	$r > k_e$	$r = k_e$
	10% < 12%	20% > 12%	12% = 12%
EPS	**15**	**15**	**15**
(*a*) When D/P ratio	$P = \dfrac{0 + \dfrac{0.10}{0.12}(15-0)}{0.12}$	$P = \dfrac{0 + \dfrac{0.20}{0.12}(15-0)}{0.12}$	$P = \dfrac{0 + \dfrac{0.12}{0.12}(15-0)}{0.12}$
is 0% D = 0	**P = 104.16**	**P = 208.33**	**P = 125**
(*b*) When D/P ratio	$P = \dfrac{3.75 + \dfrac{0.10}{0.12}(15-3.75)}{0.12}$	$P = \dfrac{3.75 + \dfrac{0.20}{0.12}(15-3.75)}{0.12}$	$P = \dfrac{3.75 + \dfrac{0.12}{0.12}(15-3.75)}{0.12}$
is 25% D = 3.75	**P = 109.37**	**P = 187.49**	**P = 125**
(*c*) When D/P ratio	$P = \dfrac{7.5 + \dfrac{0.10}{0.12}(15-7.5)}{0.12}$	$P = \dfrac{7.5 + \dfrac{0.20}{0.12}(15-7.5)}{0.12}$	$P = \dfrac{7.5 + \dfrac{0.12}{0.12}(15-7.5)}{0.12}$
is 50% D = 7.5	**P = 114.58**	**P = 166.66**	**P = 125**
(*d*) When D/P ratio	$P = \dfrac{11.25 + \dfrac{0.10}{0.12}(15-11.25)}{0.12}$	$P = \dfrac{11.25 + \dfrac{0.20}{0.12}(15-11.25)}{0.12}$	$P = \dfrac{11.25 + \dfrac{0.12}{0.12}(15-11.25)}{0.12}$
is 75% D = 11.25	**P = 119.79**	**P = 145.83**	**P = 125**
(*e*) When D/P ratio	$P = \dfrac{15 + \dfrac{0.10}{0.12}(15-15)}{0.12}$	$P = \dfrac{15 + \dfrac{0.20}{0.12}(15-15)}{0.12}$	$P = \dfrac{15 + \dfrac{0.12}{0.12}(15-15)}{0.12}$
is 100% D = 15	**P = 125**	**P = 125**	**P = 125**

Illustration 12.3 The earnings per share of a company is Rs. 8 and the rate of capitalization applicable is 10%. The company has before it an option of adopting (*i*) 50%, (*ii*) 75%, (*iii*) 100% dividend payout ratio. Compute the market price of the company's quoted share as per Walter's model if it can earn a return of (*i*) 15% (*ii*) 10% and (*iii*) 5% on its retained earnings.

[B.Com(H), DU, 2007]

Solution

Particulars	$r > k_e$	$r = k_e$	$r < k_e$
	15%>10%	10% = 10%	5 % < 10%
EPS	**8**	**8**	**8**
(*a*) When D/P ratio is 50% D= 4	$P = \frac{4+\frac{0.15}{0.10}(8-4)}{0.10}$	$P = \frac{4+\frac{0.10}{0.10}(8-4)}{0.10}$	$P = \frac{4+\frac{0.05}{0.10}(8-4)}{0.10}$
	P = 100	**P = 80**	**P = 60**
(*b*) When D/P ratio is 75% D = 6	$P = \frac{6+\frac{0.15}{0.10}(8-6)}{0.10}$	$P = \frac{6+\frac{0.10}{0.10}(8-6)}{0.10}$	$P = \frac{6+\frac{0.05}{0.10}(8-6)}{0.10}$
	P = 90	**P = 80**	**P = 70**
(*c*) When D/P ratio is 100% D = 8	$P = \frac{8+\frac{0.15}{0.10}(8-8)}{0.10}$	$P = \frac{8+\frac{0.10}{0.10}(8-8)}{0.10}$	$P = \frac{8+\frac{0.05}{0.10}(8-8)}{0.10}$
	P = 80	**P = 80**	**P = 80**

Illustration 12.4 A company earned a net profit of Rs. 10,00,000 and it has 1,00,000 equity shares. Out of the net profits the company plans to distribute Rs. 2,00,000 as dividends to the shareholders. The shareholders expected rate of return k_e = 16%. Its required rate of return is 12%. Find market price of the share using Walter's model. What will be the optimum dividend payout ratio. Find out the market price of the share when dividend is at the optimum payout ratio. What would be the minimum price of the share and at what situation?

Solution

Market price of share

Step 1

Net profit = Rs. 10,00,000

No. of outstanding share = 1,00,000

EPS = 10

Profit utilized for dividend = Rs. 2,00,000

$$k_e = 16\%$$
$$r = 12\%$$

Substituting the values in $[D + r/k_e(E - D)]/k_e = [2 + 0.12/0.16\ (10 - 2)]/0.16 = 8/0.16 =$ Rs. 50

Step 2

Since $k_e > r$, price will be maximum when D/P ratio is 100%. Substituting the values in $[D + r/k_e(E - D)]/k_e$

$$= [10 + 0.12/0.16\ (10 - 10)]/0.16 = \text{Rs. } 67.18$$

Step 3

The price would be minimum when D/P ratio is 0%.

Substituting the value when $\{D + r/k_e(E - D)\}/k_e$

$$= 0 + 0.12/0.16\ (10 - 0)/0.16 = \text{Rs. } 46.875$$

Illustration 12.5 The following data is available for a company:

The earnings per share E = Rs. 8

Rate of return on investment = 16%

Return expected by shareholders = 12%

Find price of the share according to Gordon's model when dividend payout ratio is 25% and 50%.

Solution

$$P = \frac{E\,(1 - b)}{k_e - br}$$

(*i*) When dividend payout ratio is 25% and retention is 75%

$$\text{br} = 0.75 \times 0.16$$

$$= \frac{8\ (1 - 0.75)}{0.12 - (0.75 \times 0.16)}$$

$$P = 2/0 = 0$$

The answer is indeterminate as g is higher than k_e.

(*ii*) When dividend payout ratio is 50% and retention ratio is 50%

$$br = 0.50 \times 0.16 = 0.08$$

$$= \frac{8\ (1 - 0.50)}{0.12 - (0.50 \times 0.16)} = \text{Rs. } 100.$$

Illustration 12.6 Calculate price of share by Gordon's model when D/P ratio is (*a*) 10% and (*b*) 20%, earnings per share is Rs. 20. The expected rate of return is 12% and cost of equity is 20%.

Solution

$$P = \frac{E(1-b)}{k_e - br}$$

(*a*) When D/P ratio is 10% and retention ratio is 90%.

$$P = \frac{20(1-0.9)}{0.20-0.108} = \text{Rs. } 21.73$$

$$br = 0.9 \times 0.12 = 0.108$$

(*b*) When D/P ratio is 20% and retention ratio is 80%

$$P = \frac{20(1-0.8)}{0.20-0.096} = 43.47$$

$$br = 0.8 \times 0.12 = 0.096$$

When retention ratio is more the price of the share will fall when $r < k_e$.

Illustration 12.7 Given the data:

$$\begin{aligned} \text{EPS} &= \text{Rs. } 7 \\ \text{P/E} &= \text{Rs. } 10 \\ k_e &= 12\% \\ \text{No. of outstanding shares} &= 75{,}000 \\ \text{Expected dividend} &= \text{Rs. } 5 \\ \text{Expected net income} &= \text{Rs. } 5{,}00{,}000 \\ \text{New investment} &= \text{Rs. } 8{,}00{,}000 \end{aligned}$$

Show using MM hypothesis that the payment of dividends does not affect the value of the firm.

Solution

$$\begin{aligned} \text{Market price} &= \text{P/E} \times \text{EPS} \\ &= \text{MV} = 10 \times 7 = \text{Rs. } 70 \end{aligned}$$

A. Value of the firm when dividends are paid

Step 1 To calculate price of share at the year end or P_1

$$\begin{aligned} \text{Current price} &= (D_1 + P_1)/(1 + k_e) \\ 70 &= (5 + P_1)/(1 + 0.12) \\ P_1 &= \text{Rs. } 73.40 \end{aligned}$$

Step 2 Amount to be raised $= I - (E - nD_1)$

$$= 8{,}00{,}000 - \{5{,}00{,}000 - (75{,}000 \times 5)\}$$

$$= \text{Rs. } 6{,}75{,}000$$

Step 3 No. of additional shares to be issued

$$\Delta n P_1 = (n + \Delta n)\, P_1$$

$$= 6{,}75{,}000/73.40$$

$$= 9196.19$$

Step 4 Value of the firm

$$V = (n + \Delta n)\, P_1$$

$$= (75{,}000 + 9196.19) \times 73.40$$

$$= \text{Rs. } 6180000.3$$

B. Value of the firm when dividends are not paid

Step 1 Current price $= (D_1 + P_1)/(1 + k_e)$

$$70 = (0 + P_1)/(1 + 0.12)$$

$$P_1 = \text{Rs } 78.4$$

Step 2 Amount to be raised $= I - (E - nD_1)$

$$= 8{,}00{,}000 - (5{,}00{,}000 - 0)$$

$$= \text{Rs. } 3{,}00{,}000$$

Step 3 No. of additional shares to be issued

$$\Delta n\ P_1 = (n + \Delta n)\, P_1$$

$$= 3{,}00{,}000/78.40$$

$$= \text{Rs. } 3826.53 \text{ or, Rs. } 3{,}827.$$

Step 4 Value of the firm

$$V = (n + \Delta n)\, P_1$$

$$= (78826.53) \times 78.40$$

$$= \text{Rs. } 6179999.9 \text{ or Rs. } 61{,}80{,}000$$

> ***Note:*** Rounding off value of firm when dividends are paid 6180000.3 and when dividends are not paid 61,80,000.

Illustration 12.8 A company is planning to make an investment of Rs. 10,00,000 and it expects to earn Rs. 5,00,000 by the year end. Presently, the company has 50,000 outstanding shares and the share of the company is trading at a price of Rs. 125. The company expects to pay the shareholders (*a*) Rs. 10 as dividends next year. The company's required rate of return = 15%. Find the following:

Value of the firm if dividend is declared.

(*b*) Value of the firm when dividends are not declared.

Solution

Step 1 Price of the share = P_1

$$\text{Current price} = (D_1 + P_1)/(1 + k_e)$$
$$125 = (10 + P_1)/(1 + 0.15)$$
$$P_1 = \text{Rs. } 133.75$$

When dividend is not declared P_1

$$\text{Current price} = (D_1 + P_1)/(1 + k_e)$$
$$125 = (0 + P_1)/(1 + 0.15)$$
$$P_1 = \text{Rs. } 143.75$$

Step 2 Value of the firm

Particulars	When dividends are distributed	When dividends are not distributed
Earnings	5,00,000	5,00,000
Less: Dividends paid	5,00,000	—
Total funds required	10,00,000	5,00,000
Fresh funds to be raised	10,00,000	5,00,000
Market price of the share	133.75	143.75
No. of shares to be issued	10,00,000/133.75	5,00,000/143.75
	= 7,477	= 3,478
Existing shares	50,000	50,000
Total shares	57,477	53,478
Market price per share	133.75	143.75
Value of the firm	57,477 × 133.75	53,478 × 143.75
Value of the firm	7687548.75	7687462.5

Value of the firm is almost the same, but due to fractions and rounding off for issue of new shares some slight differences occur. Hence, the value of the firm is the same whether dividends are declared or not declared.

Illustration 12.9 A company has 60,000 shares outstanding. The market price of these shares is Rs. 15 each. The company expects a net profit of Rs. 3,00,000 and has a cost of equity of 20%. The company plans to declare Rs. 5 as dividend per share for the current year. From MM model calculate

(*a*) Price of the share at the end of the year (*i*) when dividend is paid and (*ii*) when dividend is not paid.

(*b*) How many new shares should the company issue if the dividend is paid and the company needs Rs. 8,50,000 for an approved investment expenditure?

Solution

As per MM models the current market price of the share P_0 is

$$P_0 = \frac{1}{1+k_e}(D_1 + P_1)$$

(*a*) If the firm pays a dividend of Rs. 5, the price at the end of year 1 is:

(*i*) $$15 = \frac{1}{1+0.20}(5+P_1)$$

$$15 = \frac{1}{1.20}(5+P_1)$$

$$18 = 5 + P_1$$

$$\Rightarrow \quad P_1 = 13$$

(*ii*) If dividend is not paid the price will be

$$15 = \frac{1}{1+0.20}(0+P_1)$$

$$\Rightarrow \quad P_1 = \text{Rs. } 18$$

(*b*) No. of new shares to be issued if the company pays a dividend of Rs. 5:

$$= I - (E - nD_1)/P_1$$

$$= 8{,}50{,}000 - (3{,}00{,}000 - 60{,}000 \times 5)/13$$

$$= 8{,}50{,}000/13 = 65{,}384$$

Therefore the company should issue 65384 new shares at Rs. 13 to finance the proposal.

Illustration 12.10 A company earns Rs 6 per share at a capitalization rate of 10%. It has a return on investments at 15%. According to Walter's model what should be the price per share at 30% dividend payout ratio? Is this the optimum payout ratio as per Walter's model?

Solution

When dividend payout ratio is 30%, price per share is the following

$$P = \frac{D + \frac{r}{k_e}(E - D)}{k_e}$$

$$P = \frac{1.8 + 0.15/0.10(6 - 1.8)}{0.10} = 81$$

When $r > k_e$ the market price of the share will increase if dividend payout ratio is reduced and is lower than 30%. The optimum payout ratio is 0% and retention is 100%.

Illustration 12.11 The shares of a chemical company are selling at Rs. 20 per share. The firm has paid dividend @ Rs. 2 per share last year. The estimated growth of the company is approximately 5% per year.

(*a*) Determine the cost of equity capital of the company.

(*b*) Determine the estimated market price of the equity share if the anticipated growth rate of the firm (*i*) rises to 8% and (*ii*) fall to 3%.

Solution

(*a*) Determination of cost of equity capital

$$k_e = \frac{D_0(1+g)}{P_0} + g$$

$$= \frac{2(1+0.05)}{20} + 0.05 = 15.5\%$$

(*b*) Determination of estimated Market price of the Equity Share if anticipated growth rate rises or falls

$$P_0 = \frac{D_1}{k_e - g}$$

(*i*) If the growth rate raises to 8%,

$$\frac{2.16}{0.155 - 0.08} = \text{Rs. } 28.8$$

(*ii*) If growth rate of the firm falls,

$$\frac{2.06}{0.155 - 0.03} = \text{Rs. } 16.48$$

Illustration 12.12 The earnings per share (EPS) of a company are Rs. 10. It has an internal rate of return of 15% and the capitalization rate of its risk class is 12.5%. If Walter's model is used:

(*a*) What should be the optimum payout ratio of the company?

(*b*) What would be the price of the share at this payout?

(*c*) How shall the price of the share be affected, if a different payout were employed?

Solution

Calculation of share price under Walter's Model

$$P = \frac{D + \frac{R}{k_e}(E - D)}{k_e}$$

(*a*) Since $r > k_e$ (*i.e.* 15% > 12.5%), to maximize the share price the company should retain all its earnings and its optimum payout ratio is zero.

(*b*) Calculation of share price at optimum payout rate *i.e.*, if no dividend is declared.

$$P = \frac{0 + \frac{0.15}{0.125}(10 - 0)}{0.125} = \frac{12}{0.125} = \text{Rs. } 96$$

(*c*) Impact on share price, if dividend is paid @ 30%

$$P = \frac{3 + \frac{0.15}{0.125}(10 - 3)}{0.125} = \frac{11.4}{0.125} = \text{Rs. } 91.20$$

Illustration 12.13 Mr. A is contemplating purchase of 1,000 equity shares of a company. His expectation of return is 10% before tax by way of dividend with an annual growth of 5%. The Company's last dividend was Rs. 2 per share. Even as he is contemplating, Mr. A suddenly finds that due to a budget announcement dividends have been exempted from tax in the hands of the recipients. But the imposition of dividend Distribution Tax on the Company is likely to lead to a fall in dividend of 20 paise per share. A's marginal tax rate is 30%. Calculate what should be Mr. A's estimates of the price per share before and after the Budget announcement?

(CA 2004)

Solution

Price estimate before budget announcement: $P_0 = \frac{D_0(1+g)}{(k-g)} = \frac{2 \times (1 + 0.05)}{(0.10 - 0.05)}$ = Rs. 42.00

Price estimate after budget announcement: $P_0 = \frac{D_0(1+g)}{(k-g)} = \frac{1.80 \times (0.05)}{(0.07 - 0.05)}$ = Rs. 94.50

Illustration 12.14 ABC Ltd. has 50,000 outstanding shares. The current market price per share is Rs. 100 each. It hopes to make a net income of Rs. 5,00,000 at the end of current year. The company's Board is considering a dividend of Rs. 5 per share at the end of current financial year. The company needs to raise Rs. 10,00,000 for an approved investment expenditure. The company belongs to a risk class for which the capitalization rate is 10%. Show how the MM approach affects the value of firm if the dividends are paid or not paid.

(CA 2006)

Solution

Market Price if Dividend is paid = $P_1 = P_0 = (1 + k_e) - D = 100\ (1 + 0.10) - 5 =$ Rs. 105

Market Price if Dividend is not paid = $P_1 = P_0 = (1 + k_e) = 100\ (1 + 0.10) =$ Rs. 110

Particulars	Dividend Paid	Dividend not Paid
Net Income	5,00,000	5,00,000
– Dividend	2,50,000	—
Retained earnings	2,50,000	5,00,000
Fresh investment	10,00,000	10,00,000
Fresh issue	7,50,000	5,00,000
P_1	105	110
No. of new equity shares	7,142,86	4,545.45
No. of existing shares	50,000	50,000
No. of shares after fresh issue	57,142.86	54,545.45
MPS	105	110
Value of firm	60,00,000	60,00,000

Illustration 12.15 A company has 1,00,000 equity shares of Rs. 10 each and reserves are Rs. 20,00,000. Current market price is Rs. 70 per share. State the impact on (*i*) No. of shares outstanding, (*ii*) Face value of share (*iii*) Reserves (*iv*) Equity account balance, (*v*) Market price in each of the following situations:

(*a*) The company declares of bonus in the ratio 3 : 2.

(*b*) The company declares a 5 : 2 stock split.

(*c*) The company declares a 2 : 5 reverse split.

(*d*) The company buys back 10% shares at Rs. 60 per share.

Solution

Particulars	Existing	Bonus	Stock Split	Reverse Split	Buyback
Shares outstanding	1,00,000	2,50,000 (1,00,000 + 1,50,000)	250 (1,00,000 + 1,50,000)	40,000 (1,00,000 – 60,000)	90 (1,00,000 – 10,000)
Face Value	10	10	(10 × 2)/5 = 4	(10 × 5)/2 = 25	10
Reserves	20,00,000	500000 (20 – 15)	20,00,000	20,00,000	150,00,000 (20 –15)
Equity Account	30,00,000	30,00,000	30,00,000	30,00,000	30,00,000 (30 – 6)
Market price per share	70	70 × 1,00,000/2,50,000 = 28	70 × 2/5 = 28	70 × 5/2 = 175	(70 ×1,00,000) – 6,00,000/90,000 = 71.11

PROBLEMS FOR PRACTICE

Problem 12.1 The following information is provided $k_e = 15\%$, earnings per share is Rs. 4, calculate using Walter's model the value of the share when expected return is 20%, 15% and 10%. And the dividend is Rs. 4 and Rs. 2.

[**Answer:** When $r > k$, Value of the share = Rs. 26.67, Rs. 31.11. When $r = k$, Value of the share = Rs. 26.67, Rs. 26.67 and when $r < k$, value of the share is Rs. 26.67, Rs. 22.22.]

Problem 12.2 Calculate the price of a share through Gordon's model when $k_e = 15\%$, rate of return = 20%, 15%, 10%, the earnings per share are Rs. 4 and the retention ratio is 25% and 50%.

[**Answers:** When $r > k$, price of the share = Rs. 30, Rs. 40 when $r = k$, price of the share = Rs. 26.67, Rs. 26.67 and when $r < k$ price of the share = Rs. 24, Rs. 20.]

Problem 12.3 The following information is available in respect of a firm.

Capitalization rate k_e =15%. Earnings per share E = Rs. 14. Assumed rate of return on investments (*i*) 20% (*ii*) 15% (*iii*) 10%, show the effect of dividend policy on the market price of shares using Walter's model, where $r = 20\%$, *i.e.*, $r > k$. The effect of different D/P ratios is 14.2%, 28.75%, 50%, 71.43% and 100%. Corresponding to dividends per share of Rs. 0, 2, 4, 7, 10.

[**Answers:** When $r > k_e$, Rs. 124.13, Rs. 119.73, Rs. 115.53, Rs. 108.8, Rs. 102.13, Rs. 93.3 Walter's model = Dividend Policy and Valuation of Share. When $r < k_e$ Rs. 62.2, Rs. 66.9, Rs. 71.11, Rs. 77.77, Rs. 84.5, Rs. 93.3, When $r = k$ at all levels price of the share will be Rs. 93.3.]

Problem 12.4 The following information is provided

$$r = (i)\ 15\%,\ (ii)\ 14\%,\ (iii)\ 10\%$$

$$k_e = 14\%,\ E = \text{Rs. } 25$$

Determine the value of the shares by Gordon's model assuming the following:

Situations	DP Ratio (%)	Retention Ratio (%)
(*a*)	10	90
(*b*)	20	80
(*c*)	30	70
(*d*)	40	60
(*e*)	50	50
(*f*)	60	40
(*g*)	70	30

[**Answers:** When $r > k_e$, Rs. 500, Rs. 250, Rs. 214.28, Rs. 200, Rs. 192.3, Rs. 187.5, Rs. 184.4. When $r = k$ Rs. 178.57 at all levels and when $r < k$, Rs. 50, Rs. 83.33, Rs. 107.14, Rs. 125, Rs. 138.88, Rs. 150 and Rs. 159.09]

Problem 12.5 A Company's capitalization rate is 10%. It has 30,000 shares of the face value of Rs.100. Dividend per share is Rs.10. The company expects to invest Rs.10,00,000 and get a net income of Rs 5,00,000. Show that under MM hypotheses dividend payment does not affect value of firm.

[**Answer:** Value of the firm is 38,00,000 whether dividends are declared or not.]

Problem 12.6 Calculate Value of an equity share applying Walter's Formula when DP ratio is (*a*) 50% (*b*) 75% (*c*) 25%. Earnings per share is Rs. 8 and the cost of equity is 10%. Their expected rate of return = 15%, 5%, 10% what conclusions do you draw?

[**Answers:** When $r > k$; Rs. 100, Rs. 90, Rs. 110.
When $r < k$; Rs. 60, Rs. 70, Rs. 50.
When $r = k$; Rs. 80 at all levels.]

Problem 12.7 Diamond Engineering Co. has Rs. 10,00,000 equity shares outstanding at the start of the accounting year 1997. The ruling market price per share is Rs. 150. The board of directors of the company contemplates declaring Rs. 8 per share as dividend at the end of the current year. The rate of capitalization appropriate to the risk class to which the company belongs is 12%.

(*a*) Based on MM approach calculate the market price per share of the company (*i*) when dividend is declared and (*ii*) when dividend is not declared.

(*b*) How many new shares are to be issued by the company at the end of accounting year on the assumption that net income for the year is Rs. 2 crores. Investment budget is Rs. 4 crores and (*i*) the above dividends are distributed and (*ii*) they are not distributed.

(*c*) Show that the total market value of the shares at the end of the accounting year will remain the same whether dividends are distributed or not distributed. Also find out the current market value of the firm under both situations.

[B.Com(H), Delhi University 2006]

[**Answers:** (*a*) (*i*) when dividends are declared Rs. 160 and (*ii*) when not declared Rs. 168.
(*b*) No. of new shares to be issued are 1,75,000 and 1,19,048;
(*c*) (*i*)18,80,000 and 18,80,064 (*ii*) 15,00,000 and 15,00,00,057.]

Problem 12.8 Sahu & Co. earns Rs. 6 per share having a capitalization rate of 10% and has a return on investment at the rate of 20%. According to Walter's model what should be the price per share at 30% dividend payout ratio? Is this the optimum payout ratio as per Walter's model?

(CA Final, Nov. 2002)

[**Answer:** Rs. 102, 30% is not optimum payout ratio it should be reduced to make it optimum since $r > k_e$.]

Problem 12.9 A company has a total investment of Rs. 5,00,000 in assets and 50,000 outstanding ordinary shares at Rs. 10 per share par value. It earns a rate of 15% on its investment and has a policy of retaining 50% of its earnings. If the appropriate discount rate is 10%. Determine price of the share when the company has a payout of 80% and 20%.

(CS Final, 2003)

[**Answers:** (*i*) Rs. 30, (*ii*) Rs. 17 (*iii*) Rs. 15 (Negative)]

Problem 12.10 Calculate the price of shares by Walter's model when rate of investment is 15% and k_e =15%. The earnings per share is Rs. 5. Calculate when (*i*) there is 100% payout ratio (*ii*) 50% payout ratio and (*iii*) 100% retention.

[**Answers:** (*i*) Rs. 50 (*ii*) Rs. 62.5 (*iii*) Rs. 75.]

Problem 12.11 A company has a P/E ratio of Rs. 10. It plans to declare a dividend of Rs. 11. It has 50,000 shares outstanding selling at Rs. 80 each. Given MM model assumptions calculate the following:

(*i*) Price of the share at the end of the year (*a*) if dividend is declared (*b*) if dividend is not declared.

(*ii*) The company pays a dividend and has a net income of Rs. 6,00,000 and makes new investment of Rs. 12,00,000 during the period, how many new shares be issued?

[**Answers:** (*i*) When dividends are not declared Rs. 88.
(*ii*) When dividends are declared Rs. 77
(*iii*) No. of new shares to be issued Rs. 9,091.]

❑❑❑

13 Dividend Policy

LEARNING OBJECTIVES

13.1 Introduction
13.2 Types of Dividend
13.3 Buyback of Stock
13.4 Considerations for Declaring Dividends
13.5 Legal and Procedural Aspects of Payment of Dividends
13.6 Procedure for Declaring Dividend
13.7 Factors Affecting Dividend Decisions of Firms
13.8 Determinants of Dividend Policy
13.9 Dividend Payout Ratio
13.10 Stability of Dividends
13.11 Significance of Stable/Regular/Constant Dividends
13.12 Limitation on Dividend Payments
13.13 Bonus Shares
13.14 Stock Splits

13.1 INTRODUCTION

The purpose of this chapter is to discuss the different kinds of dividend policies, and how they affect the investor. Dividends paid to the shareholders are out of the firm's profits. Dividends are paid in the ordinary course of business and it refers to that part of the retained earnings of the firm which is paid to the shareholders. Dividends in a firm are paid according to the policies and decisions of the management regarding the retained earnings of the firm. A guideline gives the discretion to the directors of the firm to retain some part of the income and to give the other part as dividends to the owners of the firm called 'shareholders'.

13.2 TYPES OF DIVIDEND

There are different kinds of dividends. These are classified as cash dividend, stock dividend, scrip dividend, property dividend, bond dividend, special dividend, optional dividend, dividend from capital surplus, dividend from appreciation, and liquidation dividend.

(*i*) Cash Dividend

Cash dividend is an amount paid to the shareholders at the end of the year out of the profits of the operations of the firm. The distribution of cash reduces the net worth of the firm but these are paid to the shareholders only after, careful cash planning of the firm. As a rule the management pays cash dividends from the current earnings of the firm.

A company pays cash dividends to the shareholders by issuing dividend warrants. Since the system of DEMAT of shares has started in India and banks have become computerized, the electronic clearing system (ECS) is used to directly credit the account of the shareholder with the dividend due to him. Dividends not paid more than once in the year are called 'annual dividends'. Every year the board of directors declares the cash dividend which is to be paid to the shareholder. This dividend should be declared after the closing of the accounts of the firm. It is necessary to pass a resolution for declaring dividend at the annual general meeting.

(*ii*) Interim Dividend

Interim dividend is paid between two annual dividends. If a firm makes a high profit during the year, the shareholders are given the benefit by payment of a dividend. This dividend is not compulsory but shareholders get an extra advantage from the company. Interim dividend is useful because it does not put any financial pressure on a company continuously. It is only given when there is profitability and the firm has a surplus. This must be sanctioned at the board of directors' meeting and the Articles of Association should permit it.

(*iii*) Stock/Bonus Dividend

Shareholders do not always receive dividends in the form of cash through dividend warrants. Sometimes a firm issues dividends in the form of additional shares, called stock/bonus dividend. Stock is usually paid to the existing shareholders of the firm. The shareholders are allowed to sell this stock when they receive it. Stock dividend is paid by the firm's directors out of the retained earnings of the firm. It has a psychological effect in the minds of the shareholders that the firm is competitive and is profitable to them. Stock dividends are paid when the firm has large resources of cash for productive use. It gives the firm an effective technique of raising capital.

The investor while accepting the fact that the firm has issued stock dividend should know that stock dividend is a permanent method of capitalization of earnings. Normally, it should not be used as a method of distribution of corporate earnings because it divides the amount of existing equity into a larger number of parts of shares. Through this method there is no increase in wealth and the shareholders also do not receive any distribution in the form of cash. Stock dividend also has no effect on the assets of the firm immediately. It only represents a typical example of transfer of credit in the firm's surplus account to its capital account. The surplus amount which is distributed in the form of stock dividends becomes a permanent investment of the company. The existing shareholder's equity shares are not affected. In fact, the shareholder receives a higher number of shares than he had before. A stock dividend may be issued by a firm as a substitute of cash form of distribution of dividend. Stock dividend is also called ***bonus shares***. Stock dividend has the following limitations:

(*a*) It may lead to over-capitalization if a firm is not efficient and does not increase its rate of earnings proportionately.

(*b*) A stock dividend raises the expectation of a shareholder about the company's profitability and efficiency and his expectation about the future profits becomes high. The company may not be able to satisfy the shareholder.

(*c*) The issue of stock dividend cannot be a continuous process. It may be issued only sometimes when the firm has surpluses. Also, it can be paid only if the firm expects a higher profit in the future. Sometimes the company cannot maintain even its present rate of dividend after issuing a stock dividend.

(*iv*) Scrip Dividend

Scrip dividend is a promise to a shareholder to pay a dividend at a future date. The scrip is in the form of a promissory note with interest and it is useful as a security to bank for loans. Scrip dividend is a temporary promise made to the shareholder when the position of the firm for declaring dividends is not sound. However, the firm will be paying a dividend at a later date.

(*v*) Property Dividend

Under unusual exceptional circumstances a firm sometimes pays property dividends to a shareholder. These are non-recurring in nature and may be once in the lifetime of the firm. The directors would usually not like to issue such a dividend. Distribution as property dividend is only made when the price of the company stock falls to the extent that if the dividend is not given in this form its value will be nil.

13.3 BUYBACK OF STOCK

Buyback of share commenced in India in 2002. Sometimes the firm re-purchases its own common stock of outstanding shares. This can be done for a number of reasons. One of the main reasons is that the book value of the company is at a historical date. The company repurchases it shares to revalue itself at the market value. Another reason is for control and acquisition of another firm. This allows the firm to acquire another firm without any dilution of earnings of the firm. It is also re-purchased when the firm under contractual obligations has to retire some part of its stock. Re-purchase of stock is also resorted to fulfil certain options without in any way changing the total number of outstanding shares (*i.e.*, without increasing its own common stock).

13.4 CONSIDERATIONS FOR DECLARING DIVIDENDS

The investor should bear in mind that there are several sources for a firm to make the payment of dividends. The firm can pay the dividends from its current earnings which arise out of the regular operations of the firm. It may also pay all dividends from the past accumulation of profits. The firm is also permitted to pay dividend, out of the income from its subsidiaries. In addition, the firm is sometimes allowed to pay dividends out of other sources, but only under certain important considerations. These sources may be from the sale of a property, price of the sale being higher than the book value. It may also be paid out of the sale of securities at a premium and by conversion of some unused resources. When a company makes a surplus from mergers or purchase of subsidiaries, it may also declare a dividend.

Dividends can be declared by the board of directors only on fulfilling certain conditions. The dividend that is declared should be out of a surplus. If the firm makes a deposit, dividend should only be declared after the deposit has been absorbed. The directors should also be careful that dividend impairs the capital strength of a firm which they are managing. Sometimes directors declare dividends at the time when the firm is insolvent due to the bad conditions of business. Dividends should be avoided in such circumstances and the rights of the creditors should be protected. The dividend that is given to the shareholders is a profit which is distributed out of the profits of the firm. A dividend policy should, therefore, be carefully prepared by the management of the firm and guidelines issued for strict adherence to legal aspects. The main determinants of a good dividend policy are the dividend payout ratio, stability in dividends and procedures and legal aspects that are followed by companies.

13.5 LEGAL AND PROCEDURAL ASPECTS OF PAYMENT OF DIVIDENDS

Dividend is defined by the Income Tax Act as:

(*i*) Accumulated profits include the development rebate but not the reservations provided for depreciation. Dividend also refers to the book profits and not the accumulated profits which have been declared by the income tax authorities. 'Bonus issues' are not a part of dividend and they do not relate to any asset of the firm.

(*ii*) Any distribution of debentures, stock, deposit certificates and bonus to preference shareholders.

(*iii*) Distribution on liquidation of company.

(*iv*) Distribution on reduction of capital.

(*v*) Any payments by way of loans or advances by a closely held company to shareholders holding substantial interest provided the loan should not have been made in the ordinary course of business and money lending should not be a substantial part of the company's business.

On the basis of different decisions the following conclusions are drawn with respect to accumulated profit:

(*a*) Accumulated profits do not include current profits.

(*b*) They are computed on the basis of commercial profits and not on assessed incomes.

(*c*) Balancing charge does not form part of accumulated profit as it is not commercial profit but it is considered to be a withdrawal of depreciation after the asset is sold for a price which is higher than the written down value.

(*d*) Accumulated profits include all tax-free incomes, that is, for example, the agricultural income, but the receipts of capital nature are included in the accumulated profits if they are chargeable to Capital Gains Tax by the receiving company.

(*e*) Accumulated profit also includes general reserve.

(*f*) Provision for taxation and dividends are not considered to be a part of accumulated reserve.

(*g*) Accumulated reserve should also not include the development rebate reserve, development allowance reserve and investment allowance reserve.

13.6 PROCEDURE FOR DECLARING DIVIDEND

Dividend is declared at the annual general meeting and is considered to be the income of the previous year in which it is declared. Deemed dividend is treated as income of the previous years when it is distributed or paid but it is notional dividend under Section 2 (22). Interim dividend is the income of the previous year in which the amount of such dividend is unconditionally made available by the company to a shareholder.

Dividend can be declared after following the different procedures. These procedures are:

(*i*) Dividends should be declared out of the profits of the company.

(*ii*) Dividends can be declared only when a company has sufficient reserves for redeeming preference shares.

(*iii*) Dividends can be paid after providing for depreciation.

(*iv*) Dividends can be paid with the recommendation of the board of directors and the approval of the shareholders at the annual general meeting held by the company.

(*v*) Dividends can be paid only after transferring a percentage of profits to reserves of the company. There are certain rules for transferring an amount to the reserves of the company. (*a*) when dividends exceed 10% but not 12.5% of the company's paid up capital, the reserves should not be less than 2.5% of the profits; (*b*) when proposed dividends exceed 12.5% but not exceeding 15% of the paid up capital, reserves should be not less than 5% of the profits; (*c*) when dividends exceed 15% but not more than 20% of the paid up capital, reserves should not be less than 7.5% of the current profits; and (*d*) when the proposed dividend exceeds 20% of the paid up capital, their reserves should be not less than 10% of the current profits

(*vi*) Interim dividend is paid between two annual general meetings by passing a resolution at the board of directors' meeting, but before the finalization of their account of that year, only if it is authorized by Articles of Association.

(*vii*) Cash dividends should be paid from the revenue profits of the company, but in exceptional cases they can be paid out of accumulated profits when current profits are inadequate.

(*viii*) Dividends can be paid out of accumulated profits if the rate of dividend does not exceed the average of the dividend rates declared in the proceeding 5 years.

(*ix*) The amount which is used from the accumulated profits should not exceed one-tenth of the total of paid up capital and free reserves and that amount is first used to set off the losses before declaring dividends to preference shareholders and equity shareholders.

(*x*) The balance of the reserves should not fall below 15% of the paid up capital of the company when dividends are declared from accumulated profits.

(*xi*) The dividends that are declared should be paid within 30 days of its declaration.

(*xii*) If there is a default in payments of dividends, then within 7 days exceeding 30 days, the company must open a bank account in a scheduled bank. The account should be called 'unpaid dividend account'. If this account has any unpaid/unclaimed dividends for more than 7 years from the date on which such transfer takes place, the money can be transferred to investor education and protection fund by the company.

13.7 FACTORS AFFECTING DIVIDEND DECISIONS OF FIRMS

The following factors affect the dividend decisions of firms:

(*i*) **Expectation of Investors:** People who invest in the firms have basically done so with the view of long-term investment in a particular firm to avoid the necessity of shifting from one firm to another. The expectation of the investor has been two fold. To be able to receive income annually and have a stable investment.

(*a*) *Capital Gains:* Investors who make long-term investment do so with a view to making some capital appreciation on their investment. Capital gain is the profit, which results from the sale of any capital investment. If the investor invests in equity stock, the capital gain would be out of the sale of equity stock after holding it for more than one year.

(*b*) *Current Income:* The investor would like to have some current earnings which are also continuous in nature and it is the price of abstinence from current consumption to more profitable avenues. The expectation of the shareholder should be considered before taking any appropriate decision regarding dividends. In this sense, the company has to think of both maximization of wealth of the investor and its own internal requirements for long-term financing.

(*ii*) **Reducing of Uncertainty:** Dividends should be declared in a manner that the investor is confident about the future of his earnings. If he receives dividends annually and the amount is such that it satisfies him, the company is able to gain his confidence because it reduces his uncertainty about future capital gains or appreciation of the company's equity stock. A current dividend is the present value cash inflow to the investors. This also helps him to assess the kind of future that his investments will carry for him. The decisions for paying dividend should also be considered at this point.

(*iii*) **Financial Strength:** The payment of dividend which is regular, stable and continuous with a promise of capital appreciation, helps the company in judging its own financial strength, and also receives financial commitments from creditors and financial institutions because they are in a position to gauge the kind of working of the firm through the information they receive regarding the amount of dividend and the market value of their shares. While all investors would like to maximize their wealth, the company must also see its requirement for expansion programmes. The company also has certain limitations or environmental constraints which enable it to pay dividend in a limited form.

(*iv*) **Inflation:** Companies should balance their projects to fight against any purchasing power instability. Management should judge price level inflation, explore the possibility of gain and loss in the investments available to them. They should also try and forecast which securities will possibly appreciate. A purchase of property at the right time will lead to appreciation in time. Growth stock will also appreciate over time. An analysis of inflationary trends should be done thoughtfully with the economic and industrial factors and state of the capital market, to enable the shareholders to get good dividends. In a high inflationary period the firm will require additional funds to run the business so they will not be able to give a high dividend payout ratio. The firm will have to retain its profits to have stability in earnings.

(*v*) **State of the Capital Market:** The state of the capital market affects the profits of a company. In a boom period a firm can issue new securities and can get a premium on its issues. It will also make goods profits and consequently it will be able to give a good dividend to its shareholders, but in a recession it is necessary that the company analyses every step that it takes in making investments. While evaluating projects, the firm should realize that investments are made under conditions of uncertainty. There cannot be a magic formula which will always work. The firm should be concerned with concepts and applications that will satisfy the investment objectives and constantly evaluate the performance of his investments. If need be, the firm may consider switching over to alternate proposals. Thus state of the capital market influences liberal and controlled dividend policies. A boom period will bring about high dividends and in a recession there would be low dividends.

(*vi*) **Informational Contents of Dividends:** Dividend policy has an impact on the value of the share. When there are sudden changes in dividends it will have an impact on the price of a share of a company. When a firm increases its dividends, investors perceive that they will get higher earning in the future. If it is a decrease in dividend it is like an alarm bell that the company is not in a favourable future earning capacity. When dividend announcements are made the expectations of investors increase or decrease and the expectations in the capital market also react favourably or unfavourably depending upon whether dividend announcement is good or bad. The expectations of the market are based on the past behaviour, current earnings and dividend policy. If dividend decisions match the expectations of the market and the investors, the price of the share will not change, but when actual dividend is different to expected dividend then value of the share will change. Thus dividends are a useful tool in assessing the price of the share. Dividend policy decisions have to be made keeping in mind the price of the share.

(*vii*) **Wealth Maximization Decisions:** While the firm regards the needs of investment and expansion programmes and is guided by the decision of paying dividends as a long-term financing requirement, the other decisions that the firm may be guided by, is the prospect of paying to the shareholders a high amount of dividend to satisfy them and also to raise the price of its equity stock in the capital market. This project takes into consideration the expectation of both the investors and the shareholders. The management may adopt any one of these methods after taking into consideration the factors which affect the maximization of shareholder's wealth. Thus the most important decision relating to dividends is to maximize the wealth of the shareholders. It is one of the three most important functions of a financial manager i.e., investment decision, financing decision and dividend decision making.

13.8 DETERMINANTS OF DIVIDEND POLICY

Dividend policy is a method or technique or approach by the management of the firm towards some constant payment to the shareholders out of the profits of the company. Dividend decisions, may be for a short-term purpose, also called 'ad-hoc decisions' or may be made for a longer time period. A dividend policy should be made by the management with certain considerations in mind. It should take into account the position of the firm and the economic environment and type of industry in which it operates. It should also take into consideration the needs of the shareholders in the present position of the market and other considerations with regard to capital gain, capital increase and maintenance of levels once achieved. Apart from this, the consideration of tax should also be thought of. Dividend policy should also be oriented towards the firm's considerations, its need for future expansion, business cycle operating in the industry and the nature of business through which the firm operates.

The determinants of a dividend policy should be towards regularity of income, stability of income, and safety during the period of contingencies. The legal constraints should also be looked upon by the directors. The determinants of the dividend policy should project the factors discussed in next section.

13.9 DIVIDEND PAYOUT RATIO

The following factors about a company should be considered before dividends are declared. Two important aspects determine the dividends that should be declared. These are the dividend payout ratio and the stability in dividends to satisfy the expectations of the shareholders. Among the different aspects the most important determinants of the payout ratio is the target payout ratio or the part of earnings that should be paid to the shareholders and that part which should be kept as a reserve for future requirements.

(*i*) **Target Pay-Out Ratio:** While declaring dividends that amount should be paid to the shareholders, which can be maintained by the company. If the earning position of the firm goes down and it cannot pay the dividends in a particular year then its position in the stock market will also go down. The pay-out ratio is the rate of dividends to earnings. Although the amount will fluctuate in direct proportion to earnings the shareholders will be satisfied because if a company adopts 20% payout ratio for every year then although the percentage will continue to be the same the rupee earned will be higher. For example, if the company pays payout ratio of 40% and if it earns Rs. 1.50 per share the dividend per share will be 60 paise. If it earns Rs. 2 per share the dividend given to shareholders will be 80 paise. The earnings will, therefore, increase for the shareholders although the target payout ratio will be the same.

Dividend payout ratio is calculated by dividing the net profit with the dividends paid to the shareholders. D/P ratio should be decided after taking into consideration different aspects of the earnings position, the liquidity required by the company, its plans for expansion and the amount of funds required for additional investments.

(*ii*) **Liquidity:** A company should be careful while declaring dividend not to jeopardize the earning capacity of the firm. Liquidity is an important criterion for the working of the firm. It is important to declare dividend only after maintaining liquidity position of the firm. The company should not have too much liquidity because this means that it is not profitability investing its funds for shareholders. Proper liquidity relationship in a firm will also help to safeguard the funds of the shareholders. The firm may, however maintain less liquidity after it has the ability to borrow at short notice or if the financial institutions extend credit whenever it has a demand for it. Small companies should have a proper liquidity but large companies which are well established may be flexible about liquidity requirements because they are in a better position to get liquidity from the capital markets.

(*iii*) **Expansion Programmes:** As long-term financing decision the significance of the profits of the firm after tax is to be considered in paying dividends. Investor should know that cash dividends have the nature of reducing the funds of the firm and firm is restricted to grow or to find other financing sources. If the firm desires to fund dividend as a long-term decision then it should be guided by the following points.

(*a*) *Projects available with the firm:* When a firm has many large projects to put its investments then instead of distributing a large amount of profit it may retain earnings of the firm and advance these projects.

(*b*) *Requirement of equity funds:* A company may be able to finance itself either through long-term loans or through sourcing of capital through equity and preference shares. To raise capital the firm has to incur a large cost. The company may thus take a decision of retaining some part of the earnings of the firm and may be guided by this view at the time of paying dividends to shareholders.

(*iv*) **Control:** Those firms which have many new projects at hand would require additional funds to finance them. If internal reserves are not available with the company then new equity would be raised by company resulting in diluting the control of the management with an increased number of shares. This problem will specially arise in closely held companies.

Effects of Payout Ratio

The dividend payout ratio of a company will have certain effects in both conditions of high payout ratio and low payout ratio. Summarizing from the above discussion a ***high dividend payout ratio*** will have the following effect:

(*a*) If payout ratio is high the firm may have the problem of shortage of cash and the need for liquidity may arise.

(*b*) The company will not be in a position to start expansion programmes as there would be a high cash deficit.

(*c*) The company would be running at a loss and not be able to use its resources effectively for earning a higher profit for maximizing the wealth of the shareholder.

The problems of ***a low payout ratio*** would be the following:

(*a*) The market price of the shares may fall as the shareholders do not get the return that they expect.

(*b*) It may have a high accumulation of cash and no good projects for investments which would make the company earn a minimum rate of return.

13.10 STABILITY OF DIVIDENDS

Shareholders prefer regular and stable dividends because they perceive such dividends with certainty and upward growth. This helps to satisfy their expectations on investments made by them in a company. For stability in dividends the shareholders prefer a regular dividend which may have a constant D/P ratio, a stable, steady and fixed dividends for its shareholders and stable dividends plus extra dividends.

(*i*) **Constant Dividend Payout Ratio:** Regularity of dividends is significant for an investor, who wishes to make purchase of shares in a company. The confidence of investors is increased by taking a look at the past behaviour of companies. A regular dividend establishes the company's position in the stock market. It also provides a firm policy for taking decisions about the future of the firm with regard to its expansion programmes. It also infuses strength and confidence in the minds of creditors and it makes it easier for the firm to take loans from creditors on the strength of its regularity of dividends.

Firms who pay a regular dividend should be careful to maintain it at a rate that they are able to achieve every year. If the rate goes down, the firm's position in the stock market also falls. If too high a dividend is declared, the firm may not be able to achieve the same rate in the forthcoming years. If a company maintains a regular balance in paying dividends, it will be established and the investor can also plan to make his investments for a fairly long time. In a constant D/P ratio, the amount of dividend per share will increase or decrease with the change in earnings per share of the company. If a D/P ratio of 50% has been accepted, then when the earnings are Rs. 10,00,000 the dividend will be Rs. 5,00,000 and when it is Rs. 15,00,000 then dividends will be Rs. 7,50,000. Thus dividends will fluctuate according to the earnings per share of the company. This is depicted in Fig. 13.1.

Regularly dividends to shareholders ensure stability of income through dividends also play a major role for the satisfaction of the shareholders. Thus constant D/P ratio is a fixed percentage of the earnings of the company.

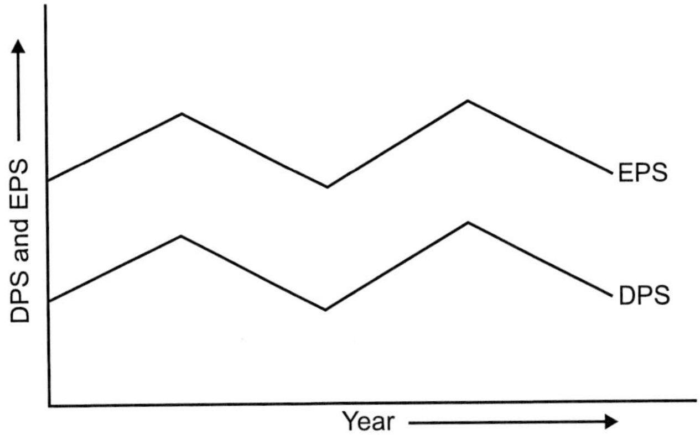

Fig. 13.1 Constant dividend payout ratio

(*ii*) **Constant Dividend per Share:** Most firms follow the constant D/P ratio method to provide for dividends. Some companies however pay a fixed and regular amount as dividend. There is no change in dividends for a fixed number of years. This is reviewed when the date of the policy closes. For example, the company may decide to pay Rs. 2 on its share of the face value of Rs. 10 for 7 years. Therefore, for the next seven years the dividend will remain at Rs. 2 without any change. On the seventh year it will be reviewed and the dividend can again be set for some number of years. This is depicted in Fig. 13.2.

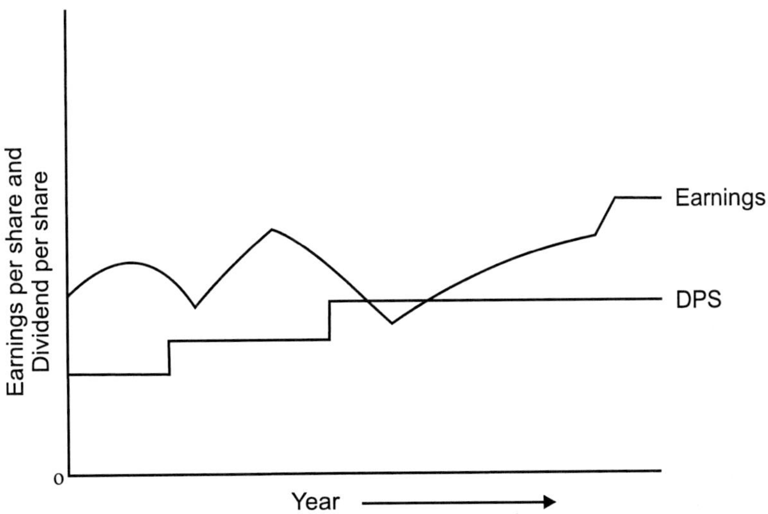

Fig. 13.2 Constant dividends per share

(*iii*) **Regular and Extra Dividend:** A company should have a policy of giving both regular incomes to its shareholders plus extra dividends whenever the firm is able to do well. An extra dividend in the form of interim dividend is a good policy because the interim dividend is not an expectation of the investors and when he receives it he is rather optimistic about the future of the company without expecting more than the stable regular income. Extra income need not be declared annually but only when the company can make an extra earning. This gives the advantage to the investor to share in the growth of the company without making it a legal restraint for continuous annual payments.

13.11 SIGNIFICANCE OF STABLE/REGULAR/CONSTANT DIVIDENDS

Stable dividends have the advantage of providing current income and financial stability to the shareholders. These issues and concerns are:

(*i*) **Current Income:** When shareholders invest in a particular company, they desire current income and capital appreciation from the company. A large number of investors believe that income received currently from the company in which they invest is a supplement to their income received from salary and other sources. This also helps in making decisions for them so that they part with some of their money which is useful for current consumption and forego it for the purpose of another investment which would give them income annually. The investor can also sell his investment from one firm to another but there are many types of costs involved in it. Costs are due to transaction or due to switching over. There may be an element of brokerage cost also. To avoid these costs the investor would like stable income so that he may continue to be a long-term investor in one firm only.

(*a*) **Information:** When a shareholder receives stable dividend the information about their shares are continuously received by the stock exchange. This gives the investor a chance to know about the future of the company. It also is able to influence a larger number of investors to continue to keep their funds in that particular firm.

(*b*) **Financial Stability:** Legally a stable dividend has many advantages. It gives to the institutional investors like financial institutions chance to qualify for investment in their corporate organizations. One of the considerations of the investment policy of the large number of financial institutions existing in India is that income should be stable over the previous years. If the firm satisfies this condition, the financial institutions like Unit Trust of India (UTI), Industrial Development Bank of India (IDBI), Industrial Credit and Investment Corporation of India (ICICI) and other Institutions would prefer such a company to make their investments.

13.12 LIMITATIONS ON DIVIDEND PAYMENTS

The firm has the following limitations in paying dividends. The management of the firm while making decision in paying out dividends to its shareholders should also analyse these problems:

(*i*) **Cash Requirements:** Many firms are unable to pay dividends regularly. A company which is going through its gestation period or is small in nature and trying to expand its business has difficulty in paying high dividends. If it does, it will be surrounded by inefficiency because of the insufficiency of cash. Sometimes a firm has the problem of tying up all resources in inventories or in the commitment of purchasing long-term investments. This acts as a restraint of the firm to pay out dividends.

(*ii*) **Limitation Placed by Creditors:** Sometimes a firm requires funds for long-term purpose and to fulfil this obligation it makes, the use of funds on long-term loans. While taking these loans the firm makes an arrangement with the creditors that it will not pay dividends to its shareholders if its debt equity ratio exceeds 2 : 1. Sometimes the firm also makes contractual obligations with its creditors to maintain a certain payout ratio till the time that it is using the loan facilities. Under these contractual obligations the firm cannot pay more than the dividends it can, or is allowed to pay, under the agreement.

(*iii*) **Legal Constraints:** In India, there are many legal constraints in payment of dividends. The payment of dividends of preference shares is subject to a limit by the legal authorities from time to time. This restraint also covers bonds, debentures and equity shares during the time when it is necessary for the authorities to do so. These legal constraints should be carefully analysed before paying dividends to the shareholders.

13.13 BONUS SHARES

Bonus shares do not affect cash and earnings position of the company nor is the ownership of stockholders changed. There will be a transfer of the amount of dividend from surplus to capital stock, which amounts to capitalization of retained earnings. The net effect is increase in number of shares of the current stockholders. It is merely an adjustment in the firm's capital structure in terms of book value and market value of common stock.

When extra dividend is paid in the form of shares, the shares so issued are termed as bonus shares. Issue of bonus shares does not affect the total capital structure of the company. It is the capitalization of that part of shareholders equity, which is represented by reserves and surplus. It does not affect the total earnings of the shareholders.

(*i*) Bonus shares are made out of free reserves built out of genuine profits or share premiums collected in cash only.

(*ii*) The residual reserve after paying bonus dividend should be at least 40% of the increased paid up capital.

(*iii*) Bonus shares can be given only on fully paid up share.

Legal Procedure of Bonus Shares

Bonus shares are also called stock dividend. They can be distributed in the following cases:

(*i*) Articles of association should permit issue of bonus shares.

(*ii*) There should be sufficient undistributed profits.

(*iii*) A resolution capitalizing profits must be passed by board of directors.

(*iv*) Resolution of board of directors should be approved by shareholders.

(*v*) When a company allots bonus shares it should file within 30 days after the allotment with the registrar of joint stock companies a return stating the number and par value of such shares comprised in the allotment and the names, addresses, and occupations of the allottees and a copy of the resolution authorizing bonus issue.

Example 13.1 Calculate the effect of the issue of bonus shares of a company. Company XYZ has the following capital structure. Assume net earnings before and after bonus issue to be Rs. 33,000.

Particulars	Amount (Rs.)
Equity share capital Rs 10 per share (30,000 shares)	3,00,000
Share Premium	3,00,000
Reserves & Surplus	1,50,000
Total net worth	7,50,000

The company issues bonus shares: 1 for every 10 at Rs. 15 per share = 30,000/10 shares = 3,000 shares. Show the new capitalization of the company. Calculate earnings per share before and after bonus issues.

Solution

Bonus Issue has effects on reserves & surplus

The reserves and surplus will reduce by 3,000 × 15 =	45,000
Share premium A/c will increase by 15,000 3,000 × 5 =	15,000
Present equity share capital A/c = 3,000 × 10 =	30,000
The new capitalization of the Co. will be equity share capital	
33,000 shares of Rs. 10 each	3,30,000
Share premium 3,00,000 + 15,000	3,15,000
Reserves and surplus 1,50,000 – 45,000	1,05,000
Total net worth	7,50,000
Earnings per share before bonus issue	
Net earnings	33,000
No. of Equity Shares	30,000
Earnings per share	Rs.1.10

[Contd...]

Earnings per share after bonus issue	
Net earnings	33,000
No. of Equity Shares	33,000
Earnings per share	Re.1

EPS has decreased from Rs. 1.10 to Rs. 1 per share. However total earnings of shareholders will not change total earnings of a shareholder holding 100 shares before bonus issue was Rs. 100 × 1.10 = 110.

After issue of bonus shares his earnings would continue to be 110 *i.e.*, 110 × 1 =110. The issue of bonus shares will not have an impact on shareholders wealth. The market value of equity shares will fall to 15 × 1/1.10 = 13.64 on account of increase in number of shares. However total market value of shareholder holdings would continue to Rs. 33,000 × 13.64 = Rs. 4,50,120.

Therefore it can be summarized that bonus issues have the following important points to be noted.

(*a*) Bonus issue is made of free reserves built out of genuine profits on share premiums collected in cash only.

(*b*) The residual reserves shall be at least 40% of the increased paid up capital.

(*c*) 30% of the average profit before tax of the Co. for the previous years should yield a rate of dividend on the expanded capital base of the company at 10%.

Bonus issues have certain advantages or the company. It increases the number of shares. It provides a saving in cash resources which can be used for starting additional projects for expansion and growth of the company. For the investor, the dividends in the current year falls but in the future he gets higher dividends because his numbers of shares have increased. A bonus issue increases the goodwill of the company and raises the confidence of the investors and shareholders. It is not taxable for the shareholder. In this manner the company gives a reward to the shareholder by utilizing a part of its profits without an effect on its liquidity position.

13.14 STOCK SPLITS

When the company pays a stock dividend it may also offer the stock split up. Effective stock split up is only an increase in the number of shares that are outstanding. The change does not affect the stated value of a stock or its surplus. It also does not affect the shareholder equity. It is only the reformation of a shareholder's equity in smaller units with the objective of providing:

(*i*) ***Reduction of the Market Price:*** A stock split helps in the stock exchange to make a round lot. By reducing the stock price the firm is able to help the small investors to purchase and sell stock with easy continuity. In the stock split, it is noticed that only the par value and the number of outstanding share are affected. The amount contributed as capital as well as earnings which are retained do not change.

(*ii*) ***Future Growth:*** Stock split gives information to the stock market of the continued improved future growth of a company.

(iii) ***Reverse Split:*** Sometimes there is a reverse split in stocks. When a firm does not increase the number of outstanding shares of stock but reduces its number it is called a reverse split which has the effect of reducing the outstanding shares. The reverse split is affected by a firm sometimes when the stock price falls far below the required level of the firm. The reversal split is an indication of financial problems faced by the firm.

Bonus shares can be distinguished from stock splits. In a stock split, the par value per share is reduced and the number of shares is increased proportionately. There is no difference between bonus issues and splits from the economic point of view but differences arise from the accounting point of view. In a bonus issue the retained earnings are reduced and paid up capital increases as well as the shape premium account. In a stock split this effect does not take place. The distinction between bonus issues and stock splits is depicted in Example 13.2.

Table 13.1 Distinction between Bonus Issues and Stock Split

Bonus Issue	Stock Split
• Par value is unchanged. • Part of reserves is capitalized. • Stockholders proportional ownership remains unchanged. • Book value, market price and earnings decline.	• Par value is reduced. • There is a capitalization of reserves. • Stockholders proportional ownership remains unchanged. • Book value, market value and earnings per share decline.

Example 13.2

Part A Equity Portion before Stock Split	
Paid up share capital	50,00,000
1,00,000 shares of Rs. 50 each fully paid up	
Reserves and surplus	1,00,00,000
Before stock split in the ratio of 5 : 1	1,50,00,000
Part B After Stock Splits	
Paid up share capital 5,00,000	
Shares of Rs. 10 each fully paid up	50,00,000
Reserves and surplus	1,00,00,000
Stock Split	1,50,00,000
Effect of bonus issue	
Part A before bonus issue	
Paid up share capital	

[Contd...]

10,00,000 shares of Rs. 10 each	1,00,00,000
Fully paid up	3,00,00,000
Reserves and surplus	4,00,00,000
Part B After Bonus issue 1 : 1	
Paid up share capital	2,00,00,000
20,00,000 shares of Rs. 10 each	
Fully paid up	
Reserves and surplus reduce by 1,00,00,000	2,00,00,000
	4,00,00,000

To conclude, dividend policy can have an effect on the price of a share. It must be made carefully after analysing the factors affecting dividend policy. It should also consider the expectations of the shareholders and offer a good payout ratio and provide stability in dividends.

POINTS TO REMEMBER

- There are many factors that affect the dividend policy of a firm. These are expectation of investors, reducing of uncertainty, financial strength, state of the capital market, inflation, informational contents of dividends, and wealth maximization of shareholders.
- There are two important determinants of a dividend policy. These are the dividend payout ratio and stability in dividends.
- There are different dividend payout ratios; these are constant D/P ratio, constant dividends and stable dividend plus extra.
- Dividends can be given in the form of cash or stock. Cash dividends can be annual dividend or interim dividend. Stock dividend is in the form of bonus from accumulated reserves.
- Bonus issues are a reward to shareholders and are not given every year.
- Stock splits and bonus issues are different. While bonus issues reduce reserves, stock splits do not have any effect on them.

OBJECTIVE TYPE QUESTIONS

State whether the following statements are true (T) or False (F).

1. Dividend is paid out of current or accumulated profits.
2. Dividend information has an affect on share prices.

3. State of capital market does not affect dividends.
4. Wealth maximization is a criterion to be adopted in dividend policy.
5. Dividend payments do not affect the liquidity of the firm.
6. Preference shareholders do not have any priority in dividends.
7. A bonus issue affects the firm in the same way as a cash dividend.
8. Interim dividend is paid every year.
9. Cash dividends are paid out of accumulated profits.
10. Capital profits cannot be distributed as dividends to shareholders.

Answers: 1. (T), 2. (T), 3. (F), 4. (T), 5. (F), 6. (F), 7. (F), 8. (F), 9. (F), 10. (F).

THEORETICAL QUESTIONS

1. What are the main determinants of a dividend policy?
2. Why do firms follow a policy of stable dividends?
3. Explain briefly the factors which affect the dividend policy of a firm.
4. 'A dividend policy of a firm has no effect on the value of the firm.' Comment.
5. What is stock dividend? How is it different from cash dividend?
6. Discuss the difference between the bonus shares and stocks splits.
7. What are the procedures for payment of dividends?
8. 'Dividend policy can be used to maximize the wealth of the shareholder'. Explain.
9. What is an informational content of dividend payment? How does it affect the value of the share?
10. Why do companies pay dividends? Discuss.
11. Explain the concepts of D/P ratio and stability in dividends.

ILLUSTRATIVE PROBLEMS

Illustration 13.1 A company expects to generate the following profits from its capital investment in the next five years.

Year	Net Income (Rs.)	Investment (Rs.)
1	60,00,000	30,00,000
2	50,00,000	25,00,000
3	40,00,000	20,00,000
4	30,00,000	35,00,000
5	25,00,000	40,00,000

The company has currently 10,00,000 equity shares and pays dividends of Rs. 6 per year.

(*i*) Determine dividends per share if dividend policy is treated as a residual decision.

(*ii*) Determine dividends per share and the amount of external financing that will be necessary if dividend payout ratio of 50% is maintained.

Solution: (*i*) Calculation of dividend per share

Year	Profit (Rs.)	Investment (Rs.)	Balance (Rs.)	DPS	External financing
1	60,00,000	30,00,000	30,00,000	3	0
2	50,00,000	25,00,000	25,00,000	2.5	0
3	40,00,000	20,00,000	20,00,000	2	0
4	30,00,000	35,00,000	—	0	5,00,000
5	25,00,000	30,00,000	—	0	15,00,000

(*ii*) Calculation of dividend per share at 50% payout

Year	Profit	Investment	Balance	DPS	External financing
1	60,00,000	30,00,000	3	30,00,000	---
2	50,00,000	25,00,000	2.5	25,00,000	---
3	40,00,000	20,00,000	2	20,00,000	---
4	30,00,000	15,00,000	1.5	35,00,000	20,00,000
5	25,00,000	12,50,000	1.25	40,00,000	27,50,000

Illustration 13.2 The earnings per share of a company for the last five years is given here.

Year	EPS
2007	50
2006	40
2005	32
2004	30
2003	34
2002	20
2001	–10
2000	4

Determine the annual dividend per year if the company pays dividend at Rs. 20 per share and increase to Rs. 25 per share when the earnings per share exceeds Rs. 30 per share for the two consecutive previous years.

Solution

Year	EPS	Dividend
2007	50	25
2006	40	25
2005	32	25
2004	30	25
2003	34	25
2002	20	25
2001	(–10)	20*
2000	4	20*

****Note:*** It is assumed that the company pays dividends out of its past accumulated profits.

Illustration 13.3 The following information is given for a company.

Equity share capital (Face Value Re. 1)	50,00,000
10% Preference capital	10,00,000
Share premium account	10,00,000
Reserves	10,00,000
Cash and bank balance	4,00,000

The profit after tax for the year 2007 is Rs. 20,00,000 the company is planning to pay dividend on equity share for the year 2007.

Prepare (*i*) EPS and Maximum DPS if 10% of the current profits are to be retained.

(*ii*) Residual dividend per share if 10% of the current year profits are to be retained and new investment proposals before the company is requires Rs. 5,00,000. No external borrowings are proposed.

Solution

Calculation of EPS	
Profit after tax	20,00,000
Less preference share dividend	1,00,000
Profits for equity shareholders	19,00,000
EPS (19,00,000/50,00,000)	0.38
Maximum DPS	

[Contd...]

Profit after tax	20,00,000
Less retained earnings	2,00,000
Profits available for shareholders	18,00,000
Less preference dividend	1,00,000
Profits for equity shareholders	17,00,000
Cash and bank balance	4,00,000

The company can distribute Rs. 17,00,000 but the company has Rs. 4,00,000 available cash. Therefore it will be Rs. 4,00,000/ 50,00,000 = 0.08

If the company plans an investment of Rs. 5,00,000; there is no cash available to pay dividends. So, the maximum DPS will be 0.08 if no investment is made.

Illustration 13.4 The following information is provided of company X and Z. The two companies are of the same industry and with identical earnings for the last 3 years. Both companies have difference in the price of their shares in the market due to their dividend to the equity shareholders. Company X pays 50% earnings as dividend and company Z pays a constant dividend per share. X's share prices are lower than Z although it paid a higher dividend in some years. Their EPS, DPS and market price is given here.

X Ltd.

Year	EPS (Rs.)	DPS (Rs.)	Market Price (Rs.)
2005	6	3	13
2006	5	2.50	12
2007	7	3.50	13

Z Ltd.

Year	EPS (Rs.)	DPS (Rs.)	Market Price (Rs.)
2005	6	3	14
2006	5	3	13
2007	7	3	14

(*i*) Calculate (*a*) Payout ratio (*b*) Dividend yield (*c*) Earnings yield.

(*ii*) What is the reason for price difference of the two companies?

(*iii*) How should X increase its market price?

Solution

Payout ratio = DPS/EPS

Dividend yield = DPS/MP

Earnings yield = EPS/MP

Year	Dividend X Ltd.	Payout ratio Z Ltd.	Dividend X Ltd.	Yield Z Ltd.	Earnings X Ltd.	Yield Z Ltd.
2005	0.50	0.50	0.23	0.21	0.46	0.42
2006	0.50	0.60	0.20	0.22	0.41	0.38
2007	0.50	0.42	0.26	0.21	0.53	0.50

Investors perceive the two companies according to the dividend received by them. The average dividend for both the companies is Rs. 3 in the last three years. The average market price of Z is Rs. 13.8 and that of X is lower at Rs. 12.66. The constant dividend model has found favour over the payment ratio method adopted by X. The market has evaluated the firms through dividends. A higher market price for shares of X is possible only through a high dividend payout ratio.

Illustration 13.5 ABC Co. had the following capital structure before issuing bonus dividends.

Common stock (Rs. 5 per share, 2,00,000 shares)	10,00,000
Capital Surplus	5,00,000
Retained earnings	5,00,000
Net Worth	20,00,000

The management issues additional stock of 10,000 shares to pay dividends at 5% market price of stock is Rs. 20. For cash 20 shares of stock the shareholders receive 1 additional share. Show the capital structure after issue of stock/bonus shares.

Solution

The capital structure after issue of stock dividends will be as follows:

Common Stock (Rs.5 per share; 2,10,000 shares)	10,50,000
Capital surplus	6,50,000
Retained earnings	3,00,000
	20,00,000

With issue of additional stock of 10,000 shares an amount worth Rs. 2,00,000 (20 × 10,000 shares) is transferred from retained earnings to capital stock and surplus account since par value remains the same common stock increases by 50,000. Residual 1,50,000 goes to capital surplus account. Earnings will decline exactly in the proportion in which shares increase. If company's assumed earnings are

5,00,000 before issue of bonus share it would be 2.50. Issue of stock dividends will result in drop in earnings per share. Thus with issue of additional stocks of 10,000 shares earnings will fall to 2,38 (5,00,000/2,10,000) total earnings available to stockholders remains unaffected earnings per share decreases in the same proportion as increase in stock.

Illustration 13.6 The following capital structure of a company is before a stock split

	Before Split
Common stock Re.1 par 4,00,000	4,00,000
Share premium A/c	3,00,000
Retained Earnings	40,00,000
	47,00,000

Show the capital structure after the company splits its shares from the face value of Re. 1 to Re. 0.50.

Solution

	After Split
0.50 per 8,00,000 shares	4,00,000
Share premium A/c	3,00,000
Retained earnings	40,00,000
	47,00,000

PROBLEMS FOR PRACTICE

Problem 13.1 Determine the annual dividend paid

(*a*) When the firm pays dividends on a constant payout ratio of 50%.

(*b*) If the firm pays Rs. 10 per share and increases to Rs. 15 per share when the firm's earnings exceed Rs. 12 per share for two consecutive years.

(*c*) If the firm pays dividend of Rs. 8 each year except when earnings exceed Rs. 12 per share, dividends equals to 80% beyond Rs. 12 will be paid.

Which dividend policy from the above will you prefer and why? The following information about the company is provided:

Year	EPS (Rs.)
1	4
2	6
3	10

[Contd...]

Year	EPS (Rs.)
4	8
5	14
6	16
7	14
8	20

[**Answers:** The dividend policy of (*b*) is recommended because of stability in dividends (*a*) has uncertainty and irregularity (*c*) is also not regular.]

Problem 13.2 The earnings of DIG Ltd. for the past 10 years is given below:

Year	EPS (Rs.)
2002	40
2001	38
2000	24
1999	30
1998	32
1997	24
1996	12
1995	38
1994	–4
1993	2

You are requested to determine the annual dividend paid each year if the company pays a dividend of Rs. 16 per share and increases it to Rs 20 per share when earnings exceed Rs. 28 per share for two consecutive previous years.

[B.Com (H), Delhi University, 2002]

[**Answers:** DPS 16, 16, 20, 16, 16, 16, 16, 16, 16, 16; Dividend in 1993 and 1994 paid out of free reserves of the firm.]

Problem 13.3

A company has capital stock	
Common shares Rs.10 per 2,00,000	20,00,000
Retained earnings	45,00,000
	65,00,000

Show its position after 2 : 1 stock split.

[**Answers:** Common stock 20,00,000 and retained earnings 45,00,000.]

❑❑❑

PART VI

Management of Current Assets

14 Working Capital Management

LEARNING OBJECTIVES

14.1 Concept of Working Capital
14.2 Operating Cycle
14.3 Adequate Working Capital
14.4 Financing Mix
14.5 Types of Working Capital
14.6 Working Capital Management and Policy
14.7 Current Assets Financing Policy
14.8 Optimum Working Capital Policy
14.9 Factors Determining Working Capital
14.10 Estimation of Working Capital
14.11 Estimation of Current Assets
14.12 Control of Working Capital

14.1 CONCEPT OF WORKING CAPITAL

Working capital refers to those assets which are required for the day-to-day working of the company. Such assets are cash, marketable securities, receivables and inventory. These assets can be converted into cash within one year without reducing their value and are also called 'current assets'. Management of working capital is very important because it can maximize the shareholder's wealth, if managed efficiently. If current assets are not managed according to the principles of financial management, the company can become insolvent and even bankrupt. The management of working capital requires a sufficient balance of current assets to run the business. Unit VI consists of study of the current assets where Chapter 14 provides the basic aspects of the theory and planning of working capital. Chapter 15 discusses cash management and the different techniques for an optimum cash balance. Chapter 16 is a study of the management of accounts that have to be received from the creditors of the company and Chapter 17 discusses some techniques for managing the inventory of the company.

The need for working capital is to generate good profits for a firm to enhance the wealth of the shareholders and to magnify their earnings per share. Profitability depends on the efficiency of a company to run its business and to emphasize on its sales. A company would find it difficult to immediately get cash on its sales. In order to increase sales the company will have to sell some of its good on credit. This means that cash will be received on a later date. This means that the company must have sufficient working capital to sustain itself till it receives cash. This movement of the company's activities and receiving of cash is called an ***operating cycle.*** This is the flow between cash, inventory and accounts receivable. It is the gap between the sales and actual realization. In order to service this flow of goods and funds working capital is required. ***The common definition of net working capital is the current assets minus current liabilities or that part of the current assets which are financed by long-term funds.***

Significance and Need of Adequate Working Capital

There are two important aspects of working capital—investment and financing. Working capital requirements must be estimated for a firm if efficiency is required and the business is expected to run on sound business principles. This will help in maximizing the wealth of the shareholders. Consequently the working capital requirements cannot be underestimated. The three important aspects of working capital are operating cycle, adequate working capital and financing mix.

14.2 OPERATING CYCLE

Working capital is required by a firm because there is a cycle between production and sales and receipt of cash. This movement from one activity to another until cash is received is called an 'operating cycle'. Due to this operating cycle working capital is required. The operating cycle consists of different phases. Each phase has a different length of time. The phases can be described as stated in the following order:

- **Phase I:** *Purchase of Raw Materials*

  This phase consists of the procurement of materials when it is a manufacturing company for production.

- **Phase II:** *Raw Materials used for Work in Progress for Manufacturing*

  In this phase goods are produced in a factory each company may have a different requirement. Some companies may have just one process, whereas other companies have more than one process during this time the money is locked up in materials. In service industries, there is no inventory for manufacture but it is a stage of providing services. During this funds are required for carrying on the business. Cash outflows will not match with cash inflows.

- **Phase III:** *Work in Progress Converted into Finished Products*

  During this phase the time is required to sell the products which may have an existing market or new demand will have to be created.

- **Phase IV:** *Sale of Finished Goods*

  Goods may be sold either on cash or on credit. A firm cannot exist if tries to sell all its goods on cash basis. Except for ready goods like bread or cakes which are immediately consumable, most trade in industries is carried out by extending credit to its customers. In order to enhance its sales a firm should extend some credit. If its gives credit, it must have its own funds to run a business until cash is received. This gap period creates the need for efficiency in the management of working capital.

- **Phase V:** *Accounts Receivable*

  Credit sales require the management of accounts of debtors of the company. During this gap period outflow continues while there is the waiting period for cash receipts. Even in service industries, after the services have been provided, time gap exists between providing services and receipt of bills.

- **Phase VI:** *Cash Received*

  This is the stage where cash is received by the company and there is an inflow of cash. While there is an inflow, outflow would continue though inflow may be higher than outflow. Thus synchronization of cash inflow and cash outflow is a continuous problem in organizations. They have to be matched with the techniques of working capital. The operating cycle is depicted in Fig. 14.1. It shows all the phases of the operating cycle.

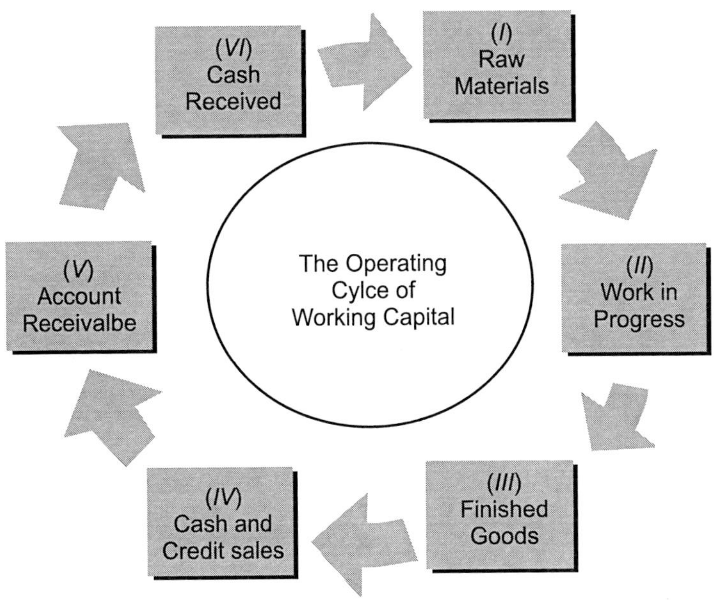

Fig.14.1 Operating Cycle

Example 14.1 The operating cycle can also be explained with the help of an example. A company provides the following information. Calculate the operating cycle in days.

Particulars	Amount (Rs.)
No. of days covered	365
Average period of credit allowed by suppliers	30 days
Average debtors outstanding	Rs. 6,00,000
Raw materials consumed	Rs. 5,00,000
Total production cost	Rs. 8,00,000
Total cost of goods sold	8,50,000
Credit sales for the year	22,00,000
Average stock maintained	
Raw materials	Rs. 3,00,000
Work in progress	4,00,000
Finished goods	3,00,000
Average creditors	1,00,000

Solution

Operating cycle of a company

(*i*) Raw material $= \dfrac{\text{Average raw material}}{\text{Raw material consumed}} \times 365$

$$= \frac{3,00,000}{5,00,000} \times 365 = 219 \text{ days}$$

(*ii*) Work in progress $= \dfrac{\text{Average work in process}}{\text{Total cost of production}} \times 365$

$$= \frac{4,00,000}{8,00,000} \times 365 = 182.5 \text{ days}$$

(*iii*) Finished goods $= \dfrac{\text{Average finished stock}}{\text{Total cost of goods sold}} \times 365$

$$= \frac{3,00,000}{8,50,000} \times 365 = 128.82 \text{ days}$$

(*iv*) Debtors $= \dfrac{\text{Average debtors}}{\text{Credit sales}} \times 365$

$= \dfrac{6,00,000}{22,00,000} \times 365 = 99.5$

(*v*) Creditors $= \dfrac{\text{Average creditors}}{\text{Total purchases}} \times 365$

$= \dfrac{1,00,000 \times 365}{3,00,000} = 121.66 \text{ days}$

> ***Note:*** Number of days is rounded off for calculating operating cycle.

∴ Operating cycle = 219 + 183 + 129 + 100 – 122 = 509 days.

Working capital is required for the firm to maintain adequate funds because the operating cycle exists. There are other important requirements for working capital such as having an adequate working capital.

14.3 ADEQUATE WORKING CAPITAL

Working capital helps in maximizing the value of money if it is used correctly. There are dangers of idle funds if there is excessive working capital and it does not earn any profit for the firm. In case funds are more than required there will be the following problems:

(*i*) In case of excessive working capital there will be a high accumulation of inventory which is not required. This would lead to losses as it is lying unused and capital is tied up.

(*ii*) Excessive working capital means that the company does not have any efficiency in its credit policy. This would lead to bad debts which would have a disadvantage in the profitability of the firm.

(*iii*) Excessive inventory leads to theft, wastage and managerial inefficiency.

When working capital is low and the requirement is more, the working is inadequate. This creates the following problems:

(*i*) The firm is unable to carry out its business and thus it results into losses as it adversely affects profits of the firm and the firm's targets cannot be accomplished.

(*ii*) If working capital is inadequate the day-to-day running of the business will become a problem, and its goodwill will be affected when it will not be able to need its obligations and liabilities in the required time.

(*iii*) Production lags will occur when there is inadequate capital to run the business. The gaps in production will create delay in finishing products and consequently sales of the firm will suffer.

(*iv*) The lack of funds is not good as the firm will not be able to use its fixed assets efficiently and as a result it will affect its profitability.

14.4 FINANCING MIX

We have analysed that the need and significance of working capital is due to an operating cycle and an adequate requirement of working capital for efficiency and profitability. Working capital significance is also due to the management of the pattern of financing of the current assets. The firm has to continuously measure and decide the source from which fund can be used for making investments. The usual sources are the long-term sources and the short-term sources. It is the efficiency with which debt and equity are combined that provides profitability of the company. Working capital financing requirements have different approaches like hedging approach, conservatives approach and aggressive approach through which decisions are taken for financing working capital requirements. Financing mix brings about an optimum working capital policy. For these reasons adequate working capital is significant in a firm.

14.5 TYPES OF WORKING CAPITAL

There are different types of working capital these are (*i*) gross and net working capital (*ii*) temporary and permanent working capital.

(*i*) Gross Working Capital

Working capital may be defined as gross working capital or net working capital. Gross and net working capital has equal significance. Gross working capital requires that a firm should have adequate investment in current assets and proper management of these assets. There should be neither excessive nor inadequate assets and it should be responsive to the changing requirements of business which depend on the level of business. Occasional changes have to be corrected so that imbalances do not occur. The gross assets should be managed with speed to see that funds do not remain idle. If there are surplus funds they should be immediately invested, and if the funds become low and the requirement is greater the financial manager should be able to get the required finance so that the commitments of the firm can be made at short notice. Thus optimum investment is desired in current assets and quick action in finding different sources for financing of short-term needs.

The gross working capital is the total of the investment of the entire current asset in a firm. Example 14.2 explains gross working capital.

Example 14.2 If a firm has the following current assets, what is the gross working capital?

Particulars	Amount (Rs.)
Raw materials	2,00,000
Finished goods	1,50,000
Cash balance	90,000
Debtors	80,000

Solution

The gross working capital of the firm is Rs. 2,00,000 + Rs. 1,50,000 + Rs. 80,000 + Rs. 90,000 = Rs. 5,20,000

(*ii*) Net Working Capital (NWC)

It is the difference between current assets and current liabilities. When current assets are higher than current liabilities NWC will be positive, but if current liabilities exceed current assets, it will result into negative NWC. The current liabilities are those which are payable in one year i.e. within the same accounting year. The liabilities are bills payable, creditors and outstanding expenses. It provides the liquidity position of a firm and also shows the requirements of working capital which should be financed by long-term sources of funds. The current assets should as a rule maintain a ratio of 2 : 1 with current liabilities. There should not be excessive liquidity but the firm should also not have negative liquidity. NWC explains the management of financing of working capital through the financing of long-term and short-term funds. To have an efficient handling of current assets the financial manager must keep a proper mix of the portion of current assets to be financed through equity capital and through borrowings.

Determination of Working Capital for the Budget Year

(A) Current Assets (CA)

(*i*) Raw materials

(*ii*) Work in progress

(*a*) Raw materials

(*b*) Labour

(*c*) Finished goods

(*iii*) Debtors

(*iv*) Cash and bank balance

Total Current Assets

(B) Current Liabilities (CL)

(*i*) Creditors

(*ii*) Wages unpaid

(*iii*) Overheads unpaid

Total Current Liabilities

Net Working Capital = (A – B)

NWC = CA – CL

Add margin for contingency = Net Working Capital required.

Example 14.3 Provides an understanding of net working capital. The following information is provided. Calculate the net working capital. Raw materials Rs. 5,00,000. Work in process consists of raw materials Rs. 2,80,000 direct labour 50,000 and overheads Rs. 8,00,000 finished goods stock is of Rs. 9,00,000 and the debtors are Rs. 20,00,000 cash at bank Rs. 1,00,000 creditors 4,00,000 wages unpaid Rs. 10,000 and 10% is for contingencies.

Solution

Particulars	Amount (Rs.)
(A) Current Assets	
(*i*) Raw materials	5,00,000
(*ii*) Work in progress	
(*a*) Raw materials	2,80,000
(*b*) Direct labour	50,000
(*c*) Overheads	8,00,000
(*iii*) Finished goods	9,00,000
(*iv*) Debtors	20,00,000
(*v*) Cash at Bank	1,00,000
Total	**46,30,000**
(B) Current Liabilities	
(*i*) Creditors	4,00,000
(*ii*) Wages unpaid	10,000
Total	**4,10,000**

$$\begin{aligned} \textbf{CA} - \textbf{CL} &= 46{,}30{,}000 - 4{,}10{,}000 = \text{Rs. } 42{,}20{,}000 \\ 10\% \text{ for contingencies} &= 42{,}20{,}000 \times 10/100 = \text{Rs. } 4{,}22{,}000 \\ \text{Net working capital} &= 42{,}20{,}000 + 4{,}22{,}000 = \text{Rs. } 46{,}42{,}000 \end{aligned}$$

Working capital is required for the firm to maintain adequate funds because the operating cycle exists. There are other important requirements for working capital. These are explained as:

(*iii*) Permanent Working Capital

The permanent working capital is the minimum level of current assets which is continuously required by a firm for carrying out its business activities. It is called 'permanent capital' because it is used continuously just like the fixed assets of a company. In low season when business activities are running at a minimum level of demand, the firm continues to maintain the assets even though there is not a requirement for production. Permanent working capital is either constant or it increases with the size of the business or its scale of operations [Fig 14.2 (*a*)].

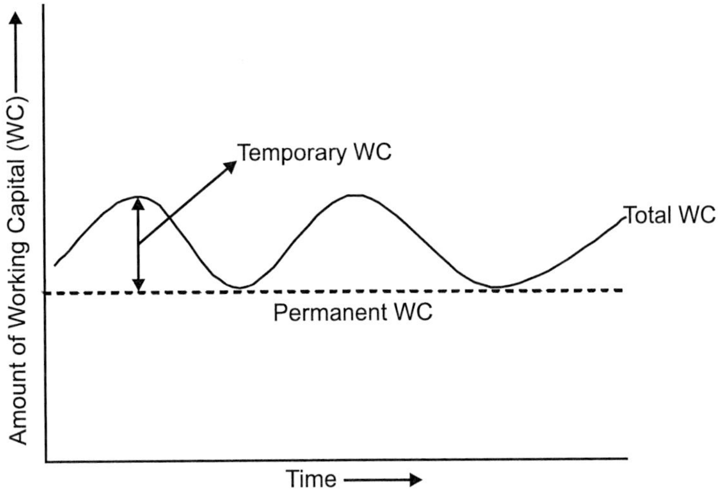

Fig. 14.2 (*a*) Permanent Working Capital

(*iv*) Temporary Working Capital

The working capital which fluctuates according to the needs and demands of the firm is called 'temporary working capital'. The extra inventory is purchased when the volume of sale increases and it can be liquidated when the volume of business falls although there is not much difference between temporary and permanent working capital, yet the difference is necessary because of the financing needs and decisions relating to funding from different sources. The permanent and variable working capital is depicted in Fig. 14.2 (*b*) the temporary/variable working capital is quick changing which means that decisions have to be taken very quickly either to raise funds or to liquidate them with the requirements of the firm.

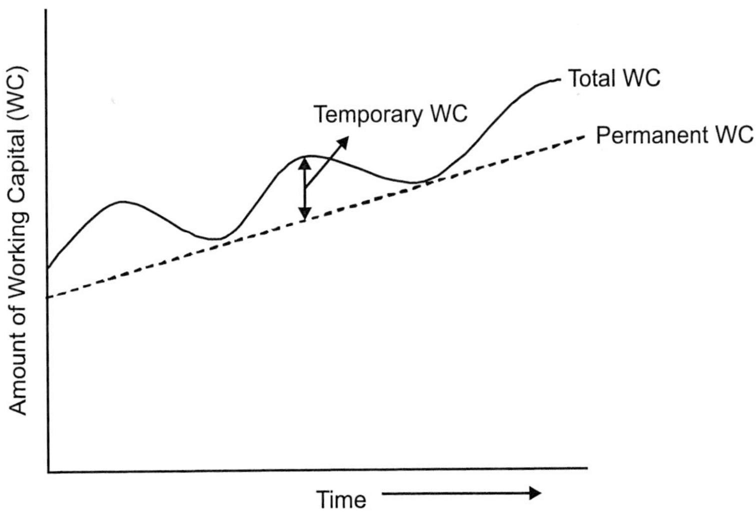

Fig. 14.2 (*b*) Temporary Working Capital

Thus the need for current assets is continuous and although an operating cycle exists, the need for working capital continues before the operating cycle, during the cycle and after the cycle when cash has already been realized by the company. The volume of capital will keep on changing. The continuous uninterrupted nature of requirement will be termed as permanent working capital and thus Fig. 14.2 (*a*) and (*b*) depict a stable rise of permanent capital whereas the temporary fluctuating variable capital is in curves moving up and down according to the liquidity requirements of the firm. The changes in the requirements of working capital may be due to a change in trend which is a long-run change or it could be seasonal changes due to sales activities. The long-term change in prices of raw materials is of a permanent nature but a seasonal change is temporary and brings about a change in temporary working capital. An increase in sales will require a higher cash balance, more inventories and the possibility of greater receivables but a fall in sales will have an effect of decline in the requirement of working capital. The need for permanent and temporary working capital would also depend upon changes in a firm's policy. A conservative policy will require a high level of investment in current asset, whereas in an aggressive policy fewer amounts of current assets will be required. Thus policy will make a great difference regarding the level of current assets.

14.6 WORKING CAPITAL POLICY AND MANAGEMENT

Working capital policy refers to two aspects:

(*i*) The effect of current assets on the profitability of a firm i.e., risk return trade off or the analysis of liquidity *vs* profitability.

(*ii*) Approaches to financing of current assets such as the use of debt and equity through hedging approach, conservative approach and aggressive approach.

(*i*) Liquidity *vs* Profitability: Risk Return Trade Off

NWC is important because it has an effect on risk and profits of a company. Profits are measured after expenses and risk is measured through NWC. When NWC is high, the firm's risk decreases and liquidity increases. It has less chances of being insolvent. When a firm increases its profitability its risk increases. Therefore, when profitability decreases risk also decreases. This is possible by changing the mix of current assets and current liabilities. While profitability risk trade off is measured there are certain basic assumptions. These are: (*a*) the NWC is being evaluated for a manufacturing company, (*ii*) that the fixed assets are more profitable than current assets, and (*iii*) the long-term funds are more expensive than short-term funds.

(*ii*) Effect of Higher Ratio of Current Assets to Total Assets

The effect of current assets on the profitability risk trade off can be depicted through the ratio of current assets to total assets. A change in ratio will reflect a change in the amount of current assets. It can increase or decrease. An increase in current assets to total assets shows fall in profitability because current assets are assumed to be less profitable than fixed assets.

When the ratio of current assets to total assets increases the effect will be the following:

(*a*) Profitability of a firm will decrease.

(*b*) The firm's risk will decrease. This will bring about a decrease in risk of the firm becoming insolvent.

(*c*) Increase in current assets with no change in current liabilities will increase net working capital, thus bringing about liquidity in the firm.

Example 14.4 From the following table calculate the effect of the ratio of current assets to total assets when the company earns 2% on current assets and 15% on fixed assets.

Balance Sheet of Co. XYZ

Liabilities	Amount (Rs.)	Assets	Amount (Rs.)
Current liabilities	35,000	Current assets	54,000
Long-term debt	50,000	Fixed assets	6,31,000
Equity capital	6,00,000		–
	6,85,000		6,85,000

(A) If a company earns 2% on current assets and 15% on fixed assets it can currently earn 2% on 54,000 and 15% on Rs. 6,31,000.

Particulars	Amount (Rs.)
(*i*) Profits on current assets	54,000
2% on current assets	1080
(*ii*) Profits on fixed assets	
15% of 6,31,000 = $631{,}000\times\left(\frac{15}{100}\right)$	94,650
	95,730
(*iii*) NWC = CA – CL = 54,000 – 35,000	19,000
(*iv*) Current to total asset ratio = $\frac{54{,}000}{6{,}85{,}000}$	0.0788

(B) Assuming that the company increases investment in current assets by investing an additional 50,000 in current assets and 50,000 less in fixed assets.

The ratio of current assets to total assets will be 54,000 + 50,000 = 1,04,000

$$\frac{\text{Current Assets}}{\text{Total Assets}} = \frac{1{,}04{,}000}{6{,}85{,}000} = 0.15 \text{ (increase in ratio)}$$

Profits on current assets

2% on current assets 1,04,000 = 2,080

Profits on fixed assets

15% on (6,31,000 – 50,000) $= 5,81,000 \times \frac{15}{100} = \underline{87,150}$

∴ Total Profit on current assets = Rs. 89,230 (87,150 + 2,080)

Profit has decreased from Rs. 95,730 to Rs. 89,230

The risk measured by amount of NWC decreases since NWC increases from 19,000 to 69,000

$$CA - CL = NWC$$

$$= 1,04,000 - 35,000 = Rs.\ 69,000$$

Decrease in the ratio of current assets to total assets will bring about:

(*i*) Increase in profitability and increase in risk.

(*ii*) A higher fixed asset will increase the profitability of the firm.

(*iii*) The current assets decrease without corresponding decrease in current liabilities so the NWC will decrease and risk will increase.

(C) Assuming that current assets decrease to Rs. 40,000 (decrease of Rs.14,000). Fixed assets increase from 6,31,000 + 14,000 = Rs. 6,45,000

The ratio of current assets to total assets will now be $\frac{40,000}{6,85,000} = 0.058$

Profits of total assets will be

Current assets	2% on 40,000	=	800
Fixed Assets	15% on 6,45,000	=	96,750
Total Profit on current assets		=	97,550

NWC will be CA – CL

40,000 – 35,000 = 5,000. (Risk increases)

The decrease in current assets to total assets leads to an increase in profitability and risk. The effect of changes in current assets of company XYZ is the following:

Particulars	Initial	Value after increase	Value after decrease
Ratio of CA to total assets	0.0788	0.15	0.058
Profits on total assets	95,730	89,230	97,550
Net working capital	19,000	69,000	5,000

(*iii*) Change in Current Liabilities on Profitability Risk Trade off

Effect of change in current liabilities can be shown by using the ratio current liabilities to total assets.

A higher ratio of current liabilities to total assets will bring:

- Increase in profitability of the firm.
- Current liabilities will increase i.e., short-term source of finance will increase and the long-term sources of finance will decrease.
- Since short-term source of finance is less expensive then long-term sources the cost will be reduced and the profitability will increased.

Increase in current liabilities with no increase in current assets will adversely affect NWC. Decrease in NWC leads to increase in risk. When current liabilities to total assets ratio increases profitability increases and also risk of the firm.

Taking the same example:

Current liabilities cost 3%

Average cost of long-term funds 10%

The cost of funds would be 3% of 35,000	1,050
Long-term funds 10% of 50,000 + 6,00,000	+65,000
	66,050

NCW = CA – CL

NCW = 54,000 – 35,000 19,000

$$\frac{\text{Current Liabilities}}{\text{Total Assets}} = \frac{35,000}{6,85,000} = 0.05$$

The Co. shifts Rs.30, 000 from long-term funds to current liabilities so that current liabilities CL will now be (35,000 + 30,000) = Rs. 65,000

CL to total assets will be $\frac{65,000}{6,85,000}$ = 0.0948 (increase)

Cost will decline

3% of 65,000 = 1,950

10% of 6,20,000 = 62,000

Cost is at a lower level = Rs. 63,950

NWC will be CA – CL

At a lower level 54,000 – 65,000 = –11,000 (Negative balance since liquidity has decreased).

(*iv*) Effect of Decrease in Ratio of Current Liabilities to Total Assets

The decrease in ratio has the opposite result of an increase.

- The firm will decrease in profitability.
- The cost will increase with the long-term use of funds.
- The risk of the firm will decrease for the current assets do not change.

Suppose current liabilities are reduced by 20,000 they will become only 15,000, then long-term funds will increase to (6,50,000 + 20,000) = 6,70,000.

The ratio of CL to total assets will be $\frac{15,000}{6,85,000} = 0.0218$

Cost will be 3% of 15,000 = 450

10% of 6,70,000 = 67,000

Cost has increased = Rs. 67,450

NWC will be CA – CL

NWC has increased = Rs. 39,000 implying liquidity.

Particulars	Initial	Value after increase	Value after decrease
Ratio of CL to total assets	0.05	0.09	0.02
Cost of financing	66,050	63,950	68,500
NWC	19,000	–11,000	39,000

(*v*) Combined Effect of Changes in Current Assets and Current Liabilities

A decrease in cost increases profitability. A firm should make changes in current assets and liabilities in such a way that it can be used for the advantage of the firm. Instead of finding out changes of current assets or current liabilities separately the combined changes should be analysed. The combined effect of changes in current assets and current liabilities would be to increase overall profitability and risk and decrease in NWC.

Combined effect of changes in current assets and liabilities of company X on profit and NWC.

(1) Particulars	(2) Change in profits	(3) Change in NWC
Decrease in current assets to total assets	+ 1,820	−14,000
Increase in current liabilities to total assets	+ 2,100	– 30,000
The net effect of the two changes taken together	3,920	– 44,000
Profits have increased by 3,920 and NWC has decreased by Rs. 44,000.		

14.7 CURRENT ASSETS FINANCING POLICY

The current assets policy has to be prepared by the profitability and risk trade off. We have discussed the effects of the increase or decrease of current assets and current liabilities to total assets and also the combination of current assets and liabilities and their effect on profitability. Besides profitability risk trade off the financing mix of current assets is important to attain the optimum level of current assets in a firm. Therefore, the costs of maintaining a level of assets must be analysed. The two costs are useful in finding out the costs of liquidity and the costs of illiquidity. If a firm has a high level of liquidity, there is idle cash increasing the cost of liquidity. The cost of illiquidity is when the firm is holding a low level of current assets. As already discussed the firm will find it difficult to honour its commitments and there will also be a loss in sales. The firm has to balance its profitability with its solvency by minimizing its total costs. Figure 14.3 illustrates that when the cost of liquidity increases the cost of illiquidity decreases. The optimum level is attained when the cost of liquidity and illiquidity are minimized. At the minimum cost the optimum level of current assets will be attained.

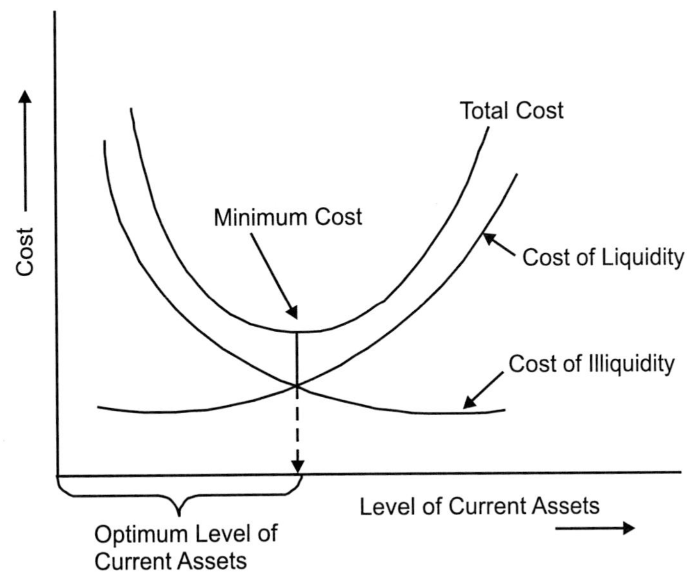

Fig.14.3 Optimum Level of Current Assets

When the optimum level of current assets is determined the firm has to decide how these current assets should be financed. What is the mix of long-term capital and short-term funds to support the current assets? We have discussed that there are two types of requirements, permanent and temporary. To simplify assets have been divided into fixed assets and current assets. Several strategies are used for policy and management of current assets. The difference in financing mix is determined through the hedging/ matching approach, conservative approach and trade off between the two. The permanent and temporary components of working capital will be financed according to the different sources of capital which are termed as long-term sources, short-term sources and sources from normal business operations. These can be described as:

(*a*) **Long-term sources:** These are share capital, retained earnings, long-term borrowings and debentures.

(*b*) **Short-term sources:** This provides funds for short-term periods of time. These are commercial papers, bank credit and public deposits.

(*c*) **Business operation sources:** This source provides funds from the normal course of business such as credit received for goods or outstanding overheads. These funds have very low cost.

The permanent and temporary portions of working capital have to be financed either by equity or by debt. The financing mix is decided according to the different approaches which are discussed here. Long-term borrowing internally generate resources, like internal retained earnings, it has to be decided as to what proportion of current assets should be financed by current liabilities and how much by long-term funds? A firm has to estimate the requirements of its current assets through the level of sales that it does. It can follow a moderate, conservative or aggressive current assets policy. If a conservative policy is adopted, then for every increase in sales there will be an increase in current assets having a safety net for current assets. This policy will reduce the risk of non-payment of its liabilities.

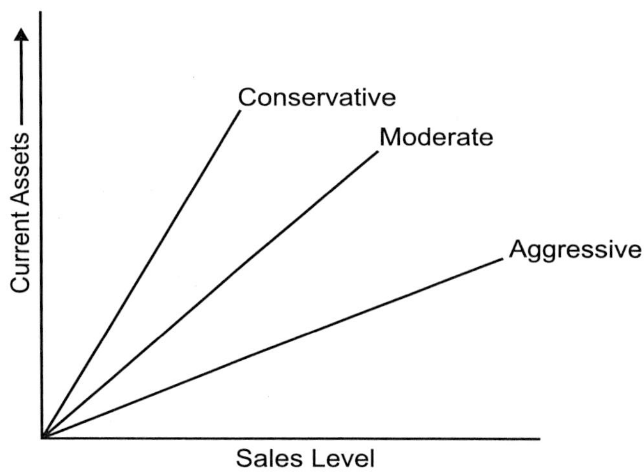

Fig. 14.4 Different Types of Working Capital Financing Policies

A conservative approach does not take risk. If an aggressive policy is followed then an increase in sales will not have a proportionate increase of current assets. Such a firm will have high risk and low liquidity. A moderate policy would be a trade off between liquidity and illiquidity to maximize its profitability. These three policies as depicted in Fig. 14.4 will be discussed through the hedging approach, aggressive approach and the risk-return trade off between the two approaches.

Hedging/ Matching/ Moderate Approach

The hedging approach is a strategy for matching maturities of debt with maturities of financial needs: The maturity of the sources of funds is matched and it is called the matching approach/moderate approach. The hedging approach states that the long-term funds should be used for financing the permanent working capital and the temporary requirements should be financed by short-term funds or current liabilities. This approach divides the permanent and seasonal requirements from different sources. The long-term financing should be used when fixed asset is required and when the business is at its peak level. When the business is less than the peak level the surplus funds can be invested in marketable securities. With this approach as depicted in the following example short-term requirements would be equal to short-term financing through current liabilities.

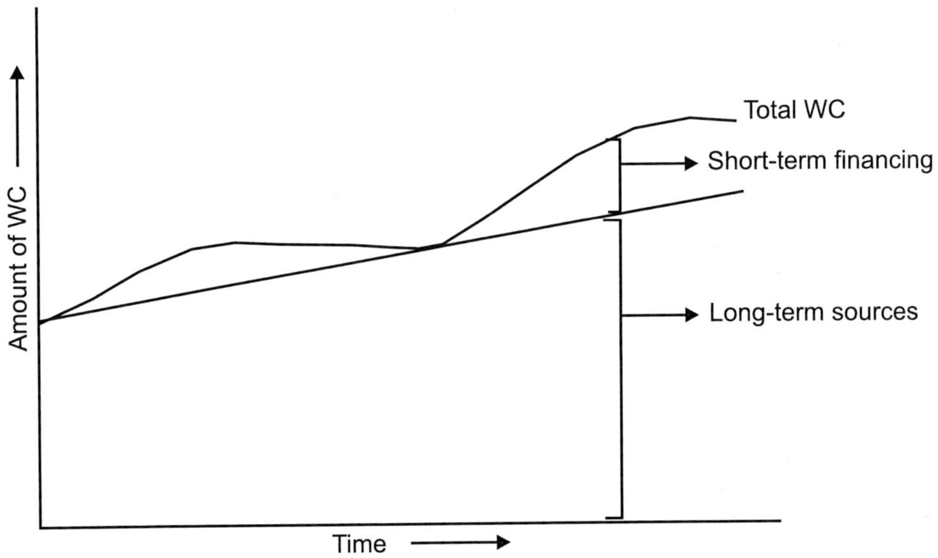

Fig. 14.5 The Hedging Approach to Working Capital Financing

The question arises as to how will current assets be financed?

Since, the timeframe work of providing finance should as a rule be according to the working life of the asset, fixed assets should be financed by long-term sources. Fig. 14.5 shows that long-term funds are for permanent requirements. Short-term funds are for seasonal variation current liabilities.

This is also explained through Example 14.5. The table on the hedging approach shows that the permanent working capital required is Rs. 10,00,000 and seasonal variations occur according to the business conducted. As seen June has the highest requirement of working capital and April has the lowest requirement of seasonal funds. The example below shows the estimated total funds acquired out of which there are permanent requirement and seasonal requirements.

Example 14.5 Hedging Approach

Month	Estimated funds required	Permanent funds (Rs.)	Seasonal requirement of funds
January	12,00,500	10,00,000	2,00,500
February	12,00,000	10,00,000	2,00,000
March	11,50,000	10,00,000	1,50,000
April	11,00,000	10,00,000	1,00,000
May	11,50,000	10,00,000	1,50,000
June	12,50,000	10,00,000	2,50,000
		60,00,000	10,50,500

Conservative Approach

In conservative approach the total funds should be from long-term sources and only in emergencies from short-term funds. Figure 14.6 (*a*) and (*b*) depicts the conservative approach. As has been explained above the conservative approach uses mainly long-term funds for its working capital requirements. The Fig. 14.6 (*a*) shows that both the short-term and long-term requirements are being financed through long-term sources and there are idle funds in many months of the year. Figure 14.6 (*b*) depicts that during the time when seasonal requirements are not there the idle long-term funds can be used for purchasing marketable securities to earn some amount of funds. During the peak season some short-term funds can be used for financing emergency conditions.

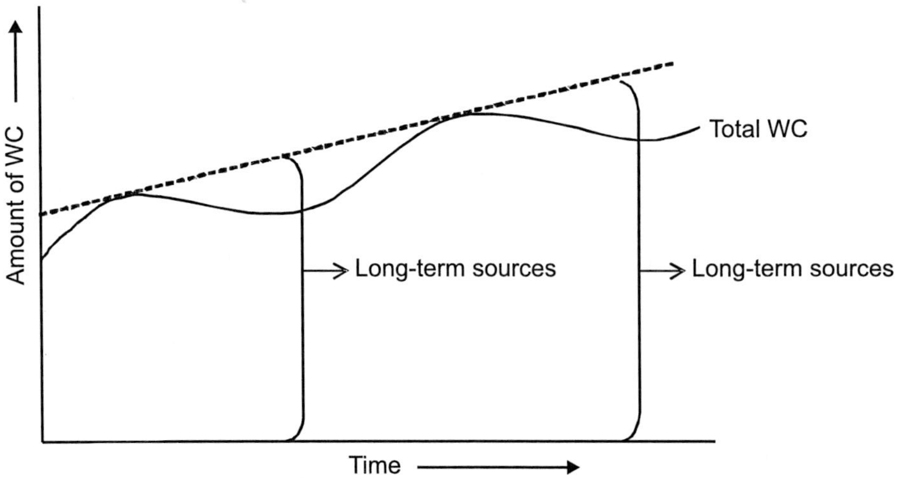

Fig. 14.6 (*a*) Financing of Working Capital (Conservative Approach)

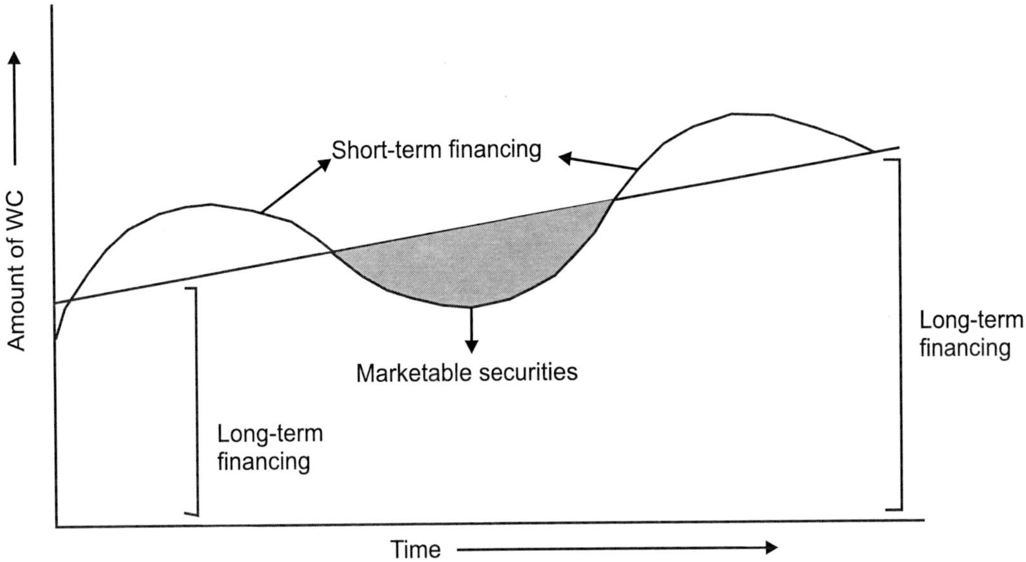

Fig. 14.6 (*b*) Short-term and Long-term Working Capital (Conservative Approach)

A comparison between hedging and conservative approach is made through ***cost consideration and risk*** taking the above example (Example 14.5).

Comparison of Hedging Approach and Conservative Approach

(*i*) On the Basis of Cost

(*a*) *Hedging Approach*

In hedging approach the cost of financing depends on the cost of long-term and short-term funds and the interest rate. As in the above example, cost of financing short-term 3% and cost of financing long-term is 10%

- The cost of long-term funds = Average annual requirement × Annual interest rate.

  = 10,00,000 × 10% = Rs 1,00,000
- The cost of short-term funds = Average annual short-term loans × Interest rate.
- Average annual short-term loans = Total monthly seasonal requirements divided by the number of months.
- Average annual short-term loans $= \dfrac{\text{Total monthly seasonal requirement}}{\text{No. of months}}$

$$= \frac{10,50,500}{6} = 175083.33$$

- Short-term cost $= \dfrac{10,50,500}{6} \times \left(\dfrac{3}{100}\right) = 5252.50$
- Total cost under hedging approach = 1,00,000 + 5,252.50 = Rs. 105252.50

(*b*) *Conservative Approach*

In conservative approach in the above example 14.5 the total requirements including the highest requirement of Rs. 12,50,000 in the month of June will be financed by long-term resources. The net working capital is highest in June Rs. 12,50,000 – Rs. 10,00,000 = Rs. 2,50,000

Any long-term financing in excess of Rs.10,00,000 in permanent financing represents the net working capital.

Under conservative approach the cost of long-term funds = Annual Average Loan × Long-term rate of interest =10% =12,50,000 × 10%

Conservative plan approach $12,50,500 \times \dfrac{10}{100}$ = Rs. 1,25,050

This shows that the conservative approach has a higher cost than the hedging approach. The reason is that the funds in the conservative approach are not utilized in some months but interest has to be paid continuously for all the months according to long-term rates of interest.

(*ii*) On the Basis of Risk

The Hedging approach is considered to be of a higher risk compare to the conservative approach. In hedging approach current assets is just equal to current liabilities because long-term funds are not used for short-term seasonal requirements. Moreover, this plan is useful then there is full utilization of short-term funds. This may not be possible always. A conservative approach is called low profit high cost low risk high NWC. It uses long-term funds for all its uses and restricts short-term funds. This has no risk because it is fully covered by funds.

(*iii*) Trade Off between Hedging and Conservative Approach

The hedging approach is considered to be of high profits but also high risk and conservative approach brings about low risk and low profits in its financing pattern. The trade off between risk and return has a financing mix between the two approaches. The trade off between risk and return will be different in each firm and will depend on the financing mix according to the cost and risk perception of the financial managers. A common and simple example to illustrate the trade off method is explained in Example 14.6 in which average minimum and maximum requirements of funds is given for every month. This level may be financed through long-term sources and for any additional financial need short-term funds may be used.

Example 14.6 Trade off between hedging and conservative approach

Month	Total Funds (Rs.)	Permanent Requirement (Rs.)	Short-term (Rs.)
1	12,00,500	11,50,250	50,250
2	12,00,000	11,50,250	49,750
3	11,50,000	11,50,250	0
4	11,00,000	11,50,250	0
5	11,50,000	11,50,250	0
6	12,50,000	11,50,250	99,750
			1,99,750

Cost of short funds = Average annual short-term funds × interest rate loan

Minimum funds required = 11,00,000

Maximum funds required = 12,00,500

$$\text{Average} = \frac{12,00,500 + 11,00,000}{2} = \frac{23,00,500}{2} = \text{Rs. } 11,50,250$$

The firm should use Rs. 11,50,250 as long-term funds and whenever short funds are required in excess of this amount, additional funds should be raised through current liabilities. Example 14.6 shows that funds are not required for short-term in months 3, 4 and 5 because the long-term funds exceed the requirement of working capital. For the 3 months in excess of the total requirements the firm will use short-term funds.

Cost of short-term funds = Average annual short-term funds required × Rate of short-term interest

$= 50,250 + 49,750 + 99,750 = 1,99,750/6 \times 0.03 = \text{Rs. } 998.75$

Cost of long-term funds = Long-term funds required × rate of interest.

$= 11,50,250 \times 0.10 = \text{Rs. } 1,15,025$

Total cost $= 1,15,025 + 998.75 = \text{Rs. } 116023.75$

The company should use Rs. 11,50,250 in the form of long-term funds and raise additional funds through current liabilities. No funds are required as short-term funds for month 3, 4, 5 as long-term funds exceed the requirements of total funds. The remaining 3 months the company will have to use short-term funds to totaling Rs. 1,99,750.

Comparison of Trade off plan with Hedging and Conservative Approach

Financial Plan	Max NWC*	Degree of Risk	Total Cost of Finance	Levels of Profits
Hedging	––	Highest	1,05,252.50	Highest
Trade off	50200	Intermediate	1,16,023.74	Intermediate
Conservative	2,00,500	Lowest	1,25,050	Lowest

* Minimum would be 0.

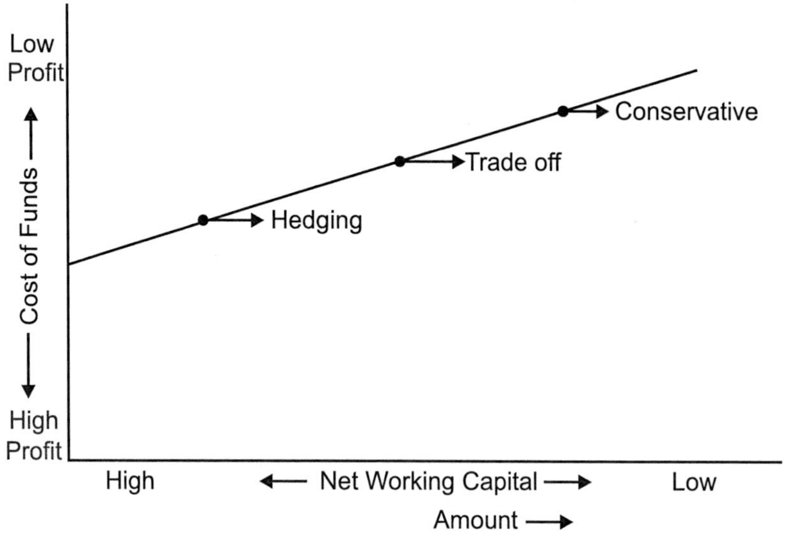

Fig.14.7 The Risk-Return Trade-off Approach

Figure 14.7 shows that the trade off approach is between the hedging approach and the conservative approach. In terms off risk, it is higher than in conservative approach but less than that of hedging approach. In terms of profitability, the conservative approach is the lowest.

Aggressive Approach

In an aggressive approach the firm finances itself with a higher amount in terms of short-term financing. Some times the permanent working capital is also financed by the short-term resources. The aggressive approach is high risk and low liquidity. This approach has the risk of insolvency. Figure 14.8 depicts the aggressive approach.

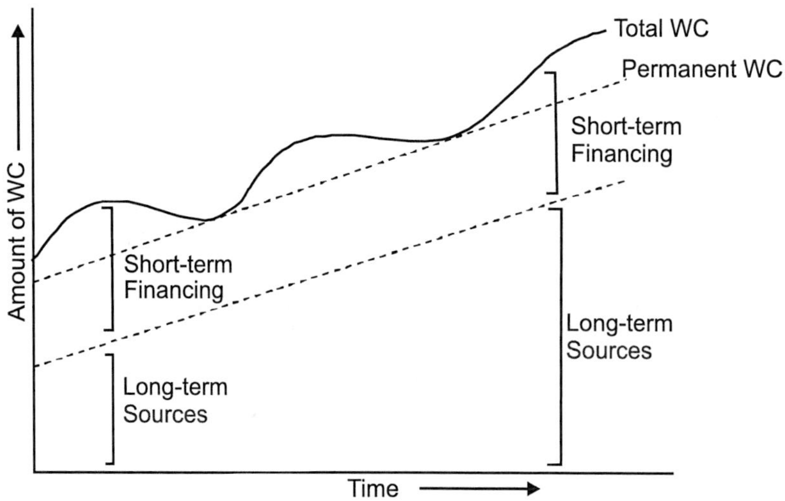

Fig. 14.8 Aggressive Approach to Financing of Working Capital

The short-term funds are considered to be of higher risk than long-term funds but it is important to have a trade off between risk and profitability and hence the financial manager should see that there is flexibility in the financial mix of short-term and long-term funds. A firm must calculate the cost of financing from both the long-term and short-term funds. It is necessary to adopt a trade off approach to achieve an optimum working capital policy.

14.8 OPTIMUM WORKING CAPITAL POLICY

An optimum working capital policy can be obtained by adopting a method whereby risk is reduced and return is high. The firm should be able to maximize its value. Working capital will increase the value of the firm but it should be increased only when it is beneficial to the firm. Whenever the benefits exceed the costs it would an optimum level of working capital for the firm. A high increase in working capital will decrease the risk of the firm but it will also have the effect of reducing its profitability. A workable solution should be considered by considering the following factors:

(*i*) **Uncertainty:** A stable firm can have low investment in working capital because its requirements of working capital are fairly predictable but a high risk firm with continuous changes and high seasonal variations should have greater investment in working capital.

(*ii*) **Systematic Risk:** A firm which remains stable in optimistic and recession conditions has less risk in terms of demand and supply and other uncertainties in the economic conditions and a minimum working capital will not have any effect on the working pattern of the firm. However companies facing changes with swings in the market forces will face insolvency, unless they have a proper reserve for their working capital requirements.

(*iii*) **Financing Sources:** A firm which is able to raise external financing at short notice without any difficulty can keep low reserves for its working capital but those firms who do not have the credibility or means for immediately raising short-term funds should maintain working capital for its liquidity.

Working capital requirements should be assessed on the basis these parameters. A moderate policy would help in preserving the conditions of liquidity and profitability. This will bring about maximum value for the firm.

14.9 FACTORS DETERMINING WORKING CAPITAL

The requirements of working capital are determined by many factors which affect a firm. These factors are different depending on the nature of business, business cycle, seasonal fluctuations, credit policy, availability of raw materials and level of profit. These factors are being discussed as:

(*i*) Nature of Business

The requirement of working capital is based on the kind of business activity being performed. A business which is based on cash sales or a business which performs services will require minimum working capital. Such businesses do not require continuous investment in inventories as they are cash rich companies. Many companies providing software services do not have any debt at all in their business operations. A truly contrasting picture arises in industries which are manufacturing different kinds of products. According to the products the working capital requirement differs. The manufacturing firms which have a long operating cycle are dependent on a large requirement of working capital.

(*ii*) Business Cycle

Working capital requirement depends on the business fluctuations or conditions in an economy. Business conditions in an upward level of economic activity will increase business activities. This shows that an economy is in a boom condition. In the upward swing in an economy it is easy to make higher profits but the need for working capital increases. The business activities will expand and the requirement of cash as well as inventories will have to be increased. It is just the opposite when an economy is in recession. In such conditions, there will be a fall in business activities and subsequently the requirement of working capital will be reduced.

(*iii*) Seasonal Fluctuations

The working capital requirements have to suit the working conditions of a firm. Those firms which have wide fluctuations during different seasons will require heavy amounts of working capital in those seasons when the demand of the product is high, more inventories will be required. In the case of wool industries in India, there is a seasonal requirement of woolen products is winter only for approximately 3 months is a year. During this time the company can make a high profit if it has an optimum working capital. Consequently the requirements of working capital in terms of inventories and cash will be higher in this season rather than in the months that follow. Other companies which have business throughout the year will have to maintain an even amount of working capital throughout the year.

(*iv*) Credit Policy

The credit policy of a company relates to purchases and sales of the company. The policy relating to credit terms provided by the firm to its customers as well as the purchasers/suppliers of its firm affect its working capital requirements. In a liberal credit policy, debtors will be high and the working capital to be maintained will also be required in a greater volume because receivables will be for a longer period of time. If the firm has a liberal credit policy from its suppliers, the requirement of working capital will be less as there will be no pressure for making payments quickly. Some firms are able to get materials on credit but they sell their own products in cash. Such firms will require a low level of working capital. It will be just the opposite if the firm was to buy on cash and sell its products on credit. In this case the volume of working capital required by it would be much higher.

(*v*) Availability of Raw Materials

The supply of raw materials has an effect on the working capital of a firm. The time period of receiving inventory decides the level of working capital with the firm. If the supply of raw materials is smooth and without any delay, the level of inventories maintain by a firm will be low, but when the time period of receiving raw materials has uncertainties and long then the inventory to be maintained will be high. The firm will have to keep a continuous storage of raw materials because it is unsure of supply of materials. In order to maintain its business with customers it will procure materials in stock for longer periods thus increasing his costs in working capital.

(*vi*) Level of Profit

The profits of a firm depend on its quality and nature of product. If a product is a monopoly item then its sales will be high and it is expected that it would have a good profit margin. If a firm is able to make a good policy it will be able to meet its expenses and cover its costs, thus its requirements of working capital will be low. Firms with low levels of profits will require a higher amount of cash for their business operations. The level of profit in products which are not monopolistic but competitive, and have a good sales volume will have to calculate the requirements of their working capital according to their cash cycles. Despite the level of profit it is important to see that the firm is able to meet its cash requirements for marketability and sale of the product. Hence working capital will depend on sales, receivable, credit and debit policies besides a high or low level of profit.

To conclude, working capital requirements depend on many factors but it is important to manage the working capital efficiently. The firm should have a good policy to continuously review its costs. A trade off between risk and profitability is desired.

14.10 ESTIMATION OF WORKING CAPITAL

A firm has to make an estimate for its working capital requirements. It has to take a decision as to the nature of working capital required. When the firm is able to decide on the quantity of permanent and temporary working capital requirements it will be clear as to the volume of funds which must be financed from long-term sources and which can be obtained from short-term sources. The three approaches through which working capital can be estimated are: (*i*) working capital as a percentage of net sales, (*ii*) working capital as a percentage of total assets or fixed assets, and (*iii*) working capital based on operating cycle.

(*i*) Working Capital as a Percentage of Net Sales

In this method the working capital is based on a sales forecast. The assumption is that higher the sales level, the greater will be the requirement of working capital in a firm.

The net working capital would be the difference between the total current assets estimated as a percentage of net sales and current liabilities as the percentage of net sales. Example 14.7 depicts the calculation of net working capital as a percentage of sales.

Example 14.7 A company provides the following information for the last two years. Calculate the working capital for next year on the estimated sales which will increase by 20% over the current year.

Particulars	2005–2006 (Rs.)	2006–2007 (Rs.)
Net sales	15,00,000	17,25,000
Total current assets	3,00,000	3,50,000
Total current liabilities	60,000	70,000
Current assets as % of sales	20%	20.29%
Current liabilities as % of sales	4%	4.06%

Solution

Step 1: Find the average for both the years of current assets as a percentage of sales

= 20% + 20.29% = 40.29/2 = 20.145%

Step 2: Find the average of current liabilities for the two years as a percentage of sales

= 4% + 4.06% = 8.06/2 = 4.03%

Step 3: Find the net working capital as percentage of sales

= 20.145 – 4.03% = 16.115% (NWC)

Step 4: If the firm expects an increase of sales at 20% next year its working capital requirements will be estimated as follows:

Expected sales Rs. 17,25,000 + 20% = Rs. 20,70,000

Net working capital as % of sales = 16.115%

= 20,70,000 × 16.115% = Rs. 333580.5

The firm is expected to have a gross working capital of 17,25,000 × 20.145%

= Rs. 347501.25

The financing by current liabilities is 4.06% of 17,25,000 = Rs. 70,035

> ***Note:*** If there is a continuous increase or decrease in current assets or liabilities, weighted average should be taken instead of simple arithmetic average of current assets and current liabilities as % of sales.

(*ii*) Working Capital as Percentage of Total Assets or Fixed Assets

The approach to finding out ***the working capital as percentage of total assets*** is reflected from the fact that the requirement of working capital is based on both fixed assets and current assets of the firm. The total current assets would represent the gross working capital and the net working capital would be associated with current assets—current liabilities. A firm which maintains 15% of its total assets in the form of current assets would have a total of Rs. 9,00,000 in current assets if its total assets comprise Rs. 60,00,000.

(*iii*) Working Capital can also be Estimated as a Percentage of Fixed Assets

Fixed assets of a firm are for long-term purposes and are planned through capital budgeting. It is expected that the working capital is develop after the fixed assets have been planned. In this sense working capital becomes part of the decision taken in capital budgeting for an optimum performance of the firm.

Both the decisions of calculating working capital as percentage of total assets or fixed assets is simple in procedure but difficult in calculation because the changes in working capital has to be made in proportion to the fixed assets. The approach becomes difficult in calculation because the exact changes in current assets with respect to the exact changes in fixed assets cannot be determined. The operating cycle approach is the most practical approach in calculation of working capital. It is explained next.

(*iv*) Working Capital based on Operating Cycle

The operating cycle makes a detailed examination of all the components of working capital. The current assets comprise raw materials, work in progress finished goods, receivables and cash and bank balance. The current liabilities consist of all the creditors for expenses and purchases. The current assets – current liabilities = net working capital. Each of these components and how they should be calculated is explained in detail. They have also been explained through the concepts of operating cycle and gross and net working capital.

According to the operating cycle method the two components of current assets and current liabilities must be calculated to find out the working capital requirements of a firm. This method states that to establish the working capital of a firm, the holding period of an inventory, the credit payment and the credit collection period are important. Moreover, it is expected that the production and the sales of a firm is usually carried out evenly and the cost incurred also accrues evenly according to the budgeted activity of a firm. In this estimation non-cash items like depreciation are excluded and the working capital requirements are based on costs and not on sales. Work in process is usually taken on 50% completion but it must be noted that sometimes it is based on 100% raw material but 50% labour and 50% overheads. Production is calculated for 1 year which is 365 days but for convenience it is some times taken for a period of 360 days. Moreover it can also be calculated in terms of weeks or months. The question usually states these aspects.

14.11 ESTIMATION OF CURRENT ASSETS

(*i*) Raw Materials

The raw material is calculated on the basis of the number of units that will be produced in a year, it is multiplied by the cost per unit and the holding period in weeks/months/days and it is divided by either 365/360 days or 52 weeks or 12 months as the case may be. This is represented in equation 14.1. Raw materials are required for manufacturing a product and it depends on the rate of consumption, time for procurement and contingencies.

$$\frac{\underset{\text{Per Units}}{\text{Production}} \times \underset{\text{Per Units}}{\text{Cost of Raw Material}} \times \underset{\text{Months / Weeks / Days}}{\text{Average Inventory Holding Periods}}}{\text{12 Months / 365 Days / 52 weeks}} \quad \text{.................. 14.1}$$

(*ii*) Work in Progress/Process

Work in progress/process can be in different stages of completion. Although completion stage may differ, for example it could be 40% or 50% or 80% completion, yet for convenience; it is usually assumed at 50%. Material is assumed at 100% but sometimes it can be taken at 50% also, but labour and overheads are usually taken at 50% of the expenses unless specified. Equation 14.2 shows the method of calculation.

$$\frac{\underset{\text{(In Units)}}{\text{Production}} \times \underset{\text{(Cost Per Unit)}}{\text{Work in progress}} \times \underset{\text{(Weeks / Months / Days)}}{\text{Average Time Span of Work in Progress}}}{\text{12 Months / 365 Days / 52 weeks}} \quad \text{.................. 14.2}$$

(*iii*) Finished Goods

When goods are manufactured, it is not possible to sell them immediately. The cost of such goods should be calculated as they have been manufactured and costs have been incurred on them. The working capital of finished goods is calculated by their unit cost, manufacturing cost, cost of carriage inwards and the locked up period or holding cost. This is depicted in Equation 14.3.

$$\frac{\text{Cost in Units} \times \underset{\text{(Excluding Depreciator)}}{\text{Manufacturing Cost per Unit}} \times \underset{\text{(Weeks/ Months / Days)}}{\text{Finished Good Holding Periods}}}{\text{12 Months / 365 Days / 52 weeks}} \quad \text{.......... 14.3}$$

(*iv*) Debtors

The working capital which is locked in receivable are due to credit sells. They are based on sales but working capital is blocked in terms of the cost incurred on them. To support this if the cost on administration and selling is provided, they must be included in the cost of debtor to estimate the working capital. This is illustrated in Equation 14.4.

$$\frac{\underset{\text{(In Units)}}{\text{Credit Sales}} \times \underset{\text{(Excluding Depreciation)}}{\text{Cost of Sales}} \times \underset{\text{(Month/ Days / week)}}{\text{Average Debt Collection}}}{\text{12 Months / 365 Days / 52 weeks}} \quad \text{................ 14.4}$$

(*v*) Cash and Bank Balance

Cash and bank balance is also required by firms for their transactions. The daily expenses and cash purchases involve the requirement of liquidity in a firm since cash balance is the least productive of all the current assets there should be a minimum balance of cash.

(vi) Current Liabilities

The current liabilities to be evaluated are the creditors of purchases. It also consists of unpaid wages and expenses in production, trade creditors wages, and overheads.

(vii) Trade Creditors

When a firm sells goods on credit, it also purchases certain materials on credit. The credit period may vary according to the terms and conditions. This is calculated in Equation 14.5. It considers the yearly production, the raw materials required and the credit period allowed by the creditors.

$$\frac{\underset{\text{(In Units)}}{\text{Yearly Production}} \times \underset{\text{(Per Unit)}}{\text{Raw Materials Required}} \times \underset{\text{Weeks/Months/Days}}{\text{Credit Periods Allowed by Creditors}}}{\text{12 Months / 365 Days / 52 weeks}} \quad \text{... 14.5}$$

(viii) Direct Wages

Direct wages and overheads which are used in the process of work are sometimes paid after a time lag like 10 days or two weeks. These are temporary working capital for the firm and must be eventually paid. Equation 14.6 and 14.7 shows that they would be calculated by taking into consideration the production in units multiplied by labour/ overheads cost per units into the time lag in making the payments.

$$\frac{\text{Production in Unit} \times \text{Direct Labour Cost Per Unit} \times \text{Time Lag in Payment of Wages}}{\text{Months / Days / Weeks}} \quad \text{........ 14. 6}$$

(ix) Overheads

$$\frac{\underset{\text{(In Units)}}{\text{Budget Yearly Production}} \times \underset{\text{(Cost Per Unit)}}{\text{Overhead}} \times \underset{\text{(Weeks/ Months / Days)}}{\text{Time Lag in Payment}}}{\text{12 Months / 365 Days / 52 weeks}} \quad \text{........... 14.7}$$

> ***Note:***
>
> ***(a)*** Depreciation is a non-cash item; it will be ignored in calculations. Cost of production-not to include selling and administration expenses.
>
> ***(b)*** Provision for contingencies is added to net working capital
>
> ***(c)*** Since taxes can be paid out of profits they are ignored. Profit is ignored in calculating NWC. Alternatively advanced payments of taxes require additional Working capital and profits are sources of working capital.

Table showing estimation of working capital

(A) Current Assets

Cash and bank balance

Raw materials

Work in process

Finished goods

Debtors

Total current assets

(B) Current liabilities

Creditors

Wages outstanding

Overheads outstanding

Total current liabilities

(C) Net working capital

Current assets – current liabilities

Add contingencies

Net working capital

14.12 CONTROL OF WORKING CAPITAL

This chapter discusses the principles of working capital and some aspects of its policies and management. To conclude this discussion, it is important to provide a synoptic view of control in working capital.

The policies made by the financial manager should be constantly reviewed and controlled as working capital is required for running a business and managing all the transactions in such a way that it maximizes the value of the shareholder's wealth. Since policies are already prepared, there should be a methodology adopted for control in working capital.

Since operating cycle determines the requirements of working capital it should be reviewed so that the number of days in the operating cycle should be managed carefully. As far as possible, operating cycle should be controlled by a careful check of raw materials, work in process, finished goods and receivables. The length of time taken to cover each of these operations should be kept according to the requirements and this length of time should not be exceeded. A good receivables policy should be prepared whereby the firm receives its payments as early as possible.

The working capital should have a trade off between ***risk and profitability***. This is possible through a continuous control of working capital. While a conservative policy brings about liquidity it reduces profits. Hedging policy is highly risky and so depending on the requirements of the firm the trade off policy may be applied. Liquidity can also be maintained by effectively using the inventories of the firm and applying a good receivables policy. Thus control should be maintained to ensure that sufficient liquidity is there without losing on its profitability.

Finally the firm should continuously keep a control on its current assets to current liabilities ratio, its liquidity ratio and its current assets to total assets and total sales ratios to indicate the liquidity position of the firm. This will bring about efficiency in a firm. Chapter 15 discusses cash management and Chapter 16 brings about some aspects of receivables management. Chapter 17 closes the discussion with inventory management techniques. These four techniques, planning and management of working capital, cash management, receivable management and inventory management help in creating an efficient day-to-day running of a business.

POINTS TO REMEMBER

- There are two concepts of working capital. These are gross working capital and net working capital. The gross working capital consists of the total of current assets. Net working capital denotes current assets minus current liabilities.
- Net working capital is important because the cash receipts and the cash payments are not synchronized and the cash inflows do not match the cash outflows creating an imbalance in the liquidity position of the firm.
- The net working capital has a bearing on the liquidity, risk and profitability of a firm.
- A need for net working capital arises because of the presence of the operating cycle which operates between purchases of materials, work in process, finished goods, sale of goods on credit and the waiting period for receivables and then the arrival of cash.
- A trade off between risk and profitability is important because if liquidity is high, risk will be low but also the profitability. Similarly when liquidity is low there is the risk of insolvency but also the advantage of a high gain. A balance is desired between the two extreme positions.
- The financing mix can be determined by the hedging approach, conservative approach, aggressive approach and the trade off between hedging and conservative approach.
- There are many factors determining working capital. These are the nature of business, business cycles in an economy, the profit level of a firm and the production requirements of the firm.
- Working capital must have a proper policy and the policy should be reviewed and controlled for efficiency at work.
- The working capital can be computed through different methods, as a percentage of sales, as a percentage of total assets and according to the operating cycle. The most practical method is an analysis of all the processes of work through the operating cycle method.

OBJECTIVE TYPE QUESTIONS

State whether the following statement is true (T) or false (F):

1. A production cycle estimates the level of the working capital required by a firm.
2. The longer the production cycle, the lower would be the requirement of working capital.
3. Hedging approach is more risky than the conservative approach.
4. Depreciation is ignored while calculating net working capital.
5. It is important to have a risk return trade off to have efficient working capital management.
6. The need for working capital arises due to the presence of an operating cycle.
7. Working capital management prepares a policy for long-term liquidity if a firm.
8. Conservative policy stress on a good short-term financing policy.
9. In working capital management there is permanent working capital and temporary working capital.
10. The net working capital is the ratio between fixed assets to total assets.

[**Answers:** 1. (T), 2. (F), 3. (T), 4. (T), 5. (T), 6. (T), 7. (F), 8. (F), 9. (T), 10. (F)]

THEORETICAL QUESTIONS

1. Discuss the factors which have a bearing on the requirements of working capital.
2. What is an operating cycle? How is it important for the management of working capital?
3. Discuss the different approaches to working capital management. What is the trade off between hedging and conservative approach?
4. Why is depreciation ignored while estimating working capital requirements?
5. Explain the risk return trade off in working capital management.
6. 'An appropriate mix and level of current assets and current liabilities brings about efficiency in working capital decisions.' Comment.
7. What is the importance of working capital management? How should it be controlled?
8. Distinguish between (*i*) gross and net working capital, (*ii*) hedging and conservative approach and (*iii*) permanent and temporary working capital.
9. What are the important characteristics of current assets?
10. How do working capital management policies affect a firm's risk and profitability?

ILLUSTRATIVE PROBLEMS

Illustration 14.1 A Company provides the following data:

Particulars	Amount (Rs.)
Cost per unit raw materials	55.00
*Direct labour	19.50
Overheads	39.00
Total cost per unit	113.50
Profit	20.00
Selling price	133.50

The following additional information is available.

Average raw material in stock is 1 month; Average materials, wages and overhead process ½ a month and 50% completion of work in process. (50% materials wages overheads to be taken for work in progress) Credit allowed to debtors 2 months. Time lag in payment of wages is 10 days. Overheads time lag is one month. 1/4th of sales are on cash basis. Cash balance is expected to be Rs. 1,50,000.

You are required to prepare a statement showing working capital required to finance a level of activity of 70,000 units of output. You may assume that production is carried on evenly throughout the year finished goods holding period is 1 month. For convenience assume 360 for one year.

Gross working capital refers to investment in current assets.

Working Capital Requirements

A. Investment in Inventory:

(*i*) Raw materials inventory

$$= \frac{70,000 \times 55 \times 30}{360} = 320833.33$$

(*ii*) Work in Progress @ 50% completion

$$\text{Materials} = \frac{70,000 \times 55 \times 15}{360} \times 50\% = 80208.33$$

$$\text{Direct Labour} = \frac{70,000 \times 19.5 \times 15}{360} \times 50\ \% = 28437.5$$

$$\text{Direct Overheads} = \frac{70,000 \times 39 \times 15}{360} \times 50\% = 56,875$$

(*iii*) Finished goods

$$= \frac{70,000 \times 113.5 \times 30}{360} = 662083.33$$

B. Investment in Debtors

$$= \frac{3}{4} \times \frac{70,000 \times 60 \times 113.25}{360} = 9,93,125$$

C. Cash Balance = 1,50,000

Investment in Current Assets (A + B + C): 1307187.49

D. Current Liabilities CA

Deferred payments

(*i*) Materials

$$= \frac{70,000 \times 55 \times 30}{360} = 320833.33$$

(*ii*) Deferred wages

$$= \frac{70,000 \times 19.5 \times 10}{360} = 37916.67$$

(*iii*) Deferred overheads

$$= \frac{70,000 \times 39 \times 30}{360} = 2,27,500$$

Total deferred payments [(*i*) + (*ii*) + (*iii*)] = Rs. 5,86,250

Net Working Capital = Current Assets – Current Liabilities

(A + B + C – D) = Rs. 17,05,312

> ***Note:*** Depreciation is a non-cash item; it will be ignored in calculations. Cost of production-not to include selling and administration expenses.

Since taxes can be paid out of profits they are ignored. Profit is ignored in calculating NWC. Alternatively advanced payments of taxes require additional working capital and profits are sources of working capital.

Illustration 14.2 Calculate the current working capital of a company with the following information:

Sales (credit)	5,00,000
Total cost of goods sold	2,50,000
Purchases	1,20,000
Average raw material stock	60,000
Average work in progress	55,000
Average finished goods stock	92,000
Average creditors	60,000
Average debtors	1,50,000

Solution

Operating cycle of a company

(*i*) Raw material $= \dfrac{\text{Average work in progress}}{\text{Total cost of production}} \times 365$

$$= \frac{60,000}{1,20,000} \times 365 = 183 \text{ days}$$

(*ii*) Work in progress $= \dfrac{\text{Average work in progress}}{\text{Total cost of production}} \times 365$

$$= \frac{55,000}{2,50,000} \times 365 = 80 \text{ days}$$

(*iii*) Finished goods $= \dfrac{\text{Average stock}}{\text{Total cost of goods sold}} \times 365$

$$= \frac{92,000}{2,50,000} \times 365 = 134 \text{ days}$$

(*iv*) Debtors $= \dfrac{\text{Average debtors}}{\text{Total credit sales}} \times 365$

$$= \frac{1,50,000}{5,00,000} \times 365 = 110 \text{ days}$$

$$(v) \text{ Creditors} = \frac{\text{Average creditors}}{\text{Total purchases}} \times 365$$

$$= \frac{60,000}{1,20,000} \times 365 = 182.5 \text{ days}$$

183 + 80 +134 +110 – 182.5 = 324.5 days

Illustration 14.3 The following information is given about total funds required, permanents funds required and seasonal requirements find out the cost of working capital under hedging and conservative plan. The cost of short-term funds is 3% and long-term funds are 10%.

Month	Estimated funds required (Rs.)	Permanent funds (Rs.)	Seasonal requirement (Rs.)
January	12,00,500	10,00,000	2,00,500
February	12,00,000	10,00,000	2,00,000
March	11,50,000	10,00,000	1,50,000
April	11,00,000	10,00,000	1,00,000
May	11,50,000	10,00,000	1,50,000
June	12,50,000	10,00,000	2,50,000
July	11,50,000	10,00,000	1,50,000
August	11,00,000	10,00,000	1,00,000
September	11,50,000	10,00,000	1,50,000
October	20,00,000	10,00,000	10,00,000
November	16,00,000	10,00,000	6,00,000
December	16,00,000	10,00,000	6,00,000
			36,50,500

Solution

Hedging plan

Total monthly seasonal requirements = 36,50,500/12 = 304208.33

$$= 304208.33 \times 0.03 \quad = \quad 9126.24$$

$$= 10,00,000 \times 0.10 \quad = \quad \underline{1,00,000.00}$$

$$= \quad 109126.24$$

Conservative approach

The cost of financing under the conservative plan = cost of long-term funds. The maximum long-term funds are in October which is 20,00,000; the total requirements including 20,00,000 in October will be financed by long-term funds. The net working capital is the highest in October which is 20,00,000 – 10,00,000 = Rs. 10,00,000.

Cost of financing = 20,00,000 × 0.10 = Rs. 2,00,000

Therefore cost of financing is higher in conservative approach compared to hedging approach.

Illustration 14.4 The following information gives the total funds required by a firm. It also gives information of permanent requirements and seasonal requirements. Calculate the cost of funds and NWC according to trade off approach between hedging and conservative approach. The cost of short-term funds is 3% and long-term funds is 10%.

Month	Estimated funds required (Rs.)	Permanent funds (Rs.)	Seasonal requirement (Rs.)
January	12,00,000	15,00,000	0
February	12,00,000	15,00,000	0
March	11,00,000	15,00,000	0
April	11,00,000	15,00,000	0
May	11,50,000	15,00,000	0
June	12,50,000	15,00,000	0
July	11,50,000	15,00,000	0
August	10,00,000	15,00,000	0
September	11,50,000	15,00,000	0
October	20,00,000	15,00,000	5,00,000
November	16,00,000	15,00,000	1,00,000
December	16,00,000	15,00,000	1,00,000
			7,00,000

Solution

The maximum fund required is Rs. 20,00,000 and minimum is Rs. 10,00,000. The average will be

(20,00,000 + 10,00,000)/2 = Rs. 15,00,000

In October, November and December funds will be required for seasonal requirements.

Cost of short-term funds is 3% of 7,00,000/12

= 58333.33 × 0.03 = Rs. 1,749.99

Cost of long-term funds is Rs. 15,00,000 × 0.10 = Rs. 1,50,000

Total cost of funds = Rs. 1,51,749.99

Net working capital = Rs. (15,00,000 – 10,00,000) = Rs. 5,00,000

Illustration 14.5 Prepare an estimate of net working capital of a company from the data given below.

Estimated cost	Rs. per unit
Raw materials	150
Direct labour	50
Overheads	100
Total	300
The following additional information is provided:	
Selling price per unit	Rs. 350
Level of activities	2,08,000 units per annum
Raw materials in stock average	4 weeks
Work in progress assume 100% completion of materials and 50% for labour and overheads average	2 weeks
Finished goods in stock average	4 weeks
Credit allowed by suppliers average	4 weeks
Credit allowed by debtors average	8 weeks
Lag in payment of wages	2 weeks
Cash at bank	Rs. 1,00,000

Assume that production is continuous for 52 weeks in the year.

Solution

Statement of working capital requirements

Current assets	Amount (Rs.)
Raw materials 4,000 × 4 × 150	24,00,000
Work in progress	
Raw materials 4,000 × 2 × 150	12,00,000
Wages (4,000 × 2 × 50) 50%	2,00,000
Overheads (4000 × 2 × 100) 50%	4,00,000
Finished goods (4,000 × 4 × 300)	48,00,000
Debtors (4,000 × 8 × 300)	96,00,000
Cash at bank	1,00,000
Total current assets	1,87,00,000
Current Liabilities	
Creditors 4,000 × 4 × 150	24,00,000
Outstanding wages 4,000 × 2 × 50	4,00,000
Total liabilities	= 28,00,000
CA – CL	= 1,59,00,000

Working Notes

(*i*) Annual production is 2,08,000 units in 52 weeks. So weekly production is 4,000 units.

(*ii*) Debtors have been taken at cost of production.

Illustration 14.6 A company plans to sell 48,000 units next year. The expected cost of goods sold is as follows:

Particulars	Rs. per unit
Raw materials	100
Manufacturing expense	30
Selling and administrating	20
Selling price	180
Cash	1,20,000

The duration at various stages is expected to be as follows:

Raw materials stage	2 months
Work in progress	1 month
Finished goods	1 month
Debtors	1 month

Estimate the gross working capital assuming monthly sales of 4,000 units. Estimate gross working capital required when work in progress is 25% complete in the manufacturing stage.

Solution

Statement of gross working capital

Current Assets	Amount (Rs.)
Raw materials = 4,000 × 2 × 100	8,00,000
Work in progress	
Raw materials = 4,000 × 100	4,00,000
Manufacturing expenses = 4,000 × 30 × 25%	30,000
Debtors = 4,000 × 150	6,00,000
Cash balance	1,20,000
Gross working capital requirements	19,50,000

Illustration 14.7 The Balance sheet of a company as on 31 March 2007 is as follows:

Liabilities (Rs.)		Assets (Rs.)	
Current liabilities	3,00,000	Current assets	2,10,000
Long-term funds	3,30,000	Fixed assets	4,20,000
Total	6,30,000	Total	6,30,000

If current assets earn 2% and fixed assets earn 15%, current liabilities cost 5% and long-term funds cost 10% calculate (*a*) total profits on assets and ratio of current assets to total assets (*b*) cost of financing and ratio of current liabilities to total assets and (*c*) net profitability of the current financing plan.

Solution

(*a*) Total profits on assets and ratio of current assets to total assets

Total profits on assets = Profit on current assets + Profit on fixed assets

(*i*) Profit on current assets = 0.02 × 2,10,000 = Rs. 4,200

(*ii*) Profit on fixed assets = 0.15 × 4,20,000 = Rs. 63,000

Total profit = 4,200 + 63,000 = Rs. 67,200

Ratio of current assets to total assets = 2,10,000/6,30,000 = 0.33

(*b*) Cost of financing and ratio of current liabilities to total assets

Total cost of financing = Cost of financing current liabilities + Cost of financing fixed assets.

(*i*) Cost of financing current liabilities = 0.05 × 3,00,000 = Rs. 15,000

(*ii*) Cost of long-term funds = 0.10 × 3,30,000 = Rs. 33,000

Total cost of financing = Rs. 48,000

Ratio of current liabilities to total assets = Rs. 3,00,000/6,30,000 = 0.476

(*c*) Net profitability = Total profit – Total cost = Rs. (67,200 – 48,000) = Rs. 19,200

PROBLEMS FOR PRACTICE

Problem 14.1 The following information is provided of a firm. Calculate its requirement for net working capital.

Particulars	Rs. per unit
Raw materials	8
Direct labour	2
Overheads	5
Total cost	15
Profits	10
Selling price	25

The additional information is the following:

The materials are in process for ½ a month total budgeted units are 1,000 and Rs. 8 is the cost per unit of raw material. Assume 50% completion stage. finished goods in stock are for 1 month. Credit is allowed by suppliers for 1 month. Credit allowed to debtors is 2 months. Average time lag in payment of wages is 3 ½ weeks, and one month in overhead expenses 1/4th of the output is sold in cash. Cash in hand and at bank are Rs. 12,000. Prepare working capital requirements for the Company.

[**Answer:** 14,519.23]

Problem 14.2 Calculate the operating cycle of a company.

Particulars	Amount (Rs.)
Raw materials consumption par annum	8,42,000
Annual cost of production	14,25,000
Annual cost of sales	15,30,000
Annual sales	19,50,000
Average value of current assets held	
Raw materials	1,24,000
Work in progress	72,000
Finished goods	1,22,000
Debtors	2,60,000

The company gets 30 days credit from its suppliers. All sales of the firm are made on a credit basis. Number of days in a year = 365 days.

[**Answer:** Operating cycle = 120 days]

Problem 14.3 A company plan to sell 30,000 units the expected cost of goods sold, and other particulars are as follows:

Particulars	Rs. per unit
Raw materials	100
Manufacturing expenses	30
Selling and administration expenses	10
Selling price	200
Cash balance	1,00,000

The duration at various stages of the operating cycle would be expected to be as follows:

Raw materials stage	2 months
Work in progress	1 month
Debtors	1 month

Assuming sales of 2,500 units every month estimate gross working capital requirements if work in progress is at 40% completion.

[**Answer:** Gross working capital = Rs. 15,55,000]

Problem 14.4 The balance sheet of a company as on 31 March 2007 is as follows:

Liabilities (Rs.)		Assets (Rs.)	
Current liabilities	1,00,000	Current assets	50,000
Long-term liabilities	2,50,000	Fixed assets	3,00,000
Total	3,50,000	Total	3,50,000

If current assets earn 5% and fixed assets 20%, current liabilities cost 3% and long-term funds cost 8%, calculate (*a*) total profit on assets and ratio of current assets to total assets, (*b*) cost of financing and ratio of current liabilities to total assets, and (*c*) net profitability of the current financing plan.

[**Answer:** (*a*) Profit Rs. 62,500, ratio CA/TA = 0.142
(*b*) Costs = Rs. 23,000 ratio CL/TA = 0.285
(*c*) Net profitability = Rs. 39,500]

Problem 14.5 Calculate working Capital requirement from the following data:

Particulars	Cost per unit (Rs.)
Raw materials	100.00
Direct labour	40.00
Overheads inclusive	80.00
Total cost of depreciation Rs. 40	220.00
Profits	40.00
SP	260.00

Average raw material in stock is for 1 month. Average material in work in wages and work 50% in progress is for half month. Credit by suppliers 30 days credit allowed to debtors 30 days. Average time lag in payment of wages 10 days average time lag in payment of overheads 30 days. 1/4th of the sales are cash sales. Cash balance for one month is Rs. 5,00,000. Finished goods are stored for 30 days. You are required to prepare WC requirements for 9,000 units. Production is carried out evenly.

[**Answer:** Net working capital = 36,65,000]

❑❑❑

Cash Management 15

LEARNING OBJECTIVES

15.1 INTRODUCTION

Cash management is the art of synchronizing cash receipt and cash payments for effective cash management in a firm. Cash is the most liquid current asset and there are motives like transaction, precaution and speculation which determine the need for cash in an organization. In order to meet the different requirements of cash, there are certain techniques, strategies and models which are adopted for optimum cash balance. Cash management consists of payments, credit sales, purchases on credit and receipt on credit. Figure 15.1 depicts the different areas of cash management. Cash budgets are prepared to avoid any future problems in cash management. Similarly forecasts cash receipts and payments are made for systematic cash management. This chapter discusses the planning, management and control of cash for efficiency in management of cash.

Cash consists of cheques, drafts, demand deposits and currency. The broader view of cash is to include those assets which are called 'near cash assets'. An example of such assets would be marketable securities and time deposits which are held in different banks. The main advantages of such assets are that it can be sold immediately, providing liquidity to a firm whenever it is required. Such assets are also used for making short-term investments when a firm has excess cash. In this chapter cash management is discussed in the sense of including both cash and near cash.

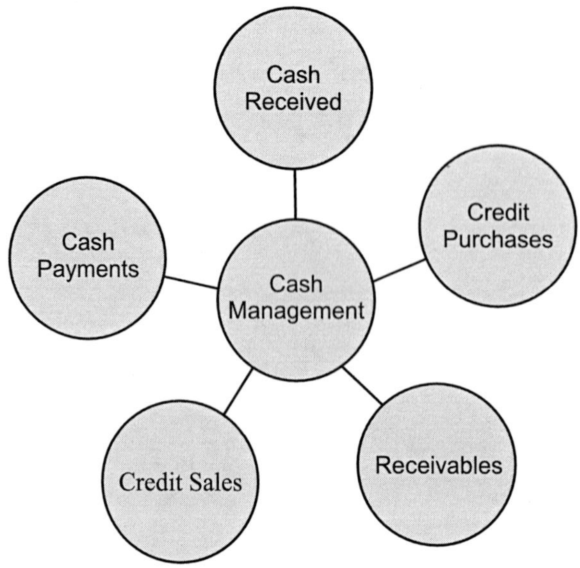

Fig. 15.1 Cash Management

15.2 MOTIVES FOR HOLDING CASH

Cash is required by a company/firm for different motives. These are (*i*) transaction motive, (*ii*) precautionary motive, (*iii*) speculation motive and (*iv*) compensation motive. These motives are depicted in Fig. 15.2.

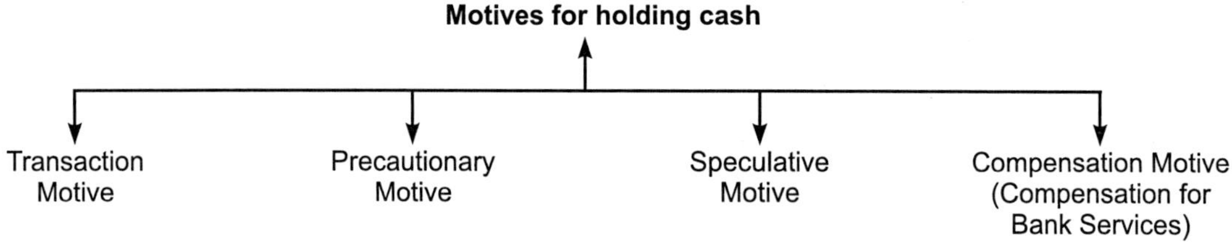

Fig. 15.2 Motives for holding cash

(*i*) **Transaction Motive:** Cash is required for carrying on the business of a firm. Transactions take place for business operations. The firm has to make its payments when it purchases products or services. Cash must be paid for all these services. Cash has also to be paid for general expenses made by the company in the form of factory expenses, office expenses and administrative charges for running the business. Other expenses include financial charges like interest, taxes, rent and dividends. A firm also receives cash for selling its own goods and services. Thus the firm has an inflow of cash as well as an outflow. Cash management consists of synchronizing the transaction inflows and outflows. Efficient cash management requires that there is no shortage of cash when it is required, to avoid loss of reputation. However cash inflows do not match cash outflows as they come in the organization or go out of the organization at different times. The financial manager is expected to have a minimum balance of cash for these normal business transactions.

Cash requirements for transaction purposes can be forecasted by the level of activity in a firm. The activity level depends on the nature of business, sales and the type of expenses. Marketable securities can be used for providing efficiency. The firm can borrow when it requires cash and sell its short-term securities to provide the adequate amount of cash. Cash budgets also have in preparing an estimation of future anticipated receipts and payments.

(ii) **Precautionary Motive:** Cash is required by a firm for future contingencies. If a firm can predict its cash flows accurately its requirements for precaution will be low. However, uncertain occasions like calamities of nature require adequate minimum cash balance to conduct business. In recent years floods, tsunami, earthquakes and landslides have created havoc and firms require funds for these unexpected contingencies. In business operations, cash is required when debtors do not pay in time or cancellations in orders arise. Sometimes creditors present unexpected bills. A firm can also face the risk of a strike or problems of raw material delivery. These conditions create imbalances. A firm has to be ready to tackle these problems quickly. If a firm has the possibility of being able to borrow at short notice, the need for precaution will be low. Similarly, if it can plan its marketable securities to be released immediately when the need arises then the firm may keep small cash balance for precaution. If the firm cannot borrow quickly and does not have proper planning of marketable securities it will have to maintain a large cash balance.

(iii) **Speculative Motive:** Speculative motive is concerned with the holding of a cash balance for making profitable investments through opportunities arising in the course of business. Opportunities arise in the stock market when prices of stocks and shares change. When the price falls the firm can buy and when it rises the security can be sold to make a profit. Managers often predict when interest rates will fall or rise and take an advantage of the situation. Decisions have to be taken quickly to exploit opportunities. Firms also make bulk purchases of raw materials by predicting fall in prices. Sometimes they delay the process of purchases when they expect to get a favourable price opportunity. The speculative motive is an aggressive approach and the opportunity can be taken only by implementing quick decisions.

(iv) **Compensation Motive:** This motive is usually related to the services provided by banks. The services rendered by banks create an indirect obligation on the firm to maintain a minimum balance with the bank. Banks provide services in the form of loans to firms. Short-term loans have fast changing interest rates. When a firm gives a specified amount as a loan and the interest rates rise the bank is at a loss. For such services it asks for compensation from the firm. The firm has to keep a minimum balance in the bank, which the bank can use for further loans. There are two kinds of cash balances which can be asked by the bank. One may be a minimum balance and the other to be an average minimum balance per month. For example a minimum balance would be very restrictive as a firm may require to keep a minimum of

Rs. 1,00,000 every month. An average monthly balance is less restrictive because a person can hold an amount which is higher than or lower than Rs. 1,00,000 provided the average remains at Rs. 1,00,000.

The two motives of cash which are most important are the transaction motive and the compensation motive. The speculation motive depends on the perception of the manager and it will differ from one firm to another. The precautionary motive can be adjusted with marketable securities and other short-term deposit.

15.3 OBJECTIVES OF CASH MANAGEMENT

The objective of cash management is to synchronize the cash inflows and cash outflows. This means that it has basic conflicting objectives. It needs to balance its payments and minimize its idle funds. The financial manager has to try and achieve the ideal cash balance for maintaining the payments of the firm on time. The financial manager has to manipulate the firm's funds in such a way that it has no loss of reputation. The firm receives cash from its revenue receipts and capital receipts. Likewise it also makes both revenue and capital payments. The main reason to make cash management effective is to keep the firm solvent and profitable. The firm must maintained good public relations with both its suppliers as well as its creditors. This should be done by cash management strategies and by the preparation of budgets to achieve the risk return trade off of the firm. From this it follows that cash management has two primary objectives:

(*i*) Meeting payments on the scheduled date.

(*ii*) Minimizing its cash balance to avoid idle funds.

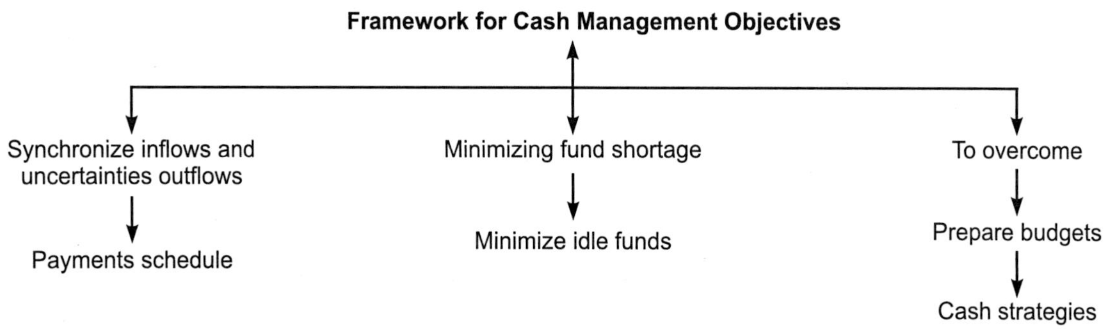

Fig. 15.3 Cash Management Objectives

(*i*) **Meeting Payments Schedule:** In a firm, the flow of cash is continuous through collections made from the debtors of the firm. Similarly payments are also continuous because business operations continue smoothly throughout the year and a firm keeps on purchasing different items required for the flow of work. The problem that happens in a firm is that when cash is received it is in abundance but payments may not be scheduled when such receipts of cash have come in the firm. When payments have to be made it must be made in time to avoid creating a problem with the suppliers of raw materials. Moreover a firm is able to avail of certain discounts if payments are made on time. If it is not able to pay on the due date, it would lose a large amount of money. The importance of meeting payments on schedule are:

(*a*) Making payments on time gives a good credit rating to a firm with its banker. Short-term loans are easy to avail as credibility becomes high.

(*b*) The creditors of the firm can trust the firm if it makes payments on time and will supply goods to it because it has confidence and trust in the firm's ability to make its payments on time.

(*c*) Meeting payments on schedule entitles a firm to cash discount and this can be a volume of funds in a year.

(*d*) The firm can take an advantage of any future favourable opportunities as it does not suffer from bankruptcy or has any fear of insolvency.

However to meet its payments schedule the firm cannot keep an excessive cash balance as the cost are high when funds are idle.

(*ii*) **Minimizing cash balance to avoid idle funds:** Idle cash should be minimized. A high level of cash will help in making the payments of the firm promptly but idle funds do not earn any returns. Too much liquidity is conservative in approach and does not use cash efficiently. Too little balance will create disturbances in the payments schedule. A firm should be able to forecast an ideal requirement of cash by adopting cash management strategies and forecasting a balanced cash flow by preparing a cash budget, cash cycles through past cash inflows and outflows to predict its nature of cash flows. This should help in keeping minimum cash balances. From this discussion the importance of minimizing cash balance are:

(*a*) Minimizing cash balance uses cash efficiently.

(*b*) It reduces locked up funds as such idle funds have a cost attached to them.

Hence an optimum cash balance should be achieved by minimizing cash balances and meeting payments on schedule.

15.4 FACTORS DETERMINING CASH REQUIREMENTS

The factors that affect the cash balances are: (*i*) cash inflows and outflows, (*ii*) cost of cash balance (*iii*) cash cycle and (*iv*) short costs.

(*i*) **Cash Inflows and Outflows:** The most important factor which affects the cash balance of a firm is non-synchronization of cash flows in a firm. Since the timing of cash flows is not matched, a cash balance is required to fill the gap so that cash is always available for payments of the firm. The firm must prepare a cash budget for one year to have with it a forecast of cash needs. This will provide a basis for developing a buffer for requirements of cash when payments arise.

(*ii*) **Cost of Cash Balance:** A cash balance has a cost in terms of interest. However, if cash is low, there is the cost of opportunity which the firm lost because of low cash. Since there is a cost 'of carrying' and the cost 'of not carrying' cash, it is important to balance both the requirements. The use of marketable securities to support excess liquidity and shortage of funds can help in maintaining a minimum cash balance for emergencies.

(*iii*) **Cash Cycle:** A cash cycle is important to find out when surplus cash is required and when there is a deficit. It will also help to bring about both liquidity and control in a firm. A cash cycle is the length of time between the purchases of materials, production, finished goods, sale of goods on cash and credit, creation of a debtor's period, collection, receipt of cash and making payments of a firm. It helps to plan and manage cash flows by investing surplus cash and borrowing deficits in cash for short purposes to maintain an optimum cash level. A cash cycle does not have perfect matching inflows with outflows but if it can be analysed, cash management techniques and strategies can be used to synchronize the inflows and outflows of cash. Figure 15.4 depicts the cash cycle.

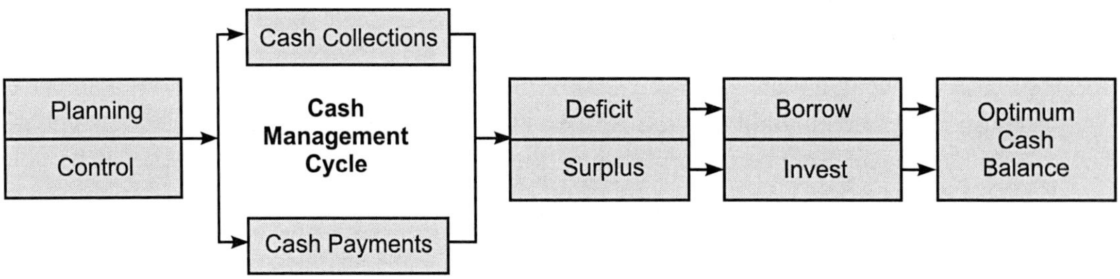

Fig. 15.4 Cash Cycle

(*iv*) **Short Costs:** Short costs are a situation when a firm has to forego its opportunities for lack of funds. Such costs arise.

(*a*) When transactions have to be made for selling marketable securities to convert them into cash or when they have to be purchased and there is a requirement of cash. Such a short cost is called a 'transaction cost'.

(*b*) When a firm loses its opportunity to avail discount because of shortage of funds it is called a 'short cost'.

(*c*) When a firm delays its payments and loses its credit rating with banks and has to pay a penalty interest rate it is called a 'short cost'.

15.5 CASH MANAGEMENT PLANNING THROUGH BUDGETING

Cash budget can be called as summary statements of cash flows over a projected time period. To synchronize cash receipts and cash payments a cash budget should be prepared. A cash budget will considered only cash receipts and cash payments and ignore the non-cash items. The objective of cash budget is to identify periods of shortage of funds and excess of requirements of cash. It helps to plan the production schedule and to find out the requirements of seasonal variations of funds. It avoids excess cash balances and arranges funds at favourable terms. Since funds can be analysed in time the opportunities of cash discounts and other advantages can be taken.

The significance of cash budgeting can be summarized in the following:

(*a*) It identifies periods of shortage of cash and periods of surplus cash.

(*b*) It helps the firm to take advantage of cash discounts.

(*c*) It prevents the firm to have excess accumulation of funds.

(*d*) It procuress funds on the most favoured terms.

(*e*) It plans the schedules of firm for an even and continuous flow of funds throughout the year so that it does not face a shortage.

It is thus an important tool for cash management of firms.

(*i*) Preparation of Cash Budget

A cash budget has certain important steps. These are called 'elements of cash budgeting system'.

The first step of cash budgeting is to select the planning horizon. This means that a time span has to be selected within which the cash budget has to be prepared. The time span should not be very long or very short because the budget will become inaccurate. In a short time period the budget cannot be accounted for all the important items to be projected. In a long budget, it becomes unwieldy. The time horizon differs from one firm to another if a firm's business is of a seasonal type. It may prepare monthly cash budgets. If business is fairly stable it should be a budget of a year. Short-term forecasts determine operating cash requirements, short-term financing and the investment of surplus cash.

The second step of cash budget is to select the cash receipts and cash payments of the firm which would affect its cash flows. The factors which generate the operations of the firm are called operating cash flows and financial cash flows. As stated above the items to be included in the budget are only cash items. Non-cash items like depreciation and amortization are ignored. Steps of budget preparation can be summarized in the following:

Steps in Preparation

- **Step 1:** Select time span – (Planning Horizon) should not be over too long or too short a period of time. In long budgets estimates become incorrect. In a short budget important details will be missed out. Planning horizon can be long if it is a fairly stable firm. It is better if it is a quartely/monthly budget.
- **Step 2:** Select factors – Those factors should be selected which have a bearing on cash flows. Cash budget includes only those items which involve cash and excludes items like depreciation.
- **Step 3:** Find opening cash balance. Then total all Cash inflows – total cash outflows. The resulting figure will be the opening cash balance for next year. This may be positive or negative.

(*ii*) **Cash Flows:** The cash flows consists of cash inflows and cash outflows. This is further bifurcated into operating cash flows and financial cash flows. These are depicted in Table 15.1.

Table 15.1 Operating and Financial Cash Flows

Operating Cash Flows	
Cash Inflows	**Cash Outflows**
Cash sales	A/c's payable
Collection of A/c's receivable	Purchase of raw material
Sale of fixed assets	Wages
	Factory expenses
	Administration and selling expenses
	Maintenance expenses
	Purchase of fixed assets
Financial Cash Flows	
Cash Inflows	**Cash Outflows**
Loans	Income Tax Payments
Sale of Securities	Loans Redeemed
Interest Received	Interest Paid
Rent Received	Repurchase of Shares
Refund of Tax	Dividends Paid
Issue of New Shares and Securities	

There are three different methods for cash budgeting:

A. Receipts and payments method
B. Adjusted net income method
C. Sensitivity analysis

A. Receipts and Payments Method

The receipts and payment method is used in most organizations. It is considered to be a very useful method. It is flexible and suitable in most firms. It analyses the periods of uncertainties through the inflow of receipts and payments. The method of preparation is simple the receipts minus the payments gives the balance for each year.

(*a*) Forecasting Receipts

Receipts on sales: Sales may be cash sales or credit sales. Cash sales will pertain to receipt of cash in the same month but credit sales will have a time lag. For example, if goods are sold for

Rs. 7,00,000 in January with a time lag of 30 days, it will become a receipt in February when cash is received. The budget should also cover the discounts given to debtors and also if the firm receives any returns of goods because the receipt of cash will be reduced when the discount is taken into account. The credit policy and the collection period should be carefully analysed.

Other Receipts: The cash budget should account for rents received, interest received, dividends received and income from royalties, sale of investments and any other receipts which may have an impact on the firm's cash balance.

(*b*) Forecasting Payments

Materials: In a manufacturing firm payment should be made for raw materials. The payments involve taking care of defective goods returned by the company and discounts received by its on timely payment. A cash budget helps in identifying the periods of heavy payments for materials ordered. A proper flow in work and planning through cash budget would help in reducing inventories. Sales of a firm and nature of business will however determine the volume of materials purchased.

Operating Expenses: Expenses of this nature pertain to manufacturing, sales and administrative expenses. This involves the forecasting of the fixed, variable and semi-variable expenses for finding out the magnitude and time period of expenses. Expenses on commission, travelling, brokerage must be analysed carefully.

Other Expenses: Cash outflows relate to payment of dividends, making payments as interest on loans or to debenture holders. It also has expenses of tax payments, purchases of assets and investments. All these are expenses and have to be indicated in the cash budget.

The receipt and payment method is first explained through Example 15.1.

Example 15.1 Prepare a Cash Budget through receipts + payments method. Cash balance on hand on 1 January, 2009 is Rs. 72,500. Prepare cash budget from January to June 2009.

Month	Sales	Materials Purchased	Salaries and Wages	Production Overheads	Office and Selling Overheads
January	72,000	25,000	10,000	6,000	5,500
February	97,000	31,000	12,100	6,300	6,700
March	86,000	25,500	10,600	6,000	7,500
April	88,600	30,600	25,000	6,500	8,900
May	1,02,500	37,000	22,000	8,000	11,000
June	1,08,700	38,800	23,000	8,200	11,500

Assume that 50% of the total sales are cash sales. Assets are to be acquired in the months of February and April. Therefore provisions should be made for the payment of Rs. 8,000 and Rs. 25,000 for the same. An application has been made to the bank for the grant of a loan of Rs. 30,000 and it is hoped that the loan amount will be received in the month of May. It is anticipated that a dividend of Rs. 35,000 will be paid in June. Debtors are allowed one month's credit. Creditors for materials purchased and overheads grant one month's credit, sales commission at 3% on sales is paid to the salesman each month.

Solution

Cash Budget for January to June 2009

Receipts	January	February	March	April	May	June	Total
Cash Sales	36,000	48,500	43,000	44,300	51,250	54,350	2,77,400
Collection From Debtors	—	36,000	48,500	43,000	44,300	51,250	2,23,050
Bank Loan	—	—	—	—	30,000	—	30,000
Payments	36,000	84,500	91,500	87,300	1,25,550	1,05,600	5,30,450
Materials	—	25,000	31,000	25,500	30,600	37,000	1,49,100
Salaries & Wages	10,000	12,100	10,600	25,000	22,000	23,000	1,02,700
Production Overheads	—	6,000	6,300	6,000	6,500	8,000	32,800
Office & Selling Over.	—	5,500	6,700	7,500	8,900	11,000	39,600
Sales Comm.	2,160	2,910	2,580	2,658	3,075	3,261	16,644
Capital Exp.	—	8,000	—	25,000	—	—	33,000
Dividend	—	—	—	—	—	35,000	35,000
	12,160	59,510	57,180	91,658	71,075	1,17,261	4,08,844
Opening Balance Beginning of month	72,500	96,340	1,21,330	1,55,650	1,51,292	2,05,767	1,94,106
Receipts-Payments	23,840	24,990	34,320	– 4,358	54,475	– 11,661	1,21,606
Total	96,340	1,21,330	1,55,650	1,51,292	2,05,767	1,94,106	3,15,712

Surplus cash should be invested in those securities which may be termed as near money or nearly liquid.

B. Adjusted Net Income Method

Cash forecasting is also done through the adjusted net income method. This method helps in controlling working capital and also in anticipating the financial requirements of a firm. It is called the sources and uses approach. Its main objective is to forecast the future requirements of cash and to identify the internal position of the firm to generate resources. It is prepared through net income statements which project the sources of cash, the uses of cash and the adjusted cash balance. It adjusts estimated earnings on an accrual basis to cash basis. It estimates dividends, net income, taxes and depreciation.

C. Sensitivity Analysis

This type of cash budget is prepared by estimating optimistic, most probable pessimistic conditions of cash flows. On the basis of these estimates a firm can increase or decrease favourable and unfavourable conditions that affect them. The analysis is based on expected or most probable values.

These cash budgets help in providing forecasts to evaluate a firm's financial planning. While cash management budgets are usually prepared for a period of one year with sub periods, they can be prepared for long-term forecasting for long-term capital investment projects.

Let us discuss some cash management strategies for control of cash.

15.6 CASH MANAGEMENT STRATEGIES

The cash management strategies consists of basic aspects like calculating cash cycles and cash turnover to find out the minimum operating cash requirements of a firm, stretching payment schedule and speedily collecting cash. The following methods explain the strategies.

(*i*) Cash Cycle and Cash Turnover Minimum Cash Balance: A cash cycle as explained is the process or path from the time cash is used to purchase materials till the time the goods of the firm are sold and cash is received for the sales of the products.

Cash cycle = Accounts receivable + Production cycle – Accounts payable

Example 15.2 Explains the calculation of a cash cycle: A firm purchase raw materials on credit of 30 days. It allows debtors 60 days. It normally takes 40 days to make payments and receives payments in 72 days. A 100 days' gap lies between purchase of raw materials and sale of finished goods. Average age of firms inventory is 100 days. Estimate the firm's cash cycle, and cash turnover, if total operating annual outlay is Rs. 82,80,000 interest cost is 10%.

Solution

Cash cycle of the firm is calculated by taking the average number of days between cash outflows with a/c's payable and cash inflows in collecting receivable.

(*a*) Cash cycle = 100 days + 72 days – 40 payments

$$= 100 + 32$$

No. of days = 132 days.

(*b*) Cash turnover = No. of days in one year/cash cycle

$$365 \text{ days in a year } = \frac{365}{132} = 2.76$$

If total operating outlay is Rs. 82,80,000 the minimum cash requirement is

$$\frac{82,80,000}{2.76} = \text{Rs. } 30,00,000$$

If the firm has Rs. 30,00,000 it will meet its requirements but Rs. 30,00,000 has an interest cost of 10%. This works out to Rs. 3,00,000.

Cash management strategy should be applied to minimize operating cash balance.

The higher the turnover less will be the cash required.

***(ii)* Stretching a/c's payable:** Efficient cash management can be performed by calculating a cash cycle and finding out the minimum operating balance of a firm. The firm can also use a strategy for extending its payments in the following way. Taking Example 15.2 as above:

If the firm can stretch its payments from 40 days to 50 days it can be reduce 10 days from its original 132 days cash cycle to 120 days. This will increase cash turn over from 2.76 to 365/120 = 3. This will lead to decrease in minimum cash requirements.

$$\frac{82,80,000}{3} = 27,60,000$$

The requirement has been reduced by 30, 00,000 – 27,60,000 = 2,40,000 (This will be a saving).

There are several cash management strategies such as increasing the raw material turnover, decreasing the production cycle and increasing the finished goods turnover. These strategies provide good production planning, inventory control and forecasting of minimum cash balance. These can be applied for managing cash. Some cash management techniques are now discussed for controlling cash inflows and cash outflows.

15.7 CASH MANAGEMENT TECHNIQUES

Cash can be managed after forecasting the requirements of the firm by applying some mechanisms for inflows and outflows so that it may results in savings to the firm.

(i) **Cash Collections/Inflows:** Cash management can be made efficient by collecting cash from debtors and by having some control mechanism. Collections can be made quickly by using certain methods like concentration banking and lock box system.

(ii) **Concentration Banking:** Firms that have many branches and at different places can collect their account receivables quickly by applying a concentration banking system. This system works on a decentralized manner whereby multiple collection points are made to expedite the collection of funds. It reduces mailing time. Collection centres are made in different geographical centres and the company has a central account called 'concentration banking'. When the customer deposits his payment to the local collection centre, it gets transferred to the central office. Concentration banking can be applied at a cost as a bank normally charges an amount for this service.

(iii) **Lock Box System:** There is another method through which collection can be made quickly. This is called 'lock box system'. In this system the firm has a locked box in a post office. The local bank is given the authority to open this box and then it is deposited in a bank. After

crediting the account of the firm the bank transfers the amount to the main bank with a deposit slip and a list of payments. For this service it charges a commission.

The main difference between concentration banking and lock box system is that in concentration banking the customer pays directly to the bank whereas in the lock box system, a locked box is kept in the post office from where it is picked up and then put in the bank. Both of them have a cost attached for the services that they provide. Although locked boxes were not popular earlier, in India, now credit cards, phone payments like Airtel, Hutch Idea and other companies are instituting their own locked boxes in central places (but not in post offices) for receiving speedy payments.

Example 15.3 A firm has an advance daily receipt of Rs. 80,00,000. It is planning Concentration Bank as this reduces collection period by 2 days. Concentration banking costs Rs. 1,00,000 annually and 10% can be earned by the firm on its investments.

A lock box system would reduce collection time by 5 days and costs 1,50,000 annually.

(*a*) Give the amount of cash released through concentration banking.

(*b*) How Much money is saved in collecting cash in two days? Should the firm institute Concentration Banking?

(*c*) How much cash will be saved?

(*d*) Which is better concentration banking or lock box system?

Solution

(*a*) Cash released by concentration banking.

(*b*) 80,00,000 × 2 days = Rs. 1,60,00,000

(*c*) Savings 10% × 1,60,00,000 = Rs. 16,00,000

The Firm saves 16,00,000 and spends 1,00,000 in instituting it.

Therefore net savings is = Rs. 15,00,000

(*d*) Cash released by lock box system = 80,00,000 × 5days = Rs. 4,00,00,000

$$\text{Saving in lock box system} = \left(\frac{10}{100}\right) \times 4,00,00,000 = \text{Rs. } 40,00,000$$

Lock box is better. Net savings are 40,00,000 – 1,50,000 = Rs. 38,50,000; whereas through concentration banking it is Rs. 15,00,000.

Its net savings 38,50,000 – 15,00,000 is higher than in concentration banking = Rs. 23,50,000. In this case the firm should adopt the lock box system as it has greater savings.

(*iv*) **Payments/Outflows:** Cash management techniques should also be adopted for making payments. A good control system will reduce the requirement of the firm. The firm should not delay its payments as it will suffer loss of reputation. It should use its resources to get maximum advantages. The firm should not make early payments. It should pay only on the due date unless it has been promised good discount terms. The bank balance should be used for maximum advantage. In certain cases payments can be delayed. As long as it possible the firm should schedule its payments from the bank by taking advantage of transit time.

(*v*) **Float:** Float is a technique which is used for delaying the disbursement of cheque payments. Cheques will be issued but by the time it is cleared there is a time gap. ***This time gap is called the float.*** The firm can use this time for making other payments because the cheques have been sent but the receiving party has not yet deposited them or inter-bank clearance has not been made. Taking advantage of the funds in the bank the firm uses it for its own purposes. Floats can be disbursement floats, collection floats and net floats.

A float has three steps. The first step is the time period when the cheque is issued and received by the other party. This is called 'transit time'. The second step consists of the cheque which is received by the payee; he has deposited it but not yet received the payment. Step three is the collection time between one bank and another and finally when it is credited to the payee's account, he can use the money. The clearing time is usually three days until which the issuer of the cheque can use the float. The advantage of using money after it has been disbursed is called playing the float or ***cheque kiting.*** While taking this advantage, the issuer should be careful that his cheque does not bounce. If it does, it is a serious offence. So playing the float has to be done carefully with some scientific calculations.

When cheques are issued but not presented by the payee it is called a ***disbursement float*** or payment float. Similarly when the cheque is received from a customer and it goes for collection but the cheque is not cleared by the paying bank it is called a ***collection float*** or a receipt float. Net float is the difference between the payment float and the receipt float. If the firm has been able to get its net float positive then it can safely play the float as its payment float is higher than the receipt float. The firm can keep a smaller cash balance and use its funds even if it has issued cheques. This is a useful technique and is applied by many firms. An example explains the floats.

Example 15.4 A company issues cheques of Rs. 50,000 per day and receives cheques of Rs. 40,000 per day the payment float is 10 days and receipt float is 4 days on an average. Find out different floats of the firm.

Solution

Different floats are as follows:

(*a*) Disbursement float = Amount × No. of days

= 50,000 × 10 = Rs. 5,00,000

(*b*) Collection float = Amount × No. of days

= 40,000 × 4 = Rs. 1,60,000

(*c*) Net float = Disbursement float – collection float

= 5,00,000 – 1,60,000 = Rs. 3,40,000

The firm's net book balance is Rs. 3,40,000 less than the actual balance there is available in the bank.

(*vi*) **Surplus Cash:** The next technique is to use surplus cash properly invested in marketable securities for short term to earn a rate of interest and to quickly convert them into cash when there is a requirement by the firm. The firm can bake a choice of marketable securities from an array of instruments available in the market. Some of these securities are treasury bills, certificates of deposit, commercial paper, repurchase (Repo) agreements, units, inter-corporate deposits and bills discounted, the financial manager has to take a decision depending on factors like financial or default risk, interest rate risk, taxes, liquidity and yield. This is a difficult decision and it is important to make the decision very carefully.

(*vii*) **Cash Shortages:** Just like surplus cash is to be invested the firm also faces shortage of funds in some seasons where work is at its peak. The firm usually requires these kinds of funds for a short time. Hence, short-term bank loans or sale of marketable securities can be arranged.

In the following paragraph discussion is related to how cash can be made at an optimum level. This is studied through two important models the Baumol's Model and Miller Orr Model.

15.8 OPTIMUM CASH BALANCE: MODELS

The strategies and techniques of cash management have indicated how shortages and surplus can arise in the course of business and in what manner they should be handled. Some models have discussed the methodology of determining optimum cash balance to have a trade off between risk and return. These models try to balance surplus and shortage of cash of a firm.

(*i*) Baumol's Model

William J. Baumol presented his model in 1952 on the same basis as an economic order quantity model for purchase of optimum number of units of inventory. He has suggested that the point where the carrying cost is equal to the transaction cost it is the optimum level of cash balance.

Assumptions of the Model

(*a*) The requirements of cash is estimated in advance.

(*b*) The cash payments are steady and do not have any changes.

(*c*) It assumes the transaction costs but not cost of precaution.

The theory states that for an optimum cash balance, a firm should invest its surplus cash in marketable securities to earn a rate of interest. However, when the firm requires funds it should be able to sell the marketable securities. While these conversions takes place the cost of brokerage, commission and other charges would have to be paid. If the firm does not want to buy or sell securities because of the transaction cost to be paid it will have to hold a higher cash balance. Therefore the firm has to balance between holding cost and transaction cost. The firm has to control both these costs. When marketable securities are sold the transaction cost should be balanced with holding cost. The model can be presented in the following way:

$$C = \sqrt{\frac{2ut}{i}}$$

C = Optimum cash balance

u = No. of units

t = Transaction cost

i = Rate of interest

This can be explained by the following example.

Examples 15.5 If monthly cash requirement is Rs. 40,000 and transaction cost is Rs. 6. Interest rate on marketable securities is 8%. Find optimum cash balance.

Solution

$$C = \sqrt{\frac{2ut}{i}}$$

$$C = \sqrt{\frac{2 \times 40,000 \times 6}{\frac{8\%}{12}}} = \sqrt{\frac{4,80,000}{0.0066}} = \text{Rs. } 8528.27$$

Holding cash is of least cost when it is Rs. 8,528.

> ***Note:*** Since cash requirement is given for a month and interest rate is given annually therefore, interest is converted at (8/12) × 100 = 0.0066.

If annual cash requirement is desired, it will be divided by 0.08. See example in illustrative problems.

This can also be explained through Figures 15.5 and 15.6. The average balance in a firm as calculated by the above equation is also depicted in Fig. 15.5, which shows that every firm can optimize its cash balance by knowing the transaction cost number of units and the opportunity cost of funds.

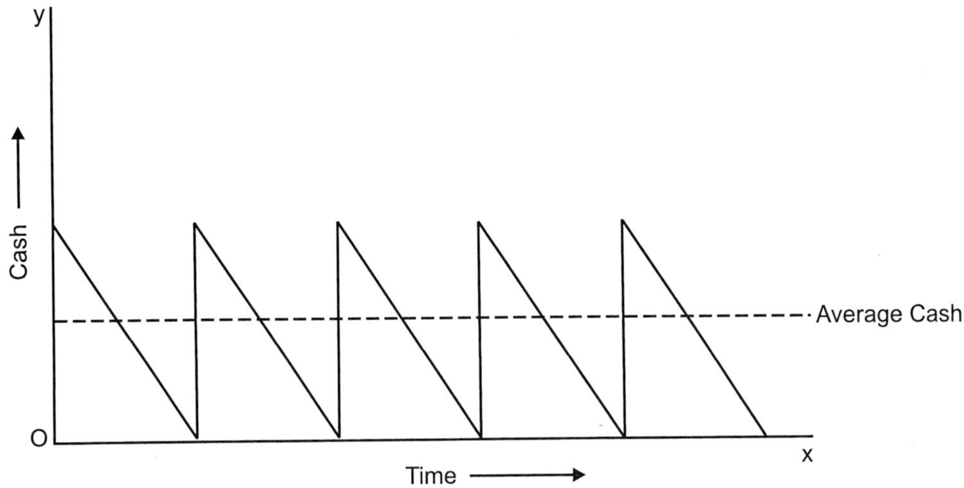

Fig. 15.5 Cash Balance – Baumol's Model

Baumol's Model shows that it should equalize the cash balance in such a way that optimum cash balance is maintained therefore holding cost and transaction cost determine the optimum level. Cash is optimum when these two costs are minimized. The average cash balance which is to be maintained by a firm is depicted in Fig. 15.6.

Limitations of the Model

(*a*) Measurement of transaction cost is very difficult because every marketable security has a different rate of return and different maturity period. Transaction cost cannot be same for all investments.

(*b*) Baumol assumes that a firm uses cash at a constant rate. Cash outflows of a firm cannot be regular or constant.

This model has many limitations but it is useful because it explains that holding cost and transaction costs have an effect on the optimum cash level of a firm.

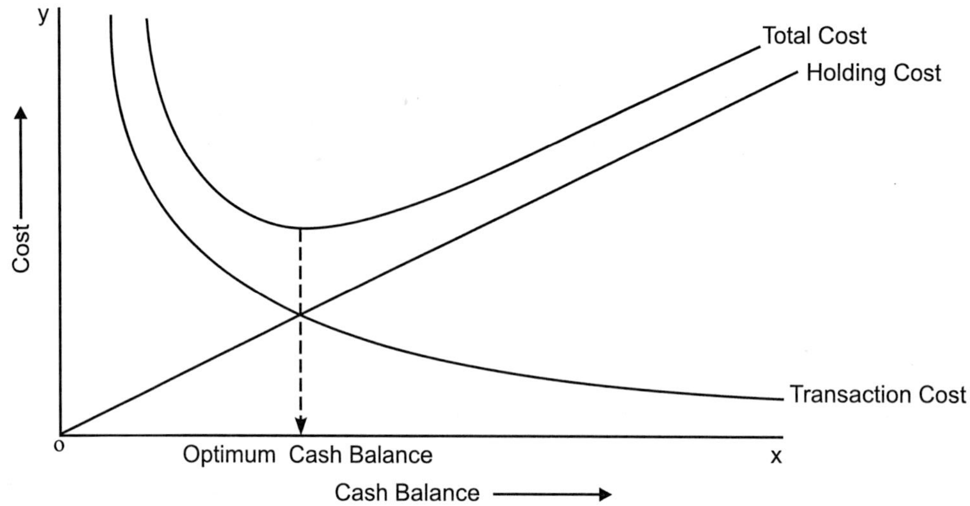

Fig. 15.6 Optimum Cash Balance—Baumol's Model

(*ii*) Miller Orr Model

Miller Orr model expands Baumol's Model and projects that the cash balance fluctuates and when the balance is high, it should be transferred into marketable securities. On the other hand, when cash is low marketable securities should be sold. They explain the model through two control limits, the upper limit and the lower limit. This is explained through Fig. 15.7.

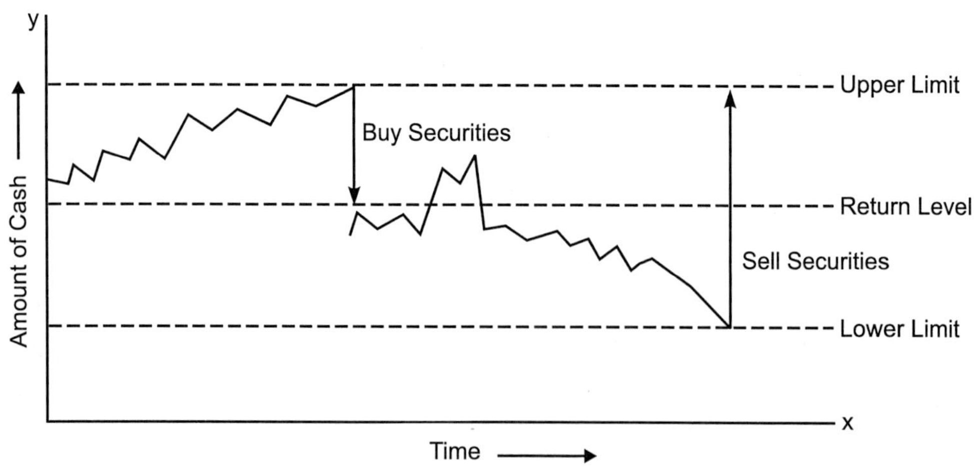

Fig.15.7 Miller Orr Model

The cash moves from upper limit to lower limit because cash flows are not steady and they move randomly. When cash reaches the lower limit, the firm should sell marketable securities so that cash is sufficient in the firm. Similarly when it reaches the upper limit there is too much liquidity in the firm and so marketable securities should be purchased to reach its optimum level. Miller Orr have also explained their model through the following equation.

$$Z = \frac{3\sqrt{2\, b\, \sigma^2}}{4i}$$

b = Fixed cost of security transaction

σ^2 = Variance of daily net cash flow

i = Interest rate per day on marketable securities

The optimal value of $h = 3z$.

Note: Cash flows given in Fig. 15.7 are random no measurement has been taken.

When cash reaches higher limit transfer of cash $h - z$ is changed to marketable securities when it reaches lower limit transfer.

The limitation of Miller Orr method is that it is mathematical and less used because of the difficulties in calculations.

This chapter has discussed the cash management strategies and techniques for optimum and efficient use of cash. The next chapter discusses another important area of working capital management—namely receivables management.

POINTS TO REMEMBER

- The objectives of cash management are to synchronize the cash inflows with the cash outflows.
- Cash management requires the meeting of payment on schedule to avoid any loss of reputation.
- It manages cash flows by finding out the cash cycle and cost of maintaining a cash balance.
- Cash inflows and outflows can be forecasted by making a summary in the form of a cash budget.
- Cash inflows can be managed through the use of concentration banking and lock box system.
- Cash outflows can be managed through float.
- Baumol's model and Miller Orr Model explain how optimum cash can be maintained.

OBJECTIVE TYPE QUESTIONS

State whether the following statement is true (T) or false (F):

1. Cash Management is the art of maintaining a large cash balance for everyday requirements of the firm.
2. Cash inflows and outflows do not happen in any sequence, they have to be synchronized.
3. Float is a method of making optimum cash balance.
4. There are different methods of cash budgeting but the most well-known one is through receipts and payments method.
5. Lock box system is operated by commission agents.
6. Concentration banking is adopted for speedy collection of receipts.
7. Baumols model explains the importance of transaction cost and the opportunity cost of marketable securities.
8. Miller Orr's model is a refinement on Baumol's model and explains the optimum cash balance within lower and upper limits.
9. Cash budgets must be made out of cash items only. Other costs must be ignored.
10. The firm has to optimize its cash management by estimation of its requirements and through a knowledge of its cash cycle.

Answers: 1. (F), 2. (T), 3. (F), 4. (T), 5. (F), 6. (T), 7. (T), 8. (T), 9. (T), 10. (T).

THEORETICAL QUESTIONS

1. What are the objectives of cash management?
2. Discuss the steps in cash budgeting through receipts and payments method.
3. What strategies can a financial manager adopt to make cash management efficient in a firm?
4. Explain Baumol's model of cash management with diagrams.
5. Why is Miller and Orr's model considered to be a refinement over Baumol's model?
6. What is a 'float'? How can it be used for efficient cash management?
7. What is 'concentration banking'? How is it different from lock box system?
8. 'Cash budget is an important technique of cash management.' Explain.
9. What are the different methods of preparing a cash budget?
10. 'The need or cash balance is due to non-synchronization of cash inflows and outflows.' Explain.
11. Write notes on:
    (*a*) Short costs
    (*b*) Playing the float
    (*c*) Lock box system
    (*d*) Concentration banking
    (*e*) Cash cycle

ILLUSTRATIVE PROBLEMS

Illustration 15.1 The following information is available of a firm:

(*i*) Debtors are collected after 30 days. Inventories have a holding period of 60 days and creditors payments period is 30 days.

(*ii*) The firm spends Rs. 90,00,000 annually at a constant rate.

(*iii*) It can earn on an average 10% on its investments.

From the above information compute (*a*) the cash cycle and the cash turnover (*b*) minimum amount of cash to meet payments when they are due (*c*) savings by reducing average inventory period by 20 days. Use 360 days for no. of days in a year.

Solution

(*a*) Cash cycle = No. of days given to debtors + Inventory period – Creditors payments
= 30 days + 60 days – 30 days = 60 days.

Cash turnover = 360 days/60 days = 6 times.

(*b*) Minimum operating cash = Total operating annual outlay/cash turnover
= 90,00,000/6 = Rs. 15,00,000

(*c*) Cash cycle = Debtors + Investment period – Creditors payment period
= 30 + 40 – 30 = 40

Cash turnover = 360/40 = 9 times

Minimum operating cash = 90,00,000/9 = Rs.10,00,000

Reduction in investments = Rs. 15,00,000 – Rs. 10,00,000 = Rs. 5,00,000

Savings = 0.10 × 5 days = Rs. 50,000

> ***Note:*** Number of days of cash cycle is reduced by 20 days making investment period 40 days.

Illustration 15.2 A firm has been offered cash management services by a bank for Rs. 1,50,000 per year. It is expected that it would eliminate excess cash on deposits of Rs. 10,00,000. It would also have the effect of reducing its administration and other costs of Rs. 7,000 per month. Assume cost of capital of 14%. Would you recommend to the firm to take the service?

Solution

Annual advantage	
Savings in interest Rs. 10,00,000 × 0.14	= Rs. 1,40,000
Reduction in administration and other costs Rs. 7,000 × 12	= Rs. 84,000
Total	= Rs. 2,24,000
Less cost of annual bank charges	= Rs. 1,50,000
Net annual benefit	= Rs. 74,000

Recommendation: It would be useful to take this service.

Illustration 15.3 A company is interested in a lock box system as it can shorten the receivables period by 3 days. Credit sales are estimated at Rs. 7,30,00,000 per year billed on a continuous basis. The firm's opportunity cost of funds is 14% the cost of lock box system is Rs. 90,000. (*a*) What would you advise the firm? (*b*) If the receivables period is reduced by 5 days what would you advise the firm?

Solution

(*a*) Cash released by lock box system Rs. 7,30,00,000/365 days	Rs. 2,00,000
Rs. 2,00,000 × saving of 3 days	Rs. 6,00,000
Savings Rs. 6,00,000 × 0.14	Rs. 84,000
Less cost of lock box system	Rs. 90,000
Net loss	Rs. 6,000

The firm should not take the lock box system as there is no benefit at all. Only a loss of Rs. 6,000.

(*b*) Cash released Rs. 2,00,000 × 5 days	Rs. 10,00,000
Savings Rs. 10,00,000 × 0.14	Rs. 1,40,000
Less cost of lock box system	Rs. 90,000
Net savings	Rs. 50,000

In this case the firm can plan to take the lock box system as there is a saving of Rs. 50,000.

Illustration 15.4 A company sells its products through distributors in east India. Its takes an average for cash receipt cheques to become available to the firm from the day they are mailed. The firm is planning to take concentration banking to reduce this period. This system would reduce collection period by three days. The daily receipts average Rs. 20,00,000. Concentration banking would cost Rs. 3,00,000 annually and the cost of funds is 14%. (*a*) Advise the firm if it should introduce concentration banking? (*b*) How would you compare it with the lock box system which would reduce the collection time by five days and its annual cost is Rs. 4,00,000.

Solution

(*a*) Cash released by concentration banking (Rs. 20,00,000 × 3)	Rs. 60,00,000
Savings (Rs. 60,00,000 × 0.14)	Rs. 8,40,000
Less: costs	Rs. 3,00,000
Net savings	Rs. 5,40,000
(*b*) Cash released by lock box system (Rs. 20,00,000 × 5)	Rs. 1,00,00,000
Savings Rs. 1,00,00,000 × 0.14	Rs. 14,00,000
Less: Costs	Rs. 4,00,000
Net savings	Rs. 10,00,000

Although there is a saving in concentration banking and lock box system, in this example the net savings is higher in lock box system. Therefore it should be adopted.

Illustration 15.5 A company XYZ issues cheques of Rs. 1,00,000 everyday and receives cheques of Rs. 50,000 everyday. The payment float is 8 days while the receipt float is 3 days on an average. Find out different floats of the firm.

Solution

The different floats of the firm are as follows:

(*i*) Disbursement float = Amount × No. of days

= Rs. 1,00,000 × 8 = Rs. 8,00,000

(*ii*) Collection float = Amount × No. of days

= Rs. 50,000 × 3 = Rs. 1,50,000

(*iii*) Net float = Disbursement float – Collection float

= Rs. 8,00,000 – Rs. 1,50,000 = Rs. 6,50,000

Illustration 15.6 A firm has a total requirement of cash of about Rs. 60,00,000 per annum. Its interest rate is 14% and transaction cost is Rs. 18. What is the optimum cash level of this firm?

Solution

$$C = \sqrt{\frac{2ut}{i}} = \sqrt{\frac{2 \times 60,00,000 \times 18}{0.14}}$$

$$= \sqrt{1,54,28,57,142} = \text{Rs. } 39279.22$$

Minimum cash balance of the firm should be Rs. 39279.22

Illustration 15.7 A firm has a monthly requirement of cash of Rs. 2,00,000 and its transaction cost is Rs. 10. Find out the optimum cash balance if rate of interest is 6% per annum?

Solution

$$C = \sqrt{\frac{2ut}{i}} = \sqrt{\frac{2 \times 20,00,000 \times 10}{0.005}}$$

$$= \sqrt{80,00,00,000} = \text{Rs. } 28284.27$$

The minimum cash balance of the firm should be Rs. 28284.27

> ***Note:*** Monthly cash requirement is given. For this interest is calculated as follows: 6%/12 = 0.005.

Illustration 15.8 A company receives cash at a steady rate of Rs. 4,00,000 per annum. If the cash is invested the firm will get a return of 12%. However every time it invests, the transaction cost will be Rs. 25 and 0.01 brokerage for the amount invested. Another investment banker has brought a new offer. He would charge Rs. 40 per transaction + 0.007 of the amount invested. Should the company accept the new proposal?

Solution

Particulars	Existing proposal	New proposal
Annual cost (Rs.)	4,00,000	4,00,000
Transaction cost (Rs.)	25	40
Brokerage	0.01	0.007
Rate of interest	12%	12%
Optimum investment (Rs.)	$C = \sqrt{\frac{2 \times 4,00,000 \times 25}{0.12}}$	$C = \sqrt{\frac{2 \times 4,00,000 \times 40}{0.12}}$
	= 12,909.94	= 16,329.93
No. of transactions yearly	= 4,00,000/12,909.94	= 4,00,000/16,329.93
	= 30.98	= 24.49
Average cash held (Rs.)	= 12909.94/2	= 16329.93/2
	= 6454.97	= 8164.965
Total transaction cost	@ Rs. 25 =774.5	@ Rs. 40 = 979.6
Interest cost @ 12% (Rs.)	774.59	979.6
Brokerage (Rs.)	@ 1% = 4,000	@ 0.007 = Rs. 2,800
Total cost (Rs.)	5549.09	4759.3

The cost is lower in the new scheme so the company should select the new proposal.

Illustration 15.9 Prepare a monthly forecast for the company for the quarter July–September 2009.

(*i*) Opening balance as on 1 July is Rs. 1,00,000.

(*ii*) It is estimated that the sale for July and August is Rs. 10,00,000 each and for the month of September it will be Rs. 15,00,000. The sale for May and June was Rs. 10,00,000 in each month.

(*iii*) Cash and credit sale is estimated at 25% and 75% respectively.

(*iv*) The receivables from credit sales are expected to be collected as follows. 50% of the receivables on an average of 1 month from the date of sale and balance 50% after 2 month from date of sale. There are no bad debts on the realization of sales.

(*v*) Rs. 5,00,000 is expected from the sale of a machine in September.

The forecast of payments is as follows:

(*a*) Purchase of materials worth Rs. 3,00,000 each in July and August and materials worth Rs. 4,50,000 in September.

(*b*) The payments for these purchases will be made 1 month after the purchase. The purchases of June were materials worth Rs. 4,00,000 the payment of which will be made in July.

(*c*) There are miscellaneous cash purchases of Rs. 50,000 per month.

(*d*) The wage payments are expected to be Rs. 70,000 per month.

(*e*) Manufacturing expenses are Rs. 40,000 every month.

(*f*) General selling expenses are expected to be Rs. 40,000 per month.

(*g*) A machine worth Rs. 7,50,000 is proposed to the purchased in September.

Solution

Cash budget for the period July–September 2009

Particulars	**July (Rs.)**	**August (Rs.)**	**September (Rs.)**
Opening cash balance	1,00,000	5,00,000	10,00,000
(A) Cash inflows			
Cash sales	2,50,000	2,50,000	3,75,000
Collection on credit sales	3,75,000 (June)	3,75,000 (June)	3,75,000 (June)
	3,75,000 (May)	3,75,000 (July)	3,75,000 (August)
Sale of machine	—	—	5,00,000
Total cash (A)	11,00,000	15,00,000	26,25,000
(B) Cash outflows			
Cash purchases	4,00,000	3,00,000	3,00,000
Cash expenses	50,000	50,000	50,000
Wages	70,000	70,000	70,000
Manufacturing expenses	40,000	40,000	40,000
Selling expenses	40,000	40,000	40,000
Purchase of machine	—	—	7,50,000
Total outflows (B)	6,00,000	5,00,000	12,50,000
Cash balance (A–B)	5,00,000	10,00,000	13,75,000

Illustration 15.10 A company sells 20% of its products in cash and the remainder 80% of goods on credit for 30 days. It is estimated that 1% of credit sales are bad debts. 50% of the credit sales are collected in the following month, 25% in the second month and 24%in the following month.

Sales in the preceding 3 months is as follows: January Rs. 1,00,000; February Rs. 1,20,000; March Rs. 1,60,000.

Sales for the next 3 months are estimated as follows: April Rs. 2,00,000; May Rs. 1,80,000; June Rs. 1,50,000.

Prepare a schedule showing expected cash collections during the month of April, May and June.

Solution

Cash receipts	Jan (Rs.)	Feb (Rs.)	Mar (Rs.)	April (Rs.)	May (Rs.)	June (Rs.)
Total Sales	1,00,000	1,20,000	1,60,000	2,00,000	1,80,000	1,50,000
Cash sales 20%	20,000	24,000	32,000	40,000	36,000	30,000
Credit sales 80%	80,000	96,000	1,28,000	1,60,000	1,44,000	1,20,000

Collection	April (Rs.)	May (Rs.)	June (Rs.)
1st month following sales 50%	64,000	80,000	72,000
2nd month following sales 25%	24,000	32,000	40,000
3rd month following sales 24%	19,200	23,040	30,720
Total estimated cash receipts	1,07,200	1,35,040	1,42,720

Illustration 15.11 From the following information prepare the cash budget for the month of June.

(*a*) The firm makes 30% cash sales credit sales are collected 40%, 30%, 20% in the month of sales, 1 month after sales and 2 months after sales respectively. The remaining 10% becomes bad debts.

(*b*) The firm has a policy of buying enough goods each month to maintain its inventory at 2 ½ times of the following months budgeted sales.

(*c*) The firm is entitled to 2% discount on all purchases if bills are paid within 15 days and the firm avails of all such discounts. Monthly purchases are made in two equal lots on a fortnightly basis.

(*d*) Cost of goods sold while considering the 2% discount is 50% of selling prices. The firm records inventory net of discount.

(*e*) Additional information is as follows:

March actual sales	Rs. 2,00,000
April actual sales	Rs. 2,40,000
May actual sales	Rs. 3,00,000
June budgeted sales	Rs. 3,50,000
July budgeted sales	Rs. 3,00,000
Inventory on May 31	Rs. 3,50,000
Cash on May 31	Rs. 1,00,000
Gross purchases in May	Rs. 3,00,000

Selling, administrative expenses budgeted for June Rs. 70,000 (includes Rs. 15,000 depreciation).

Solution

Cash budget for the month of June

Particulars	Amount (Rs.)
(A) Cash inflows	
Opening balance on June 1st	1,00,000
Collection from sales	
Cash sales 30% × 3,50,000	1,05,000
Collection for credit sales	
April (0.20 × 1,68,000)	33,600
May (0.30 × 2,10,000)	63,000
June (0.40 × 2,45,000)	98,000
Total cash inflows (A)	3,99,600
(B) Cash outflows	
Payment for purchases	
May Rs. 3,00,000 × 0.50 × 0.98	1,47,000
June Rs. 1,89,000 × 0.5	94,500
Selling and administrative expenses 70,000 – 15,000	55,000
Total payments (B)	2,96,500
Budget for June (A–B)	1,03,100

Purchase budget	Gross (Rs.)	Net (Rs.)
Inventory	3,00,000 × 0.50 × 2.5	3,75,000 × 0.98
	= 3,75,000	= 3,67,500
Add cost of sales in June	3,50,000 × 0.5	1,75,000 × 0.98
	= 1,75,000	= 1,71,500
Total requirements	5,50,000	5,39,000
Less: Opening inventory-gross	3,50,000 × 100/98	
	= 357142.85	349999.99
Required purchases	192857.15	189000.01

PROBLEMS FOR PRACTICE

Problem 15.1 The following information is available of a trading company.

(*i*) Debtors are collected after 90 days, inventories have a holding period of 120 days and creditors payment period is 60 days.

(*ii*) The firm spends a total of Rs. 1,00,00,000 annually.

(*iii*) The firm can earn on an average 10% on its investments.

From the above data compute (*a*) Cash cycle and cash turnover (*b*) Minimum cash to be maintained (*c*) Savings by reducing inventory holding period by 30 days.

[**Answers:** (*a*) Cash cycle 150 days, cash turnover 2.43 times (*b*) Minimum cash Rs.4115226.33 (*c*) Cash cycle 120 days, cash turnover 3.04 times reduction in cost Rs. 825752.46, savings Rs. 82575.26.]

Problem 15.2 A firm has been offered a cash management service by a bank for Rs. 2,00,000 per year. This system would reduce an estimated sum of Rs. 16,00,000 and administration costs of Rs. 8,000 per annum. If cost of capital is 15%, should the firm take the offer?

[**Answer:** Net annual benefit is Rs. 1,36,000. The firm should take this proposal.]

Problem 15.3 A company feels that a lock box system can shorten its accounts receivables collection period by 6 days. Credit sales are estimated to be Rs. 10,95,00,000. the opportunity cost of funds is 15% the cost of lock box system is Rs. 3,00,000.

(*a*) Should the firm adopt lock box system?

(*b*) If the firm reduces collection period by 9 days should the company adopt the lock box system?

[**Answers:** (*a*) Net loss Rs. 30,000 bank should not take the lock box system (*b*) There is a gain of Rs. 1,05,000. Lock box system should be adopted.]

Problem 15.4 A company sells its products in south India. It takes 10 days for cash receipt cheques to become available from the day they are mailed. The firm is planning concentration banking to reduce this period. It is expected to reduce 5 days with this method. The daily cheque receipt average Rs. 25,00,000 and concentration banking would cost Rs. 2,00,000 annual and cost of funds is 15%.

(*a*) Should the firm adopt concentration banking?

(*b*) If a lock box system is undertaken it will reduce the days by 6 days and the cost would be Rs. 2,50,000 which of the two systems should the firm adopt?

[**Answers:** (*a*) Net savings Rs. 16,75,000 adopt concentration banking. (*b*) Net savings Rs. 20,00,000 prefer lock box system.]

Problem 15.5 A firm issues cheques of Rs. 4,00,000 per day. The payment float is 5 days. It receives cheques of Rs. 3,00,000 per day and the receipt float is 2 days on an average. Find out different floats of the company.

[**Answers:** Disbursement float = Rs. 20,00,000, Collection float = Rs. 6,00,000, Net float = Rs. 14,00,000.]

Problem 15.6 A firm has a total cash of Rs. 40,00,000 per annum. Its interest is 10% and it has a transaction cost of Rs. 20. Calculate the optimum cash required by it.

[**Answer:** Rs. 40,00,000.]

Problem 15.7 The sales forecast for 5 months is as follows:

(*a*)	January	Rs. 1,00,000
	February	Rs. 1,20,000
	March	Rs. 1,50,000
	April	Rs. 1,60,000
	May	Rs. 1,55,000

Further information as follows:

(*b*) Debtors balance is Rs. 50,000 and creditors balance is Rs. 20,000 which are yet to be provided. Unpaid sales commission is Rs. 2,500 and cash balance is Rs. 10,000; opening stock of materials is Rs. 80,000.

(*c*) 50% sales are on cash. Credit sales are collected after 30 days. Now 5% commission is to be given to salesmen when cost is realized from credit sales.

(*d*) The trade creditors are paid 30 days from the date of purchase. Stock is 70 % of sales of the current one. Stock is Rs. 70,000 for January; Rs. 80,000 for February; and Rs. 1,00,000 for March.

(*e*) Fixed cost is Rs. 8,000 including depreciation.

You are required to prepare a cash budget for January, February and March.

[**Answers:** Cash balance: January Rs. 87,500; February Rs. 1,25,000 and March Rs. 1,77,000.]

❑❑❑

Receivables Management 16

LEARNING OBJECTIVES

16.1 INTRODUCTION

Working capital management is concerned with making policies and controlling the day-to-day working of a firm. Chapter 14 has introduced the concept of working capital management and the different strategies like hedging, conservative approach and aggressive approach towards the management of current assets. Chapter 15 gives an explanation on cash management and strategies and techniques for an effective policy. This chapter discusses another important area, namely receivables management. This is an analysis of sales made by a company on credit. It is inevitable that a firm makes both cash and credit sales to get a favourable position in the market. Pure cash sales do not get a good return for a firm. When a firm sells on credit, it has to consider costs attached to it and the risk of bad debts. In order to streamline its credit sales it must make certain policies. These policies are based on collection costs, credit standards, investment in receivables and sales volume of the firm. Finally in order to efficiently collect its cash it has to make certain collection policies. An efficient credit management can be made by good policies. Let us evaluate the costs and the policies leading to such decisions.

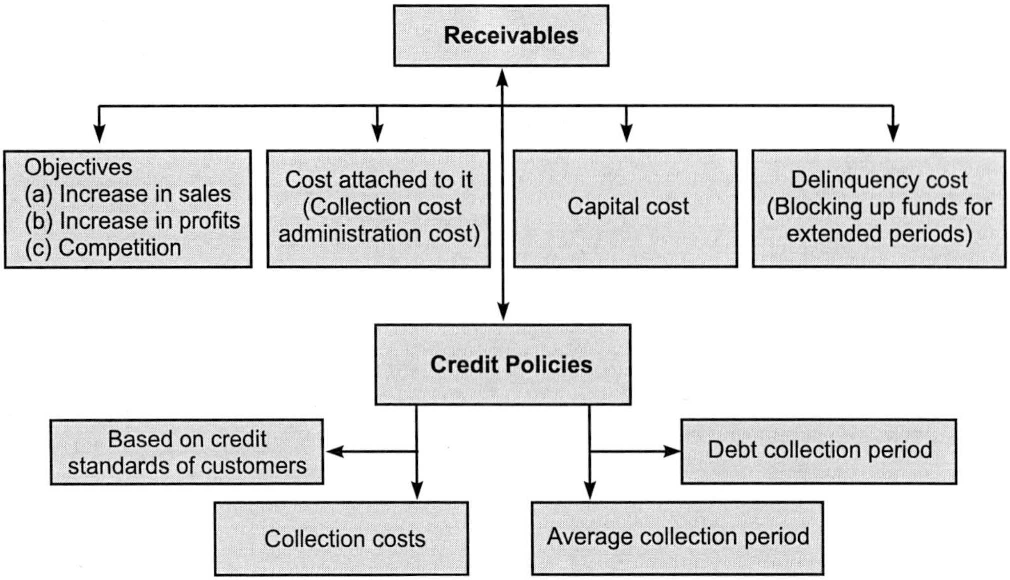

Fig.16.1 Receivables Management

16.2 OBJECTIVES OF RECEIVABLES MANAGEMENT

The objective of receivables management is to have certain gains for the firm. These benefits can be achieved by having an effective receivables management. It is a study to establish certain procedures for making collection of debts efficient in the organization.

The objectives of receivables management is to:

(*i*) Analyse the costs of receivables.

(*ii*) Evaluate the benefits of receivables by establishing a cost benefit analysis.

(*iii*) Have a trade off between profitability and liquidity.

(*iv*) Prepare a credit policy by analysing credit standards and credit terms like credit period and discount.

(*v*) Evaluate and control receivables.

Costs of Receivables

When goods are given on credit there are several kinds of costs associated with them. These costs can be classified into (*a*) cost of financing (*b*) collection cost (*c*) delinquency cost, and (*d*) cost of default.

(***a***) **Cost of Financing:** Goods sold on credit delays the process of receiving cash. Since funds get locked in transactions for period of extension of credit, the firm has to create additional resources to maintain its level of production and sales. The firm's expenses continue while it is waiting for its own funds to be released by customers. As we have analysed in cash management that cash inflows and cash outflows are not synchronized. Therefore, the firm has to look for short-term resources. The cost of financing the receivables is thus both explicit and implicit cost.

(*b*) **Administration Cost:** The collection cost is the cost of administration of funds which have to be received in the future. Before the sale of the product the administrative costs begin and they can be called 'part of collection cost'. The firm has to find out the credit standards of people to whom credits have to be extended. After the sale, information has to be recorded about the different customers and when their debts become due. Some firms have a separate department for maintaining their accounts receivables. Hence additional costs are involved in collecting and maintaining of credit sales.

(*c*) **Delinquency Cost:** When a firm provides credit facility to its customers, it expects that it will receive its funds on the specified date. Some customers do not pay on that date. Instead, they ask for an extension of the period. This extended period causes delay to the firm and creates a disturbance in its receipt and payments position. This delay causes a loss of interest to the firm for the delayed period from the due date. This is called the 'cost of delinquency'.

(*d*) **Cost of Defaults:** A firm cannot survive without making credit sales. There are many benefits attached to making sales on credit. Credit sales however have the problem of bad debts or funds which cannot be realized because the customer is not reliable. The customer may not have the capacity to repay its debt or its reputation is of poor credibility. Thus every customer must be analysed carefully before credit is extended to him. The cost of default is thus a risk attached to credit sales. Figure 16.2 shows the different types of costs of receivables.

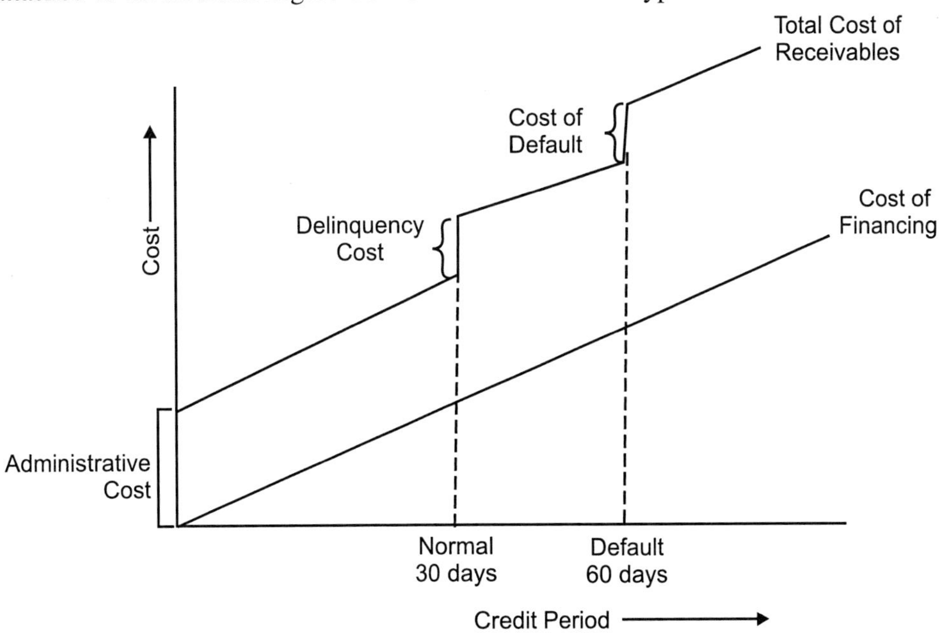

Fig: 16.2 Costs of Receivables

16.3 ADVANTAGES OF RECEIVABLES

Receivables have many benefits in terms of sales and profits. While making credit sales, there are costs of financing, administration, delays and defaults by customers. Benefits also accrue in making sales on credit. For this reason, firms prefer to relax their terms in credit period, discount and other terms and evaluate their costs and benefits. The benefits of receivables are:

(*i*) ***Increased sales:*** Most firms have to sell on credit because it helps their sales. Cash sales are difficult to sustain in a competitive market. Most goods are sold through extension of credit. Goods of daily need like bread and eggs can be sold on cash but trade credit is normally expected by distributors and dealers of goods. Liberal credit and easy payment terms provides the benefit of growth in a firm and higher profits.

(*ii*) ***Increased profits:*** Easy credit terms will increase sales and the firm will be able to attain its break-even position and also recover its fixed cost. When sales increase it is expected that profits will also increased.

16.4 COST BENEFIT ANALYSIS

The credit policies of a firm will have an effect on the volume of sales and profits; however the credit policy will have both costs as well as benefits. For an optimum policy, there should be a ***trade off between costs and profits.*** An optimum credit policy is one which will maximize the value of the firm. Although the maximum operating profit is desired, this is not an optimum credit policy. An optimum policy is the incremental rate of return of an investment equal to the incremental cost of capital. This is also called the 'marginal cost of capital'.

When a firm liberalizes its credit policy, it becomes risky because the payment of customers is over an extended period and this may result into a delinquency cost or cost of default of customers. In addition, the costs of collection are also increased.

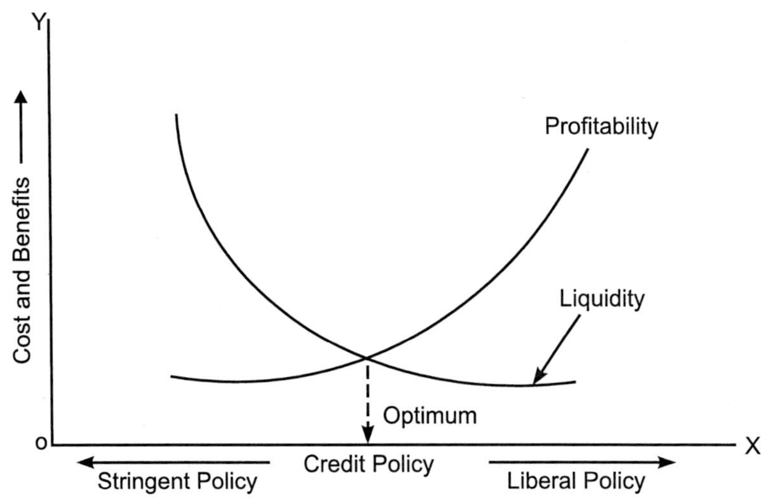

Fig. 16.3 Credit Policy

Figure 16.3 shows that as trade policy becomes liberal, the profitability of a firm increases but in the process the liquidity decreases. If the firm follows a tight credit policy, liquidity increases but profitability falls. For this reason there has to be a trade off on receivables to reach an optimum credit policy.

To maximize the value of the firm it is necessary to make an estimate of incremental operating profits, incremental investment in accounts receivables and incremental rate of return on investments and compare the incremental rate of return with the required rate of return. This is the position of an optimum credit policy and the position of trade off between liquidity and profitability.

The following section discusses credit policy, evaluation and control of receivables management.

16.5 CREDIT POLICY

A credit policy has to be effective in conducting the credit sales of the firm. To make the policy effective a decision has to be taken on the relaxation of the credit period and the terms offer to the customers on such policy. In order to take decision a firm has to find out the credit standards of the customers, before any credit is granted and take a decision on the credit terms to be granted.

(*i*) Credit Standards

Credit standards consist of examining the creditability of a customer. The firm has to take a decision on the basis of references, credit rating and financial information of the customer. Decision is influenced by the quality of the customer. The firm is interested in receiving its payments on time and is also keen that the default rate is low. The firm can assess an existing customer through its past dealings with it to find out if the customer is reliable. The 5C's are used as a parameter for judging the credit standards of a customer. The 5C's pertain to the character, capacity, condition, capital and collateral provided by the customer. On the basis of these limits the credit policy can be decided. Character means the willingness of the customer to make the payment. Capacity pertains to the ability of a customer to make his payments depending on his financial position and condition refer to the kind of economic factors which can affect the customer's ability to pay. Capital is the financial position of the customer. The source of information on this aspect would be the financial statements provided by the customer and collateral refers to the security offered by a customer for getting benefits of extension of credit from the firm.

Numerical ranking is a new method for evaluation of customers. The 5 C's is a traditional method and also subjective. Now attributes are ranked numerically to find out the worth of the customer.

(*ii*) Credit Terms

The terms of credit extended to a customer may be an individualistic approach or a band covering all the customers. Hence it can be an exclusive or an inclusive approach depending upon the customer's stability and difference between existing customers and new customers, as well as on the volume of purchases made by them. The credit terms consists of the length of the credit period and the terms of discounts provided to the customers. Therefore credit terms may be discussed on the basis of (*a*) credit period and (*b*) discounts.

(*iii*) Credit Period

The credit period is the extension of time given to a customer for making a payment on the sale of goods. It is usually stated on a ***net date***. This means that if the firm extends a period of net 60 it means that the customers are required to pay not later than 60 days. Every trade has some common norms and some which are dependent on the firms own nature of business. For example, the cloth trade in India extends credit for 90 days to its distributors, whereas a trade for selling car tyres extends 45 days.

The credit period is relaxed in order to increase sales but the cost of the extended credit period should be less than the incremental operating profit when sales increase, the firm also makes an investment in receivables. Therefore incremental sales also have incremental receivables. Thus there is a cost attached to receivables. The costs are of additional investment and the cost of collection.

An example may be given to calculate the profit on incremental sales. This can be calculated in two ways the long method and the shortcut method.

Long method: The costs and profits of the present and proposed sales are calculated and the difference between the two will be the incremental profit.

Example 16.1 A firm sells its products for Rs. 100 per unit currently. Its takes annual sales is Rs. 3,00,000 in units. The variable cost per unit is Rs. 60, the average cost per unit is Rs. 80 and the fixed cost of the firm is Rs. 8,00,000. The collection period is 30 days. The firm plans to relax credit standard, which will bring about at least 20% increase in sales. The collection period as suggested would be increased to 60 days. The firm requires a return on its investments of 15% should the firm relax the credit standard. Calculate:

(*a*) Cost of incremental investments

(*b*) Cost of incremental investments in receivables. (Sales are expected to increase by 20%)

Marginal Profits

(*i*) Proposed Plan		
Sales Revenue	3,00,000	3,60,000 × 100 = 3,60,00,000
Increase by 20/100	60,000	
	3,60,000	
***Less*: Costs**		
(*a*)	Variable costs	3,60,000 × 60 = 216,00,000
(*b*)	Fixed costs	8,00,000 = 8,00,000
	Profit from sales (*i*)	= 1,36,00,000
(*ii*) Current Plan		
(*a*) Sales Revenue	= 3,00,000 × 100	= 3,00,00,000
***Less*: Costs**		
(*a*) Variable	= 300,000 × 60	= 1,80,00,000
(*b*) Fixed		= 8,00,000

[Contd...]

	Profit from sales (*ii*)	= 1,12,00,000
	Marginal profits; In new plan 1,36,00,000 – 1,12,00,000 (*i* – *ii*)	24,00,000
	Marginal cost in a/c's receivable	
	Average investments Proposed plan	= 46,00,000
	Average investments present plan	= – 20,00,000
	Marginal investments	= 26,00,000
(*iii*)	**Marginal Profit with New Plan**	(*i* – *ii*) = Rs. 24,00,000

Cost of Marginal/Incremental Investment in Receivables

Find cost carrying receivables before and after proposed relaxation.

(*a*) Turnover of a/c's receivables

$$\text{Proposed Plan} = \frac{\text{No. of days in the year}}{\text{Average collect period}}$$

$$\text{Collection period has increased to } \frac{360}{60} = 6$$

$$\text{Present Plan} = \frac{360}{30} = 12$$

(*b*) Total cost of sales

Present Plan = No. of Units × Average cost per unit

$$\text{Present Plan} = 3{,}00{,}000 \times 80 = \text{Rs. } 2{,}40{,}00{,}000$$

$$\text{Average investments present plan} = \frac{2{,}40{,}000}{12} = \text{Rs. } 20{,}00{,}000$$

Proposed plan = (No. of units × Average cost per unit) +

(Investment in new units × Cost per units)

$$\text{Proposed Plan} = (3{,}00{,}000 \times 80) + (60{,}000 \times 60)$$

$$= 2{,}40{,}00{,}000 + 36{,}00{,}000 = \text{Rs. } 2{,}76{,}00{,}000$$

$$\text{Average Investment} = \text{Rs. } 2{,}76{,}00{,}000$$

$$\text{Proposed plan} = \frac{2{,}76{,}00{,}000}{6} = \text{Rs. } 46{,}00{,}000$$

Cost of marginal profits in account receivables is the difference between average in proposed plan and present plan $= 46{,}00{,}000 - 20{,}00{,}000 = \text{Rs. } 26{,}00{,}000$.

Marginal Investment is the additional cost of Rs. 26,00,000 if credit standards are relaxed. The additional cost of Rs. 2,60,000 will have to be made.

Given 15% of as required rate of return on investments of firm $\frac{26,00,000 \times 15}{100}$

$$= \text{Rs. } 3,90,000$$

This is the opportunity cost which the firm would earn if funds were not tied up in additional a/c's.

Since additional Profits is Rs. 24,00,000. It is more than the cost of incremental investment in a/c's receivables *i.e.*, Rs. 3,90,000. The firm should relax its credit standard. This would lead to an overall increase of 24,00,000 – 3,90,000 = Rs. 20,10,000

Shortcut Method: In this method the difference between the sale price per unit and the variable cost per unit = 100 – 60 = Rs. 40.

The marginal profits would be Rs. 40. The total marginal profits from incremental sales will be 60,000 × 40 = Rs. 24, 00,000.

(*iv*) Discounts

A discount offer to the customers reduces the inflow of cash. It also provides timely payment from the customer. Thus a trade off between timely payment and discount is desired. The discount terms consist of the period extended for discounts and the rate of discount. 4/10 net 40 means that a 4% discount will be offered if the customer pays within 10 days. If he does not pay within that period then he should make his payment within 40 days without any discount.

A discount is provided by a firm to attract timely payment by its customers. It is also used to reduce the cost of collection. Discounts have a cost for example if a firm offers 4% discount if the payment is received within the 10 days, then the firm receives only Rs. 96 and not Rs. 100. Therefore the cost as given above is Rs. 4. The annual cost of this discount will be Rs. 4/ 96 × 365/ 30 × 100 = 50.6%. The firm will receive Rs. 96 on the 10th day and will continue to have the amount for a period of (40 – 10) = 30 days.

An example can also be given on how discounts affect the sales of the firm.

Example 16.2 Discount Policy: A firm has annual credit sales of Rs. 25, 00,000. It grants 2 months credit to its customers with no cash discount facility. It intends to offer a discount of 2/10 net 60. It is expected that this will reduce average collection period to one month and 50% of the customers (in value) will take advantage of this benefit the selling price per unit is Rs. 25 while average cost per unit is Rs. 20.

You are required to advise the firm in the new scheme presuming required rate of return on investment is 25% and one month is of 30 days.

Solution

Annual Credit Sales = Rs. 25, 00,000

Cash Discount allowed 50% will take advantage

$$25{,}00{,}000 \times \frac{50}{100} \times \frac{2}{100} = \text{Rs. } 25{,}000$$

$$\text{Present Investment in receivables} = \frac{\text{Holding Period}}{\text{Months in a year}} \times \frac{\text{Average cost}}{\text{Selling Price}}$$

$$25{,}00{,}000 \times \frac{2}{12} \times \frac{20}{25} = \text{Rs. } 333333.32$$

Expected Investment in receivables

$$25{,}00{,}000 \times \frac{1}{12} \times \frac{20}{25} = \text{Rs. } 16666.66$$

Decrease in Investment in receivables Rs. 166666.66

Savings in capital cost

$$166666.66 \times \frac{25}{100} = \text{Rs. } 41666.65$$

$$\text{Net Savings} = 41{,}666.665 - 25{,}000 = \text{Rs. } 16666.66$$

Company should allow 2% discount.

It means 2% discount of payment is made within 10 days net 60 means full payment by the end of 60 days from date of sale.

16.5 CREDIT EVALUATION

The relaxed credit terms and discounts should not be extended to all the customers. A strict evaluation policy should be prepared and only those customers who qualify for easy credit terms and discounts should be allowed the benefits. The reason for this is the risk of default. After the customers qualify for easy terms they should still be monitored and on the basis of their continued evaluation support should be extended to them. We have already discussed that the 5 C's should be used to find out the worthiness of the customers. After that the highest importance should be given to the financial information of the customer. This information can be collected from the following sources.

(*i*) **Bankers References:** A bankers reference is of great value as it provides a credit rating to a customer. Although banks do not show the financial records of their customers, they do give information whenever it is required.

(*ii*) **Published Financial Statements:** Large companies have published balance sheet and profit and loss account and other information. In this case it is easy to evaluate a customer. However, when small firms approach the firm for credit and discount personal inspection and analysis of audited balance sheet provide information about the customer.

(*iii*) **Inspection to the Office Premises:** The firm can send its representatives to inspect the offices, store and factory and take an estimate of the credit worthiness of the customer and make an evaluation according to the 5 C's.

(*iv*) **Credit Agents Report:** Credit rating is possible by hiring a credit agent to give a report of the customer. A credit agent would make an evaluation on behalf of the firm. On the basis of this evaluation credit can be extended by the firm.

16.6 CONTROL OF RECEIVABLES

The last process of receivables management consists of control in receivables. When a firm has made a credit policy it has to follow rigorous procedure. If the firm becomes lenient in its collection procedure the cost of delinquency will increase. The firm should build a system in collecting receivables. It should send continuous reminders to customers. They should send their sales staff to make person visits for collection of the amount on credit sales. Sometimes a firm may have to initiate legal action if the customer does not pay in time.

(*i*) Monitoring Receivables

(*a*) The firm has to prepare the average collection period by calculating the average receivables and the credit sales per day. Monitoring has to be done on a weekly basis.

$$\text{Average collection period} = \frac{\text{Average receivables}}{\text{Credit sales per day}}$$

The average receivables turnover should be calculated by the following formula:

$$\text{Average receivables turnover} = \frac{\text{Number of days}}{\text{Average collection period}}$$

(*b*) Receivables can also be monitored by preparing an aging schedule. This is calculated through the number of days of default. For example, if a firm has a policy for allowing 15 days credit then the ageing schedule can be prepared in the following way:

Ageing Schedule of Receivables

Age Group	% of Total Outstanding Receivables
Above 15 days	20
15 – 30 days	10
30 – 45 days	5
45 – 60 days	1

This shows that the firms monitoring process is good because there is hardly any debt between 45 days and 60 days. 1% may be due to bad debts of the firm. However, the firm should try to see that there are no collections left between 30–45 days because the policy of the firm is to grant a discount of 15 days only.

(*c*) The degree of credit means the maximum credit to grant to a customer. Those customers which are of a high risk group should be given less credit compared to those who are of a lower risk group. Hence, customers should be classified to see if credit facilities should be provided or not.

Example 16.3 A firm is considering pushing up its sales by extending credit facilities to following categories of customers.

5% risk of non-payment in category 'A'

25% risk of non-payment in category 'B'

The increase in monthly sales expected in category A is Rs. 35,000 while in category B are Rs. 40,000.

The cost of production and selling costs are 60% of sales while collection costs amount to 5% of sales in category A and 10% of sales in category B.

You are required to advise the firm about extending credit facilities to different risk groups of customers.

Extending credit facilities to 5% risk group of customers

A.	Incremental sales	35,000
	Less: Risk of non-payment 5% on gross	1,750
	Net Sales realized	33,250
	Less: Production + Selling cost 60% of sales 21,000	
	Less: Collection Costs 5% 1,750	22,750
	Incremental income	10,500

Extending credit facilities to 25% non-payment risk group

B.	Incremental Sales	40,000
	Less: Risk in non-payment 25%	10,000
	Net Sales realized	30,000
	Less: Production + Selling cost 60% of sales Rs. 24,000	
	Less: Collection Costs 10% 4,000	28,000
	Incremental Income	2,000
	Risk is too high	

(*d*) *Accounting Ratios*: The firm should monitor the collection of credit by the use of accounting ratios to find out the change in the pattern of receivables. Some of these ratios are the receivable turnover ratio as well as the average collection period.

(*ii*) Evaluation of Credit Policy

To conclude the discussion it may be stated that the credit policies must be evaluated carefully on the basis of both profit and cost. The cost of each proposal should be analysed. Further, the incremental cost and the incremental profits should be evaluated.

Since the firm will invest in the higher amount of receivables, the funds that are blocked due to the increase in receivables should be analysed because there is cost which has to be calculated on it. When credit facilities are extended bad debts will occur, therefore policies must be constantly reviewed.

POINTS TO REMEMBER

- A firm sells goods on credit to increase its volume of sales and also its profitability.
- The extension of credit creates both risks and costs.
- It is important to have a trade off between profitability and costs while credit sale reduces liquidity it increases profitability but costs also increase. This has to be balanced.
- Receivables involve credit policies, credit terms and collection policies.
- Policies must be framed according to the credit standards of customers. Only if they pass the 5 C's test, they should be extended credit.
- There are two different kinds of customers: high risk customers and low risk customers. Only low risk customers should be extended credit.

OBJECTIVE TYPE QUESTIONS

State whether the following statement is true (T) or false (F).

1. Receivables management is concerned with optimum inventory.
2. The cost and benefits trade off help to optimize receivables policy.
3. Cost of delinquency refers to the extended period of credit beyond the due date.
4. The objective of the credit policy is to provide support to a firm to liberalize its terms for benefits.
5. Ageing schedule helps to monitor receivables.
6. Receivables should be minimized for maximum benefits.
7. Cash discounts help a firm to expedite its cash collections.
8. A customer should be analysed before providing relaxation in credit terms.
9. Receivables policy extends to cash sales, collection of cash from credit sales and inventory management.
10. The credit period should be decreased and collection procedures should be controlled to decrease the level of receivables.

[**Answers:** 1. (F), 2. (T), 3. (T), 4. (F), 5. (T), 6. (F), 7. (T), 8. (T), 9. (F), 10.(T)]

THEORETICAL QUESTIONS

1. What is a credit policy? Discuss the objectives of a credit policy of a large firm.
2. What are the costs and benefits of a credit policy?
3. How do you evaluate a policy to find out whether it is useful for a firm?
4. What are the consequences of increasing and decreasing the credit period of a firm?
5. Discuss some of the techniques for control of receivables.
6. Write short notes on:
   (*a*) Credit terms
   (*b*) Credit standards
   (*c*) Collection procedure in receivables management
   (*d*) Credit evaluation of customers
   (*e*) Optimum credit policy
7. What is the importance of an ageing schedule? Prepare a schedule?
8. Discuss the costs of receivables. How is the average age of receivables important in receivables management?

ILLUSTRATIVE PROBLEMS

Illustration 16.1 A company has a sales level of 20,000 units @ Rs. 600 per unit. It has a fixed cost of Rs. 6,00,000 and variable costs of Rs. 200 per unit. The credit allowed by the company is 30 days. The company proposes to relax the present credit period to (*a*) 60 days and (*b*) 90 days. The following estimates are provided:

Particulars	Existing	Proposal (A)	Proposal (B)
Credit period	30 days	60 days	90 days
Increase in sales	—	20%	30%
Bad debts	1%	1%	1%

The fixed costs increase by Rs 60,000 beyond an increase of 25% of the current sales. The company plans to have a pretax return of 20% on its investments in receivables. Advise the firm as to which of the proposals it should adopt.

Solution

Evaluation of 3 proposals for extension of credit

Particulars	30 days (Rs.)	60 days (Rs.)	90 days (Rs.)
Sales in units	20,000	24,000	26,000
Sales revenue	1,20,00,000	1,44,00,000	1,56,00,000
Less: variable costs	40,00,000	48,00,000	52,00,000
Total contribution	80,00,000	96,00,000	1,04,00,000

[Contd...]

Particulars	30 days (Rs.)	60 days (Rs.)	90 days (Rs.)
Less: other costs			
Fixed costs	6,00,000	6,00,000	6,60,000
Bad debts	1,20,000	1,44,000	1,56,000
*Investment cost	76666.66	1,80,000	2,93,000
	796666.66	9,24,000	11,09,000
	7203333.34	86,76,000	92,91,000

The firm gets maximum return with 90 days extension of credit.

*Investment cost			
Investment in debtors	**30 days**	**60 days**	**90 days**
Variable cost + Fixed cost/Debtors turnover	46,00,000/12	54,00,000/6	58,60,000/4
	= 383333.33	= 9,00,000	=14,65,000
Cost of Investment in debtors × 0.20	76666.66	1,80,000	2,93,000
Debtors turnover ratio =	360/30 = 12	360/60= 6	360/90 = 4
90 days proposal is the best			

Illustration 16.2 A company has annual sales of Rs. 30,00,000. The selling price per unit is Rs. 8 and variable cost is Rs. 2 per unit of selling price. The required rate of return on investment is 20%. Average cost per unit is Rs. 5 the credit terms are 2 months. The annual collection expenditure is Rs. 30,000 and default risk is 2%. The company wants to change its policy by following one of the new proposals. The information is as follows:

Particulars	Proposal (1)	Proposal (2)
Average collection period	1.5 months	1 month
Annual collection expenditure	60,000	1,00,000
Percentage of default	1%	1%

Which of the credit policies should the firm follow?

Solution

Evaluation of credit policies

Particulars	Existing policy (Rs.)	New policy (1) (Rs.)	New policy (2) (Rs.)
Sales	30,00,000	30,00,000	30,00,000
Annual collection cost	30,000	60,000	1,00,000
Less bad debts	60,000	30,000	30,000
*Debtors investment cost	37,500	28,125	18,750
Total costs (Rs.)	1,27,500	1,18,125	1,48,750

* Cost of investment in debtors			
Investment in debtors (Rs.)	11,25,000/6	11,25,000/8	11,25,000/12
[Sales – (No. of units × Average cost)]	= 1,87,500	= 1,40,625	= 93,750
Debtors investment cost @ 20% (Rs.)	37,500	28,125	18,750
Debtors turnover ratio	360/60 = 6	360/45 = 8	360/30 = 12

The new policy (1) has a minimum cost of operation, so it should be selected.

> ***Note:*** Average cost = Fixed cost + Variable cost = Rs. 5 (given above in Question).
> No. of units = Sales/price per unit = 30,00,000/8 = Rs. 3,75,000.

Illustration 16.3 A company sells its goods on credit but does not have a policy of offering any discounts. It is planning to give 3% discount, if payment is made within 15 days. The firm's current collection period is 60 days. Sales are 5,00,000 units and selling price is Rs. 50 per unit. Variable cost is Rs. 20 and average cost is Rs. 25 per unit.

The company wants to change its credit terms. It expects to increase its sales by 50,000 units and the average collection period will reduce to 45 days. Due to increase in sales an additional capital will be required of Rs. 80,000. Assuming 50% of the total sales will be on cash discount and 20% is required rate of return. Should the proposal be accepted?

Particulars	**Amount (Rs.)**
Increased sales revenue 50,000 × 50	25,00,000
Less: variable costs 50,000 × 20	10,00,000
Incremental contribution	35,00,000
Add: savings in cost due to decrease in debtors	79166.66
	3579166.666
Less: cost of additional capital required 1,00,000 × 0.20	20,000
Less: cost involves in cash discount 0.03 × 5,50,000 × 50 × 0.5	4,12,500
Profit	3146666.666

> ***Note:*** Savings due to decrease in average collection without cash discount = 5,00,000 × 25/8
> = Rs. 2083333.33

Expected investment in debtors with cash discount = (5,00,000 × 25) + (50,000 × 20)/ 8 = 16,87,500

Decrease in investments = 395833.33

Savings in costs = 395833.33 × 0.20 = Rs. 79166.66

Illustration 16.4 A company manufactures a small part of a computer. The part is sold for Rs. 1000 and its variable cost is Rs. 700. The company sold on an average 300 units every month in 2006. At present the company grants one month credit to its customers. The company plans to extend the credit to 2 months on account of which the following is expected:

Increase in sales is 20%

Increase in stock Rs. 1,50,000

Increase in creditors Rs. 60,000

Should the company extend the credit terms if

(*a*) All customers avail of the extended period of 2 months.

(*b*) If new customers avail of 2 months credit. The assumption is that the increase in sales is due to new customers.

The company expects a minimum rate of return of 30% on its investment.

Solution

(*a*) Incremental profit

Particulars	Amount (Rs.)
Incremental sales revenue 75 × 12 × 1,000	9,00,000
Less: Increased variable costs 9,00,000 × 0.70	6,30,000
Incremental contribution	2,70,000
Less: Cost of additional working capital	1,21,500
Incremental profit	1,48,500

Note: (*i*) Present investment in debtors

$300 \times 12 \times 700/12 = \text{Rs. } 2,10,000$

(*ii*) Proposed investment in debtors

$375 \times 12 \times 700/6 = \text{Rs. } 5,25,000$

Additional investment in debtors (*ii*) – (*i*) =	3,15,000
Add: Increase in stock	1,50,000
	4,65,000
Less: Increase in creditors	60,000
Additional working capital required	4,05,000
Minimum return expected 4,05,000 × 0.30	1,21,500

(*b*) Incremental profit

Particulars	Amount (Rs.)
Incremental sales revenue 75 × 12 × 1,000	9,00,000
Less: Increased variable costs 9,00,000 × 0.70	6,30,000
Incremental contribution	2,70,000
Less: Cost of additional working capital	58,500
Incremental profit	2,11,500

Note: Additional investment in debtors = 300 × 12 × 700/6= Rs. 4,20,000

Add: Increase in stock	Rs. 4,20,000
	Rs. 4,65,000
Less: Increase in creditors	Rs. 2,55,000
Additional working capital required	Rs. 1,95,000
Minimum return expected 1,95,000 × 0.30	Rs. 58,500

Illustration 16.5 A company is planning to tighten its credit policy. It has an annual sales of Rs. 50,00,000. The proposed new policy would reduce the sales to Rs. 42,00,000. However, the average age of receivables would reduce to 40 days from the present 60 days. The sale price of the product is Rs. 50 and the variable cost is Rs. 25 on the volume of 1,00,000 units, the average cost is Rs. 40. Assume 1 year to be 360 days. Advise whether the proposed credit policy should be implemented. The firm's required rate of return is 20%.

Solution

Step 1: Calculate average investment in accounts receivable.

Number of units presently manufactured = Rs. 50,00,000/50 = Rs. 1,00,000

Fixed costs = (Average cost per unit – Variable costs per unit) × Number of units

= (40 – 25) × 1,00,000 = Rs. 15,00,000

Step 2: Evaluation of proposed policy – investment in receivables

Particulars	Present policy (Rs.)	Proposed policy (Rs.)
Total no. of units	1,00,000	84,000
Fixed cost	15,00,000	15,00,000
Variable cost	25,00,000	21,00,000
Total cost of sales	40,00,000	36,00,000
Debtors turnover ratio	360/60 = 6	360/40 = 9
Average investment in accounts receivable	666666.66	4,00,000

Savings = Reduction of investment × Required rate of return = 266666.66 × 0.20 = 53333.33

Step 3: Evaluation of profit of proposed policy

Particulars	Present policy (Rs.)	Proposed policy (Rs.)
Selling price per unit	Rs. 50	Rs. 50
Sales	50,00,000	43,00,000
Total cost	40,00,000	36,00,000
Profit	10,00,000	7,00,000
Reduction in profit	3,00,000	—

Since profits have reduced the firm should not accept the proposal.

Illustration 16.6 A company has an annual sale of Rs. 12,00,000 currently and its average collection period is 45 days. The product is manufactured with a variable cost of Rs. 10 and is sold at Rs. 50 per unit. The fixed expenses of the firm are Rs. 1,00,000. The firm plans to offer a discount of 2% if payment is made within 10 days of sale. 80% of the customers would take advantage of this offer. Sales turnover is likely to increase by 30% and average collection period will reduce to 25 days. Should the firm implement the proposal if the required rate of return of the firm is 20%.

Solution

Make a cost benefit analysis.

No. of units in present policy = Sales/Selling price per unit = 12,00,000/50 = 24,000

No. of units in proposed policy = Sales/Selling price per unit = 15,60,000/50 = 31,200

Step 1: Cost of cash discount

Discount to customers for making payment within 10 days = 15,60,000 × 0.02 × 0.80 = Rs. 24,960

Step 2: Benefits of cash discount

Increase in profits is due to increased sales.

Particulars	Present Policy (Rs.)	Proposed Policy (Rs.)
Sales	12,00,000	15,60,000
Less: Variable cost	2,40,000	3,12,000
Less: Fixed cost	1,00,000	1,00,000
Profit	8,60,000	11,48,000

Incremental profits = Rs. 11,48,000 – 8,60,000 = Rs. 2,88,000

Step 3: Investment in accounts receivable

Particulars	Present Policy (Rs.)	Proposed Policy (Rs.)
Variable Cost + Fixed Cost	3,40,000	4,12,000
Average collection period	45	25
Total in accounts receivables	8	14.4
Average investment	42,500	28,611.11

Decrease in investment 42,500 – 28611.11 = 13888.89

Cost of funds saved = Rs. 13888.89 × 0.20 = Rs. 2777.778

Total benefits = Incremental profits + Savings

= 2,88,000 + 2777.778 = Rs. 290777.78

Net benefit = Total profit – Total cost

= 290777.78 – 24,960 = Rs. 265817.778

The firm should implement the proposal.

Illustration 16.7 A company has the following options to change its credit policy.

Particulars	Present (Rs.)	A (Rs.)	B (Rs.)	C (Rs.)	D (Rs.)
Sales	9,00,000	9,50,000	10,00,000	10,50,000	11,00,000
Variable costs 80% of sales	7,20,000	7,60,000	8,00,000	8,40,000	8,80,000
Fixed cost	1,00,000	1,00,000	1,00,000	1,00,000	1,00,000
Average collection period	30 days	45 days	60 days	75 days	90 days

Firm's expected rate of investment = 20%. Which of the above is the best option?

Solution

Evaluation of different policies:

Particulars	Present (Rs.)	A (Rs.)	B (Rs.)	C (Rs.)	D (Rs.)
Sales	9,00,000	9,50,000	10,00,000	10,50,000	11,00,000
Variable costs 80% of	7,20,000	7,60,000	8,00,000	8,40,000	8,80,000
Fixed cost	1,00,000	1,00,000	1,00,000	1,00,000	1,00,000
Profit	80,000	90,000	1,00,000	1,10,000	1,20,000
Total cost	8,20,000	8,60,000	9,00,000	9,40,000	9,80,000
Average collection period	30 days	45 days	60 days	75 days	90 days
Debtors turnover ratio	12	8	6	4.8	4
Total cost of sales/ Debtors turnover ratio	68,333.33	1,07,500.00	1,50,000.00	195833.33	2,45,000
Investment in accounts receivable	—	39,166.67	81,666.67	127500	176666.67
Cost of additional investment @ 20%		7833.334	16333.33	25,500	35333.33
Increase in profit		10,000	20,000	30,000	40,000
Incremental profit		2166.67	3666.67	4,500	4666.67

Option D is the best.

Illustration 16.8 The credit manager of XYZ Ltd. is re-appraising the company's credit policy. The company sells its products on terms of net 30. Cost of goods sold is 85% of sales and fixed costs are further 5% of sales. XYZ classifies its customers on a scale of 1 to 4. during the past five years, the experience was as under:

Classification	Default as a percentage of sales	Average collection period—in days for non-defaulting accounts
1	0	45
2	2	42
3	10	40
4	20	80

The average rate of interest is 15%. What conclusions do you draw about the Company's Credit Policy? What other factors should be taken into account before changing the present policy? Discuss.

(CA Final May 2001)

Solution

Working Notes

If selling price is taken as Rs. 100, cost of goods sold is 85% of selling price i.e., Rs. 85.

∴ Gross profit = 100 – 85 = Rs. 15

Interest cost = 15% of cost of goods sold in proportion to the average collection period. Calculation of Interest cost for different categories:

$$I = 85 \times 15 / 100 \times 45 / 365 = \text{Rs. } 1.57$$

$$II = 85 \times 15 / 100 \times 42 / 365 = \text{Rs. } 1.47$$

$$III = 85 \times 15 / 100 \times 40 / 365 = \text{Rs. } 1.40$$

$$IV = 85 \times 15 / 100 \times 80 / 365 = \text{Rs. } 2.80$$

Gross	I	II	III	IV
Gross profit	15.00	15.00	15.00	15.00
Less: Bad debts	—	2.00	10.00	20.00
Interest cost	1.57	1.47	1.40	2.80
Net profit	13.43	11.53	3.60	7.80
Strategy	Accept	Accept	Accept	Reject

Before changing the present policy, the company should keep in view the past performance and creditworthiness of the customers.

PROBLEMS FOR PRACTICE

Problem 16.1 A firm presently sells on credit but without any discount facility. It is planning to give a discount of 2.5% cash discount if payment is made within 15 days. The firm's current average collection period is 60 days. Sales are 3,00,000 units. Selling price is Rs. 60 per unit. Variable cost per unit is Rs. 10 and average cost per unit is Rs. 25 at the current sales level. The cash discounted is estimated to increase sales by 30,000 units and the average collection period will fall to 40 days. The working capital will increase by Rs. 1,00,000. Should the firm offer the discount if 70% of the total sales will be on cash discount and the firm's required rate of return is 20%.

[**Answers:** Since benefits are higher than costs the proposal should be accepted. Total benefits = Rs. 15,76,666; total cost = Rs. 97,750.]

Problem 16.2 A firm has an annual credit sales of Rs. 30,00,000. It grant 2 months credit to it customers with the 2% discount. It is expected that this will reduce average collection period to 1 month and 50% pf the customers in value will take advantage of this benefit. The selling price per unit is Rs. 30 while average cost per unit is Rs. 20. You are required to advise the firm of the new scheme presuming rate of return on investment is 20% and 1 month is of 30 days.

[**Answer:** This scheme should be accepted as the net savings in receivables is Rs. 26666.66]

Problem 16.3 A firm is considering pushing up its sales by extending credit to the following categories of customers.

10% risk of non-payment in category A

20% risk of non-payment in category B

The increase in monthly sales which is expected in category A are Rs. 3,00,000 and category B are Rs. 4,00,000.

Cost of production and sales are 50% of sales while collection cost are 5% in A and 10% of sales in B. You are requested to advise the firm if the required rate of the firm is 6% on sales.

[**Answer:** The firm should extend credit to A category. It can extend credit to B category also but the risk is higher. The benefit is higher in A.]

Problem 16.4 A firm presently has credit terms of net 30 days. It has Rs. 50,00,000 in credit sales and its average collection period is 45 days. To stimulate sales the company plans to give credit net 60 days. This is expected to increase sales by 15% the average collection period will become 75 days. Variable costs are 80% of account receivables. The company requires a return of 20% on its investments. Should the firm extend the credit period?

[**Answer:** Since the increase in net profit on sales is Rs. 1,50,000 and the incremental costs are Rs. 91666.66 proposal should be accepted.]

Problem 16.5 The following are details of operations of a firm during a period of 12 months.

Sales	Rs. 10,00,000
Selling price per unit	Rs. 10
Variable cost per unit	Rs. 6
Total cost per unit	Rs. 8

Credit period to customers 1 month. The firm proposes a more liberal credit policy by increasing credit from 1 month to 2 months. Relaxation is expected to increase sales by 20% from its existing level.

Advise the firm for adoption of new policy presuming a return of 25%.

[**Answer:** Required rate of return is 25% while actual return on additional investment in receivables comes to 66% the proposal should be accepted.]

❑❑❑

Inventory Management 17

LEARNING OBJECTIVES

17.1 Introduction
17.2 Objectives of Inventory Management
17.3 Types of Inventory
17.4 Benefits of Holding Inventory
17.5 Cost of Holding Inventory
17.6 Techniques of Inventory Management
- ABC Analysis
- Economic Order Quantity (EOQ) Model
- Recorder Level and Minimum Level Stock
- Ageing Schedule

17.1 INTRODUCTION

Inventory consists of raw materials; work in process and finished goods. Raw materials are the basic materials used for manufacturing a product. Usually raw materials are purchased for production from different sources to get a maximum benefit of price and quality. Firms usually find the sources where such materials actually exist and purchase from there after calculating their own requirements of inventory. Such items are put into production and when they are manufactured, they are sold as finished goods. The financial manager has to assess the right quantity of inventory required by a firm. Inventory must be controlled because losses arise if it is not safely and properly stored. Losses also arise if too much inventory has been purchased. Inventory can be stolen or it can be wasted. The techniques of inventory management may be applied to reduce such kinds of losses. Inventory should be purchased in the right time and the right quantity and it should be controlled to have efficient inventory management. This chapter covers the basic objectives of inventory management. It discusses costs and benefits of managing inventory. It also gives an explanation of some techniques like the ABC analysis, EOQ model and the reorder level of units. There are different objectives of inventory management. These are discussed ahead.

17.2 OBJECTIVES OF INVENTORY MANAGEMENT

The objectives of inventory management are to provide adequate inventory for the requirements of the firm in the process of work. This can be called the conservative objective of inventory management. This will ensure abundant inventory but high investment in inventory. Efficient inventory management requires that investment is at a minimum level and at the same time it is able to satisfy production use and requirements of sale of the finished product. This means that inventory management has conflicting objectives. However, an optimum level of inventory is desired in a firm. Thus there has to be a continuous balance between the costs and benefits of storage of inventory. Inventory has the cost of storage as well as the cost of not storing it. This is called the cost of carrying and the cost of not carrying inventory. The storage of inventory has a benefit for all types of firms such as trading and manufacturing firms. The objectives of inventory management (Fig. 17.1.) are:

(*i*) To minimize firm's investment in inventory.

(*ii*) To ensure smooth flow of materials in production and sales operations.

(*iii*) To have an optimum level of inventory through a trade off between costs and benefits of storing and not storing inventory in a firm.

Let us first see the different kinds of materials used in a firm. The materials may be classified into raw materials, work in process and finished goods.

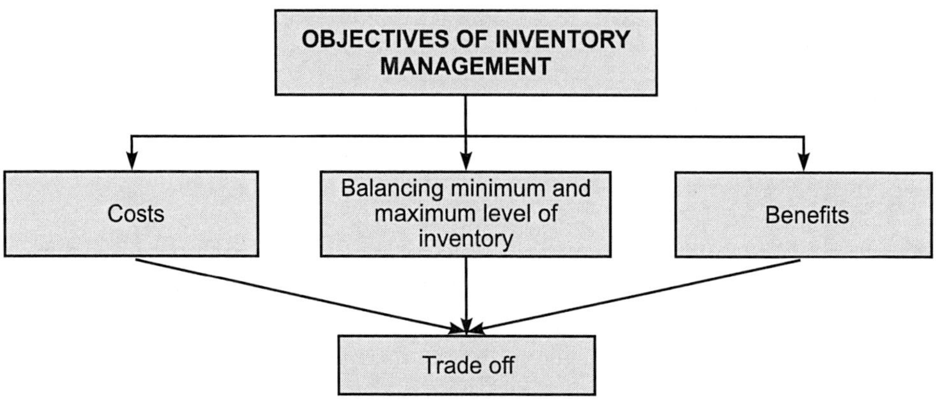

Fig 17.1 Objectives of Inventory Management

17.3 TYPES OF INVENTORY

Inventory required by a manufacturing firm will be different to that of a trading organization. A manufacturing firm will require inventory from the stage of acquiring raw materials for manufacturing goods. A trading firm will acquire material only after they are manufactured to sell or distribute them.

(*i*) ***Raw Material:*** Inventory relating to raw materials is very sensitive because not only should it be bought by the right supplier and the right quantity; it should also be stored with care. Raw materials should be priced correctly when sending them in the manufacturing process. It is useful to make an ageing schedule to see that raw materials are not left unused for a long time. In the stores, they should be managed carefully through the system of bins to make it easy for the manager to assess the minimum and maximum quantity lying with it in the store. The raw materials should be looked after by the manager through storage system of ABC analysis. Raw materials should also be protected by having a stores ledger and day book to record all the transactions of raw materials which leave the store and new purchases which are brought into the store. Raw materials relating to goods returned because they are defective should also be entered in the stores journal.

(ii) ***Work in Process/Progress:*** Such materials are those which are in a semi-finished state. Work in progress may be at a completion of 40%, 50%, 80% or even 90%. Every manufacturing firm has its own cycle of production. Production may vary according to length of time taken for completion of a product. It may also vary according to the volume of materials required for the process. Material should be in abundance as costs of not carrying material are very high. The work in process can close, if timely material is not received. The correct pricing of materials will help in efficient use of resources.

(iii) ***Finished Goods:*** These goods are ready for sale to the customers. Optimum inventory management requires that firms have the opportunity of selling the products as soon as there is a demand for them. Firms ensure that there will be a continuous demand by forecasting sales and finding ready customers so that finished goods do not lie unnecessarily in the store. A large stock of finished goods would mean that stores should be efficiently controlled. It also means that there is high investment in goods. One of the objectives of the financial manager is to see that there are optimum uses so that the finished goods are realized into cash quickly. The benefits and costs of holding inventory can be seen by a discussion.

17.4 BENEFITS OF HOLDING INVENTORY

Inventory is of great importance in production and in marketing of goods. The benefits of inventory are multiple. It is useful in production and sales and it is also useful in trading and in manufacturing firms.

(i) ***Benefits in Production:*** A manufacturing firm will have an uninterrupted production schedule if there is a smooth flow of raw materials. In firms which have a peak season and an off season can take advantage of making purchases in bulk and at a discount and use it in production when required by the firm. Other firms which have a continuous flow of work will be able to deliver goods in time and thus acquire a good reputation of quality as well as timely production.

(ii) ***Benefits in Purchase:*** The purchase of materials in bulk will entitle a firm to discounts and relaxation in credit period. A firm will also be able to purchase goods in advance of production to allow time for raw materials to reach the destination in time. This will help a firm to put its material into production whenever the process begins.

*(iii) **Benefits in Sales:*** A large quantity of inventory in the form of finished goods will enhance sales in a company. It will be able to step up its demand by pushing sales through personal efforts and advertisement. It will be able to deliver the products as soon as there is demand and its comparative position will rise in the market. Thus it will be able to establish a good reputation in the market.

Although there are many benefits of holding inventory, there are many costs associated with it. A firm should invest in inventory after considering all its costs. It has costs which can be identified and those costs which are termed as 'hidden costs'.

17.5 COST OF HOLDING INVENTORY

The objective of inventory management is to see that there are no shortages in the supply of material for work in progress, but the objective is also to minimize the cost of inventory. Thus an efficient management and control is required. To manage inventory it is important to find out the various costs of inventory by estimating the right quantity and the time when it should be ordered. We will first analyse the costs and then discuss the techniques for efficient management of inventory.

There are different costs in purchasing and storing of inventory. These costs are classified as carrying costs, costs of ordering and hidden costs.

(i) **Carrying Costs:** The costs which are incurred for maintaining inventory in a firm are called carrying costs. Such costs vary with size or volume of inventory. Most firms find out the economic order quantity for an efficient order of inventory so that costs are at a minimum level.

The two most important carrying costs are the cost of storage and the costs of financing:

(a) The storing cost consists of rent paid for space for maintaining of inventory. It includes costs like insurance, cost of security of inventory, costs of infrastructure, air-conditioning, and installation of fireproof and theft proof conditions.

(b) Carrying costs also consists of the costs of financing of inventory which may not be used immediately. The expenses of locking up of funds also create costs of opportunity lost for investing funds.

(ii) **Ordering Costs:** There are many costs involved while ordering of goods. Such a cost is fixed per order irrespective of the volume of the order. Such costs include the cost of purchasing and handling an order such as requisition costs, costs of transporting, clerical and administration costs. Such costs are increased with the number of orders. Hence, if the firm maintains a high level of inventory the number of orders will reduce but carrying cost will increase.

(iii) **Hidden Costs:** The costs of ordering and the cost of carrying have to be balanced. When inventory increases in a firm then cost of carrying increases and the costs of ordering decreases. A trade off between carrying costs and ordering cost will bring about optimum inventory level in a firm.

Hidden costs arise when a demand for a material arises but the level of inventory of that material is completely finished. This is called a stock-out. When such costs arise it can be said that it is an opportunity lost because of not carrying inventory. A stock out position is unlikely if safety stock is kept with a firm. For example, if the firm has the experience that it is short of inventory only once in 100 times if it has 400 units in stock then 400 units becomes its safety stock. If it maintains an inventory of 300 units then there is a possibility of the firm being short of 100 units. The size of the stock out increases when the level of safety stock decreases. The probability of stock out is usually calculated in a firm. If for example 400 units is safety stock and the firm has only 300 units then there is a probability of 0.01 or 1% chance of a stock-out in the firm. The cost of stock-out is quite expensive. Hence sufficient quantities of stock should be maintained. When inventory is kept above the required level the hidden cost of carrying arises because the firm does not immediately require the inventory but it is lying in its store and hence other opportunities of investing are lost. The benefits and costs of maintaining optimum inventory is given in Fig. 17.2.

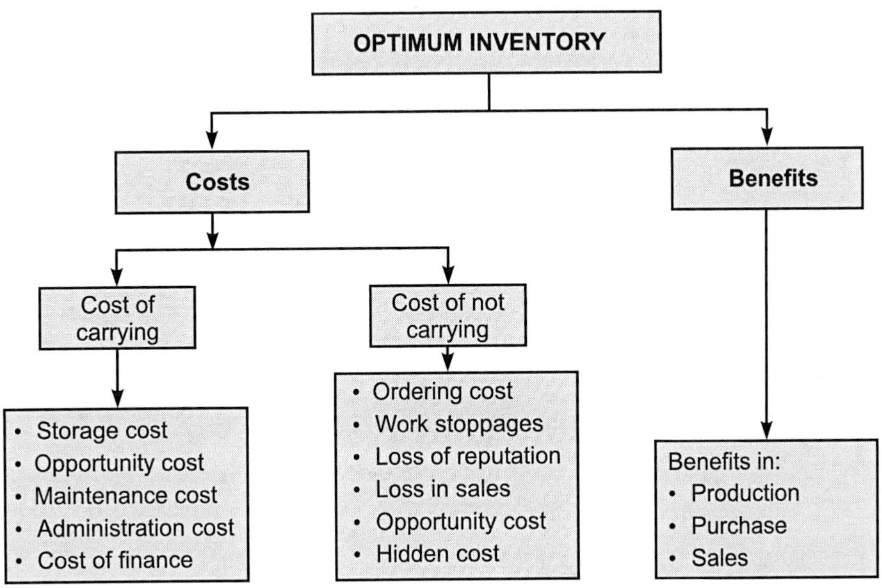

Fig. 17.2 Benefits and Costs of Inventory

17.6 TECHNIQUES OF INVENTORY MANAGEMENT

Inventory management involves the balance between the benefits and the costs of maintaining inventory. The financial manager achieves this task by following certain important techniques like the ABC-Analysis, Economic Order quantity and the correct reorder level of materials. Let us analyse each of these techniques.

I. ABC Analysis

This technique classifies inventories into different types and then controls them. The objective of ABC analysis is to find out those items which most expensive but they are used in small quantity. Such items would be called 'A' class of inventory. Those items which are less expensive and also their requirement is higher would be given less security than 'A' class inventory and 'C'. The 'C' groups are relatively low in investment although in number and volume it may be quite high. This can be summarized in the following way.

Classification of ABC Analysis:

A Control most Expensive Items — Tight Security

B Control Less Expensive Items — Medium Security

C Control Least Expensive Items — Low Security

This can be explained through an example. A firm has three different items. Item A is the most expenses but in volume of items only 10 out of 100 is required. This item requires security and the store requires inspection and control. Item B has less investment value than item A and the volume is 20 items which is more than item A and its investment value is Rs. 2,00,000. C involves large number of items but the investment value is low. From point of security control must be least required but in terms of production it may be required crucially but limitations of ABC is that it does not consider this. It gives priority according to investment value

The table below shows the classification of different items.

ABC Analysis

(1)	No. of Items (2) (Rs.)	% of Column (3) (Rs.)	Inventory Value(4) (Rs.)
A	10	70	7,00,000
B	20	20	2,00,000
C	80	10	1,00,000
		100	10,00,000

An example may be given to explain the ABC analysis in greater detail.

Example 17.1 A firm has seven different items in its inventory. The average number of each of these items with the unit cost is given below. The firm wants to introduce the ABC inventory system.

Item No.	Annual Consumption	% of Total Units (%)	Rate per Unit	Total Value (Rs.)
1	5,000	6	100	5,00,000
2	9,000	10	60	5,40,000
3	4,000	7	50	2,00,000
4	20,000	6	6	1,20,000
5	50,000	30	3	75,000
6	15,000	7	10	1,50,000
7	20,000	10	6	1,20,000
8	25,000	24	2	50,000

Solution

The ABC analysis indicates the items in decreasing total value and finding out the percentage of cumulative values and then classifying them into ABC. In this case classification is made through investment value.

Item No.	Annual Consumption	Costs (Rs.)	Total Costs (Rs.)	% to Total Cost	Classification & % to Consumption
1	5,000	5,00,000	10,40,000	59.26	16% (A)
2	9,000	5,40,000			(A)
3	4,000	2,00,000			30% (B)
4	20,000	1,20,000			(B)
6	15,000	1,50,000	5,90,000	33.6	(B)
7	20,000	1,20,000			(B)
5	50,000	75,0000	1,25,000	7.14	54% (C)
8	25,000	50,000			(C)

Thus the above items are classified according to their investment value and then security is provided to them in terms of their investment value.

II. Economic Order Quantity (EOQ)

After making an analysis on the basis of ABC categories, the financial manager should focus his attention to the quantity of inventory which is to be purchased. In particular, it is important to assess the annual requirements and then to find out the economic order quantity or the number of times materials should be bought in one year and the quantity which should be purchased in each lot. The economic order quantity would help to provide a trade off between costs and benefits. It identifies the level of inventory which minimizes the total cost of inventory. Economic order quantity considers both ordering costs and carrying costs. The minimum level of total cost is considered to be the EOQ.

EOQ can be calculated either by the trial and error method or a simple shortcut formula.

The assumptions of EOQ technique are:

(*i*) The firm can forecast its annual consumption of the materials required by it.

(*ii*) The usage of inventory is even and steady.

(*iii*) The orders that are placed are received by the firm when their inventory stock is completely finished.

(*iv*) The ordering and carrying costs are constant when a range of inventory levels are being considered.

(*v*) There are only two costs: these are the cost of ordering and the cost of carrying the inventory.

(*vi*) There is no time gap between order and supply of inventory.

Figure 17.3 depicts a graphical view of the EOQ model. It shows that when the size of the orders increases, then the total cost decreases. It also shows that the carrying costs increases with order size. The total costs will decrease initially when the size of order increases but then the cost increases with the increase in the size if the order. The trade off between the order cost and carrying costs arises at that point where the cost is at the minimum. This is the EOQ.

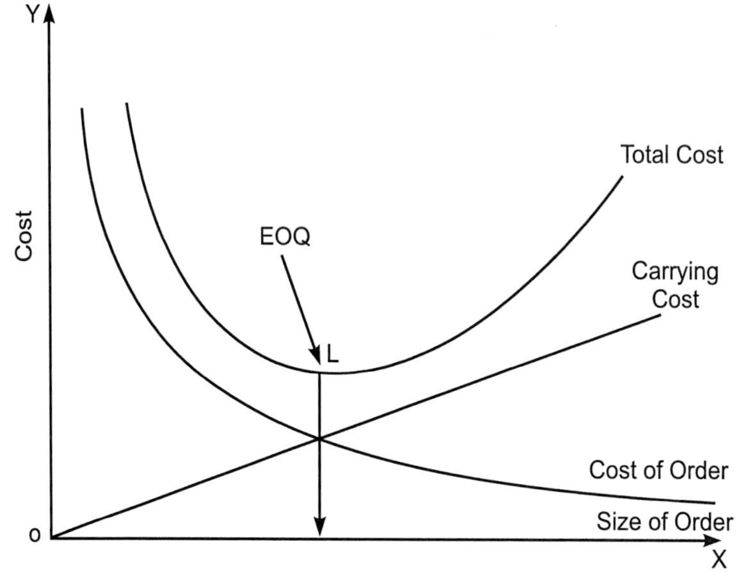

Fig. 17.3 Economic Order Quantity

EOQ can be explained by trial and error method, simple mathematical model and graphical method. These are explained next.

Example 17.2 A firm is planning its annual consumption its annual requirements are 12,000 units. The carrying cost per unit is Rs. 10 and its ordering cost per unit is Rs. 40. The firm can order inventories various lots such as 12,000; 6,000; 4,000; 3,000; 2,000; 1,500; 1,200; 1,000; 500; 300; 200; 100. Which of these quantities is the economic ordered quantity? Find using (*a*) trial and error analytical approach (*b*) mathematical shortcut approach.

Solution

Trial and error method showing economic order quantity

Order Size	Average Inventory (Rs.)	No. of Orders (Rs.)	Annual Costs Carrying (Rs.)	Annual Ordering Costs (Rs.)	Total Costs (Rs.)
12,000	6,000	1	60,000	40	60,040
6,000	3,000	2	30,000	80	30,080
4,000	2,000	3	20,000	120	20,120
3,000	1,500	4	15,000	160	15,160
2,000	1,000	6	10,000	240	10,240

[Contd...]

Order Size	Average Inventory (Rs.)	No. of Orders (Rs.)	Annual Costs Carrying (Rs.)	Annual Ordering Costs (Rs.)	Total Costs (Rs.)
1,500	750	8	7,500	320	7,820
1,000	500	12	5,000	480	5,480
500	250	24	2,500	960	3,460
300	150	40	1,500	1600	3,100
200	100	60	1,000	2400	3,400
100	50	120	500	4800	5,300

Thus EOQ shows how much inventory should be bought in one lot *i.e.*, the appropriate quantity.

Mathematical model

$$\text{EOQ} = \sqrt{\frac{2uo}{c}}$$

EOQ = Economic Order Quantity

u = Quantity of units purchased or required in a year

o = Cost of placing an order

c = Cost of carrying one unit

$$\text{EOQ} = \sqrt{\frac{2 \times 12{,}000 \times 40}{10}} = 309.8 \text{ units}$$

Thus trial and error method is approximate. It shows 300 units as the optimum size whereas the shortcut method shows 309 units.

The EOQ as explained above can be depicted graphically as shown in Fig. 17.3.

The Limitations of the Model are:

(*i*) It assumes that the firm makes an exact estimate of its future requirements. It is difficult to predict the exact usage of items because consumption fluctuates with demand as well as with seasonal variations.

(*ii*) The model assumes a very unrealistic issue when it states that there is no time gap between order of an item and its future supply. Supply is not always efficient as it depends on transportation and other human limitations.

(*iii*) The EOQ dies not consider the order of units in fractions. Goods can be ordered only in multiple figures.

(*iv*) The EOQ model assumes that order costs do not change. This means that they do not consider the economies of scale or discounts that are offered for bulk purchases.

III. Reorder Level and Minimum Level Stock

Since EOQ has many limitations the firm should maintain a safety stock so that if supplies are not received in time, such stock can be used as a buffer. A firm should also maintain its inventory in such a way that the reorder point is defined and stock is immediately replenished. At least the order should be sent for replacement of inventory. Reorder level is calculated on the basis of the daily use of the inventory and the lead time which is necessary between placing of order and receiving of delivery of materials. Therefore reorder level can be calculated by the following formula:

Reorder level = Average daily usage of inventory × Lead time

For example if the average daily usage of a firm is 4,000 units and the lead time is 30 days, then the reorder level = 4,000 × 30 = 1,20,000 units.

Just like the reorder level the minimum level or safety stock can be calculated to avoid being out of stock. Safety stock is the minimum level which the firm would require to keep with it because of the time lag between demand and supply.

The discounts on the purchase price are offered to customers by many firms. Although EOQ does not consider these discounts, it is worth considering them if the savings exceed the cost of holding stock. For reorder level, minimum level and advantage of discounts can easily be done by following the ***Bin Card Method*** in stores management which will indicate the level of stock.

IV. Ageing Schedule

It is necessary to prepare an ageing schedule for inventory to prevent stock piling or increasing carrying costs. The ageing schedule helps to identify the date of purchase and slow moving items.

An ageing schedule of inventory

Age classification	Date of Purchase	Amount (Rs.)	(%)
Product 4 up to 15 day	Jan 16	25,000	25
Product 5 (15 - 1 Month)	Jan 12	10,000	10
Product 2 (1 Month - 45 days)	Dec 26	30,000	30
Product 1 (45 days to 2 months)	Dec 10	20,000	20
Product 3 (Above 2 months)	Nov 25	15,000	15
		1,00,000	

The above schedule indicates that 15% of total stock in the firm is still unused. The firm should investigate into its carrying costs. An example of bin card method is given below.

V. Bin Card

A bin card is a card attached to a materials shelf which indicates lead time, reorder level and minimum level of stock.

Example 17.3 Bin Card Method

Reorder quantity	= 500 units
Lead time	= 4–6 weeks
Maximum weekly usage	= 400 units
Minimum weekly usage	= 200 units
Normal usage	= 300 units

Weeks of safety desired by firm 2

Calculate (*a*) reorder level (*b*) minimum level (*c*) maximum level (*d*) average stock level.

Solution

(*a*) Reorder level = Maximum usage × Maximum delivery time

$= 400 \times 6 = 2{,}400$ units.

(*b*) Minimum level = Reorder level – Normal usage × Average delivery time

$= 2{,}400 - (300 \times 5) = 900$ units.

(*c*) Maximum level = Reorder level – Minimum usage × Minimum delivery period + Reorder quantity

$= 2{,}400 - (200 \times 4) + 500 = 2{,}100$

(*d*) Average stock level = Minimum level + Reorder quantity/2

$= 900 + (500/2) = 1{,}150$ units.

Alternative method for Average stock level = Minimum level + Maximum level/2

$= (900 + 2{,}100)/2 = 1{,}500.$

In conclusion, it may be stated that inventory management forms a very important issue in a firm. The right quantity of units should be ordered at the right time to get the maximum benefit. The benefits and costs should be analysed before inventory should be purchased because the costs of carrying are very high. Since costs of not carrying have several costs therefore firms must plan optimum level of inventory.

POINTS TO REMEMBER

- Inventory consists of raw materials; work in process and finished goods.
- Inventory management is the technique of balancing costs and benefits of maintaining inventory.
- The costs of inventory include cost of ordering, cost of carrying and hidden costs.
- The techniques of inventory management are to maintain stock through ABC analysis and to buy stock at the right quantity through EOQ analysis.
- Inventory management also consists of proper management of existing stock to find out the right time to purchase materials. This can be done through bin card method in stores which show the lead time for procuring units, the maximum and minimum usage, the reorder level and the reorder quantity.
- An ageing schedule can be prepared to have a control on usage of stock. It indicates the time period in which the stock has been purchased but not used. As stock becomes old and piled up, it adds to the cost. This cost must be eliminated.

OBJECTIVE TYPE QUESTIONS

State whether the following statement is true (T) or false (F):

1. Inventory management is a study of the costs of inventory.
2. Ordering cost decreases with the increase in the quantity of materials.
3. Carrying cost is due to the expense of storing each unit of material.
4. The cost of carrying and the ordering cost provide the total cost of purchasing materials.
5. ABC analysis explains maximum usage of materials.
6. Since cost of maintaining inventory is high, it should be purchased immediately when it is required.
7. EOQ assumes a forecasted number of units that a firm will require in one year.
8. Carrying costs and cost of ordering are opposite forces.
9. The financial manager has the objective of finding a trade of between benefits and cost of inventory management.
10. Maintaining high inventory level reduces risk but increases cost.

Answers: 1.(F), 2.(T), 3.(T), 4.(T), 5.(F), 6.(F), 7.(T), 8.(T), 9.(T), 10.(T)

THEORETICAL QUESTIONS

1. Discuss the costs and benefits of maintaining inventory.
2. Discuss the objectives of inventory management.
3. Write notes on stock out, re-order level, ageing schedule.
4. What is EOQ model? Discuss its assumptions and limitations.
5. What is ABC analysis? Prepare a table to show how it works.
6. What is ordering cost? Distinguish between ordering cost and carrying cost.
7. What is a stock out position? Discuss the trade off between carrying cost and tock out position of inventory.
8. Briefly discuss the techniques of inventory management.
9. What is safety stock? Show its usefulness in inventory management.
10. What is the importance of inventory management? Discuss the neat for storing inventory by a firm.

ILLUSTRATIVE PROBLEMS

Illustration 17.1 Cost per unit Rs. 30

Annual requirement = 5,000 units

Carrying cost = 10% of cost per unit

Ordering cost = Rs. 50 per order

Discount = 10% on an order of 1,000 units

Solution

Evaluation of the proposals

Annual requirements = 5,000 units

Carrying cost = Rs. 3

Ordering cost = Rs. 50 per order

$$\text{EOQ} = \sqrt{\frac{2 \times 5{,}000 \times 50}{3}} = 408.24 = 408 \text{ units}$$

Comparative evaluation of EOQ and discount offer

Particulars		EOQ	Discount Offer
1. Annual requirement (units)		5,000	5,000
2. Size of order		408	1,000
3. No. of orders (1/2)		12.25	5
4. Cost per order		50	50
5. Total ordering cost (3 × 4) (A)	(Rs.)	612.5	250
6. Carrying cost per unit	(Rs.)	3	3
7. Average inventory		204	500
8. Total carrying cost (6 × 7) (B)	(Rs.)	612	1,500
9. Purchase price	(Rs.)	30	27*
10. Total price of purchase (1 × 9) (C)	(Rs.)	1,50,000	1,35,000
Total cost A + B + C	(Rs.)	1,51,224.5	1,36,750

*Discount 10% on purchase price = 30 – 10% = Rs. 27

The total cost of discount is less than the cost of EOQ. The company should avail of the discount.

Illustration 17.2 The following information is provided

Cost per unit = Rs. 60

Annual requirement = 10,000 units

Carrying cost = 20% of cost per unit

Ordering cost = Rs. 50 per order

Discount = 2% on an order of 2,000 units

Evaluate the proposal. Should the order be placed according to EOQ or should the company avail of the discount offered?

Solution

Step 1: Calculate EOQ

Annual requirement = 10,000 units

Carrying cost = Rs. 12

Ordering cost = Rs. 50 per order

$$\text{EOQ} = \sqrt{\frac{2uo}{c}} = \sqrt{\frac{2 \times 10,000 \times 50}{12}} = 288.67 = 289 \text{ units}$$

Step 2: Comparative evaluation of EOQ and discount offer

Particulars		EOQ	Discount Offer
1. Annual requirement (units)		10,000	10,000
2. Size of order		289	2,000
3. No. of orders (1/2)		35 (34.6)	5
4. Cost per order		50	50
5. Total ordering cost (3 × 4) (A)	(Rs.)	1,750	250
6. Carrying cost per unit	(Rs.)	12	12
7. Average inventory		144.5	1,000
8. Total carrying cost (6 × 7) (B)	(Rs.)	1734	12,000
9. Purchase price	(Rs.)	60	58.8
10. Total price of purchase (1 × 9) (C)	(Rs.)	6,00,000	5,88,000

Illustration 17.3 A company requires 100,000 units of an item annually. The cost per unit is Rs. 10. The cost per purchase order is Rs. 500 and inventory carrying cost is Rs. 5 per unit:

(*a*) What is the EOQ?

(*b*) What should the firm do if the suppliers offer discount?

Further information:

Order Quantity	Discount
4,500–5999	3%
6,000 & above	3.5%

Solution

(*a*) $$\sqrt{\frac{2uo}{c}} = \sqrt{\frac{2 \times 1,00,000 \times 500}{5}} = 4,472 \text{ units}$$

(*b*) Determination of optimum order quantity

Particulars	EOQ (No discount)	Discount Offer 3%	Discount Offer 3.5%
1. Order size units	4,472	5,500	6,500
2. Average inventory	2,236	2,750	3,250
3. Annual requirements	1,00,000	1,00,000	1,00,000
4. No. of orders	22	18	15
5. Price per unit	10	9.7	9.65
6. Cost of purchase	10,00,000	9,70,000	9,65,000
7. Carrying cost @ Rs. 5 per unit	11,180	13,750	16,250
8. Total ordering cost (2 × 4)	49,192	49,500	48,750
9. Total cost (6 + 7 + 8)	10,60,372	10,33,250	10,30,000

The total cost is lowest at 6,500 units and so the firm should place that order.

Illustration 17.4 The following information of two kinds of materials A and B are as follows.

Normal usage: 60 units each per week

Minimum usage: 100 units each per week

Reorder quantity: A = 400 units, B = 500 units

Reorder period: A = 4 – 6 weeks, B = 2–4 weeks

Calculate (*a*) reorder level (*b*) minimum level (*c*) maximum level (*d*) reorder level.

Solution

(*a*) Reorder level = Maximum usage × Lead period

$$A = 100 \times 6 \text{ weeks} = 600 \text{ units}$$

$$B = 100 \times 4 \text{ weeks} = 400 \text{ units}$$

(*b*) Minimum level = Reorder level – Normal usage × Average delivery time in weeks

$$A = 600 \text{ units} - (60 \text{ units} \times 5 \text{ weeks}) = 300 \text{ units}$$

$$B = 400 \text{ units} - (60 \times 3 \text{ weeks}) = 220 \text{ units}$$

(*c*) Maximum level = Reorder level – Minimum usage × Minimum delivery time + Reorder quantity.

$$A = 600 \text{ units} - (30 \times 4) + 400 \text{ units} = 880 \text{ units}$$

$$B = 400 \text{ units} - (30 \times 2) + 500 \text{ units} = 840 \text{ units}$$

(*d*) Average stock level = Minimum level + Reorder quantity/2

$$A = 300 + 400/2 = 500 \text{ units}$$

$$B = 220 + 500/2 = 470 \text{ units}$$

Illustration 17.5 A manufacturer buys equipment from a supplier for Rs. 50 per unit. Total annual requirements are 1,000 units. The following information is available:

Annual return on investment = 10%

Rent insurance taxes per unit = Rs. 2

Cost of placing an order = Rs. 80

Determine EOQ

Solution

$$\text{EOQ} = \sqrt{\frac{2uo}{c}} = \sqrt{\frac{2 \times 1{,}000 \times 80}{7}} = 151.18 = 151$$

$$\text{Total interest cost} = \frac{1{,}000 \times 50 \times 10}{100} = \text{Rs. } 5{,}000$$

Interest cost per unit = Rs. 5,000/1,000 = Rs. 5

Carrying cost = Rs. 5 + Rs. 2 as rent insurance and taxes = Rs. 7

Illustration 17.6 A company requires 3,000 units of a certain item per year. The purchase price is Rs. 40 per unit. The carrying cost of inventory is 25% of the unit cost and cost per order is Rs. 500.

You are required to compute (*i*) EOQ (*ii*) what is the total size of ordering and cost of carrying inventories when 4 orders of equal size are placed.

Solution

(*i*) $\sqrt{\frac{2uo}{c}} = \sqrt{\frac{2 \times 3{,}000 \times 500}{10}}$ = 547.72 = 548 units

(*ii*) Cost of ordering 4 orders of equal size

Order cost = 4 × 500 = 2,000

Order size = 2,000

Average inventory = 1,000

Average carrying cost = 1,000 × 10 = Rs. 10,000

Total cost = 2,000 + 10,000 = Rs. 12,000

Illustration 17.7 A company buys 60,000 units on a material every month to supply steady demand for material in production. Order costs are Rs. 100 per order and carrying costs are Rs. 2 per unit per month.

Calculate EOQ. Should the company accept a quantity discount for the material if he buys in lots of 30,000 units.

Solution

$$\text{EOQ} = \sqrt{\frac{2uo}{c}} = \sqrt{\frac{2\times 7,20,000\times 100}{12}} = 3,464 \text{ units.}$$

If EOQ is 3,464 number of orders will be 7,20,000/3,464 = 208 orders.

The discount offer may be evaluated in the following manner:

Annual cost of maintaining 3,464 units

Order cost	= 100 × 208	= 20,800
Carrying cost	= (12 × 3,464)/2	= 20,784
Total cost of existing policy		= 41,584
No. of orders = 24 and average stock is 30,000/2		= 15,000
Ordering cost 100 × 24		= 2,400
Carrying cost	= 12 × 15,000	= 1,80,000
Total annual cost		= 1,82,400
Discount		= 14,400
		= 1,68,000

The firm should not accept the discount offer.

Illustration 17.8 From the following data for the year ended 31 March 2006, calculate (*i*) inventory turnover ratio of the two items, and (*ii*) their average stock holding in terms of number of days.

Particulars	Material A (Rs.)	Material B (Rs.)
Operating stock 1-4-2005	20,000	18,000
Purchases during the year	1,04,000	54,000
Closing stock 31-3-2006	12,000	22,000

(ICWA Inter June 2001)

Solution

Material Consumed	=	Operating stock + Purchases – Closing stock	
A	=	20,000 + 1,04,000 – 12,000	= Rs. 1,12,000
B	=	18,000 + 54,000 – 22,000	= Rs. 50,000
Average stock	=	(Opening stock + Closing stock)/2	
A	=	(20,000 + 12,000)/2	= Rs. 16,000
B	=	(18,000 + 22,000)/2	= Rs. 20,000

(*i*) Inventory Turnover Ratio

= Raw material consumed/Average stock

A = 1,12,000/16,000 = 7

B = 50,000/20,000 = 2.5

(*ii*) Average Stock Holding in terms of number of days

= 365/Inventory turnover ratio

A = 365/7 = 52.14 days

B = 365/2.5 = 146 days

PROBLEMS FOR PRACTICE

Problem 17.1 The following information of a firm is provided

Inventory requirements = 2000 units

Cost of placing an order = Rs. 50

Carrying cost per unit = Rs. 2

Calculate EOQ.

[**Answer:** 316 units (no fractions to be taken)]

Problem 17.2 A company provides the following information:

(*i*) Carrying cost per unit is Rs. 6

(*ii*) Fixed cost Rs. 15

(*iii*) No. of units required per year is 20,000

Calculate EOQ, total number of orders per year and time gap between two orders.

[**Answer:** 316, 92 orders, 4 days time gap.]

Problem 17.3 A company purchases 10,000 units of spare parts for its annual requirements ordering one month usage at a time. Each spare part costs Rs. 25. The ordering cost per order is Rs. 20 and carrying costs are 15% of unit costs. The firm wants a more economical order. Evaluate it.

[**Answer:** The firm can save 1802.5 – 1231.25 = 571.]

Problem 17.4 The following information has been provided of two items of materials:

Normal usage = 55 units each per week

Minimum usage = 20 units each per week

Maximum usage = 70 units each per week

Reorder quantity A = 250 units, B = 450 units

Reorder period A = 4–6 weeks, B = 2–4 weeks.

Calculate (*a*) reorder level (*b*) minimum level (*c*) maximum level and (*d*) average stock level.

[**Answers:** (*a*) 420,280 units (*b*) 145,115 units (*c*) 610,690 units (*d*) 145,245 units.]

Problem 17.5 A manufacturer buys an equipment from a supplier at Rs. 20. The total requirements are 1,000 units. Additional information is as follows:

Annual return on investment = 10%

Rent, insurance, taxes per unit = Rs. 2

Cost of placing an order = Rs. 70

Determine EOQ.

[**Answer:** 167.33 or 167 units]

Problem 17.6 A company produces a product which has a demand of 60,000 units annually. The product requires a material which can be purchased for Rs. 30. The ordering cost is Rs. 100 per order. Holding cost is 10% per annum.

Calculate (*a*) EOQ, (*b*) if minimum lot size is 5,000 units what is the extra cost to the company and (*c*) what is the minimum carrying cost?

[**Answers:** Extra cost to be incurred is 8,700 – 6,000 = Rs. 2,700 when order size is 5,000 units.]

There is a positive relationship between carrying cost and size of average inventory. Average size of inventory is positively related to size of order. The minimum carrying costs of a firm are 3,000 at an average level of 1,000 units.

❑❑❑

PART VII

Financial Restructuring

Chapter 18: Corporate Restructuring

Corporate Restructuring 18

LEARNING OBJECTIVES

18.1 BACKGROUND

In India the new economic reforms took place in 1991. Since then its economic policy has changed from a controlled economy to a liberal deregulated and globally participative environment. There has been a complete corporate restructuring from government controlled to private enterprise. This has brought about competition in industry leading to mergers and acquisitions, consolidation, divestitures, takeovers and liquidations to bring about change in operations, capital structure and ownership of a company.

18.2 CORPORATE RESTRUCTURING

Corporate restructuring encompasses all forms of change in an organization. It is a comprehensive term which is used to mean changes in the company's structure. There can be many reasons for such structural change. The main essence is to make the company more powerful, productive, profitable and economically viable. Corporate restructuring has a background history in United States of America since 1890, when the first merger took place. Mergers in the US are quite common as most corporate organizations have corporate wars to achieve the position of power. In India, corporate restructuring is becoming a very important way of business both for companies which are financially weak and for financially strong companies.

Reasons for Restructuring

A corporate organization may be restructured due to some selected reasons:

(*i*) **Change in Government Policy:** One of the most important reasons is change in government policy. When major policy changes occur, the business environment completely changes and those businesses which were profitable and useful suddenly become non-existent. Uncontrollable socio-economic factors will increase risk and in a dynamic environment the company may not be able to sustain itself. In this event the company will restructure itself either internally or externally, or both.

(*ii*) **Competition:** When an economy has competition from different countries and large international companies like multinationals are able to produce good quality products at low prices due to economies of scale, a company has to resort to restructuring. Change in consumer choices and high expectation of customers will change the complexion of the business of the company. Survival in an international world may become difficult. In such situations, a company may expand itself by merging with other companies to become a large company or by acquiring another company through takeover.

(*iii*) **Technology Changes:** New technology requires more investment which a company may not be able to do in isolation because of high expenses involved. It may decide to become part of a larger company. This may have a holding company and a subsidiary company. Through this form it will survive technology changes and yet retain some of its original flavour for business. Shifts in methods of production from traditional environment to modern and scientific methods will bring about a more powerful organization. Innovations and change in technology are thus an important factor for restructuring a corporate organization.

(*iv*) **Inflation:** Countries which face persistent price rise leading to inflation will have an impact on their business environment. Some industries do not function in the same manner as in normal conditions. Small individual firms find it difficult to survive because the production costs become high and the demand for the product falls. Trends show that corporate organizations increasingly have to restructure themselves to be able to survive the pressure of raising prices. They make arrangements for voluntary settlements, liquidation or reorganization formulating changes in their corporate policies and control function.

18.3 TYPES OF REORGANIZATION

Reorganization takes some of the following forms:

(*i*) Mergers

(*ii*) Acquisitions

(*iii*) Takeovers

(*i*) **Merger:** Two or more companies decide to combine to form one company. This form of the reorganization is called 'merger'. In India, mergers are popularly called 'amalgamation'. Merger can take place through absorption or consolidation. There is a difference between absorption and consolidation.

Absorption is the combination of two or more companies to become a single company. Such a merger results into loss of identity of merging companies. Only one of the companies retains its identity and the others are merged in it.

Consolidation is a combination of two or more companies to form into a single newly created company. All the companies lose their identity. The ownership shares, liabilities and assets are transferred by the acquired company to the acquiring company. Amalgamation and consolidation are used interchangeably in India. There can also be reverse mergers. Such mergers takes place to give strength to a sick company in business, situation where a smaller company takes over a larger one. In this situation the profitable company loses its identity and merges with the sick unit.

Mergers take place for enhancing the value of the company. It helps in maximizing the growth of the company. The company expects that merger will bring about an increase in sales and profitability of a company.

(*ii*) **Acquisition:** An acquisition means to takeover the control of another company. Sometimes in an acquisition the two companies desiring consolidation may have independent identity but the amalgamating company will have control over amalgamated company. Acquisition can be through either absorption or consolidation. The new company which is formed through acquisition takes over the asset and liabilities of the other companies.

(*iii*) **Takeover:** A company sometimes obtains control of another company through takeover of its management. The control may be effective. If a company decides to invest more than 10% of the subscribed capital of another company it can result into a takeover. Section 372 of the Companies Act states that approval of government and the shareholders through an annual general meeting is required for subscriptions in excess of 10% of the subscribed capital.

Acquisition and Takeover Distinction

Takeover can be distinguished from acquisition. An acquisition of companies is when two or more companies decide mutually to merge together, but a takeover is a strong reaction or a movement to acquire another company. In an acquisition, the merging between two companies is on a friendly basis to reap the benefits of becoming strong brain in the market. A takeover is like a hostile merger when strong company forcibly takes over a weak company. However, both acquisition and takeover have certain benefits. They create operating or financial synergy. Their main objective is to create economies of scale, become powerful through greater pricing power, combine different functional strengths and have higher growth in new or existing markets.

18.4 FORMS OF REORGANIZATION

Reorganization through mergers, takeovers or acquisitions can have three basic forms:

(*i*) **Horizontal:** When two or more firms having similar types of business, production or distribution of products combine together to become powerful, it is called a 'horizontal reorganization'. For example, two software companies decide to merge to capture the market size of an economy would be a horizontal merger. Example of horizontal merger in India is Hyderabad Allwyn Ltd., Voltas Ltd.

(*ii*) **Vertical:** When two or more firms combine through backward or forward merger, it is called a 'vertical merger'. A forward merger is the combination of a customer with the manufacturing house of a product. For example, a leather coat manufacturer and exporter from India combined his business with a customer to achieve higher sales. This is called 'forward merger'. Sometimes a manufacturing house combined with the supplier of material. This is called 'backward merger'. For example, the leather coats manufacturer combines with the raw material supplier of leather to the factory. Therefore vertical merger happens between people in different stages of production. In India, one of the popular examples can be of Maruti Suzuki Car manufacturers. The company combines different small units for making small parts for the company. A manufacturer makes gears for the car. Another manufacturer makes glass especially for Maruti Suzuki Cars. Thus, it combines many small units to work for it. In effect it does not have full legal control over such small companies but it exerts control over them as these companies have to adhere to Maruti Company's demands, rules and regulations for its own benefit.

(*iii*) **Conglomerate:** When two companies combine for some benefit in unrelated areas of business activity it is called a 'conglomerate merger'. Take the example of Godrej & Boyce which manufactures and distributes of a wide range of consumer durables and industrial products. Another example is of a group companies headed by Anil Ambani with business interests in the sectors of energy, telecommunications, finance, health and media. Similarly, Oswal group of companies offer a range of products including electrical goods, diamonds, financial services, and web services.

18.5 STEPS IN MERGERS AND ACQUISITIONS

Mergers and acquisitions are made through certain evaluations made by the companies. The companies merging together for financial benefits, diversification of risks or operational economies have to first project the kind of benefits they will receive through the synergy of combining the firms. For this to take place the companies have to plan, analyse and evaluate the positive advantages as well as the negative limiting factors to find out the value created by merger. There are three steps in mergers and acquisitions. These are: planning, analysis and calculation of value creation.

(*i*) **Planning:** The acquiring company has to make a SWOT analysis. This analysis should include government policies, the profile of the products that are to be introduced, location of the factory and the type of economies of scale that can be imbibed with the merger. To plan the company's future information must be gathered about the products of the company, the areas of marketing and sales required and plan proper budgets and control systems for long-term and short-term to achieve high returns and create value through synergy.

***(ii)* Analysis:** The merger has to be analysed like a project. In the analysis the company will have to do an economic evaluation of the project, a social cost benefit analysis, and a financial evaluation. This is required in order to make the merger successful. Analysis includes screening of products, new areas of exploration for marketing of goods, analysing, internal control systems and external limiting factors. The company will also have to use ratio analysis especially trend analysis of the company's past profitability, returns on assets, shareholders earnings, dividends financial leverage and debt equity position. Such an analysis will help in creating value of the combined firms.

***(iii)* Value Creation:** Value creation means the benefit that will arise from the synergy of two firms on their merger. The firm that is acquiring another firm must pay cash which is equal to the value of the acquired firm. This will bring about economic advantage to the shareholders. The firms can create value by calculating the cost of the merger and how much advantage each firm will have after the acquisition takes place. Value of creation can be done through estimation of the cost of capital of each company, projecting cash flows, calculating the net present value of the companies and the impact on the earnings per share of the shareholders through acquisition. Therefore for value creation the companies wanting to merge or go in for acquisition or takeover should calculate the following:

(*a*) Estimation of the cost of capital

(*b*) Exchange value of shares

(*c*) Impact on earnings per share or shareholder

The effects of mergers should be calculated to determine pre- and post-merger benefits and disadvantages. In addition to the above, both the companies have to determine the intrinsic value of the company, determine revised capital structure and give importance to recasting of the new capital structure.

18.6 PROCEDURE FOR MERGERS, ACQUISITIONS OR TAKEOVERS

Once the financial analysis is done, there are importance steps to be taken for actual merger to take place. The following approvals have to be taken for effecting a restructure of the existing company:

***(i)* Board of Directors Approval:** When the decision has been taken to merge because distinct advantages can be seen with the changes in the existing structure into a new restructured organization it is necessary that the proposal is put before the directors of the company. At the meeting the directors have to accept and approve the proposal. This is supposed to be a routine event in any restructuring movement which is internal or external. However, most companies take long-term loan from banks and financial institutions. In such cases the interests of the financial institutions have also to be taken care of. The procedure is that these parties have to be informed and only after their approval the next step can be taken.

***(ii)* Sanction of Shareholders:** In addition to the annual general meeting of shareholders, in case of merger a special meeting of the shareholders will have to be convened. The details of the proposal have to be placed before then. The shareholders of both the companies should have the details as specified in the Companies Act 1956 (Section 73). In this meeting it is necessary that at least three fourth of the shareholders should approve the merger. Shareholder approval will be require by bringing to their notice the cash offer given by the acquiring company, the exchange price of shares, the impact of earnings per share and the merger negotiations that have taken place with both companies. The shareholders sanction the merger and then the next step is to get the approval of the court.

***(iii)*Information to Stock Exchange:** In case of merger or acquisition the stock exchanges in which the companies are registered have to be informed about the decision to merge or the acquired.

***(iv)* Creditors Meeting:** If a company has a large number of creditors both of long term and short term, it must hold a creditor meeting informing the situation and taking an approval. This is necessary because their rights of payment have to be protected and sometimes it may not be acceptable to them to be informed only. They would like to participate, give their opinion and also restrict the new company from certain aspects which do not suit them. Therefore, they should be given a chance to present their restrictive clauses or covenants before the transfer of assets and liabilities of the company.

***(v)*Approval by Court:** When the shareholders sanction the merger/acquisition/takeover, it is important that an application is made to the court giving details of the desired change from the present form of company. The acquisition gives the details regarding share exchange, impact on earnings per share, intrinsic value of the companies, the revised capital structure and the recasting of the present capital structure.

***(vi)* Satisfaction of the Court:** The court is interested in finding out whether the shareholders interests have been kept intact and the merger will actually benefit them. They are keen to see that there is an equitable and fair exchange of shares between both the companies. They also carefully analyse whether the exchange and reorganization is within the permissible levels of the Companies Act. According to the Companies Act, an individual or a company cannot invest or acquire more than 25% of the total paid of capital in the acquiring company together with the shares that it holds earlier. The Central Government also has to approve its holding if it exceeds 10% of subscribed capital. The court analyses that all the Sections of the Companies Act have been complied with and approvals have been taken from the directors and the shareholders. Thereafter, when they are satisfied with the genuineness of the case, they will give their approval through a court order.

***(vii)* Transfer of Assets and Liabilities:** When the court order is received, the acquiring company will transfer the acquired company's shares and restructuring as decided by both the companies will take place.

(*viii*) **Exchange of Payment:** The acquiring company will pay cash to the acquired company and in exchange the acquired company will give its shares and debentures to the acquiring company. A new listing on the stock exchange will be required by the reorganized structure of the companies.

18.7 DEFENSIVE STRATEGIES OF COMPANIES

Some companies adopt defensive strategies at the time of mergers/acquisition/takeovers to get a better bargain while restructuring into a new company. These strategies consist of divestiture or spin of strategies for higher return to shareholders. The sell-off is done either as a whole company or a part of it. Sometimes it is a merger by choice of both the companies and sometimes it is a question of distress restructuring when the company does not have any means of making a profit and the intrinsic value of the company is below expectations. The following strategies are adopted.

(*i*) **Divestiture:** When a company decides on to divestiture its business it sells off or spins off some part of its business into an independent subsidiary company. Spin-off strategy helps the company in retaining the identity of the company as a separate division or a subsidiary. In spin-off a company becomes a separate company and the business unit does not get sold for cash. It distributes the shares of the company to the shareholders on a pro-rata basis. The company which is taking over and buying this company can use its managerial capacity for the other unit to make it profitable. In such a situation, the parent company retains control over the company but some equity shares are transferred to the other company. Acquiring company expects a higher profitability by using the assets of the acquire company.

(*ii*) **Crown Jewels:** In a takeover situation, many companies sell some of their shares through divestiture strategy. This strategy is called by the term 'selling of crown jewels'. In UK, this spin-off is not allowed as the strategy is in favour of one company, whereas two or more companies have to make a deal between them in restructuring their capital structure.

(*iii*) **Poison Pill:** The poison pill strategy is used by the buyer company when it is bidding for another company for acquiring it. The acquiring company itself faces a threat from stronger companies for being taken over. In this situation it uses the strategy of 'poison pill' by showing itself as an unattractive company. It tries to dilute the voting control of a company by different methods. One such method is to have a larger number of shares by making a fresh issue of shares. Another strategy is to issue convertible debentures to their existing shareholders. This will reduce the attractiveness of the company unless the takeover company is very strong and does not find it difficult to erode the poison pill strategy.

(*iv*) **White Knight:** It is the term used when a company steps in to help another company. This is a company's strategy to avoid a hostile takeover. It is the most cost-effective method of avoiding a takeover which the company does not find favourable for its operations. The 'black knight' is an unfriendly bidder and a 'grey knight' is more favourable than a black knight/unfriendly bidder. The most favourable is the white knight which is a friendly takeover of another company.

The intention of the white knight is to prevent the unfriendly bidder by offering a higher and better bid to strike a favourable deal with the management for acquisition of the company. Example of a white knight would be when company T, which is the target is to be acquire by company H a hostile firm. Company A which is friendly with company T offers a higher return and thus acts as a white knight.

(*v*) **Golden Parachutes:** It is an agreement between the employer and the employees that they will receive a good amount of severance money if the company decides on a takeover bid by another company. It can be called a compensation that is given if employees are terminated due to merger acquisition or takeover. This compensation is usually given to senior executives. The employees do not resist the takeover/merger/acquisition because it is an attractive form of compensation. Through this strategy the company is able to get its objective without resistance from employees.

(*vi*) **Greenmail:** It is a strategy used by an acquiring company for higher gains. It looks for an incentive by the company which wants to avoid the takeover. It asks for a substantial premium from the company it wants to takeover. It gives the company to repurchase its own shares and prevent the takeover. Greenmail is also known by the terms **Bon Voyage Bonus** or **Goodbye Kiss**.

18.8 ACCOUNTING PROCEDURE OF FIRMS—MERGERS/ACQUISITIONS

There are two methods of accounting in merger/acquisitions. These are—pooling of interests method and purchase method.

(*i*) Pooling of Interest Method

The pooling of interest method consists of the combination of balance sheet and profit and loss account of both the companies without making a record of the effect of merger. The assets liabilities and other items of both the acquiring and the acquired companies are added at the book values without any adjustments. In this method, there is no revaluation of assets or liabilities. Example 18.1 explain this method.

Example 18.1 Pooling of Interests Method of Firms X & Z

(Rs. in Crore)

Column I Particulars	Column II Firm X	Column III Firm Z	Column IV Combined Firms
Assets			
Net fixed assets	20	30	50
Current assets	12	16	28
Total	32	46	78
Shareholders fund	9	16	25
Borrowings	15	20	35
Current liabilities	8	10	18
Total	32	46	78

In this example firm X has merged with firm Z. Firm Z has issued shares of Rs. 12 crore to firm X's shareholders. The balance sheet of both the firms is shown in Example 18.1. The book values are added of their assets and liabilities. Even though Z has issued shares to X's shareholders they are recorded at the book values. The combined values are shown in column IV.

(*ii*) Purchase Method

In the purchase method the assets and liabilities of the acquiring firm are adjusted with price paid to the acquired firm. The assets and liabilities after the merger are revalued. When the acquirer pays a higher price than the market the excess amount is recorded as goodwill. If the value of assets and liabilities is less than the purchase price that is paid then the difference will be added to capital reserve. This is shown in Example 18.2.

Example 18.2 Take the Balance Sheets of Example 18.1 with the additional points. The market value of X's fixed assets are Rs. 22 crore and current assets are Rs. 10 crore. Current liabilities are at book value and the fair value of borrowing is Rs. 14 crore. Firm Z issues shares to its shareholders by Rs. 14 crore to pay excess shareholders.

Solution

Adjustments are made in the following way:

Firm Z after merger

Calculation of goodwill

Payment to X's shareholders	Rs. 14 crore
Add: Fair value of fixed assets	22
Add: Fair value of current assets	10
Less: Fair value of borrowings	14
Less: Fair value of current liabilities	8
	Rs. 10 crore
	Rs. 4 crore

Example 18.3 depicts how the accounting procedure of merger/acquisition takes place.

Example 18.3 Firm A is planning to acquire firm B. The relevant financial details of the two firms prior to merger announcement are as follows:

Particulars	Firm A	Firm B
Market price per share (Rs.)	75	30
Number of shares	10,00,000	5,00,000
Market value of the firm (Rs.)	7,50,00,000	1,50,00,000

The merger is expected to bring gains which have present value of Rs. 1.50 crore. Firm A offers 2,50,000 shares in exchange for Rs. 5 lakh shares to the shareholders of firm B.

You are required to calculate:

(*i*) True cost of firm A for acquiring firm B.

(*ii*) Net present value of the merger to firm B.

You may state your assumptions, if any. **(June 1993, CS)**

Solution

$$\text{\% of shares Firm B gets in New Company} = \frac{2{,}50{,}000 \text{ shares}}{10{,}00{,}000 \text{ shares} + 2{,}50{,}000 \text{ shares}} = 20\%$$

Present value of A & B = Market Value of A + Market Value of B + Gain on merger.

= Rs. 7.50 crore + Rs. 1.50 crore + Rs. 1.50 crore

= Rs. 10.50 crore

20% being given to B = Rs. 2.10 crore

Less value of Firm B (Market value) = Rs. 1.50 crore

Cost of Firm A = Rs. 0.60 crore

Benefit or gain to Firm A = Rs. 1.50 crore

Net Present value of Firm A = Rs 0.90 crore (Rs. 1.50 crore – Rs. 0.60 crore)

Similarly, NPV of Firm B = Rs. 1.50 crore – Rs. 0.90 crore

= Rs. 0.60 crore

Thus net present value of merger to Firm B = Rs. 0.60 crore.

POINTS TO REMEMBER

- A merger is a combination of two or more firms by reorganization of capital structure or ownership of capital or recasting of capital structure.
- The different types of reorganizations are mergers, acquisitions and takeovers.
- In India mergers are called 'amalgamation'.
- There are different forms of mergers. These are horizontal mergers, vertical mergers, and conglomerate mergers.
- Mergers can be through absorption or consolidation.
- Horizontal mergers are a combination of two or more companies in similar types of activities. Vertical mergers combine different stages of production or distribution and conglomerate mergers combine unrelated types of business.

[Contd...]

- It is expected that mergers will bring about the benefits of economies of scales, utilization of under utilized resources. It would also help in creating value to brand image. The maximum benefit would arise in higher profitability, growth and increase in earnings per share.
- Some of the strategies used as a defensive mechanism by companies are divestiture, crown jewels, white knight, greenmail, poison pill and golden parachutes.
- The important steps in mergers are planning, analysis and value creation through financial evaluation.
- The procedure for merger/acquisition/takeover is to first have a directors meeting and take an approval. Then a meeting of the shareholders should be conducted and the aspects relating to the mergers should be discussed. If there are a large number of creditors a separate meeting of the creditors is desired. After their approval an application has to be sent to court. When the court approves of the merger, the stock exchange has to be informed and previous listing is to be removed and application for new listing on the stock market must be done. Then the assets and liabilities have to be transferred and payment and exchange of shares has to be made.
- Cash flows, cost of capital, exchange value of shares and impact on earnings per share are some of the important aspects of analysis.
- There are two accounting procedures. These are called 'pooling of interests method' and 'purchase method'.

OBJECTIVE TYPE QUESTIONS

State whether the following statements are true (T) or false (F).

1. Horizontal merger means combination of two or more companies in different types of business activities.
2. Vertical merger take place in different stages of production and marketing or distribution.
3. A white knight is a friendly company whereas a black knight is hostile company.
4. A greenmail is a green signal for takeover of a company.
5. A golden parachute is given to company executives in the form of money equivalent to the price of gold.
6. The benefits of merger are to create brand image, become a powerful organization and to reap the benefits of experience from each other.
7. The court approval is given after finding out the profitability of merging into one company.
8. The maximum share a company can take from the acquiring company is in terms of 30% of its shares.

9. The assets of the acquired company are transferred to the acquiring company according to the approved scheme and consensus between the two companies.
10. Pooling of interests method reorganizes the balance sheet at the time of acquisition.

[**Answers:** 1. (F), 2. (T), 3. (T), 4. (F), 5. (F), 6. (T), 7. (F), 8. (F), 9. (T), 10. (F).]

THEORETICAL QUESTIONS

1. What is a merger? Discuss the different forms of reorganization—vertical, horizontal and conglomerates.
2. What are the defensive strategies taken by companies to avoid takeovers?
3. What is the procedure for carrying out a merger/acquisition?
4. What are the three important steps for merger/acquisition?
5. Right notes on:
   (*a*) Conglomerate merger
   (*b*) Divestiture
   (*c*) Poison pill
   (*d*) Accounting methods in mergers/acquisition
6. Distinguish between pooling of interests method and purchase method of accounting in mergers and acquisitions.

ILLUSTRATIVE PROBLEMS

Illustration 18.1 A Ltd. is considering takeover of B Ltd. and C Ltd. The financial data for the three companies are as follows:

Particulars		A. Ltd.	B. Ltd.	C. Ltd.
Equity share capital of Rs. 10 each	(Rs. millions)	450	180	30
Earnings	(Rs. millions)	90	18	18
Market price of each share (Rs.)		60	37	46

Calculate:

(*i*) Price earnings ratios

(*ii*) Earning per share of A Ltd. after the acquisition of B Ltd. and C Ltd. separately.

Will you recommend the merger of either/both of the companies? Justify your answer.

(CS Final, December 1995)

Solution

Calculation of P/E Ratios

Particulars		A. Ltd.	B. Ltd.	C. Ltd.
Earning	(Rs. millions)	90	18	18
Number of equity shares	(millions)	45	18	9
EPS	(Rs.)	2	1	2
Market price per share	(Rs.)	60	37	46
P/E Ratio	(Market price/EPS)	30	37	23

Calculation of EPS of A Ltd. after acquisition of B Ltd. and C Ltd.

Exchange ratio or rate = Buyer's P/E ratio/Seller's P/E ratio

Particulars	A. Ltd.	B. Ltd.	C. Ltd.
Exchange ratio in A Ltd.	—	0.81	1.30
Value of shares (Rs. millions)	2,700	666	414
Number of A Ltd.'s shares to be given (millions)	—	666/60	414/60
EPS (Rs.)	—	11.11	6.9
Total earning after acquisition (Rs. million)	—	108	108
Total number of shares (millions)	—	56.1	51.9
EPS after acquisition (Rs.)	—	1.93	2.08

Analysis: After merger of C Ltd. with A Ltd., C Ltd's. EPS is higher than A Ltd. (Rs. 2.08). Hence merger only with C Ltd. is suggested to increase the value to the shareholders of A Ltd.

Illustration 18.2 East Co. Ltd. is studying the possible acquisition of Fost Co. Ltd. by way of merger. The following data are available in respect of the companies.

Particulars	East Co. Ltd.	Fost Co. Ltd.
Earning after tax (Rs.)	2,00,000	60,000
Number of equity shares	40,000	10,000
Market value per share (Rs.)	15	12

(*i*) If the merger goes through by exchange of equity share and the exchange ratio is based on the current market price, what is the new earnings per share for East Co. Ltd.

(*ii*) Fost Co. Ltd. wants to be sure that the earnings available to its shareholders will not be diminished by the merger. What should be the exchange ratio is the case.

(CS Final, December 2000)

Solution

(*i*) Calculation of New EPS of East Co. Ltd.

Number of equity shares to be issued by East Co. Ltd. of Fost Co. Ltd.

= 10,000 shares × Rs. 12/Rs. 15 = 8,000 shares

Total number of shares in East Co. Ltd. after acquisition of Fost Co. Ltd

= 40,000 + 8,000 = 48,000 shares

Total earning after tax after acquisition = 2,00,000 + 60,000 = Rs. 2,60,000

$$\text{EPS} = \frac{\text{Rs. } 2{,}60{,}000}{48{,}000 \text{ equity shares}} = \text{Rs. } 5.42$$

(*ii*) Calculation of exchange ratio which would not diminish the EPS of Fost Co. Ltd. after its merger with East Co. Ltd.

Current EPS

$$\text{East Co. Ltd.} = \frac{\text{Rs. } 2{,}00{,}000}{40{,}000 \text{ equity shares}} = \text{Rs. } 5$$

$$\text{Fost Co. Ltd.} = \frac{\text{Rs. } 60{,}000}{10{,}000 \text{ equity shares}} = \text{Rs. } 6$$

Exchange ratio is to be = Rs. 6/5 = 1.20

Number of new shares to be issued by East Co. Ltd. to Fost Co. Ltd

= 10,000 × 1.20 = 12,000 shares

Total number of shares after acquisition = 40,000 + 12,000 = 52,000 shares

EPS after Merger = Rs. 2,60,000/52,000 shares = Rs. 5

Total earnings of Fost Co. Ltd. = No. of Shares × EPS = 12,000 × Rs. 5 = 60,000

Illustration 18.3 Summarized balance sheet of R. Co. Ltd. as on 31 Dec., 1993 is given below:

Liabilities	Amount (Rs.)	Assets		Amount (Rs.)
Equity share capital		Fixed assets		19,00,000
(2,00,000 @ Rs. 10 each)	20,00,000	Investments		1,00,000
		Current assets		
		Inventories	5,00,000	
13% Preference share capital	1,00,000	Debtors	4,00,000	
		Bank	1,00,000	10,00,000
Retained earnings	4,00,000			
12% Debentures	3,00,000			
Current liabilities	2,00,000			
	30,00,000			30,00,000

Negotiations for takeover of R. Ltd. result in its acquisition by A Ltd. The purchase consideration consists of (*i*) Rs. 3,30,000 13% debentures of A Ltd., for redeeming the 12% debentures of R Ltd., (*ii*) Rs. 1,00,000 12% convertible preference shares in A Ltd. for the payment of the preference share capital of R Ltd., (*iii*) 1,50,000 equity shares of A Ltd. to be issued at its current market price of Rs. 15, and (*iv*) A Ltd. would meet dissolution expenses of Rs. 30,000. The break up figures of eventual disposition by A Ltd., of un-required assets and liabilities of R Ltd. are: investments—Rs. 1,25,000; debtors—Rs. 3,50,000; inventories – Rs. 4,25,000; and payment of current liabilities—Rs. 1,90,000.

The project is expected to generate yearly operating CFAT of Rs. 7,00,000 for 6 years. It is estimated that fixed assets of R Ltd. would fetch Rs. 3,00,000 at the end of 6th year.

The firm's cost of capital is 15%. As a company secretary, comment on the financial prudence of merger decision of A Ltd. (PV at 15% rate of discount is—1st year: 0.870. 2nd year: 0.756, 3rd year: 0.658, 4th year: 0.572, 5th year: 0.496 and 6th year: 0.432).

(CS, December 1994)

Solution

Acquisition of R. Ltd. to A. Ltd.

Year	PV Factor at 15%	CFAT (Rs.)	PV (Rs.)
1	0.870	7,00,000	6,09,000
2	0.756	7,00,000	5,29,200
3	0.658	7,00,000	4,60,600
4	0.572	7,00,000	4,00,400
5	0.496	7,00,000	3,47,900
6	0.432	10,00,000	4,32,000
		Total PV	27,79,100
		Less: Cost of Acquisition	19,00,000
			NRV = 8,79,100

Comment: A Ltd. is expected to benefit from the merger R. Ltd. as the NPV is positive.

Illustration 18.4 X Ltd. is considering takeover of Y Ltd. and Z Ltd. The financial data for the three companies are as follows:

Particulars	Z Ltd.	Y Ltd.	Z Ltd.
Equity share capital of Rs. 10 each (Rs./million)	450	180	90
Earnings (Rs./millions)	45	9	9
Market price of each share (Rs.)	60	37	46

Calculate:

(*i*) Price earnings ratios.

(*ii*) Earning per share of A. Ltd. after the acquisition of B Ltd. and C Ltd. separately. Will you recommend the merger of either both of the companies? Justify you answer.

Solution

Calculation of Price Earning (PE) Exchange ratio and EPS after Acquisition

Particulars	X Ltd.	Y Ltd.	Z Ltd.
Earning (Rs./million)	45	9	9
No. of shares (million)	45	18	9
EPS (Rs.)	1	0.5	1
Market price per share (M.P.) (Rs.)	60	37	46
PE ratio	60	74	46
PE Exchange ratio or rate		1.62	1.30
Value of Shares (Rs. million) [No. of shares × MP]	2,700	1332	414
No. of A's shares to be given (million)	—	1332/60	414/60
		22.2	6.9
Earning per share			
Total earning after Acquisition (Rs. million)	—	54	54
Total number of shares (million)	—	67.1	51.9
EPS after acquisition (Rs.)	—	0.80	2.08

Since for X, EPS after merger is higher (Rs. 2.08) in case of Z only, so the merger of company Z in X is recommended.

PROBLEMS FOR PRACTICE

Problem 18.1 Company X acquires Company Y on "Share exchange" basis. The position before takeover was as follows:

Particulars	Company X	Company Y
No. of shares	10,000	5,000
Total earnings (Rs.)	1,00,000	50,000
Market price of share (MPS) (Rs.)	20	15

The shareholders of Company Y are offered 3 shares of Company X for 4 shares Company Y.

You are required to calculate the EPS of the amalgamated company vis-a-vis before takeover position, of the two companies and gain/loss of the shareholders of both the firms consequent to amalgamation.

(ICWA Final, June 1994)

[**Answer:** Gain of Company X = 9100, Company Y = 9087.50.]

Problem 18.2 X Ltd. wants to takeover Y Ltd. and the financial detail of both are as follows:

Particulars	X Ltd. (Rs.)	Y Ltd. (Rs.)
Preference share capital	20,000	—
Equity share capital of Rs. 10 each	1,00,000	50,000
Share Premium	—	2,000
Profit and Loss A/c	38,000	4,000
10% Debentures	15,000	5,000
	1,73,000	61,000
Fixed assets	1,22,000	35,000
Current assets	51,000	26,000
	1,73,000	61,000
Profit after tax and preference dividend	24,000	15,000
Market price	24	27

What should be share exchange ratio to be offered to the shareholders of Y. Ltd., based on (*i*) net assets value, (*ii*) EPS, and (*iii*) market price. Which should be preferred from the point of view of X Ltd.

(CS Final, June 1994)

[**Answers:** (*i*) 4,060, (*ii*) 6,250 and (*iii*) 5,625 shares to be issued.]

❑❑❑

APPENDIX

TABLES

Table A-1
Factor for Compounded Value of an Amount *i.e.*, CVF $_{(r\%, n)}$

Period (n)	1%	2%	3%	4%	5%	6%	7%	8%	9%	10%
1	1.010	1.020	1.030	1.040	1.050	1.060	1.070	1.080	1.090	1.100
2	1.020	1.040	1.061	1.082	1.102	1.124	1.145	1.166	1.188	1.210
3	1.030	1.061	1.093	1.125	1.158	1.191	1.225	1.260	1.295	1.331
4	1.041	1.082	1.126	1.170	1.216	1.262	1.311	1.360	1.412	1.464
5	1.051	1.104	1.159	1.217	1.276	1.338	1.403	1.469	1.539	1.611
6	1.062	1.126	1.194	1.265	1.340	1.419	1.501	1.587	1.677	1.772
7	1.072	1.149	1.230	1.316	1.407	1.504	1.606	1.714	1.828	1.949
8	1.083	1.172	1.267	1.369	1.477	1.594	1.718	1.851	1.993	2.144
9	1.094	1.195	1.305	1.423	1.551	1.689	1.838	1.999	2.172	2.358
10	1.105	1.219	1.344	1.480	1.629	1.791	1.967	2.159	2.367	2.594
11	1.116	1.243	1.384	1.539	1.710	1.898	2.105	2.332	2.580	2.853
12	1.127	1.268	1.426	1.601	1.796	2.012	2.252	2.518	2.813	3.138
13	1.138	1.294	1.469	1.665	1.886	2.133	2.410	2.720	3.066	3.452
14	1.149	1.319	1.513	1.732	1.980	2.261	2.579	2.937	3.342	3.797
15	1.161	1.346	1.558	1.801	2.079	2.397	2.759	3.172	3.642	4.177
16	1.173	1.373	1.605	1.873	2.188	2.540	2.952	3.426	3.970	4.595
17	1.184	1.400	1.653	1.948	2.292	2.693	3.159	3.700	4.328	5.054
18	1.196	1.428	1.702	2.026	2.407	2.854	3.380	3.996	4.717	5.560
19	1.208	1.457	1.753	2.107	2.527	3.026	3.616	4.316	5.142	6.116
20	1.220	1.486	1.806	2.191	2.653	3.207	3.870	4.661	5.604	6.727
21	1.232	1.516	1.860	2.279	2.786	3.399	4.140	5.034	6.109	7.400
22	1.245	1.546	1.916	2.370	2.925	3.603	4.430	5.436	6.658	8.140
23	1.257	1.577	1.974	2.465	3.071	3.820	4.740	5.871	7.258	8.954
24	1.270	1.608	2.033	2.563	3.225	4.049	5.072	6.341	7.911	9.850
25	1.282	1.641	2.094	2.666	3.386	4.292	5.427	6.848	8.623	10.834
30	1.348	1.811	2.427	3.243	4.322	5.743	7.612	10.062	13.267	17.449
35	1.417	2.000	2.814	3.946	5.516	7.686	10.676	14.785	20.413	28.102
40	1.489	2.208	3.262	4.801	7.040	10.285	14.974	21.724	31.408	45.258
45	1.565	2.438	3.781	5.841	8.985	13.764	21.002	31.920	48.325	72.888
50	1.645	2.691	4.384	7.106	11.467	18.419	29.456	46.900	74.354	117.386

[Contd...]

Period (n)	11%	12%	13%	14%	15%	16%	17%	18%	19%	20%
1	1.110	1.120	1.130	1.140	1.150	1.160	1.170	1.180	1.190	1.200
2	1.232	1.254	1.277	1.300	1.322	1.346	1.369	1.392	1.416	1.440
3	1.368	1.405	1.443	1.482	1.521	1.561	1.602	1.643	1.685	1.728
4	1.518	1.574	1.630	1.689	1.749	1.811	1.874	1.939	2.005	2.074
5	1.685	1.762	1.842	1.925	2.011	2.100	2.192	2.288	2.386	2.488
6	1.870	1.974	2.082	2.195	2.313	2.436	2.565	2.700	2.840	2.986
7	2.076	2.211	2.353	2.502	2.660	2.826	3.001	3.185	3.379	3.583
8	2.305	2.476	2.658	2.853	3.059	3.278	3.511	3.759	4.021	4.300
9	2.558	2.773	3.004	3.252	3.518	3.803	4.108	4.435	4.785	5.160
10	2.839	3.106	3.395	3.707	4.046	4.411	4.807	5.234	5.695	6.192
11	3.152	3.479	3.836	4.226	4.652	5.117	5.624	6.176	6.777	7.430
12	3.498	3.896	4.335	4.818	5.350	5.936	6.580	7.288	8.064	8.916
13	3.883	4.363	4.898	5.492	6.153	6.886	7.699	8.599	9.596	10.699
14	4.310	4.887	5.535	6.261	7.076	7.988	9.007	10.147	11.420	12.839
15	4.785	5.474	6.254	7.138	8.137	9.266	10.539	11.974	13.590	15.407
16	5.311	6.130	7.067	8.137	9.358	10.748	12.330	14.129	16.172	18.488
17	5.895	6.866	7.986	9.276	10.761	12.468	14.426	16.672	19.244	22.186
18	6.544	7.690	9.024	10.575	12.375	14.463	16.879	19.673	22.901	26.623
19	7.263	8.613	10.197	12.056	14.232	16.777	19.748	23.214	27.252	31.948
20	8.062	9.646	11.523	13.743	16.367	19.461	23.106	27.393	32.429	38.338
25	13.585	17.000	21.231	26.462	32.919	40.874	50.658	32.669	77.388	95.396
30	22.892	29.960	39.116	60.950	66.212	85.850	111.065	143.371	184.675	237.376

[Contd...]

Period (n)	21%	22%	23%	24%	25%	26%	27%	28%	29%	30%
1	1.210	1.220	1.230	1.240	1.250	1.260	1.270	1.280	1.290	1.300
2	1.464	1.488	1.513	1.538	1.562	1.588	1.613	1.638	1.664	1.690
3	1.772	1.816	1.861	1.907	1.953	2.000	2.048	2.097	2.147	2.197
4	2.144	2.215	2.289	2.364	2.441	2.520	2.601	2.684	2.769	2.856
5	2.594	2.703	2.815	2.392	3.052	3.176	3.304	3.436	3.572	3.713
6	3.138	3.297	3.463	3.635	3.815	4.001	4.196	4.398	4.608	4.827
7	3.797	4.023	4.259	4.508	4.768	5.042	5.329	5.629	5.945	6.275
8	4.595	4.908	5.239	5.590	5.960	6.353	6.767	7.206	7.669	8.157
9	5.560	5.987	6.444	6.931	7.451	8.004	8.595	9.223	9.893	10.604
10	6.727	7.305	7.926	8.549	9.313	10.086	10.915	11.806	12.761	13.786
11	8.140	8.912	9.749	10.657	11.642	12.708	13.862	15.112	16.462	17.921
12	9.850	10.872	11.991	13.215	14.552	16.012	17.605	19.343	21.236	23.298
13	11.918	13.264	14.749	16.386	18.190	20.175	22.359	24.759	27.395	30.287
14	14.421	16.182	18.141	20.319	22.737	25.420	28.395	31.961	35.339	39.373
15	17.449	19.742	22.314	25.196	28.422	32.030	36.062	40.565	45.587	51.185
16	21.113	24.084	27.446	31.243	35.527	40.357	45.799	51.923	58.808	66.541
17	25.547	29.384	33.758	38.741	44.409	50.850	58.165	66.461	75.862	86.503
18	30.912	35.848	41.523	45.039	55.511	64.071	73.869	85.071	97.862	112.454
19	37.404	43.735	51.073	59.568	69.389	80.730	93.813	108.890	126.242	146.190
20	45.258	53.357	62.820	73.864	86.736	101.720	119.143	139.380	162.852	190.047
25	117.388	144.207	176.857	216.542	264.698	323.040	393.628	478.905	581.756	705.627
30	304.471	389.748	497.904	634.820	807.793	1025.904	1300.477	1645.504	2078.208	2619.937

Table A-2

Factors for Compounded Value of an Annuity *i.e.*, $CVAF_{(r\%, n)}$

Period (n)	*1%*	*2%*	*3%*	*4%*	*5%*	*6%*	*7%*	*8%*	*9%*	*10%*
1	1.000	1.000	1.000	1.000	1.000	1.000	1.000	1.000	1.000	1.000
2	2.010	2.020	2.030	2.040	2.050	2.060	2.070	2.080	2.090	2.100
3	3.030	3.060	3.091	3.122	3.152	3.184	3.215	3.246	3.278	3.310
4	4.060	4.122	4.184	4.246	4.310	4.375	4.440	4.506	4.573	4.641
5	5.101	5.204	5.309	5.416	5.526	5.637	5.751	5.867	5.985	6.105
6	6.152	6.308	6.468	6.633	6.802	6.975	7.153	7.336	7.523	7.716
7	7.214	7.434	7.662	7.898	8.142	8.394	8.654	8.923	9.200	9.487
8	8.286	8.583	8.892	9.214	9.549	9.897	10.260	10.637	11.028	11.436
9	9.369	9.755	10.159	10.583	11.027	11.491	11.978	12.448	13.021	13.579
10	10.462	10.950	11.464	12.006	12.578	13.181	13.816	14.487	15.193	15.937
11	11.567	12.169	12.808	13.486	14.207	14.972	15.784	16.645	17.560	18.531
12	12.683	13.412	14.192	15.026	15.917	16.870	17.888	18.977	20.141	21.384
13	13.809	14.680	15.618	16.627	17.713	18.882	20.141	21.495	22.953	24.523
14	14.947	15.974	17.086	18.292	19.599	21.015	22.550	24.215	26.019	27.975
15	16.097	17.293	18.599	20.024	21.579	23.276	25.129	27.152	29.361	31.772
16	17.258	18.639	20.157	21.825	23.657	25.673	27.888	30.324	33.003	35.950
17	18.430	20.012	21.762	23.698	25.840	28.213	30.840	33.750	36.974	40.545
18	19.615	21.412	23.414	25.645	28.132	30.906	33.999	37.450	41.301	45.599
19	20.811	22.841	25.117	27.671	30.539	33.760	37.379	41.446	46.018	51.159
20	22.019	24.297	26.870	29.778	33.066	36.786	40.995	45.762	51.160	57.275
25	28.243	32.030	36.459	41.646	47.727	54.865	63.249	73.106	84.701	98.347
30	34.785	40.568	47.575	56.805	66.439	79.058	94.461	113.283	136.308	164.494

[Contd....]

Period (n)	11%	12%	13%	14%	15%	16%	17%	18%	19%	20%
1	1.000	1.000	1.000	1.000	1.000	1.000	1.000	1.000	1.000	1.000
2	2.110	2.120	2.130	2.140	2.150	2.160	2.170	2.180	2.190	2.200
3	3.342	3.374	3.407	3.440	3.473	3.506	3.539	3.572	3.606	3.640
4	4.710	4.779	4.850	4.921	4.993	5.066	5.141	5.215	5.291	5.368
5	6.228	6.353	6.480	6.610	6.742	6.877	7.014	7.154	7.297	7.442
6	7.913	8.115	8.323	8.536	8.754	8.977	9.207	9.442	9.683	9.930
7	9.783	10.089	10.405	10.730	11.067	11.414	11.772	12.142	12.523	12.916
8	11.589	12.300	12.757	13.233	13.727	14.240	14.773	15.327	15.902	16.499
9	14.164	14.776	15.416	16.085	16.786	17.518	18.285	19.086	19.923	20.799
10	16.722	17.549	18.420	19.337	20.304	21.321	22.393	23.521	24.709	25.959
11	19.561	20.655	21.814	23.004	24.349	25.733	27.200	28.755	30.404	32.150
12	22.713	24.133	25.650	27.271	29.002	30.850	32.824	34.931	37.180	39.580
13	26.212	28.029	29.985	32.089	34.352	36.786	39.404	42.219	45.244	48.497
14	30.095	32.393	34.883	37.581	40.505	43.672	47.103	50.818	54.841	59.196
15	34.405	37.280	40.417	43.842	47.580	51.660	56.110	60.965	66.261	72.035
16	39.190	42.753	46.672	50.980	55.717	60.925	66.649	72.939	79.850	87.442
17	44.501	48.884	53.739	59.118	65.075	71.673	78.979	87.068	96.022	105.931
18	50.396	55.750	61.725	68.394	75.836	84.141	93.406	103.740	115.266	128.117
19	56.939	63.440	70.749	78.969	88.212	98.603	110.285	123.414	138.166	154.740
20	64.203	72.052	80.947	91.025	102.44	115.380	130.033	146.628	165.418	186.688
25	114.413	133.334	155.620	181.871	212.793	249.214	292.105	342.603	402.042	471.981
30	199.021	241.333	293.199	356.787	434.745	530.321	647.439	790.748	966.712	1181.882

[Contd...]

Period (n)	*21%*	*22%*	*23%*	*24%*	*25%*	*26%*	*27%*	*28%*	*29%*	*30%*
1	1.000	1.000	1.000	1.000	1.000	1.000	1.000	1.000	1.000	1.000
2	2.210	2.220	2.230	2.240	2.250	2.260	2.270	2.280	2.290	2.300
3	3.674	3.708	3.743	3.778	3.813	3.843	3.883	3.918	3.954	3.990
4	5.446	5.524	5.604	5.684	5.766	5.848	5.931	6.016	6.101	6.187
5	7.589	7.740	7.893	8.048	8.207	8.368	8.533	8.700	8.870	9.043
6	10.183	10.442	10.708	10.980	11.259	11.544	11.837	12.136	12.442	12.756
7	13.321	13.740	14.171	14.615	15.073	15.546	16.032	16.534	17.051	17.583
8	17.119	17.762	18.430	19.123	19.842	20.588	21.361	22.163	22.995	23.858
9	21.714	22.670	23.669	24.712	25.802	26.940	28.129	29.369	30.664	32.015
10	27.274	28.657	30.113	31.643	33.253	34.945	36.723	38.592	40.556	42.619
11	34.001	35.962	38.039	40.238	42.566	45.030	47.639	50.399	53.318	56.405
12	42.141	44.873	47.787	50.985	54.208	57.738	61.501	65.510	69.780	74.326
13	51.991	55.745	59.778	64.110	68.760	73.750	79.106	84.853	91.016	97.624
14	63.909	69.009	74.528	80.496	86.949	93.925	101.465	109.612	118.411	127.912
15	78.330	85.191	92.669	100.815	109.687	119.346	129.860	141.303	153.750	167.285
16	95.779	104.933	114.983	126.011	138.109	151.375	165.922	181.868	199.337	218.470
17	116.892	129.019	142.428	157.253	173.636	191.733	211.721	233.791	258.145	285.011
18	142.439	158.403	176.187	195.994	218.045	242.583	269.885	300.252	334.006	371.514
19	173.351	194.251	217.710	244.033	273.556	306.654	343.754	385.323	431.868	483.968
20	210.755	237.986	268.783	303.601	342.945	387.384	437.568	494.213	558.110	630.157
25	554.230	650.944	764.596	898.092	1054.791	1238.617	1454.180	1706.803	2002.608	2348.765
30	1445.111	1767.044	2160.459	2640.916	3227.172	3941.953	4812.891	5873.231	7162.785	8729.805

Table A-3
Factors for Present Value of a Future Amount *i.e.*, $PVF_{(r\%, n)}$

Period (n)	*1%*	*2%*	*3%*	*4%*	*5%*	*6%*	*7%*	*8%*	*9%*	*10%*
1	0.990	0.980	0.971	0.962	0.952	0.943	0.935	0.926	0.917	0.909
2	0.980	0.961	0.943	0.925	0.907	0.890	0.873	0.857	0.842	0.826
3	0.971	0.942	0.915	0.889	0.864	0.840	0.816	0.794	0.772	0.751
4	0.961	0.924	0.889	0.855	0.823	0.792	0.763	0.735	0.708	0.683
5	0.951	0.906	0.863	0.822	0.784	0.747	0.713	0.681	0.650	0.621
6	0.942	0.888	0.838	0.790	0.746	0.705	0.666	0.630	0.596	0.564
7	0.933	0.871	0.813	0.760	0.711	0.665	0.623	0.583	0.547	0.513
8	0.923	0.853	0.789	0.731	0.677	0.627	0.582	0.540	0.502	0.467
9	0.914	0.837	0.766	0.703	0.645	0.592	0.544	0.500	0.460	0.424
10	0.905	0.820	0.744	0.676	0.614	0.558	0.508	0.463	0.422	0.386
11	0.896	0.804	0.722	0.650	0.585	0.527	0.475	0.429	0.388	0.350
12	0.887	0.788	0.701	0.625	0.557	0.497	0.444	0.397	0.356	0.319
13	0.879	0.773	0.681	0.601	0.530	0.469	0.415	0.368	0.326	0.290
14	0.870	0.758	0.661	0.577	0.505	0.442	0.388	0.340	0.299	0.263
15	0.861	0.743	0.642	0.555	0.481	0.417	0.362	0.315	0.275	0.239
16	0.853	0.728	.0.623	0.534	0.458	0.394	0.339	0.292	0.252	0.218
17	0.844	0.714	0.605	0.513	0.436	0.371	0.317	0.270	0.231	0.198
18	0.836	0.700	0.587	0.494	0.416	0.350	0.296	0.250	0.212	0.180
19	0.828	0.686	0.570	0.475	0.396	0.331	0.276	0.232	0.194	0.164
20	0.820	0.673	0.554	0.456	0.377	0.312	0.258	0.215	0.178	0.149
25	0.780	0.610	0.478	0.375	0.295	0.233	0.184	0.146	0.116	0.092
30	0.742	0.552	0.412	0.308	0.231	0.174	0.131	0.099	0.075	0.057

[Contd....]

Period (n)	*11%*	*12%*	*13%*	*14%*	*15%*	*16%*	*17%*	*18%*	*19%*	*20%*
1	0.901	0.893	0.885	0.877	0.870	0.862	0.855	0.847	0.840	0.833
2	0.812	0.797	0.783	0.769	0.756	0.743	0.731	0.718	0.706	0.694
3	0.731	0.712	0.693	0.675	0.658	0.641	0.624	0.609	0.593	0.579
4	0.659	0.636	0.613	0.592	0.572	0.552	0.534	0.516	0.499	0.482
5	0.593	0.567	0.543	0.519	0.497	0.476	0.456	0.437	0.419	0.402
6	0.535	0.507	0.480	0.456	0.432	0.410	0.390	0.370	0.352	0.335
7	0.482	0.452	0.425	0.400	0.376	0.354	0.333	0.314	0.296	0.279
8	0.434	0.404	0.376	0.351	0.327	0.305	0.285	0.266	0.249	0.233
9	0.391	0.361	0.333	0.308	0.284	0.263	0.243	0.226	0.209	0.194
10	0.352	0.322	0.295	0.270	0.247	0.227	0.208	0.191	0.176	0.162
11	0.317	0.287	0.261	0.237	0.215	0.195	0.178	0.162	0.148	0.135
12	0.286	0.257	0.231	0.208	0.187	0.168	0.152	0.137	0.124	0.112
13	0.258	0.229	0.204	0.182	0.163	0.145	0.130	0.116	0.104	0.093
14	0.232	0.205	0.181	0.160	0.141	0.125	0.111	0.099	0.088	0.078
15	0.209	0.183	0.160	0.140	0.123	0.108	0.095	0.084	0.074	0.065
16	0.188	0.163	0.141	0.123	0.107	0.093	0.081	0.071	0.062	0.054
17	0.170	0.146	0.125	0.108	0.093	0.080	0.069	0.060	0.052	0.045
18	0.153	0.130	0.111	0.095	0.081	0.069	0.059	0.051	0.044	0.038
19	0.138	0.116	0.098	0.083	0.070	0.060	0.051	0.043	0.037	0.031
20	0.124	0.104	0.087	0.073	0.061	0.051	0.043	0.037	0.031	0.026
25	0.074	0.059	0.047	0.038	0.030	0.024	0.020	0.016	0.013	0.010
30	0.044	0.033	0.026	0.020	0.015	0.012	0.009	0.007	0.005	0.004

[Contd...]

Period (n)	21%	22%	23%	24%	25%	26%	27%	28%	29%	30%
1	0.826	0.820	0.813	0.806	0.800	0.794	0.787	0.781	0.775	0.769
2	0.683	0.672	0.661	0.650	0.640	0.630	0.620	0.610	0.601	0.592
3	0.564	0.551	0.537	0.524	0.512	0.500	0.488	0.477	0.466	0.455
4	0.46	0.451	0.437	0.423	0.410	0.397	0.384	0.373	0.361	0.350
5	0.386	0.370	0.355	0.341	0.328	0.315	0.303	0.291	0.280	0.269
6	0.319	0.303	0.289	0.275	0.262	0.250	0.238	0.227	0.217	0.207
7	0.263	0.249	0.235	0.222	0.210	0.198	0.188	0.178	0.168	0.159
8	0.218	0.204	0.191	0.179	0.168	0.157	0.148	0.139	0.130	0.123
9	0.180	0.167	0.155	0.144	0.134	0.125	0.116	0.108	0.101	0.094
10	0.149	0.137	0.126	0.116	0.107	0.099	0.092	0.085	0.078	0.073
11	0.123	0.112	0.103	0.094	0.086	0.079	0.072	0.066	0.061	0.056
12	0.102	0.092	0.083	0.076	0.069	0.062	0.057	0.052	0.047	0.043
13	0.084	0.075	0.068	0.061	0.055	0.050	0.045	0.040	0.037	0.033
14	0.069	0.062	0.055	0.049	0.044	0.039	0.035	0.032	0.028	0.025
15	0.057	0.051	0.045	0.040	0.035	0.031	0.028	0.025	0.022	0.020
16	0.047	0.042	0.036	0.032	0.028	0.025	0.022	0.019	0.017	0.015
17	0.039	0.034	0.030	0.026	0.023	0.020	0.017	0.015	0.013	0.012
18	0.032	0.028	0.024	0.021	0.018	0.016	0.014	0.012	0.010	0.009
19	0.027	0.023	0.020	0.017	0.014	0.012	0.011	0.009	0.008	0.007
20	0.022	0.019	0.016	0.014	0.012	0.010	0.008	0.007	0.006	0.005
25	0.009	0.007	0.006	0.005	0.004	0.003	0.003	0.002	0.002	0.001
30	0.003	0.003	0.002	0.002	0.001	0.001	0.001	0.001	0.000	0.000

Table A-4

Factors for Present Value of a Future Annuity *i.e.*, PVAF $_{(r\%, n)}$

Period (n)	*1%*	*2%*	*3%*	*4%*	*5%*	*6%*	*7%*	*8%*	*9%*	*10%*
1	0.990	0.980	0.971	0.962	0.952	0.943	0.935	0.926	0.917	0.909
2	1.970	1.942	1.913	1.886	1.859	1.833	1.783	1.783	1.759	1.736
3	2.941	2.884	2.829	2.775	2.723	2.673	2.624	2.577	2.531	2.487
4	3.902	3.808	3.717	3.630	3.546	3.465	3.312	3.312	3.240	3.170
5	4.853	4.713	4.580	4.452	4.329	4.212	4.100	3.993	3.890	3.791
6	5.795	5.601	5.417	5.242	5.076	4.917	4.767	4.623	4.486	4.355
7	6.728	6.472	6.230	6.002	5.789	5.582	5.389	5.206	5.033	4.868
8	7.652	7.326	7.020	6.733	6.463	6.210	5.971	5.747	5.535	5.335
9	8.566	8.162	7.786	7.435	7.108	6.802	6.515	6.247	5.995	5.759
10	9.471	8.983	8.530	8.111	7.722	7.360	7.024	6.710	6.418	6.145
11	10.368	9.787	9.253	8.760	8.306	7.887	7.499	7.139	6.805	6.495
12	11.255	10.575	9.954	9.385	8.863	8.384	7.943	7.536	7.161	6.814
13	12.134	11.348	10.635	9.986	9.394	8.858	8.358	7.904	7.487	7.103
14	13.004	12.106	11.296	10.563	9.899	9.295	8.746	8.244	7.786	7.367
15	13.865	12.849	11.938	11.118	10.380	9.712	9.108	8.560	8.061	7.606
16	14.718	13.578	12.561	11.652	10.838	10.106	9.447	8.851	8.313	7.824
17	15.562	14.292	13.166	12.166	11.274	10.477	9.763	9.122	8.544	8.002
18	16.398	14.992	13.754	12.659	11.690	10.828	10.059	9.372	8.756	8.201
19	17.226	15.679	14.324	13.134	12.085	11.158	10.336	9.604	8.950	8.365
20	18.046	16.352	14.878	13.590	12.462	11.470	10.594	9.818	9.129	8.514
25	22.023	19.524	17.413	15.622	14.094	12.783	11.654	10.675	9.823	9.077
30	25.808	22.397	19.601	17.292	15.373	13.765	12.409	11.258	10.274	9.427

[Contd...]

Period (n)	*11%*	*12%*	*13%*	*14%*	*15%*	*16%*	*17%*	*18%*	*19%*	*20%*
1	0.901	0.893	0.885	0.877	0.870	0.862	0.855	0.847	0.850	0.833
2	1.713	1.690	1.668	1.647	1.626	1.605	1.585	1.566	1.547	1.528
3	2.444	2.402	2.361	2.322	2.283	2.246	2.210	2.174	2.140	2.106
4	3.102	3.037	2.974	2.914	2.855	2.798	2.743	2.690	2.639	2.589
5	3.696	3.605	3.517	3.433	3.352	3.274	3.199	3.127	3.058	2.991
6	4.231	4.111	3.998	3.889	3.784	3.685	3.589	3.498	3.410	3.326
7	4.712	4.564	4.423	4.288	4.160	4.039	3.922	3.812	3.706	3.605
8	5.146	4.968	4.799	4.639	4.487	4.344	4.207	4.078	3.954	3.837
9	5.537	5.328	5.132	4.946	4.772	4.607	4.451	4.303	4.163	4.031
10	5.889	5.650	5.426	5.216	5.019	4.833	4.659	4.494	4.339	4.192
11	6.207	5.938	5.687	5.453	5.234	5.029	4.836	4.656	4.487	4.327
12	6.492	6.194	5.918	5.660	5.421	5.197	4.988	4.793	4.611	4.439
13	6.750	6.424	6.122	5.842	5.583	5.342	5.118	4.910	4.715	4.533
14	6.982	6.628	6.303	6.002	5.724	5.468	5.229	5.008	4.802	4.611
15	7.191	6.811	6.462	6.142	5.847	5.575	5.324	5.092	4.876	4.675
16	7.379	6.974	6.604	6.265	5.954	5.669	5.405	5.162	4.938	4.730
17	7.549	7.120	6.729	6.373	6.047	5.749	5.475	5.222	4.990	4.775
18	7.702	7.250	6.840	6.467	6.128	5.818	5.534	5.273	5.033	4.812
19	7.893	7.366	6.938	6.50	6.198	5.877	5.585	5.316	5.070	4.843
20	7.963	7.469	7.025	6.623	6.259	5.929	5.628	5.353	5.101	4.870
25	8.422	7.843	7.330	6.873	6.464	6.097	5.766	5.467	5.195	4.948
30	8.694	6.005	7.496	7.003	6.566	6.177	5.829	5.517	5.235	4.979

[Contd...]

Period (n)	21%	22%	23%	24%	25%	26%	27%	28%	29%	30%
1	0.826	0.820	0.813	0.806	0.800	0.794	0.787	0.781	0.775	0.769
2	1.509	1.432	1.474	1.457	1.440	1.424	1.407	1.392	1.376	1.361
3	2.074	2.042	2.011	1.981	1.952	1.923	1.896	1.868	1.842	1.816
4	2.540	2.494	2.448	2.404	2.362	2.320	2.280	2.241	2.203	2.166
5	2.926	2.864	2.803	2.745	2.689	2.635	2.583	2.532	2.483	2.436
6	3.245	3.167	3.092	3.020	2.951	2.885	2.821	2.759	2.700	2.643
7	3.508	3.416	3.327	3.242	3.161	3.083	3.009	2.937	2.868	2.802
8	3.726	3.619	3.518	3.421	3.329	3.241	3.156	3.076	2.999	2.925
9	3.905	3.786	3.673	3.566	3.463	3.366	3.273	3.184	3.100	3.019
10	4.054	3.923	3.799	3.682	3.570	3.465	3.364	3.269	3.178	3.092
11	4.177	4.035	3.902	3.776	3.656	3.544	3.437	3.335	3.239	3.147
12	4.278	4.127	3.985	3.851	3.725	3.606	3.493	3.387	3.286	3.190
13	4.362	4.203	4.053	3.912	3.780	3.656	3.538	3.427	3.322	3.223
14	4.432	4.265	4.108	3.962	3.824	3.695	3.573	3.459	3.351	3.249
15	4.489	4.315	4.153	4.001	3.859	3.726	3.601	3.483	3.373	3.268
16	4.536	4.357	4.189	4.033	3.887	3.751	3.623	3.503	3.390	3.283
17	4.576	4.391	4.219	4.059	3.910	3.771	3.640	3.518	3.403	3.295
18	4.608	4.419	4.243	4.080	3.928	3.786	3.654	3.529	3.413	3.311
19	4.635	4.442	4.263	4.097	3.942	3.799	3.664	3.539	3.421	3.311
20	4.657	4.460	4.279	4.110	3.954	3.808	3.673	3.546	3.427	3.316
25	4.721	4.514	4.323	4.147	3.985	3.834	3.694	3.564	3.442	3.329
30	4.746	4.534	4.339	4.160	3.995	3.842	3.701	3.569	3.447	3.332

Table A -5

Z-Table Value of the Standard Normal Distribution Function

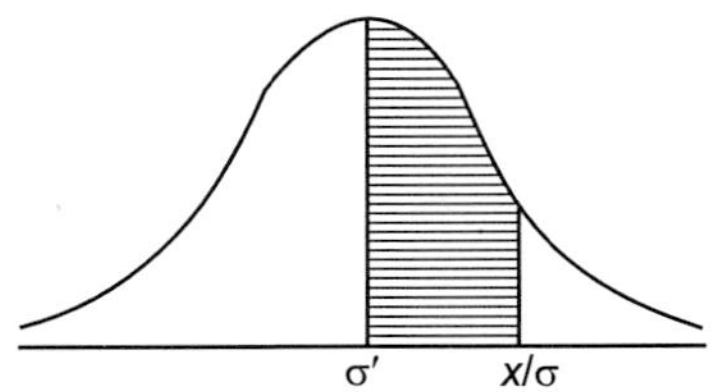

x/σ	.00	.01	.02	.03	.04	.05	.06	.07	.08	.09
0.0	.0000	.0040	.0080	.0120	.0160	.0199	.0239	.0279	.0319	.0359
0.1	.0398	.0438	.0478	.0517	.0557	.0596	.0636	.0675	.0714	.0753
0.2	.0793	.0832	.0871	.0910	.0948	.0987	.1020	.1064	.1103	.1133
0.3	.1179	.1217	.1255	.1293	.1331	.1363	.1406	.1443	.1480	.1515
0.4	.1554	.1591	.1628	.1664	.1700	.1736	.1772	.1808	.1844	.1570
0.5	.1915	.1950	.1935	.2019	.2054	.2088	.2123	.2157	.2190	.2324
0.6	.2257	.2291	.2324	.2357	.2389	.2422	.2454	.2486	.2518	.2549
0.7	.2580	.2612	.2642	.2673	.2704	.2734	.2764	.2794	.2823	.2892
0.8	.2881	.2910	.2939	.2967	.2995	.3023	.3051	.3078	.3106	.3185
0.9	.3159	.3186	.3212	.3238	.3264	.3289	.3315	.3340	.3365	.3389
1.0	.3413	.3438	.3461	.3485	.3508	.3531	.3554	.3577	.3599	.3621
1.1	.3648	.3665	.3686	.3708	.3729	.3749	.3770	.3790	.3810	.3830
1.2	.3849	.3869	.3888	.3907	.3925	.3944	.3962	.3980	.3997	.4015
1.3	.4032	.4049	.4066	.4082	.4099	.4115	.4131	.4147	.4162	.4177
1.4	.4192	.4207	.4222	.4236	.4251	.4265	.4279	.4292	.4305	.4319
1.5	.4332	.4345	.4357	.4370	.4382	.4394	.4406	.4418	.4429	.4441
1.6	.4452	.4463	.4474	.4484	.4495	.4505	.4515	.4525	.4535	.4545
1.7	.4554	.4564	.4573	.4582	.4591	.4599	.4608	.4616	.4625	.4633
1.8	.4641	.4649	.4656	.4664	.4671	.4678	.4686	.4693	.4699	.4706
1.9	.4713	.4719	.4726	.4732	.4738	.4744	.4750	.4750	.4761	.4767

[Contd...]

x/σ	.00	.01	.02	.03	.04	.05	.06	.07	.08	.09
2.0	.4772	.4778	4783	.4788	.4793	.4798	.4803	.4803	.4812	.4817
2.1	.4821	.4826	.4830	.4834	.4838	.4842	.4846	.4850	.4854	.4857
2.2	.4861	.4864	.4868	4871	.4876	.4878	.4881	.4884	.4887	.4890
2.3	.4893	.4896	.4898	.4901	.4904	.4906	.4909	.4911	.4913	.4916
2.4	.4918	4920	.4922	.4925	.4927	.4929	.4931	.4932	.4934	.4936
2.5	.4938	.4940	.4941	.4943	.4945	.4946	.4948	.4949	.4951	.4952
2.6	.4953	.4955	.4956	4957	.4959	.4960	.4961	.4962	.4963	.4964
2.7	.4965	.4966	.4967	.4968	.4969	.4970	.4971	.4972	.4973	.4974
2.8	.4974	.4975	.4976	.4977	.4977	.4978	.4979	.4979	.4980	.4981
2.9	.4981	.4982	.4982	.4983	.4984	.4984	.4985	.4985	.4986	.4986
3.0	.49865	.4987	.4987	.4988	.4988	.4989	.4989	.4889	.4990	.4990
3.1	.49903	.4991	.4991	.4991	.4992	.4992	.4992	.4992	.4993	.4993
3.2	.4993129	.4993	.4994	.4994	.4994	.4994	.4994	.4995	.4995	.4995
3.3	.4995166	.4995	.4996	.4996	.4996	.4996	.4996	.4996	.4996	.4997
3.4	.4996631	.4997	.4997	.4997	.4997	.4997	.4997	.4997	.4998	.4998
3.5	.4997674	.4998	.4998	.4998	.4998	.4998	.4998	.4998	.4998	.4998
3.6	.4998409	.4998	.4999	.4999	.4999	.4999	.4999	.4999	.4999	.4999
3.7	.4998922	.4999	.4999	.4999	.4999	.4999	.4999	.4999	.4999	.4999
3.8	.4999277	.4999	.4999	.4999	.4999	.4999	.4999	.5000	.5000	.5000
3.9	.4999519	.5000	.5000	.5000	.5000	.5000	.5000	.5000	.5000	.5000
4.0	.4999683									
4.5	.4999966									
5.0	.4999997133									

Glossary

ABC Analysis	: An inventory management technique. Different kinds of material are classified according to value. Emphasis is given to high value investment products.
Accounting Rate of Return	: The rate on an investment defined as accounting profit divided by book value of investment. It is also called average rate of return.
Accounts Payable	: Money which is to be paid by a firm to its suppliers, since goods are purchased on credit.
Accounts Receivable	: Cash to be collected by a firm from its customers on account of goods sold on credit.
Agency Theory	: It is a theory about the relationship between a financial manager and shareholders, creditors of the company and management.
Ageing Schedule	: A statement showing the distribution of debtors on particular dates.
Amortization	: To write-off of expenditure, for example, the issue cost of shares over a period of time.
Annuity	: A stream of uniform periodic cash flow.
Average Collection Period	: It is the average length of time to collect cash after credit sales.
Benefit Cost Ratio	: This is also called 'profitability index'. It is a technique of capital budgeting.
Bond	: This is an instrument for long-term debt. It gives a fixed rate of interest.
Bonus Shares	: Shares issued to existing shareholders as a result of capitalization of reserves.
Book Value	: The cost price of an asset less accumulated depreciation is called 'book value'.
Break-Even Analysis	: It determines the level of activity at which revenues and costs are equals and how profit varies with volume.
Budget	: A plan expressed usually in financial terms.
Budgeted Expenses Method	: It is a method for preparing proforma financial statements which are based on information pertaining to a future period.
Business Risk	: This risk arises from variation in profit before interest and taxes.
Call Provision	: A bond or preference share which has the feature of enabling the issuing firm to 'call back' or repurchase the outstanding bonds or preferred stock at a predetermined price.

Capital Asset Pricing Model (CAPM) : This is a theory, which shows the relationship between risk and return for efficient and inefficient portfolios.

Capital Budgeting : It is the process of analysing, appraising, and taking decisions about projects of long-term nature and involving heavy investment.

Capital Gains : Gains arising from sale of long-term assets is called capital gains. If there is a loss on long-term assets it is called a capital loss.

Capital Structure : It is the composition of a firm's financing, consisting of equity, preference, and debt.

Carrying Cost : Costs connected with storing of inventory for smooth functioning of production and sales. The costs can be both operational and financial.

Cash Budget : A statement which depicts the forecast of cash receipts, cash disbursements, and net cash balance over a period of time.

Cash Cycle : The time period between the dates, a firm pays its supplies and the date it receives cash from its customers.

Cash Discount : A discount given to buyers for cash payment.

Collection Float : The amount of cheque deposited by the firm in the bank but not cleared. It is a technique of receivables management.

Compound Interest : Interest payable and receivable on interest.

Compounding : It is the process of determining the final value of an amount when compound interest applies.

Contribution : This is the difference between revenue and variable cost. It is used in techniques of operating leverage.

Cost of Capital : The minimum rate of return the firm must earn on its investments in order to satisfy the expectations of investors who provide the funds to the firm.

Coupon Rate : It is the rate of interest stated on a bond.

Covenant : A provision or an agreement between a lender and a borrower in a loan contract. It has to be abided by the borrower.

Credit Period : The lengths of time that customers are allowed for their credit purchases.

Credit Policy : It is the firm's policy regarding its credit standards, cash discount, credit period and collection procedures.

Credit Risk : The risk that a party to a contract may default.

Cum Dividend : It is a scrip with dividend.

Cumulative Dividends : It is a feature of preference shares which requires that all unpaid past dividends on preferred stock to be paid before any equity dividends are paid.

Current Assets : These are assets, which normally get converted into cash within a year or during the operating cycle of the firm.

Current Liabilities : Liabilities that is normally payable within a year.

Current Ratio : It is a measure of liquidity. It is defined as current assets divided by current liabilities.

Current Yield : This is the current annual interest or divided received, divided by current market price.

Debenture : It is an instrument for long-term debt. Debentures in India are usually secured.

Debt Asset Ratio : A leverage ratio which is calculated as total debt divided by total asset.

Defensive Security : A security, which has a beta of less than one.

Degree of Financial Leverage : It is the percentage change in earnings per share as a result of one per cent change in profit before interest and tax.

Degree of Operating Leverage : It is the percentage change in profit before interest and taxes as a result of one per cent change in sales.

Degree of Total Leverage : The percentage change in earnings per share as a result of one per cent change in sales.

Depreciation : It is a charge on an asset for using it. The value of the asset is reduced every year until its lifetime.

Discounting : It is the process of finding the present value of a future cash flow of a series of future cash flows.

Dividend Discount Model : A model that calculates the value of equity share as the present value of future dividends expected from it.

Dividend Payment : It is a payment made by a company to its stockholders on its profits.

Dividend Yield : It is an annual dividend stated as a percentage of a share's market price.

Economic Order Quantity (EOQ) : This is a model which shows the optimum level of inventory which the firm should purchase to have a trade off between carrying costs and order costs.

Equity : This is the net worth of a firm. It consists of paid up equity capital plus reserves and surplus.

Face Value : It is the amount a firm promises to pay to its bondholder or preference stockholder at the time of maturity. It is also referred to as the par value or principal value.

Financial Intermediaries : Financial institutions which serve as intermediaries between savers and users of funds, for example, commercial banks, development banks, mutual funds.

Financial Risk : It is the risk which arises from the use of debt capital.

Financial System : It is a network of markets and institutions to facilitate the exchange of assets and risks.

Fixed Charge : It is a payment made by a firm which is required under a contract or a legal system. For example, rent, depreciation, taxes and managerial perquisites.

Float : These are those funds which are issued by cheques but have not been collected.

Goodwill : These are intangible assets that are represented by the excess of purchase price over book value.

Hurdle Rate : It is an investment decision making rate. It is the minimum acceptable rate of return on a project.

Initial Public Offering : The first public issue of a company's equity.

Insolvency : It is the inability of a firm to meet its debt obligations.

Intangible Assets : These are non-physical but valuable resources like goodwill, patents and copyrights which are owned by the firm.

Internal Financing : These are the funds which are generated internally. It consists of retained earnings plus depreciation and other non-cash charges.

Internal Rate of Return : This is the rate of discount that equates the present value of future cash flows to the initial investment on the project. At this point the net present value of an investment is zero. It is also called 'yield on investments'.

Intrinsic Value : The intrinsic value of an asset is the present value of the stream of benefits expected from it. It is also called 'fair value' or 'reasonable value' or 'investment value'.

Letter of Credit : This is an official document issued by a bank on behalf of the customer, stating the conditions under which the bank will honour the commitments of the customer.

Liability : It is a claim on the assets of a business.

Liquidity : A firm's liquidity refers to its ability to meet its obligations in the short run, usually one year. An asset's liquidity refers to how quickly it can be sold at a reasonable price.

Listed Securities : These are securities which are admitted for trading on a recognized stock exchange. In India the firm has to apply to SEBI for listing.

Market Risk : It is called 'systematic risk' or 'non-diversifiable risk'.

Money Market : It is a financial market which deals in short-term funds.

Net Present Value (NPV) : It is a method for evaluating investment proposals. NPV is defined as the present value of benefits minus the present value of costs.

Nominal Interest Rate : It is the interest rate as expressed in money terms.

Non-diversifiable Risk : The part of total risk, which cannot be eliminated by diversification. It is also referred to as 'market risk' or 'systematic risk'.

Normal Distribution : It is the systematic, bell-shaped probability distribution that is completely defined by its mean and standard deviation.

Operating Cycle : The operating cycle of a firm begins with the acquisition of raw materials and ends with the collection of receivables.

Operating Leverage : It is the relationship between sales and EBIT due to the presence of fixed operating costs.

Opportunity Cost : The rate of return that can be earned on the best alternative investment.

Paid Up Capital : This is the share capital which has been paid up by the shareholders.

Par Value : This is also called 'face value'. It is the value of the share, bond, preference share which is the actual value of the scrip.

Payback Period	: This is the time which is required for an investment to generate cash flows equal to the initial outlay of the project.
Payment Float	: These are cheques issued by a firm but not yet paid by the bank.
Payout Ratio	: This is the proportion of earnings paid by a company to its shareholders out of the profits of the firm as dividends.
Perpetuity	: This is an annuity in which a fixed sum is received annually and perpetually.
Required Rate of Return	: This is the rate of return which an investor is interested in receiving for the money that he has invested.
Retained Earnings	: This is that part of after tax profits which is not paid to the shareholders as dividends and it is ploughed back into business.
Return on Equity	: This is the ratio of earnings to network.
Risk	: This is the variability of returns associated with a project. It is also called 'uncertainty'.
Safety Stock	: This is the minimum level of inventory which the firm keeps as a reserve to protect itself from variations in sales, production and procurement time.
Salvage Value	: This is the amount or the expected value of a depreciated asset at the end of its useful life.
Sensitivity Analysis	: This is a technique of risk analysis. Its studies and analyses the effect of changes in certain variables on an outcome to estimate a project.
Sinking Fund	: This is an amount which is paid at periodic intervals to retire a debt of a firm.
Stock Split	: A stock split means that the par value per share is reduced and the numbers of shares are increased proportionately.
Sunk Costs	: These are costs which have been incurred by a firm and cannot be reversed.
Working Capital	: It is the analysis of current assets and current liabilities. It deals with the day today working of a firm. Working capital can be gross or net. Gross working capital is the total of current assets. Net working capital is the difference between the total of current assets and current liabilities.
Yield to Maturity	: This is the rate of return which is received by an investor if he actually holds a security until its maturity date.
Zero Coupon Bond	: This bond does not pay any interest. It is issued at a price which is less than the maturity value. It is issued at a discount over its face value.

❑❑❑

Index